TRAVEL CAREER DEVELOPMENT

ELEVENTH EDITION

TheTravelinstitute®

SINCE 1964

TheTravelinstitute®

SINCE 1964

Dear Future Travel Professional:

Congratulations on your decision to enter the travel and tourism industry. We, at The Travel Institute, applaud your decision and wish you a fulfilling and prosperous career.

As you can imagine, travel and tourism evolve as quickly as the world and technology change. Politics, economics, geography, weather, cultural events, and a host of other factors continually affect travel and tourism businesses. Accordingly, the paramount role of The Travel Institute is to encourage and facilitate professional development and continuous learning for individuals at all career stages.

The Travel Institute's professional designation and certification programs address core and advanced knowledge requirements needed by all travel professionals.

The Travel Institute maintains a unique position in the world of travel and tourism. We are the only professional, not-for-profit industry organization that is politically neutral and open to all. We strive to remain at the forefront of change and evolution as we advance the industry one professional at a time.

Visit www.thetravelinstitute.com to learn about membership and all of the benefits available to each and every member of our Institute family.

Sincerely,

Brian D. Robb, CTIE
Chairman of the Board of Trustees
The Travel Institute

Diane Petras, CTIE
President
The Travel Institute

The Travel Institute
945 Concord Street - Framingham, MA 00701
P: (800) 542-4282 - F: (781) 237-3860
www.thetravelinstitute.com

Acknowledgments

A collaborative industry effort created in 1964, The Travel Institute® has continuously evolved to maintain its role as the global leader in industry education and certification while staying true to its mission: dedicated solely to advancing the professionalism of both agents and industry leaders in support of individual and industry success. A non-profit, independent organization, The Travel Institute also works with leaders throughout the industry to create and deliver relevant, meaningful, and rigorous coursework. A trusted partner to industry suppliers and educational institutions, The Travel Institute has trained hundreds of thousands of travel professionals through introductory training, certification, specialist courses, webinars, and in its online Premium Access for members. Throughout North America, many successful agents and high-profile leaders credit their success to coursework from The Travel Institute.

The Travel Institute relies on the expertise, generosity and collaboration of our industry subject matter experts to ensure educational excellence for students and partner organizations. We want to acknowledge the generosity and dedication of the following individuals who provided content, expertise, suggestions, and edits for this new edition that were of invaluable help in making *Travel Career Development* the leading textbook in the industry:

- Don Capparella, CTC, Quality Travel Solutions
- Richard D'Ambrosio, Hudson Valley Communications
- Tom Ogg, Ogg Marketing Group
- Joanie Ogg, CTC, Ogg Marketing Group
- Andy Ogg, CTIE, Ogg Marketing Group
- Peter N. Lobasso, American Society of Travel Advisors
- Ana Zecevic, The Travel Agent Next Door
- Heather Kindred, CTIE, Travel Leaders of Tomorrow
- Patricia J. Gagnon, CTC, The Travel Institute, Independent Consultant
- Guida Botelho, CTIE, The Travel Institute
- Lisa Owers, CTIE, The Travel Institute
- Marty Sarbey de Souto, CTC, Independent Consultant
- Jim Prchlik, Rail Europe

- Terry Regan, CTC, Berkeley's Northside Travel
- Steve Shields, CTC, Orinda Travel

The Travel Institute
945 Concord St.
Framingham, MA 01701

thetravelinstitute.com

Brief Contents

Table of Contents

Preface

Hundreds of thousands of students in the United States and Canada have used *Travel Career Development* as a key to unlocking a career in the travel/tourism industry. Since its introduction, *Travel Career Development* has been widely used as a core text in survey courses, as an office reference for new employees, and as the centerpiece for various programs on specific aspects of the travel/ tourism industry. The eleventh edition continues to provide a systematic, comprehensive overview of the travel and tourism industry. Its content is organized into four parts:

- Part One, Exploring the World of Travel, sets the foundation for the rest of the book, introducing students to basic concepts and topics.
- Part Two, The Travel Product, examines the key sectors of the travel industry one by one: Air Travel, Ground Travel, Accommodations, Cruises, and Tours and Packages.
- Part Three, Marketing Travel, provides both an overview of basic principles and a discussion of effective practices for selling travel products.
- Part Four, The Travel Workplace, gives a practical introduction to key aspects of working in the travel and tourism industry. It discusses the essential tasks of communicating and managing money in travel offices and the operation of home-based travel businesses. It also offers guidelines for finding employment and building a successful career.

Travel professionals have experienced changes since the tenth edition of Travel Career Development was published, and this eleventh edition has been thoroughly updated to reflect the current realities and many opportunities facing the industry.

Special Emphases

To address the needs and interests of future travel professionals, *Travel Career Development* offers a real-world focus, bridging the gap between the classroom and the workplace. Several features of the textbook address this goal.

- Each chapter includes On the Spot features, which present scenarios of situations faced by travel professionals; these should help students sharpen their critical thinking and problem-solving skills.
- Close-Up boxes give a personal account of day-to-day work on the job in the travel industry; these invite students, in effect, to step out of the classroom and learn about the challenges and rewards experienced by travel professionals.

- Marketing, selling, and customer service receive attention throughout *Travel Career Development*. Chapter 1 introduces these topics, and they are the subject of Chapters 9–11. In addition, Chapters 2–8 include Close-Up boxes that focus on selling and customer service, and sections of Chapters 4–8 discuss how the travel product discussed in that chapter can be sold successfully.
- Careers in all segments of the travel industry are explored. Close-Up boxes throughout the book describe specific positions in the industry. In addition, Chapters 15 and 16 are devoted to the subjects of finding employment and building a career. These chapters include such key topics as how to prepare for and apply for that first travel job, career advancement, professionalism, ethics, skill-building, and continuing education.

Learning Aids

Any comprehensive introduction to the travel industry must consider a broad range of subjects as well as many technical details. To help students master this content more easily, *Travel Career Development* includes several special elements:

- *Chapter outline and questions.* Each chapter opens with a general outline of the chapter, including the key question(s) addressed by each major section of the chapter.
- *Objectives.* Numbered objectives appear at the beginning of each chapter, giving students a framework and a set of goals to use as they begin their reading.
- *Check-Up.* Each major section of the chapter ends with a brief review, encouraging students to check that they have mastered key points in the section before they move on.
- *Chapter Wrap-Up.* Each chapter ends with a section that provides (1) a summary of the chapter's key points organized by the numbered Objectives listed at the beginning of the chapter; (2) a list of the chapter's key terms; and (3) questions for review and discussion.
- *Images, lists, tables, and figures.* These features throughout the book highlight key points, provide supplementary information, and help illuminate points in the text.

Special Features

To enhance interest and emphasize key themes and skills, the text also includes these special features:

- *Close-Up: On the Job.* This feature provides personal accounts of what particular travel jobs are like day to day. Included are such varied positions as an intern in a travel agency and a group tour leader.
- *Close-Up: Careers.* This feature, which appears in Chapters 1–8, supplements the discussion of careers in Chapters 1, 15, and 16. Each Close-Up: Careers focuses on one segment of the travel industry and gives typical job descriptions and the requirements for selected positions.
- *Close-Up: Selling.* Appearing in Chapters 2–8, this feature focuses on the selling and customer service skills needed when dealing with particular travel products and provides supplementary information and tips.
- *On the Spot.* Realistic cases put students in the position of travel professionals, inviting them to apply the discussion in the text to situations and problems encountered by industry professionals in their daily work. Each On the Spot includes recommendations for dealing with the scenario presented.

Key Topics in the Eleventh Edition

Every chapter in the Eleventh edition has been updated and revised. Updates address some of these important changes in the travel and tourism industry:

- The dramatic trend toward specialization, offering careers in fields such as cruising, family travel, adventure travel, honeymoon/wedding planning, meetings/event planning, women-only travel, luxury travel, LGBT, and many others.
- The recognition of inbound (receptive) travel as an important contribution to a country's economic health and a new awareness of careers in this sector.
- The growing recognition of the importance of marketing in all facets of travel and tourism and how all employees, whatever their positions, must participate in ongoing marketing within their job descriptions.
- Continued changes brought about by world-wide safety concerns and their costs since 9/11 and today's political realities.
- The growth of social media and how successful travel/tourism companies are learning to incorporate it in their marketing plans and budgets.
- The increase in consumers' dependence on experienced, well-trained travel advisors to help them choose the best travel experience.
- The emergence of locally based destination management companies or organizations (DMCs or DMOs) to service inbound travel.
- The changes in U.S. federal regulation mandating proof of identification and U.S. citizenship—specifically, the requirement of enhanced driver's licenses (EDLs) and compliance with the Federal Real ID program—to be presented by travelers at U.S. airport TSA security checkpoints and entrances of secure federal buildings.
- The growing recognition of the need for smaller classes of ships to manage the number of tourists visiting environmentally sensitive areas.
- The changes in aircraft design, baggage policies, classes of service, and amenities to enhance fuel efficiency, safety, and comfort for travelers.
- The increased popularity of ground travel provided by private vehicle owners, including peer-to-peer car sharing services and ridesharing.
- The trend of lodging companies to consolidate through mergers and acquisitions, resulting in large companies creating distinct classes of accommodations and many different brands.
- The emergence of room and home rentals, ranging from a shared room in someone's home to a private luxury estate.
- The increased use of tablets, laptops, and smartphones for home-based and other travel professionals who need a virtual office with them at all times.
- The trend toward agents using technological tools other than the Internet, including video editing software and their computers' web-based software.
- The growth in the use of multiple marketing platforms through social media companies and website providers, along with software in the cloud marketing tools, allowing agents to find new sales leads and book more business.
- The increased use of e-mail as an effective form of marketing due to the ease in content customization based on customer preference and the effective measurement of success through digital "bread crumbs."
- The evolution of contact management software for agents to track customers and prospects in ways never before possible.
- The sharp increase in customers' expectations that travel counselors use digital communication and provide digital customer service.
- The continued growth of home-based agents as a cost-cutting effort by businesses (by saving on salaries, office space, health insurance, etc.), as an attractive alternative to commuting, and as a path to a better work-life balance.

Organization and Content

To provide an engaging and comprehensive introduction to the travel industry, *Travel Career Development* includes 16 chapters, divided into four parts.

In Part One, Chapters 1–3 introduce the key topics covered in the book. Chapter 1 presents an overview of the travel industry, the travel market, and travel careers. Basic geographic terms and concepts as well as issues unique to international travel are introduced in Chapter 2. Chapter 3 gives the background that students will need in order to understand later discussions of how the Internet and other technologies are used throughout the industry.

In Part Two, Chapters 4–8 present the building blocks of travel, from air travel and hotels to cruises and tours. Each chapter in Part Two discusses a different sector of the travel industry, examining how businesses in that sector are organized; the products and services they offer; how to sell them; and how suppliers, sellers, and travelers interact.

In Part Three, Chapters 9–11 examine key concepts and skills needed to market travel. The basic elements of marketing, steps in selling, how to close a sale, the role of outside agents, and the importance of customer service and specialized travel markets are considered. Corporate travel, meeting and incentive travel, and selling to groups and to travelers with special needs receive particular attention.

In Part Four, Chapters 12–16 discuss issues pertaining to the travel workplace. Chapter 12 discusses how to communicate effectively. Chapter 13 focuses on the financial aspects of operating a retail travel agency. Home-based work and basic issues in setting up a business at home are examined in Chapter 14. Chapters 15 and 16 discuss how to find jobs in the travel industry and how to turn these jobs into satisfying careers. Sample résumés, advice regarding interviews and career advancement, and a description of opportunities for continuing education are all included. Also discussed are important issues related to professionalism and ethics in the travel industry.

The Glossary defines the terms that appear in bold italic in the chapters.

The Student Workbook

The *Student Workbook* is an important learning resource specifically designed for use with *Travel Career Development*. Its worksheets and practical exercises emphasize hands-on learning and will help students

- Understand key terms.
- Find information on the Internet.
- Analyze tour brochures.
- Increase their knowledge of geography.
- Compare travel products.
- Develop critical analysis and problem-solving skills.
- Become familiar with resources and practice finding up-to-date information.
- Go beyond the text to apply concepts to current and anticipated future conditions in the travel industry.

The Instructor's Resource Manual

Instructors can use *Travel Career Development*'s resource manual to plan lectures and to reinforce their teaching strategy. Among the tools included are

- Answers to the Review Questions in the text.
- Answers to *Student Workbook* exercises.
- Suggestions for classroom activities.

- Test banks and answer keys.
- Additional information about The Travel Institute's testing and certification programs.

The Travel Institute's Testing Programs

Travel Career Development is the primary resource text for the national TAP® Test developed by The Travel Institute and ASTA. This entry-level proctored and closed-book competency test consists of 100 multiple-choice questions that measure entry-level knowledge of all segments of the travel industry.

Instructors who would like more detailed information about the TAP Test are encouraged to visit www.thetravelinstitute.com or contact The Travel Institute's testing department at 1-800-542-4282.

Welcome

You're cordially invited to join us in one of the most exciting industries in the world. Why is it exciting? For many, many reasons. Those of us who work in this field do so for some of the following reasons:

- We love that it's a global industry and that we meet people from all over the world.
- It's a "people" job—talking and dealing with the public—rarely locked away in our own little box.
- It's an upbeat job as most clients are looking forward to a trip. And when they are traveling for unhappy reasons, it can be gratifying to help them in a difficult situation.
- It's a satisfying job as we often feel we help people realize a dream or a personal goal.
- It's an education—we are constantly learning something new, building our storehouse of knowledge and our career.
- And lastly, we enjoy our own opportunities for personal travel, visiting parts of the world we might never visit if we were in another career.

If those are reasons that appeal to you, then please join us on this career journey.

Prepare Yourself

In many years past, one might walk into a travel agency, an airline office, a hotel or other tourism company and find employment easily without previous training. Today, travel-related companies are more diversified, and reading this book is a good start toward preparing yourself to qualify for some of the many, varied positions the industry offers.

Who Are You?

You may be the re-entry mom who left the workforce to raise her family and now wants to return to work in a new field. You may be a recent college graduate with a good education who has traveled a bit and wants to find an interesting and challenging career path. Perhaps you're a recent retiree with years of business experience and some personal travel and looking for a second career. Maybe you've just completed high school and find the excitement of travel beckoning. Or perhaps you're an international student away from home and planning to return to your country to practice your career. Wherever you are in life, there's probably a place for you in this fascinating and rewarding world-wide industry.

We're an industry of all ages, all nationalities, all walks of life. This study program will help you prepare yourself and analyze your own strengths and weaknesses to see where you may be a "good fit" and where you may need to sharpen personal skills.

Job Requirements

While each industry position may require knowledge of specific subject matter (which you'll be studying here), most segments of the industry look for candidates who possess the following attributes:

- A pleasant, gracious telephone demeanor—with clients, colleagues and suppliers.
- The ability to meet the public, speak with clients in a positive, upbeat and friendly manner, and a willingness to be patient if they are indecisive.
- Knowledge of basic office skills and appropriate industry protocol.
- The ability to read, write, spell, and speak English correctly.
- An understanding of world geography and a bit about the various nations.
- Basic math competency.
- An attention to detail.
- The ability to research—on the Internet, in trade publications, and elsewhere.
- The ability to get along with co-workers and often work as a team.
- The ability to work alone and solve problems thinking on your feet.
- Dependability.
- Time management skills and knowing how to prioritize.
- A willingness to "go the extra mile."
- The ability to multi-task.
- The ability to see the big picture—pull lots of facts and pieces together into a whole.

In certain areas of the industry, one may find other attributes helpful. For example, a tour operator who specializes in Latin America might find you more valuable if you speak some Spanish and have traveled in Spanish-speaking countries. An adventure company offering challenging trips that include hiking and whitewater rafting would be more likely to hire an outdoor person who knows how to pitch a tent rather than one who prefers gambling at a luxury hotel in Las Vegas. With so many specialty travel companies now, applicants can focus their employment search on companies that match their particular lifestyle, interests, and personal qualifications.

Ready, Set, Go

So, we invite you to prepare for a wonderful journey ... the journey through life in an incomparable field.

—Diane Petras, CTIE

Part 1:
Exploring the World of Travel

Chapter 1
Overview of the Travel and Tourism Industry

Chapter 2
Geography and International Travel

Chapter 3
Using Technology

Overview of the Travel and Tourism Industry

CHAPTER 1

If you love the travel/tourism business and work hard at it, success can be yours in the largest industry on the planet. The industry includes businesses as diverse as airlines and theme parks, huge international hotel chains and small neighborhood retail travel agencies, cruise lines and campground operators, outdoor adventure operators, and online booking sites. What are the major segments of this industry, how do they interrelate, and which segment may be the best match for you? What should you know about the travel/tourism market to succeed? What are the career opportunities; what skills are required? In this chapter, a brief industry overview addresses these basic questions.

Our Industry: Past and Present

■ WHAT ARE THE MAJOR PARTS OF THE TRAVEL INDUSTRY?

From Moses' journey to the Promised Land, to Marco Polo's trip to the Far East, to the migrations to the Americas, travelers have shaped history. The first business travelers may have been people who went to another

FIGURE 1.1

Milestones in the History of the U.S. Travel Industry

1829 First U.S. luxury hotel, the Tremont House in Boston, opens.

1869 Railroad across the U.S. is completed, cutting travel time to six days; hotels begin appearing in towns along railroad routes.

1903 Wright brothers take the first flight at Kitty Hawk, North Carolina.

1926 First motel opens, in California.

1927 Pan Am is the first U.S. carrier to operate scheduled international service.

1938 U.S. government establishes agencies to promote safe air travel.

1939 First commercial flight crosses the Atlantic.

1946 Avis opens a rental car counter at an airport.

1958 First U.S. commercial passenger flight is put in service. More travelers fly across the Atlantic than sail by ship.

1970 First wide-bodied jets are put in service.

1971 Amtrak begins service.

1976 First airline computer reservation systems are established.

1978 Airline Deregulation Act introduces a new era of competition among airlines and travel agencies.

1988 Royal Caribbean and Carnival cruise lines christen the first megaships.

1994 Airlines introduce electronic ticketing.

1995 Major airlines initiate caps on travel agency commissions.

2000 Internet emerges as vital force.

2001 September 11 terrorist attack on New York City and Washington, D.C. damages all parts of the industry.

2002 Major U.S. airlines eliminate travel agency base commissions.

2004 Cunard's *Queen Mary 2*—the largest and most expensive passenger vehicle at the time—replaces *QE2* for luxury transatlantic crossings.

2005 The number of independent contractors joining the industry begins to explode, changing the travel landscape dramatically.

2010 Some airlines eliminate meal service and free baggage.

2011–2012 The earthquake/tsunami in Japan and the *Concordia* accident off the coast of Italy deal blows to tourism.

2014–2015 Fatal air accidents in Asia frighten potential travelers.

2020 The Coronavirus pandemic brings global travel to a standstill.

encampment to sell their produce. Other people traveled just to find out what was on the other side of the hill. For business or pleasure, people have sought out every corner of the globe. Only in modern times, however, have masses of ordinary people been able to travel for pleasure. And today, whether travelers from our country are visiting abroad, or those from other countries are coming to visit us, travel is a two-way street, outbound and inbound.

The Difference between Travel and Tourism

Throughout this text, the terms "travel" and "tourism" will be frequent. What do they really mean, and is there a difference between the two? *Merriam-Webster's Dictionary* refers to travel as "to go from place to place, to journey, to move in a given direction or path, to traverse...." On the other hand, tourism is defined as "the practice of traveling for recreation, the guidance or management of tourists, the promotion or encouragement of touring."

In the industry, tourism is usually perceived as the larger of the two terms, implying both inbound (often called receptive services) and outbound visitors. In terms of statistics, tourism brings business into a city, town, hotel, or given business and is seen favorably in a country's balance of payments. On the other hand, outbound travel involves participants purchasing services for going away, such as airline tickets or hotels in another city or country.

In many countries, travel agencies may operate both inbound and outbound services. First-floor windows of a travel agency in London may advertise sun destination trips to Greece or Madeira or Miami, designed to catch the eye of a British client walking by. On the other hand, upstairs in this same agency, the company may be operating a receptive office to handle groups and individuals coming into London. In the United States, most travel offices handle only outbound travel—that is, travel to other spots in the United States, as well as to overseas destinations. Inbound services are usually handled by separate companies called *Destination Management Companies (DMCs)*.

Evolution of the World's Largest Industry

While we don't know exactly who built the first roads or inn, we *do* know that people were traveling on religious journeys, to trade their goods, and to pay their taxes in biblical times. In medieval Europe, wealthy landowners and prosperous merchants made religious pilgrimages. In the 15th and 16th centuries, young English aristocrats spent one to five years on a trip through Europe known as the *Grand Tour*.

By the 19th century, thousands of Europeans and Americans were traveling for pleasure or for self-improvement. The coming of railroads allowed them to expand their horizons. Because rail travelers needed lodging, the railroads also spurred the growth of hotels along the route (see Figure 1.1). Hotel porters helped travelers arrange for train trips and future lodgings and, thus, became the forerunners of the modern travel counselor.

The golden age for train travel extended from the late 1800s through the early 1900s. By the middle of the 20th century, both automobiles and airplanes were competing with the railroads, and the railroads fell into a long decline in the United States. After the end of World War II, pent-up consumer spending led to Americans buying homes, automobiles, and durable goods, like refrigerators and televisions. In the 1950s, as auto travel became extremely popular in the United States, motels (motor hotels) sprang up across the country to meet the needs of long-distance travelers. In the 1960s and 1970s, jets and wide-bodied aircraft reduced the time and cost of air travel, putting it within reach of millions of Americans. Europe and Asia, now well recovered from the damages of World War II, became popular markets for business and vacation travel.

The growth of air travel challenged the shipping lines that had carried passengers across the Atlantic between Europe and North America. To survive, some lines adapted by converting oceangoing vessels into cruise ships.

The new cruise industry illustrated a simple law of business life: To sell its product or service, a business must provide customers with some *value*. Once airlines could transport people across the seas faster than ships, transportation by ship could survive only if the ships provided some value in addition to transportation, and that is what cruises do. Rather than simply transporting people from point to point, cruises offer complete vacations.

Today, consumers depend more heavily than ever on experienced, well-trained travel advisors to help them choose the right cruise experience. For example, Royal Caribbean alone has eight classes of cruise ships, with each designed to deliver a different experience based on which ports it can enter, the variety of dining venues, and onboard entertainment.

In general, the industry's "Contemporary Class" ships are topping out at around 5,500 guests and are more like floating resorts, or "Vacations at Sea," with everything from atriums to wave pools, Broadway-style entertainment, and go-kart racing.

Smaller classes of ships are targeting destinations that require managing the number of tourists visiting what could be environmentally sensitive areas. For example, ships for a company like Lindblad Expeditions accommodate a little more than 100 guests and sail to places like the Galapagos Islands.

Many cruise lines also have started offering personal enrichment classes on board with a lineup of speakers, instructors, and activities targeted to passengers' interests.

Even the most impressive cruise ships would not have succeeded without other changes that encouraged the growth of travel in the 1990s. The number of people with the time and money to travel soared. Global corporations emerged and sent employees on business trips around the world. And travel businesses became more skillful at creating alluring services for travelers.

Myths and Realities

Myth You can't get a job in travel/tourism without experience.

Reality Most employers would like to hire experienced people. (Wouldn't you?) But where were these "experienced" people a year ago? Everyone in the industry started without experience.

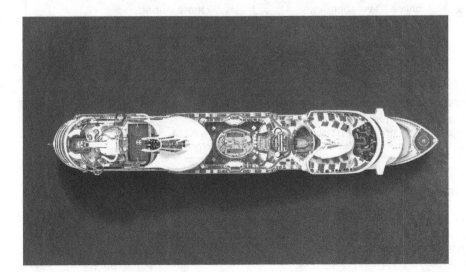

Cruise ships like the *Royal Caribbean Navigator of the Seas* have become floating resorts.

Technology played a major role in this story. In the 1970s and 1980s, computerization allowed airlines to keep track of the ever-growing numbers of flights, accommodations, and passengers. In the 1990s, personal computers and the Internet sparked more change. These tools allowed increasing numbers of travel professionals to work out of their homes. They gave all travel professionals easier ways to obtain information and communicate with one another and with clients.

The Internet also made it easier for consumers to obtain information and book travel arrangements on their own without going to a travel agency. Today, an estimated 80% of Americans book their own trips directly on their home laptops, smartphones, and tablets. However, a growing share of consumers are gradually returning to travel agencies to handle their arrangements once they learn how complex and time-consuming travel planning can be. Today, Internet-savvy travelers expect travel professionals to not only book their travel arrangements to save them time but also to be able to enhance their travel experience with additional knowledge and services. These heightened expectations provide new career opportunities for professionals who can adapt and acquire additional sales and customer service skills to act as true travel counselors.

As the 21st century began, terrorism, wars, and economic downturns discouraged travelers. However, as the century progressed, new destinations opened to travelers, consumers sought out different styles of travel, and the industry fostered growth through innovation.

Today's Travel Industry and Its Segments

Millions of people now have the time, money, motivation, and means to travel, whether for pleasure or business. A complex industry has evolved to promote travel and to serve the needs of travelers. There are many segments of the industry; however, there are three principal categories: suppliers, distributors, and supporting organizations (see Figure 1.2).

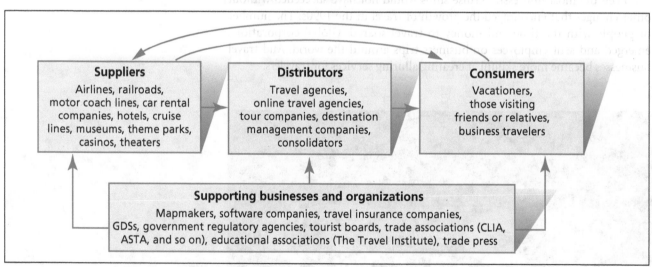

FIGURE 1.2 The Travel/Tourism Industry

This diagram lists some of the key groups involved in the travel/tourism industry. It puts them in categories based on their key relationships to one another and to travelers, but the boundaries among groups often are blurred: Suppliers, for example, can also be distributors, selling directly to the public and bypassing the retail travel agency

- **Suppliers** own the goods and services that travelers use, including transportation, food, shelter, entertainment, and attractions. Airline and railroad companies, car rental companies, hotels, and cruise lines—all are major suppliers. Examples of suppliers include Royal Caribbean and Disney. Restaurants, nightclubs, museums, theaters, and others also may be considered suppliers, though on a smaller scale.
- **Distributors** act as intermediaries between suppliers and travelers, helping travelers obtain the goods and services owned by suppliers and helping suppliers promote their products in the marketplace where travelers can find them. Examples of distributors include tour operators/packagers and travel agencies, such as Classic Vacations and Travel Impressions.
- **Supporting businesses and organizations** either provide travel-related services, such as maps and travel insurance, or aid or regulate the travel industry. For example, the **American Society of Travel Advisors (ASTA)** is a trade association that lobbies governments and promotes agents to the public. **National tourist offices (NTOs)** are government agencies that promote travel to their countries; for example, the German National Tourist Board promotes travel *to* Germany *from* other countries.

These three segments of the travel industry are closely linked, and the divisions among them are not sharp. For example, airlines supply the seats and service for air travel, but they also distribute their products, marketing and selling directly to consumers through their websites and smartphone apps, as do most suppliers. Furthermore, a few large corporations may own companies in each segment of the industry; for example, one corporation may own hotels, rental car companies, travel agencies, and companies that make software for the travel industry. Let's take a quick look at some major participants in the industry and how they intersect. (Later in Chapters 4–8, we will examine each of these segments in detail.)

Travel Agencies.

A **travel agency** sells travel products and services directly to the public. We like to think of them as retail stores with a wide selection of products on the shelves, just like a supermarket. We may sometimes refer to

Agencies sell both leisure and business travel all around the world.

them as full-service agencies. These agencies usually sell products produced by other sectors of the industry, rarely producing their own products. Agencies sell two major types of travel: leisure travel (also referred to as vacation travel) and business travel (also referred to as corporate travel). Some agencies sell both; others may specialize in one or the other. There are also many sub-types. For example, some vacation travel agencies may specialize in adventure travel only. There are some corporate travel agencies that may concentrate on handling meetings and conventions. We'll learn more about specialization in Chapter 11.

CLOSE-UP: ON THE JOB WITH LISA SYNOWIECZ, TRAVEL COUNSELOR

Lisa Synowiecz is a travel counselor at Vacations Unlimited, an agency with four full-time and two part-time employees. Lisa has been with the agency for almost five years.

"What's an average day like for me? Well, that's easy to answer because there is no average day. The following are my notes from one day.

"This morning I attend a breakfast seminar given by a cruise line. Coffee and rolls come from 7:15 to 7:45 a.m.; then a breakfast plate arrives, and the program begins. A video on their newest ships, a few sales techniques, a look at the new brochures, questions and answers, and they are done at 8:30 a.m. Though I don't like getting up at 6:00 a.m. to make this meeting, I'm glad I came. I'm learning more about cruises and trying to decide if it's an area I want to specialize in. I meet a nice agent from another agency, and we exchange cards. I'll give a report on the seminar at our Friday morning 'quick meeting.'

"I get to the agency a little after 9:00. I work on some basic airline reservations for two travelers from our small commercial accounts. One of them goes all over the face of the earth—well, the United States anyway. He gives seminars in college towns, and that makes for tricky connections. If he finishes a talk in Poughkeepsie and has his next one in Peoria, it's Poughkeepsie to LaGuardia to O'Hare to Peoria. He never does the same trip twice. I hadn't even heard of half these places the first time he called.

"At 11:00, I have an appointment with a lady who is planning a cruise for her husband and herself for their anniversary. Often, Muriel handles our cruise clients. She's cruised many times and has gone to Miami for seminars and cruise ship inspections in port. But I've handled this client before and we seem to hit it off. Besides, if I'm going to specialize in cruises, I need to jump in and learn, and I can always get help from Muriel. We pick out an itinerary, a ship, a date, a cabin—the whole works, subject to the OK from her husband (but we both know it's her decision).

"This morning was productive, but the afternoon is not going so well. The Poughkeepsie guy (that isn't where he is going this time) e-mails me asking if I can get him an earlier connection. Back to the drawing board—well, the computer, actually. The phones start ringing, and I am the only one who's not talking to a client already, so I start answering all the calls.

"An hour later and I haven't gotten much done except two messages for Muriel (who is on the phone), one for the manager, and two shoppers who didn't seem impressed with my best selling techniques. I've got to get Mr. P. a hotel and car in each of his destinations.

"It's almost 3:00 p.m. and I haven't looked at my e-mails, except the ones I know are from regular clients. I also need to send messages requesting commissions that a hotel and a car rental company never sent. My uncle calls and wants to go to Las Vegas again. Maybe I'll take some brochures home, see what's on the Internet for Vegas, and work on his trip tonight.

"Chris, our receptionist, brings a client back to me who just walked in. She wants to send her son a ticket to fly from San Diego back to our town but wants to make sure that he can't cash it in because then he won't come. 'Not to worry,' I tell her. After she pays by credit card, she starts telling me her life story, explaining that she can't send a ticket to the correct address or her ex-husband might find it first. Finally, the phone rings, and I extend a 'thank you, come again' to my current client, who leaves.

"It's getting late, but I'm determined to finish all of Mr. P.'s bookings today, answer or file my e-mail messages, and complete at least one of the things that have been sitting on my desk for a few days.

"Well, that's one day. Tomorrow is likely to be completely different. I might be booking Europe or researching China. And this is the slow season. As we start to specialize—one of us will do most of the domestic leisure travel, another will take care of international travel, another one (or two) will sell cruises—things should be easier. In the meantime, I'm coping—and I wouldn't give it up for the world."

The people who do the selling in travel agencies go by several names, including *travel agent or advisor, travel manager, sales representative, travel consultant,* and *travel counselor.* We prefer the title **travel counselor** because those who sell travel to the public should be able to offer professional advice to the client, above and beyond just booking the needed travel arrangements. Some travel counselors work in the physical agency itself (a brick-and-mortar agency). However, more and more agents work from their homes while linked to the agency—whether the agency is in the same town or hundreds of miles away. (See Chapter 14 about entrepreneurs and home-based agents.)

Travel counselors have complicated relationships with the public and with the rest of the travel industry. They act on behalf of travelers, but they also represent suppliers to the public. To a great extent, suppliers control who may sell their products and how they are sold. For example, some travel products are sold through a **conference system,** which is an arrangement where an organization of suppliers appoints travel agencies to sell their products. The Airlines Reporting Corporation (ARC) is an example of a conference. Travel agencies must meet certain standards (discussed in later chapters) in order to receive an appointment from conferences and thus be authorized to sell their products.

Travel counselors earn their income from both the traveling public and suppliers. Most counselors charge clients directly for their services through fees or markups. They also earn income when suppliers pay a **commission**—a fee or percentage of the sale—for selling their products to the public. Some years ago, airlines generally paid retail agencies an automatic commission for selling their product. That is no longer true today. Many travel agencies or individual counselors must negotiate the right to receive a commission from an airline or belong to a consortium of agencies that negotiates commissions on behalf of their members. In fact, many agencies no longer issue air tickets; they buy them on behalf of their clients directly from the airline or through an airline consolidator (more about this in Chapter 4).

In addition, travel agencies earn income from suppliers by establishing **preferred supplier relationships,** which are commitments from the travel agency to certain suppliers to maximize their use of those suppliers. For example, an agency might consolidate all client tours to England under one operator. In turn, the suppliers may offer the agencies higher commissions and/or **overrides,** which are an extra payment for a large volume of sales, as well as other benefits, such as training programs and even familiarization trips (fam trips) for the agency's sales staff. The majority of travel agencies have lists of preferred suppliers that they want their counselors to use with clients, whenever possible, if the travel product is suitable for the particular client. In this way, the agency maximizes its profit and builds its relationship with the supplier, often benefiting the client with added value and special attention.

What do travel agencies offer in return for these payments by travelers and suppliers? Airlines and railroads provide transportation; hotels provide lodging. What is the value provided by travel agencies? What do they add to the travel product that makes it worthwhile for the supplier or the traveler to pay them?

Skilled travel counselors save time for travelers by understanding their needs, doing all the research and matching the best supplier products and services to their clients. They can also offer clients the advantages of a personal relationship. Travel counselors who add value to the travel product are those who know what to book, when to do so, and what other possibilities exist.

They know, for example, how to find discounts and special perks; they can help a couple choose the ideal hotel for their honeymoon; they can curate a group trip based on hobbies and interests, such as exploring ruins in Peru or

Myths and Realities

Myth A career in travel means a life at low pay.

Reality Hundreds of thousands of people make a career in the travel/tourism industry and enjoy excellent financial rewards as they become more experienced. But the pay for most entry-level positions is low. Of course, pay scales differ in different parts of the industry. Experienced people see their salaries rise, some slowly and some more rapidly, depending on their willingness and ability to find or create opportunities for advancement. Today, most travel counselors who make high earnings work on a base salary plus commission or may work totally on commission and control their own clientele, rather than serving the agency's clientele.

taking cooking lessons in Italy. They also keep up to date on trending destinations, a company's latest product offering, and the most recent visa regulations or airline baggage rules. Experienced counselors know which products are most appropriate for certain ages, budgets, and lifestyles, as well as a supplier company's reputation in the industry. And anyone can mount a convincing website for a new travel company, so an experienced counselor can provide an important service of investigating new companies before a client makes a purchase.

Online Travel Agencies. Most travel agencies have their own websites, but the term *online travel agency (OTA)* refers to a travel agency that exists *only* online (e.g., Travelocity and Expedia). OTAs typically offer everything from airline rickets to hotel rooms and villa rentals, car rentals, and cruises.

Airlines. The world's major airlines and hundreds of regional carriers, as well as airports, air traffic controllers, and federal aviation agencies, are all part of the complicated air travel industry. Nearly every facet of the travel industry interacts with air travel. Car rental sales rely on travelers who fly to destinations and then need a private car. Cruise passengers fly to their embarkation ports. Air passengers spend tens of billions of dollars at hotels when they arrive at their destinations. Everyone in the travel industry should be knowledgeable about air travel whether or not they actually book air reservations for clients.

Until recently, airline tickets accounted for most of the income earned by U.S. travel agencies. The airlines paid travel agencies commissions for tickets sold. In the late 1990s, travel agencies handled more than 80 percent of domestic air travel bookings and 85 percent of international air sales. Seeking to increase profitability, airlines intensified their efforts to sell seats directly to consumers, bypassing travel agencies, and, in 1995, began cutting the commissions paid to agencies. Most airlines no longer automatically pay commissions to agencies for selling air tickets, which is why most agencies now charge a service fee for air reservations. Some governments underwrite their national air carriers financially, whereas airlines must stand on their own in the United States.

During the 1990s and early 2000s, the airline industry went through a significant period of consolidation, with major carriers merging to the point where, today, there are only three classic "mainline" carriers with the lion's share of U.S. air passengers.

Some startup airlines—including carriers like Southwest Airlines and JetBlue—have survived by carving out niches based on lower cost structures, affordable fares, and fiercely loyal customers. More recently, ultra-low-cost carriers—like Allegiant, Frontier, and Spirit—offer low base fares but charge for nearly any other traditional service (including advance seat assignments, checked bags, and inflight food and beverage). This has forced the mainline carriers to restructure their pricing and offer similar base fares, stripped of any additional services.

Many of these low-cost carriers do not make their seat inventory and fares readily available to travel agents through networks like the GDS.

Rail Travel. As air and automobile travel soared after World War II, U.S. rail travel declined. In fact, U.S. passenger train service was saved from extinction in 1970 only when the government set up and subsidized Amtrak as a corporation to operate passenger rail service between U.S. cities. In many other countries, however, railroads remain a crucial means of travel, including the government-financed high-speed rail systems *TGV* in France and Japan's *Bullet Train*.

U.S. travel agencies sell tickets and passes for European rail travel as well as group tours and independent packages linked with rail travel. But for years, selling Amtrak tickets to the U.S. domestic market was a money-losing proposition for travel agencies, and many refused to do so. Today, many agencies sell Amtrak tickets for travel along the Boston–New York–Washington corridor, which is important to business travelers, as well as for Amtrak tours and packages. Many agencies market and sell Amtrak packaged vacations. They must determine whether the commission or goodwill earned is worth the time and effort involved. If not, they may charge a fee for helping a client plan a schedule, book the reservations and handle the tickets.

On the other hand, special train journeys are making a comeback. Entrepreneurs are refitting and designing elegant railroad cars and attaching them to various rail lines to provide upscale rail journeys that can be sold as part of a trip or as a trip unto itself. Grandparents are proudly taking their grandchildren on train rides, remembering the great days of U.S. trains with names like the *California Zephyr* or the *City of New Orleans*. American travelers are now intrigued with trips on famous trains, such as the *Orient Express*, *Blue Train*, and *Glacier Express*. And some innovative companies are coupling rail travel with a cruise, advertising "No Air Travel Necessary" to a public wary of flying and tired of standing in long airport security lines.

The *Glacier Express* travels from Zermatt, Switzerland, to Davos or St. Moritz through 291 bridges and 91 tunnels.

Other Ground Transportation. Most trips in the United States are by car, and more than a million rented cars, vans, and other vehicles are on the road each day, a large percentage booked by travel agencies. Most car rentals occur at airports.

Travel agencies also handle car rentals for overseas vacations and business travel and receive commissions from well-known auto rental companies like Hertz, Avis, Auto-Europe, and many more. They also make arrangements for limousine service, motor coaches, and private cars with a driver/guide. Overall, only a small percentage of U.S. motor coach tickets are sold through travel agencies, whereas motor coaches and vans are a key component of many group tours.

Accommodations. Every year, Americans spend more than $100 billion on hotel stays. The industry that supplies this service is known as the ***hospitality industry,*** sometimes referred to as the lodging industry. It is a worldwide business and is the most people-intensive part of the travel/tourism industry, said to employ more than two million people in the United States alone. Many of these people have mastered such specialized fields as managing room inventories, food service, meeting/convention handling, event handling, and security.

Like the airline industry, lodging companies recently have undergone significant consolidation through mergers and acquisitions. This has meant that a company, such as Marriott International, can have five distinct classes of lodging and 30 different brands. With more negotiating leverage and frequent guest programs representing millions of members, the largest chains have been exercising their muscle to try to reduce the commissions they pay to OTAs and traditional agents. Also, all of them recently have engaged in prominent marketing campaigns to persuade consumers to book directly with the chains through their websites, phone apps, and call centers.

While the lodging industry has consolidated like the airline industry has, it also has experienced the emergence of a group of independent startup chains with distinct brands, often focusing on properties that immerse the consumer in local neighborhoods.

As a result of the consolidation and new chains, hotels can vary greatly in the experience a guest receives. Because the choice of lodging is often critical to the success of a trip, once again, the professional travel counselor's expertise has become very valuable in selecting accommodations. Nevertheless, travelers make more than half of the bookings for these rooms directly on their own. This segment includes other accommodation types, such as villas in Tuscany, ski lodges in the Rockies or Alps, campgrounds in national parks, beach resorts, home/room rentals (e.g., Airbnb), and bed & breakfasts, known as B&Bs.

Cruise Lines. From Antarctica to Alaska, Maine to Tahiti, and just about everywhere in between, travelers can find a cruise. The cruise business probably ranked as the most successful part of the travel industry in the last years of the 20th century and into the 21st. Cruise lines built the market for their product as they launched new and bigger ships. Today, large cruise ships are like small cities. Other cruising options include smaller, intimate ships for river and coastal cruising.

Some cruise lines have set up their own websites and their own travel agencies, so-called "cruise stores," to fill their ships. Still, most cruise cabins, particularly the more upscale ones, are purchased through travel agencies. And there are many agencies that only handle cruises or have departments devoted to selling cruises with specialists who have personally traveled on many of the great cruise lines of the world and can bring their personal experience to the sale.

Tours/Packages. Tour companies are in the business of packaging various aspects of a trip, such as transportation, accommodations, and attractions. The packages they create come in all lengths and types. On some, participants travel together as a group and are escorted by an expert tour leader. On others, travelers are on their own and never see anyone connected with the tour operator. Some tours include air and ground transportation, lodging, food, and attractions, such as theme parks or museums; others include only air transportation, a hotel, and a rental car. There are tours arranged around special events, such as the Olympics, and tours devoted to special interests, such as golf, bird watching, classical music, or archaeology. However, one thing all tours and packages have in common is that they are sold as a unit and prepaid at a set package price. The traveler does not pay each hotel or each service as the trip progresses. Many tours do not actually tour; they go to one place and stay there, taking local side trips from their headquarters hotel.

Because there are so many tours and packages to choose from and so many tour companies, consumers often need help deciding which tour or package is best for their particular interest, needs, and budget. A large percentage of tours and packages are sold through retail travel agencies. Some tour companies, however, sell directly to the public, and many retail travel agencies create their own tours, even selling them through other travel agencies—in effect, becoming tour operators themselves.

If the client is willing to commit to the dates, hotels, and other features in the package, tours and packages are usually considered a better deal financially than buying the component parts separately. Extremely independent clients may find buying a package is too constraining for their independent natures. For these clients, many innovative travel agents will sell a basic package augmented with additional services, such as theater tickets, side trips, and custom activities.

Destination Marketing. As travel has grown, governments, as well as businesses, have found it lucrative to encourage tourism.

Countries, regions, states, cities, and even groups within cities have created organizations to promote tourism to their area. National tourist offices, local tourist bureaus, and city convention centers, for example, publish marketing materials, host websites, participate in industry trade shows and consumer travel expos, and help groups organize events to the destination. For example, international travel into the United States from abroad has consistently been one of the country's leading imports and helps the country's balance of payments. It is linked heavily to the exchange rate between the U.S. dollar and the international currency involved.

✔ CHECK-UP

The modern travel industry includes
✔ Suppliers, which develop, own, and sell their travel products.
✔ Distributors, which act as intermediaries between the traveling public and suppliers.
✔ Businesses and other organizations that provide travel-related services, support businesses in the travel industry, or regulate that industry.

Retail travel agencies earn their income from
✔ Commissions and overrides paid by suppliers.
✔ Fees, service charges, or markups paid by travelers.

Major suppliers include
✔ Tour operators (packagers).
✔ Airlines.
✔ Rail lines.
✔ Car rental companies.
✔ Hotels and other accommodations.
✔ Cruise lines.

The Travel Market: Basic Concepts

■ HOW DO TRAVEL BUSINESSES ATTRACT TRAVELERS?

■ WHAT ARE SOME KEY DIVISIONS WITHIN THE TRAVEL MARKET?

If you wait for customers to come to you, a competitor is likely to find them first. A successful travel business works to bring in the clients who are inclined to purchase travel, become loyal repeat customers, and refer their friends and family. Meeting these goals requires skill in marketing, selling, and customer service, as well as expert knowledge of the buyers and products.

Marketing Fundamentals

Marketing is a series of decisions and actions taken by a seller to create a match between consumers' preferences and a product or service. The match is not likely to happen by chance; businesses research and analyze the marketplace in order to develop a marketing plan.

One key element of a marketing plan is the definition of the **target market**—the consumers that the business will try to reach. Some companies try to serve the needs of the greatest possible number of clients; others try to appeal to particular *market segments* or **niches**, clusters of individuals who have similar wants and needs. *Market segmentation* is the process of identifying these clusters.

There are many ways of segmenting the market, including:

■ *Demographic segmentation* categorizes people according to characteristics, such as age, sex, geography, or marital status. For example, senior citizens might form one market segment and singles another.

■ *Price segmentation* divides a population into segments based on how much people are able and willing to pay for a product.

■ *Psychographic segmentation* groups people with similar attitudes, interests, and beliefs into distinct target markets. White-water rafters and art lovers, for example, might each form a market segment.

■ *Usage segmentation* divides people according to the purpose for which they would buy a product. For example, some travelers are taking a trip for business; some for a vacation, others, for education.

Young singles can be considered a demographic segment.

Besides defining a target market, a marketing plan describes basic decisions about how a business will be structured. What will be sold and where? How will it be promoted and distributed? What price will be charged?

Chapter 9 discusses the elements of marketing plans. Suppose you are offering a new travel product. Should you promote it on the basis of price or convenience or service? Products are not equally suitable to each of these approaches. To the extent that people view a product as a *commodity*—an item that varies little—they are likely to buy it wherever it is most convenient or least expensive, unless they are very loyal to a particular seller. Airline seats, for example, are usually considered a commodity; cruises are not.

Essentials of Selling

Marketing skills bring people to your doorstep or website. *Selling* is an aspect of marketing to encourage a customer to purchase your product and/or service. Making a sale requires the ability to meet three goals:

- *Identify the customer's needs.* For example, suppose John Smith wants to travel from Charleston to Chicago. Is he looking for the quickest way to get to a business meeting or the most scenic route to a tourist attraction? Is luxury or economy important to him? How long will he stay?
- *Identify the products or services that will meet those needs.* What types of transportation, accommodations, or other services are most likely to meet and exceed the client's needs? Qualifying the client requires expert knowledge, solid questioning skills, and active listening.
- *Translate the features of products and services into benefits for the customer.* A *feature* is an inherent characteristic of a product or a service; a *benefit* is the positive result a client experiences from that product or service. For example, being located just outside an industrial park may be a feature of one hotel. For travelers interested in a city's nightlife, this feature might bring no benefit at all, but for many business travelers, this location brings the benefit of convenience. To sell the hotel to a business traveler, you would describe the convenience it offers.

Making a sale is more art than science, but people can and do learn how to sell. When selling is conducted through person-to-person contact—a process called *personal selling*—it helps to think of the sale in terms of eight steps, which are detailed in Chapters 10 and 11.

Understanding Travelers and the Travel Product

To sell a product, you must identify clients' needs. To do that, the most basic question to answer is why they are traveling. Is it because they choose to travel or because their work requires traveling? In other words, is the trip *nondiscretionary* or *discretionary*? Those are the two very broad types of travel.

Business (Nondiscretionary) Travel. Nondiscretionary travel is usually *business travel,* also called *corporate travel.* This category includes all trips that are purchased by individuals, companies, and other organizations principally for the purpose of conducting business. In selling business travel, you must meet the needs of the business paying for the travel, the person who is doing the traveling, and the person arranging the trip (often an administrative assistant). Two distinct types of business trips include meeting travel and incentive travel. ***Meeting travel*** consists of trips to organized gatherings, such as conventions. ***Incentive travel*** is offered by an organization as a reward, often for meeting goals, such as sales quotas.

Meeting and incentive travel involve a host of special needs. Arranging a meeting, for example, requires selecting a site and planning transportation to, from, and around the site, as well as activities at the site, schedules, food and beverage, registering participants, and numerous other details. Incentive travel involves not only the details of the trip itself but also the goals of the incentive program and the rules for determining and announcing the winners. These types of travel are discussed in Chapter 11.

Discretionary Travel. More than three-fourths of the trips taken by Americans are discretionary. These trips fall into two broad categories:
- ***VFR travel,*** which is travel to visit friends or relatives.
- ***Leisure travel,*** which is travel for pleasure or vacation travel. Some leisure travel can be classified as ***special-interest travel,*** which consists of trips devoted to a particular activity or interest, such as shopping, golf, or art.

Analyzing Leisure Travelers. Unlike business travelers and those on VFR trips, leisure travelers choose where they travel. Can you predict whether a person would enjoy Tonga more than Miami Beach for a vacation? Stanley Plog, a travel researcher, developed one influential way of analyzing why people choose particular destinations (see Figure 1.3).

Plog suggests that psychological differences predict where people can be to visit exotic places or familiar ones. According to Plog, all travelers can be placed on a spectrum, with venturers at one end and dependables at the other.

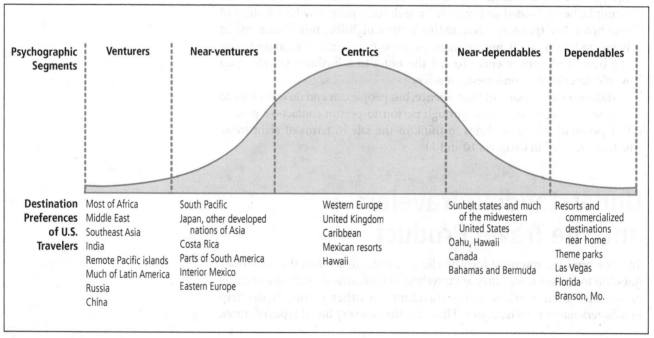

FIGURE 1.3 American Travelers: A Psychographic Analysis

Stanley Plog proposes that psychological characteristics predict the types of destinations that leisure travelers are likely to prefer. He places travelers on the spectrum of psychological types shown here. Examples of some preferred destinations by traveler type are listed here.

Venturers center their lives on varied interests. They are outgoing, confident, curious, and eager to be among the first to discover a new vacation spot. In contrast, *dependables* focus on everyday problems and value familiarity and comfort. They like predictability and prefer places that offer reassuring signs of home.

Plog's analysis suggests that most international travelers are likely to be venturers and near-venturers. Dependables take almost no international trips.

Of course, both the popularity of a destination and the needs of travelers change throughout the year. For the tourism industry, there are three basic seasons: *high season*, when rates and traffic peak; *low season*, when rates and traffic are at their lowest; and *shoulder season*, a period between high and low seasons. In Europe, for example, the high season is generally June, July and August, which is their summer. However, these same months are winter (low season) in Argentina, where the seasons are reversed, and the beaches are empty as locals and vacationers head for ski resorts.

✔ CHECK-UP

Market segmentation
- ✔ Identifies clusters of individuals who can form target markets.
- ✔ May be based on characteristics, such as demographics, price, psychographics, or usage.

Success in selling requires the ability to
- ✔ Identify the customer's needs.

- ✔ Identify the products or services that will meet those needs.
- ✔ Translate the features of products or services into benefits.

The main types of travel are
- ✔ Business or corporate travel, which includes meeting/convention travel and incentive travel.
- ✔ VFR travel.
- ✔ Leisure travel, which includes special-interest travel.

Travel Careers: Paths to Success

■ WHAT SKILLS ARE NEEDED FOR WORKING IN TODAY'S TRAVEL/TOURISM INDUSTRY?

■ WHAT IS YOUR REALITY?

Most positions in this industry are challenging, exciting, and satisfying. They also tend to be exhausting, stressful, and intense. Travel careers are for people who like dealing with others, have a passion for travel, and for helping others to travel as well. And they are for people who enjoy hard work. Just ask the flight attendant who wakes up at 4:30 a.m., drives to the airport, "crews" six takeoffs and landings in turbulent weather, serves hundreds of drinks and snacks by 6:00 p.m., and still has a smile for the departing passengers on her last flight.

Many paths are available to a person who wants to have a career in the travel industry. A travel worker may be the CEO of a major company or may be the baggage handler at the airport; he or she may be self-employed or work for a worldwide corporation. Careers in computer programming, website design, accounting, law, marketing, and other fields may also be pursued in travel-related companies. Table 1.1 lists some of the many employment opportunities that make up this huge industry.

TABLE 1.1 Careers in Travel: A Sampling

Industry	Positions	Industry	Positions	Industry	Positions
Travel agencies/ travel counselors	Agency manager Corporate travel counselor Cruise specialist Group agent Leisure travel counselor Meeting planner Outside sales agent Webmaster	Car rental companies	City manager District sales manager Rental agent Reservationist Sales manager Station manager	Cruise lines	Accountant Account executive Cabin steward Human resources Marketing Public relations Purser Reservationist Sales representative Social director
Airlines	Accountant Account executive Baggage handler Flight attendant Human resources Marketing Pilot Reservationist Ticket agent	Rail and bus companies	Area sales manager Customer service agent Marketing manager Onboard attendant Reservationist Station manager	Tour companies	District sales manager Group supervisor Product coordinator Quality assurance manager Reservationist Sales director Sales representative Step-on guide Tour guide or director Tour planner Webmaster
Travel trade and tourism organizations	Convention and visitors' bureau representative Convention sales manager Group travel coordinator Marketing director Travel photographer Travel writer	Hotels	Catering manager Concierge Convention sales director Executive housekeeper Food and beverage manager Front desk clerk Front office manager Group services manager Human resources Reservationist Sales representative		

Starting Out

It is not too soon to begin thinking about your own career path. On the one hand, you may have a fixed idea as to what segment of the industry you'd like to work in. On the other hand, you may not have any idea as to where you'd fit in best. Throughout this course, you will learn about new possibilities and may change your mind several times. We suggest you look at Table 1.1 for the broad view of some of the diverse career possibilities throughout the industry's many sectors.

You may wish to think through some basic life decisions around these possibilities. Do you live in an area where all these possibilities exist? Or are you willing to relocate? For example, the majority of employment opportunities with cruise lines are in Florida where most cruise companies have their headquarters. If you can't relocate to Florida, you might consider becoming a cruise specialist within a retail travel agency in your town. Can you work full-time or only part-time? If so, you might prefer to become a tour guide and work as an independent contractor only at certain times. Can you be away from home to take advantage of some of the many familiarization trip possibilities to help you enhance your learning? Or would it be difficult to leave home and family for a five-day familiarization trip to Paris?

In addition, you should analyze your strengths and weaknesses. Do you have the following attributes, or can you work on developing them in preparation for your new career?

- *Interpersonal relationships.* Successful travel professionals must be empathetic. In other words, you must be able to understand your clients' needs and to communicate that understanding. In addition, enthusiasm, patience, and a positive outlook will smooth your way through tough situations.
- *Language.* The ability to speak and write clearly with correct spelling, grammar, and pronunciation is very important. Knowledge of a second language may be a requirement for a few positions (particularly in receptive tourism or companies that deal in the ethnic market) but is not mandatory for most others.
- *Math.* Computers handle much of the basic math requirements today. Nevertheless, many positions still require enough fluency with basic math to understand and, in some cases, to calculate fares, rates, and commissions; to convert currencies and measurement units; and to handle money. In addition, it's important to understand financial terms, including net, gross, and markup.
- *Technology.* Most businesses use technology extensively; many promote, sell, and work with clients through the Internet and e-mail, and many have their own websites.
- *Ability to learn.* In any position in any company, there will be routines and procedures to learn, as well as changing facts and new skills to master. Flexibility will be expected of employees because the industry changes daily. The ability to research will prove important as well.

All of these are considerations. You may find that once you begin your career, you will move from one sector of the industry to another as your life changes. Many industry employees have grown in the process. But at the outset, your primary concern is to find entry-level employment and to know what skills you need to bring to the position.

You might also ask yourself if you are willing to intern or spend the first year of your new career in an entry-level position, such as receptionist or clerk. Many travel counselors begin their careers by answering phones, greeting clients, delivering travel documents, and doing research for others in the office, for example. Tour operators need beginners to produce hotel rooming lists, help prepare the tour leader for departure, or handle computer records. Remember, beginners in all professions need experience; even top graduates of the best medical schools serve as interns. The fact that you may already have traveled to 79 countries and are an expert on the wines of France may eventually be a boon to your employer, but what management needs first may be something much more mundane, such as greeting the public graciously.

Building a Career

If you begin your career in an entry-level position, how do you advance to a position with more responsibility? To win trust and advance in your career, professionalism is essential. **Professionals** are people who train themselves to become experts in a field, use that expertise to benefit clients, and do so in an ethical manner.

Courses like this one are a first step toward becoming a professional, providing the basics for developing expertise. By itself, however, a basic education will not allow you to meet professional standards. Personal travel will help, but no one can go everywhere. Moreover, the travel/tourism industry changes quickly, with new destinations, new technology, new tastes and trends, new competition, and new selling techniques. One year,

CLOSE-UP: CAREERS WITH TRAVEL AGENCIES

Each travel agency is a business with sales and marketing functions and administrative tasks to be performed. In small agencies, one person may perform all these tasks, acting as owner/manager as well as travel counselor. The larger the agency is, the greater the specialization.

Opportunities and jobs vary tremendously. Generally, the smallest agencies and the largest corporations offer the best opportunities for those just starting their careers. Many people work for travel agencies as independent contractors; Chapter 14 is devoted to home-based agents.

■ **Position** Leisure travel counselor

Description This job entails an amazing array of activities: In the span of an hour, the leisure travel counselor may plan an African safari, book an airline ticket to Boston, and answer an e-mail from a client wondering about spring in Heidelberg. The counselor helps clients select travel arrangements, after researching destinations and travel products; helps clients obtain the best possible value for their travel dollar; and makes bookings.

Qualifications A travel counselor must have good selling skills and know about destinations and travel products. The job also requires patience, close attention to detail, and an ability to listen and enjoy dealing with people.

■ **Position** Corporate travel counselor

Description This counselor books travel services for business travelers. Typically, the corporate travel counselor does not have face-to-face contact with the traveler and may often communicate through an assistant. The counselor provides information about fares and availability, makes and changes reservations, and handles many bookings, at a fast pace, throughout the day. Service, rather than advice, is key. The counselor sometimes works on-site at the client company.

Qualifications This very fast-paced job requires a lot of stamina, skill at communicating on the telephone, the ability to handle details and enter data with speed and accuracy, and professionalism. Agencies and corporate travel departments often require experience with a computer reservations system, called a GDS. A beginner with good computer skills may be able to become a productive corporate travel counselor in a short time.

■ **Position** Outside sales agent

Description The job of an outside sales agent is to bring new clients to the agency. The person goes into the community to promote and sell travel services, perhaps giving presentations to clubs, hosting cruise nights, and offering travel seminars. Some outside agents handle all aspects of the transactions for their clients; others just make the sale while the agency handles travel details. Most outside agents work on a commission basis; many are independent contractors, not employees.

Qualifications Excellent communication and interpersonal skills, including the ability to conduct public presentations, as well as creativity and resourcefulness, are required for this job. The person must be able to find leads and do promotions and follow through on projects. An ability to manage a database is desirable.

■ **Position** Webmaster

Description This professional is responsible for building and maintaining a company's website. The job involves not only the creation of web pages but also constant efforts to improve the site and streamline the process of entering and exchanging data. The webmaster may also provide software support, handle hardware updates, and provide general technical assistance.

Qualifications This position requires a solid background in software and software languages as well as web design and management. The webmaster should be able to work with databases, spreadsheets, and data migration. An understanding of relevant hardware is an asset.

■ **Other positions** Cruise (or destination) specialist; database administrator; group sales agent; meeting planner; sales administrator/coordinator.

knowledge about ancient sites in Mexico may be in demand; the next year, you may need expertise in finding accommodations for the Olympics. Even after years in the industry, travel professionals are likely to encounter questions they cannot answer or problems they do not know how to solve at first. Is it safe, for example, for a client to travel to Belize? Is transportation available from the airport in Belize City to the archaeological site of Caracol?

Of course, travel professionals cannot know everything, but they can and should know where to look for the answers. Chapter 16 discusses opportunities for continuing education and the additional skills that are important for travel professionals. The Travel Institute (publishers of this book) offers continuing education and the well-recognized CTA®, CTC®, and CTIE® certifications.

Is transportation available from the airport in Belize City to the archaeological site of Caracol?

The many changes in the travel industry during the 1990s and the first part of the 21st century highlighted the importance of continuing education and the ability to adapt. Less than three decades ago, for example, almost no one except scientists and academics used the Internet. Successful travel professionals met the challenge of building a new travel world in which websites, e-mail, and social media are everyday tools. They now are looking to technologies, such as artificial intelligence, for the next generation of marketing, sales, and customer service.

Once you are employed, you will be expected to continue on the learning curve, and there are many opportunities to help you do so. Some suppliers offer seminars or webinars as they launch each year's new products.

Finally, membership in professional organizations often means access to special training and insider knowledge. Networking opportunities abound where you can exchange ideas with your peers. Webinar invitations come in almost daily—some excellent, some not so. In short, the industry is always making continuing education opportunities available; it's only up to you to find the time, energy, and dedication to become involved.

In short, to be successful in the travel industry, you need to learn all that you can about your business as soon as you can, learn while on the job, and then prepare to learn more as the industry and the world change.

CHAPTER WRAP-UP

CHAPTER HIGHLIGHTS

Those who work in the travel/tourism industry are helping people meet a very important need. In this chapter, we have given an overview of the industry and the role of its true professionals. Here is a review of the objectives with which we began the chapter.

1. **Describe the major segments of the travel industry and how they are related.** The industry can be divided into suppliers, distributors, and supporting organizations. The major suppliers are the airlines, rail companies, cruise lines, car rental companies, and lodging companies. Major distributors are travel agencies and tour companies. Supporting organizations include trade associations, such as the American Society of Travel Advisors (ASTA) as well as national tourist offices (NTOs) and businesses and organizations that sell travel-related products or regulate the industry.

All parts of the industry are interdependent, and the line between suppliers and distributors is often blurred. Many suppliers, for example, also distribute their products to the public. As distributors, most travel agencies earn their income from both travelers and suppliers. Most agencies charge travelers through fees or markups. They earn commissions from some suppliers, and many agencies establish preferred supplier relationships and earn overrides as a result.

2. **Outline basic techniques for marketing and selling travel.** As the travel industry has become more competitive, marketing, selling, and service have become ever more important to success. Like other businesses, travel businesses develop marketing plans for their products. These plans define a target market, often through market segmentation. Ways of segmenting the market include demographic segmentation, price segmentation, psychographic segmentation, and usage segmentation.

   To ensure that interested consumers become actual buyers, travel professionals need skill in selling techniques, such as qualifying clients, translating features into benefits, and closing the sale. And they need knowledge of their products and customers in order to give high-quality service.

3. **Describe key characteristics that shape a traveler's needs.** Psychographics and demographics are important, but usage provides the key division in the travel market. That is, some travel is nondiscretionary and is for the purpose of business; other travel is discretionary. Different needs are associated with each type of travel. Business or corporate travel includes meeting travel and incentive travel. Discretionary travel includes VFR travel and leisure travel. Psychological characteristics—such as whether people can be characterized as venturers or dependables—shape whether leisure travelers prefer exotic or popular destinations.

4. **Describe the skills needed for most positions in the travel industry.** People in almost all entry-level positions need skills in interpersonal relationships and in language. In addition, they must be able to handle basic math and to use standard office technology. Finally, they require skill in learning itself so that they can master the routines of specific positions and adapt to changes. To win greater responsibility and advance in a travel career, professionalism is required. One component of professionalism is a commitment to continuing education.

KEY TERMS

A list of key terms introduced in this chapter follows. If you do not recall the meaning of these terms, see the Glossary.

American Society of Travel Advisors (ASTA)	low season
	marketing
benefit	market segmentation
business travel	meeting travel
commission	national tourist office (NTO)
commodity	online travel agency (OTA)
conference system	override
corporate travel	personal selling
demographic segmentation	preferred supplier relationship
dependables	price segmentation
destination management company (DMC)	professional
	psychographic segmentation
distributor	selling
familiarization trip	shoulder season
feature	special-interest travel
high season	supplier
hospitality industry	supporting businesses and organizations
incentive travel	target market
leisure travel	travel agency

travel counselor
usage segmentation

VFR travel
venturers

REVIEW QUESTIONS

1. Name at least 10 major developments in the history of the U.S. travel/tourism industry.

2. How would you describe the role of technology in the past and in the future of the travel/tourism industry?

3. What value can a travel counselor add to a travel product?

4. Applying usage segmentation, identify several target markets for travel, and suggest what travel products might be appropriate for them.

5. Would you describe yourself as a venturer or a dependable? Why? How would these psychological characteristics affect your needs as a traveler?

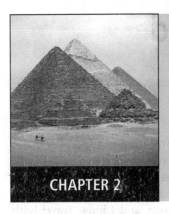

Geography and International Travel

CHAPTER 2

OBJECTIVES

After completing this chapter, you should be able to

1. Identify the characteristics that shape the appeal of destinations, ensuring that people want to visit.

2. Explain how to locate a destination and how to calculate time differences.

3. Outline the major factors that shape the climate of a destination.

4. Describe at least five key sources of information about destinations.

5. Outline the requirements that governments place on international travelers visiting their countries.

6. Identify reliable sources of information about possible dangers abroad and common problems encountered by international travelers.

7. Suggest four methods of handling currency exchange for an international trip.

OUTLINE

LOCATIONS AND DESTINATIONS
- What makes a location a popular destination?

LOCATIONAL AND PHYSICAL GEOGRAPHY
- How do you describe the location of a destination and calculate time differences?
- What determines a destination's climate?

LEARNING ABOUT DESTINATIONS
- What are good sources of information about destinations?

CROSSING BORDERS
- What rules and regulations govern international travelers?

HEALTH AND SAFETY ABROAD
- What are reliable sources of information about dangers when traveling abroad, and what health precautions should travelers take?

DEALING WITH MONEY AND OTHER DIFFERENCES
- How are foreign currencies and measurements converted, and what other everyday differences should travelers be ready to handle?

If a client wants to find a place where she can go horseback riding during the day and attend a top-notch opera at night, where would you send her? If a colleague says that a trip from the pyramids of Giza to the pyramids of Teotihuacán is just an easy day's journey, does he know what he's talking about? Are you likely to get a chance to practice your Spanish in São Paulo? Can someone who likes gambling at casinos find a destination that also provides opportunities for time at the beach and water sports?

These questions touch on aspects of *destination geography,* the study of those characteristics of locations that influence travel. This knowledge is essential to help understand sites and destinations that would appeal to different travelers. It also helps to understand and to narrow down choices for clients as they describe the type of art tour, extreme adventure experience, or city environment that they may want. In this chapter, we consider some basic terms and concepts necessary for learning destination geography. We also consider other information that travel professionals should master, such as passport and visa requirements, customs regulations, and health and safety issues to help travelers going abroad.

Locations and Destinations

■ WHAT MAKES A LOCATION A POPULAR DESTINATION?

Not every place on earth is a destination. A ***destination*** is a location that a traveler chooses to visit. According to the U.S. Travel Association, in 2018, the United States received 79.6 million international visitors. Leisure travelers spent a total of $762 billion in 2018. The top five international markets to the USA were Canada, Mexico, United Kingdom, Japan, and China. Travel both domestically and internationally continues to grow, making the need for

---

CLOSE-UP: CAREERS IN DESTINATION MARKETING AND PROMOTION

Businesses and governments alike aggressively develop destinations and promote tourism. The task has many facets—from researching potential sites for a new resort to publishing promotional materials to finding volunteers who will make conventioneers feel welcome and coordinating travel arrangements for incoming travelers and groups.

Among the many destination marketing organizations are local tourist bureaus, city convention and visitors' bureaus, state travel offices, regional travel organizations, and associations created by businesses, such as ski resorts. A new specialty is sports commissions, charged with bringing major sporting events to a destination. These marketing organizations are frequently divided into departments devoted to convention sales, tourism sales, and membership services; often there is a division between domestic and international markets. In places that are just beginning to focus on tourism, even those with little experience may find excellent opportunities to begin work at a relatively high level. The best place to start is your hometown, but often the way to advance is by moving from city to city and from state to state.

■ **Position** Senior staff assistant

Description The person in this position provides administrative support while learning the fundamentals of the sales, tourism, or communications department. The job includes work on special projects, such as helping to coordinate familiarization trips.

Qualifications This is an entry-level position. It requires good communication skills, common sense, and attention to detail.

■ **Position** Agent (for a national tourist office)

Description To promote travel to their countries, many foreign nations have tourist offices in major U.S. cities. Agents who staff these offices help to raise awareness of the country, promote a positive image of it, and assist potential travelers. They answer questions, send out information, greet visitors, and conduct seminars for travel professionals.

Qualifications Enthusiasm for the NTO's country, knowledge about the country, and interpersonal and communication skills are needed for this position. Knowledge of the nation's language is also usually required. Many of these employees are natives of the country concerned.

■ **Position** Special events coordinator

Description This specialist develops, prepares, and manages events and related programs designed to increase tourism to a destination. Attendance at functions, which sometimes occur on a weekend or in the evening, might be required.

Qualifications Though the coordinator is often an entry-level position, prior experience in putting together events—perhaps at a hotel or a meeting planning company—is desirable. A similar position focused on organizing sporting events is becoming more prevalent.

■ **Position** Convention sales manager

Description Opening new markets for meetings, conventions, and trade shows is the responsibility of this position. The convention sales manager makes sales calls, attends trade shows, and implements sales blitzes in order to develop leads and help to close sales on behalf of a local convention center or convention bureau and the local hospitality industry. This person also has responsibility for the marketing budget.

Qualifications Typically, these positions are filled by people coming from hotel sales. The position requires the ability to make presentations to high-level decision makers, to provide top levels of service, and to be creative in finding leads. The job also involves considerable travel, possibly even internationally.

(continued on next page)

educated travel professionals that much greater. Projections and reality can be very different. Factors such as terrorism, major weather occurrences (tsunamis or earthquakes), or military conflicts can be stumbling blocks to high-volume tourism to any destination.

Key Characteristics of Destinations

What turns a location into a popular destination? Attractions alone do not guarantee success. The UNESCO World Heritage site of Great Zimbabwe National Monument is one of the most important archaeological sites in Africa. Here, as early as 350 A.D., Shona-speaking farmers first settled an area, leading to the formation of the Great Zimbabwe state and eventually to the building of a great city of towers and stone walls 35 feet tall and 15 feet thick built without mortar. Yet fewer than 20,000 people visit the ruins annually. Why? Perhaps it's because this fascinating site has little promotion and is far away and expensive to visit. Perhaps it's because the country has had an unstable government and other safety issues. Other interesting competitive sites are easier and less expensive to access.

CLOSE-UP: CAREERS IN DESTINATION MARKETING AND PROMOTION (cont.)

■ **Position** Convention services manager

Description The person in this position works with the organizers of conventions and meetings, finds out what they need, and then notifies convention bureau members (such as hotels, restaurants, ground transportation companies) so they can bid for the business. The manager is responsible for keeping costs to a minimum; for recommending amenities, venues, speakers, and themes; and for being sure that contracts with the convention bureau are fulfilled. Responsibilities may also include handling housing and assigning registration personnel. Attendance at functions on weekends and evenings might be required. Over time, the convention services manager develops relationships with local businesspeople.

Qualifications Interpersonal and communication skills, as well as knowledge of the destination, are needed.

■ **Position** Group tour specialist/coordinator

Description This specialist locates groups or organizations that are potential visitors as well as those that generate group travel (such as travel agents, tour operators, civic organizations, special-interest groups). Once the group is sold on the destination, the specialist hands the booking over to members of the hospitality industry. In order to stimulate tourism, this specialist may also create packages and itineraries that travel agencies or tour operators can sell.

Qualifications Experience in sales, hotels, or other areas of the travel industry is usually required. This position demands creativity, tenacity, excellent communication skills, the ability to relate to people, and excellent follow-through and attention to detail. Previous experience in tour packaging is helpful.

■ **Position** Public or destination information officer

Description This professional develops programs designed to increase the number of visitors and to enhance the destination's image. Other responsibilities include planning; writing and disseminating information through various media, including the Internet; and designing and producing official publications distributed to residents, tourists, businesses, and media representatives. The public information officer may also organize media events and familiarization trips.

Qualifications Prior experience in public relations or marketing is usually required; budgeting and the ability to analyze cost-effectiveness may also be necessary.

■ **Position** Global sales agent (for a corporate travel management company or a destination marketing organization)

Description The person in this senior sales position is responsible for securing foreign companies or foreign-based divisions or subsidiaries of U.S.-based multinational companies as clients. The sales agent must travel a great deal, sometimes 80 percent of the time, building relationships abroad and following through on the sale to be sure all aspects of the contract are understood.

Qualifications Knowledge of the regulations and customs for doing business in other countries and the ability to understand a client's needs are essential, along with follow-up abilities, professionalism, excellent communication skills, and the ability to travel frequently. Foreign language ability is a strong asset.

■ **Other positions** Cartographer; marketing manager; market research analyst; travel photographer; travel writer; webmaster.

In contrast, in 1963, a U.S corporation took an area of citrus groves and cattle ranches in Florida and turned it into a tourist mecca that now attracts over 19 million visitors each year—Walt Disney World Resort. Similarly, in the late 1960s, Fonatur, a Mexican government agency, searched for an ideal site to create a beach resort and succeeded spectacularly with Cancún and the Riviera Maya that now hosts over eight million travelers each year.

What makes a successful destination? Destinations are distinguished from each other primarily by climate, attractions (both natural and man-made), costs, standard of living, accessibility, culture, and competition:

- *Climate.* The **climate** is the average weather over a long time, and it greatly affects the appeal of a destination.
- *Attractions.* What is there to see or do at a destination? Does it have natural attractions, such as magnificent scenery, or created attractions, such as an unusual amusement park?
- *Costs and standard of living.* What kinds of food and lodging are available and at what cost? How expensive is it to get to the destination? Can visitors obtain the day-to-day services to which they are accustomed, such as a good cup of coffee or dry cleaning? Will they be able to go on the Internet or watch television? Is quality health care available in an emergency? The more exotic a destination, the more prepared the traveler must be to forgo some services that are commonplace at home or to pay an exorbitant price for them.
- *Accessibility.* How far away is the destination, and how do travelers get there? Can they fly directly to the location on a reliable, well-known air carrier? Both the physical features of a location and the transportation available locally influence its accessibility. For example, you can travel the 4,000 miles from London to Nairobi, Kenya, in less time than it takes to go the 200 or so miles from Nairobi to the gorilla preserve in Bwindi, Uganda. Not everyone believes that "getting there is half the fun."
- *Culture.* Are there customs or laws that would make a visit difficult? Are there cultural differences that the traveler will enjoy? Does the destination offer art or dance or music or architecture with special appeal? Does the destination have historical significance?
- *Competition.* Are there other destinations that may be just as interesting but are less difficult and expensive to visit and have better publicity?

Some characteristics of destinations can change suddenly. Political conflict may make a destination temporarily inaccessible; fluctuations in the

Fonatur, a Mexican government agency, developed Cancun, Mexico, as a beach resort in the 1960s.

exchange rates for currency may alter the affordability of a destination; a hurricane may destroy a key attraction. Changes like these may drastically alter an area's popularity.

The appeal of a destination may also shift with little apparent cause. Sometimes, destinations grow in popularity like a fad. Adventurous travelers find a place off the beaten track, and word of its appeal spreads, luring the less adventurous. Thus, some destinations may begin as exotic places for the few and eventually become familiar to almost everyone. Jamaica, for example, was once an exclusive retreat; now it is a popular destination for tours, cruises, resorts, and all-inclusives.

Like clothing, destinations go in and out of fashion. Some destinations, like denim jeans, manage to retain their popularity. Others, like hemlines, rise and fall cyclically. Still others, like starched collars, disappear, seemingly forever. Ultimately, popularity depends on people and their changing tastes. Whether the culture or climate or other characteristic of a destination draws visitors depends on how travelers view these features, what travelers are looking for, and what competitive sites may offer. Likes and dislikes also can vary based on the demographics of your clients. Millennials might be attracted to a particular destination or travel style, while Gen X, Gen Y, and baby boomers might all have different destinations in mind.

Destination Management

Persuading people that a particular destination is worth visiting is one of the tasks of people who work in the field of *destination management and promotion.*

CLOSE-UP: ON THE JOB WITH MANDY HALLET, CONVENTION AND VISITORS' BUREAU REPRESENTATIVE

Mandy Hallet has worked for the convention and visitors' bureau of a major city on the West Coast for almost two years. She is currently assistant manager of its downtown public facility. During the summer, she supervises a staff of six to eight, most of whom are seasonal employees or interns in tourism and public relations.

"I work in a tourist office on the ground level of a downtown building. After going in and meeting the marketing director of our convention and tourism bureau, I left my résumé and a letter explaining how much I loved our city and what it offered, even though the bureau had no positions at that time. I kept in touch afterward, too, and when there was an opening, I got an interview. The pay wasn't great to start, but I was in a supervisory role very quickly. At slow times, I do some research and planning for the busier season.

"We all love to talk to people who come in because they are genuinely seeking information about our city. They want to be sold on it. I especially enjoy talking to international visitors. I never thought about it before, but it's amazing that we have the whole world visiting us. Still, the majority of our walk-ins are other Americans from out of town. We ask them where they are from and usually have them sign a register to help keep track.

"Individual tourists are fine, but bringing in conventions and people by the hundreds or even thousands is where the expansion is. More and more hotels are being built, and more and more conventions are choosing our area. It's the convention and tourism bureau's job to enhance the possibility of that happening as often as possible.

"Our office talks to convention managers and meeting planners and sells them on our city for dates years into the future. We coordinate this with the other groups that are coming in, and especially with the hotels and convention center or other meeting places. Once we think they are on a course to come here, we step aside and let the groups and hotels negotiate with each other to set up the details. But we are always ready to give backup support.

"This seemed like just fun at first, but now I can see an entire career in it. I enrolled in evening business and communication courses and should have a chance to move into the marketing part of the office in the future."

People in this field communicate knowledge about destinations, develop and promote destinations, and help tourists when they come to those destinations. *National tourist offices (NTOs)*, for example, are organizations established by governments to promote travel to their countries. Most NTOs do not sell travel arrangements but work to attract travelers and to present the country in the best light to potential travelers from around the world.

Similarly, smaller political units—states, provinces, cities, and so on—fund offices that try to attract visitors to the area and to serve travelers once they arrive. There are *tourist bureaus, visitors' information centers,* and *convention and visitors' bureaus,* which aim to bring meetings, conventions, trade shows, and tourists to an area and promote its convention centers. Often, businesses are members of these organizations and help fund them.

Finally, destination management companies or organizations (DMCs or DMOs) are locally based for-profit tourism businesses whose function is to provide groups and individuals with services to meet their travel, meeting, and entertainment interest and needs at a specific time and place. Private groups, such as chambers of commerce, tour operators, and city hotels, also set up their own marketing organizations.

✔ CHECK-UP

Characteristics that distinguish one destination from another include
- ✔ Climate.
- ✔ Attractions.
- ✔ Costs and standard of living.
- ✔ Accessibility.
- ✔ Culture.
- ✔ Competition.

Locational and Physical Geography

■ HOW DO YOU DESCRIBE THE LOCATION OF A DESTINATION AND CALCULATE TIME DIFFERENCES?

■ WHAT DETERMINES A DESTINATION'S CLIMATE?

People who develop and promote particular destinations obviously need expertise about those destinations, but all travel professionals need knowledge of their products and the travel industry. Destinations *are* products. Knowledge about them comes from *geography*—the science that studies the earth, its features, its life, and how these interact.

In particular, travel and tourism professionals need some understanding of the three types of geography: *locational geography,* which covers the location of places; *physical geography,* which examines natural features, such as terrain and climate; and *cultural geography,* which studies how people and their environments interact. As a first step, travel professionals should know how to find the answers to three of the most often asked questions about destinations: Where is it? How long does it take to get there? And what will the weather be like?

Where Is It?

Every place on earth has a unique address based on a *grid,* or network of lines, created by geographers. The two basic lines of this grid are the equator and the prime meridian:

- The *equator* is an imaginary line that circles the globe halfway between the North and South Poles. The distance measured in degrees north or south of the equator is the *latitude* of a location.
- The *prime meridian* is an imaginary line running through Greenwich, England, that connects the North and South Poles. The distance measured in degrees east or west of the prime meridian is the *longitude* of a location.

New York City, for example, is located at 40°45′ north latitude, 74° west longitude (or 40°45′N, 74°W); no other place on earth has this particular address. However, if you were trying to explain New York City's location to someone, it's not likely you would quote the latitude and longitude.

In fact, few people know the latitudes and longitudes of different locations. For the traveler and travel professional alike, this precise address or *absolute location* is less important than relative location. Where, for example, is Cancún? Its latitude and longitude are 21°N, 87°W. But for most people a more meaningful answer would describe the location of Cancún by giving its *context—a beachside resort on the tip of the Yucatan Peninsula of Mexico.* Where is it in relation to larger natural features? Answering this question requires the use of a few basic geographic concepts and terms, such as the terms for large areas of land and water.

The prime meridian in Greenwich, England

Describing the Earth. Most of the earth is occupied by a huge body of salt water with four major divisions known as *oceans:* the Arctic, the Atlantic, the Indian, and the Pacific. At the borders of these oceans are *seas,* which are smaller bodies of salt water surrounded by land (such as the Mediterranean and the Caribbean Seas), and *gulfs,* which are bodies of salt water bordered by a curved shoreline (such as the Gulf of Mexico). The oceans embrace seven large landmasses called *continents:* Africa, Antarctica, Asia, Australia, Europe, North America, and South America. (Some people consider Europe and Asia as one continent, Eurasia.)

The continents are used by some geographers to define even larger areas of the globe: the Eastern and Western Hemispheres. North and South America constitute the *Western Hemisphere;* the other continents make up the *Eastern Hemisphere.* Geographers use the equator to divide the earth into a *Northern* and a *Southern Hemisphere.* Thus, we can locate Cancún by saying it is in the Northern and Western Hemispheres on the North American continent, bordering the Caribbean Sea.

More specific descriptions of the location of a destination distinguish smaller bodies of land and water. Cancún, as mentioned before, is on the Yucatán peninsula. A *peninsula* is a body of land with water on three sides. In contrast, an *island* is a body of land completely surrounded by water, and an *isthmus* is a narrow body of land connecting two larger bodies of land. A *strait* is a narrow channel of water connecting two larger bodies of water, whereas a *sound* is a long, wide body of water connecting two larger bodies of water. A *river* is a natural-moving channel of fresh water that flows over the land and empties into a body of water, such as an ocean or lake. The end point is referred to as the *mouth.*

Reading a Map. A map is the key tool for locating places, an invaluable source of information about destinations. Remember, though, that every map is a simplified picture of reality. No map can show everything; every map reflects choices about what to include and what to omit. Furthermore, maps must distort reality because a map is flat and two-dimensional; the earth is spherical and three-dimensional. It is impossible to represent a spherical object on a flat surface without distortion.

FIGURE 2.1

24-Hour Clock

On the 24-hour clock, each day begins at 0000 (midnight) and progresses through each hour of the day from 0100 (1:00 a.m.) to 2300 (11:00 p.m.). The last two digits give the minutes. To convert 24-hour time to a.m./p.m. time, subtract 1200 from hours greater than noon. To convert a.m./p.m. time to the 24-hour clock, add 1200 to hours after noon.

a.m./p.m. Time	24-Hour Time
Midnight (12 a.m.)	0000
1 a.m.	0100
2 a.m.	0200
3 a.m.	0300
4 a.m.	0400
5 a.m.	0500
6 a.m.	0600
7 a.m.	0700
8 a.m.	0800
9 a.m.	0900
10 a.m.	1000
11 a.m.	1100
Noon (12 p.m.)	1200
1 p.m.	1300
2 p.m.	1400
3 p.m.	1500
4 p.m.	1600
5 p.m.	1700
6 p.m.	1800
7 p.m.	1900
8 p.m.	2000
9 p.m.	2100
10 p.m.	2200
11 p.m.	2300

Many maps include the grid that shows latitude and longitude. The east-west lines that measure latitude are called *parallels*. The north-south lines that mark off longitude are called *meridians*. (Recall that *latitudes* are distances north and south of the equator; *longitudes* are distances east and west of the prime meridian.)

Most maps offer several aids to help readers understand them:

- An *index* lists in alphabetical order the places and features that are noted on the map.
- A *legend* (or *key*) explains the symbols that are used on the map, such as a star for the capital of a country.
- *Compass points* show where north, south, east, and west are in relation to the map. Usually, north is at the top of the map.
- A *scale* indicates how the size of the map is related to real-world distances. For example, one inch on a map might represent 700 actual miles (or 1,126 kilometers).
- A *relief key* shows how **altitude,** or elevation above sea level, is represented on the map. Often, changes in altitude are indicated by changes in color or shading.

When Will I Get There?

Knowing where a place is does not answer one of the most frequently asked questions: When will I get there? Sometimes, determining the answer requires use of both the 24-hour clock and a map of the world's time zones.

Figure 2.1 shows the **24-hour clock.** It eliminates the a.m./p.m. distinction, providing a different numeral for each hour of the day. It is used often by airlines and the military. Many people in the travel industry prefer to use it as it avoids errors, although computers in the United States are programmed to show a.m. and p.m. because so many Americans are not accustomed to using the 24-hour clock in their daily lives. For example, many flights that leave around midnight are scheduled to leave at 23:59 (one minute before midnight) or at 00:01 (one minute after midnight)—note, only two minutes apart but actually two different dates!

Figure 2.2 shows how the world is divided into 24 time zones, starting from the prime meridian at Greenwich, England. There is a one-hour time difference between most adjacent time zones. The time at Greenwich is called **Greenwich mean time (GMT)** or **universal time coordinated (UTC),** and the time elsewhere in the world is expressed as plus or minus GMT or UTC. New York, for example, is –5 GMT—in other words, five hours earlier than GMT.

About 12 time zones from Greenwich, on the opposite side of the world in the Pacific Ocean, is the **international date line.** It is an imaginary line roughly corresponding to 180° longitude that, by international agreement, separates one calendar day from another. When it is noon in Greenwich, England, on the prime meridian, it is midnight on the international date line. West of the international date line, toward Asia, it is one calendar day later than east of the line.

Figure 2.2 also describes how to use a map of time zones to calculate both time differences and the duration of a trip. Note, though, that these calculations get more complicated at certain places and times. A few countries do not follow the international time zones in setting their clocks. China, for example, uses only one time zone throughout the entire country; the time is the same no matter where you are in China. Furthermore, most countries adjust their clocks during the summer to create *daylight saving time,* and places have varying rules about when they move their clocks forward and backward. The computers used in travel agencies called GDSs (Global Distribution Systems) and many websites are set to calculate time differences and travel times for you. Even within the United States, there are some locations that do not observe daylight saving time, such as in Arizona and parts of Indiana.

Airline schedules indicate the local time in a particular place on a particular date. In some cases, you may arrive at your destination before you left home! For example, in flying eastward from Asia to the United States, you

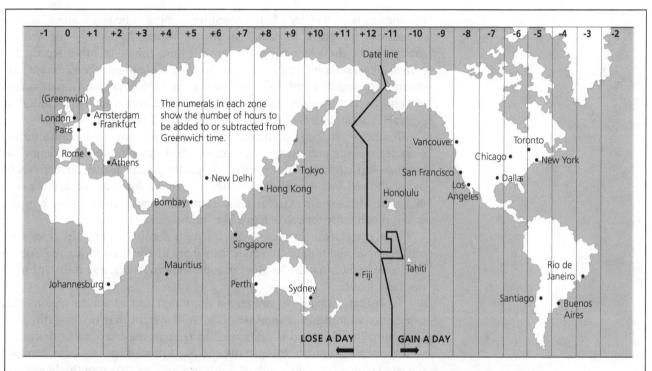

To calculate the time difference

1. For each location, find the local time and its relationship to GMT on an international time chart.

2. If both locations are either ahead of GMT (GMT+) or behind GMT (GMT–), subtract the smaller from the larger figure.

   For example, Toronto is GMT –5 and San Francisco is GMT –8. Subtracting 5 from 8 gives 3, so there is a 3-hour time difference between the two locations.

3. If the local time is ahead of GMT (GMT+) at one location and behind GMT (GMT–) at the other location, add the figures.

   For example, New York is GMT –5 and Rome is GMT +1. Adding 5 plus 1 gives 6, so there is a 6-hour time difference between the two locations.

To calculate the elapsed travel time

1. Convert departure and arrival times to 24-hour clock time.

2. Subtract the departure time from the arrival time.

3. When traveling east, subtract 1 hour for every time zone crossed. When traveling west, add 1 hour for every time zone crossed. The result is the actual travel time.

   For example, suppose the departure time from Paris is 12:15 p.m. and the arrival time in New York is 1:25 p.m. Converted to 24-hour time, the departure time is 1215 and the arrival time is 1325. The difference is 1 hour and 10 minutes. Because 6 time zones are crossed going west from Paris to New York, add 6 hours to the result. Thus, the elapsed travel time in this case is 7 hours and 10 minutes.

FIGURE 2.2 Time Zones

There is a one-hour difference between most adjacent time zones. But the 12th time zone is two half zones, as the map shows. The international date line crosses this zone at about 180° from Greenwich. East of the date line, it is a day earlier than it is west of the line.

might leave Singapore and arrive in the United States earlier on the same date you left Singapore. Another factor affecting flight schedules is wind. For example, flights from New York to San Francisco take longer than flights from San Francisco to New York, due to prevailing tail winds flying eastward and headwinds flying westward. It is important that travel professionals are aware of the exact departure and arrival dates and times because other travel plans (i.e. tours and hotel reservations) need to correspond accordingly.

What Is the Climate Like?

No one can tell a traveler what the weather is going to be at a destination on a certain day, but travel professionals should be able to describe the weather that prevails, the average weather over a long time—in other words, the climate. For example, areas with what is called a *Mediterranean climate* have warm, dry summers and mild, wet winters. A Mediterranean climate occurs not only in countries along the Mediterranean but also in southern California, central Chile, and parts of the southern coasts of Africa and Australia.

Temperature, precipitation, atmospheric pressure, winds, humidity, altitude, and the percentage of cloudiness and sunshine together define the weather and climate. Temperature is often the salient feature, but it can be overshadowed by other characteristics. Humidity, for example, has a major effect on whether a particular temperature is comfortable. A very hot, dry area is much more tolerable than a hot, humid one.

In many places, patterns of precipitation dominate life. Arid deserts are one example. Major deserts include the Sahara in northern Africa, the Gobi in Mongolia and China, the Kalahari in southwestern Africa, and the Atacama in northern Chile.

Precipitation patterns are also a dominant fact of life in regions that experience monsoons. A *monsoon* is a wind system that reverses direction seasonally, but the word is often used to refer to the heavy rains that come with the wind. In northern Australia and parts of southern Asia, for example, the wind comes from the south or southwest for about six months, blowing in moisture from the Indian and Pacific Oceans and bringing torrential rains. For the next six months, the winds reverse direction, and little rain falls.

What creates differences in climate? Many factors interact, but the key ones include a location's latitude, altitude, proximity to bodies of water, and winds.

Latitude. All year, because of the way the earth tilts on its axis, the equator receives the most direct rays of the sun; the North and South Poles get the least amount of direct sun. Thus, the closer a place is to the equator, the warmer it tends to be. Also, the closer a place is to the equator, the less difference there is likely to be between seasons. North of the equator, winter occurs during December, January, and February and summer during June, July, and August. The seasons are reversed south of the equator.

Latitude is the basis for one ancient and very simple classification of the world's climates. This classification describes five zones that circle the globe. In the far north, at the Arctic Circle, is a *frigid polar zone*, where summers are cool despite up to 24 hours of sunlight and winters are cold with 24 hours of darkness. South of the polar zone is a *temperate zone*. Next, straddling the equator, lies the *tropical zone*, where the average temperature every month is about 80°F. South of the tropical zone is another temperate zone and then another polar zone.

This very broad picture of the world's climates can be useful, but dramatic differences occur within climate zones. Places at about the same latitude (such as Seattle, Washington, and Fargo, North Dakota) often have very different climates because latitude is not the only key to climate.

It also should be noted that sunrise and sunset times vary greatly during the seasons at the extreme north and extreme south zones. However, close to the equator there is little difference between the time the sun sets in the winter and in the summer. This can affect tourism greatly, as long periods of light in the evening can make for additional opportunities for sightseeing activities, driving times, and social events.

Altitude. One factor that may overshadow the influence of latitude is the altitude. The higher the altitude, the cooler the climate is likely to be. The temperature along a beach at sea level may be 85°F (29°C), while just a few miles away, on top of a high mountain, the temperature may be only 40°F (4°C). If you are at the equator but in the mountains 9,000 feet high (as in Ecuador, for example), it may be very cool. Many travel industry novices make the mistake of assuming it's always hot if you are near the equator—not so! Among the most famous peaks on earth are Mount Everest (at 29,028 ft) in the Himalayas on the border of Tibet and Nepal, Denali (at 20,320 ft) in Alaska, Mount Kilimanjaro (at 19,340 ft) in Tanzania, and Mount Fuji (at 12,388 ft) in Japan.

It is important that travel professionals become aware of high-altitude destinations because many travelers have health issues at altitudes of 9,000 feet and above. And adventure travelers need to be reminded that, if climbing Mt. Kilimanjaro, they will start their climb wearing light summer clothing and continually add clothing as they approach the summit.

Because of warm Atlantic winds, London, England, rarely drops below 40 degrees in the winter.

Proximity to Bodies of Water. Water usually moderates temperature. In summer, the closer you are to a body of water, the cooler it will be. In winter, the closer you are to the water, the warmer the temperature.

Winds. Paris and London do not experience many days below freezing, even though they are at the same latitude and altitude as places in central Canada where the temperature may be −40°F (−40°C) during the winter. Why? Prevailing winds bring warm Atlantic air to western Europe for many miles inland from its coast. The air is warm because it passed over the *Gulf Stream,* which is a warm ocean current that flows north from the Caribbean through the Atlantic. In contrast, winds that blow across ocean currents coming from the polar regions can bring cooler temperatures.

Mountain ranges often create interesting variations in climate by blocking the prevailing winds. As air passes over mountains, it rises and is cooled; it also loses moisture. Thus, the climate on the *windward* side of the mountains, which is the side exposed to the wind, will differ from the climate on the *leeward* side, the side sheltered from the wind. For example, if a mountain range blocks a warm ocean wind, then its leeward side will have a cooler and drier climate than its windward side.

Conclusions. Understanding the geographic characteristics we have discussed can lead to educated guesses about where to look for a certain type of climate, as well as the wisdom not to jump to conclusions. Some areas have weather that rarely changes; in other places, the weather varies considerably. In some places, one climate prevails over hundreds of miles; elsewhere, the climate changes within just a few miles. San Francisco may be foggy and cool in the summer, for example, while a few miles inland skies may be clear, and the temperature can be hot. How to find good information about the climate and other characteristics of a specific destination is the topic of the next section.

✔ CHECK-UP

The largest features of the earth are its
✔ Four oceans: Atlantic, Arctic, Indian, and Pacific.
✔ Seven continents: Africa, Antarctica, Asia, Australia, Europe, North America, and South America.

The earth's time zones
✔ Are measured from the prime meridian, which is at Greenwich, England.
✔ Are one hour apart.

The weather is defined by
✔ Temperature.
✔ Precipitation.
✔ Atmospheric pressure.
✔ Winds.
✔ Humidity.
✔ Percentage of cloudiness and sunshine.
✔ Altitude.

Learning about Destinations

■ WHAT ARE GOOD SOURCES OF INFORMATION ABOUT DESTINATIONS?

No one can be an expert on all destinations, but every travel professional should be acquainted with the most popular ones and should know how to find other information when it is needed. Personal travel, general education, and formal courses on travel provide the foundation for this knowledge. Travel industry publications and websites also are important for advisors to stay educated on destination knowledge and on other news that can impact destinations.

Travel and Education

There is no substitute for a personal visit as a way of learning about a destination. Governments, as well as suppliers, such as tour operators, sponsor *familiarization trips (fam trips).* These are trips offered to bona fide travel professionals at a reduced rate so they can inspect hotels and restaurants, sample attractions and experience the local culture, as well as learn about the services of the sponsoring companies. They are usually short, concentrated learning trips in a business format. Cruise lines also offer similar trips, known as *seminars at sea.*

A brief visit, however, cannot provide a comprehensive picture of a destination, and places may change rapidly. Travel professionals must go beyond their limited personal experience and learn from others.

Almost anything that contributes to your general education can also build your knowledge about destinations. Conversations with other people, books, magazines, newspapers, websites, blogs, online videos, documentaries, even movies and novels—all these sources help travel professionals enrich their understanding of the world and keep in touch with the latest trends and events. Many travel professionals continue their learning after they are employed by speaking with their clients when they return from a trip, by talking with colleagues, and by attending industry seminars and participating in familiarization trips. More discussion of these opportunities may be found in Chapter 16.

Making sense of this flood of information can be difficult. The backbone of a travel professional's knowledge about destinations comes from references, such as maps, guidebooks, textbooks, industry news, the Internet, and personal research. Mastering all the information they offer becomes far easier with the help of the systematic, formal study offered by colleges, travel schools, professional associations, and suppliers. For example, *The Travel Institute,* the educational organization for travel professionals and the publisher of this book, offers Destination Specialist courses that examine specific areas of the world in depth.

Chapter 16 describes such opportunities for further education. Our focus here is slightly different: If you need an answer to a specific question about a location to solve a problem, where do you turn? You might find help from the following sources:

ON THE SPOT

After a glance around the room of the town's tourist office, the middle-aged man strode to the counter and simply blurted out, "What's the best restaurant in town?" If you are the representative at the bureau, what do you say?

In this, as in many interactions with clients, you need to ask questions before you can answer one. In this case, you might ask questions such as, What types of food are your favorites? Will you be bringing children? Do you want something casual? Where are you staying?

Once you have some idea of the client's tastes and needs, you might be able to recommend some appropriate restaurants. You will want to make several suggestions, not just one. (The representative's job, after all, is to fairly promote all the companies in the area.) You might choose to emphasize a few that seem most likely to interest this client.

CLOSE-UP: SELLING THROUGH KNOWLEDGE

The idea that travel professionals need to know where to find answers, rather than the answers themselves, can be taken too far. To make a good first impression and to gain the confidence of a new customer, travel professionals should be able to talk to the customer about a destination, at least briefly. And to plan a trip, travel counselors will need to answer the following basic questions:

- *Where is the destination located?* Suppose a couple wants to go to Kaanapali. Do you know where it is?
- *How does a traveler get there?* How easy or difficult is the trip? Are there nonstop flights to Kaanapali, Maui? Direct flights? How many connections will the traveler need to make? How long will the entire trip take, including the transfer from the airport to the destination?
- *What is the climate at the destination?* Does it vary much throughout the year? Are there particularly unpleasant times, or are there weeks best suited to particular activities? What type of clothing do I recommend my clients pack?
- *When are the best times to go?* The answer depends on more than the climate. For example, crowds and prices might vary greatly—and might be worst when the climate is best. Of course, the clients' interests may shape what type of weather is "best."

- *What are the health conditions, safety concerns, culture, and people like at the destination?* Is the novice traveler likely to be comfortable there, or is this a place better suited to experienced and sophisticated travelers?
- *What are the major reasons people go to the destination?* What activities are available there? What are the major sights?
- *How does a traveler get around at the destination?* What local transportation is available?
- *Where would the traveler stay and eat?* Are there a lot of choices? Can travelers find the brand names they are accustomed to? Can they find unusual types of lodging and food?
- *What is the price range of a trip?* Can travelers on every budget find transportation and accommodations, or is the destination too expensive for most? Are there accommodations that would suit travelers looking for a luxurious destination?

To help yourself prepare to sell a trip to a destination, plan a trip for yourself and a loved one as if you were going to make the journey. If you feel as if you are actually making the trip, you will remember the information for a very long time. The more knowledge you gain, the easier it is to sell that destination.

- *Colleagues.* Your colleagues can be helpful, especially if they are experts on the destination and have seen the specific spot you are asking about.
- *Tour operators.* These companies usually have employees who are very familiar with the destinations they offer in their many tour packages and itineraries and are often willing to share their knowledge with their travel industry colleagues.
- *Government tourist offices.* Their staffs include people with an intimate knowledge of the destinations they represent, and many can provide leads to other knowledgeable people as well as promotional aids, such as guides to the destination or contacts with receptive operators in their specific country.
- *Other government sources.* As we discuss later in this chapter, government agencies, such as the U.S. State Department and Centers for Disease Control and Prevention, are the best source for some types of information on destinations, particularly information about safety and health issues.

Often, however, finding answers requires the use of references—in print or online—such as atlases, guidebooks, newspapers, magazines, brochures, and websites. These sources are worth a closer look.

Some Key References

Maps and Atlases. You can answer many kinds of questions by finding the right map. Besides maps that focus on physical features, there are also maps that give historical and cultural information. A compilation of maps is called an **atlas.** A good atlas should be visited frequently, like an old friend. You can find atlases in both print and online versions.

Guidebooks. Hundreds of guidebooks have been published. Leading series of guidebooks include the following:
- *DK Eyewitness.* These highly visual guidebooks are very attractive, and they include mini-essays on all aspects of a destination's culture.
- *Fodor.* This is a comprehensive series of guides. Most books in the series cover sightseeing, walking tours, attractions, nightlife, and shopping and provide hotel and restaurant reviews.
- *Frommer.* This series includes country and regional guides that provide pricing, maps, and sightseeing information, as well as the authors' insights, recommendations, and advice. Their day-by-day guides offer itineraries showing how to see destinations in a short time.
- *Insight.* These books offer superb photography and essays that provide excellent background on a country or area.
- *Let's Go.* This series emphasizes budget travel. It is geared toward student travelers, and much of it is written by students but is used by many others.
- *Lonely Planet* and *Moon Publications.* Designed for the budget traveler, these series give in-depth commentary on the local scene.
- *Michelin.* Michelin's *Red Guides* list hotels, restaurants, and garages (for tires); the *Green Guides* provide detailed historical and sightseeing information, as well as maps.
- *Rick Steves' Europe.* These city and regional guidebooks also include tips on preparing for a trip.
- *Rough Guide.* This is a practical, analytical, and down-to-earth series.

Keep in mind that no book is infallible and that much of the information in guidebooks is not updated frequently and must, therefore, be augmented by computer research. Most of the guidebooks maintain an online presence to help keep you informed of new or updated information about a location.

Multiple sources of information are available when planning trips.

Newspapers and Magazines. Newspapers and magazines are often excellent sources; many have both online and print editions. Four categories of publications are most useful: (1) consumer magazines devoted exclusively to travel, (2) general consumer publications not devoted exclusively to travel but with occasional helpful travel columns, (3) specialty consumer publications, and (4) travel industry trade publications. Below are some samples of these publications for readers in the United States. Similar publications are available in many other countries as well.

Consumer magazines devoted exclusively to travel include *National Geographic Traveler, Travel + Leisure, Condé Nast Traveler,* and *Afar.*

General consumer magazines with occasional travel articles or columns include *Harper's, New Yorker, The Atlantic, Elle,* and *Sunset.* The Sunday travel sections of some key U.S. newspapers are also a good source. Particularly notable are *The New York Times,* the *Los Angeles Times, The Boston Globe,* and the *Chicago Tribune.* The *Wall Street Journal* is also noted for its business travel coverage and, in particular, its reports on the airline industry.

Several travel trade resources and business publications are aimed specifically at those who work in the industry. They are a great way to stay current on the latest news, trends, and issues in the travel industry. *Travel Agent, Travel Weekly, TravelAge West,* and *Luxury Travel Advisor* all feature news and supplier and destination information, geared at helping travel agents sell more effectively, while *Agent@Home* gives home-based agents the information about how to run a successful home-based travel business.

Travel Market Report and *TravelPulse* provide coverage and analysis of trends affecting leisure and corporate travel agents. *Travel Research Online* offers free marketing tools and content for use in social media. Finally, *Insider Travel Report, Travel Professional News,* and *The Compass by VAX VacationAccess* are publications that provide resources, insights, and news.

Brochures. Brochures, most of which are in digital format, are far from objective; tour operators and suppliers create them to present destinations in the best possible light. Still, brochures often present useful information about local customs, health precautions, visa requirements, currency, shopping, and sightseeing activities in the area. Sometimes the quickest way to get an overview of the attractions of a destination is to read the itinerary of an escorted tour in a tour operator's brochure or catalogue. The brochures also can provide insight in terms of relative distances, modes of transportation that might be involved, and other logistical ideas as you match the perfect supplier to your clients' travel needs.

Websites. Much of the time and money that companies once devoted to creating brochures now go to designing and maintaining websites. In fact, you can find just about everything about destinations online. Every national tourist office has a site, as do many tourist offices representing regions, cities, states, provinces, and other entities. A major advantage of a website over print media is that it can be updated frequently with current information, as it becomes available. However, print media may offer more in-depth coverage.

Beyond these standard references, the Internet offers innumerable other sources of information about destinations. The sites of many suppliers and online travel agencies include destination guides. Often you can find useful sites by searching under a topic—castles or skiing, for example. We cannot underestimate how searching for information has changed since being able to 'Google' just about any question one has.

How do you sift through and use all this information? Here are two suggestions:

1. *Remember to be skeptical.* Identify the source and its date and judge the information accordingly. Is the source likely to be biased? Does the information come from someone with first-hand, recent experience of the location? Many websites have names and addresses that make them sound as if they were created by tourist offices when, in fact, they are maintained by private companies selling their services or by individuals describing places they love. Many are not current.

2. *Develop a list of favorite websites and other sources that you know to be reliable and easy to access.* Travel professionals who know how to search efficiently for reliable information can save valuable time and money for their companies and their clients. Periodically review broad topics in a search engine as new, reliable, informative websites continue to be created and can expand your list of sources.

✔ CHECK-UP

You can develop a foundation of knowledge about destinations through
- ✔ Travel, including personal travel and fam trips.
- ✔ General education.
- ✔ Systematic courses of study offered by colleges, travel schools, and professional associations.
- ✔ Seminars usually sponsored by suppliers, such as government tourist office, tour operators, and cruise lines, among others.

- ✔ Webinars—online seminars, also usually sponsored by suppliers.
- ✔ Colleagues and friends

Key references for finding specific information about a destination include
- ✔ Maps and atlases.
- ✔ Guidebooks.
- ✔ Newspaper and magazine articles.
- ✔ Brochures.
- ✔ Websites.

Crossing Borders

■ WHAT RULES AND REGULATIONS GOVERN INTERNATIONAL TRAVELERS?

McDonald's may well be on the street corners of Tokyo, Paris, and Moscow, but international travel is still unlike domestic travel in whatever country you live. If you travel through Papua New Guinea, for example, you could come across 862 local languages. Visitors in the Gobi Desert might be invited to spend the night in white tent-like homes called *gers*. Travel abroad can bring both exotic experiences and perplexing challenges. Government regulations and differences in currencies, customs, and languages of the many nations making up our world can be frustrating for the unprepared traveler.

The flow of citizens between countries reflects the relationship between these nations. Each country decides whether to welcome or not welcome visitors from other nations and establishes laws accordingly. Many times, such laws are based on reciprocity between two countries. Economic, social, political, medical, and natural events can all influence the number of people willing and able to visit other lands.

Every country has rules that restrict the passage of people and goods across its borders, through its airports, and into its ports. Is a Ukrainian citizen who is a resident of the United States allowed to enter Guatemala without a visa? Can U.S. travelers buy ivory in Africa and bring it home? The travelers themselves are responsible for determining and following the rules, but the travel professionals who counsel them should be able to help them with answers to such questions. And the answers often require research. There are companies and organizations that can assist with learning about specific travel requirements. For example, CIBTvisas is a company that can help you understand visa and passport requirements for US citizens and residents traveling internationally. Foreign embassies and consulates also can be a good resource for doing research about international travelers coming to the U.S.

Disasters—such as the March 2011 earthquake and subsequent tsunami in northeast Japan, the 9/11 attacks, the 2015 terrorist attack in Paris, Hurricane Katrina in New Orleans, the worldwide financial downturn with massive loss of employment, and the fear associated with outbreaks of certain diseases—all take their toll on world tourism and complicate issues of travel documentation. Nevertheless, the tremendous growth of international travel in past years (both for vacation/leisure and business) requires that travel professionals understand the documentation requirements of travelers and know where to find answers to often-complicated situations.

Today, many people may be *residents* of a country but not necessarily be *citizens* of that same country. For example, a citizen of Australia may be living and working in the United States and planning to visit Brazil on vacation. While living in the United States, that person must have a *residency card* (often called a *green card*). It's important that the travel counselor verify that client's citizenship/nationality to provide accurate information regarding entry requirements for Brazil as well as re-entry requirements for the United States. The counselor should never assume the traveler's citizenship. Let's look at some of the documentation terminology and requirements.

ON THE SPOT

Luigi Catania, a U.S. citizen and member of your church, calls you. He needs to fly to Italy as soon as possible because his mother is ill. He has never had a U.S. passport. Can you help Mr. Catania?

You should be able to tell Mr. Catania how to obtain an emergency passport. In addition to the usual documents, he will need to present proof of his flight itinerary and any other proof he might have that the trip is an emergency, and he will have to pay the extra fee for expedited applications. If possible, he should apply at a passport agency, available only by advance appointment. But if he lives too far from a passport agency, he must apply at the nearest post office or court that is authorized to accept passport applications; he should then arrange to have the application sent and the passport returned by overnight delivery. Information about the procedures can be obtained from the State Department.

Entry Documents

Enhanced Driver's Licenses. As the name suggests, an enhanced driver's license (EDL) is a driver's license with a few extra perks. The EDL is similar to a passport card in that it provides proof of identification and U.S. citizenship. It allows you to re-enter the U.S. from Canada, Mexico, and the Caribbean. An EDL is accepted only at land and sea border crossings—not for air travel. It also contains radio-frequency microchipping that uniquely identifies you in Customs and Border Protection (CBP) databases, which should promote a more expeditious cross. Unfortunately, not all U.S. states (or Canadian provinces) issue EDLs—yet. The best way to find out if your state offers an enhanced driver's license is to contact your state's motor vehicle agency.

Up-to-date information on passport requirements is available from the U.S. State Department.

In addition to enhanced driver's licenses, there is the Federal Real ID program, which is intended to set national standards for state-issued identification cards, like driver's licenses and non-driver IDs. When the REAL ID act is fully implemented, US citizens, residents, and visitors will need to show a REAL ID-compliant document to go through TSA security at the airport or to enter secure federal buildings. The REAL ID is available to both US citizens and to legal US alien residents. The enhanced driver's license is available only to US citizens.

Passports. A *passport* is a document issued by a government that establishes an individual's identity and nationality of that particular country and requests protection for the citizen while abroad. For example, a U.S. passport is issued to U.S. citizens by the State Department's Bureau of Consular Affairs and is valid for 10 years from date of issue (except for those younger than 16 when they apply; their passports are valid for only five years). In the past, U.S. citizens did not need a passport for some international travel, such as to the Caribbean, Mexico, or Canada. Today, most U.S. citizens need a passport any time they leave the United States, with the exception of those traveling to approved destinations using an enhanced driver's license. Note that some countries require that passports are still valid for six months after entering the country; some have increased that to nine months, and a few require only three months.

When leaving the United States by air, passengers must prove to airline personnel at check-in that they have proper documentation to enter the destination country when their plane arrives. The airline is subject to a fine and must provide return transportation to any passenger not allowed to enter the destination. Therefore, airline personnel check travelers' documents carefully and do not allow people with incomplete documentation to board.

Where and How to Obtain a Passport. The following information pertains to U.S. citizens only. Citizens of other countries should follow the instructions of their individual countries.

For U.S. citizens, current information is available from the U.S. State Department's Bureau of Consular Affairs. Its website (www.travel.state.gov) includes full information on passport books versus passport cards, where to apply, items needed for applying, fees, special rules for minors, and first-time passports versus renewals, among other information. Below are a few basic points from the website, but please note that information can change, sometimes with little or no notice.

An adult (age 16 or older) can obtain application forms at many U.S. Post Offices, court houses, and other stipulated sites. The completed application form must be accompanied by: (1) a birth certificate that is certified with the registrar's signature and has a raised, impressed, embossed, or multicolored seal (or if born abroad, a certificate of naturalization); (2) evidence of U.S. citizenship, such as previous passport, certified birth certificate, or naturalization certificate (not a drivers' license, draft certificate, Social Security card, or a voting card); (3) one photo in color 2x2 inches in size, full-face view on white background, taken within the last six months; (4) payments of $110 application fee, $35 execution fee, and added fees for expedited services, if any.

Rates for minors vary, and effective April 1, 2011, birth certificates for a minor applicant must have the names of both parents. Young people under age 18—traveling alone or with someone—are under special scrutiny when traveling internationally. Some countries, notably Mexico, require written, notarized approval by one or both of the nontraveling parent or legal guardian for minors to enter another country. Travel professionals should be sure to notify clients accordingly.

Travelers should apply for a passport three months in advance, if possible, although the State Department's website indicates that passports usually arrive within four to six weeks for routine service or three weeks for expedited service. However, the backlog can reach three months at busy times.

It's good practice for travel counselors to ask the client to send them a copy of the inside data page of the passport. Because the name of the passenger listed on the air ticket must match exactly the name spelled on the passport, this doublecheck avoids check-in problems at the airport. This also gives the travel counselor an opportunity to verify the expiration date and other important details. It is suggested that travelers make several photocopies of the inside data page of the passport—one to keep at home and one to carry on the trip. One photocopy should be kept with them or in a safety deposit box in their hotel. Having a copy and an extra set of passport photos helps facilitate replacement if the passport is lost or stolen. If necessary, the nearest overseas U.S. embassy or consulate can provide a temporary replacement for urgent travel, but it has limited validity. (*Embassies* are the offices of the ambassadors who represent a nation in another country; *consulates* are regional offices of embassies.)

Visas. Whereas a passport is required to travel abroad and is issued by the country of one's citizenship, a *visa* is issued by a country and allows the individual to *enter* that country. Visas are generally stamped on a page of the passport, although in certain cases they may be issued on a separate paper. Not all countries require visas, however.

For example, a U.S. citizen visiting many central and northern African countries would require two things: a U.S. passport *and* a visa issued by the government of the country they will be visiting. Visa requirements do change. For example, until 2019, Brazil required both a U.S. passport and a visa. It now has implemented a visa-exempt program in which U.S. citizens can stay for up to 90 days without a visa, although travelers still need to have a blank visa page in their passports upon arrival.

Different types of visas allow visitors to enter a country for varied purposes and periods of time. Each has different governing rules, length of permitted stay, and cost. For example, visitors who travel to study in another country and stay for an academic year may need a *student visa*; businesspeople entering to conduct business may need a *business visa*. Some countries require all visitors, even those who are just passing through, to obtain a *transit visa*. Many countries do not require a visa if a traveler is staying for less than

24 hours or is making a flight connection and does not leave the airport. For most tourists, the appropriate visa is a *tourist* or *visitor visa*. Visitor visas are usually valid for a specific period but can often be renewed without leaving the country. Some tourist visas permit multiple entries. Most tourist visas do not permit the traveler to work in the country concerned.

Requirements for obtaining a visa vary. Some countries charge a fee. Other requirements for a typical visitor visa include

- A passport signed and valid for a minimum of six months after arrival in the country concerned.
- A completed visa application form signed by the applicant.
- A passport-size photograph taken within the past six months.
- A printout of the traveler's flight reservations.
- A specified number of blank pages in your passport.

Requirements for obtaining a typical business visa might include everything required for a visitor visa plus letters from the host company being visited and from the employer. The employer's letter states the purpose of the trip, the company's guarantee of financial and moral responsibility while the employee is in the country, and the name and address of a reference.

Although some countries, Egypt and Turkey, for example, offer tourist visas upon arrival, many experienced travel counselors believe that travelers should obtain their visas before leaving home. If the traveler is taking a prearranged tour, the tour operator might take care of the process. Travelers who are obtaining their own visas should apply to the consulates or embassies of the countries they plan to visit. Application forms from many countries can now be obtained online.

Travelers must submit their passport with each visa application one at a time, so obtaining visas for several countries might take months. An alternative is to use a visa service company, which can obtain several visas in a relatively short time. They are usually well worth the fees they charge, particularly when time is short or when several different visas are required for a complicated trip. Their service fee is *in addition to* the consulate's fee, if any, and any additional fees for expediting the process. There are companies—available to travel professionals—that specialize in passport and visa processing services.

To summarize, up-to-date information on the requirements for U.S. citizens to enter each country is available from the State Department's Bureau of Consular Affairs. Rules vary from nation to nation and often change, sometimes with little or no notice. Depending on the country visited, travelers may need to provide proof of citizenship, a passport, a visa, or a tourist card.

Tourist Cards. Some countries, such as Mexico, require a **tourist card** for entry instead of a visa. Often, these are "landing cards"—cards given to travelers when they check in for the flight, part of which they must turn in on arrival at their destination airport, and the other part that they must surrender when they leave their destination. They are often used by the country as a way of keeping visitor arrival statistics.

Conclusions. The need to check for changes in the requirements for entering and leaving a country cannot be overstated. Since 2001, the United States has been revising and tightening rules and procedures to keep closer track of all kinds of people. For example, particular controversy has surrounded proposals about encoding information on electronic chips on U.S. passports and about procedures that make it more difficult for people to obtain visas to enter the United States. As the United States tightens the rules on international visitors, other nations sometimes threaten to retaliate, making it more difficult for U.S. citizens to enter other countries.

Customs Regulations

Every country in the world restricts the items that can be brought across its borders and assesses a charge, called a **_duty_**, on items whose value exceeds a certain allowance. Travel counselors should alert clients to the regulations published by the U.S. Customs and Border Protection service. All returning residents of the United States, citizens or not, must observe these rules.

Articles Free of U.S. Duty. Anything taken from home can be brought back into the United States duty-free. However, the traveler may have to prove to a U.S. Customs officer that some items were bought in the United States. For example, a Japanese-made camera bought in the United States is liable for duty if the traveler cannot provide proof of purchase. Owners of internationally made articles should take the bill of sale with them or register the item with a U.S. Customs office well before departure. Similarly, travelers should bring a bill of sale or appraisal for valuable items, such as furs or jewelry.

To stimulate the economies of developing countries, some products from certain countries are exempt from any duty. This is the Generalized System of Preferences (GSP) policy. More information can be found at https://www.cbp.gov/trade.

Travelers who are overseas can mail home to themselves personal clothing or articles that they do not need without paying duty if the items were not bought abroad. Also, travelers may mail home items that do not exceed a market value of $200. Gifts purchased abroad and mailed back to friends or relatives are not subject to duty if their fair retail value in the country where they were purchased does not exceed $100. No recipient can receive more than $100 worth of items in one day. Such packages should be marked "Unsolicited Gift" and the value noted on the outer wrapper. You may not send such gifts to yourself.

The Personal Exemption. Each U.S. traveler may bring back into the United States as accompanied baggage items valued up to $800 in duty-free purchases if one has been out of the country at least 48 hours and has not had a similar exemption within the past 30 days. This duty-free exemption is called the _personal exemption_. If travelers bring back goods worth more than the personal exemption, they must pay duty of a flat 3 percent on the next $1,000. Items to be sent later may not be considered accompanied baggage and may not be included in the $800. The value of each item is based on its fair market value in the country where it was purchased. Antiques that are at least 100 years old and fine art may enter the United States duty free, but folk art and handicrafts are generally not exempt. Certain differences apply when returning from U.S. insular possessions (the U.S. Virgin Islands, American Samoa, or Guam) as well as some Caribbean countries. Check the "Know Before You Go" section of the U.S. Customs and Border Protection website carefully.

U.S. federal regulations allow the personal exemption to include up to 100 cigars and 200 cigarettes. Also, it may include up to one liter of alcohol if the passenger is at least 21 years of age. However, some states prohibit the importation of alcohol or tobacco products regardless of federal regulations. Information on these state regulations is available from U.S. Customs and from local alcoholic beverage control commissions.

On the flight or cruise back to the United States, passengers complete a customs declaration form that U.S. Customs inspectors examine upon arrival. All items acquired abroad beyond the personal exemption must be listed, and receipts are requested for substantial purchases. Receipts should be presented with the declaration form.

Forbidden and Restricted Items. Some items cannot be brought into the United States at all. These include narcotics and dangerous drugs, fireworks, switchblade knives, dangerous toys, automobiles that do not conform to standards set by the Environmental Protection Agency, endangered species, and most threatened species. The United States also forbids the importation of any articles made from whale teeth, African ivory, tortoise shell, alligator skin, and many kinds of furs, except for certain limited purposes with advance permission. These articles are regarded as contraband, and they will be seized *without reimbursement* by U.S. Customs officers. Importing them is a felony and may result in a heavy fine.

Severe restrictions exist on other items, including firearms and ammunition; fruits, vegetables, and plants; meat, livestock, and poultry; money; and pets. Detailed information is available from the U.S. Department of Agriculture's Animal and Plant Health Inspection Service (APHIS).

If travelers must carry prescribed medicines, they should:

- Be sure that cough medicines, diuretics, heart drugs, tranquilizers, sleeping pills, antidepressants, and similar medicines are in their original containers and are clearly labeled.
- Carry only the amount needed for the trip.
- Have a copy of the prescription with a doctor's statement that the medicine is necessary.

Duty-Free Ports. To attract tourist dollars, many countries have *duty-free ports.* These are ports in which no duty or tax is charged on goods either entering or leaving the country. For example, in St. Thomas in the U.S. Virgin Islands, Swiss watches are imported without any duty; they can then be sold to visitors, who can take them out of St. Thomas without duty or tax.

Duty-free ports can theoretically offer goods at lower prices than they cost elsewhere. In reality, this does not always happen. The traveler contemplating a spending spree in other countries would be wise to comparison-shop at home first.

Remember that an item bought in a duty-free port is only duty-free at the place of purchase. When it is brought back to the United States, the normal regulations regarding duties apply. Duty-free ports are not to be confused with duty-free airport shops.

Duty-Free Airport Shops. When leaving the United States, travelers may wish to make some purchases before boarding their outbound aircraft. Liquors, perfumes, cameras, and other luxury items on which there is normally a high U.S. tax are particularly good buys. If purchasing something that will be used completely while abroad, there's no need to be concerned

---

✔ CHECK-UP

Depending on the country visited, a U.S. traveler may need to supply
- ✔ A passport, which is issued by the U.S. government to its citizens.
- ✔ A visa, which is issued by the foreign government to those wishing to enter its country.
- ✔ A tourist card.

For U.S. residents returning to the United States, duty-free articles include
- ✔ Items taken from home and brought back.
- ✔ Items mailed home to one's self by the traveler that do not exceed a market value of $200.
- ✔ Gifts mailed home to friends or relatives that do not exceed $100 in value.
- ✔ Goods produced by certain countries, as may be specified by government agreements.
- ✔ Items purchased abroad up to the personal exemption.

about paying import taxes on it when returning to the states. However, if a partially used or never-used item purchased at a U.S. duty-free airport shop is brought back into the United States, it counts as part of the duty-free allowance or it is taxed by U.S. Customs officials on re-entry.

Health and Safety Abroad

■ WHAT ARE RELIABLE SOURCES OF INFORMATION ABOUT DANGERS WHEN TRAVELING ABROAD, AND WHAT HEALTH PRECAUTIONS SHOULD TRAVELERS TAKE?

No one can guarantee that a traveler will have a safe and healthy trip, but there are many ways that travel professionals can help travelers avoid unnecessary problems and be prepared for unavoidable difficulties. Just by knowing where to go for expert advice and by understanding some commonsense precautions, the travel professional can provide invaluable help.

Finding Out What Is Safe

Travel counselors have a responsibility to tell clients about potential hazards of certain destinations, methods of travel, and activities. For information, the U.S. government is often the best source. In particular, the **Centers for Disease Control and Prevention (CDC)** provides advice for travelers and information about specific diseases abroad, such as malaria, about recommended or required immunizations, and about current health risks by region.

The U.S. Department of State also has information about serious disease outbreaks, natural disasters, and political conditions. It distributes (in print and online) three types of information for international travelers:

■ *Travel warnings.* The U.S. State Department issues a travel warning when it decides to recommend that Americans avoid travel to a specific country.

■ *Public announcements.* Whenever the U.S. State Department perceives a short-term threat to the security of American travelers, it issues a public announcement. Past announcements have included bomb threats to airlines and the anniversaries of terrorist attacks.

■ *Consular information sheets.* For every country in the world, the U.S. State Department posts consular information sheets online. These usually do not give advice, but they do give important information, such as the health conditions, minor political disturbances, crime, and areas of instability.

Once U.S. travelers are abroad, U.S. embassies and consular offices overseas can provide invaluable help in emergencies. These officials replace passports; help travelers find medical assistance; relay emergency messages to and from home; and help travelers who have lost money to contact family, friends, or employers. However, they do not lend monies to travelers who may be in financial difficulty. They also visit U.S. travelers who have been arrested and work to protect their rights and interests, and they notify families in case of death. U.S. citizens traveling independently overseas should register with the nearest U.S. embassy or consular office. Travelers of other nationalities similarly would turn to the embassy or consular office of their own country. U.S. citizens traveling and living abroad should register with The Smart

Palazzo Margherita is the home of the U.S. Embassy in Rome, Italy.

Traveler Enrollment Program (STEP), which is a free program to notify the nearest U.S. embassy or consulate about a trip. More information on this program can be found at https://step.state.gov/.

International organizations are another important source of information about health and safety abroad. The **World Health Organization (WHO)** has information about every country in the world, detailing health risks, health-related certificates required to enter the country, its recommended vaccinations and medications, and other health precautions.

Vaccinations

Usually, vaccinations are not required for direct travel from the United States to most countries, and the United States currently does not require any vaccinations for incoming or returning travelers. But some nations do require visitors to present documentation stating that they have received a specific vaccination or that they are free of HIV, the AIDS virus.

The Bureau of Consular Affairs at the U.S. State Department can provide the current requirements of various countries. In addition, information about immunizations is available from the CDC, and most cities with major airports have a division of the federal Department of Health and Human Services that provides up-to-date information on vaccinations.

Note: Just because a vaccination is not required in order to enter a country does *not* indicate that travelers will be safe from contracting the disease within the country. Governments require vaccinations in order to protect their own citizens against incoming travelers. In contrast, the World Health Organization (WHO) and governments recommend vaccinations to protect travelers. Thus, the difference between a recommendation and a requirement does *not* indicate a difference in the degree of risk to travelers.

Yellow fever, cholera, meningococcal meningitis, typhoid, tetanus, and hepatitis A are among the diseases against which immunizations may be recommended. All vaccinations have an incubation period before they become effective, and some require a series of shots spaced several days apart. Thus, travelers should plan to receive shots well before departure. Because many doctors do not have the necessary vaccines in their offices, travelers must often go to major hospitals, to the Department of Health, or to travel clinics that specialize in pertinent diseases. Because some hospitals and clinics may offer certain inoculations only on certain days, it's important to plan ahead and schedule accordingly. For each immunization, the doctor issues a certificate standardized by WHO.

Seeking Medical Advice and Aid

If travelers have high blood pressure, should they climb the steps at Machu Picchu? Is there a risk of malaria in Nepal? Technical medical questions such as these should be addressed to doctors in the field of travel medicine. They keep current with health conditions worldwide and can provide predeparture counseling, inoculations, preventive medications, and treatment for maladies that result from international travel. They are often affiliated with medical centers or universities. Other doctors, health departments, the CDC, and the International Society of Travel Medicine can provide referrals.

To prepare for an emergency, travelers can obtain updated lists of English-speaking doctors around the world from several organizations. One of the best known is the International Association for Medical Assistance to Travelers (IAMAT), a Canadian organization that lists English-speaking doctors in many countries with a pre-determined fee schedule.

Neither Medicare nor most private health insurance will cover the cost of medical care for travelers abroad. Before departure, travelers should check with their insurance carriers to determine whether their policies cover travel-related medical expenses and should then decide whether they need to purchase additional coverage. The Health Insurance Association of America offers information about travel insurance, as do most travel agencies. It is strongly encouraged that all travelers have travel protection that includes comprehensive medical coverage.

Today, fast-moving changes in the world's medical scenarios can mean the sudden arrival of disease, epidemics and the like, such as the Ebola 2014 outbreak or the Zika Virus epidemic in 2015. The Atlanta-based CDC should be a primary resource for all travel professionals.

If travelers have high blood pressure, should they climb the steps at Machu Picchu?

Other Health Precautions and Problems

Here are a few simple steps for travelers to take before going overseas to avoid or minimize medical problems during a trip. Travelers should:

- Have any necessary dental work done.
- See their doctors if they have a health condition or take medications to be sure they're in good health and have enough of their prescriptions to cover the time they're away.
- Obtain recommended and required vaccinations.
- Carry a small first-aid kit containing adhesive bandages, aspirin, antiseptic, and any over-the-counter drugs they normally require. Those traveling independently or to undeveloped areas should take more extensive medical supplies than those who are part of a tour group or cruise.
- Carry prescription drugs in original, clearly marked containers to avoid any suspicion that they might be illegal.
- Carry extra eyeglasses or contact lenses or a copy of the prescription.
- Carry a copy of their medical coverage and their doctor's phone number.

To minimize the dangers of serious illness and the discomfort of minor disorders, it helps to know something about the most common health problems encountered by travelers abroad. Here is an overview.

Malaria. A serious and sometimes fatal disease, malaria is mosquito-borne. No vaccination is available, but drugs—along with insect repellents and bed nets—can help prevent it. It can linger in the bloodstream for many months before it flares up.

Contaminated Food and Drink. Where hygiene and sanitation are poor, travelers should avoid unpasteurized milk and milk products, such as cheese. Cooked food is preferable to raw vegetables and fresh fruit, which should always be peeled by the traveler. However delicious they look, salads may contain invisible contaminants.

It is usually safe to drink the water in major cities where it is treated with chlorine. Wherever chlorinated water is not available, travelers should substitute carbonated drinks, bottled water, beer, wine, or beverages made with boiling water. If the water is questionable, ice should be avoided.

Contaminated food or water is usually the cause of diarrhea. The disorder is rarely serious or incapacitating, but severe cases may require medical attention, and children are at particular risk. Fruit juices, hot tea, or carbonated drinks can be helpful to the sufferer. Over-the-counter drugs treat some symptoms at the risk of aggravating others.

Motion and Altitude Sickness. Travelers with a history of motion sickness can choose from many over-the-counter remedies that can be taken before departure. Most induce drowsiness and react with alcohol. *Sea-Bands* are wristbands that exert subtle pressure on a point inside the wrist, quelling the disconcerting sensation of motion sickness. There are also patches worn behind the ear.

At altitudes of more than 9,000 feet, even healthy people may suffer from *altitude sickness.* Its symptoms include severe headaches, chest pain, shortness of breath, and intense fatigue. Doctors can prescribe drugs to overcome the symptoms, but elderly people and those with heart or respiratory problems should consult their doctors before traveling to high altitudes. All travelers should rest and take it easy the first day when visiting high-altitude destinations, and itineraries should be planned accordingly.

Travel counselors should learn the altitudes on a passenger's itinerary to properly advise him/her when first planning the trip.

Side Effects of Flying. Flying itself contributes to fatigue. The combination of a high ozone content, low humidity, and constant pressurization in the cabin has a draining effect. Drinking alcohol or overeating worsens the effect; drinking plenty of nonalcoholic fluids can help.

Long flights bring special hazards. First, sitting in one position for a long time may increase the risk of thrombosis (blood clots). To decrease the risk, passengers on long flights should try to exercise in their seats or walk around the plane cabin; they should avoid sleeping through the entire flight. They also may wish to consider compression socks.

Second, long flights may lead to *jet lag* (or *dyschronism*). Its symptoms include the disruption of normal sleeping and eating patterns and mental and physical exhaustion. These may be caused by the fact that a person flying east to west finds a normal day extended; the passenger flying west to east loses hours of sleeping time in the middle of the night. Usually, the worst effects of jet lag are felt on the second or even third day of a trip. Generally, each hour of time differential requires one day of recovery time.

The following steps can minimize the effects of jet lag:

- If possible, schedule arrivals close to the travelers' normal bedtime.
- Schedule time after arrival so that travelers who arrive short of sleep do not immediately have to rush into hectic schedules. Even a short nap may help.
- Before departure, travelers should adjust their eating and sleeping schedules to the time zone of the country to be visited.
- Most important, travelers should not rush around on the day of departure and should arrive at the airport in plenty of time. Many experienced travelers arrange to stay at an airport hotel the night before their departure flight, and some hotels have packages that include keeping passengers' cars while they are traveling. And some travelers, planning a somewhat strenuous trip, may prefer to arrive at the tour's starting point several days ahead of time to adjust to the new time zones.
- If possible, travelers should avoid travel sickness medicines and other drugs that aggravate jet lag.

Doctors may prescribe sleeping medications to ease the insomnia that accompanies jet lag. Some people claim that melatonin, which is available at health food stores, prevents the insomnia, but the scientific verdict on its effectiveness is still to come. Meanwhile, production of melatonin is not regulated by the Food and Drug Administration (FDA), so the quality and strength of the product vary.

✔ CHECK-UP

The U.S. State Department provides three forms of information about countries around the world:
- ✔ An online consular information sheet for each country.
- ✔ A travel warning when the U.S. State Department is recommending that Americans avoid travel to a particular country.
- ✔ Public announcements about specific threats.

To increase their chances of a healthy trip, travelers should
- ✔ Verify their medical, dental, health—and possibly travel—insurance coverage before departure.
- ✔ Obtain recommended as well as required vaccinations.
- ✔ Bring along a basic first-aid kit, a list of doctors abroad, and whatever medications or health aids normally used.
- ✔ Avoid food or water that might be contaminated.
- ✔ Arrange their schedule to minimize the discrepancy between their eating and sleeping schedules at home and at their destination.

Dealing with Money and Other Differences

- HOW ARE CURRENCIES AND MEASUREMENTS USED IN OTHER COUNTRIES CONVERTED, AND WHAT OTHER EVERYDAY DIFFERENCES SHOULD TRAVELERS BE READY TO HANDLE?

If five liters of gasoline costs 200 pesos in Cancún, is gas expensive there? Travelers abroad often come up against a question like this. To answer it, at least three issues must be considered.

First, how much is a liter? Many Americans don't know because it is part of the *metric system,* a measurement system used by most countries but unfamiliar to many Americans. See Table 2.1 for key metric measurements.

TABLE 2.1 Metric Units

Unit	Description	Formula
Liter (l)	A liter is a little more than a quart. For example, 4 liters is about 1 gallon and 5 ounces. Most liquids that tourists buy (such as gasoline, wine, or water) are sold by the liter.	1 l = 0.264 gallon
Meter (m)	A meter is somewhat more than a yard; 100 meters is somewhat longer than a football field. Someone might tell a visitor, "It's about 200 meters past that next street."	1 m = 3.28 feet
Kilometer (km)	A kilometer is 1,000 meters or a bit more than six-tenths of a mile. Highway distances are given in kilometers. If the next city is 100 kilometers away, then it is 62 miles farther.	1 km = 0.62 mile
Gram (g)	There are approximately 28 grams in 1 ounce.	1 g = 0.035 ounce
Kilogram (kg)	A kilogram is 1,000 grams and equals about 2.2 pounds. Thus a 20-kilo baggage allowance would permit 44 pounds. Most market items such as produce and meats are measured in kilos. A quarter-kilo (250 grams) of sausage is a bit more than half a pound.	1 kg = 2.21 pounds
Celsius (C)	The freezing point of water is 0° Celsius (C), or 32° Fahrenheit (F). For example, 100°C (212°F) is the usual boiling point for water at sea level. Normal body temperatureis about 37°C (98.6°F).	°C = (°F − 32) ÷ 1.8

Second, what is a peso worth? How many dollars does it take to buy 200 pesos? The answer depends on the current *exchange rate,* the rate at which the currency of one nation can be exchanged for the currency of another.

Third, to evaluate the cost of a product or service, you need to gauge it against other prices in the country. A dollar may fetch 18 pesos in Mexico, but the cost in dollars for a product or service may be higher in Mexico. Purchasing power is what counts.

Travel professionals should understand how differences like these in measurements, exchange rates, and prices can affect travelers. They should be able to alert travelers to the kinds of things they need to know and to help them evaluate the cost of a trip.

Currencies and Exchange Rates

One thing travelers should know is that governments have rules about their currencies. For example, anyone entering or leaving the United States with more than $10,000 in cash or negotiable securities must report that on a U.S. Customs form. Information about the currency regulations of other nations can be obtained from the national tourist office, consulate, or embassy of the country in question.

Most countries accept only their own currencies, not necessarily U.S. dollars or euros. For illustration purposes, Table 2.2 lists a few of the world's major currencies and the exchange rates that may have applied in July 2019. Two simple rules describe how to convert currencies:

- To convert dollars into a local currency, multiply the current value of the local currency unit per dollar times the number of dollars.
- To convert a local currency into dollars, divide the amount of the local currency by this exchange rate.

Most large-city newspapers and GDSs publish the exchange rates for major currencies, which also can be obtained from the international exchange department of your bank. Many websites provide currency converters with instant quotes. Fortunately, international travelers today deal with fewer differences in currency than they did just a few years ago, thanks to the number of countries that have adopted the euro, the currency of the European Union.

TABLE 2.2 Exchange Rates, July 2019

Country	Currency Unit (Code)	Value of Each Unit in US$	Value of US$1
Australia	Australian dollar (AUD)	US$1.42	00.70 Australian dollars
Canada	Canadian dollar (CAD)	US$0.76	01.30 Canadian dollars
European Union members*	euro (EUR)	US$1.12	00.88 euros
United Kingdom	pound (GBP)	US$1.25	00.79 pounds
India	rupee (INR)	US$0.01	68.75 rupees
Japan	yen (JPY)	US$0.009	1.07 yen
Mexico	peso (MXN)	US$0.05	19.02 pesos

*As of July 2019, 19 countries and territories use the euro as their national currency.
Note: Rates are based on the Universal Currency Converter found at www.xe.com.

Normally, the changes in exchange rates from day to day are not dramatic, but they can be large during the time between booking and departure or during a lengthy trip. Also, when a country is experiencing very high inflation or a crisis, even day-to-day changes can be significant.

Getting Money Abroad

To pay for purchases abroad, travelers have four basic options—cash in the local currency of a country, travelers' checks, ATM cards, and credit cards. It's recommended that travelers not depend on only one of these options but plan to use several, depending on circumstances.

- Obtain some destination currency before leaving home. In the United States, only large banks or special banks at gateway airports stock other currencies. Many national banks will accommodate currency exchanges if the order is placed in advance and up to two weeks are allowed for delivery of the currency. Currencies or drafts in international currencies can also be ordered online through a limited number of sources. However, it is unwise to carry a lot of cash in any currency; travelers should have enough for the first few days and then have other methods of paying as the trip progresses. Travelers with local currency left at the end of the trip should spend the money to avoid having to exchange the money at higher rates upon returning home.
- Obtain traveler's checks, although they rarely are used anymore as consumers turn more and more to credit and debit cards instead, but for those who prefer them they should be bought before leaving home. American Express, the company that started circulating them more than a century ago, is among the few issuers still offering them, along with Visa. The advantage is that they are quickly replaceable in case they are lost or stolen. However, because traveler's checks are increasingly less common, using them is becoming more difficult and time consuming.
- Use an ATM card. Many banks make it possible to obtain money with an ATM card. The traveler should check with his/her own bank before considering this option and be sure to memorize a four-digit PIN (numbers, not letters). A client may want to ask the bank to increase the amount that may be withdrawn daily before leaving. Withdrawals made while traveling will be in the local currency and at an exchange rate stipulated by that bank.

- Use credit cards because they are accepted at many locations, are easy to use for major purchases and provide a record of expenses. It's suggested that travelers check with the credit card companies before leaving home to see which card has the lowest international exchange charge. It's also recommended to inform the credit card company about the travel plans so an unusual spending pattern will not trigger an alert and a halt to honoring purchases. Credit cards also may be used for cash advances.

A modified version of a credit card, called a prepaid or preloaded card, is also worth considering. It can be loaded with a limited amount of money, which cannot be exceeded if the card is lost or stolen. Special fees apply with these cards. Parents find them a helpful way to give travel monies to children who may be traveling apart from the parents.

Everyday Culture

Music, painting, sculpture, architecture, and crafts all form part of the culture that may draw tourists to a country. Everyday life is also filled with the products of a people's culture—rules of etiquette, language, forms of dress, law courts, and technology. These aspects of culture may confront travelers whether they are looking for them or not.

Social Behavior and Laws. Mongolians consider it rude to show surprise or enthusiasm at a guest's arrival. In contrast, travelers arriving on the Marquesas Islands might be crowded by local people greeting them with flowers, songs, and dances. In Saudi Arabia, restaurants, stores, and other public places close for about half an hour when the call for prayer is heard, which happens five times a day.

Variations like these in customs and etiquette are virtually endless. Some differences can be more problematic, however. For example,
- Some countries restrict what can be photographed or what antiques can be bought.
- Alcoholic beverages and other drugs that are legal in the United States are illegal in some countries, and the penalties for using them may be severe.

Traditional clothing and dance reflect Thailand's culture.

- In Saudi Arabia and some other Islamic nations, adult males and females are not free to congregate together in public places, and it is considered inappropriate to touch women. Even intense eye contact that we may use in sales situations in western countries, for example, may be misunderstood.

Religion, history, and the political system provide the soil and seeds for many of these cultural products. On a very practical level, however, differences in electricity, electronic communications, taxes, and language may be most important to the traveler.

Electricity. Electric current in the United States is 110–120 volts. In Europe, Africa, and many countries elsewhere, it is generally 220–240 volts. As a result, travelers who want to use small electrical appliances (including chargers for cell phones and laptop computers) that were designed for use in the United States will need a transformer that converts voltages unless the appliance works on dual voltage. They will also need an adapter for the appliance so that the plug will fit in the wall outlet; the shape of plugs varies around the world.

Although many major hotels throughout the world have adapter plugs available on request, they rarely offer a transformer to convert voltage. Failure to convert the voltage will ruin an appliance. Before leaving, travelers can purchase converter kits that include a transformer and a variety of adapter plugs at U.S. electronics stores. Some of the more modern hotels may have the 110-120 volts in the bathroom for shavers but not necessarily throughout the rest of the hotel room. Cruise lines generally offer both 110 and 220 voltage.

Computers and Internet Connections. Travelers who want to use their laptop computers or handheld devices to connect to the Internet while abroad should be aware of the following:
- The power adapter on most laptop/notebook computers, unlike many other electronic devices, can convert the voltage. People will need to check the information on their current power adapter. Be sure to have a plug adapter only, not a plug adapter/transformer combination.
- It's a good idea to check in advance with the hotel to see what options they provide to connect to the Internet.

Most airports and hotels offer hotspots, areas in which computers with wireless access can connect to the Internet. And if travelers have the right equipment and mobile phone service plan, they can plug their mobile phones into their laptops to go online. Alternatives for going online while abroad include Internet cafés, which charge a fee based on the time spent online on their computers. There are devices available that can serve as mobile hotspots so that travelers can have internet access wherever they travel.

Phones. Making international phone calls from a hotel room may be very expensive. Travelers can purchase an international calling card before leaving the United States, but they should verify that the card will work in the country they are visiting. Many popular tourist locations have phones specially equipped for international calls. The traveler purchases a phone card from a nearby store and inserts the card into the phone.

A mobile phone service may be the best option for making international telephone calls. In several countries, however, many U.S. cellular phone plans will not work. The Global System for Mobile telephone (GSM) is a standard that is used in 200 countries. Travelers may want to rent a GSM or a satellite phone that provides service in the country they are visiting. Some mobile phone providers offer international calling plans that can be activated for a temporary period.

Taxes. Many nations use a form of tax unfamiliar to most Americans, the value-added tax. It is based on the fact that each stage of manufacture or distribution adds to the market value of a product or service. A ***value-added tax (VAT)*** levies a tax on this added value at each stage of manufacture or distribution and adds the total to the ultimate cost of the product. For the consumer a VAT resembles a sales tax, but the amount of the tax is included in the price charged. The VAT rates in European countries can be as high as 25 percent of the total purchase price.

Some European countries encourage tourists to shop by offering a refund of VATs. The procedures vary from country to country. Travelers should always ask about the procedures and the minimum-purchase requirements for obtaining a refund at the stores where they make purchases. Unless making fairly large purchases or all in one store, it's often not worth the time and paperwork needed to obtain the refund. It often requires packing those items in a special area in your suitcase and taking it to the refund counter at the airport before check-in. This means arriving at the airport especially early to handle this transaction.

Languages. These days, some knowledge of English is widespread in major metropolitan areas around the world. Unless travelers go off the beaten path, their ignorance of local languages may create few difficulties. But in a medical emergency or business negotiation or whenever something important and precise must be conveyed, even those who enjoy dealing with other languages should consider contacting someone to interpret.

Travelers who want to be courteous and prepared should learn at least a few words in the local language. Most useful to know are numbers, names of common things they might need (train station, water, and so on), and basic phrases, such as "Hello," "Do you speak English?" "Please," "Thank you," "Where is . . . ?" "Pardon me," and "Good-bye." This is particularly important for those traveling independently. Those traveling on escorted group tours have a tour leader to assist them in emergencies or difficulties.

CHAPTER WRAP-UP

CHAPTER HIGHLIGHTS

To give advice to their clients, plan trips, or construct itineraries, travel professionals need a working knowledge of world geography and an understanding of differences among destinations. They need to be aware of the political, economic, and physical factors and events that influence travel to destinations around the world. In addition, travel professionals should be well versed in the procedures and requirements that international travelers face when entering and leaving countries and the health, safety, and cultural issues related to international travel. The discussions in this chapter represent the first steps in acquiring this knowledge. Here is a review of the objectives with which we began the chapter.

1. **Identify seven characteristics that shape the appeal of destinations, ensuring that people want to visit.** Among the key characteristics of a destination are its climate, natural and man-made attractions, accessibility, costs, culture, competition, and safety.

2. **Explain how to locate a destination and how to calculate time differences and travel times.** A destination can be located precisely by giving its distance from the equator and the prime meridian—in other words, by citing its latitude and longitude. Usually, though, places are located by describing their location relative to natural features, such as continents, islands, oceans, and rivers.

   The world is divided into 24 time zones, starting at the prime meridian, which is at Greenwich, England. The time at Greenwich is known as Greenwich mean time (GMT) or universal time coordinated (UTC). The time changes by one hour at most time zones. To the west, one hour is subtracted at each zone crossed; to the east, one hour is added at each zone. Halfway around the world from Greenwich in the Pacific is the international date line, where, by international agreement, the calendar day changes. It is one day later west of the line than it is to the east.

3. **Outline the major factors that shape the climate of a destination.** Wind, pressure, temperature, humidity, clouds, and precipitation are atmospheric conditions that define the weather and hence the climate. Among the key geographic factors that interact to create the climate are latitude, altitude, proximity to bodies of water, and prevailing winds. As a result, particular types of climate recur at varying places around the globe. For example, northern Australia and southern Asia experience monsoons, and a Mediterranean climate is characteristic of parts of California and Spain and many popular resort spots. Variations in climate may occur over short distances—for example, between the windward and leeward sides of mountains.

4. **Describe at least five key sources of information about destinations.** Firsthand experience, whether through personal travel or fam trips, general education, and formal courses represent sources of both information and the background necessary to understand and evaluate information about destinations. For specific questions, sources include colleagues, tour operators, tourist offices and other government offices, travel websites, and references—in print or online—such as atlases, guidebooks, newspapers, magazines, and brochures.

5. **Outline the requirements that governments place on international travelers visiting their countries.** Governments restrict the movement of both people and goods across their borders. The requirements on travelers vary with the country and the citizenship of the traveler, and they may change with little notice. To enter another country, travelers may be required to produce proof of citizenship, a passport, a visa, or a tourist card. In addition, vaccination certificates may be needed. Travelers also must obey local laws and customs regulations, and they may owe a duty on goods purchased abroad. Many governments encourage tourism by setting up duty-free ports. International travelers may seek help from their own government through its embassies and consulates.

6. **Identify reliable sources of information about dangers abroad and common problems encountered by international travelers.** Government agencies and international organizations (such as the CDC, State Department, and WHO) are usually the best sources of information on health and safety issues abroad. Among the most common health problems encountered by international travelers are diarrhea, motion sickness, altitude sickness, and jet lag. Travelers can often alleviate or avoid these by taking common-sense precautions. Travelers to regions where serious illnesses—such as malaria, cholera, and yellow fever—are a danger should protect themselves with the appropriate medications or vaccinations. Travelers to potentially volatile countries should also check U.S. State Department recommendations.

7. **Explain how to convert one currency into another and outline other differences that international travelers should be prepared to handle.** To convert a currency, check a GDS, a website, a major newspaper, or the international department of your bank to determine the current exchange rate. Next, to convert dollars into the local currency, multiply the exchange rate of the local currency per dollar by the number of dollars. To convert the local currency into dollars, divide the amount in the local currency by the exchange rate.

Besides planning how to pay for items abroad, international travelers should be prepared to deal with differences in measurement systems, with possible difficulties in phone and electronic communications, with language differences, and with local customs and laws.

KEY TERMS

A list of key terms introduced in this chapter follows. If you do not recall the meaning of these terms, see the Glossary.

24-hour clock	latitude
altitude	leeward
atlas	longitude
CDC	Mediterranean climate
climate	metric system
consulate	monsoon
continent	NTO
destination	ocean
destination geography	passport
destination management and promotion	peninsula
duty	prime meridian
duty-free port	river
embassy	sea
equator	sound
exchange rate	trait
familiarization trip (fam trip)	tourist card
geography	The Travel Institute
Greenwich mean time (GMT)	universal time coordinated (UTC)
gulf	value-added tax (VAT)
international date line	visa
island	WHO
isthmus	windward

REVIEW QUESTIONS

1. What is the difference between latitude and longitude?

2. When it is 1:00 p.m. in San Francisco, what time is it in London?

3. What sources would you consult in order to determine the attractions of a visit to Tonga?

4. What are the three main types of identifying documents that travelers need, and how would they obtain each of them?

5. What is a duty-free port?

6. What two websites would you go to first for advice about the health and safety conditions in another country?

Using Technology

Thirty years ago, most travel companies did not have fax machines. Now the Internet, e-mail, smartphones, and tablets have changed how business is done; most travel professionals could not work without these and other technologies. For many travelers, too, travel and technology go hand in hand; many use their own computers to plan or buy their trips.

The Close-Up on Careers in Technology describes a few of the many jobs in the travel industry created by new technologies. We focus in this chapter particularly on three: personal computers, GDSs, and the Internet. We also mention a few new devices that can enhance the travel professional's working experience.

Personal Computers and GDSs

■ WHAT ROLE DO PERSONAL COMPUTERS AND GDSs PLAY IN THE TRAVEL INDUSTRY?

Computers are at the heart of the technologies that have transformed the travel/tourism industry. It was the marketing of the personal computer in the 1980s that sparked a revolution in our lives. A *personal computer* is a computer that has its own *central processing unit (CPU)*, a collection of electronic circuitry that allows a single computer to run a great variety of software. Depending on the software used, a personal computer can perform a vast array of specialized tasks, such as creating graphs, keeping financial records, researching destinations, and many more.

Software for the Office

Personal computers use two basic types of software: an operating system and applications software. An *operating system* is the software that manages the computer system; Microsoft's Windows, Macintosh's OS, and Linux are examples.

The earliest operating systems had a ***command interface,*** which means that users communicated with the computer by typing commands. Users memorized strings of keystrokes to tell the operating system what to do. Computers became much easier for novices to use when operating systems were created that had a ***graphical user interface (GUI),*** which means that users control the computer by using a pointing device, such as a mouse, to click on

---

CLOSE-UP: CAREERS IN TECHNOLOGY

More money is spent on travel than on any other category of goods and services sold on the Internet. Every supplier and retailer has been affected by this revolution in the industry. Most now have their own websites or link with others who do. The result is a myriad of new professional positions, generally requiring a technical and analytical background, but with a travel bent.

■ **Position** Manager of database marketing, planning, and analysis

Description This position is responsible for ensuring that information about past and potential customers can be retained and analyzed and for devising direct marketing campaigns (by mail or online) in a cost-effective manner. Formulating strategies and executing direct marketing campaigns are also the job of this manager.

Qualifications This position requires proven success with direct marketing, database management, response analysis, and management. A B.A. in marketing is required, in addition to five years' experience in direct marketing.

■ **Position** Programmer analyst

Description This position is responsible for evaluating and implementing new technologies and products. The programmer analyst often develops specifications and design documentation, oversees the project and must be able to communicate the status of projects.

Qualifications A B.S. degree and two to three years' hands-on experience with appropriate hardware and software are required. The person in this position needs solid problem-solving and analytical skills, the ability to organize and meet deadlines, strong attention to detail, and capability to work both independently and with a team.

■ **Position** Technology planning specialist—interactive marketing

Description This professional serves as a member of the team responsible for the operation, infrastructure, and security of the company's website. Responsibilities include working with a development team to gather infrastructure requirements, managing external vendors, and analyzing technical recommendations. This professional uses expertise in technology, along with project management skills, to manage infrastructure projects.

Qualifications The technology planning specialist must be able to work in a fast-paced, changing environment; to set priorities; and to manage multiple projects. The person in this position must have excellent communication skills, project management experience, and a strong technical background.

■ **Position** Digital marketing manager

Description This position is responsible for using the Internet (especially social media) as a marketing vehicle, for overseeing strategies for maximizing revenues through the use of websites, and for developing new websites.

Qualifications Requirements for this position are likely to include a B.S. degree, strong experience in interactive marketing, and a record of successfully evaluating, creating, and executing marketing programs. The person in this position needs an ability to succeed in a fast-paced, changing environment, as well as financial acumen and strong communication, leadership, and management skills.

■ **Other positions** Database administrator; online community manager; project manager; software design engineer; webmaster.

commands that are displayed on the computer screen. Compared with a graphical interface, a command interface takes much longer to learn, but once learned, it allows the user to find and enter information much more quickly.

Applications software is software that allows the computer to perform specific types of tasks, such as writing letters, creating brochures, managing budgets, or drawing graphs. The basic types of applications used in offices include the following:

- *Word processing software* makes it easy to draft, revise, print, and store letters, and other documents. Microsoft's Word is the best-known example.
- *Desktop publishing software* goes beyond word processing to allow users to integrate text and graphics in sophisticated formats for publications, such as brochures and books. Examples are Adobe's InDesign, Microsoft Publisher, and an array of online applications (e.g., Canva.com, Adobe Spark).
- *Presentation graphics software* creates high-quality displays of images, charts, and numerical information. Corel Draw, Adobe Illustrator, and PowerPoint, for example, let you create graphics for presentations to groups.
- *Database management software* stores and sorts organized collections of data, which are called **databases** or **customer relationship management (CRM)** systems. Examples include Microsoft Access. With programs like these, you can create profiles of clients and then retrieve client lists with particular characteristics, such as a love of cruising.
- *Cash and office management software* provides up-to-the-minute reports of a business's cash flow and financial well-being. Quicken and Sage 50 are examples.
- *Internet applications* allow users to send and receive e-mail, to connect to the Internet and to design websites.

There are also many programs specifically designed to meet the needs of travel professionals. Very large travel agencies may design their own software or have it custom-made, but even small agencies can buy travel-specific software. Software of particular interest to travel businesses includes the following:

- Database programs, such as ClientBase (a Sabre CRM offering) and TESS by Travel eSolutions, not only organize lists with the usual information (names, addresses, phone numbers, e-mail addresses, and so on) but also make it easy to store and retrieve information about clients' travel history and their likes and dislikes (see Figure 3.1).
- Back-office systems handle functions related to accounting and marketing, such as tracking sales by agents, commission receivables, clients' invoices and payments. Trams Back Office, a Sabre offering, connects reservation systems with back-office functions, such as accounting.
- Integrated software links programs that handle back-office functions with client databases. ClientBase and WinCruise are examples. Thanks to the integration of systems, when a travel counselor enters a client's name and makes a booking, the computer can automatically bring up on the screen information about the client from the agency's database and immediately transfer information about the booking to the accounting system and the database.
- Specialized Internet applications make it easy for travel agencies to book online. One example of these *booking engines* is VAX VacationAccess, which travel agencies use to book tours and cruises online. Some booking engines now allow *dynamic packaging*, which makes it easy for travel sellers to create and book travel packages themselves. From one online site, they can research and book several travel components (such as a hotel as well as air travel and a rental car) and offer them to the client as a package for a single price. Additional tools include itinerary management from Travefy and Umapped.

These and other software packages designed for the travel industry are providing a supplement and even an alternative to what has been the key electronic tool for travel counselors—global distribution systems.

Global Distribution Systems (GDSs)

Years before computers were on desks in travel/tourism offices, travel professionals were using computer technology every day and communicating with distant computers. The airlines were the driving force behind this automation. In the 1950s, they began to use computers to keep track of fares, reservations, and the seats available on their own flights. In the 1970s, United Airlines and then American and TWA began to install computerized systems in travel agencies. These systems allowed travel agencies to obtain information and make reservations for several airlines. They were the first airline computer reservation systems. A *computer reservation system,* or *CRS,* is a

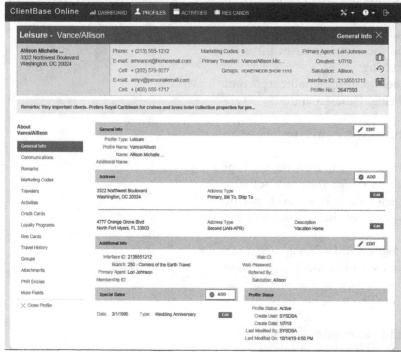

FIGURE 3.1 ClientBase Profile and ResCard

The Client Base Profile screen will hold all of your clients' information, from dates of birth to credit cards. The ResCards will hold any and all trip segments you are working on, making it easy to track, look up and invoice. There are many components when making a reservation; it is very helpful to have it all in one place.

Source: Reprinted by permission of TRAMS, Inc.

computerized system that links distributors and suppliers to a centralized storehouse of information for the primary purpose of making reservations. It is designed to create and maintain a database concerning reservations. CRSs originally handled only airline reservations.

From CRSs to GDSs. For almost two decades, nearly 80 percent of the CRSs in travel agencies came from two companies—Sabre (then owned by American Airlines) and *Apollo* (then owned by United Airlines).

Today, GDS systems unite word processing, accounting, and database management functions.

Reservations on hundreds of major airlines throughout the world could be made on any of the systems. Travel agencies leased the CRS, including the hardware, from the airline. The system looked much like a personal computer does today, but it was different in an important way. It was a *dumb terminal*; that is, it could exchange information with the airline's central computer, but it could not do any processing of its own.

The 1990s brought many changes to CRSs, partly because of the spreading use of personal computers and the Internet. The systems themselves are now commonly called *global distribution systems,* or *GDSs,* and most systems are owned and run by companies independent of the airlines. Other changes in GDSs are more obvious to users. Dumb terminals are a thing of the past; on today's GDS, users can run a host of programs to perform tasks, such as word processing, accounting, and database management. Both command interfaces and graphical interfaces are available. And GDSs offer a wealth of information on all travel products, not just air travel.

With today's GDSs, travel counselors can, for example,

- Check the schedule and seat availability of flights on any of the world's major carriers nearly a year in advance, including connecting service between cities.
- Quote fares.
- Price most itineraries and book flight reservations.
- Check hotel room rates and availability and confirm hotel reservations.
- Confirm car rental reservations.
- Reserve and ticket Amtrak rail travel.
- Find information on international rail service.
- Obtain information on tours, packages, and cruises and book them.
- Find information about a destination, such as its weather conditions, theater offerings, and convention facilities.
- Order theater tickets and arrange limousine service.
- Keep files on frequent travelers and their preferences.
- Access the GDS through their laptops and be travel counselors anywhere.
- Use the Internet to send confirmation to clients and access reservations that were made in the GDS.

The companies that run GDSs are sometimes called *hosts* or *vendors.* They obtain revenue from suppliers that pay to have their services included in the system, as well as from travel agencies that subscribe to the system.

Whether the GDS continues to be the travel counselor's best friend or not remains to be seen; some suppliers (like airlines) are rebelling at the fees they must pay the vendor and are looking to circumvent the GDS.

Suppliers, Travel Agencies, and GDSs. Many suppliers have their own CRSs but still participate in a GDS. They have the choice of various levels of participation at various costs. For example, an airline might have its schedule displayed on the GDS, but not information about the availability of seats on its flights; this is the least expensive level of participation. At more expensive levels, the GDS also indicates the availability of the supplier's product (such as available seats) and allows reservations to be made through the GDS. At the most expensive level of participation, there is a *direct link* between the supplier's own computer system and the GDS.

When a direct link exists, GDS users receive up-to-the-minute information about the supplier's product. When there is no direct link, the information displayed on the GDS may be out-of-date. The difference is critical if you are interested in whether a seat is available on a flight or whether a room is still available at a particular price. Travel counselors must determine by experience, on a case-by-case basis, when the information about a supplier on the GDS is likely to be reliable.

CLOSE-UP: ON THE JOB WITH DEE DEE DANKAUSKAS, GDS TECHNICIAN

Following her natural interest, Dee Dee Dankauskas began taking advanced classes in computers even before she completed her travel training. She wound up uniquely qualified for emerging jobs because few techie job seekers know anything about how the travel industry works.

"One day in early 2001, dozens of potential travelers went on the Internet and looked up the airfare between two major cities and found that the fare was a dollar. Surely, they all knew that the fare was a mistake, but the more enterprising booked the fare and the ticket. The airline was advised by its lawyers that it should honor the fare, and so it did. This just shows the importance of the hundreds of people who are putting information into computers every day. Garbage in, garbage out, as they used to say. In this case, garbage in and an almost free ticket out—out of the airline's pocket, that is.

"My first travel job was as an agent at a discount ticket seller/consolidator in Chicago. We dealt directly with clients and with travel agencies. I don't like to be idle for a second, and I found that what I could do best was figure out prices, churn out tickets and make my computer hum. At least I enjoyed those things better than counseling clients who weren't sure what they wanted or where they wanted to go. I'm not the patient type.

"When I heard from a friend about a position at Galileo, I asked for an interview and got the job and a hike in salary. The work was just as interesting, and I was on the cutting edge of what was happening with computers in travel.

"I started out inputting fares. We all had our own airline that we were responsible for, and we'd send changes to the Galileo mainframe system three times a day. We could change fares three times a day on the same route for that airline, though of course that didn't always happen. But when there was a fare war, our supervisor would just say, 'Plan on working late.'

"In recent years, surcharges, airport taxes, landing fees, customs and immigration fees, and other amounts also changed frequently. They all had to be changed and monitored. Airline ticket agents and travel agents in New Delhi, Cape Town, or Buenos Aires would be charging those fees seconds after I entered them. And if I made a mistake, they'd be charging that wrong amount until it was corrected.

"As a matter of fact, for a while I worked on auditing fares, too. If another airline claimed a mistake had been made in a ticket three months ago, I had to trace the history of what that fare was at the exact moment it was issued. Then if an error was found, we had to determine if it was Galileo's error. Somebody had to pay for it.

"Now I'm at the Help Desk at the Data Center. I help suppliers who are on our system. If any glitch occurs in the computer linkup between Galileo and Hertz, shall we say, a code yellow flashes on my screen, and I monitor it. Usually the connection comes right back on, and everything is fine. But if other codes are flashed, they are more serious. On a code red, I call the supplier immediately because some problem has broken the connection, and agents will not be able to book them.

"Of course, there are quality control people monitoring everything I do. Advancement to this area is always a possibility, but so is the possibility of computer jobs with other companies."

Travel agencies generally sign multi-year contracts to gain access to a GDS. There may also be a monthly payment with a small fee for each transaction. The agency may choose to

- Lease the system, including the hardware, with a direct link to the GDS.
- Use its own computer hardware and contract with the GDS for the system's database and reservation capability, with a direct link to the GDS.
- Use its own computer hardware, contract with the GDS for the system's database and reservation capability and reach it through the Internet.

As their contracts with GDSs run out, travel agencies are looking at other options. They might contract with a third party or host agency that provides access to multiple GDSs, or they might bypass the GDSs by making reservations on suppliers' own websites. They might use systems, such as VAX VacationAccess, which is free to travel agencies, to book online. Relations between GDS companies and travel agencies are in a state of flux.

GDSs Today. When the airlines owned the forerunners of today's GDSs, people worried that an airline could use its control of a reservation system to gain an unfair advantage in selling tickets. The U.S. Department of Transportation issued and enforced rules to prevent bias in how information was displayed on reservation systems and to prohibit unfair practices in contracts with suppliers. In 2004, however, the government ended its regulation of GDSs.

Today, the four major GDSs are *Sabre, TravelPort's Galileo, Amadeus,* and *Worldspan* systems (see Table 3.1). When people go on the Internet to visit sites hosted by airlines and by online travel agencies, the prices, schedules, flights, hotels, etc. come from the GDSs. As a result, the companies that own the major GDSs are a huge force throughout the travel industry.

TABLE 3.1 Global Distribution Systems

Global Distribution System	Originators of System	Current Ownership
Amadeus	Four European airlines	Amadeus IT Holdings
Galileo (known as Apollo in the United States and Japan)	United Airlines (in partnership with foreign airlines)	Travelport IT Holding
Sabre	American Airlines	Sabre Holdings
Worldspan	Delta, Northwest, and TWA	Travelport IT Holding

✔ CHECK-UP

Important uses for applications software in travel offices include
- ✔ Word processing.
- ✔ Database management.
- ✔ Cash management.
- ✔ Presentation graphics.
- ✔ Internet applications.

The major GDSs are
- ✔ Sabre.
- ✔ Galileo.
- ✔ Amadeus.
- ✔ Worldspan.

Major uses of GDSs include
- ✔ Checking the schedules, availability, and fares for flights around the world.
- ✔ Booking flights.
- ✔ Finding information about and booking hotel rooms, car rentals, and rail tickets.
- ✔ Finding information about the weather and attractions at a destination.

The Internet

Years ago, the connection from a travel agency's CRS to an airline's computer hundreds of miles away seemed a rare and wonderful thing. Today, millions of people connect to distant computers as easily as they turn on their TV set by going on the Internet. The ***Internet*** is a worldwide network of thousands of computer networks; it allows any computer or smartphone on one of the networks to communicate with any other device also on any of the networks. Computers, called *servers*, store and distribute the messages at nodes in the networks.

The Internet began in 1969 as a U.S. Defense Department project, but the ideas that turned it into a tool that could be used by the general public only date to 1989. It was then that researchers at a European physics laboratory (CERN) began to circulate the proposals that led to the creation of the ***World Wide Web,*** a system that makes it easy to present and to retrieve information on the Internet. Most every household in the United States is now connected to the Internet, and hundreds of millions of Americans not only communicate but also buy and sell online daily.

Using the Internet

Internet Security. The beauty of this industry is that it allows many people the flexibility to work from the beach, their homes, and local coffee shops. However, it is imperative that all users exploring the Internet adopt policies for online security and data protection. This applies not only to protecting clients' files. It also applies to protecting personal laptops and systems from malware and viruses, and it applies to keeping passwords secure.

WiFi networks are available at many sites, including airports, hotels, businesses, restaurants, and some cities.

Many people don't realize that using public WiFi is not secure. This means that, anytime you make a transaction (storing a credit card, making a payment, etc.), you are exposing that information to hackers and identity thieves. Tips to protecting yourself and your clients include using a *virtual public network (VPN)*—which provides a secure Internet connection so users can share information across insecure public WiFi—and using a password manager—a software application that safely stores passwords in an encrypted format. When collecting and processing clients' personal information, you should consult your attorney to make sure you are complying with the *General Data Protection Regulation (GDPR)*—for clients residing in the European Union (EU)—and with any applicable consumer privacy laws of your state. Finally, when handling clients' sensitive credit card information, be sure to follow PCI compliance standard regulations. View Chapter 12, in the Digital Communications section, for more detail on the *Payment Card Industry Data Security Standard (PCI DSS).*

Accessing the Internet to Conduct Business

The ability to communicate instantaneously, share and edit documents, and access software have radically altered the way travel counselors operate. Electronic mail, *e-mail,* alone has enabled travel counselors to conduct mass and targeted marketing, to communicate directly and quickly with suppliers, clients, and co-workers. (Chapter 12, on communications, discusses tips on when and how to use e-mail.)

Here are some other important uses of the Internet:

- Agents can work from anywhere. As long as their location has internet/ *WiFi* access, travel advisors always can care for their clients. *WiFi* (short for "wireless fidelity") is a wireless network that broadcasts over a different part of the electromagnetic spectrum than cellular networks do.
- Advisors can manage multiple marketing platforms through social media companies, like Facebook, Instagram, LinkedIn, and Pinterest, as well as through dozens of website providers (e.g., Squarespace, Wix, and Wordpress). Additionally, software in the cloud marketing tools, like Active Campaign and Constant Contact, provide agents with the ability to find new sales leads and book more business.
- Companies can set up *intranets,* which are communications systems within an organization that are accessible only by people within that organization.
- Companies and other organizations can also set up *extranets,* which are intranets that are partially accessible to authorized outsiders. These "portals" allow business partners to exchange information and perform interactions online.
- Cruise line travel agency portals, for example, provide authorized travel agencies with itinerary and ship information, marketing and training materials, and special client offers.

Exploring the Internet

Today, almost all that people need to do is point and click with a mouse in order to find the text, images, video, or sounds they are looking for. These billions of pieces of information are organized in a series of interconnected pages, called *websites.* The first page of a website is known as its *home page.*

Several innovations made this possible:

- *Hypertext,* a process that embeds connections between documents. It creates an electronic link between related pieces of information stored in different documents. Thanks to hypertext, users can click on a highlighted word or image in a document and be taken to a related website. For example, on the websites of many travel agencies, users can click on a link that takes them to the website of a supplier, such as a hotel.
- *Hypertext transfer protocol,* or *HTTP,* which defines rules for sending and receiving information, something like a secret handshake that lets a document in the door.
- *Hypertext markup language,* or *HTML,* the code that makes documents readable by computers that use different operating systems and other software.
- *Web **browsers,*** software that translates HTML documents and displays them in a readable form on a computer. Microsoft's Internet Explorer, Google's Chrome, and Apple's Safari are popular browsers, but, as with everything in the world of technology, new tools constantly are being developed.
- ***Uniform resource locators,*** or ***URLs,*** a standardized system for identifying documents. In other words, URLs give addresses to websites.

These tools together make information from the Internet easily accessible.

URLs. To get to a website, the user simply types its address, its URL. For example, the URL for The Travel Institute's home page is http://www.thetravelinstitute.com. This address illustrates the two main parts of a URL:

1. The *protocol:* http://. This tells the browser that the information is located on a server that uses the HTTP protocol.
2. The *domain name:* www.thetravelinstitute.com. The host of a site pays to register a domain name; a nonprofit organization (ICANN) regulates the companies that sell the names. Most sites today use the suffix ".com" in their domain names; it was originally used to indicate that a website was a commercial site. Other common suffixes are ".org" (for a nonprofit organization) and ".gov" (for a government-run site).

After the domain name, URLs may also include a *path* and *filename,* which point to a particular part of the website. For example, typing http://www.thetravelinstitute.com/membership will take you directly to The Travel Institute's membership page.

Search Engines. If you do not know the address for a website, you can go for help to a search engine like Google, Bing, or Yahoo. **Search engines** are websites that provide indexes of websites. If you go to a search engine and type the topic you are looking for, the search engine lists websites and URLs related to that topic (see Figure 3.2). Clicking on a URL makes that web page appear on your screen.

Not all search engines are created equal—far from it. Search engines have (1) different databases, (2) different ways of retrieving information from Web pages, (3) different indexes, or ways of organizing Web documents, and (4) different ways of ranking their results. If you conduct the same search on different search engines, you will obtain different results.

As use of the Internet soars, variations of standard search engines, such as meta-crawlers and travel search engines, have been created. *Meta-crawlers,* also called *meta-search sites,* allow a single query to be sent to several search engines simultaneously. Examples include Kayak and Trivago. One query produces a search of numerous search engines, compiling the results on a single page.

Travel search engines, also called *travel aggregators,* specialize in searching supplier travel sites. Travelocity, Expedia, and Cheapflights are examples.

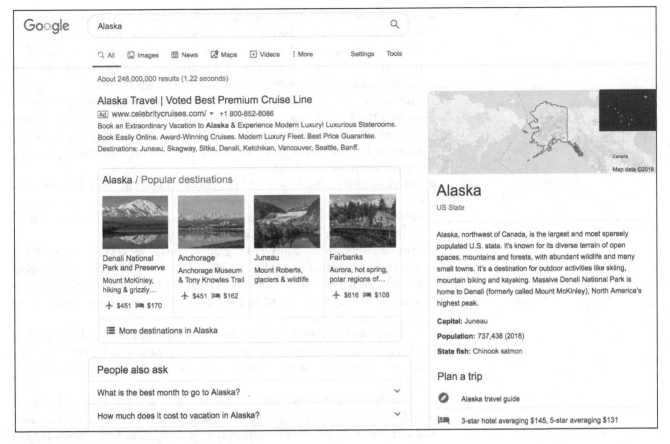

FIGURE 3.2 Searching for Alaska

When "Alaska" was entered as the topic to be searched by Google, this search engine listed about 294,000,000 websites. Usually, search engines list the most relevant sites first, but listings also can depend on payments to the search engine by website hosts. Google lists suggestions relating to your topic when you type your subject in the search box. Learning to conduct effective searches will put relevant information at your fingertips quickly. You also can click on News, Images, Maps, and Videos for more information.

Aggregators for specific travel products are increasingly popular, like Airbnb for home rentals and Squaremouth.com and TravelInsurance.com for travel insurance.

With the help of search engines, people with little expertise or experience can use the Internet to access travel information from just about anywhere in the world.

Researching Online

The Internet is an incomparable research aid; it puts the equivalent of millions of libraries on your desktop. What kinds of sites are most useful to travel professionals, and what skills are necessary to use them effectively for research?

Sources on Travel. Suppose you are a travel counselor and Jane Doe decides to book the flights you recommended, but she has questions about the trip. She asks about the weather, sightseeing, hotels, car rentals, restaurants, documentation requirements, driving distances, currency conversions, theaters, and parks. You can find answers to her questions online through the following ways:

- *Government entities.* National tourist offices, countries, states, provinces, counties, cities, and many other government agencies have websites. Often these are the most authoritative, reliable sources available. Information from the U.S. State Department, for example, offers reliable updates on travel security, and its website (www.travel.state.gov) is the place to go for information on topics, such as documentation requirements for travel outside the United States. Information from government tourist offices, such as the Bahamas Tourist Authority (www.bahamas.com), is usually accurate. But remember that tourist offices are in the business of putting a destination in the best light.
- *Travel industry associations.* ASTA, ARC, CLIA, The Travel Institute—organizations for just about every imaginable segment of the travel industry have websites, and many of these provide a wealth of information on the industry or destinations, or both.
- *Printed publications.* Many hotel guides, consumer travel reports, trade magazines, and other printed materials used by travel agencies and travelers are also available online. Leading periodicals have websites that include much of the material found in their printed versions. Many websites are replacing print publications.
- *Suppliers and distributors.* Airlines, hotel chains, car rental companies, railroads, cruise lines, ferry companies, tour operators, and every other type of supplier and distributor publish schedules and reservation information online.

Keep in mind that the goal of these sites is to sell; the information must be judged accordingly. But don't avoid using these sites. Very often, suppliers and distributors present information that is difficult to find elsewhere, and their sites are often easier to use and more attractive than those from noncommercial sources.

- *Individuals.* Many people create their own websites for no reason except their interest in or dedication to a topic. These sites (travel blogs, for example) reflect their owners' tastes and opinions. Some look like tourist office sites at first glance. They can be chock-full of information, or they can be noninformative, irrelevant impressions about one person's trip.

Many websites restrict access to certain parts of the site. Some sections may be open only to people who have registered with the site or to people who are members of a certain organization or who have other credentials. Many suppliers, for example, restrict access to part of their site to travel counselors, which strengthens the bond between suppliers and travel agencies and allows for discussion of some confidential information, such as commissions and other matters to which the client traveler does not have access.

At the same time, most travel websites are linked to other sites. For example, many have links to sites that will produce maps of just about any place on earth or give conversions for currencies from around the world. The number of possible sources, as well as the amount of information on each site, can be overwhelming.

Keys to Effective Research. To use the Internet effectively as a research tool, you need to be able, first, to conduct effective searches. That requires learning how to make the most of search engines. Although their features vary, the basic steps in conducting a search are similar in all search engines.

The key step in conducting an effective search is to use the correct combination of keywords and commands in your queries. Figure 3.2 demonstrates a search that is too broad. The searcher typed "Alaska" and

Sources of information about travel sites are plentiful.

received almost 300 million relevant sites! The Help section on search engines indicates commands that you can use to refine your searches. Learn to use the advanced search features of your favorite search engines so the engines will give you a short list of the most relevant websites. Learn to be more specific, such as "Alaska Inside Passage," for example.

In addition, for effective online research, you need to exercise the same thinking skills that should be applied to any information. Websites must be examined at least as critically as printed material. In particular,

- *See who is sponsoring the site.* Does the host of the site have an interest in pushing a certain point of view? Is it likely to be an unbiased source of information? Note that the vast number of online travel sites can give both consumers and travel professionals the impression that there is much more competition for their business than actually exists. In fact, many online companies have little known close ties with each other; one may even own the other.
- *Check when the information was last updated.* Finding this information may require a few clicks and scrolling to small type at the bottom of a page.
- *Go directly to the official source.* If you find information at a secondary source, validate the information with a primary source. For example, if you read on one site that the U.S. government has a new regulation about airport security, you can check that information on the site of the government agency in charge of airport security (the Transportation Security Administration or TSA). Perhaps the best feature of the Internet is that it gives you access to official resources; you no longer have to rely on out-of-date information from third parties.

Advertising and Marketing Online

Anyone who has gone online and seen the streams of ads that appear, unbidden, on computer screens understands the World Wide Web is a major advertising medium. (In fact, if companies were not willing to pay to advertise online, the Internet could not offer so much information for free.) Some travel companies advertise online, but most are more likely to market themselves by hosting their own websites.

You are a travel counselor who just gave your business card to a friend of a friend. She mentions that she's planning to go to the Caribbean for her honeymoon and expects that she and her fiancé will check the Internet and reserve the trip themselves to save some money. How would you respond?

You almost always want to respond to a person by finding an area of agreement. "Yes, it's amazing what you can do on the Internet," you might say. "We know all the best honeymoon hotels on each island. I'd love to tell you about the ones our clients have raved about to make sure you don't book at one they were disappointed with. If you two would like to come in next week and describe your dream getaway to me, I can tell you which ones might fit."

If she seems responsive, follow up with, "What day would be best for you?" If she seems reluctant, you might ask for her phone number or e-mail address. You want to keep as personal a connection as possible, so a meeting or phone number is better than an e-mail address. Your object in the future will be to have another face-to-face meeting to plan her honeymoon—hardly a trip she would want to leave to chance.

Even grade school children can create a website, particularly with the templates available today. But the host of a successful site must accomplish three more difficult tasks:

- The site itself must be designed so it is simple for people to use, yet complex enough to meet its objectives.
- The site must be promoted so that people visit it. In order to attract people to their sites, businesses need to advertise or to pay search engines to feature their sites when people ask for certain types of information. They can also become so expert in one specific area that search engines list them as top choices when someone searches for sites related to that area.
- The site must be maintained continuously.

The difficulty and expense of these tasks depend greatly on the goals set for the site. For example, should an agency's site do anything beyond providing information about the agency and its counselors? How much information should it give about the products that the agency sells? Should it accept bookings online? Chapter 9 discusses these and other questions about marketing online.

Booking Online

The Internet also offers travel professionals additional ways to book online. They might go online and then book by using specialized software or accessing a GDS or going directly to suppliers' sites. To encourage travel counselors to book through their sites, many suppliers have agency-only portals, and some suppliers hook up their most productive travel agencies directly to their own booking software.

As a travel advisor, if you sell air, there are options for you to book air travel outside a GDS. It is important that you research different booking methods with your agency, host agency, or consortium.

The Internet and GDSs. Does the Internet make direct access to a GDS unnecessary? Although travel counselors have increasingly booked directly online, GDSs remain the electronic tool of choice for booking. Using a GDS is still the most efficient way, for example, to switch quickly from one airline's schedule to another, to find the best connecting cities and the lowest airfares available on alternate dates, and to book itineraries with multiple stops or gaps between flights. In addition, using a GDS is likely to be easier than booking online in two situations:

- If you want to book several elements of a trip, such as a rental car, hotel, and flights.
- If you need information about a certain category of travel from different companies. A GDS, for example, will instantly list each major hotel that has rooms available this weekend in Philadelphia—whether it is a Marriott, Westin, Holiday Inn, or Wyndham.

These advantages of GDSs may be short-lived, however, as new products and approaches make it easier to book online. The owners of GDSs themselves are in the forefront of offering Web-based tools for assembling travel packages.

Travelers Online. Of course, travelers can also book online themselves. They might book online with a ***bricks-and-clicks agency***—a travel agency that has not only a website but also a traditional walk-in brick-and-mortar office—but they can also bypass traditional travel agencies when they book online directly. Travelers might go to one of the online travel agencies, such as

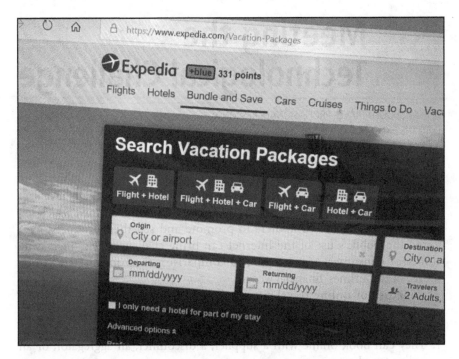

FIGURE 3.3 An Online Travel Agency: Expedia

The website for Expedia illustrates the wide range of offerings available from online travel agencies.

Expedia and Travelocity (see Figure 3.3). Or they might go to an online discounter or directly to supplier websites. Some suppliers encourage online booking; airlines, for example, offer discounts or extra frequent-flyer miles for booking online. Hotels promise the lowest rates at their sites and in their smartphone apps. Other suppliers encourage people who visit their websites to contact a travel agency.

In competition with hotels, aggregators, like Airbnb and VRBO, offer homeowners, apartment building managers, and vacation rental companies the ability to offer whole homes or single rooms online for purchase by business and leisure travelers. Other sites, like Luxury Retreats, offer similar capabilities for high-end villa-style vacation rentals.

Recent trends seem to indicate that more and more U.S. travelers have been booking their own travel plans via the Internet, particularly simple air and hotel reservations. However, it also appears that a number of those who have been researching and booking their own trips are turning to travel counselors (or returning to them) because many don't have the time, energy, and interest in DIY travel reservations. That seems to hold especially true for more complicated vacations, such as cruises, escorted group tours, and custom-designed vacations requiring more local knowledge.

✔ CHECK-UP

Common ways of going online today include
✔ Broadband connections via DSL, cable, or satellite.
✔ Broadband wireless access via cellular networks or WiFi.

Key uses of the Internet include
✔ E-mail.

✔ Communicating with clients, suppliers, and colleagues.
✔ Researching information.
✔ Advertising and marketing.
✔ Booking.

Meeting the Technological Challenge

The Internet has certainly revolutionized the travel industry. Travel ranks first among all types of products and services bought online.

All travel professionals today use the Internet, but it is not only a tool: It is also a challenge and the home of competitors. Even the airlines, which led the way in the use of computers to promote and sell their products, have found the public's use of the Internet can bring challenges. The increasing ability of consumers to go online to comparison-shop for airfares is one source of the airlines' financial woes.

The use of online travel sites has posed a special challenge to travel agencies. Thanks to the Internet, travelers with computers now have four choices for booking travel:

1. They can book online with a supplier, a discounter, an aggregator, or an online travel agency.
2. They can call a supplier directly.
3. They can book online with a bricks-and-clicks travel agency.
4. They can call or visit a travel agency's office or work with a home-based counselor.

Still, not everyone has a computer, and not everyone likes using computers. Even among those who go online in search of travel information, many are just lookers, not bookers. They might not book online because they prefer to talk to a live person or because they are worried about privacy or about the security of credit card transactions or because they want advice or other help from a trusted advisor.

The complexity of all but the simplest trips means that most travelers will continue to use a travel agency at some point. But agencies must offer services that travelers want and need so that clients will want to consult an agency, even if they found information about their trip online.

Learning to use new technologies effectively is key to providing those services. Travel counselors must be as informed as their clients about resources available online. In a world overflowing with information, travel counselors should be prepared to become their clients' "cyberspace tour guide," in the words of Jeff Hoffmann, former Priceline CEO. For the vast majority of people, anything more than a simple transaction can take hours of research online. Armed with the best sites and the knowledge of how to use them, the travel counselor can save clients hours of time, a value those clients will pay for.

Furthermore, misinformation is widespread online. Many people suffer from information overload and uncertainty regarding information they find on the Internet; they may turn to travel professionals to validate and verify it. Travel counselors have the following tools they can use to validate information found online:

■ *Knowledge, experience, and expertise.* Travel professionals view the information found online through trained eyes. Extensive knowledge of the industry, suppliers, products, and destinations should enable you to help clients sort through the massive amounts of information available online and to identify the most relevant, accurate, and useful information.

- T*ravel industry resources.* Travel professionals have access to many industry resources that the public does not. For example, travel counselors can access the travel-agent-only section of the CLIA (Cruise Lines International Association) website if their agency is a member. Or to learn about a tour operator, they can contact the National Tour Association or the United States Tour Operators Association.
- *Relationships with suppliers.* Clients may benefit from the relationships that travel counselors and travel agencies have built with travel suppliers, especially trusted **business development managers (BDMs)** assigned to work with agents. These relationships enable a travel counselor to validate information from the Internet as well as to provide clients with quality products and services that consumers may be unable to obtain on their own.

CLOSE-UP: SELLING WITH TECHNOLOGY

The technologies that have revolutionized the travel industry can be used in many ways to sell travel services and serve clients more effectively. Here is one example.

Suppose you are a travel counselor, and one of your clients is going to London, where he hopes to indulge a love of East Asian food, theater, and Dickens. If you know how to search online efficiently, you could create a proposed itinerary, custom-made to match the client's needs and interests. You might include
- The client's travel itinerary.
- A diagram of the airport to show how to get to the tube (subway).
- The tube schedule and prices.
- A map of the neighborhood near the tube stop where the client's hotel is located.
- Information from the hotel's website.
- A list of East Asian restaurants and the menu from one of those restaurants.
- A list of theaters and their phone numbers, including a map showing the theater for which the client has tickets, and a list of pubs near the theater that will be open when the play ends.
- Maps of locations mentioned in Charles Dickens's books, a short biography of Dickens, and a menu from one of Dickens's favorite pubs.

The document might also include practical information to make the trip easier, such as currency exchange rates and time differences, comments about reaching the Internet and using small appliances, and the local phone number of the airline.

The point is to meet the client's needs and help make the trip as enjoyable as possible. Technology makes it easier to provide the service that delivers real value to clients and earns their loyalty.

Videos hosted on an agent's website or social media platforms can be particularly effective in persuading clients to select a more expensive option, to encourage them to add another destination, and to finalize the sale of lesser-known destinations.

Many travel videos from tour operators and suppliers contain practical information, showing places to stay, attractions to see, and souvenirs to buy. Other videos emphasize the "flavor" of the destination; these are often produced by tourist bureaus or independent production houses, but user-generated (i.e., agent- or client-generated) videos are extremely popular, too.

The abundance of travel videos can be intimidating if you are trying to select one for a client. Keep these tips in mind:
- It should be relatively short and feature practical information, such as maps. Undecided clients should usually be given videos no more than 15 minutes long.
- Music and narration should reflect the culture of the destination but should not obscure the message of the film.
- The video should sell the destination and experience, not the sponsors' products.

As helpful as videos are, they are only tools that can help to make a sale; they cannot replace your own presentation. You must first ensure that you have considered the client's needs and desires and know what point the video should make with that client.
In summary, to use videos effectively,
- Preview all videos to make sure they are interesting, accurate, and relevant.
- Offer a video when it will prove certain sales points, show features or benefits you have presented to the client, or enhance a client's enthusiasm about a destination that you believe will meet his or her needs.
- Follow up on the video, elaborating on points it made.

Prospective travel professionals should begin creating their own dossiers of information by keeping lists of favorite websites for different categories of information—such as industry news, destinations, airlines, hotels, car rentals, and travel tips.

Travel professionals today also need to know how to use technological tools besides the Internet. Important examples include video editing software, social media, and web-based software.

For those dealing extensively with international contacts, the telephone service *Skype* offers free calling, including video chat. Your smartphone's built-in camera allows you to photograph and produce videos of your own journeys, including fam trips, and then post this content on your website, Facebook page, or YouTube channel. Tablets and laptops are a boon to home-based travel professionals who need to have a virtual office with them at all times. And for group leaders, being able to store travel guidebooks on a light-weight *electronic reading device,* such as Amazon's Kindle or Barnes and Noble's Nook, frees up luggage space.

Knowing when to use a particular technology is also a key to effective selling and service. The information on DVDs or thumb drives, for example, is often also available on the Internet or YouTube. And, as Chapter 12 discusses, sometimes a phone call is a better way to communicate with a client than an e-mail; sometimes, a letter is better. Will you find an answer faster by looking in a book or by talking to someone or by going online? The answer varies, and experience will teach you which source to turn to first.

Travel counselors have always been information sifters, problem solvers, advisers, and sales clinchers. Clients look to them for ideas, creative itineraries, and reassurance. Technology can never replace people who are able and willing to understand a client's needs and to help solve problems with specialized expertise and a smile. And even if you are not a techno-wiz, you can become knowledgeable enough to use technology as a tool for selling travel effectively. Companies need people who can learn to use a technology, continue to learn, change as their industry changes, and even think up new ways of using technology. The new uses do not have to be earth-shattering sparks of genius; even simple new applications of technology in the right market are enabling small companies in out-of-the-way places to sell to the world.

CHAPTER WRAP-UP

CHAPTER HIGHLIGHTS

Technology has dramatically altered the way travel professionals conduct research, communicate with clients and market their services. This chapter has described some of the fundamental concepts needed to prepare professionals to meet the resulting challenges. Here is a review of the objectives with which we began the chapter.

1. **Describe how personal computers and GDSs are used in the travel industry.** Like other businesses, travel professionals use personal computers for word processing, database management, presentation graphics, cash management, and Internet applications. They also use software created specifically for the travel industry, such as databases designed to handle client profiles, software packages that integrate back-office systems with reservation systems and client databases, and Internet booking engines. The most-used

electronic tools, however, are the GDSs. These are the descendants of the reservation systems known as CRSs, which were created in the 1970s. The major GDSs are Sabre, Galileo, Amadeus, and Worldspan. Travel counselors today can gain access to a GDS in several ways, and they use GDSs not only to make airline reservations but also to find information about and to book other types of travel arrangements.

2. **Outline four major ways that travel professionals use the Internet.** E-mail is probably the most popular application of the Internet; travel professionals use it to communicate more efficiently with both clients and colleagues. But the World Wide Web opened the way to other uses of the Internet. Just by knowing a website's URL or by using a search engine, travel professionals can find information about destinations and suppliers around the world, making the Internet an incomparable research tool. Travel professionals also advertise and market themselves on the Internet; many travel companies allow travelers to book travel on their websites. In addition, travel counselors use the Internet to make bookings for their clients.

3. **Mention three technology devices that have come into the marketplace and how they might be used in the industry by travel professionals.** Many technology devices have become available that may be helpful to travel counselors and others in the industry. Among those could be the Skype telephone service and smartphones with cameras for photographing personal travels to show to potential clients. Outside travel counselors and sales representatives will appreciate tablets, which allow them to carry a virtual office with them. And tour leaders will appreciate being able to download travel guidebooks into a light-weight electronic reading device to carry with them on tour.

4. **List at least four reasons why travelers would seek out a travel professional despite the existence of online travel services.** Travel professionals should see online travel sources as tools they should master and a possible source of new opportunities. For travel counselors in particular, however, online travel services can be a major competitor. But travelers will continue to seek contact with a travel counselor if they dislike using computers, worry about the privacy or security of online transactions, want a personal interaction, want advice, or believe that using a travel counselor can save them time or money. Travel counselors can verify information the public finds on the Internet by using their expertise and experience, their knowledge of travel industry resources and their reliability, and their relationships with suppliers.

KEY TERMS

A list of key terms introduced in this chapter follows. If you do not recall the meaning of these terms, see the Glossary.

Amadeus	Galileo
Apollo	General Data Protection Regulation (GDPR)
bricks-and-clicks agency	global distribution system (GDS)
browser	graphical user interface
business development manager (BDM)	Internet
command interface	Sabre
computer reservation system (CRS)	search engine
customer relationship management (CRM)	Skype
	uniform resource locator (URL)
database	virtual public network (VPN)
direct link	WiFi
electronic reading device	Worldspan
e-mail	World Wide Web

REVIEW QUESTIONS

1. The forerunners of today's GDSs were built to sell air travel. For what other arrangements are GDSs useful today?

2. How does the integration of travel software allow travel counselors to be more efficient?

3. How does the ability of clients to book airline tickets from their own computers affect travel agencies?

4. Some believe that the use of computers makes business less personal; others say it frees people from mechanical tasks and gives them the time to be more personal. What do you think? Explain your opinion.

Part 2:
The Travel Product

Chapter 4
Air Travel

Chapter 5
Ground Travel

Chapter 6
Accommodations

Chapter 7
Cruises

Chapter 8
Tours and Packages

Air Travel

OBJECTIVES

After completing this chapter, you should be able to

1. Outline how the airline industry is regulated and coordinated by the government and suppliers.

2. Describe how airlines differ and know the codes for some major airlines and airports in the United States, Canada, and abroad

3. Explain three types of flights, five types of journeys, and the different classes of service.

4. Describe at least five factors that are likely to affect the cost of a passenger's flight.

5. Outline the procedures involved in taking a flight and common questions and problems that come up in air travel.

6. Show why a good travel counselor needs to know about airline ticketing and how airline tickets can be an income source if handled properly.

OUTLINE

ORDER IN THE SKIES:
RULES AND REGULATIONS
- What is the role of government in the airline industry, and how do suppliers regulate the travel market?

AIRLINES AND AIRPORTS
- What are the major airlines and airports?

SERVICE IN THE AIR:
VARIATIONS IN AIR TRAVEL
- What are the most significant variations in the flights and services available to airline passengers?

AIRFARES
- What are the most important factors determining the cost of an airline ticket?

SELLING AIR TRAVEL:
POLICIES AND CHALLENGES
- What are the key policies and challenges related to air travel?

"Flying," said American astronomer Simon Newcomb in 1903, "is one of that class of problems with which man will never be able to cope." But before the year was out, Orville and Wilbur Wright *had* coped with it. Over the windswept dunes of Kitty Hawk, North Carolina, they completed the first manned, powered flight on December 17, 1903. The 12-second flight, with Orville Wright manning the controls, managed to stay airborne for 120 feet.

The air transportation industry has progressed tremendously since then; it is now the key long-distance mover of people. Every day, the FAA's Air Traffic Organization provides service to more than 44,000 flights and 2.7 million airline passengers across more than 29 million square miles of airspace. This chapter examines both international air travel, transborder, and *domestic air travel*, which includes flights between and within the continental United States and parts of Alaska, Hawaii, Puerto Rico, the Virgin Islands, and Canada. We look first at how the air travel industry is coordinated and regulated. Next, we examine the suppliers of air travel—the airlines—and airports and variations in the airlines' products and prices. Finally, we discuss some of the procedures, policies, and problems that most concern the sellers of air travel.

Order in the Skies: Rules and Regulations

■ WHAT IS THE ROLE OF GOVERNMENT IN THE AIRLINE INDUSTRY, AND HOW DO SUPPLIERS REGULATE THE TRAVEL MARKET?

Air travel is amazingly easy. You can buy a ticket for a flight from, say, San Francisco to Vancouver on one airline, from Vancouver to Montréal on another, to New York on a third, and then back to San Francisco. You might board a different type of aircraft for each leg of this journey, and your life

---

CLOSE-UP: CAREERS IN AIR TRAVEL

People who are interested in a career in air travel tend to focus on the biggest airlines, but there are also opportunities with regional airlines, private airlines, and international carriers—as well as jobs in airport management, air traffic control, and the Federal Aviation Administration (FAA). Many in-flight and technical positions require licensing by the FAA, but there are plenty of other career opportunities related to sales, marketing, administration, operations, information technology, e-commerce, and security. Many airline employees begin their careers as reservationists or flight attendants.

■ **Position** Reservations agent

Description Reservations agents may work at large airline reservations centers, in city ticket offices, or at airports. At reservations centers, they handle telephone requests for tickets as well as questions about fares, seating, schedules, availability, special requests, escorts for juveniles, and ticket policies. Reservationists also reserve and confirm seats on domestic and international flights and research and resolve passenger problems. Reservation agents also may assist in selling travel packages the airlines create in partnership with hotels, along with other auxiliary travel products.

Qualifications This position demands skill in communicating and problem solving. A pleasant voice, a ready smile, the ability to be clear and concise, tact, and good humor are important assets. Training involves mastering the airline's computer system, rules, and policies.

■ **Position** Customer service representative/passenger services agent

Description Providing customer service is the pivotal responsibility of this position. The job is typically fast-paced and physically demanding, with long and inconvenient hours. Duties include answering questions about schedules and fares, initiating and completing flight transactions, maintaining security by checking passengers' ID, helping customers in the check-in and boarding process and aiding those who have baggage-related questions or who require special help (such as those dealing with missed connections). At some airports, duties also include baggage handling, aircraft cleaning, and other ramp services. Much of the work involves computers.

Qualifications On-the-job training is usually provided for this position. Experience as a reservations agent or ticket agent is helpful. Good people skills, an unflappable personality, and patience are needed. The flexibility to work weekends and holidays is required.

■ **Position** Flight attendant

Description Flight attendants' primary responsibility is passenger safety, but most of their time is spent providing for the comfort of travelers—offering food and beverages, assisting passengers with baggage, helping sick passengers or those with disabilities and answering questions. Behind the scenes, they attend preflight briefings, check the cabin for supplies, give first aid, take special care of unaccompanied children and write postflight reports. Flight attendants may have little choice of home base, schedules, or routes until they have gained seniority.

(continued on next page)

would be in the hands of different mechanics, flight attendants, and pilots. But, at each step on your trip, you could feel confident that your flight would be honored and that the equipment, procedures, and people had all met certain standards and were worthy of your trust.

In just one stop, you will have ordered and paid for services from hundreds of people; the Close-Up on Careers in Air Travel describes some of the jobs they perform. In this section, we look at how the efforts of all these people are coordinated and regulated.

The U.S. Government and the Airlines: A Brief History

From the start, the airline industry and the U.S. government have had a complicated relationship. Its history divides into three eras: from the birth of the industry until 1978, from 1978 to 2001, and the present.

CLOSE-UP: CAREERS IN AIR TRAVEL (cont.)

Qualifications Prior customer service experience is desired. Airlines look for poise, personality, a well-groomed appearance, good sense, physical stamina, rapport with people, grace under pressure, and the ability to work as part of a team. In addition, flight attendants must meet requirements regarding vision, ability to lift objects, and other physical requirements as determined by each airline. Candidates must complete a 4- to 6-week training course. For international services, foreign language capability is a must; the ability to travel in and out of the country is essential.

■ **Position** Airline sales representative

Description This position provides a liaison with travel counselors, tour operators, and corporate accounts. Responsibilities include selling new accounts, building sales from existing accounts and servicing special requests. Sales representatives are in the field much of the time calling on agencies, making presentations and participating in civic functions, seminars, and trade shows. They may become involved in promoting the airline's image and the destinations it serves.

Qualifications Selling and presentation skills are required for this position, along with knowledge of your airline— its strength, policies, and destinations.

■ **Position** Account executive, corporate sales

Description Responsibilities of this position include marketing airline services to companies within an area and negotiating volume-based agreements; helping corporations to prepare Requests for Proposals from travel agencies; and working with meeting sales and group sales.

Frequently, account executives also coordinate arrangements with those car and hotel vendors that are the airline's partners.

Qualifications Typically, the person in this position is promoted from a job as a reservations or passenger services agent or from a business-to-business sales position in another airline or related travel company.

■ **Position** Marketing automation software developer

Description This professional is responsible for special projects and new technologies, including Internet-related marketing activities. The position involves a variety of tasks related to system and software engineering, from analysis to design, coding, testing, and maintenance of software. Airlines now have many technology-related positions opportunities, and many of these positions are specialized due to the numerous technologies used to operate an airline.

Qualifications This position typically requires a minimum of a B.S. in computer science or equivalent experience as well as at least two years' experience in software development and support. An understanding of database design and implementation, organizational and communication skills, and the ability to handle multiple tasks simultaneously are needed. The job may require working evenings or weekends.

■ **Other positions** Advertising and sales promotion for foreign flag carrier; aircraft mechanic; customer relations for frequent-flyer programs; gate agent; station manager; strategic market planning analyst; yield management analyst.

The Era of Regulation. At first, the only way for airlines to make money was to obtain a contract from the government to fly the U.S. mail. By 1938, American, Eastern, TWA, and United had emerged as major airlines, and the government had set up the Civil Aeronautics Authority (CAA) to regulate the new industry. The CAA was soon reorganized and renamed the *Civil Aeronautics Board,* or *CAB.*

The CAB had two goals: to promote the new airline industry and to protect the interests of passengers. It decided whether an airline was fit to fly, which routes it flew, and how much the airline could charge. Airlines received subsidies from the government to serve remote areas.

As the airline industry grew and changed, so did the government's regulatory structure. The government allowed the airlines to work together through the *Air Traffic Conference (ATC)* to establish a standard sales contract, appoint travel agencies to sell air travel and set up ways to transfer baggage and handle reservations. In 1958, the government established the **Federal Aviation Administration,** or **FAA,** to license pilots, certify aircraft as safe and enforce rules regarding passenger safety. In 1967, the **National Transportation Safety Board (NTSB)** was created to investigate accidents, and the FAA became part of the Department of Transportation (DOT).

Market Control. In 1978, the *Airline Deregulation Act* ended the government's economic control of U.S. airlines. Airlines were given the power to determine their own routes, fares, and commissions. The CAB and ATC were phased out of existence.

The effects of deregulation came quickly. New airlines were established, competing with old carriers. Some airlines expanded; some merged; some went bankrupt. Of the 50 new jet airlines that started after deregulation, 35 had gone out of business 15 years later.

For travel counselors and travelers alike, deregulation brought uncertainty and confusion. Before deregulation, there might have been three possible fares for one route; now there might be hundreds. Schedules changed frequently; fares changed daily, sometimes hourly.

There were other dislocations. Some small towns and cities lost air service. Travelers who could not adjust their schedules faced high fares. Service before and during flights deteriorated. And, beginning in 1995, the airlines began cutting or eliminating the commissions paid to travel agencies for selling air tickets. Airlines and travel agencies, once seen as partners, became competitors.

But deregulation also delivered important benefits. Entrepreneurs tried out new ideas. Travelers with flexible schedules could find bargain fares. U.S. airlines made impressive innovations, such as using electronic ticketing and selling tickets online. By 2000, record numbers of Americans were flying; that year the airlines carried more than 730 million people.

In 2000, most of the complaints about air travel seemed to reflect the industry's success. As more and more Americans took to the air, flight delays and cancellations soared. The airlines fought off calls for new government regulation by promising to improve service.

Then the hijackings of September 11, 2001 by terrorists pushed concerns about service into the background and threw the airline industry into turmoil. Demand plummeted. The industry needed the federal government to bail it out financially and to reassure the public that it was safe to fly.

Economic deregulation obviously had not abolished the need for rules and agreements to keep order in the skies. Today, both the federal government and the airlines themselves play important roles in keeping this complicated industry in shape.

The U.S. Government's Role Today. Even after economic deregulation, the federal government retained the authority to protect airline passengers and to police unfair practices by airlines. The key issue still regulated by the government was safety, but, until September 11, 2001, implementing many safety procedures—including screening passengers and their baggage—was the responsibility of the airlines. This arrangement seemed to work. In every year of the last two decades of the 20th century, fatalities at U.S. railroad crossings far outnumbered fatalities in the air. But, when terrorists hijacked four U.S. planes on September 11, 2001 and used them to attack New York and Washington, D.C., weaknesses in the system were tragically exposed.

Concerns focused on security at airports. After a wave of hijackings in the 1970s and early 1980s, U.S. airports had hired security guards and installed metal detectors. The FAA provided guidance about security procedures to airlines and airports, and, in the largest airports, federal security managers oversaw procedures for protecting passengers. Generally, though, airlines and airports were responsible for planning and carrying out security measures, subject to FAA approval. That changed after September 11, 2001.

Two months after the attacks, federal legislation established the *Transportation Security Administration (TSA)*. For the first time, airport security became a direct federal responsibility. Congress provided additional funds for new personnel, including baggage screeners to ensure that all passengers and carry-on bags are thoroughly inspected. In 2002, the Department of Homeland Security (DHS) was established, and the TSA became part of this department, along with other government agencies that are responsible for protecting the nation's transportation systems and supervising the entry of people and goods into the United States.

Table 4.1 summarizes the federal agencies that play important roles in air travel today. In particular,

- The FAA licenses commercial pilots, oversees maintenance programs and procedures for all aircraft and certifies the airworthiness of planes.

- The NTSB investigates all accidents involving aircraft.

- The FAA also runs the air traffic control system.

- The TSA is responsible for developing policies to ensure the safety of U.S. transportation, including airport security and the prevention of hijacking.

- The federal government also enforces rules regarding issues, such as liability for lost and damaged baggage, treatment of travelers with disabilities, and compensation when boarding is denied.

In addition to U.S. rules and regulations, North American agents should familiarize themselves with the **Canadian Aviation Regulations (CARs),** *which* are a compilation of regulatory requirements and rules governming civil aviation in Canada. The authority for the establishment of the CARs is the Aeronautics Act. Both the Act and the CARs are the responsibility of the Minister of Transport and his department, Transport Canada.

TABLE 4.1 The Key Regulators of U.S. Domestic Airlines

Government Body	Description
Department of Transportation (DOT)	The cabinet-level department of the federal government that is responsible for mass transportation. It oversees the formulation of national transportation policy. Other responsibilities range from negotiating international transportation agreements to enforcing airline consumer protection regulations, including how to compensate travelers for significantly delayed flights while passengers are on board an aircraft.
Federal Aviation Administration (FAA)	An agency of DOT. The FAA has primary responsibility for airline safety regulations. It develops, maintains and operates the air traffic control system; reviews the design, manufacture, and maintenance of aircraft equipment; sets minimum standards for crew training; and establishes operational requirements for airlines.
Transportation Security Administration (TSA)	Part of the Department of Homeland Security. The TSA is responsible for developing policies to ensure Administration (TSA) the safety of U.S. transportation, including airport security and the prevention of hijacking.
National Transportation	An independent federal agency. The NTSB investigates all aviation accidents (as well as significant Safety Board (NTSB) accidents in other modes of transportation) and recommends enhancements for safety. It also tracks aviation fatalities, publishes annual safety statistics and conducts special studies of transportation safety issues.
U.S. Department of Justice	Has become involved in partnership with the DOT on issues of consumer protection.

Sources: Air Transport Association, (www.air-transport.org), FAA, (www.faa.gov); TSA (www.tsa.gov).

Interline Agreements and ARC

Many aspects of air travel are governed by agreements among the airlines themselves—*interline agreements.* Airline ticketing is one important example. After deregulation, the airlines worked together through the *Air Transport Association (ATA),* the trade association of major North American airlines, to adopt a system remarkably similar to the one that existed during the era of government regulation. This system has two key features.

First, the ATA created a *standard ticket,* which let passengers fly on many airlines with just one ticket. As we discuss later in this chapter, purchase of an airline ticket brings into force a contract between the airline and the passenger. The exact terms of the contract vary from one airline to another, but the standard ticket identifies the important areas, such as airline liability in cases of delays, injury, or death.

Second, the ATA created *ARC,* the *Airlines Reporting Corporation,* to regulate the distribution of airline tickets and to provide a centralized system for processing sales. ARC, which is owned by major North American airlines, accredits travel agencies. Any nonairline company that issues airline tickets must have ARC accreditation.

ARC sets the requirements that allow a travel agency to sell airline tickets. Among other things, the agency must:

- Be located in and authorized to do business in the United States, U.S. Virgin Islands, or Puerto Rico. (It may be in a private residence, as long as it meets the local jurisdiction requirements).
- Provide a bond, a letter of credit, or a cash deposit of at least $20,000.
- Meet the personnel standards of Section IV-B of the Agent Reporting Agreement, which includes different responsibilities and training requirements.
- Meet ticketing security standards of Attachment 8 of the Agent Reporting Agreement.

Many travel professionals today work with agencies that already are ARC accredited, saving them the time and money of becoming accredited. It is still important that travel professionals are aware of the sensitivities and regulations that apply to issuing airline tickets.

International Rules of the Skies

Each nation owns the right to the sky above it, and it has the right to protect that airspace and to say whether airplanes can fly into its skies. The ability of travelers to zip from nation to nation depends on the fact that countries have agreed on rules that balance two goals: preserving the sovereignty of nations over their skies and enhancing the freedom of people to travel.

One milestone occurred in 1944, when 52 nations signed the Chicago Convention. Among other things, this agreement set out principles called *freedoms of the air* that describe what a carrier of one nation may do in another nation; other freedoms were agreed to later. These freedoms have provided the basis for negotiations among nations about how their airlines will operate.

Over the years, much of the negotiating about international air traffic has occurred through **IATA,** the ***International Air Transport Association.*** Founded in 1919 and reorganized after World War II, IATA is an association of 290 international airlines, representing 117 countries, that aims to create order and stability in international aviation.

Ultimately, however, governments must approve the decisions of IATA. In fact, the U.S. government has periodically challenged the authority of IATA and turned to *bilateral agreements* (agreements between two countries) to supersede IATA. Thus, international fares reflect agreements between governments, which also negotiate agreements regulating the carriers, routes, frequency, and number of seats on international flights.

In recent years, many governments have backed away from regulating air travel. During the 1990s, the U.S. government led the way in urging an ***open-skies policy*** under which carriers can fly where they choose, charge what they wish and make deals with each other. It reached open-skies agreements with several European nations. It also granted immunity from antitrust laws to several U.S. airlines so they could form alliances with airlines of other nations. Continued deregulation seems likely, but, ultimately, political decisions will determine the power corporations will have over the international skies.

IATAN

Like sales for domestic flights, selling seats on international flights also requires coordination and regulation. Since 1945, IATA has a screening program to approve travel agencies that can serve international airlines. It still operates this network outside the United States. But in May 1985 **IATAN,** the ***International Airlines Travel Agent Network,*** replaced IATA as the organization that appoints U.S. travel agencies to sell tickets for international airlines serving the United States.

IATAN operates as a subsidiary of IATA and links its members with U.S. travel agencies. IATAN serves three primary functions:

- It endorses travel agencies that meet specific standards of financial stability, security, professional integrity, and experience.
- It acts on behalf of its subscriber airlines and other suppliers to appoint agents to sell their products according to the suppliers' standards.
- It promotes professional practices within the international travel industry.

IATAN also sponsors the *IATAN ID Card,* which identifies those carrying the card as industry professionals (see Table 4.2).

TABLE 4.2

Qualifications for the IATAN Identity Card

To qualify for the ID card, applicants must

- Be an owner, employee, or independent contractor of an IATAN-accredited location.
- Be registered with IATAN.
- Devote at least 20 hours per week to the business of selling travel.
- Have earned at least $5,000 in salary and/or commission in the previous 12 months.
- Be at least 18 years of age.

The card is valid for one year. A new card costs $40 online or $45 by mail.

After the Airline Deregulation Act of 1978,
- ✔ U.S. airlines were free to set their own fares and routes.
- ✔ The federal government continued to enforce rules to regulate safety and to ensure fair treatment of passengers.
- ✔ The airlines themselves established rules and policies to govern the ticketing of air travel.

Key roles in the system that coordinates and regulates domestic air travel are played by
- ✔ The airlines.
- ✔ ATA, the trade association of major airlines, and ARC, which is owned by the major airlines.
- ✔ The Department of Transportation, which has primary responsibility for enforcing airline consumer protection regulations.

- ✔ The FAA, an agency of the Department of Transportation that has primary responsibility for safety regulations.
- ✔ The NTSB, an independent agency that investigates all accidents.
- ✔ The TSA, an agency in the Department of Homeland Security that has primary responsibility for security.
- ✔ The U.S. Department of Justice, which gets involved in consumer issues.

Key roles in the system that regulates international air travel are played by
- ✔ IATA, which is an association of international airlines.
- ✔ Airlines.
- ✔ Governments.
- ✔ IATAN, which appoints travel agencies to sell tickets for international airlines serving the United States.

Airlines and Airports

■ WHAT ARE THE MAJOR AIRLINES AND AIRPORTS?

The world of aviation includes military aviation and *general aviation* (that is, crop dusters, corporate jets, and other planes not used by commercial airlines) as well as **civil aviation,** which includes all air service that is offered to the public for hire, whether for passengers or for cargo. Passenger service includes both **charters,** which are specially scheduled flights reserved by a private group or tour operator, and **scheduled service,** which consists of flights for designated routes offered to the public according to a published timetable.

The first years of the 21st century were not kind to the airlines and airports that provide scheduled service. First, fears of terrorism and an economic slowdown dampened demand for air travel; then war and rising fuel and security costs and taxes put new financial pressures on the industry. (Chapter 9 says more about the strategies that some airlines have used to survive in this environment.) Who are the major players in the airline industry?

Canadian Airlines

Canada is the second largest country in the world by total area. The total population is approximately 37 million, which is relatively small for a large territory. The majority of the population, about 80%, resides in urban areas. The small population does not allow massive airline business growth, which is the reason why in Canada there are only two major airlines, Air Canada and WestJet. There are several chartered airlines that are used primarily to reach popular vacation spots and, used in conjunction with land arrangements, form popular all-inclusive packages.

Air Canada Air Canada is Canada's largest domestic and international airline, serving nearly 220 airports on six continents. It is one of the 20 largest airlines in the world and, in 2018, served nearly 51 million customers. Air Canada provides scheduled passenger service directly to 63 airports in Canada, 56 in the United States, and 100 in Europe, the Middle East, Africa, Asia, Australia, the Caribbean, Mexico, Central America, and South America.

Air Canada's predecessor, Trans-Canada Air Lines (TCA) inaugurated its first flight on September 1, 1937. The 50-minute flight aboard a Lockheed L-10A carried two passengers and mail between Vancouver and Seattle. By 1964, TCA had grown to become Canada's national airline; it changed its name to Air Canada. The airline became fully privatized in 1989.

Air Canada's four hubs—Toronto Pearson International Airport, the primary global hub; Montréal-Pierre Elliott Trudeau International Airport, the gateway to French international markets; Vancouver International Airport, the airline's premier gateway to Asia Pacific; and Calgary International Airport—offer Air Canada customers a simple, customer friendly experience, easy security clearance and smooth connections to Air Canada's global network, all under one roof.

Canada's geography and Air Canada's worldwide Network make its Canadian hubs excellent transfer points for travel to points throughout the world. Air Canada, Air Canada Express, and Air Canada Rouge operate a fleet of more than 340 aircraft combined, with seat capacity ranging from 37 seats to 450+ seats. The airline's recent international fleet renewal of state-of-the-art Boeing 787 Dreamliners creates one of the world's youngest, most fuel efficient. and simplified airline fleets. With a choice of Business, Premium Economy, and Economy class, Air Canada offers a full range of products to meet your clients' needs.

WestJet WestJet Airlines is a Canadian airline founded in 1996. It began as a low-cost alternative to the country's competing major airlines. WestJet provides scheduled and charter air service to more than 100 destinations in Canada, the United States, Europe, Mexico, Central America, and the Caribbean.

WestJet currently is the second-largest Canadian air carrier, behind Air Canada, operating an average of 777 flights and carrying more than 66,130 guests per day. In 2018, WestJet carried 25.49 million passengers, making it the ninth-largest airline in North America by passengers carried.

WestJet is a public company with more than 14,000 employees and is not part of any airline alliance. It operates three variants of the Boeing 737 Next Generation family—the Boeing 737 MAX, as well as Boeing 767 and Boeing 787 aircraft—on select long-haul routes. The airline's headquarters is located adjacent to the Calgary International Airport.

U.S. Airlines

The United States is home to the largest civil aviation system in the world. Table 4.3 lists some of the best-known U.S. airlines offering scheduled service. As the table shows, every airline is assigned a two-letter code, which is used on GDSs (global distribution systems), schedules, and tickets.

U.S. airlines offering scheduled service do not fit neatly into simple categories. The average traveler probably divides them into (1) major airlines, such as United or American, (2) commuter lines, such as Mesa or ComAir, and (3) budget lines, such as Allegiant or Spirit. The government takes a different approach. It categorizes airlines with scheduled service into three types based on the amount of revenue generated.

- *Major airlines* generate annual operating revenues of more than $1 billion. They provide service nationwide (and sometimes worldwide).

TABLE 4.3

A Sampling of Some Major U.S. Airlines and Their Codes

Airline	Code
Alaska Airlines	AS
American Airlines	AA
Delta Airlines	DL
Frontier Airlines	F9
Hawaiian Airlines	HA
JetBlue Airways	B6
Southwest Airlines	WN
Spirit Airlines	NK
United Airlines	UA

- *National airlines* generate annual operating revenues of $100 million to $1 billion. Many of these airlines serve specific regions of the country, but some offer long-haul or even international service.
- *Regional airlines* generate annual operating revenues of less than $100 million. Most regionals offer service only to one region of the country. The government further classifies regional airlines into large, medium, and small regionals based on their revenue. *Small regionals* are also called **commuter airlines.**

Most regional lines today either are owned by major airlines or have **code-sharing agreements** with them. Major airline alliances, such as The Star Alliance, oneworld, and SkyTeam, also use code sharing. These agreements allow an airline to use the code of a larger, better-known airline. Many code-sharing agreements also call for the companies to coordinate their schedules and marketing efforts, including mile sharing. When there is code sharing, travel advisors are required to inform clients in writing which airline they actually are flying. Also, when travel advisors are handling air, it is crucial to fully understand the airlines' regulations and policies. Many of these regulations and policies change often, so it is advisable always to reach out to each airline to fully understand the code-sharing regulations.

The Hub-and-Spoke System

Since economic deregulation allowed the airlines to determine their own routes, they have increasingly used a **hub-and-spoke system**, in which an airline uses certain cities as connecting centers, or hubs, for as many flights to and from outlying cities as possible. Passengers from outlying cities must fly first to the hub and from there catch connecting flights to their destinations.

Figure 4.1 shows an example. In this case, by using two hubs—Dallas and Chicago—along with 11 shorter feeder routes, the airline offers 42 route combinations. The airline could not profitably operate daily flights from, for example, Jackson, Mississippi, to Omaha, Nebraska, because the **passenger load factor**—the percentage of available seats sold on a flight—would be extremely small. Instead, it flies travelers between Jackson and Omaha through the Dallas and Chicago hubs. That way, the airline maximizes passenger loads from small cities and saves fuel by operating fewer small-city departures.

FIGURE 4.1

A Hub-and-Spoke System

This sample hub-and-spoke system creates 42 possible route combinations.

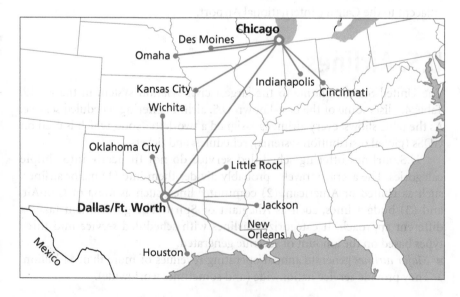

For the airlines, the hub-and-spoke system is a strategy for serving as many passengers as possible while maximizing efficiency. For travelers, though, the hub-and-spoke system means fewer direct flights, more connections, and an increased risk of delays. By decreasing competition, the hub-and-spoke system may also lead to high fares. At some hubs, one airline is so dominant that there is little competitive pressure on fares.

The hub-and-spoke system also creates winners and losers among airports. Airport hubs often host administrative and maintenance centers for the airlines, generating jobs and revenues. But for airports that are only spokes or that lose air service, the system can be disastrous.

There are some airlines that avoid this hub-and-spoke system and instead operate point-to-point service from smaller airports. For example, Allegiant Air operates flights out of Mesa, Arizona, about 30 minutes from the Phoenix Airport, which is a hub for American Airlines and Southwest Airlines. Allegiant can offer lower prices by using a smaller airport and also flies directly to airports not otherwise served in a nonstop capacity from the Phoenix airport. Several airlines are adjusting their business models to offer similar services for cities with limited air service.

Canadian Airports

There are 17 international airports in Canada. An international airport is any airport situated as an airport of entry and departure for international air traffic, where the formalities incident to customs, immigration, public health, animal and plant quarantine, and similar procedures are carried out. Through bilateral agreement, transborder commercial air transport operations conducted from within the United States to Canadian air transport ports of entry are not deemed international. Toronto Pearson International Airport is the largest and busiest international airport in Canada; Montréal-Pierre Elliott Trudeau International Airport, however, serves a higher percentage of international passengers.

U.S. Airports

Table 4.4 lists some of the busiest North American airports. Every city and airport worldwide served by an airline is known by a three-letter code. If a city has only one airport, the same code is often used for both the city and the airport. Cities served by more than one airport have one code for the city and others for the airports. The codes are easily found in reference books, online, and GDSs, but many employers check to see if prospective counselors know their codes.

Today, many employees new to the travel industry do not know their airport codes because they depend on the GDS for them. However, experienced counselors will tell you how important knowing the codes is to assure accuracy and avoid making fateful errors.

For example, Portland, Oregon, (PDX) is a long way from Portland, Maine, (PWM) and San Jose, California, (SJC) should definitely not be confused with San Jose, Costa Rica (SJO). Many cities have more than one airport, such as New York City (NYC) with Kennedy (JFK), La Guardia (LGA) and nearby Newark, New Jersey (EWR). It would be essential for a passenger flying from California through New York and then to Europe to make connections in and out of the same New York airport.

Even worse can be confusion over international airports. One letter different, and you're in a different country. For example, landing at Iguassú Falls on the Brazilian side (IGU) would be an error if the traveler's destination were the Sheraton Iguazú Resort and Spa in Argentina (IGR).

Major U.S. airports are owned by public authorities (city, county, or state). The airlines rent space from the airport and pay landing fees for each flight. The airports get their revenues from these payments and from concessions, such as restaurants, rental car counters, newsstands, and other shops.

TABLE 4.4

A Selection of Major North American Airports

Airline	Code	Airline	Code	Airline	Code
United States		Lihue, Kauai, HI	LIH	San Francisco, CA	SFO
Albuquerque, NM	ABQ	Little Rock, AR	LIT	San Jose, CA	SJC
Anchorage, AK	ANC	Long Beach, CA	LGB	Seattle/Tacoma, WA	SEA
Atlanta, GA	ATL	Los Angeles, CA/ Burbank	BUR	Sioux Falls, SD	FSD
Baltimore, MD	BWI			St. Louis, MO	STL
Bismarck, ND	BIS	Los Angeles, CA/ International	LAX	Tampa, FL	TPA
Boston, MA	BOS			Tulsa, OK	TUL
Buffalo, NY	BUF	Los Angeles, CA/Ontario	ONT	Washington, DC/Dulles	IAD
Charleston, SC	CHS	Louisville, KY	SDF	Washington, DC/ Reagan-National	DCA
Charlotte, NC	CLT	Memphis, TN	MEM		
Chicago, IL/Midway	MDW	Miami, FL	MIA	West Palm Beach, FL	PBI
Chicago, IL/O'Hare	ORD	Milwaukee, WI	MKE	Wichita, KS	ICT
Cincinnati, OH	CVG	Minneapolis/St. Paul, MN	MSP		
Cleveland, OH	CLE	Nashville, TN	BNA	**Canada**	
Columbus, OH	CMH	New Orleans, LA	MSY	Calgary, Alb	YYC
Dallas/Fort Worth, TX	DFW	New York, NY/ Kennedy	JFK	Montreal, Que/Dorval	YUL
Daytona Beach, FL	DAB	New York, NY/LaGuardia	LGA	Montreal, Que/Mirabel	YMX
Denver, CO	DEN	New York/Newark, NJ	EWR	Ottawa, Ont	YOW
Des Moines, IA	DSM	Oakland, CA	OAK	Toronto, Ont/Pearson	YYZ
Detroit, MI/Wayne County	DTW	Omaha, NE	OMA	Vancouver, BC	YVR
El Paso, TX	ELP	Orlando, FL	MCO	**Mexico and the Caribbean**	
Fairbanks, AK	FAI	Philadelphia, PA	PHL	Acapulco, Mexico	ACA
Fort Lauderdale, FL	FLL	Phoenix, AZ	PHX	Bermuda	BDA
Hartford, CT	BDL	Pittsburgh, PA	PIT	Cancún, Mexico	CUN
Hilo, Hawaii, HI	ITO	Portland, ME	PWM	Guadalajara, Mexico	GDL
Honolulu, Oahu, HI	HNL	Portland, OR	PDX	Mexico City, Mexico	MEX
Houston, TX/ Bush-Intercontinental	IAH	Providence, RI	PVD	Montego Bay, Jamaica	MBJ
Houston, TX/Hobby	HOU	Raleigh/Durham, NC	RDU	Nassau, Bahamas	NAS
Indianapolis, IN	IND	Rapid City, SD	RAP	Puerto Vallarta, Mexico	PVR
Jacksonville, FL	JAX	Richmond, VA	RIC	San Juan, Puerto Rico	SJU
Kahului, Maui, HI	OGG	Sacramento, CA	SMF	St. Croix, USVI	STX
Kansas City, MO	MKC	Salt Lake City, UT	SLC	St. Maarten, Netherlands Antilles	SXM
Kona, Hawaii, HI	KOA	San Antonio, TX	SAT		
Las Vegas, NV	LAS	San Diego, CA	SAN	St. Thomas, USVI	STT

Amenities and Design. Some large airports offer far more than the traditional newsstands and gift shops. They also feature health clubs, business service centers, WiFi, mini-hotels, nail salons, and more. Many airports now resemble luxury shopping malls with upscale dining and shopping options.

For greater comfort, travelers willing to pay $350 to $695 a year, plus an enrollment fee or frequent-flyer miles, can join an airline-sponsored club that has members-only lounges at many large airports. The lounges provide comfortable chairs and sofas, a relaxed atmosphere, newspapers, magazines, televisions, and a place to store coats and baggage while passengers shop or dine. There are also bars, facilities for making telephone calls and cashing checks, computer ports or WiFi, and meeting rooms. Members can receive boarding passes at the lounge and enjoy complimentary soft drinks, coffee, or light snacks. Complimentary alcohol is available at numerous clubs. To many travelers, none of these comforts is as important as easy access.

How quickly can they get to the gate for a flight, especially a connecting flight? Where do they pick up transportation? You can find diagrams depicting the layouts of many airports online.

Many airports use a *satellite design*, which means central buildings are attached to boarding areas by passageways. This design minimizes the distances that travelers must cross to reach their planes. Some airports, like those in Orlando, Tampa, and Denver, are connected by light rail systems; most have moving sidewalks and electric carts.

Security. After the attacks of 9/11, many new rules went into effect to tighten airport security. Here are some of the rules that directly affect passengers.

- Air travelers may take onboard only one carry-on bag and one personal item (such as a purse or a briefcase).
- Travelers must show a government-issued picture ID when they check in. They may be asked to produce this ID at several points before boarding, and the name on their air ticket must match exactly the name on their IDs.
- Only ticketed passengers are allowed beyond screening checkpoints except for those with specific medical or parental needs.
- Parking and curbside check-in are subject to new controls, which vary among airports and airlines.
- Knives of any length, cutting instruments, and most metal scissors are among the items that cannot be carried onboard. (Tweezers, safety razors, and nail clippers are permitted.)
- All visitors (noncitizens) must be finger-scanned and digitally photographed upon entering the United States. (*Finger scanning* is digitized, inkless fingerprinting.)

The TSA Pre✓®, begun in 2011, is a program allowing qualified low-risk passengers traveling in the United States to receive expedited screening at the airport. After completing a background check, being finger printed and paying a fee, participants will receive a Known Traveler Number (KTN) to use when making flight reservations. Participating airlines will then print an indicator on the boarding pass. Those passengers can proceed through designated lanes and will not need to remove shoes, jackets, or laptops.

Global Entry is another program offered by TSA that allows expedited clearance for pre-approved, low-risk travelers upon arrival in the United States.

Note that security procedures may change with little or no notice. The government has increased passenger searches and pat-downs and has revised rules for its no-fly lists—people stopped from flying. See the Transportation Security Administration website for current airport security information.

International Airports and Airlines

In many airports abroad, security procedures have long been tighter than those in the United States. Passengers may be interviewed extensively and searched before boarding. Even before the terrorist attacks of 2001, check-in times were usually one and a half to two hours before flight time; they may be as long as three hours. The U.S. government requires foreign airlines and airports to meet certain standards of security in order for flights to serve U.S. airports.

Airports at major international *gateways* (cities that are arrival or departure points for international travel) are listed in Table 4.5. Almost all the listed airports are served by major U.S. carriers, as well as international carriers.

Aircraft that fly internationally must be registered in and accountable to a particular nation. The flag of that nation is painted somewhere on the plane, and it is known as a *flag carrier*. Table 4.6 lists many of the major foreign flag carriers.

Outside the United States, many countries owned major airlines. In recent years, however, many governments have gotten out of the airline business. Some experts predict that, in the future, airlines of different countries will merge to form multinational carriers that will dominate international skies.

In the meantime, airlines based in different nations have been forming code-sharing and marketing alliances. To the prospective traveler, it may look as if one airline offers service to a far-flung city when, in fact, the trip to that city might require several connections and flights on different airlines.

Alliances among international airlines now number in the hundreds. As part of their agreements, allied airlines often market and sell each other's flights, link their frequent-flyer programs, and pool revenues and divide profits for the routes involved. In a small percentage of alliances, one airline actually acquires stock in the other.

The airlines argue that these alliances give travelers more choices, easier booking and smoother service between destinations. Critics respond that travelers will ultimately have fewer choices and face higher fares. Lack of interline agreements between rival airline alliance groups often limits interline ticketing and baggage acceptance.

✔ CHECK-UP

The large regional airlines
- ✔ Typically fly shorter routes than the major carriers.
- ✔ Are governed by the same safety standards as the major and national carriers.
- ✔ Are often owned by major airlines or have code-sharing agreements with them.

Trends that have greatly influenced U.S. airports in recent years include
- ✔ The popularity of the hub-and-spoke system.
- ✔ The use of a satellite design.
- ✔ Increased security measures.

Service in the Air: Variations in Air Travel

■ WHAT ARE THE MOST SIGNIFICANT VARIATIONS IN THE FLIGHTS
AND SERVICES AVAILABLE TO AIRLINE PASSENGERS?

When Western Air Express flew from Los Angeles to Salt Lake City for the first time in April 1926, passengers rode on folding seats in the mail compartment. By 1928, Western's passengers on a flight from Los Angeles to San Francisco were served meals prepared by a first-class Los Angeles restaurant. But airlines could not make money on passenger service until American Airlines introduced the DC-3 in 1936. It could carry 21 passengers, could travel coast to coast in 16 hours and had seats set in rubber to decrease vibrations.

Today's travelers have easier, faster trips and more choices than those early fliers did. In this section, we look at variations in the trips travelers might take, the planes they fly on, and the amenities they are offered.

TABLE 4.5 A Selection of Major Airports Outside North America

Airport	Code	Airport	Code
Amsterdam, Netherlands	AMS	Madrid, Spain	MAD
Athens, Greece	ATH	Manchester, U.K.	MAN
Auckland, New Zealand	AKL	Milan (Malpensa), Italy	MXP
Bangkok, Thailand	BKK	Moscow (Vnukovo), Russia	VKO
Barcelona, Spain	BCN	Munich, Germany	MUC
Beijing, China	PEK	Nairobi (Jomo Kenyatta), Kenya	NBO
Berlin (Tegel), Germany	TXL	Oslo (Gardermoen), Norway	GEN
Bogotá, Colombia	BOG	Paris (De Gaulle), France	CDG
Brussels, Belgium	BRU	Paris (Orly), France	ORY
Buenos Aires (Ezeiza), Argentina	EZE	Prague, Czech Republic	PRG
Cairo, Egypt	CAI	Quito, Ecuador	UIO
Caracas, Venezuela	CCS	Rio de Janeiro (Jobim International), Brazil	GIG
Copenhagen (Roskilde), Denmark	RKE	Rome (Da Vinci), Italy	FCO
Delhi, India	DEL	San José, Costa Rica	SJO
Dublin, Ireland	DUB	Seoul, South Korea	SEL
Frankfurt (International), Germany	FRA	Shannon, Ireland	SNN
Geneva, Switzerland	GVA	Singapore	SIN
Helsinki, Finland	HEL	Stockholm (Arlanda), Sweden	ARN
Hong Kong, China	HKG	Sydney (Kingsford Smith), Australia	SYD
Istanbul, Turkey	IST	Tel Aviv (Yafo), Israel	TLV
Johannesburg (Jan Smuts), South Africa	JNB	Tokyo (Narita), Japan	NRT
Lima, Peru	LIM	Vienna, Austria	VIE
Lisbon, Portugal	LIS	Warsaw, Poland	WAW
London (Gatwick), U.K.	LGW	Zürich, Switzerland	ZRH
London (Heathrow), U.K.	LHR		

Note: Some cities have more than one airport, each with a separate code.

Types of Flights

For most people traveling by air, about the only things that matter is that their flight is safe, on time, and as fast and simple as possible. Its simplicity depends on the stops.

A *stop* occurs whenever a plane lands, and there are different types. A *connection* is a stop that occurs when the passenger gets off a plane with the sole purpose of boarding another plane. A *stopover* is a planned break in a journey. Stops count as stopovers whenever the traveler stays at a domestic location for more than four hours—or, for international flights, 24 hours—unless no flight to the destination is available on that airline. If such a flight is available, the passenger must take the next available flight to avoid paying for a stopover.

Depending on the stops involved, travelers might take three different types of one-way flights, as Figure 4.2 illustrates.

- A *nonstop flight* has no intermediate stops.
- A *connecting flight* has a stop that requires the passenger to change planes.
- A *direct,* or *through, flight* has one or more stops at which the passenger does not have to change planes. In fact, some so-called direct flights change

TABLE 4.6 Some Major International Airlines

Name of Airline	Code	Country
Aer Lingus	EI	Republic of Ireland
Aeroflot	SU	Russia
Aeromexico	AM	Mexico
Air Canada	AC	Canada
Air France	AF	France
Air India	AI	India
Air Jamaica	JM	Jamaica
Air New Zealand	NZ	New Zealand
Alitalia	AZ	Italy
Asiana	OZ	South Korea
Austrian	OS	Austria
Avianca	AV	Colombia
BahamasAir	UP	Bahamas
British Airways	BA	United Kingdom
Cathay Pacific	CX	Hong Kong, China
China Airlines	CI	Taiwan
Egypt Air	MS	Egypt
El Al	LY	Israel
Emirates	EK	Dubai
Eva	BR	Taiwan
Finnair	AY	Finland
Iberia	IB	Spain
Icelandair	FI	Iceland

(continued on next page)

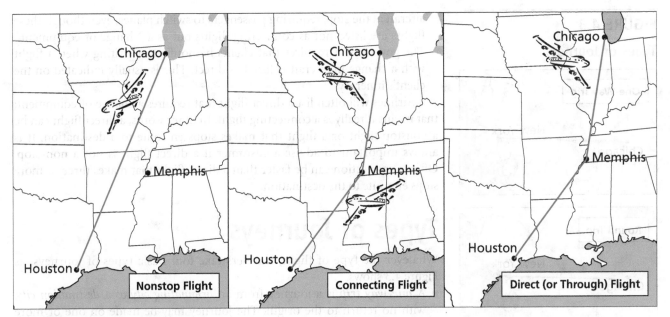

FIGURE 4.2 Types of Flights

The difference between nonstop and direct flights can be very important to travelers, who often confuse the two.

TABLE 4.6 Some Major International Airlines

Name of Airline	Code	Country
Japan (JAL)	JL	Japan
KLM	KL	The Netherlands
Korean Air	KE	South Korea
LAN	LA	Chile
Lot Polish	LO	Poland
Lufthansa	LH	Germany
Olympic	OA	Greece
Philippine Airlines	PR	Philippines
Qantas	QF	Australia
Qatar Airways	QR	Qatar
Royal Air Maroc	AT	Morocco
Royal Jordanian	RJ	Jordan
Ryan Air	FR	Ireland
Saudia	SV	Saudi Arabia
Scandinavian Airlines System (SAS)	SK	Denmark, Norway, Sweden
Singapore	SQ	Singapore
South African Airways	SA	South Africa
Swiss	LX	Switzerland
TAP-Air Portugal	TP	Portugal
Turkish Airlines	TK	Turkey
Virgin Atlantic	VS	United Kingdom

FIGURE 4.3

Types of Journeys

For an itinerary to qualify as an open-jaw journey, the distance between the cities unconnected by a flight must be less than the distance of the shortest flight segment. Otherwise, the flights may not be eligible for the usual discounted fares.

aircraft at the stop, requiring passengers to switch planes, even though these flights are listed not as connecting flights but as a "change of equipment." The government requires that clients be notified in writing when a flight with a change in aircraft is listed as direct. This is usually indicated on the client's itinerary.

Airlines will often list a direct flight that requires a change of equipment; that means it really is a connecting flight. In other words, a direct flight can be a nonstop flight or a flight that makes stops en route to a destination. It is always important to advise a customer if a direct flight is not a non-stop. Often a connection can be faster than a direct flight that makes three or more stops en route to the destination.

Types of Journeys

Whatever the type of flight, travelers take four basic types of journeys, as Figure 4.3 shows.

- A *one-way trip* is a journey from an *originating city* to a *destination city*, with no return to the origin. The journey may be made on one or more flights and may or may not require the passenger to change planes.
- A *round-trip* is a journey that returns to the city where it began, without additional stopovers. Thus, the ultimate destination is the originating city, with the same route used going and coming.
- A *circle trip* is like a round-trip except that the route on the return trip differs from the route on the outgoing trip. The journey involves two or more stopovers and returns to the originating city.
- An *open-jaw trip* is like a round-trip except that the passenger either (1) returns to a city different from the point of origin or (2) departs for the return trip from a city other than the original destination. For example, a passenger might go from Seattle to Boston by plane, then to New York by car, and then return to Seattle by plane from New York. Thus, the traveler uses some form of transportation in addition to air.
- A *double open-jaw trip*. Often for fare purposes, airlines will allow a double open-jaw, often found in itineraries where there is more than one airport in a city. One example is Oakland to La Guardia, returning Newark to San Francisco. Some international airlines allow an *APEX (Advance Purchase Excursion) fare* with a double open-jaw, such as San Francisco to Frankfurt, returning from Munich to Los Angeles.

Types of Aircraft

Most modern aircraft have two to four jet engines for propulsion. Basically, there are three types of jet engines: *turbojets; turbofans,* an improved version of turbojets; and *turboprops (propjets),* which use the jet engine to turn a propeller. Turboprops fly more slowly and at lower altitudes than other jet aircraft. On all jets that fly at high altitudes, the air pressure inside the plane is artificially increased to approximate the air pressure at ground level.

Jet aircraft come in two broad types: *wide-bodied planes,* with two aisles and a middle section of seats, and *narrow-bodied,* with seats on either side of a single aisle. For each aircraft, several models or series are likely to exist, as the manufacturer makes improvements on the original plane. For example, there are 15 models of the Boeing 747.

The largest commercial airplane is the Airbus A380. The initial version is designed to carry up to 555 passengers, but it could eventually hold up to 800.

Airlines are continuing to design and introduce new aircraft that are more fuel efficient, can travel longer distances, have new safety mechanisms and are more comfortable for the travelers.

It is important to know the kind of aircraft and to communicate this to your clients. Most GDS systems have a way to decode the aircraft listed for a flight. Clients must be advised if they are flying on a turbojet. There are big differences between traveling on a 30-seat plane with limited space for seating and carry-on luggage and a 300-passenger jet aircraft.

Classes of Service

Some budget airlines offer only one class of service. But on most aircraft, movable partitions, called *bulkheads*, divide the plane into compartments, and the airline offers different classes of service in the different compartments. Most airlines offer two *classes of service* on most flights: first class and coach. For long flights (particularly international flights), many airlines offer a third option, business class, and now some have four classes, including premium economy.

Most passengers (including those flying on discount fares) travel *coach* class. On international flights, coach class is more often known as *economy class.* Large jets have several compartments for coach seating. Coach passengers may receive free soft drinks and sometimes free snacks, but they usually must pay for alcoholic beverages. If movies are shown, coach passengers often pay for the use of headsets. The seating in coach has become steadily less comfortable as more and more U.S. flights feature fewer amenities and crowd more and more coach seats into the cabin. For an additional fee, some airlines offer a coach seat with extra leg room, and some airlines also provide additional amenities, such as complimentary beverages and checked luggage. Most airlines are now charging standard coach passengers for both their seat assignments and checked luggage.

The *first-class* section is located at the front of the plane and features more legroom and seats that are wider and, usually, more heavily padded than those in the coach compartment. First-class passengers receive personalized service, such as separate check-in desks and more flight attendants per passenger, as well as free alcoholic beverages and free headsets on flights with movies. Meals are elaborate, and passengers are offered more choices, often served on china with cloth napkins, rather than plastic and paper. Many of the seats on long-haul international fights convert into lay-flat beds, making traveling much more comfortable for their first-class travelers.

Business or *executive class* falls between first class and coach in the amenities. Drinks may be free and the seating is in a quieter area than the coach section; sometimes the seats are more comfortable and the meals better. Some airlines offer business class in addition to first class and coach; others substitute it for first class.

International flights often provide amenities beyond those we have described. Some even have on-board showers and bars for their first-class customers.

A newly introduced class of service is premium economy, which is offered on many long-haul international routes. The seats are located in the front of the economy section, and just behind business or first class. The seats are larger than the standard economy, recline a great amount, and offer upgraded meals and beverages, without having to pay the cost of a business or first-class ticket.

Aircraft Seating

The layout of the cabin has much to do with passenger comfort. Airline policies, not the manufacturer, determine seat space. Even when airlines use the same type of aircraft, seat space varies from flight to flight. It is determined by a combination of three factors: seat pitch, seat width, and configuration of the aircraft.

Pitch (often referred to as leg room) is the term for the front-to-rear spacing of seat rows. On U.S. domestic routes, seat pitch in coach averages between 31 and 35 inches. The average pitch in first class is 40 inches, although in wide-bodied aircraft it may be as much as 57 to 60 inches. Seats are mounted on tracks in the floor, which the airline uses to adjust the spacing.

Seat width is the total side-to-side space at seat cushion or chest level. Like seat pitch, it is determined by airline policy, but it cannot be adjusted as easily as pitch.

The *configuration,* or layout, of seats in each row also influences comfort and the feeling of roominess. At any given width, seats installed in pairs provide the most comfortable arrangement; this configuration puts every passenger beside either an aisle or a window. If seats are installed in groups of three or more and the plane is full, then at least one passenger in each row is in a middle seat between two other passengers. Most jet aircraft have a seating configuration of three across; some may have two across. Wide-bodied planes may seat four or five across in the middle section.

In the first-class compartment, all seats should be equally comfortable. In coach, where people sit can make a difference, especially on flights of long duration such as Los Angeles to Sydney, Australia.

- Seats over the wings generally provide a smoother ride, but the view is obscured, and the area may be noisy because of the engines.
- Seats in emergency exit rows often have extra legroom because the pitch must provide access to the exit. For the same reason, seats in front of the exit row do not usually recline. (To sit in emergency exit rows, passengers must be physically capable and willing to perform emergency actions, such as opening the exit door.)
- Aisle seats provide easy access to the bathrooms and a chance to stretch cramped legs.
- Bulkhead seats offer extra legroom, but they have no space below the seat to stow carry-on luggage. Often, bulkhead seats are reserved for families with babies and bassinets or for anyone with service animals.

A good source to help your clients choose the best seats and in-flight amenities is seatguru.com.

Checked Baggage

Regulations on the baggage that can be taken without charge vary somewhat from airline to airline and even from flight to flight. In the past, it generally was assumed that passengers could check through two standard-size suitcases per person, but that is no longer the case. Many airlines now permit only one bag free of charge plus additional bags at a per-bag fee. Some airlines charge a fee for the first checked bag.

There are also limits on the size and weight of baggage. Usually, no piece of luggage may weigh more than 50 pounds, and the largest piece should not measure more than 62 inches in total dimensions. To determine a case's total dimensions, add its length, height, and width. For example, if a suitcase's longest side measures 28 inches and it is 20 inches high and 5 inches deep, then the case's total dimensions are 53 inches. Outside the United States, the standard limit is 44 pounds (20 kilos) and 60 pounds for first class.

All checked baggage must bear an identification tag on the outside giving the owner's name and address. It is advisable to put another tag inside the luggage in case the outside tag comes off. Checked bags can be opened and inspected by TSA security.

There are exceptions, and the fees vary with different airlines. Baggage allowances, size, weight and fees can vary by flight and by airline. Travel professionals must advise their clients of the baggage policy for each of the flights on their clients itinerary. The airline's website is the most reliable source of current information.

If passengers have unusual baggage, the airline should be alerted beforehand. If a person has more baggage than permitted, an extra fee is charged. The **excess baggage charge** varies from airline to airline but has been about $50 per extra bag. The amount of excess baggage permitted is limited, but a passenger is unlikely to reach that limit. Most airlines accept sporting equipment—such as bicycles, surfboards, skis, and golf clubs—for the same excess baggage charge, but always check the website of the airline concerned.

Other Services on Domestic Flights

Travelers who save money by flying on a budget airline may find that they must do without conveniences standard on most airlines. Their luggage may not be transferred automatically to other carriers; they may not be able to obtain a seat assignment; and they may fly into small airports with very limited connecting flights. But some budget airlines actually offer *more* service and better amenities than the major airlines, as Chapter 9 (on marketing) discusses.

Seat Assignments. Most airlines allow passengers to choose a seat when making a reservation, but there are important limitations. Sometimes passengers booked at discount fares cannot make advance seat selections, and some airlines do not allow seat assignments to be made more than 30 days in advance of the flight. If passengers have not selected a seat in advance, they may make a choice when they check in at the airport, but their desired seating may not be available at this late date. Many airlines provide the option for passengers to pay for seats located in premium sections of the aircraft, such as the bulkhead, emergency row, or towards the front of the aircraft. The airlines can limit the number of advanced seat assignments that are free of charge at the time of booking.

No matter when a seat is selected, passengers may be disappointed with the results. Airlines reserve many seats for their frequent flyers and hold some seats to be assigned at the airport, so passengers might not be able to reserve a particular seat on a particular flight.

Assistance for People with Disabilities. Under the 1986 Air Carrier Access Act and the 1990 Americans with Disabilities Act, travelers with disabilities are guaranteed the same service and access as other travelers on domestic flights. Airport terminals, for example, must have telephones equipped with telecommunication devices for the deaf (TDDs) for those with hearing or speech impairments.

Wheelchairs are available for those who need them and must be requested in advance at the time of booking; the same is true with passengers who want to take their own wheelchairs or who have other special needs. Also, they should ask for a wheelchair to meet their arriving flight.

Special Meals. Few meals are now offered on domestic U.S. flights. Passengers can bring their own food, and increasingly airlines are selling meals onboard. Depending on the airline, when meals are offered with a flight, travelers may be able to order children's meals, seafood platters, low-calorie meals, pasta dishes, or vegetarian and lacto-vegetarian (no dairy or egg products) meals. There are also meals to meet the medical restrictions for diabetics and the religious requirements for Hindus, Muslims, and Jews. Special meals must be ordered at least 12 to 24 hours in advance; extremely unusual meals should be ordered at least a week in advance. Many airport restaurants prepare boxed meals that travelers can buy to carry onboard.

Pets. Advance reservations are needed for pets. Some airlines will transport animals either in the passenger cabin or in the pressurized cargo hold. However, other airlines will not take pets or will limit pets in cargo to certain seasons. There is an extra charge for pets transported as cargo. Check with the specific airline about their pet policy.

Service animals are exempt from the rules forbidding large pets in the cabin. Passengers with service animals should have bulkhead seats so the animal has room to lie down. Each airline has rules about service animals and which ones are accepted on its aircraft. It is important to verify this information on the airline's website.

Electronic Gadgets. Passengers who want to stay "wired" into their earthbound lives may use their own computers, cellular phones, or other electronic devices when a plane is at its cruising altitude. But electronic devices must be turned off while the plane is on a runway, while it is climbing, and while it is descending below 10,000 feet.

More and more planes are equipped with WiFi, another source of revenue for the airlines. Cell phones may be used only when the plane is on the ground before take-off and after landing.

Some airlines offer special electronic devices for entertainment. Again, check with the specific airline concerned as to what entertainment features are available on specific flights and whether they are complimentary or have a cost.

✔ CHECK-UP

Among the most basic variations in a traveler's trip are
✔ The type of flight, which might be nonstop, connecting, or direct (through).
✔ The type of journey, which might be a one-way trip, round-trip, circle trip, open-jaw trip, or double open-jaw.
✔ The type of aircraft, which might be turbojets, turbofans, or turboprops and might be wide-bodied or narrow-bodied.

Other variations that influence the comfort or convenience of a flight include
✔ The class of service, which might be first class, coach, business, or premium economy.

✔ Seat space, which depends on pitch, seat width, and configuration of the aircraft.

Special services that passengers might request include
✔ Checking of excess or unusual baggage.
✔ Wheelchair assistance.
✔ Special meals, which should be ordered at least 24 hours in advance.
✔ Reservations for animals, which require a special charge that will vary by airline.

Airfares

To those new to air travel, nothing may be more bewildering than the fares. Two persons sitting next to each other in coach on a flight from Los Angeles to New York may be holding round-trip tickets, one at $399 and the other at $2,200. A 500-mile trip at noon tomorrow may cost $400; a 1,000-mile trip may cost $99.

Once upon a time, before deregulation, fares could be looked up in published lists called *tariffs*. Now the fares may change at any moment. A fare is guaranteed only when the ticket is purchased. Some airlines do allow reservations to be put on hold for 24 hours, guaranteeing that airfare until the actual purchase happens. Still, we can make some useful generalizations about airfares.

Domestic Fares

Some variations in domestic airfares are straightforward. The airlines set different fares for (1) different routes and (2) different classes of service. In addition, though, the airlines offer an ever-changing array of discounted fares. In fact, on average, more than 80 percent of passengers fly on some sort of discount.

Routes and Classes of Service. The fare for a flight depends first on the route. In theory, the airlines charge the same fare for connecting as for direct flights—for example, for a one-way nonstop flight from New York to Los Angeles and for a one-way flight from New York to Los Angeles with a connection in Chicago. In practice, however, discount fares on the nonstop flight would sell out first. Knowing this, the airline may set a lower fare on the flight with a connection.

The fare through a connecting point is called a **through fare** when it involves a connection between flights of the same airline. When the connection involves different airlines that have agreed on one published fare, that fare is called a **joint fare.**

If a passenger makes a stopover anywhere along the route, the situation changes. Fares from one stopover point to another are called **point-to-point fares,** and they are usually more expensive than through or joint fares. Thus, flying from Boston to Washington with a required connection at New York, the fare charged will be a through fare from Boston to Washington. But, if the client wants to fly from Boston to New York with an overnight stay in New York and then fly on to Washington, the trip will involve point-to-point fares from Boston to New York and from New York to Washington.

Airfares also depend on the class of service selected. Coach fares are sometimes called *straight coach, normal,* or *straight Y fares* (because the code used for coach when booking a flight is *Y*). A client who arrives at the airport without a reservation and wishes to travel at the last moment will usually pay the straight coach fare. First-class fares (for which the primary code is *F*) may be only 10 to 20 percent higher than straight coach fares. Business-class fares (coded as *C*) may be 5 to 10 percent higher than straight coach fares.

Discounts for Selected Demographic Groups. Variations in fares begin to get complicated once discounts are considered. Airlines may offer special fares to specific age groups or to people in specific situations. The availability of these special fares is becoming limited because many airlines discount seats strictly based on supply and demand. Each airline has its own rules and fare levels, but special discounts may be available to

- Seniors (with varying definitions; minimum age may be 62 or 65).
- Active members of the armed forces.
- The bereaved—that is, those attending funerals or traveling to be with close relatives who are seriously ill.
- Children. The fares and rules for children vary with the age of the child. They also vary from airline to airline.
- Children under the age of two are considered infants, and one infant per adult travels free on domestic flights. The infant is not guaranteed a seat, but airlines often try to assign an empty seat next to the parent, if available.

CLOSE-UP: ON THE JOB WITH NADIA JONES, AIRPORT TICKET AGENT

For two years, Nadia Jones has worked as an airport ticket agent at a large regional airline. Here is how she describes her job.

"Although many of my days have become routine, I never lose the excitement of coming to the airport every day. Hearing the planes overhead as I am driving in and just being there dealing with person after person flying to places far off—it gives me a thrill every day.

"I work the ticket counter, so I'm the first person from the airline most travelers deal with face-to-face. The pilots, reservationists, accountants, baggage handlers, mechanics—the many, many behind-the-scenes employees all depend on us to present a good image to the public and give good customer service.

"Most of my job consists of checking in and tagging luggage, issuing boarding passes to those who don't have them, writing down the gate number for the traveler, checking that the customer's ID matches the reservation before going to airport security and answering questions.

"I learned that good customer service is more than just the technical functions of the job. We need to smile at each traveler, use their names when we can, make eye contact and be ready to be extra helpful if they have special needs. Sometimes we can notice or anticipate customers' needs before they even ask.

"So, it sounds pretty routine—until flight delays occur. Then the entire job changes. You can feel the mood in the crowd change. Actually, 99 percent of the travelers are understanding, but there is usually at least one who gets somewhat nasty when things aren't going right. And there isn't a darn thing we can do.

"Once we had to cancel the last flight out because a fog rolled in and practically closed the airport. There wasn't much we could do except send everyone home or suggest hotel space. 'Well, I'm sorry that you just have to be there early tomorrow morning, but you should have left yourself more leeway in planning' is what I'm thinking of telling a traveler who just stands there not believing that he can't go. But I just calmly explain the situation again and try to be as helpful as possible without being too apologetic.

"Of course, other times it's a mechanical delay, which theoretically is our fault—though it happens to all airlines. We try to keep travelers aware of exactly what is happening with the flights. We had a special seminar on 'giving people the bad news' as soon as possible and keeping them informed of changes. People hate 'no news' more than 'bad news.'

"What is really tough, though, is then trying to reroute them on other flights when one flight is canceled. Of course, the next flight out is already almost full. And we have to put them on a standby list, with no guarantee they'll get on that next flight—it's that uncertainty again that people don't like. I'm almost surprised how well most people take it.

"I got this job starting with a group interview. There were about 20 people there. I knew from my travel classes that they look for assertive, friendly, and communicative people, so I spoke up as soon as I could.

"They called me back for a personal interview, and I was conditionally hired to start training. Training was fun but intensive. They gave us a list of city codes to have memorized before we started training. The test was on the second morning. My roommate said she only missed one code. She was sent home; she was history as far as the airline was concerned.

"I was a little scared when I faced my first travelers at the counter, but I was assisting another agent and eased into it. On the first day, I was taking care of many of the passengers on my own already. And now I get that thrill of heading out to the airport every day."

To reserve a seat for an infant, parents pay the cost of a child's fare; some airlines have infant seats.

- Children two through 11 years old who fly with an adult may qualify for a fare discount.

Unaccompanied children, however, are charged the adult fare plus a fee. If an unaccompanied child is taking a flight with a connection, a higher fee is charged because of the need for an escort between the flights. Children must be above a certain age (often, age five) to be allowed to fly unaccompanied. When booking an unaccompanied child, always check with the airline in question as to their procedures.

Promotional Fares. Other discounts are even less predictable than those for specified groups. An airline may offer a lower fare known as a *promotional fare* or *discount fare* when it opens a new route; when it wants to promote travel between particular destinations during the off-season, if at certain times of the day, or on certain days of the week; or when a competitor has offered a discount. For example, airlines usually offer promotional fares between the Northeast and Florida during the summer. A promotional fare may be only half the cost of a straight coach fare, or even less. Some of the larger airlines also introduce these promotional airfares to compete with the low-cost carriers that operate similar travel routes.

Promotional fares come with a variety of restrictions. For example, to obtain the promotional fare, passengers may be required to purchase the ticket several weeks in advance, and often they cannot take advantage of other discounts (such as children's fares). Table 4.7 describes some common types

TABLE 4.7 Restrictions on Promotional Fares

Minimum/maximum stay Many promotional fares are round-trip fares and require the traveler to stay a minimum amount of time at the destination, such as a Saturday night; some set a maximum stay, such as 30 days. Thus, a traveler might depart on a Sunday and return the following Sunday or depart on a Saturday and return the next day. One-way discounts are not governed by this rule. (Most round-trip fares can be used on open-jaw itineraries or circle trips; the fare is then calculated by taking half of each of the round-trip fares.)

Advanced booking The reservation must be made in advance, such as seven or 14 days before departure.

Advanced ticketing The ticket must be paid for in advance. Often, it must be paid within 24 hours of making the reservation, but the restriction may specify a certain number of days before the flight. Some fares require instant ticketing and are capacity-controlled.

Cancellation and change fees Promotional fares are nonrefundable, and a fee is charged for changes. The fee may be anywhere from 100 percent of the fare to cancel a reservation to $50 to change it. If the ticket is changed, there will be an additional charge if the fare has been increased or if the old fare no longer exists. Even some full-fare airfares now have penalties for cancellation and changes. The rules are constantly changing.

Effective dates of fare sale Fare sales are often advertised suddenly and are then good only for a short time, such as two weeks. Tickets must be purchased within that time, but sometimes the time limit is extended at the last minute. Generally, other restrictions apply to the date of travel (see next item).

Effective dates of travel A fare may be good only for travel within certain calendar dates. Usually, travel must start and end within these time limits. For example, tickets bought in a fare sale that is in effect only between September 1 and September 14 may require that travel occur between September 15 and December 15.

Blackout dates Many discounts do not apply during busy travel periods, such as holidays. Thus, many promotional fares will be blacked out certain days of the week on the day preceding and the Sunday after Thanksgiving, around Christmas, or even around school holidays, such as Presidents' Day. Careful planning may find holes in blackout times; for example, December 25 is often not blacked out.

Capacity control (Inventory control) Only a certain percentage of seats (a percentage known to the airline) is offered at the discount fare. Even though a fare is not blacked out, it may be sold out because of high demand or because only a small number of discounted seats were available in the first place. (Some controversy exists as to how many seats a carrier must make available when advertising such a discount fare.)

No interlining On many discount fares, the itinerary must use only one carrier or partner carrier.

Discount levels Fares may be slightly higher or lower on different days of the week (for domestic flights, cheaper days generally are Tuesday, Wednesday, and Saturday) or even at different times of the day. These restrictions can vary greatly.

Routing Some promotional fares require stopovers; others require that travelers fly direct.

of restrictions on promotional fares; the details vary from airline to airline and change frequently.

Many of the restrictions on promotional fares exist simply to ensure that discount-fare passengers travel when the airline would otherwise have empty seats. For example, promotional fares on shuttle flights between New York and Boston, which primarily serve business travelers, may be available on weekends but not on weekdays, when the flights are likely to be full without the lure of discounts. In effect, passengers who travel at the full fare are paying for the freedom of flying without such restrictions.

Airlines usually introduce promotional fares with no warning and implement them as speedily as possible. Sometimes, travelers hear about a new fare before travel counselors or even the airline's own reservations agents are aware of it.

Some promotional fares are available only if passengers book tickets online. These purchases save the airlines money because they bypass the airlines' phone reservationists, travel agencies, and GDS fees. Airlines periodically offer reduced fares online to encourage clients to buy tickets that way.

The Whys of Airfares

Is there some logic to the bewildering array of fares and discounts? Sometimes, airlines offer discount fares to attract new clients for future travel or to generate a quick increase in sales in order to meet cash commitments. More generally, airline fares reflect the same simple goal that drives prices in similar businesses. They aim to sell the most they can at the highest possible price, which may be limited by competition or concerns about the effects of the price on consumer behavior. For the airlines, this strategy translates in its simplest terms to "Let's try to fill the planes up as much as possible at the highest possible fares."

At a more sophisticated level, the airlines' fare structure, including promotional fares, can be explained as a strategy of *yield management. Yield* is the average amount of revenue earned per passenger mile; it is computed by dividing total passenger revenue by the total number of passenger miles flown. The airlines' fare structure is an effort to manage the yield in a way that produces the most revenue. To achieve this aim, the airline may need to offer promotional fares in order to increase the passenger load (the percentage of available seats on a flight that is actually sold).

Thus, the promotional fare is the airlines' version of a sale. But unlike many businesses, airlines cannot wait to put their product on sale after it fails to sell at a high price. If they wait, it will be too late, because each seat on each flight is *perishable;* that is, if a seat remains empty for a particular flight, that revenue is lost forever. The opportunity to sell a seat on that flight occurs only once; once the flight has departed, it's too late!

Successful promotional fares rely heavily on the airlines' ability to predict which flights would have a large number of unsold seats at the regular fare. Airlines can adjust the frequency of flights and the size of aircraft to match broad seasonal changes, but they cannot make these changes from day to day. They cannot fly a large plane one day and a small one the next. The restrictions on promotional fares represent an attempt to direct discount-fare-buying passengers to flights that might otherwise remain unsold and, thus, to avoid diluting revenue from full-fare passengers. The rules may be bizarre and complicated, but they reflect an effort to achieve the rather simple goal of increasing revenue.

Frequent-Flyer Programs

Bonus programs that reward consistent patronage are another technique for increasing revenue over the long haul. Although each airline has a different name for its bonus program, these programs are known generally as *frequent-flyer plans.* For example, after traveling 40,000 miles on an airline, a client might be rewarded with a free unrestricted domestic ticket; 10,000 miles might earn a free upgrade from coach to first class.

All frequent-flyer plans generally work the same way. The traveler signs up with an airline and then makes sure that the mileage for each flight is credited to his or her account. Depending on the plan, this means that the traveler might submit a certificate at the gate, show a membership card, or (most commonly) provide a number when making a reservation or checking in. The airline records the mileage on the participant's account and sends the participant periodic summaries of accumulated credits.

Frequent-flyer programs have become so popular that businesses of all kinds have established tie-ins with the programs. Airlines have formed partnerships with hotel chains, car rental companies, credit card companies, online shopping companies, and telephone companies. These partnerships allow frequent-flyer members to earn air miles by buying these services or to cash in their air miles for these services.

For example, members of one frequent-flyer program can cash in 10,000 to 12,000 air miles for a three-day car rental with any of several car rental companies, and they can earn air miles by taking a cruise, obtaining a mortgage, or buying a specialty cake with one of the airline's mileage partners.

Some people use a bank credit card that has a tie-in with an airline—for example, the Chase Bank credit card with United. They then try to put as many of their monthly expenditures as possible on that specific card, from groceries to college tuition, in an effort to build their mileage points even though they haven't actually flown anywhere that month.

To some extent, frequent-flyer programs have become victims of their own success. They are costly to operate, and they no longer give a competitive edge because every major airline has one. Most frequent-flyer members today belong to several frequent-flyer plans, and they collect miles on whatever airline they can.

Flights are capacity controlled as to the number of travelers on board who are flying on frequent flyer miles that day. Therefore, many travelers are often disillusioned when they wish to use their earned miles and find that it may take many, many months for them to be able to get the desired seat to fly to the destinations of their choice.

Domestic Taxes and Surcharges

Often, an airline's advertisement might say, for instance, "The fare is $398 plus tax," instead of noting that the fare is $438.73 including all taxes and service charges. Airline fares are subject to several taxes and surcharges. Although a computer can calculate the total cost, sales agents should understand the basic taxes. Current taxes on domestic flights include (1) a federal transportation tax, (2) a segment tax, (3) an airport passenger facility charge at some airports, and (4) a security fee.

The federal transportation tax is known as the *U.S. ticket tax.* It is charged on tickets purchased within the United States when air travel meets one of the following conditions: it is (1) within the continental United States or (2) within the states of Alaska and Hawaii or (3) between the continental United States and a 225-mile **buffer zone** that extends from the U.S. border into Canada and Mexico or (4) within this buffer zone, which is shown in Figure 4.4.

For flights from the continental United States to Alaska or Hawaii, travelers pay only a portion of the U.S. ticket tax based on the percentage of the flight that occurs across the continental United States and Alaska or Hawaii. (Travelers to Alaska and Hawaii are also assessed the U.S. international travel facilities tax.)

The **segment tax** is charged for each takeoff and landing. This tax has been increasing yearly since its inception in 1997.

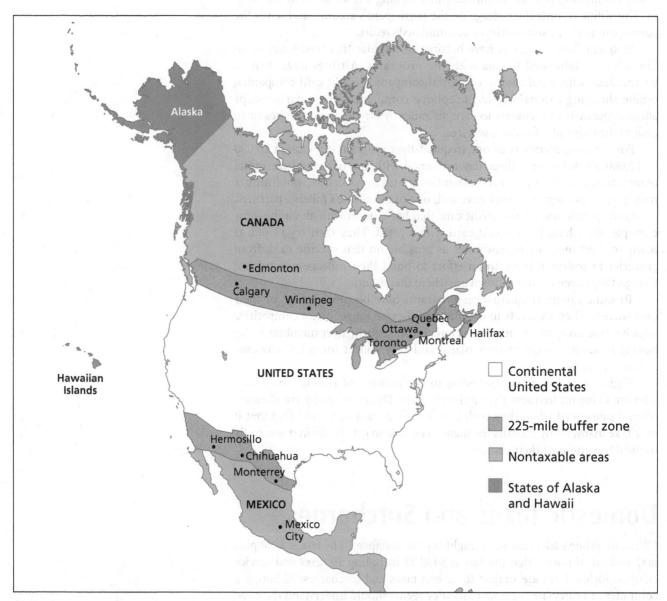

FIGURE 4.4 Buffer Zone

Notice that the only large Canadian city outside the buffer zone is Edmonton, Alberta. The only large Mexican city within the buffer zone is Monterrey. Thus, international taxes apply to airline tickets from the United States to Edmonton and domestic taxes apply to airline tickets from the United States to Monterrey.

A *passenger facility charge (PFC)* is levied at almost all U.S. airports. The FAA allows airports to collect this surcharge for airport improvements. There are limits on the number of PFC charges that can be incurred per itinerary.

The *security fee* was established in 2001 to pay for increased security measures.

Airlines also add fuel surcharges at times when the price of oil increases, but those are considered part of the fare.

International Airfares

Like U.S. domestic fares, international airfares vary with the class of service, the time, the day of the week, and the season. As in the case of domestic travel, some discounts are available on international fares for travelers who can meet certain restrictions.

In other important ways, international airfares are very different from domestic fares. They are based on agreements between governments and, broadly speaking, are set by one of two systems:

- A *routing system,* in which the fare depends on the specific route flown.
- A *mileage system,* in which the fare generally depends on (1) the origin, (2) the farthest point on the trip, and (3) the number of miles flown.

Fares based on the routing system are much simpler than those based on mileage, and we begin with them.

Fares Based on Routing. When an international fare is based on the route, the traveler must go to specific connecting or stopover cities. For example, a fare may be cited for a flight from New York to Nice, France, with a connection in Paris.

Most international discount fares use the routing system and feature many of the same restrictions as domestic discount fares. The lowest fares to Europe generally allow no stopovers, but discount fares to Asian and South Pacific destinations may allow stopovers. The most frequently used discount fare for international travel is the APEX fare (for Advance Purchase Excursion).

Fares Based on Mileage. Most economy, first-class, and business-class fares apply the mileage system, which ties the fare to the number of miles flown. Basically, when the mileage system is used, the fare depends first on the through fare for a flight from the origin to the farthest point of the trip, which is called the *destination city.* Stopovers are usually allowed.

Taxes and Surcharges. Taxes and fees add to the cost of international flights and can be considerable. For flights to or from the United States, possible taxes and fees include the following:

- The U.S. international *departure tax* on individuals flying out of the United States or any of its possessions.
- The U.S. international *arrival tax* on individuals flying into the United States or any of its possessions.
- The passenger facility charge levied by certain U.S. airports.
- The U.S. security fee.
- International departure taxes levied by many foreign governments. They usually collect the tax at the airport before the departing flight, and often it must be paid in the local currency. Occasionally, the ticket includes this tax.

Consolidators and Other Sources of Discounts

For international travelers looking for low fares, consolidators may be the answer to their prayers. ***Consolidators*** are distribution companies that negotiate with airlines to buy seats on international flights at bargain rates and then sell the tickets to consumers, either directly or through travel agencies. They typically buy their seats in bulk to get the lowest prices available on the flights. They are called *bucket shops* in Britain. Their agreements with airlines allow consolidators to offer international tickets for substantially less than normal discount fares. Their fares often appear in tiny newspaper ads that show a list of cities with fares but no airline names.

Evaluating Consolidators. For the airlines, consolidators offer the guaranteed sale of large blocks of seats or a way of selling at the last-minute seats that would otherwise go unsold—without officially lowering their fares. The airline sets aside a portion of its inventory of seats to be available only to the consolidator. It makes a specific agreement with the consolidator to sell the seats at a reduced price but does not lower its fares across the board. The airline may also allow the consolidator to bypass some restrictions on discounted fares, such as requirements for advance booking.

For the traveler, consolidators offer low fares, sometimes on short notice. But even when travelers buy tickets from consolidators through travel agencies, using a consolidator has drawbacks. In particular, when a ticket is sold through a consolidator,

- Severe penalties may apply for any changes in travel plans.
- Routings may be unusual and time-consuming, requiring several connections.
- Travelers may be required to use an airline with which they are not familiar.
- Frequent-flyer plans may not be offered or may not apply.
- Seat assignments may not be possible until the day of the flight.
- Funds paid for flights may be tied up or lost altogether if the consolidator goes out of business.
- Travel insurance offered by the traveler's credit card company may not apply.
- A fee may be charged for using a credit card.
- The ticket may be totally non-refundable and non-changeable.

Rules change and vary among consolidators; check the conditions of purchase each time with a consolidator, and travel insurance is important.

For travel agencies, consolidators represent an opportunity to serve clients who might otherwise find international travel too expensive, and the results can be profitable. Some consolidators pay commissions to travel agencies; in some cases, the consolidator quotes the agency a net rate with no commission, and the agency sets its own markup on the ticket, instead of receiving a commission. Also, travel agencies can negotiate with an airline to become consolidators themselves. In light of reduced and eliminated commission being paid directly from the airlines, there are great revenue earning opportunities for agencies.

Obviously, consolidators should not be used blindly; nor should they be rejected out-of-hand. Travel counselors should be sure that

- The consolidator is reputable and reliable.
- The consolidator's ticket meets the client's needs.
- The client understands the advantages and disadvantages of purchasing a ticket through a consolidator.

Charters. Whereas consolidators purchase seats on scheduled flights, *charter* companies own or lease entire planes and then sell seats to the public or to tour operators. Consolidators have reduced the market for charters, but hosted tours (discussed in Chapter 8) often use charters. Some tour operators charter and fill entire planes weekly to popular destinations, such as the Caribbean, Hawaii, and Mexico, packaging the cost of the charter flight into the total tour package rate for opaque pricing.

Charters offer reasonable prices and direct flights to destinations that require connecting flights on regular scheduled service. But charters also bring many of the same disadvantages as consolidators, plus the following:

- Because charters want to fill every seat, some may be more crowded or provide less service than other flights. (Others provide superior service.)
- Charters generally provide little flexibility in schedule. They may offer only weekly flights; travelers cannot extend their stay for a day or two.
- Because charter tickets are not accepted by scheduled airlines, a passenger who must change plans during the trip usually has no options.
- Any delays may be prolonged because replacement aircraft may not be available and because scheduled flights are usually cleared to take off first after delays caused by weather.
- The charter may only partner with specific hotels in a destination, reducing the options that some traveler may prefer.

Fare Sales. Bargain hunters have yet another option for low international fares: online sales by the airlines. Some airlines post special low international fares online, just as they do for domestic tickets. Generally, these extra-low fares are available for only a limited number of tickets, to specific destinations, on short notice, and for brief stays.

✔ CHECK-UP

A passenger's fare is affected by
- ✔ The route taken.
- ✔ The class of service selected.
- ✔ Whether the passenger qualifies for a discount based on his or her age or special situation.
- ✔ Whether the passenger can accept restrictions that permit a promotional fare.

Among the major restrictions on promotional fares are
- ✔ Minimum stay.
- ✔ Advance booking and ticketing.
- ✔ Lack of refundability.
- ✔ Effective dates.
- ✔ Limited availability in the booking inventory.
- ✔ Routing.

Federal taxes on domestic air travel include
- ✔ The U.S. ticket tax.
- ✔ The segment tax.
- ✔ The airport passenger facility charge (PFC).
- ✔ The U.S. security fee.

Taxes that apply only to international flights include
- ✔ The U.S. international departure tax for individuals flying out of the United States.
- ✔ The U.S. international arrival tax for individuals flying into the United States.
- ✔ The U.S. Customs fee, immigration (INS) fee, and animal and plant health inspection service fee.
- ✔ International departure taxes levied by foreign governments.

Sources for low fares for international flights include
- ✔ Traditional discount fares from the airlines, such as APEX, which usually are based on the routing system.
- ✔ Consolidators.
- ✔ Charters.
- ✔ Internet-only fares offered by airlines.

Selling Air Travel: Policies and Challenges

■ WHAT ARE THE KEY POLICIES AND CHALLENGES RELATED TO AIR TRAVEL?

For decades, some writers have predicted that automation would make people redundant in selling air travel. As discussed in Chapter 3, travelers can now find detailed information about the availability of flights online and buy those flights without talking to anyone. But flights are still sold with the help of travel counselors or reservations agents. Salespeople are far from obsolete, especially when it comes to international and complex itineraries.

What do these people do? Their job is to

- Listen carefully to the customer.
- Gather all relevant information concerning travelers and their needs. (The Close-Up on Selling by Identifying Needs looks at this step in more detail.)
- Determine the best schedules and fares for the client.
- Close the sale, book the flight and determine whether any additional services are needed.
- Provide the client with the documents and information needed to make the journey as smooth as possible. This includes airport connections, baggage limitations, and additional fees for services and amenities.

In this section, we introduce some of the procedures and policies that travel professionals must understand in order to carry out these tasks.

Finding a Flight

Finding the schedule and fare that match a client's needs best is the most important service provided by the sales agent. A study by the Public Interest Research Group dramatized the difference that good travel sellers can make. When travel counselors in the Boston area were asked to find the lowest fare available for 23 trips all over the country, no two counselors came up with the same fares. The highest fares quoted were often more than twice the cost of the lowest ones.

Using a GDS, sales agents can search out airfares by giving the GDS the command to show all fares for all airlines or fares for a particular airline; they might even use software that automatically searches multiple GDSs and the Internet for the lowest possible and lowest available fares. They can also look online, just as the general public can, to check for low fares offered only online by the airlines, discounters, or auction houses. But sales agents must still interpret the results and explain the advantages and disadvantages of each fare to their clients.

Making a Reservation

To make a reservation, the sales agent needs to know

- The full, legal names and titles of all travelers, matching the names on their travel IDs.
- The ages of any children or senior citizens.
- The address and work or home phone number of at least one traveler.
- The departure and return dates and the origin and destination cities.

- The class of service desired.
- The form of payment for the tickets.

When using a GDS to make the reservation, the agent enters into the computer a *PNR,* or *passenger name record,* which is the complete record of a reservation stored by the airline's reservation system. (Multiple passengers may be on the same PNR if their itineraries are exactly the same.) The *mandatory fields,* or required parts, of a PNR are the following:

- **Phone number** of the passenger(s), including the area code.
- **Record** of the person requesting the reservation.
- **Itinerary,** with complete information on the travel segments booked. (The travel segment may be not only a flight but also a car rental, hotel, tour, and so on.)

CLOSE-UP: SELLING BY IDENTIFYING NEEDS

One key to success in selling is the ability to size up a client's needs by asking the right questions. If you are selling air travel, what are those questions?

In order to search for a schedule to meet a client's needs, you need to know
- The number of persons traveling.
- The destination.
- The preferred dates of departure and return.
- The desired class of service. A client who is leaning toward an unrestricted coach fare is a good candidate for being upgraded to business or first class because the difference in prices for these classes of service is usually relatively small.

To find the lowest fare for the client, you also need to know the ages of any children who are traveling, and you might ask questions, such as:
- Do you have any flexibility in your departure or arrival date in case fares are lower on those dates?
- Can you return on Sunday instead of Saturday? Or can you leave on Saturday instead of Sunday?
- Do you need a nonstop, or would you be willing to take a connection if one is available at a lower fare?
- Can you leave earlier in the day? Later? On a different airline?

Knowing when, how, and to whom to ask these questions takes some experience and judgment. Asking these questions of many business travelers might be a waste of your time and theirs. Asking these questions of a student trying to get home for the holidays may be absolutely necessary.

With repeat clients, you might verify that they have e-mail and online access. If so, you might tell them about how to receive postings of special fares.

In addition, you should ask
- Whether the client has a seating preference. Although this information is optional, asking for it is a standard service. Ask whether the client prefers an aisle or a

window seat (no one prefers a middle seat). If two clients are flying, give one the preferred seat and the other the middle seat. If three are flying, assign them three seats across, if possible.
- Whether the client will need a car rental, hotel room, and other auxiliary services.

Other services that you might suggest in appropriate situations include
- Assistance for the disabled.
- Special meals.
- Reservations for service animals.
- Airport transfers.
- A tour package.
- Travel insurance.

For international travel, travel sellers must consider additional needs, as discussed in Chapter 2. Here is a checklist of basic questions regarding each overseas destination.
- Is a visa required? How much is the fee? How long is the visa valid and for how many entries?
- Are financial data required in order to enter the country? Must the traveler have an onward or return ticket?
- Are immunizations or medical certificates required?
- What are the currency regulations?
- What are the restrictions on imports and exports?
- Is there a departure tax? (The traveler should be sure to have enough cash in the local currency to pay it.)
- Is the airline or airport known for any particular problems?
- Is the reservation confirmed in writing?

In addition, the International Society of Travel Medicine concluded that travel counselors should
- Inform travelers of immunizations required for entry into a country and advise them to seek expert advice regarding recommended immunizations.
- Warn clients if there is a risk of malaria at a destination.
- Advise clients to consult a health care provider or an expert in travel medicine. They may need information about food and beverage precautions and protection against insect bites, for example.
- Be able to discuss the availability of travelers' health insurance policies.

- **N**ame of the passenger(s) exactly as it appears on the ID.
- **T**icketing arrangements, such as the date by which the passenger must pay for the ticket. (Discount fares may require almost immediate payment, but for some fares clients may wait to buy the ticket up to an hour before flight time.)

You might remember these fields by the first letter in each name, which spells *PRINT.* But the computer arranges the fields in the order *NIPTR.*

The itinerary field of the PNR in the computer includes the following information in the following order:
- Airline name.
- Flight number.
- Class of service.
- Date of departure.
- Departure city/airport.
- Destination city/airport.
- Number of seats.

For each PNR, the computer assigns a ***record locator number,*** a combination of six numbers or letters that is used to retrieve the PNR. But if a traveler forgets his or her record locator number, the PNR can also be retrieved by using the traveler's name and flight number or date of flight.

Flights are said to be ***confirmed*** when they are reserved. In fact, the airline must respond in order to confirm the flight, but this usually occurs instantaneously. When the airline's computer does not respond instantaneously, the flight is said to be *on request.*

If space is not available on a particular flight, clients may choose to be ***waitlisted,*** which means that they are on a list of people seeking a sold-out service. As other people cancel, waitlisted clients are confirmed in the order in which their reservations were received. Waitlisted clients usually reserve another flight in case the first flight is never confirmed. Waitlisting is seldom allowed on discount fares.

A person without a confirmed reservation is referred to as waitlisted only until the day of the flight; once at the airport, a person who was waitlisted is called a ***standby*** or is said to be flying *space available.* That person may get on the flight because of ***no-shows***—people who do not cancel or change their reservation but who, nevertheless, do not appear for the flight.

For non-GDS users, it is important to gather similar information to enter in your booking engines. While systems vary, all airlines require similar information to allow a passenger to travel.

Tickets and Boarding Passes

After reservations are made and paid for, sales agents issue the ticket as an electronic ticket. An ***electronic ticket*** (or e-ticket) exists only as a computer record; the information is stored in the computer but not printed on a conventional ticket. The "ticketless travel" provided by electronic tickets saves money for the airlines and saves passengers from worrying about lost, forgotten, or stolen tickets. A passenger with an electronic ticket is given a record locator number and a printed itinerary or confirmation, as well as a receipt if the ticket is purchased at a travel agency.

Most travelers now use electronic tickets, and many airlines charge fees as high as $50 for paper tickets. But a few passengers still prefer a conventional ***paper ticket***, particularly for international travel and to less-developed areas. Having the conventional ticket does save time if passengers must change airlines at the airport.

An airline ticket, whether electronic or printed provides:

- Authorization to travel.
- Evidence of payment.
- An accounting link between the distributor and the airline (discussed in Chapter 13).
- Acceptance of the contract between the airline and the passenger. When people purchase air tickets, they enter into a contract and accept the airline's terms and conditions for transporting them and their baggage.

But a ticket does not allow a passenger on a flight; a *boarding pass* does. Travelers obtain a boarding pass at the airport ticket counter, at curbside check-in from skycaps, or at e-ticket counters, which are self-check-in kiosks. Most airlines allow online check-in up to 24 hours prior to departure to print their boarding passes from home. Many airlines also accept digital boarding passes accessed on the passenger's phone. Some restrictions do apply for international travel.

Passengers' Rights and Responsibilities

In the ideal situation, clients have their tickets and seat assignments before reaching the airport. If they have only carry-on luggage, they arrive at the airport, check a monitor for the gate assignment of the flight, obtain their boarding pass, go through security and board the plane. Passengers with luggage check it at the airline's ticket counter or with the skycap outside, if permitted. Clients who do not have a ticket or who wish to change anything about their tickets must wait in line at the ticket counter.

Reality, of course, is often more complicated. What is the liability of the airline when things go wrong? When does it owe the traveler some type of compensation? The answers depend in part on the contract that the traveler has with the airline.

The Ticket as Contract. Each airline has its own contract. The airline ticket does not include an actual copy of the terms of the contract but is available online. The standard ticket printout only identifies the important issues covered in the contract.

Issues covered in the contract include the airline's liability for personal injury and death; restrictions and procedures for filing claims; the right of the airline to change the terms of the contract without advance notice; the airline's rights and liabilities for delays, schedule changes, reroutings, or failure to operate; the limitation of liability for lost or damaged baggage; and the availability of excess valuation insurance. Here we discuss a few of the issues that frequently affect travelers.

Airline Default. Serious problems may arise even before a flight if an airline files for bankruptcy and ceases operations, leaving travelers with useless tickets and travel agencies with unhappy customers. Travelers may seek recompense in the bankruptcy courts. If they paid for the tickets by credit card, many credit card companies will protect them, ensuring that they do not pay for services not received. Also, some travel insurance policies cover defaults; these policies are discussed in Chapter 11.

Check-In Times. Passengers sometimes cause problems themselves by ignoring check-in times. After September 11, 2001, passengers on domestic

"Let's just go to the lounge and relax," Jeannie Rogers had suggested when she and Bill Rogers arrived at the airport. They had received their seat assignments from their travel counselor and did not bother to check in. Now, 10 minutes before departure, they arrive at the gate. The flight is oversold, and their seats have been reassigned. As the gate agent, what do you do?

Try to get the couple reserved on the next available flight. Without lecturing them, you should explain that check-in times are important, even for those with assigned seats.

flights were told to be at the airport two hours before their flights, but check-in times may be changed at any time. In practice, the airlines hold clients' seats until 15 to 20 minutes before flight time; then they may release seats to standby passengers, and late passengers lose their rights to their reserved seats. The airlines will try to get full-fare passengers aboard confirmed flights. But if they cannot seat late arrivals, those travelers are put on the next available flight of that same airline.

Check-in times are longer for international flights. Even before the 2001 terrorist attacks, international passengers were usually told to check in one and a half to two hours before flight time, but check-in times now are usually three hours, particularly because of lengthy security check-ins.

Overbooking and Bumping.
Having a ticket is no guarantee that it will be honored. Airlines often *overbook* their flights; in other words, they sell more tickets than there are seats in order to compensate for no-shows. (Ticket contracts announce that they do so.)

Generally, the number of no-shows equals or exceeds the number of overbooked passengers, and everyone gets on the plane. But occasionally the number of confirmed passengers who show up for a flight exceeds the number of seats. At that point, the flight is said to be *oversold*. The gate agents then ask for volunteers who will give up their seats on the flight in return for both (1) passage on the next flight and (2) either a free ticket in the future or a voucher for varying amounts of money to be applied against the cost of a future ticket.

Occasionally, even the offer of free tickets does not produce enough volunteers to make up for overbooking. As a result, some confirmed passengers cannot get on the flight; they are said to be *bumped*. For every 10,000 passengers on U.S. airlines, one is likely to be bumped.

If the airline cannot get a bumped passenger to his or her destination within one hour of the originally scheduled time, the person is entitled to *denied boarding compensation*. The amount of compensation depends on how much the ticket cost and on how quickly the airline can deliver the passenger to the destination. The amount also depends on the airline and on whether the flight is domestic or international. Each airline has its own policy.

For international flights, different rules specify how much compensation is due for involuntary bumping, and they vary from country to country. Each airline's policy regarding denied boarding compensation can be found in the Contract of Carriage section of its website.

Cancellations and Delays.
Note that flight cancellations due to weather or mechanical difficulties do not constitute bumping. Airlines are not required to compensate customers for cancellations and delays. They do try to rebook passengers from canceled flights as soon as possible. Sometimes airlines pay for a passenger's hotel room when a flight delay strands a passenger overnight, but they are not required to do so.

Unfortunately, flight cancellations and delays are far from rare. Flights are counted as being on time if they operate fewer than 15 minutes after their scheduled time. Most GDSs show how often a particular flight has been delayed during the most recent reported month; the website of the U.S. Department of Transportation's Aviation Consumer Department also offers information about on-time performance.

Liability for Baggage.
Lost or damaged baggage continues to be a problem. Passengers should report baggage problems immediately to the office in the airport's baggage claim area. The airline will not assume liability

for damage to bags that the passenger carried onboard or for damage to checked luggage caused by the passenger (for example, by overstuffing bags or packing fragile items improperly).

If luggage seems to be lost, the traveler fills out a form, presents the ticket and baggage claim check, and describes the luggage and its contents. At the discretion of the airline's airport station manager, a small cash advance may be offered to allow the passenger to buy emergency articles until the baggage is found. Any cash advance is deducted from the final liability settlement.

In fact, the vast majority of bags reported lost are only delayed and are delivered the same day or the next day. If the luggage is located, it is delivered to the passenger's home or destination as soon as possible. Most major airlines allow three to five days to trace lost baggage; then the luggage is officially declared to be lost. At that time the passenger submits a claim, which is forwarded to the carrier's central office. Most claims are settled within six weeks to three months.

The airline makes its own assessment of the depreciated value of lost or damaged luggage. For domestic flights, the airline can invoke a ceiling of $3,300 per fare-paying passenger on the amount it will pay for lost or damaged luggage. If the value of luggage and its contents exceeds this limit, the passenger may want to declare a higher valuation when checking the baggage and pay an additional charge. But the airline may refuse to sell excess valuation on especially valuable or breakable items such as cash, jewelry, bank notes, antiques, and negotiable securities. Passengers may still be covered for the loss by their homeowner's or renter's insurance, by their credit card company, or by baggage insurance, as discussed in Chapter 11.

The Role of Travel Counselors

Even though travelers can make their reservations and purchase tickets themselves on their own computers, many still look for advice from travel counselors before they complete their transactions. Good salespeople can convert these people into long-term clients by providing good service and a personal touch.

Travelers may need help with any number of questions and possible snafus. Travel counselors should be prepared, for example, to

- Serve as a guide to useful websites.
- Answer questions about the rationale for a fare. Although they need not understand the subtleties behind specific fares, travel counselors should be able to discuss the general strategy behind airfares.
- Explain the layouts of the most commonly used airports and use their knowledge of these layouts to evaluate connections and to give clients tips on parking, restaurants, and other services.
- Point out connections and layover times to be sure the client is comfortable with them.
- Recognize a code share in the computer, and let clients know that they will be connecting to or from a different line and what type of aircraft is being operated.
- Sign up to receive information about online-only fare sales and other offers so that they can provide clients the best available fares as often as possible.
  Countless other items could be added to this list.

Although travel agencies no longer receive automatic base commissions from airlines for selling tickets, they can still earn revenue from air travel and do receive commissions from preferred airline relationships. Most agencies

ON THE SPOT

Mr. Roundtree is worried. "I can't leave on Friday because I have meetings scheduled, but I have to be there at noon on Saturday. After all, I'm giving the bride away. You're sure that flight will get me there on time?" You know that the scheduled arrival will leave enough time for Mr. Roundtree to get to the church on time. As his travel counselor, how do you answer his seemingly rhetorical question?

You might be tempted to say, "Oh, sure, that flight will get you in with time to spare. No problem." But as much as you want to meet the client's needs, you have no control over the airline's performance. A better answer would be, "I certainly can't guarantee the flight will arrive on time. This flight has an 85 percent on-time performance rating, but that means it's late 15 percent of the time. You'll probably make it, but do you want to gamble when it's so important? Are you sure you can't rearrange your Friday schedule?" Regardless of what Mr. Roundtree decides, it's his decision and his gamble.

now charge clients a service fee for handling their air travel (see Sample Travel Agency Service Fee Schedule, Table 13.1 in Chapter 13). Also, while many agencies may book international air and control the booking, they may ultimately negotiate with a consolidator to issue the ticket to save the client money and to assure a reasonable markup to protect reasonable earnings for the agency. This is only feasible with the client's permission as consolidator-issued tickets may have restrictions not in the client's best interest.

One key service is providing information about the special requirements of international travel. These requirements (discussed in Chapter 2) can seem like a maze to novice travelers. Travel counselors should make sure that travelers who are planning to leave the United States will be permitted to enter the countries they wish to visit, that they will be allowed back into the country, and that they do not unknowingly break any laws regarding the import or export of goods. Travel counselors also have the responsibility to warn travelers when they are planning trips to areas with known medical risks. The previous Close-Up on Selling by Identifying Needs includes a checklist of basic questions that should be considered for each overseas destination.

An important role of the travel counselor that must not be overlooked is the accuracy with which airline tickets are issued, especially for reservations made using a GDS. Tickets must be issued that comply with all of the rules for that particular fare, including the fare basis code, class of service, applicable taxes, and ticketing deadlines. In instances when a ticket has been issued by an agent that does not comply with all of the rules and regulations, the airlines can issue the agency a *debit memo*. This debit memo requires the agency to pay a penalty or the difference in airfare between the ticket that was issued and how the ticket should have been issued. This sometimes can be a costly learning lesson for travel counselors. It is important for agents issuing tickets to fully understand all applicable fare rules and regulations.

CHAPTER WRAP-UP

CHAPTER HIGHLIGHTS

The first years of the 21st century brought many challenges to the airline industry and to those who sell their products, but the growth of the global marketplace has reinforced the importance of air travel to the travel industry as a whole. Here is a review of the objectives with which we began the chapter.

1. **Outline how the airline industry is regulated and coordinated by the government and suppliers.** Since the Airline Deregulation Act of 1978, U.S. airlines have been free to set their own fares, routes, and commissions. But the federal government continues to set rules to ensure airline safety and to prevent unfair practices, particularly through the work of the TSA, FAA, NTSB, DOT, and DOJ. Many other aspects of airline travel are governed by policies set by the airlines themselves through interline agreements and groups such as ATA, which created a standard ticket, and ARC, which determines who can sell domestic airline tickets.

    International air travel is regulated through international agreements and IATA. In the United States IATAN, a subsidiary of IATA, appoints travel agencies to sell international airline tickets.

2. **Describe how airlines differ and know the codes for major airlines and airports.** Passenger airlines may offer scheduled service or charters. Airlines with scheduled service include major, national, and regional airlines. (Small regional

airlines are often called commuter airlines.) Regional airlines often join with larger carriers in code-sharing agreements.

3. **Explain three types of flights, four types of journeys, and the different classes of service.** The type of flight depends basically on whether the stops include connections or stopovers; flights may be nonstop, connecting, or direct (also called through). Journeys may involve one-way trips, round-trips, circle trips, open-jaw trips, or double open-jaw trips. Classes of service include first class, coach, and business or executive class, and premium economy. Bulkheads typically divide compartments set aside for each class. One key advantage of first-class over coach service is its greater seat space, which depends on pitch, seat width, and configuration. Some flights substitute business class for first class or offer only first class and coach; budget airlines may offer only one class of service. On international flights, coach class is often known as economy class. Many long-haul international routes offer premium economy class. International flights often provide amenities beyond those available on domestic flights.

4. **Describe at least five factors that are likely to affect the cost of a passenger's flight.** A passenger's fare is affected first of all by the route flown and whether there are stopovers. The resulting fare may be a through fare, joint fare, or point-to-point fare. Other factors are class of service and whether the passenger is applying a bonus from a frequent-flyer plan, fits into a category eligible for a discount (such as children), or can accept the restrictions placed on a promotional fare (also known as a discount fare). Taxes—including the U.S. ticket tax, departure and arrival taxes (for international flights), PFCs, and the segment tax—and surcharges and fees (such as security, immigration, and customs) also influence the cost of a flight.

For U.S. domestic flights, the fare structure is set by the airlines and reflects sophisticated yield management strategies. For international flights, governments play a role in setting the fares.

5. **Outline the procedures involved in taking a flight and common questions and problems that come up in air travel.** When a passenger's planned flight is confirmed, the reservation record in the computer is known as a PNR. A client who cannot obtain a reservation may wish to be waitlisted and may even go to the airport as a standby in the hope that no-shows may make a seat available. Clients may receive either a paper ticket or an electronic ticket. The ticket entitles the client to a boarding pass, which is needed to board the plane. Passengers who do not arrive within the specified check-in time lose their right to a seat. They may also lose their seats if the airline's overbooking leads to an oversold flight. But if passengers are bumped, the airline must either get them to their destination within an hour of the originally scheduled arrival or pay denied boarding compensation. The airline is also liable for lost or damaged luggage that has been checked. Rules regarding liability and compensation for lost luggage and other problems vary for domestic and international flights.

KEY TERMS

A list of key terms introduced in this chapter follows. If you do not recall the meaning of these terms, see the Glossary.

Airline Deregulation Act	bumped
Airlines Reporting Corporation (ARC)	business class
Air Transport Association (ATA)	Canadian Aviation Regulations (CARs)
APEX fare	charter
arrival tax	circle trip
boarding pass	civil aviation
buffer zone	classes of service
bulkhead	coach

ON THE SPOT

Suppose you are a travel counselor. One of your clients, Raoul, who is a U.S. citizen, is booking a trip back to his original homeland in Costa Rica with his companion, Irina, who came from Bosnia but is a U.S. resident. How does Raoul's destination affect your responsibilities?

Your professional and legal duty is to advise Raoul and Irina of the documents required for their trip. If you do not sell tickets to Costa Rica frequently, odds are you may not know what documents Raoul needs, and (unless you are Bosnian yourself) you probably do not know what documents Irina needs.

The first question you should ask is if either has a passport and what country issued it. By contacting the State Department and looking at its consular information sheet (in print or online), you will see the required documents for U.S. citizens to enter Costa Rica. The State Department's website also gives a link to the Costa Rican embassy in the United States, where you should find information on the documents that Irina needs. That information, however, could be incomplete or unclear. You should have the clients sign disclaimers stating that they are responsible for obtaining the documents. But you might continue to help them by giving them numbers to call or arranging expedited service through a visa company.

Remember that you also have a responsibility to warn travelers if their destination poses health risks. Check the consular sheets from the State Department as well as information from WHO and the CDC.

code-sharing agreements
commuter airlines
configuration
confirmed
connecting flight
connection
consolidator
construction principle
debit memo
denied boarding compensation
departure tax
direct flight
discount fare
domestic air travel
double open-jaw trip
economy class
electronic ticket
excess baggage charge
executive class
Federal Aviation Administration (FAA)
first class
frequent-flyer plan
gateway
hub-and-spoke system
interline agreement
International Air Transport Association (IATA)
International Airlines Travel Agent Network (IATAN)
joint fare
mileage system
National Transportation Safety Board (NTSB)
nonstop flight

no-show
one-way trip
open-jaw trip
open-skies policy
overbook
oversold
paper ticket
passenger facility charge (PFC)
passenger load factor
passenger name record (PNR)
pitch
point-to-point fare
premium economy class
promotional fare
record locator number
round-trip
routing system
scheduled service
seat width
security fee
segment tax
standard ticket
standby
stop
stopover
through fare
through flight
Transportation Security Administration (TSA)
U.S. ticket tax
waitlisted
yield
yield management

REVIEW QUESTIONS

1. Name three important airlines in your area. List their codes.

2. From an airline's point of view, what are the advantages of the hub-and-spoke system?

3. Why would a travel agency avoid using a consolidator to obtain air tickets for a particular client?

4. Airline websites, discount travel sites, and other online sources sell air tickets directly to the public. How can travel counselors use these as tools to serve their clients?

5. How would you summarize the most important differences between domestic and international air travel?

Ground Travel

CHAPTER 5

OBJECTIVES

After completing this chapter, you should be able to

1. Describe rail service in Canada, the United States and Europe.

2. Outline the services provided by car rental companies and the requirements that renters should expect to meet.

3. Identify the functions played by motor coaches.

4. Explain the comparative advantages of traveling by rail, rental car, ridesharing, or motor coach.

5. Discuss the roles of transfers, ridesharing services, and other ground services that travel counselors might offer.

The second most popular attraction in the Washington, D.C., region (after the Air and Space Museum) is Potomac Mills, a mega-mall in Virginia. It attracts more than four million visitors each year, including more than 3,000 groups and chartered tours. In fact, around the country, millions of tourists flock to shopping malls. And in Canada, the largest shopping mall is The West Edmonton Mall, which also currently is the largest shopping mall in all of North America. West Edmonton Mall is the home of an indoor amusement park, rollercoaster, water park, and an NHL-size hockey ring, and all these attractions bring millions of visitors each year. These visitors go by bus, and they go by car. If travelers never took a train or bus or car, their travels would be limited indeed.

More than 90 percent of the trips Americans take involve some form of ground transportation. Most of these trips do not require professional travel planning, but ground transport is vital to the travel/tourism industry. Without the motor coach, for example, tours would find it difficult to operate, and, without rental cars, most traveling business people would be at a loss. Ridesharing has also become a viable option for both business and leisure travelers, impacting both the taxi and car rental industries.

For travelers, ground transportation can provide a pleasant, relaxing, and often inexpensive alternative to air transportation, as well as access to places not served by airlines. For countless motels, restaurants, and attractions, an efficient ground transportation industry is a key ingredient to success. And for hundreds of thousands of Americans, the ground transportation industry is a source of employment. (The Close- Up on Careers in Ground Transportation describes a few of the positions in the industry.) In this chapter, we look at three major elements of ground transportation: intercity and international train service, car rentals or ridesharing, and motor coaches.

Rail Transportation

■ WHAT IS THE STATE OF RAIL TRAVEL TODAY?

"Empire Builder now departing for Fargo, Devils Lake, Rugby, Wolf Point, Cut Bank, Glacier, Spokane, and points west on Track Four," drones the stationmaster. "Aaaall aboard!" To some who hear that sound, the romance of the rails still lives, and travel by train is their first choice.

Trains offer many potential advantages. Compared with air travel, they provide a more leisurely trip. Travelers can sit back, enjoy the scenery, and meet other passengers. Train travel is also an alternative for those who fear flying, and sometimes it is cheaper than flying. Sometimes it is more convenient, partly because many train stations sit in the heart of a city, whereas airports lie on the fringes. Procedures for traveling by train are often simpler and faster than those required for air travel. And, of course, some places served by train do not have regular air service.

In much of the world, trains are popular or essential or both. Japan has one of the fastest, safest, and most punctual rail systems in the world. Its high-speed passenger trains, known as **bullet trains** *(Shinkansen),* reach speeds of more than 200 miles per hour (320 km). But Asia's largest railway system belongs to India; its railroads blanket the country. Our focus in this chapter, though, is primarily on rail transportation in North America and western Europe, plus some unique Amtrak train trips famous around the world.

Amtrak

Freight trains and commuter trains, as well as passenger trains, make up the U.S. railroad industry, but only intercity passenger service represents a key part of the travel industry. That service is just a shadow of what it once was.

A Brief History. The first steam locomotives made their appearance in 1825 in England and 1830 in America. Rail travel developed rapidly, thanks in part to land given up by the government in order to promote the railroad industry. Between the 1860s and the 1930s, the railroads were the dominant means of transportation and one of the mightiest industries in the United States. Fortunes were made from the railroads; thousands of towns and world-famous hotels grew near the tracks. Rail was king.

Beginning in the 1920s, Americans' love for driving their own cars helped push passenger trains toward the fringes of the transportation market. Train travel dropped further after World War II when air travel became more affordable. By the late 1950s a trip from Chicago to Los Angeles took 40 hours by train and just four hours by jet. By 1960, passenger miles by air surpassed those by rail. While government-owned and -subsidized trains in Europe were constantly modernizing, the privately owned passenger trains in the United States became less competitive with other transportation. By 1970, while freight business remained strong, railroad companies were eliminating passenger trains. It began to look as if passenger rail travel might disappear from the United States.

To keep passenger trains running, the federal government in 1970 established the National Railroad Passenger Corporation, known as Amtrak. Today, *Amtrak* is a private corporation that operates medium and long

CLOSE-UP: CAREERS IN GROUND TRANSPORTATION

The ground transportation industry is not as glamorous as the airline industry, but it offers more career opportunities. There are thousands of car rental and motor coach companies. Like other parts of the travel industry, these companies have jobs in marketing and sales, international sales, e-commerce, and franchising. There are also fascinating positions related to logistics and the acquisition of fleets. Openings at Amtrak are few because turnover is low among its unionized employees, but opportunities exist for employment with specialty trains.

■ **Position** Car rental agent

Description Most car rental agents work at airport locations and deal directly with customers. They greet renters, complete the paperwork and check credentials before handing over the car keys. Sales of insurance or upgrades may also be part of the job. The starting salary may be little over the minimum wage, but the position is often a stepping-stone to other positions.

Qualifications This entry-level position requires a professional manner, excellent interpersonal and communication skills, and a customer-service orientation.

■ **Position** Car rental customer service representative

Description Customer service representatives are responsible for resolving rental complaints, answering inquiries from customers and solving problems concerning rates.

Qualifications This entry-level position requires articulate, personable individuals with the ability to communicate well. Common sense, patience, and tact, and the ability to work under pressure are also needed.

■ **Position** Onboard attendant, Amtrak

Description Like airline flight attendants, train attendants serve the needs of their onboard clients and watch out for their safety. Seniority governs choice of routes.

Qualifications This position is ideal for individuals with a background in food or transportation service.

■ **Position** Revenue manager

Description Many ground transportation companies need a professional to implement pricing tactics to spur sales without cutting into profitability. The revenue manager works with marketing, sales, and reservations departments to identify market opportunities and to design and implement products. The revenue manager must also keep abreast of what competitors are doing.

Qualifications A B.A. or B.S. in economics, finance, marketing, or statistics or equivalent experience is necessary; an M.B.A. is a strong plus. This position also requires two or more years' experience with pricing tactics, excellent analytical skills, strong communication and organizational skills, and the ability to work independently.

■ **Position** Marketing coordinator

Description Responsibilities of this position include managing the frequent-renter club, direct-mail or online marketing to members, and promotions of discounts, vacation packages, and the like. The marketing coordinator verifies that criteria are met for those being enrolled in the frequent-renter club, provides customer support for members, works with programmers to create and enhance the customer database, and helps book reservations for members.

Qualifications This is a step up from a sales representative and requires knowledge of both marketing methods and list acquisition and management, as well as the ability to analyze results.

■ **Position** Customer service manager (also called station manager)

Description The person in this position hires, trains, schedules, supervises and evaluates staff—including service agents, rental sales agents, and shuttle bus drivers—and ensures efficient daily operation of the station. Responsibilities also include servicing customers, overseeing fleet control, monitoring daily computer reports and undertaking local marketing programs.

Qualifications This position requires attention to detail and excellent organizational and managerial skills, along with analytical ability.

■ **Other positions** Account executive; account manager; fleet manager; motor coach driver.

distance intercity passenger rail service with the help of funding from the federal government. Its board of directors is appointed by the president of the United States, and the U.S. Department of Transportation holds the majority of its stock.

When Amtrak began operating in 1971, it immediately cut routes and services but also began to modernize. It improved tracks, cars, and onboard amenities, and it introduced a national reservation system. In 2000, it finally launched a train—the *Acela Express*—similar to the high-speed trains that have long operated in Europe and Japan. This service operates on the Northeast Corridor of the United States between Boston and Washington, DC. Amtrak continues to plan upgrades to improve equipment and services. But, for decades, Amtrak has struggled to deal with changes in the marketplace and declining federal subsidies. In 2017, it was announced that former Delta and Northwest Airlines CEO Richard Andersen would become the next President & CEO of Amtrak.

Rail has been the stepchild as U.S. government subsidy to the rail industry is dwarfed by that granted to air and road traffic. Nevertheless, ridership has been increasing, particularly since the 9/11 terrorist attacks when many U.S. travelers avoided air travel in favor of ground travel, and some innovative tour operators developed packages combining rail travel with cruises, motor coach travel, and other industry sectors.

Routes and Equipment. Figure 5.1 shows Amtrak's major routes. One of the longest routes, the *Sunset Limited* between New Orleans and Los Angeles, covers nearly 2,000 miles. The long-distance routes, such as Chicago to Los Angeles and New York to Miami, are used mainly by leisure travelers; the short-distance, or *corridor,* routes serve a high percentage of business travelers. Many states are working to develop plans for regional and privatized high-speed service. Whether these plans will be carried out depends on the potential for riders and on support from Congress and the states, which can be difficult.

There is currently one privatized train option in South Florida operated by Virgin Trains USA, with service from Miami to West Palm Beach. Phase Two, which will extend service to Orlando, currently is under construction with a projected completion of 2022. When completed, it will be the only modern high-speed passenger train privately operated in the United States.

Fleet Amtrak's fleet includes single-level and bi-level trains, coach cars and sleeping cars, food service cars, and lounges (see Table 5.1). The trains that are used vary with the route. Among Amtrak's modern trains are

- The *Acela Express,* which offers high-speed service between Boston, New York, and Washington, D.C. The 150-mile-per-hour Acela can make the trip between New York and Boston in 3 hours and 18 minutes and between New York and Washington in 2 hours and 43 minutes.
- The *Pacific Surfliner,* a double-decker train that travels the San Diego–Los Angeles–Santa Barbara, San Luis Obispo route.
- The *Auto Train,* which carries cars and their passengers from a Virginia suburb of Washington, D.C., to Florida.
- The *Cascades,* fast Talgo-manufactured trains (with many amenities) operating in the Pacific Northwest: Vancouver, Seattle, Portland.

Onboard Services. Amtrak offers several classes of service: first class, business class, coach class, and sleeping accommodations, as well as club class—an extra level of service for coach passengers. *Coach* class features two reclining seats on each side of an aisle. Usually seats have fold-down trays, leg rests, and individual reading lights. There are restrooms at the

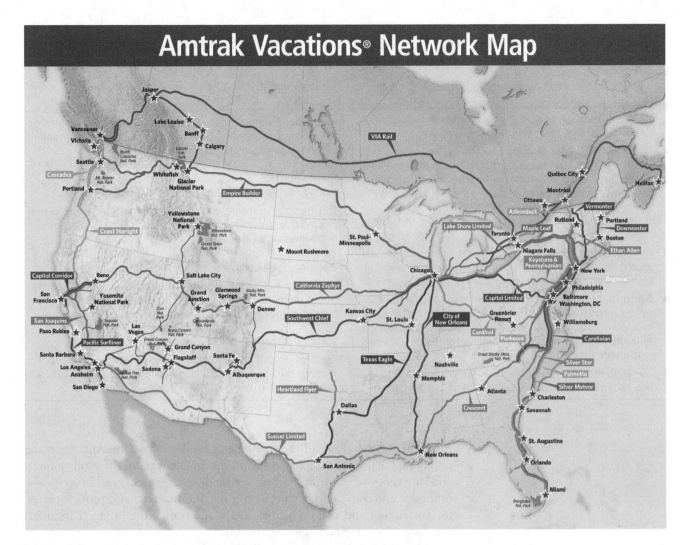

Amtrak Vacations® Network Map

FIGURE 5.1 Major Passenger Rail Routes of North America

This map shows major routes offered by Amtrak and by VIA Rail of Canada. On Amtrak, the busiest routes include the Northeast corridor from Washington to Boston and the California coastal route from San Francisco to San Diego.

ends of the cars. Power outlets for laptop computers are also available on some trains. Club service brings amenities, such as a complimentary beverage and newspaper.

Travelers willing to pay more than coach fare may be interested in *business class,* which offers a private car, complimentary nonalcoholic beverage, and newspaper on the *Acela* only. *First class* provides deluxe reserved seats, meals and beverages served at the seat by an attendant, hot towels, and complimentary daily newspapers. *Sleeping accommodations* represent first class on long-distance trains. The traveler receives a private room in a sleeping car, personal service, complimentary meals, and other amenities. Table 5.1 describes the variety of sleeping accommodations available.

Not all classes are available on all trains. What you get on Amtrak depends on where you are going and when. Generally, long-distance trains provide more amenities than trains on corridor routes. The services available on specific trains are indicated on Amtrak schedules, which are viewable on Amtrak's website (amtrak.com).

TABLE 5.1 Selected Trains on Amtrak

SLEEPING CARS

Viewliner Single-level cars, with standard and deluxe bedrooms.

- The standard bedroom has two reclining seats that convert to a bed plus an upper berth that pulls down from the ceiling. A sink and toilet are in the room; a shower is nearby.
- The deluxe bedroom features an armchair and a sofa that converts to a bed. An upper berth folds down from the wall. Shower, sink, vanity, and toilet are all in the room. Two deluxe bedrooms can be combined to create a suite for four people.

Superliner Bi-level cars with standard, deluxe, and family bedrooms.

- The standard bedroom features two reclining seats that convert to a bed; an upper berth pulls down from the wall. Restrooms and a shower are nearby.
- Deluxe bedrooms are on the upper level and feature an armchair and a sofa that converts to a bed; an upper berth folds down from the wall. Sink, vanity, shower, and toilet are all in the room. Some deluxe bedrooms can be combined to form a suite.
- The family bedroom features windows on two sides. A sofa and two seats convert to two lower berths, and upper berths fold

down from the wall, to provide total sleeping room for two adults and two children. Restrooms and a shower are nearby.

Note: Both Viewliners and Superliners also have bedrooms designed to be accessible to those with special mobility requirements, including space for a wheelchair.

SELECTED DAY TRAINS

Acela Express A single-level high-speed train.

This train's features include plush seats, movable armrests and headrest, laptop computer outlets, conference tables, deluxe restrooms, and a café car.

Talgo A single-level train.

Known for its European style, this train offers plush seating, laptop computer outlets, onboard movies, bicycle and surfboard racks, luggage cars, a bistro car, and a dining car.

Surfliner A spacious bi-level train.

Features on this train include panoramic windows, spacious seating, outlets for laptop computers, bicycle and surfboard racks, and a café car.

Most Amtrak trains offer some type of food service. On some, there are dining cars that serve complete sit-down meals. Other trains offer only lounge and café cars—where travelers can buy sandwiches, snacks, and beverages—or dinette and club cars, which offer tray meals. These cars also provide places for socializing and playing games. On some trains, the lounge cars offer movies or domed windows for sightseeing.

Checked baggage service is available at many Amtrak stations. Passengers may check up to two bags at no additional cost, depending on size. Two additional bags may be checked for $20 each. Bags may not weigh more than 50 pounds each.

Other Services. Amtrak's Guest Rewards program lets riders earn points every time they travel on Amtrak. Riders also can earn points by spending money at their travel partners, including hotels, car rentals, cruises, and other retail providers. The rewards program works very similarly to those the airlines offer. As points accumulate, they may select from a variety of rewards: free travel on Amtrak, hotel and car rental awards, airline miles and gift certificates from nationally known retailers, restaurants, and entertainment venues. Frequent travelers on the *Acela Express* and on New York's Empire trains (running from Buffalo to Albany to New York City) may register for the complimentary Executive Privileges program, which offers special incentives and discounts.

First-class passengers with a same-day ticket may use Amtrak's Metropolitan lounges and ClubAcela facilities. The Metropolitan lounges, in Chicago, Portland (Oregon), and Los Angeles, provide comfortable seating, complimentary soft drinks and coffee, and ticketing assistance. ClubAcela facilities also have free use of photocopy and fax machines and conference rooms. All have Internet access. ClubAcelas are in Boston, New York, Philadelphia, and Washington, D.C. First-class lounges (separate waiting rooms) are in St. Paul/Minneapolis, St. Louis, New Orleans, and Raleigh, NC.

For some cities not served by Amtrak, the railroad offers Amtrak Thruway Bus Service, which guarantees connections to bus service from the Amtrak station. The cost of the bus trip is included in the rail fare.

Customized vacation packages are also available from Amtrak and can be reserved online. With one type of package, Amtrak reserves and books rental cars and hotel rooms along with the train ticket. Another type of package includes a motor coach tour with a professional tour director, as well as hotel accommodations and meals. You can even charter your own private train for retreats or conventions, based on the size of your group. Prices vary by equipment, origin, and destination.

Fares/Products. Amtrak has two major types of fares/products to choose:
- Basic *Point-to-Point tickets* vary in price based on a number of factors, such as advance purchase, time of day, number of changes, and type of equipment on the route. The price includes either seat or sleeper accommodations.
- *USA Rail Pass* comes in a variety of options: up to eight segments within 15 days, up to 12 segments within 30 days, and up to 18 segments within 45 days. Purchase of the rail pass does not constitute a reservation; space in this category is limited each day. Reservations for specific dates must be booked well in advance to assure confirmation of the dates desired for each segment. Reservations must be booked within 180 days of the pass purchase date. Note: A segment means one trip without stopping over; if a stopover is made in the middle of a segment, it counts as two segments.

Like the airlines, Amtrak also offers promotional discounts on certain routes at certain times of the year to fill seats that would otherwise go empty. Amtrak also offers year-round discounts for children ages two to 12, people age 62 and over, people with disabilities, military personnel and families, veterans with a VetRewards® card, high school and college students in Amtrak's Student Advantage program, international students, groups of 20 or more, and members of AAA and the National Association of Railroad Passengers.

Union Station in
Washington, D.C.

For sleeping accommodations, travelers pay the rail fare plus an accommodations charge. Discounts apply only to the rail fare. Although the rail fare is charged per person traveling, the accommodations charge is calculated per accommodation. Thus, if three people share a bedroom, the total cost includes three rail fares plus one accommodations charge.

Even with the accommodations charge, the cost of traveling overnight by train can be very reasonable because it covers transportation, accommodations, and meals. Budget-minded travelers can buy a coach fare, purchase reasonably priced food onboard, and—at no extra cost—sleep in seats that recline to an almost-horizontal position.

Ticketing, Reservations, and Commissions. Reservations are necessary for sleeping accommodations, first class, business class, and long-distance trains. For coach seats on certain trains, reservations are not required. But seats at discount fares are limited, and reservations may be sold out months ahead during the summer.

Travel counselors may book Amtrak service in one of three ways:
1. By calling Amtrak directly
2. By using the travel agency's GDS (requires an ARC or CLIA appointment)
3. By booking with tour operators that specialize in U.S. rail packages. Many will book rail packages in conjunction with special events or unique destinations.

When booking directly with Amtrak or using a GDS, Amtrak pays only base commissions to Amtrak National Account Partner Agencies. These include AAA Travel Agencies and agents that are part of the Travel Leaders Network. Other agencies may opt to charge a service fee for selling individual rail tickets or passes.

Train Travel in Canada and Mexico

Both Amtrak and *VIA Rail*, Canada's passenger train network, operate routes that cross the border between the two nations. (Look again at Figure 5.1.) Travelers can go from the United States to Canada and return, without changing trains, on at least four routes: (1) between Vancouver and Seattle and points south on the West Coast, (2) between Toronto and New York, (3) between Toronto and Chicago, and (4) between Montreal and New York.

VIA Rail links more than 400 Canadian communities from the Atlantic to the Pacific, offering intercity as well as transcontinental journeys. Of particular interest are

- The *Canadian,* Canada's best-known train, which takes a 2,800-mile, (4,506 km) three-day journey from Toronto to Vancouver, passing through northern lakelands, prairies, and the Rocky Mountains—one of the world's great train trips. The train has been restored to its 1950s style and features observation cars, dining car, bar, and lounge. Luxury class offers private sleeping compartments and intimate dining.
- The *Winnipeg-Churchill* train, which travels north to Churchill, the "polar bear capital of the world," on Hudson Bay and the edge of Canada's Arctic.
- The *Ocean,* which goes from Montreal through rural communities to New Brunswick and Nova Scotia.

Dining service and sleeping accommodations are available on some VIA Rail routes, and there are connections to bus and ferry service at selected points. With 24 hours' notice, those planning an adventure in Canada's wilderness areas can arrange to be dropped off or picked up at points where there is no scheduled stop. (But checked baggage service is not available on all trains.)

VIA Rail offers discount and rail pass programs for seniors, children, and groups, as well as a frequent-traveler program. Because VIA Rail is a member of ARC, U.S. travel agencies can make reservations and issue tickets conveniently through a GDS. Reservations can also be made by calling VIA Rail or by visiting its website.

In Mexico, the highlight of train travel is the ride on the Chihuahua al Pacífico Railway through the Copper Canyon. The train travels between the desert city of Chihuahua to Los Mochis for about 13 hours, through spectacular mountain scenery over the Sierra Madre and through coastal plains. There are travel journey options that range from nine to 16 hours in length. The journey includes 86 tunnels, 37 bridges, and many hairpin turns from elevations ranging from 8,000 feet to sea level. It has been described as the most dramatic train ride in the Western Hemisphere, and some tour operators have developed interesting rail/motor coach tours that include stays at lodges along the way and visits to the Tarahumara Indians.

Otherwise, travel by train in Mexico appeals mostly to dedicated train fans or those with plenty of time on their hands. It is generally slow and often irregular; most local people take the bus. Tourists who want to take the train anyway should be advised to travel first or luxury class. Local travel agencies in Mexico as well as a few U.S. tour operators offer information and reservations.

Mexico's Copper Canyon

European Rail

From its origins in the first half of the 19ᵗʰ century, rail travel in Europe grew rapidly to become the dominant mode of transportation. Even through the 20ᵗʰ century, trains remained popular—thanks in part to political and economic factors that slowed the purchase of private automobiles, to the short distances between major European cities, and to the high cost of air travel for short European flights. Furthermore, European governments continually subsidized and improved their rail systems, modernizing tracks and trains. Thus, European train travel escaped the decline that occurred in the United States.

Today, travelers in continental Europe can use the train to take a quiet, swift, businesslike journey from one city center to another or to enjoy an intimate experience of the land, its people, and its customs. *InterCity (IC) trains* are domestic trains running within a country's borders; major international trains are called *EuroCity (EC) trains*. The trains are fast and dependable. When travel to and from airports is taken into account, it may be faster to go from the heart of one city to another by train than by plane. France's **TGV** (*train à grande vitesse*) and Germany's *ICE* (InterCity Expresses) travel close to 186 (300 km) miles per hour. Other high-speed trains include *Frecciarosa* in Italy, *AVE* in Spain, *X2000* in Sweden, and *Thalys Paris* to Amsterdam and Cologne.

In addition, there are now an enormous range of two-country and regional passes (Scandinavia and Eastern Europe, for example) plus many one-country passes. Since 1994, travelers can take a train from England to continental Europe. **Eurotunnel** and **Eurostar** operate through the **Chunnel**, the tunnel beneath the English Channel that links England and France. Eurotunnel operates from terminals at Folkestone and Calais. Their trains

Gare du Nord in Paris

carry cars, coaches, trucks, motorbikes, and bicycles; you may stay in your car for the 35-minute trip. Eurostar operates the passenger trains from London St. Pancras station, Ashford and Ebbsfleet in England to Paris, Brussels, Lille or Eurodisney, and other European destinations. About 20 minutes of your trip is in the Chunnel itself.

Onboard Services. Some European trains still offer traditional compartments (small rooms) that have six seats arranged in two rows of three seats facing each other; the compartments open to a corridor that runs along one side of the car. Virtually all new and high-speed trains have *bank seating* like that on most American trains and buses, with seats on each side of a central aisle. Typically, the first-class configuration is two seats, an aisle and then one seat. Second-class is two seats, an aisle, and then two more seats. Restrooms are located at the ends of most train cars.

Most European trains have first-class and second-class seating and compartments. Seats in second class are usually perfectly comfortable, but first-class compartments are roomier, and the seats have more cushioning. The cost of the extra comfort that first-class provides means that fares tend to be 30 to 60 percent more than those for second-class.

Sleeping accommodations require the payment of a supplement in addition to the basic fare. On most overnight trains, there are sleeping cars that offer private compartments with single or double berths. The cost may be the same as for a moderate hotel room, depending on the country. Sleeping cars usually have a washbasin, towels, and linens; toilet facilities are at the ends of each car.

Another form of sleeping accommodation is the ***couchette,*** which is a compartment with six bunk beds (three on each side); it has little headroom and not much luggage space. Couchettes are not private, and beds are assigned without regard to gender. (Some trains have four berths and may be reserved for families or members of the same gender.) Linen for the berth and a pillow are provided. Couchettes are inexpensive but should be described very carefully to travelers to avoid unhappy clients.

For food, travelers may just pack a lunch and bring something to share with their compartment neighbors. But many long-distance, international day trains have dining cars, which are sometimes quite elegant and serve good and not-too-expensive meals, although menus are often not in English. Most high-speed trains and many overnight trains do not have dining cars. Those that don't often have café cars with drinks and light food options. Many trains have trolley service where vendors pass through the train selling drinks and snacks.

Drinking water must be purchased separately from vendors or brought along by the traveler. Tap water from sinks is not for drinking.

It is important to travel light on European trains. On most of them, the traveler must stow his/her luggage personally either in overhead storage racks or in luggage areas at each end of the car, and most European rail stations do not have porters. Traveling with a suitcase on wheels is highly recommended.

Stations and Procedures. Travelers on European railways need to check not only that they get on the right train at the correct platform but also that the car is going to their destination. Cars that start out on the same train may end up at different destinations. Casually changing seats and cars during the ride could bring the traveler to an unexpected destination or separate the traveler from his or her luggage. Many advance-purchased train tickets include both seat assignments and rail car assignments. The rail cars are clearly marked outside the entry door of the train. It is also wise to keep all tickets and passports handy because they are often inspected during the trip and sometimes collected upon arrival.

Many members of the European Union now allow border crossings with no document checks, but travelers should be prepared to produce any required travel documents. Officials may board the train to check these documents while the train is en route, even on simple one-day excursions.

Travelers also need to check the specified station for their departure or arrival location. Many large cities, and even some small ones, have multiple train stations.

Larger stations are mini-malls. They feature the usual ticket counters, information desks, waiting rooms, and newsstands. But there are also currency exchange booths, post offices, and shops. Many have baths and showers, a hotel-finding service, cafés, restaurants, supermarkets, hair salons, and hotels attached to the station. Rome's Termini has a chapel and even a morgue.

Ticketing and Reservations. Reservations are necessary for all sleeping accommodations as well as for all high-speed trains and certain other trains. On most local trains, reservations are not required. But travelers who are taking a long trip, who are traveling at peak times, or who want to be assured of a seat should make a reservation if it is possible; not all trains take reservations. There is always an extra charge for a reservation.

The European Rail Timetable (www.europeanrailtimetable.eu) gives rail schedules for trains in Europe (and Britain). Information is also available from *Rail Europe,* a company owned by Swiss and French railroads that acts as a Canadian or U.S. booking agent for virtually all trains in Europe.

Rail Passes

For train travelers seeking the freedom to change their itineraries on a whim and add extra trips, a rail pass may be ideal. *Rail passes* allow train travel for a specified time and region with unlimited stops and unlimited mileage. They can provide savings as well as convenience. A pass does not guarantee a seat, however, unless a reservation has been made. Even with a pass, all high-speed trains tightly control reservations.

To determine whether a rail pass will bring savings, add up the point-to-point rail fares on an itinerary and then compare that figure to the cost of the pass. Usually, the pass will not turn out to be cheaper if the traveler is taking just one long trip. To get the best use of an unlimited mileage pass, plot an itinerary that follows a continuous loop. Or take a hub-and-spoke approach, setting up several base cities and fanning out from each city on a series of one-day trips.

Rail passes are available in many nations. Each rail pass has its own advantages and restrictions. Some are available to anyone; some only to youths. Some are valid only in one country; others in several. Some must be bought outside the country in which they are used. BritRail passes are an example; they may be purchased only outside the United Kingdom. The granddaddy of rail passes is the European pass, known as the Eurailpass for years, and now called the Eurail Pass.

Eurail Pass. Introduced in 1959, and formerly known as Europass or Eurorail Pass, the **Eurail Pass** allows unlimited first-class travel through 31 European countries on nearly all railroads and several shipping lines. The Eurail Pass is available for non-European residents, and the Interrail Pass (introduced in 1972) is available to European residents. There are two types of passes: The *Eurail Global Pass* and *The One Country Pass*.

The Eurail Global Pass is valid in all 31 participating countries; as of 2020, they were Austria, Belgium, Bosnia and Herzegovina, Bulgaria, Croatia, Czech Republic, Denmark, Finland, France, Germany, Hungary, Ireland, Italy, Lithuania, Luxembourg, Montenegro, the Netherlands, North Macedonia, Norway, Poland, Portugal, Romania, Serbia, Slovakia, Slovenia, Spain, Switzerland, Turkey, and the United Kingdom. A Global Pass fare is dependent on the number of days it is valid in a specific period. Fare categories include:

- 3, 5 or 7 days in 1-month (flexi)
- 10 or 15 days in 2 months (flexi)
- 15 or 22 continuous days
- 1, 2, or 3 continuous months

The One Country Pass permits travel on the national rail networks of one country, with unlimited trips on each travel day. The pass is available in Austria, Benelux, Bulgaria, Croatia, Czech Republic, Denmark, Finland, France, Greece, the Greek islands, Hungary, Ireland (the Republic of Ireland and Northern Ireland), Italy, Norway, Poland, Portugal, Romania, Scandinavia, Serbia, Slovakia, Slovenia, Spain, Sweden, and Turkey. The passes are available for travel on three, four, five, six or eight travel days in a 1-month period.

Up to two children, aged four to 11, can travel free of charge when accompanied by a full-fare adult. Eurail passes also are available in these age-based categories:

- Child: under the age of 12
- Youth: ages 12 to 27
- Senior: over the age of 60

Eurail passes are also good for free or reduced-rate passage on many steamers and scenic bus trips. The passes are often used for trips on ferries connecting Ireland and France, Greece and Italy, or Sweden and Finland as well as for steamers on the Rhine, the Danube, and Lake Lucerne. Certain passes also provide a discount for fares on Eurostar.

For decades, Eurail passes could be purchased only outside Europe. Today, the passes can be purchased in Europe at special Eurail offices, but the charge is 10 percent higher, and few travelers will want to wait until arrival to plan their itineraries. In effect, Eurail passes remain an excellent and almost exclusive marketing tool for North American travel sellers. They can be purchased through Rail Europe in the same way as Eurail tickets.

Before boarding, passengers must have their passes validated and passport numbers inscribed; this can be done at a ticket or information window at any railway station. Eurail passes are nontransferable, and passengers may be required to show their passports along with the pass. Passes do not include seat-reservation fees, meals, sleeping accommodations, or port taxes. Very important: Even with a rail pass, all high-speed trains require a seat reservation, and increasingly the number of seats for rail pass holders are limited because of capacity controls. Although it diminishes the historical legacy of flexibility, it is essential for travelers to make reservations as far in advance as possible. Currently, most trains can be reserved up to 90 days in advance.

For travelers visiting only one European country, the one country rail pass offered by that country may be a better bargain than a global pass.

BritRail Pass. A **BritRail pass** allows travel throughout England, Scotland, Wales, and Northern Ireland. The pass can be purchased for periods ranging from three days to one month; either first-class (on many trains) or second-class service is available. Other variations include the following:

FIGURE 5.2 Participants in the Eurail pass and the BritRail Pass

Thirty-one countries are part of the Eurail pass system. Ireland, Greece, and the three countries of Scandinavia are reached by ferry, which is included in passes at no extra cost.

- Children and those 60 years or older are eligible for discounts through the BritRail Family Pass and Senior Pass.
- The BritRail Flexipass allows travel on a specific number of nonconsecutive days within a one-month period.
- Access is allowed on Airport Express trains to central London.

Other passes are available for people who plan to visit only certain parts of Britain or to travel in Ireland along with Great Britain. There is also a package that combines a trip on Eurostar with a special Flexipass.

BritRail passes must be purchased outside Britain. They are distributed by BritRail Travel International.

Canrailpass. Anyone can purchase a *Canrailpass*, offered by VIA Rail, regardless of residence. Sleeping accommodations must be purchased separately, but the cost is reasonable.

Many options are available, including the Corridor pass, which allows travel between Québec and Ontario for 21 consecutive days, and the System pass, which allows travel across Canada for 60 consecutive days. You also can choose among seven, 10, or unlimited one-way trips to your choice destination.

Specialty Rail

Travelers take **specialty trains** mainly for the experience, not the transportation. Getting there isn't half the fun; it's almost all the fun.

In the United States, a modest growth industry exists in small railroads that offer local sightseeing tours. One of the best known is the *Durango and Silverton Railroad* in southwestern Colorado. This narrow-gauge, coal-burning train has been operating since 1882 and travels through superb scenic mountains and valleys on a three-hour journey between two historic mining towns. The *Napa Valley Wine Train* is a privately owned excursion train between Napa and St. Helena, California.

The Durango and Silverton Railroad in Colorado

In Canada, since 1990, *Rocky Mountaineer* has grown to become the largest privately-owned passenger rail service in North America. Rocky Mountaineer offers unique Canadian vacation packages and four spectacular rail routes from British Columbia, Alberta, and Washington State. This luxury train travels by daylight and is the best way to experience the majestic Canadian Rockies. Rocky Mountaineer's newest rail route is Coastal Passage—a seamless coastline connection between Seattle, Washington, and Vancouver, British Columbia, to the heart of the Canadian Rockies. Coastal Passage can be added on to the beginning or the end of any Rocky Mountaineer package of two days or more. Rocky Mountaineer has been honored with eight World Travel Awards. Scenic valleys, lush forests, and plentiful wildlife create a truly memorable Canadian vacation. There are two levels of service, Gold Leaf and Silver Leaf, but both include glass domes for the best views of the Canadian Rockies. Onboard a Rocky Mountaineer, each guest will enjoy gourmet cuisine, complementary drinks and snacks, as well as luggage handling.

Other specialty trains can be found all over the United States. Some are dinner trains to the beach or mountains; some can be leased; and on some, private cars can be chartered.

Abroad, many international specialty trains use restored equipment to evoke nostalgia for a past era and feature elegant meals and deluxe service.

Fares should be compared to the cost of a deluxe tour or a cruise. Some famous specialty trains of Europe include

- The deluxe *Venice Simplon-Orient-Express,* named after one of the most famous trains of the past, which journeys between Venice and London.
- The *Royal Scotsman,* which features vintage carriages, ornately decorated Pullman sleeping cars, and an observation car with an open veranda on which to sit and watch the Highlands pass by.

Among the trains in Asia and Africa that offer chances for unique journeys are the following:

- India's *Palace on Wheels* travels for eight days, with modern facilities and luxurious service, past marble palaces, temples, and colorful markets.
- South Africa boasts two deluxe trains: the *Blue Train*—which travels between Cape Town and Johannesburg (Pretoria), a distance of 994 miles (1,599 km) in 27 hours—and *Rovos Rail,* which covers various itineraries.

The world's longest overland train trip, Russia's *Trans-Siberian Railroad* from Moscow to Vladivostok, is far from deluxe. It covers 5,778 miles (9,298 km) in seven days. This fascinating journey ranges from an adventure to an ordeal. An alternate route goes through Mongolia to Beijing, China.

✔ CHECK-UP

Passenger rail service in the United States
- ✔ Is provided by Amtrak.
- ✔ Includes busy corridor routes that serve many business travelers as well as long-distance routes used mainly by leisure travelers.
- ✔ Features amenities and service options that vary from route to route.

Unlike Amtrak trains, on European trains
- ✔ Some of the seating is in compartments, rooms of six passengers.

- ✔ Most trains have first- and second-class compartments.
- ✔ Cars are often switched from one train to another during the trip, and many cities have more than one train station.

Rail passes
- ✔ Do not by themselves guarantee a seat.
- ✔ Usually will be cheaper than point-to-point fares only if the traveler is taking more than one long trip.
- ✔ Can be most efficiently used by plotting an itinerary that follows a continuous loop or that takes a hub-and-spoke approach.

Rental Cars

■ WHAT SERVICES DO CAR RENTAL COMPANIES PROVIDE, AND
WHAT REQUIREMENTS SHOULD CAR RENTERS EXPECT TO MEET?

A car is an expensive nuisance in cities that have excellent public transportation or extreme congestion. On long trips, taking a car is exhausting for the driver, and it may be uncomfortable for the passengers. Often, though, these disadvantages pale beside the advantages of renting a car. Car rentals offer

■ Freedom to change an itinerary. Business travelers can pursue a new lead or rearrange appointments. Vacationers can follow their whims and take the road less traveled.

■ Flexibility to combine different modes of transportation, such as flying and then renting a car rather than driving many hours.

■ Access to destinations unreachable by other means. Car rentals permit vacationers to stay at country inns, farmhouses, or less expensive hotels hidden in the countryside. In a great many places, such as Florida and California, getting around without a car is extremely difficult.

■ Room for baggage. A car is like a huge extra suitcase, enabling travelers to carry loose items such as books, food, or sports gear without difficulty.

■ Economy. The larger the group traveling together and dividing the cost of the vehicle, the more economical the rental becomes.

North American Car Rental Companies

The history of car rental companies goes back to 1916, but it was the expansion of air travel that transformed car rental into the major enterprise it is today. The great majority of North American car rentals occur at airport locations, and most of the jobs are there, too. Some companies, though, do most of their business not with people at airports, but with people who rent cars in their hometowns because their own cars broke down or were stolen. Enterprise, for example, rents most of its cars to this *replacement market*.

Three rental car companies dominate the industry, although dozens of small and local companies also compete successfully. These three are Enterprise Holdings (which includes Alamo and National), Hertz (which includes Dollar and Thrifty) and Avis (which includes Payless).

For a car rental company, the ups and downs of economic life are tied to the state of the auto industry. When auto manufacturers are hungry for sales, car rental companies can obtain their cars on favorable terms. Boom times for the auto industry translate into tough terms for the car rental companies and declining profits.

Competition among car rental firms is stiff, but there is little difference in the cars they offer. To distinguish themselves in the marketplace, some companies emphasize full service (Hertz, Avis, and National) and others emphasize savings (Thrifty and Dollar). The categories are far from absolute, however. "Full-service" companies may try to compete on the basis of price and sometimes cost less than those that emphasize savings, and "economical" companies often give good service. Also, companies may change strategies.

Budget, for example, has been categorized as a company that targets customers looking for savings, but in the late 1990s it emphasized its service in order to attract business travelers. Generally speaking, business travelers expect high levels of service from a car rental company, whereas many leisure travelers are willing to sacrifice service to save on the rate.

Fleets and Services

Companies use slightly different terms to describe their fleets, but generally the cars fall into six classes:

- *Economy* or *subcompact,* which are small cars that are suitable for one or two persons and have few options.
- *Compact,* which are slightly larger than subcompacts and may have a few more options.
- *Intermediate* or *midsize,* which are suitable for three or four persons for short distances and may include amenities.
- *Standard* or *full size,* which can seat four persons comfortably.
- *Luxury* or *premium,* which are expensive deluxe models.
- *Sport utility vehicles (SUVs) and vans,* which seat seven or have extra cargo area.

Car renters can reserve a particular class but usually not a specific make or model. If the customer has a reservation and the confirmed class is not available at the time of rental, the customer is usually given the next higher class at the rate of the confirmed class.

Large companies usually have convertibles, SUVs, and minivans in their fleet. They may or may not be able to meet requests for sports cars, jeeps, and other specialty cars. Some companies specialize in motor home rentals.

If travelers want child safety seats, four-wheel drive, bike racks, ski racks, or tire chains, they must request these and pay extra. Hand controls are another option. Computerized navigational systems are available as both standard and optional features in most cities, depending on the car rental company and the model of the car.

Full-service companies might aim to provide

- Speedy handling of phone reservations.
- Speedy check-in, pickup, and drop-off procedures.
- More convenient locations.
- Drop-off freedom (renting the car in one city and returning it in another).
- New cars with few miles.
- Cars with more amenities.
- Clean cars.
- More locations to switch cars (in case something is wrong with the first one rented).

To promote customer loyalty, car rental firms have three types of programs:

- *Service clubs,* which give members preferential treatment. For example, National offers the Emerald Club. Members can reserve a car an hour in advance, and they can bypass the rental counter and personally select their own cars.
- *Frequent-renter plans,* which reward renters with free upgrades or rentals after a certain number of paid rentals. For example, Alamo's Insiders program gives renters points for each rental; they can use their points for rentals and priority service.
- *Tie-ins* with frequent-traveler programs offered by airlines and hotels. For example, for each rental day with Alamo, members of Alaska Airlines'

Mileage Plan earn 50 air miles. Most major rental companies have partnerships with numerous frequent-flyer programs.

Requirements and Procedures

A hotel room does not move away from its rental location, and an airline chooses its own extremely qualified "drivers." In contrast, the car rental firm loses control over its expensive investment the moment the unknown client drives it away. This difference is reflected in the conditions that car renters must meet.

The renter must

- Have a valid driver's license.
- Be at least 25 years of age, ordinarily. Those who are 18 to 24 years old may qualify with certain companies under certain conditions, such as if they hold a credit card or if an employer or parent fills out certain forms.
- Be creditworthy. Holding a major credit card usually satisfies this requirement. If the traveler does not have an acceptable credit card, a travel counselor may issue a prepaid voucher. A person who has neither a credit card nor a prepaid voucher may still be able to rent a car, but it may take several days to make the arrangements. The company may need to verify the renter's address, telephone number, employment, bank account, and even references.

CLOSE-UP: ON THE JOB WITH FRANK SCIATA, CAR RENTAL AGENT

Frank Sciata works for one of the largest car rental companies in the country. It emphasizes economy first and serves a higher percentage of leisure customers than other big car rental companies. Most of Frank's day is spent behind the rental counter dealing with people who have just flown into the city.

"I started out 'hiking cars,' or that's what I called it—it was transferring cars from one location to another, usually from downtown to the airport, part-time. If there was nothing to be driven, I'd help out cleaning the cars. Then I started driving the van from the airport to the agency and back. This was fun because I've always liked to drive.

"After a while, though, I realized there wasn't much advancement unless I got to work in the office, and there weren't many openings. When there was one and they hired an outsider, I figured maybe they'll just always think of me as a driver, so I applied somewhere else and got hired right away at a larger company. They sent me for sales and computer training and then put me right to work as a rental agent.

"My experience was an advantage. I knew little things about the cars, how they were serviced, and the inventory, and I could discuss the aspects of each car with clients. I have to check each person's driver's license and credit card. Most people have a reservation when they come in. If their license and credit card check out, they get the car. If they don't have a credit card, they may not get the car unless they've made prior arrangements for us to check out their job and credit. But there's a lot more to it than that.

"I have to make sure the client understands the rental agreement and charges. Better they understand it now than after they are finished using the car. It happens quite a few times that people come in after the rental and argue about the bill. They didn't bother to take a good look at it when they got it. And some people bring the car in early and then wonder why their bill isn't less. Sometimes it is, but if they got a special discount for a weekend or week, it may even cost more if it's returned early. A deal is a deal. Bring the car in early and it's a different deal and a different rate. They can't believe it; I wonder what business they are in.

"A lot of people make a reservation for the best price they hear but might not actually want that car when they arrive. A lot of times it's for the least expensive car, which is not as strong and safe and not as large as the car they're used to driving. It's my job to see if a better car would suit their needs.

"Usually business travelers have reserved the car they want and stick with it. But the vacationers are all over the lot on this. They think they're going to fit seven kids into a compact car. So, I always explain the next size or two larger to them and how much it will cost. Often, we have a special if they upgrade their car then and there. It may not cost them that much more.

"I'm fairly good about selling larger cars, waivers, and fuel options. I always reach my monthly quota. The business has been growing every year, and I'm looking for advancement to shift manager and maybe station manager in the long run, if I stick with it. I'm also going to school taking business classes."

In addition, in some states the potential car renter's driving record will be checked—but not until the person appears at the counter. Drivers with serious violations, such as driving while using alcohol or leaving the scene of an accident, will be denied the rental.

Other terms and conditions may apply at different times and places; for example, there may be restrictions regarding what state lines may be crossed, and violators may face substantial fees. Satellite positioning systems allow rental companies to track their cars. Some car rental companies have a 'no rent' list based on the customers prior rental history with the company.

Rental Rates

Cars are rented on a 24-hour basis. If you pick up the car at 3:45 p.m. on one day and drop it off by that time the next day, a one-day rental will be charged. There is usually a 59-minute grace period, after which additional charges apply.

The cost of renting a car varies widely among cities; it may even change with the pickup point within a city. Generally, companies offer different rates for different classes of cars and for daily, weekly, and weekend rentals. Weekly rates are usually substantially lower than seven times the daily rate. Weekend rates are usually less than weekday rates.

In addition to the charge for the time rented, there may be a mileage charge. The different ways of handling mileage yield three types of rental rates:

- *Time plus mileage.* The car renter is charged a fee for a certain amount of time plus a fee per mile driven; for example, the rate might be $19 a day and three cents per mile.
- *Time with mileage cap.* The car renter is charged per day, with a certain number of miles allowed; for additional mileage, there is a charge. For example, the rate might be $29 a day with 100 included miles and 29 cents per mile above 100 miles. If the car is rented for one day and driven 120 miles, the charge would be $34.80.
- *Time with unlimited mileage.* The car renter can drive any number of miles for the same price. If the rate is $29 per day, and the car is driven 500 miles, the charge is still $29.

Car renters may obtain discounts on the standard rates if they belong to frequent-renter plans, certain organizations such as the American Association of Retired Persons (AARP), or motor clubs. The best-known motor clubs are the **American Automobile Association (AAA)** and **Canadian Automobile Association (CAA),** which offer members a variety of travel and motoring services. Also, renters may receive discounts if their companies participate in a corporate discount program.

Rental rates generally cover oil, minor repairs, public liability insurance, and property damage insurance. But because of additional charges, the car renter's final fee may be more than double the quoted rental price. Additional charges might include

- Drop-off charges. Dropping the car at a location different from the pickup point usually brings an extra charge, if it is permitted at all.
- Special equipment. Bike racks and ski racks are examples.
- Fuel. If the gas tank is not full when the renter returns the vehicle, a charge of close to double the regular cost of fuel may be applied. To avoid this fee, some companies offer clients the option of buying a full tank in advance at current prices; the renter gets no credit for gas left in the tank upon return.
- Additional drivers. Nonregistered drivers may void the car rental contract and make the renter liable for any damages or injuries.

ON THE SPOT

A client returns from a trip and says to you, "I did check my insurance like you said and found out that my package includes rental cars, but the rental car agent said that I would be responsible if I didn't buy the company's waiver. I didn't know what to do and I was in a hurry, so I took it. It added more than $83 to my weekly rental, but I didn't want to have to pay for a $20,000 car if something happened. What gives?" How would you explain the situation?

"The rental agent is technically right to say that you'd be responsible. But, because your insurance covered rentals, that really means that your insurance company would have had to pay for any damage or theft if you hadn't bought the car rental company's waiver. Because you did buy the waiver, the car rental company would have had to pay for any problems, and your insurance company would not be involved. In effect, you bought double insurance for the time you had the car. If anything had happened, at least your insurance premiums wouldn't have been affected, so that was a plus. In the future, though, you might want to check with your insurance agent to see if you should decline the waiver. For what you're getting, the rate is high."

■ Taxes. Up to three local taxes, including an airport surcharge, are added to the car rental in some cities.

One other important possible cost covers insurance. Rates and rules are complex and vary from state to state and from company to company. We take a closer look at this sometimes-confusing topic in the next section.

Insurance and Waivers

Car rental agreements include—at no extra charge—liability for damage to persons, to other cars, or to property. But who pays for damage to or theft of the rented car itself? Rental agreements state how much the company will pay. In many cases, the agreement leaves the renter liable for thousands of dollars or for the entire cost of the car.

For an additional charge, car rental companies in many states offer

■ A *collision damage waiver (CDW),* which waives the rental company's right to charge the renter for damages if the rental car is involved in an accident.

■ A *loss damage waiver (LDW),* which waives the company's right to recover damages resulting from theft or vandalism as well as from collisions.

■ *Personal accident insurance (PAI),* which covers bodily injury to the car renter. PAI is sometimes included with a CDW or LDW or is offered at a low rate.

■ *Additional liability insurance (ALI)* or *extended liability insurance (ELI),* which adds insurance for injuries to persons or property up to $1 million above what is covered by the renter's own car insurance and what the rental company is mandated by state law to cover.

State laws differ regarding the amount of insurance that car rental companies must themselves provide. In some states, laws prohibit the sale of some of these forms of insurance. The cost of CDWs and LDWs has traditionally been very high.

In fact, many travelers do not need any of this coverage, or they can get it more cheaply elsewhere. Often, the renter's own car insurance or the credit card used for the rental will cover any damage to the rented car. However, this coverage may not be in effect for special situations (such as antique automobiles, certain vans, motorcycles, or recreational vehicles) or if the car is rented for more than two weeks.

In any event, a travel insurer may offer the same coverage for less than half the cost of a CDW or LDW from the car rental company. For example, car renters can purchase CDW-equivalent coverage over the phone or online through several travel protection providers, such as Travel Guard International. Similarly, the car renter's own health and life insurance is likely to provide the coverage offered by PAIs.

Traffic jams can be part of a city vacation, as seen in Istanbul, Turkey.

Whether car renters need additional insurance coverage should be determined ahead of time. Renters are very likely to find it difficult to read and understand all the fine print of the car rental agreement while standing at the rental counter, and it may be impossible at that point for them to determine whether their personal insurance is adequate. It is the client's responsibility to determine whether the coverage provided by a CDW, LDW, PAI, or ALI/ELI is needed. But travel counselors should explain the matter as clearly as possible so that the client will know what information is needed.

International Car Rentals

Cars can be rented practically anywhere in the world. In fact, in much of the world you can find offices of the major U.S. car rental companies. Auto Europe, Europcar and Sixt are other well-known companies that arrange rentals with various car companies in Europe. These companies offer a number of helpful services. For example, Auto Europe offers maps with estimated drive times between cities, rather than just listing mileage.

Driving Abroad. Travelers who want to drive while abroad should check whether their U.S. driver's licenses allow them to drive at their destinations. Major European countries accept U.S. driver's licenses. Some countries elsewhere require an ***International Driver's Permit (IDP),*** which is essentially a translation of the bearer's driver's license into an internationally recognized format. The IDP is available from the American Automobile Association (AAA) at a fee of $20 plus the cost of photos. To obtain an IDP, travelers must present a valid license, pay a fee, and submit two passport-size photos. Some countries, however, require local driver's permits, and a few allow only chauffeur-driven service. The car rental company should be able to provide information about these regulations.

Driving in certain countries is more confusing than in others. For example, cities observing the typical Mediterranean work schedule have four major rush hours; drivers are bound to get caught in one rush hour or another. The German autobahn has no speed limits. Driving is on the left side of the road in Japan, Thailand, Britain, and most members of the British Commonwealth. Those who plan to drive while abroad should familiarize themselves with international signs before their departure (see Figure 5.3).

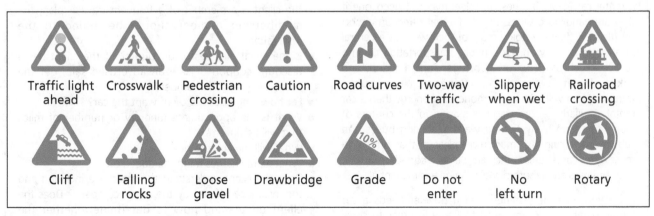

FIGURE 5.3 International Signs

The American Automobile Association and any good road atlas have a complete list of international signs.

Traffic abroad often moves faster and more aggressively than in the United States, and, in some countries, the injury and death rates for auto collisions are far higher than in the United States. Drunk-driving regulations in most countries are stricter than those in the United States, ranging from prison to death. Note that American insurance is not valid in Mexico whether driving a rental car or one's own car.

Rentals Abroad. Perhaps the most important point to keep in mind about international car rentals is that they should be reserved in advance. In most cases, car rentals are substantially less expensive if they are booked or paid for before the traveler leaves the United States or Canada.

Procedures for renting a car abroad are similar to those in the United States. Only the type of car, not the model, can be guaranteed. Rental fleets vary from country to country. Cars familiar to Americans may be given different names abroad. To help renters, most firms renting European cars publish pictures of their fleets in their brochures and on their websites. For travelers staying in city locations, it can many times be more efficient to rent from a city (non-airport) location. Keep in mind that many cities can be quite congested, with steep parking fees. It can be easier to rent the car only when you are ready to depart a city to visit other regional destinations.

There are some other differences between renting a car in the United States and abroad.

- Luggage space will generally be somewhat smaller than in cars in the United States. If a roof rack is needed, it must be ordered in advance.
- Automatic transmission must be specifically requested in advance; the cost varies greatly.

CLOSE-UP: SELLING AND QUALIFYING

Because cars are so familiar, it may seem as if renting one would not require much thought. But clients who reserve a car that is too small or who do not understand drop-off restrictions or fuel charges could end up with an uncomfortable or unnecessarily expensive trip. Not informing clients about insurance regulations could have worse consequences.

A first and most obvious question is whether a client needs a rental car at all. Business travelers may not need one if they are handling business at a hotel that offers an airport shuttle or if they are doing most of their work at a central location in a city with good public transportation or limo service—such as New York, Chicago, Paris, London, and Tokyo. In cities like these, taking a taxi or public transportation will cost less in money and energy than a car rental. Similarly, leisure travelers staying in the centers of many cities are likely to find walking, taking buses and subways, or taking taxis much more pleasant than driving. In most other cases, unless they are being escorted on a tour, both business and leisure clients will find a car essential.

Once you have determined that a traveler needs a car rental, what else do you need to know in order to serve the customer? Here are the key questions.

- Does the client meet the requirements for renting a car?
- When and where will the client pick up the car and drop it off?
- What kind of car does the client want to rent? (A good way to match car and driver is to ask what type of car the client owns and then ask if he or she wants a similar one.)
- Is the client a member of a frequent-traveler plan? (The possibility of earning points or air miles, or of using the rewards from one of these programs to rent the car, might determine the choice of rental company. Also, if the client is a member of a frequent-traveler plan, the membership number should be added to the reservation.)
- Is the client eligible for discounts? (If the client has a discount coupon or saw an advertised sale, get the accompanying code number.)
- For how long does the client want the car?
- What is the approximate itinerary or number of miles that will be driven?
- What will the charges be?
- What extra charges might be added on?
- Does the client understand the insurance included and the insurance offered by the rental company? Does the client understand how to determine whether the additional insurance offered is needed?
- Is the client also traveling by air on the trip? (If so, note the arrival time and flight number.)

- Air conditioning must be specifically requested. It may not be available in many countries or on mini, compact, economy, and intermediate cars; it probably will be available only on the largest and most expensive cars.
- Fuel prices may be significantly different. In some popular destinations, they can be two to four times those in the United States.
- Value-added taxes (VATs) may not be included in the general rates and can range from 10 to 25 percent of the total rental charge. (Travel counselors should quote the rate and add the tax for the client.)
- Cars rented in one country may not be taken across a border into another country. Or special documents may be needed to do so.
- U.S. and Canadian auto insurance policies usually do not cover rentals abroad.
- Some rental companies in a few countries may have a maximum age limit as well as the usual minimum age requirements.

International Alternatives to Car Rentals. Renting may not be the best solution for everyone who wants access to a car when abroad. Clients who need a car for a month or more might instead consider *leasing,* which is essentially a prearranged purchase/repurchase plan. Leased cars come new from the factory and usually cost less than long rentals. Furthermore, a leased car is not subject to the high taxes levied on rentals in European countries. Insurance is usually completely covered in the lease rate.

International car purchase may offer advantages for those on a lengthy overseas trip, depending on the currency exchange rate. The car must meet visa regulations, however. Also, U.S. regulations often change regarding whether the car is considered used when shipped to the United States—an important point for tax purposes. It is wise to use a company that specializes in factory-delivered cars in order to obtain the latest choice of purchase plans and the latest shipping and import information.

Alternative Options and Ridesharing

In recent years, there have been new transportation options available to travelers. An alternative option to renting a car from a traditional car rental agency are peer-to-peer car sharing services, such as Turo. For travelers looking to rent a vehicle, this can be a cheaper and more flexible option. Turo (and similar services) are web applications that allow you to rent a car from a private owner, who will many times deliver the car to your specific location. Services like this are available in many cities around the globe. It also provides travelers an opportunity to rent specific types of vehicles, such as pick-up trucks, ultra-luxury sports cars, and even Vespas. Renting through the alternative options also provides comprehensive insurance for renters who might not otherwise be covered or have their own policy. A valid drivers license and background check is required to book cars through these platforms.

Another transportation option is ridesharing, which is a car service with which a person can use a smartphone app to arrange a ride, usually in a privately-owned vehicle. The most commonly known apps are Uber and Lyft. They are available in many cities around the world and provide travelers an easy way to request a ride from a specific location, along with the ability to charge rides directly to their credit cards. Often, the cost of the service is significantly less than local taxi services. This has benefits for both the leisure and corporate traveler, saving significantly on car rentals. It is important to verify that a ridesharing service is available in the travelers' destinations and that it is reputable and reliable.

While peer-to-peer car sharing services and rideshare services might not be commission-earning opportunities, they still can be a value-add for travel professionals to present to their travelers. If you can save your clients time and money, other earning potential opportunities will arise.

✔ CHECK-UP

North American car rental companies may be roughly classified according to whether they emphasize
- ✔ Rentals to air travelers or to those who rent from their hometowns.
- ✔ Competing through full service or through price.

Rental fleets generally include six types of cars:
- ✔ Economy or subcompact.
- ✔ Compact.
- ✔ Intermediate or midsize.
- ✔ Standard or full size.
- ✔ Luxury or premium.
- ✔ Sport utility vehicles (SUVs) and vans.

Motor Coaches

■ WHAT ARE THE VARIOUS USES OF MOTOR COACHES?

For many Americans and Canadians, bus transportation is the last resort. They expect buses to be slow and uncomfortable. Today, however, many buses are equipped with large picture windows, plush seats, restrooms, bars, and even video players with multiscreens throughout the coach. Specially designed coaches intended for a small number of passengers may have lounge chairs, sofas, and tables. This upgrading is reflected in the fact that buses are now called *motor coaches;* the term *bus* usually connotes a vehicle with few amenities that is used only for short trips, such as the buses used for public transportation within cities, school buses, and so on.

In thousands of American communities, buses are the only alternative to cars; no other public mode of transportation serves these communities. For those who do have a choice among bus, rail, and plane, intercity bus service traditionally offered the advantage of being the cheapest way to travel. But bus companies have had difficulty maintaining this competitive advantage. Although about 100 privately owned companies still provide regularly scheduled bus service between U.S. cities, Greyhound Bus Lines is now the only nationwide bus carrier.

Intercity travel represents only one of the uses of motor coaches. Others include
- *Transfers*—that is, transportation between hotels and airports, docks, or railroad stations. Motor coaches and shuttle vans often are the most efficient transportation for transfers and for trips from a hotel to a restaurant or to a special activity, such as skiing. It is important to know the details of the transfer as it relates to wait times, pick-up and drop-off locations, cost, and other terms outlined by the travel supplier.

- Sightseeing within a city and its surrounding area.
- Tours run by bus companies themselves or by travel agencies or tour operators. (Chapter 8 covers tours in detail.)
- Charters by private groups, such as church organizations and clubs. Trips to dinner theaters, casinos, historic sites, and shopping malls are especially popular.

More than 4,000 independent motor coach companies offer charters and local sightseeing. Many local sightseeing lines have connections with two of the largest sightseeing companies, Gray Line and Sightseeing.com (formerly American Sightseeing International, a worldwide association of sightseeing tours and charter companies).

Selling Ground Transportation

- WHAT ARE THE ADVANTAGES OF EACH FORM OF GROUND TRANSPORTATION?
- WHAT ARE SOME OTHER GROUND TRAVEL SALES OPTIONS?

Each form of ground transportation has an important place in travel. Rail offers opportunities for meeting other passengers and for relaxing—viewing the scenery, walking about, eating and drinking comfortably. Auto travel provides flexibility—the opportunity to drive to and from almost all lodgings, restaurants, or places of interest—and the ability to carry much more luggage. For transfers, though, a motor coach is often the best means of transportation.

Although the sale of domestic ground transportation is not known for its glamour, these forms of transportation are certainly significant to travelers. For example, more than one-fifth of all business trips involve use of a rental car. Ground transportation represents a market opportunity that travel professionals cannot afford to overlook.

Funicular from the port on Capri, Italy, up to Marine Granda mountain

For travel counselors, selling ground transportation offers chances both for earning revenue directly from the sale and for giving the kind of service that earns the loyalty of clients. With little extra effort, for example, travel counselors can increase sales by suggesting rental cars to their air travelers. Providing good service, however, might be more important in the long run. Arranging for transfers and preparing travelers for their arrivals represent two important services provided by travel counselors.

Transfers

Because of their small cost and brief duration, transfers are easy to overlook when planning a trip. Unfortunately, the result can be memorable. Arriving in a strange city half asleep from jet lag, loaded down with luggage, and confused about what to do next is no way to begin a journey.

Sometimes it might be appropriate to have clients met and helped by interpreters or to sell clients vouchers for transfers. In some cases, arranging for limousine service may be the best option for clients. International Chauffeured Service is one of the fastest-growing limousine services in the United States; it also offers service at many international destinations. Carey International is a well-known service since 1921, offering ground transportation services with limo, van, mini-bus, SUVs, and motor coaches.

Just giving information may be a significant service. For example, a travel counselor might want to tell travelers ahead of time that, after arriving on Capri, they will transfer by *funicular* (a cable railway), with porters wheeling their bags in carts. This bit of information can both enhance the travelers' trip and heighten their esteem for the travel counselor.

Taking the extra step to find out if their hotel provides shuttle service (vans) to and from the airport will contribute to clients' feeling that they are well taken care of by their travel counselor. When hotels don't provide shuttle service, they often have information regarding local, independent shuttle services that make regular stops at their property. Many of these local companies allow advance reservations.

If taxi service is the best choice for a transfer, a travel counselor can provide clients with approximate taxi rates in advance. Armed with this information, travelers will know how much money to have ready and will be confident that they are paying a reasonable fare.

Additional Services

Technology offers ways of improving service. Travel counselors can use the Internet to obtain for their clients a local map, a description of ground transportation from the airport, and schedules for public transportation or (for clients who are driving) exact directions from one destination to another. Travel counselors can reserve a seat on a train in Australia as easily as one on Amtrak. They can meet travelers' needs before the travelers are even aware of those needs. Consider the many passes offered by Rail Europe, for example, and imagine a new traveler trying to decide among them. Travel counselors can help clients choose the right pass—and, along the way, can sell other products as well.

Other services counselors can provide to their clients could include a car and driver, an airport meet and greet, a translator, and other offerings from a variety of specialty companies.

Except for car rental companies, Rail Europe, and Amtrak, most ground transportation companies are not included on GDSs but might be found online. Look for the section of the website that is reserved for travel agencies; it will offer inside information and indicate if and how services are commissionable. If the site does not have such a section, call or e-mail the company to establish a relationship.

CHAPTER HIGHLIGHTS

Smooth transportation by rail, car, or motor coach can be critical to the success of any traveler's journey; knowing about ground transportation and how to sell it can be key to a travel professional's success. Here is a review of the objectives with which we began the chapter.

1. **Describe rail service in the United States, Canada and Europe.** Amtrak provides almost all of the passenger train service available in the United States. Amtrak offers coach, business, and first class, as well as sleeping accommodations, but not all classes of service are available on all trains. Reservations are always required for all classes of service except coach. Food service is available on most routes, and meals are included with sleeping accommodations. Types of fares include basic Point-to-Point tickets, the USA Rail Pass, and numerous discounts and promotional fares. Amtrak also offers many vacation packages.

   The railroads of continental Europe are known for their high-quality service and high-speed trains (such as France's TGV and Eurostar). Accommodations include compartments and *couchettes* as well as private sleeping accommodations. For many tourists, rail passes are a convenient, economical way to travel.

   Amtrak offers a rail pass known as USA Rail. Unlike the Canrailpass from VIA Rail of Canada, which can be bought in Canada, the USA Rail pass can be purchased only outside the United States. The Eurailpass is good for unlimited first-class train travel in 31 European countries for specified periods. There are also variations of the pass including the Global Pass and One Country Pass. Discounts are also available based on the age of the traveler.

2. **Outline the services provided by car rental companies and the requirements that renters should expect to meet.** There is little difference in the cars offered by different car rental companies, and renters usually can reserve only a particular class of car, not a specific make or model. Some companies emphasize the service they provide—such as cars with the latest gadgets, speedy check-in, or drop-off freedom. The car renter must have a valid driver's license. Possession of a major credit card is important and often necessary; renting a car without one requires either a prepaid voucher or a thorough credit check. Those under 25 years of age must also make special arrangements to qualify for a car rental. Rental companies may refuse cars to those with poor driving records. The renter might pay daily, weekend, or weekly rates. Most companies offer unlimited mileage, but some add a charge for each mile driven over a certain number or for all miles driven. Renters may incur extra charges for drop-off fees, special equipment, fuel, additional drivers, or various taxes. Car rental companies also sell collision damage waivers (CDWs), loss damage waivers (LDWs), personal accident insurance (PAI), and additional liability insurance (ALI) or extended liability insurance (ELI), but many renters are adequately covered without these.

   Overseas, car fleets may be different, and familiar cars may appear under different names. Cars are likely to offer less luggage space. Automatic transmission and air conditioning must be requested and paid for, and fuel is likely to be significantly more expensive than in the United States. In some countries travelers will need an International Driver's Permit (IDP), which can be obtained from AAA. In most cases, booking the overseas rental before leaving the United States is much less expensive than booking it when abroad.

3. **Identify the functions played by motor coaches.** In many American communities, motor coaches are the only form of public transportation available. Motor coaches are used not only for intercity travel but also for transfers, sightseeing, tours, and chartered trips by groups, such as church organizations.

4. **Explain the comparative advantages of traveling by rail, car, or motor coach.** Rail provides the opportunity to meet other passengers, to walk around, and to relax. Auto travel provides flexibility and the ability to carry much more luggage, and if several people are traveling together and sharing car expenses, it can be very viable financially. For transfers, though, a motor coach is often the best means of transportation.

5. **Discuss the roles of transfers and technology in the selling of ground travel.** Arranging transfers provides an opportunity not only to gain revenue but also to provide an important service that can help gain a client's loyalty. In different circumstances, motor coaches, limousines, shuttles, or taxis might be the best choice for a transfer; some destinations offer unusual options such as a funicular. Learning to find information about these options online is just one way that travel counselors can use the Internet to improve the service they offer clients.

KEY TERMS

A list of key terms introduced in this chapter follows. If you do not recall the meaning of these terms, see the Glossary.

Acela Express	extended liability insurance (ELI)
additional liability insurance (ALI)	International Driver's Permit (IDP)
American Automobile Association (AAA)	loss damage waiver (LDW)
Amtrak	motor coach
BritRail pass	personal accident insurance (PAI)
bullet train	Rail Europe
Canadian Automobile Association (CAA)	rail pass
Canrailpass	ridesharing
Chunnel	specialty train
collision damage waiver (CDW)	TGV
couchette	transfers
Eurail Pass	USA Rail pass
Eurostar	VIA Rail
Eurotunnel	

REVIEW QUESTIONS

1. What kinds of clients might prefer to travel by Amtrak rather than by car or plane?

2. What types of clients might benefit from a Eurailpass?

3. In which situations or places might a car rental be necessary?

4. An economy car rental is advertised at $99 per week with unlimited mileage. For what kinds of clients might this car be inappropriate? What extra charges might be applied to this rental?

5. Why might a client refuse to buy a collision damage waiver or personal accident insurance?

6. Explain how you can use the Internet and e-mail to obtain information on additional ground services for independent travelers.

7. What is ridesharing, and when would you recommend it to your client?

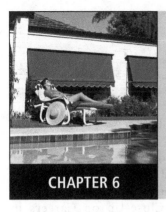

Accommodations

What does this word *accommodations* mean? In the travel/tourism industry it generally is recognized as somewhere to sleep. Other terms are **lodging**, the **hospitality industry**, or the *hotel* industry. Or, as one author put it succinctly, "It's a home away from home."

Within the overall tourism industry, this sector is the largest employer, with the largest number of opportunities, and often provides young people with their first jobs. Best of all, the sector is found worldwide with many different types of properties making up this multi-billion-dollar industry. And employees interact with many other parts of the travel/tourism industry, such as travel agencies, tour operators, restaurants, meeting and event planners, and the entertainment industry.

Accommodations may be found in big cities and in the countryside, in the mountains and at the seashore, in campsites and in private homes, in dormitories and in apartments. But regardless of the many different kinds of properties, all must meet basic requirements. They must be:
- clean
- quiet
- secure
- comfortable
- attractive

This chapter first explores the characteristic of the hotel industry then looks at accommodations themselves and how to sell them.

FIGURE 6.1

U.S. hotels have kept pace with the country's rising living standards, progressing from rooms with telephones to rooms with computers.

1829 Tremont Hotel in Boston is the first U.S. hotel to offer indoor toilets and private bedrooms with locks on the doors.

1907 E.M. Statler opens his first hotel in Buffalo with individual rooms, private baths and catering to business travelers.

1907 The Plaza Hotel in New York City installs telephones in each room.

1919 Conrad Hilton opens his first hotel, the Mobley, in Texas.

1925 The first motel, Mo-Tel Inn, opens in San Luis Obispo, California.

1927 Radio reception is made available to guests at the Boston Statler.

1929 The first U.S. airport hotel is built at the Oakland Municipal Airport.

1934 The Detroit Statler is the first hotel to air-condition every room.

1945 Sheraton becomes the first hotel company to be listed on the New York Stock Exchange, and Travelodge becomes the first economy hotel corporation.

1946 The first casino hotel, the Flamingo, opens in Las Vegas.

1947 New York City's Roosevelt Hotel installs television sets in every room.

1949 Hilton becomes the first international hotel chain.

1952 The first Holiday Inn opens in Memphis.

1958 Sheraton installs a centralized reservation system.

1964 Holiday Inn establishes a computerized reservation system.

1968 The first all-inclusive resort, Club Med, begins marketing to Americans.

1981 In-room movies are available in 500,000 U.S. guestrooms.

1995 Radisson and Holiday Inn go online, allowing Internet bookings.

1999 Choice International becomes the first chain to test making in-room PCs a standard amenity.

2004 Ninety-eight percent of hotel rooms offer cable or satellite television.

2008 Airbnb launches worldwide home-stay program.

2011 Many U.S. hotels offer guests Internet access.

2016 Marriott and Starwood Hotels merge to create the world's largest hotel chain.

The Business of Accommodations

■ WHAT ARE THE DOMINANT TRENDS IN HOW ACCOMMODATIONS ARE OWNED, MANAGED, AND MARKETED?

According to the 2015 Lodging Industry Trends Report prepared by the **American Hotel and Lodging Association** (AH&LA), the U.S. hotel industry has close to five million guestrooms, generating $176 billion in sales and employs almost two million people. The Close-Up on Careers in Accommodations describes some of the job opportunities. How did this economic giant develop, and what keeps it running?

A Brief History

The history of accommodations goes back at least to the times described in the Bible, which includes many references to lodgings. Travelers from ancient Rome were required to carry official documents that granted them permission to travel and stay in private *mansionis*. In medieval Europe, inns for travelers in dangerous regions were often run by monks. More than 400 years ago, the Incas of South America kept inns (called *tambos*) along a road thousands of miles long. But it was only in the late 1700s that large, comfortable lodgings like today's hotels appeared. Figure 6.1 describes some milestones in the history of hotels in the United States.

Over the years, transportation and accommodations have evolved together. In the United States, when cities in the Northeast became transportation centers, for example, they also became home to the first luxurious hotels. As trains opened up the West to travelers in the late 1800s, railroad companies built some of Canada's grandest hotels. And in the early 20th century, the growing popularity of automobiles paved the way for the rise of motels (short for *motor hotels*).

It was in 1925 that the word *motel* was coined. Arthur Heineman gave the name Mo-Tel Inn to his long one-story establishment on Route 101 in San Luis Obispo, California. Motels introduced many Americans to steam heat, tile bathrooms, sliding glass doors, and radio—features that were promoted on hundreds of motel signs along the highways. Motels caught on because they allowed motorists to be close to their vehicles and belongings, to park easily, and to avoid dealing with hotel lobbies after a tiring, dusty drive. Also, motels usually cost less than hotels because motels were built on less expensive land on the outskirts of town and did without large lobbies.

The 1930s Depression devastated the hotel business; after World War II, the U.S. industry was rebuilt as Americans took to the road and to the air. The railroads were deteriorating, air travel was expanding, and, in 1956, the federal government began building the interstate highway system. City hotels suffered from both the loss of railroad travelers and their inability to provide enough parking for the increasing number of motorists. Travelers on the new highways looked for lodging more convenient than the downtown hotels. Motels sprang up everywhere. Many were built by chains and offered swimming pools, televisions, and convenient reservation systems. The small mom-and-pop cabins, called **tourist courts**, built in the 1920s could not compete.

Economic changes during the 1970s and 1980s produced other

innovations in accommodations. As air travel boomed, new hotels were built near airports. As major American cities were revitalized, large hotels came back to the downtown areas. In fact, by the late 1980s, there were too many

CLOSE-UP: CAREERS IN ACCOMMODATIONS

Mobility is excellent in the accommodations industry, the segment of the travel industry that employs the most people. Pay levels tend to be low for entry-level positions, but you can rise rapidly to better positions. Opportunities are greatest at the largest chains and smallest hotels. The best way to get in the door is by working part-time, on weekends, or on the night shift. But be prepared to give service. The accommodations industry puts great demands on your time and personal life. To climb the career ladder, you may have to relocate frequently or work long hours.

■ **Position** Front desk clerk

Description The front desk clerk checks guests in and out, makes reservations and handles requests from guests. At some hotels, the clerk may also perform office duties, such as posting payments and maintaining records.

Qualifications Typically, this is an entry-level position that is part of the hotel's management training program. Companies look for a person with some background in customer service, a polished appearance, and a personable manner. Foreign-language skills may be an asset at some properties.

■ **Position** Sales manager

Description Soliciting and booking business is the heart of this job. Depending on the hotel, it might involve dealing with corporate accounts, convention organizers, tour operators, travel counselors, international clients, and so on. The sales manager participates in trade shows, makes sales calls and delivers presentations. The sales manager usually has latitude to spot and pursue untapped markets and to help fashion packages or pricing programs. Sales managers must be able to meet revenue and hotel occupancy goals.

Qualifications Employers look for prior sales experience. A sales assistant might move up to this job.

■ **Position** Food and beverage manager

Description Directing the production and service of food and beverages is the essence of this position. It involves training dining room and kitchen staff, ensuring quality control, planning menus, budgeting and purchasing ingredients and selecting wine and liquor.

Qualifications Usually, this position requires experience in management and training from a hospitality or culinary arts program. It also demands a keen interest in food and wine, knowledge of food trends and guests' tastes, and a willingness to work long hours under pressure and ability to supervise and work collaboratively with food and beverage personnel.

■ **Position** Catering manager

Description This manager sells food and beverages and related services for banquets. The job involves working directly with the staff and the clients—such as convention organizers and local groups—as well as supervising the banquet service.

Qualifications Sales experience, interpersonal skills, a talent for details, and a flair for entertaining are needed.

■ **Position** Executive housekeeper

Description This key position brings responsibility for training, scheduling and supervising all housekeeping personnel and for purchasing supplies.

Qualifications Housekeepers may be promoted to this position, but, in some hotels, it requires management experience. Leadership ability and knowledge of inventory control, scheduling, hiring, and training are needed.

■ **Position** Concierge

Description The concierge recommends and makes reservations for restaurants, activities, and attractions and answers guests' questions about how to get around, what is open and when, and where to find just about anything. The concierge also arranges limousines and babysitting services, books accommodations in other cities and provides information on an incredible variety of subjects. In short, the concierge aims to satisfy a guest's every wish.

Qualifications Prior experience is not essential, but the concierge must possess a wealth of knowledge and great resourcefulness, as well as a polished, professional demeanor and can-do attitude. Other prerequisites include personal knowledge of the destination, excellent interpersonal skills, understanding of the hotel industry, and proficiency in two or more languages.

■ **Position** Programmer analyst (for a hotel company)

Description This professional is responsible for the day-to-day operation and support of the forecast management system as well as programming enhancements.

Qualifications Employers look for two to three years of programming experience, experience in developing web-based applications, and a thorough understanding of relevant technical subjects, such as relational database design.

■ **Other positions** Convention sales director; engineering and facility maintenance specialist; resident manager; sales representative; security specialist.

rooms and too few guests. When the economy weakened, the hotel industry lost money for six straight years.

In the 1990s, the lodging industry responded to economic challenges by expanding overseas and competing with many of the world's most famous hotels (see Figure 6.2), by developing new forms of ownership and management, and by marketing itself aggressively. As the U.S. economy boomed, the 1990s became the most profitable era ever for the hotel industry. It took advantage of new technology to improve management, marketing, and services. For example, most hotels of any size set up their own websites. They put computers, fax machines, and photocopiers in office centers for guests and installed data ports in rooms. And, increasingly, hotels used computers to track the preferences of frequent guests and to personalize services, such as in-room snacks and the kinds of pillows requested previously.

Today, the U.S. landscape features motor hotels around small cities and towns, large downtown city hotels, airport lodgings of all kinds, and resorts for every budget. Two trends that helped spark the industry's growth in the 1990s continue today: (1) consolidation of ownership and management and (2) specialization in the product offered, as a result of aggressive marketing.

FIGURE 6.2 A Sampling of Some of the World's Great Hotels

City	Hotel	Comments
Athens	Grande Bretagne	Built in 1842, originally a private mansion. Fabulous views of the Acropolis and Parthenon.
Bangkok	Mandarin Oriental	Opened 1876. List of celebrities who have stayed here reads like Who's Who. On the banks of the Chao Phraya River.
Cairo	Marriott Mena House	Built in 1886. Lies at foot of Pyramid of Cheops. Former royal hunting lodge turned luxury resort.
Hawaii	Halekulani	Much-loved Waikiki Beach hotel, known as "House Befitting Heaven" in the Hawaiian language.
Hong Kong	Peninsula	Opened 1928. Flagship property of Peninsula Hotels. Rooftop heliport for guests, famed for afternoon tea in the lobby.
London	Savoy	Opened 1889. Built with profits from Gilbert & Sullivan operas. Famous for its dance bands and Art Deco jazz era.
New York	Plaza	Founded in 1907. Landmark property, setting of *Eloise* children's books and many films. Afternoon tea a must.
Paris	Ritz	Opened 1898. Fashion designer Coco Chanel and author Ernest Hemingway lived here for years. Diana, Princess of Wales, dined here before her 1997 death in a car crash.
Québec	Château Frontenac	Opened 1893. Overlooks St. Lawrence River. Built by Canadian Pacific Railway, managed by Fairmont.
Rio de Janeiro	Copacabana Palace	Opened 1923. Home of rich and famous, including Elton John, the Rolling Stones, and Madonna. Faces Copacabana Beach.
Singapore	Raffles	Opened 1887. Singapore Sling cocktail originated here. Hangout for authors Ernest Hemingway and Somerset Maugham.
Vienna	Danieli	Formerly 14th-century home of noble Venetian family. Handmade Murano glass chandeliers, carved marble columns.

Private room and home rentals continue to take hold of the industry, creating competition for traditional lodging types. Companies, such as Airbnb, VRBO, and HomeAway, provide opportunities to private home owners to list and rent their properties to the traveling public. These options can range from a shared room in someone's home, to a private luxury estate that can sleep 30+ guests. They have given other lodging types a big opportunity to compete in terms of pricing, location, and service.

Ownership and Organization

Some of the world's finest hotels still operate independently, and travelers can still find *properties* (lodging establishments) with a unique character. But much as the local coffee shop has given way to Starbucks and the family diner to McDonald's, large companies dominate the lodgings market. Chains of one sort or another have spread around the globe.

Hotel Affiliations. A *chain* consists of a group of affiliated properties that bear the same name, follow the same operating procedures and standards, and share a reservation system. Holiday Inn, Sheraton, Hilton, Marriott, Ramada, and Days Inn are familiar examples. Chains of every size and kind are available.

The success of chains is easy to understand. A chain is like a *brand* name: people expect consistency from one example of the brand to the next. Travelers who go to a motel with the same name at an airport in Topeka and at the seaside in Galveston expect to get the same level of service and the same amenities, in a similar atmosphere, at similar prices relative to other motels in the area. To the travel counselor, the chain represents an easily accessible inventory of rooms with predictable standards. Reservations can be easily confirmed. Tour operators love the consistency of rooms for groups so that all tour participants receive equal rooms. Thus, a chain provides a sense of security: The seller knows what is being sold, and the client knows what is being purchased.

More difficult to understand than the popularity of chains is the variety of ways they are organized. Some chains are owned by other chains or by a conglomerate (see Table 6.1). For example, Marriott Hotels, Courtyard by Marriott, and Ritz-Carlton are all owned by Marriott, catering to different market segments. Many fast-growing chains are franchise operators. The *franchise company* provides the use of the name, a central reservation system, advertising, and training. The *franchisee* owns the hotel but pays a fee to the parent company and must meet its standards.

Management contracts represent another approach to ownership and management. Hotel companies manage hotels under contract with the owners. The management contract gives the operator the right to manage the property without the owner's interference; the owner is responsible for operating and financing costs.

Best Western International is an example of yet another arrangement: a *membership organization*. The members are individually owned and operated hotels that share a reservation system as well as marketing, purchasing, and other services. Member properties retain their independence and individuality, but they benefit from their identification with the image of Best Western, which is marketed to the public.

Hotel Representative Firms. Whatever its type of ownership and management, a hotel might turn to a hotel representative firm for help in staying competitive. ***Hotel representative firms,*** or ***repping firms,*** accept reservations and provide marketing and sales help. Rep firms in the United States include Leading Hotels of the World, Preferred Hotels, and Utell.

For hotels, repping firms provide

- Reservation systems that use toll-free numbers.
- A staff that works extended hours.
- Tie-ins with the major GDSs (global distribution systems, discussed in Chapter 3).
- Pooled marketing, including direct mail, advertising, and participation at trade shows.
- The enhanced image that comes from being represented by a well-known firm.

Thus, a hotel repping firm acts like a large sales force. These firms can be especially helpful to individually owned or remote hotels that cannot afford their own sales force.

For travel agencies, repping firms may provide

- Up-to-date information on what's new at a given hotel.
- Information about what rooms are available in a city.
- An easy way of making reservations for overseas hotels.
- Confirmation of reservations immediately or within 24 hours for remote properties.
- Substantial discounts in many cases.
- A personal, perhaps local, face to a property.
- Speedy commission payments to the booking travel agency.

TABLE 6.1 A Sampling of Largest Hotel Companies and Their Brands, 2018

Organization/Web Site	Properties	Major Brand Names
Accor www.accor.com	4,300 in 92 countries	Ibis, Novotel, Pullman, Mercure, Sofitel, Adagio, Fairmont, Raffles, MGallery, and others
Best Western www.bestwestern.com	4,200 in 100 countries	All hotels independently owned but carry Best Western name. They have different collections, including BW Signature, Best Western Plus, and Best Western Premier.
Choice Hotels www.choicehotels.com	6,600 in United States and abroad	Clarion, Comfort Inn, Econo Lodge, Mainstay Suites, Quality Inns, Rodeway, Sleep Inns, Suburban Extended Stay, Ascend, and Cambria.
Hilton Worldwide www.hiltonworldwide.com	5,400 in 94 countries	Conrad Hotels & Resorts, Doubletree, Embassy Suites, Hampton Inns, Hilton Garden Inn, Hilton Hotels & Resorts, Homewood Suites, Waldorf Astoria Hotels, and others
Intercontinental Hotels Group www.ichotelsgroup.com	5,400 in nearly 100 countries	Candlewood Suites, Crowne Plaza, Holiday Inn, Holiday Inn Express, Hotel Indigo, Kimpton, Intercontinental Hotels and Resorts, Staybridge
Marriott International www.marriott.com	6,900 in United States and over 100 countries	Courtyard by Marriott, Marriott Hotels, Resorts and Inns, Renaissance Inns, Ritz-Carlton, Springhill Suites, Townplace Suites, Fairfield Inns + Suites, Ritz Carlton, St. Regis Collection, Gaylord Hotels, Westin, Sheraton, W Hotels, The Luxury Collection, and others.

Source: Individual Web sites for each firm listed.

Some repping firms are, in effect, consolidators for hotels in many big cities. **Hotel consolidators** buy up blocks of rooms from hotels at favorable prices and then resell them at discounted rates; Hotel Reservations Network is an example. Consolidators may be able to provide rooms when a hotel is sold out or offer rooms at prices lower than those offered by the hotel itself.

Similar to hotel repping firms, there are hotel booking engines geared toward the travel industry that provides similar services. Agents can access these sites to find pricing and make reservations for different lodging types around the globe. These sites pull pricing from multiple sources, such as GDSs, online travel agencies, and directly from the hotels' inventory. Travel professionals then can confirm reservations with ease, manage the bookings and track their commissions. Examples of these booking tools include CCRA and ABC Global Services.

Marketing Segments

Aggressive marketing has been another response of the lodging industry to increased competition. The industry has created an ever-wider variety of specialized types of accommodations, targeting more specific *market segments*. What are these segments?

The accommodations market can be segmented in numerous ways, including the following:

- *By location.* A company might aim to attract travelers needing accommodations at airports, downtown, or at the beach, for example.
- *By purpose of the usage.* Figure 6.3 applies this type of market segmentation, analyzing whether guests at U.S. hotels are traveling for business, pleasure, or other purposes.
- *By current needs.* Honeymooners, families with children, and people attending a religious convention, for example, are likely to look for different things in a hotel.
- *By attitudes and interests*—in other words, *psychographics.* People who enjoy scuba diving and those who want to spend their time shopping are likely to be attracted by different features.
- *By price,* probably the most often used basis of segmentation. Analyzed by price, the lodging market can be divided into six segments: strict budget, economy, budget luxury, mid-priced, first class, and luxury. Table 6.2 describes accommodations that target each of these segments.

Many large hotel companies target specific market segments by developing or buying up brands for different market segments. The Marriott chain is one example. It operates Fairfield Inn for the economy segment; Courtyard for the mid-priced segment; Marriott Hotels, Resorts, and Suites for first-class lodging; and Ritz-Carlton for luxury.

Successful companies adapt to changes in market segments, as the history of Club Med illustrates. Established shortly after World War II as a tent village on the Mediterranean island of Majorca for a French clientele, Club Med introduced vacations featuring fun, sun, and *joie de vivre* for one fee covering transportation, lodging, three meals a day, and a multitude of sports and leisure activities. It first catered to young singles and couples. As its clientele aged and had children, Club Med adapted. At many locations, it set up activity centers for children of different ages (including Baby Clubs, Petit Clubs, and Mini Clubs). Parents can drop their children off at the centers for the day. Today, Club Med has over 60 villages and all-inclusive resorts in 28 world destinations.

FIGURE 6.3

U.S. Lodging Customers, 2015: Segmentation by Usage

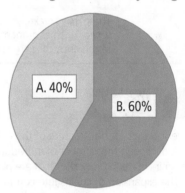

| A. Business travelers | 40% |
| B. Leisure travelers | 60% |

This chart shows the main purposes for the trips being taken by guests at U.S. hotels.

Source: Data from *AH&LA 2016 Lodging Profile.*

TABLE 6.2 Segmentation of Hotels by Price

Segment	Description	Examples
Strict budget	Basically, these are no-frills hotels that offer the lowest rates. They have only a small lobby or no lobby, no restaurant, and few amenities in the rooms. There may be just a rack to hang clothes and limited drawer space and furniture.	Motel 6, Microtel
Economy	Compared with strict-budget properties, these offer slightly expanded amenities—such as slightly upgraded decor, an extra chair, larger double-bed rooms, and sometimes a continental breakfast. Many have a restaurant and an outdoor pool.	Super 8, Red Roof Inn, Fairfield Inn, Travelodge
Budget luxury	These may have only small lobbies and few facilities. However, the rooms may have more furniture and be slightly larger than those in economy lodgings. They are more likely to have outdoor swimming pools and room amenities, such as shampoo and lotion, and they may have more offerings for continental breakfast.	Comfort Inn, Hampton Inn
Mid-priced	Compared with budget-luxury lodgings, these provide more room amenities and facilities, a 24-hour desk attendant, restaurants, lounges, and room service. Often, mid-priced hotels are located near convention facilities.	Holiday Inn, Quality Inn, Ramada Inn, Courtyard Inn
First class	These offer tastefully furnished, very comfortable, and well-designed public areas and rooms; a choice of restaurants and bars; 24-hour room service; and health clubs. Some have an indoor swimming pool and concierge service.	Sheraton, Hilton, Marriott, Embassy Suites
Luxury	These may be extravagantly lavish or exceptionally tasteful and elegant. They have impeccable service, lobbies of marble and brass, health clubs, spas, in-room minibars, haute cuisine restaurants, concierge service, and many suites.	Ritz-Carlton, Westin, Four Seasons, Hyatt, Wyndham

✔ CHECK-UP

Recent trends in the structure of the lodging industry include
✔ A decline in the number of individually owned properties.
✔ An increase in properties that are part of chains.
✔ The expansion of chains into countries around the globe.
✔ Private home ownership rentals creating competition for traditional lodging options.

For customers and sellers, the advantages of lodgings that are part of a chain include

✔ Predictable standards.
✔ Readily confirmed reservations.

Two important ways of segmenting the accommodations market are segmentation
✔ By the purpose of the guest's trip.
✔ By price, which yields six segments: strict budget, economy, budget luxury, mid-priced, first class, and luxury.

Evaluating Accommodations

■ WHAT ARE THE MAIN TYPES AND KEY CHARACTERISTICS OF ACCOMMODATIONS?

While the world may be getting smaller, what a lodging should provide differs in many countries. Many Europeans, for example, might not expect a private bath but would be shocked to find no bidet (a fixture useful for bathing the genitals and posterior parts of the body). On the other hand, many Americans might be surprised to find no elevator or baggage service in some of the less expensive European lodgings. Likewise, Americans who rent a car in Europe are often frustrated to find their lodging has no garage or parking lot. So, travel counselors well informed about the different types of worldwide accommodations are better equipped to match their clients' needs with an appropriate property.

But giving good advice can be challenging, largely because (1) accommodations vary tremendously and (2) judgments about accommodations are unusually subjective. Travelers often develop expectations that can be hard to define and even harder to match. A good first step in learning to evaluate accommodations is to become familiar with some of the major types of lodgings that are available.

Kinds of Accommodations

1. **Commercial hotels** are generally located in a city. They are most used by business travelers, particularly during the week, and by leisure travelers more often on weekends, both individually and as part of package tours.

2. **Convention hotels** cater to business travelers and groups that do not need to leave the property to conduct their business. Convention hotels are usually first class and up. Sometimes they are directly attached to or connected to a city's convention center, or, sometimes, they may have trade/exposition space available within the hotel itself.

3. **Airport hotels** are convenient for travelers departing on early-morning flights and for those not needing to go downtown. Many offer parking packages for travelers who may like to leave their car at the hotel for a week or two while they are traveling. Most airport hotels have complimentary shuttle service between the property and the nearby airport. Many airport hotels are members of major chains.

4. **All-Suites** offer rooms that have separate sleeping and living areas. The typical all-suite unit provides a living room, sleeping area, and kitchenette. Some all-suites are termed **extended-stay hotels**. These cater to people intending to stay for weeks or even months and offer such services as weekly housekeeping and coin laundromats but may eliminate amenities, such as daily maid service. They are popular with businesspeople planning to be in a sales area or territory for some time or for families that are relocating to a different city but have not yet found permanent housing. An example would be Residence Inn by Marriott. In Europe, all-suites are sometimes called self-catering apartments.

5. **Bed and Breakfasts** (B&Bs) appeal to travelers looking for lodging with a unique character and a taste of the local life. The concept began in Britain, where the B&Bs are best suited for budget travelers. In the United States, a beautiful old home that offers a full breakfast in the morning is usually thought of as a B&B. In practice, the building can be almost anything; but to be called a B&B, it should be a small establishment that emphasizes personal attention and offers individually decorated rooms with some special character. Usually, they are individually owned and operated, often by retired couples.

   B&Bs have the advantage of being homey and friendly, but they may allow less privacy than other accommodations. Guests may have to share bathroom facilities and follow the rules of the house, such as when to play the television (if there is one). Sometimes the hosts will offer complimentary afternoon tea or perhaps a glass of sherry in the evening. Also, some B&Bs have evening lock-out hours.

6. **Inns** are generally somewhat larger than B&Bs, offer a dining room and function more like hotels. Still, a true inn provides a great deal of local character and personal service. In practice, however, the term is used very loosely.

Hostels frequently feature bunk beds and basic accommodations.

7. **Hostels** are usually dorm-like accommodations and used to be called youth hostels, with rather rigid rules, hours, and the like. Today, they are usually open to those of all ages in most of the world.

8. **Motels** (short for motor hotels) cater to motorists. The classic motel is a building with just one or two stories, ample parking (usually at the guestroom door) and very limited food service, if any. Today's motels are often more elaborate than the classic model. When they consist of several stories and offer food service and recreational facilities, they are sometimes classified as **motor inns.** Other classifications distinguish motor hotels and motor lodges, but the differences among all these are rather slight and the various names are often used interchangeably.

9. **Resorts** provide a vacation in themselves. These are not places just to spend the night. They are meant to attract guests for a lengthy stay. In fact, many resorts, especially in the Caribbean, will not accept guests for fewer than three nights, and many resort packages are sold in one-week segments only. Most resorts are in the first-class or deluxe category. They may have wide-ranging facilities for daytime entertainment, nightlife, dining, shopping, and special activities, such as golf, tennis, skiing, water sports, or gambling.

CLOSE-UP: ON THE JOB WITH TAMMY JOHNS, FRONT DESK CLERK

Tammy Johns's hotel is a first-class establishment but one without luxuries, such as a huge lobby. Tammy handles the check-in process, but employees are trained to take responsibility for anything a guest might need. Most of her time is spent behind the check-in desk.

"My basic job is to rent rooms. But my real job is to be as pleasant as possible, so people will enjoy their stay from the moment they enter. Even if people don't look too friendly when they walk in, I've got to remember they may be tired from working all day or even from traveling and sightseeing.

"I greet them and ask for their name. I ask them how their day or trip was while looking up their reservation. I assign them a room, have them sign a charge slip, and give them their key or coded door card. I give directions to the room and ask if there's anything else they need.

"If they don't have a reservation, I ask how many persons are with them, how many beds they need, and so on, and then quote them a rate. This is usually fairly routine, but not always. At certain times, we have a lot of empty rooms, and I'm graded on how many walk-ins I can convert and at what price. I'm given a sample rate, which is already lower than our regular rate. I can then go down from there if I think the client will walk out. A lot depends on the time of day the client comes in.

"Sometimes you can tell just by how people walk in that they are staying at this hotel no matter what. Others, you are not too sure of, especially if they ask about the rate as their first question. When you lower your rate, you give

some reason—maybe they get a corporate rate or belong to a motor club. Then again, maybe they're not and you say, 'I can give you that motor club rate anyway tonight because of such and such.' Or, 'Oh, I see I have a room on the lower floor toward the back for only X dollars; it's the last one left there. It's a good value if you don't mind being at the end of the corridor.'

"The important thing is that you don't want them to walk out. On the other hand, there is a limit to what we can do with the rate, and we can't go below a certain level. Our manager keeps records of how many walk-ins we sell and what the average rate is and compares us to each other.

"We help out on phones when the reservationist is out to lunch, update computer records, and try to answer clients' questions. I like clients who ask questions about where they are because then I can play concierge. Our hotel is fairly large, but it's nowhere near the point where it would have a concierge. We visited with one on a trip to Phoenix. I decided that that is something I would really like to do.

"Anyway, just ask me about places to eat in my town, and I'll be ready with an answer and make a reservation for you. And I'm ready with information on the city or the airport. We have information in racks, but I'm ready with schedules and updates at the desk. I've compiled many of them myself, and I leave it for the others at the front desk. There's usually a front desk cashier who handles checkout. But when she's busy, I can do that also.

"I was hired directly after graduating from a hotel program at a two-year college. I plan to make this my career."

Group and convention business is a staple for many resorts; new ones are built with special facilities for meetings.

10. ***All-inclusives*** are resorts that charge one basic rate for just about everything. Meals, entertainment, sports, educational classes, and the room are usually included in the price. The pioneer of all-inclusives is Club Med. Other popular all-inclusives are AMResorts (Secrets, Zoetry, Dreams, etc.) and Sandals, to mention just a few of a wide selection of properties. Some cater to special markets, such as families, newlyweds, adults only, and so on. One specialty all-inclusive is the ***dude ranch*** found in many U.S. western states. Such facilities include horseback riding excursions and classes, hayrides, square dancing, and other ranch-style activities.

11. ***Spas*** are a special type of resort that emphasizes health, diet, and fitness. They have a long history in Europe, often built near mineral springs. (The name comes from the first letters of the Latin phrase *salus per aqua*, meaning "health through water.") European spas typically have a medical focus; visits may be prescribed as treatment for illnesses and may be paid for by health insurance. Throughout history, many royal families and bon vivants took to the spa to compensate for a social season of over-eating, and names like Bath, Baden-Baden, Marienbad, and Saratoga Springs came to be known in literature. In the United States, spa popularity has soared. Many resorts feature spa treatments, and day spas have come of age as well.

12. ***Pensions*** (pronounced *pahn-see-ohn*) are usually small, family-run lodgings in Europe that may be operated much like a hotel or B&B. In German-speaking countries, a pension might be called a *gasthaus*; in Italy, a *pensione*. Other countries have different names. They usually serve three meals a day included in the price (***full pension*** or board) while some operate on the basis of breakfast and dinner (demi-pension or half-board). Similar lodgings in Japan are called ***minshukus*** and follow Japanese traditions.

13. ***Châteaux***, ***castles***, and ***villas*** might be described as very upscale inns. Visitors might stay in one room of a medieval castle or rent an entire villa. Villa rentals, with chef and private swimming pool, have become very popular in Italy, Mexico, and other areas and are an attractive offering for small groups of friends or extended families.

14. The ***parador*** in Spain and the ***pousada*** in Portugal are specialized inns that may be housed in a castle, palace, or fortress. These are government-owned and -run and carry ratings from mid-priced to luxury. Puerto Rico also uses the parador designation for a limited number of its local inns, often simpler than those in Spain.

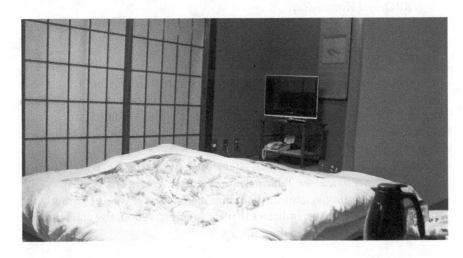

Ryokan inn in Japan with tatami mats for sleeping

15. **Ryokan** are found in Japan and are local upscale inns that retain many Japanese traditions, such as sleeping on futons on the floor on tatami mats, wearing *yukatas* (cotton sleeping kimonos), and featuring Japanese cuisine. Beautiful gardens or natural scenery often surround the ryokan. Usually only Japanese is spoken. Traditional baths, geisha entertainment, and massage are often available.

16. **Tented camps** and **tree lodges** are for travelers on safari. They consist of structures built on stilts, usually above an animal watering hole, and can be found in eastern Africa. Some can be simple and rustic; others are extremely deluxe, complete with oriental carpets on the floor. In southern Africa, circular lodgings known as **rondavels** may provide inexpensive accommodations. Some offer neither bedding nor bath; others are comfortable, air-conditioned cottages with fully equipped kitchens.

17. **Boatels** are motels for those who may arrive by private boat, rather than by car, obviously located on rivers, inland waterways, and so on. The lodging itself may be on boats as well.

18. **Casinos** are often operated in conjunction with hotels or major resorts, such as in Las Vegas and other areas where gambling may be legalized.

19. **Retreat-Style Accommodations** are often a full complex designed for organizations or companies that wish to have a retreat for meetings, educational activities, and the like. Often, they are somewhat rustic in nature, perhaps with cabins surrounding a central meeting house and dining facility. An example would be Asilomar Conference Grounds overlooking the ocean at Pacific Grove on the Monterey Peninsula in Northern California.

20. **Lodges** may often be found in U.S. National Parks, usually historic and rustic in appearance, but not necessarily inexpensive. Examples are the Ahwahnee Hotel in Yosemite, Grand Canyon Lodge on the north rim of the Grand Canyon, or Old Faithful Inn in Yellowstone Park. These lodgings are heavily booked during the summer months, often a year in advance.

21. **Self-catering rental apartments and home rentals** are furnished flats or apartments, available in some major cities, such as London, Paris, Sydney, Istanbul, and in some beach communities, such as Spain's Costa del Sol. They can be found anywhere around the world. They provide a good option for families and business people seeking a more home-like atmosphere when on a business trip or on a lengthy vacation in one location. They can range from a furnished room in someone's home to private luxury estate rental. There are several companies that provide owners that opportunity to list and market their apartments and homes. These include Airbnb, VRBO, and HomeAway.

Emerald Lake Lodge in Yoho National Park in the Rocky Mountains, British Columbia, Canada

Rating Systems

In some countries, the government runs a formal rating system for accommodations. For example, both Spain and Italy rate their hotels from one star (strictly budget) to five stars (deluxe). The United States has no official rating system, but many references and guidebooks publish their own. Among the best known are

- The 10-category classification system used by Northstar Travel Group's *Hotel & Travel Index* (see Table 6.3) (www.travelweekly.com/Hotels).
- The five-star rating system in the online *Forbes Travel Guide* (formerly the *Mobil Guides*). One star indicates that the lodging is good; five stars indicate that it is one of the best in the country.

- A similar five-diamond rating system in the *AAA Guidebooks,* which are available to any member of AAA.

What Affects the Price of a Room?

The variations in accommodations are at least matched by the variety in their prices. The **rack rate** is the "regular" posted or "off-the-street" price of a room. It is generally the highest rate charged for that room except during special events, such as the Olympics. However, a standard twin-bedded room of the same chain may run $450 per night in London or $109 in a suburb of Akron, Ohio. Although the two rooms are not identical, why the huge difference? The difference in rate is often based on location. At any given hotel, people will be paying many different rates within the same hotel for identical rooms on the same night.

Like the airlines, hotels practice *yield management* (discussed in Chapter 4): They aim to maximize rates and occupancy to produce the highest daily average revenue for all rooms on any given day. Computer reservation systems permit them to adjust prices on a day-to-day, often

---

TABLE 6.3 Hotel & Travel Index Classification System

1. **Superior Deluxe** An exclusive and expensive luxury hotel, often palatial, offering the highest standards of service, accommodations, and facilities; elegant and luxurious public rooms; and a prestigious address. Establishments in this category are among the world's top hotels.

2. **Deluxe** An outstanding property offering many of the same features as Superior Deluxe. May be less grand and offer more reasonable rates than the Superior Deluxe properties, yet in many instances may be just as satisfactory. Safe to recommend to most discriminating clients.

3. **Moderate Deluxe** Basically a Deluxe hotel, but with qualifications. In some cases, some accommodations or public areas may offer a less pronounced degree of luxury than that found in fully Deluxe properties. In other cases, the hotel may be a well-established famous name, depending heavily on past reputation. The more contemporary hotels may be heavily marketed to business clients, with fine accommodations and public rooms offering Deluxe standards in comfort, but with less emphasis on atmosphere and/or personal service.

4. **Superior First Class** An above-average hotel. May be an exceptionally well-maintained older hotel, but more often a superior modern hotel specifically designed for the First-Class market, with some outstanding features. Accommodations and public areas are expected to be tastefully furnished and very comfortable. May be a good value, especially if it is a commercial hotel. May be recommended to average clients and, in most cases, will satisfy the discriminating ones.

5. **First Class** A dependable, comfortable hotel with standardized rooms, amenities, and public areas. May have a superior executive level or wing. May be safely recommended to average clients not expecting Deluxe facilities or special services. Should also be satisfactory for better groups.

6. **Limited-Service First Class** A property offering full First-Class quality accommodations but limited public areas, food service, and facilities. Usually moderate in size, the hotel often uses a residential scale and architecture, and many offer complimentary breakfast and evening cocktails in the lobby or in a small, informal restaurant. Geared to the individual business/pleasure traveler.

7. **Moderate First Class** Essentially a First-Class establishment with comfortable but somewhat simpler accommodations and public areas. May be lacking in some features (e.g., restaurant). Some of the rooms or public areas, while adequate, may tend to be basic and functional. Usually suitable for cost-conscious clients.

8. **Superior Tourist Class** Primarily a budget property with mostly well-kept, functional accommodations, some up to First-Class standards. Public rooms may be limited or nonexistent. Often just a place to sleep but may have some charming or intimate features. May be good value. Should satisfy individuals (sometimes even discriminating ones) or groups on a budget.

9. **Tourist Class** Strictly a budget operation with some facilities or features of Superior Tourist Class, but usually no (or very few) First-Class accommodations. Should not be recommended to fussy or discriminating clients.

10. **Moderate Tourist Class** A low-budget operation, often quite old and may not be well maintained. Should only be used in a pinch if no others are available. Clients should always be cautioned what to expect.

Source: Northstar Travel Group's *Hotel & Travel Index*

moment-to-moment basis. As demand weakens, the hotel offers lower prices or discounts requiring advance bookings. As demand builds, consumers must pay more for the same product.

In fact, accommodation rates can vary almost as much as airline rates. Airlines will at least have particular rules in effect at a given moment. Accommodation rates sometimes depend on a decision by the person taking the reservation. Still, there are some constant factors that affect the price of a room. In this section, we look first at the factors that influence the room price and then at different types of rates. Note that the prices quoted by hotels may or may not include taxes, various fees, and service charges, which can be significant and should be queried. For example, some properties may automatically charge an additional resort fee whether or not the client chooses to use the pool, beach, or other such offerings.

Location of the Lodging. Location within a city or area is the single most important factor influencing the cost of a room. Commercial hotels located in the heart of a city close to convention facilities will be more expensive than those on the fringes of the city. Resort hotels on a beautiful beach can command top prices; an identical room one block from the beach would cost much less. If a hotel is the only lodging in sight in a popular area, it can charge high prices. In some countries, the government controls the number and variety of hotels in resort areas to ensure that overdevelopment does not produce either a low *occupancy rate* (the percentage of rooms occupied) or damage to the environment.

Location of the Room. Another factor affecting price is the location of a room within a hotel, which may influence the guest's convenience, view, and exposure to noise. Often, the most expensive rooms are those with the best views. An ocean view on a high floor may command top price; rooms with parking-lot views and rooms on lower floors may be the least expensive. Sometimes proximity to sources of noise influences the price. Rooms on upper floors—far from public areas, such as the lobby and pool—tend to be quieter. Rooms close to elevators are noisier, because of the opening and closing of doors and the sounds of guests in the halls.

Room Size and Furnishings. Old hotels tend to have rooms of many different sizes, and luxurious hotels usually have suites that are much like small apartments. In these hotels, the price reflects the size of the room. But in new hotels, almost all rooms are the same size; for these rooms, types of fixtures or decor, rather than size, shape the price.

Most Americans expect a hotel room to contain a comfortable bed, chairs, a dresser, a desk, good lighting, a closet with hangers, a television set, a telephone, a private bathroom with sink, a toilet, a bathtub with shower, and, of course, heat and air conditioning. Beyond these items, amenities—such as balconies, WiFi, and ergonomic chairs—may add to the price of a room.

Occupancy. Different rates may be cited, depending on the number of beds as well as the number of occupants. A room with one double bed, one queen- or king-size bed, or two twin beds usually has two rates: *single* (one person) and *double* (two persons). A room with two double or two queen- or king-size beds may have four rates: single, double, *triple* (three persons), and *quad* (four persons). Or the hotel may simply have an add-on rate for each extra person in a room. Triple may often be a twin room for two with a rollaway brought in for the third person. Rates for more than four persons in a room are usually not offered.

Most hotel rooms are designed for two people. When a room is rented as a single, a hotel loses revenue, not only on the room, but also on possible purchases of food, drink, and activities. Thus, hotels may charge as much for a single room as for a double room—which means that the person with a single room is paying twice as much on a per-person basis as those in a double room. Some hotels, particularly older hotels, may actually have single rooms, but such rooms should not be sold as being better. Often, they are the maid's room made over or similar inferior rooms or location within the property.

Friends or family members may ask for **adjoining rooms,** which are rooms located next to each other that have separate entrances and no means of going directly from one room to the other, or they may ask for **connecting rooms,** which are linked by a common door inside the rooms. There is no extra cost for adjoining or connecting rooms, but travel counselors must be careful to be sure the client understands the different terminology.

For little or no extra cost, most hotels provide cribs or rollaway beds for small children sharing a room with their parents. Many chains have a "kids-free" policy: there is no extra charge for children occupying the same room as long as no additional beds are needed.

Meals. Room rates in the United States usually do not include meals unless specifically stated. Outside the United States, hotels usually offer the following choice of meal plans:

- **European plan (EP).** No meals are included.
- **Continental plan (CP).** A light, or continental, breakfast is included.
- **Bermuda plan (BP).** A fully cooked breakfast is included.
- **Modified American plan (MAP).** Breakfast and one other main meal, usually dinner, are included. This plan is called **demi-pension** in Europe. Some hotels provide a **dine-around plan**; it gives MAP guests a credit toward dinner at other hotels or restaurants within the same resort property or around town.
- **American plan (AP).** Usually three meals are included. This is also called **full board** or **full pension**.

Table 6.4 describes these plans in more detail. EP and BP are desirable when various affordable restaurants are nearby; AP and MAP may be attractive if a hotel is isolated or if nearby restaurants are expensive. MAP makes it easier to predict the total cost of a vacation, and the plan saves guests the cost and inconvenience of transportation to and from restaurants. Also, it is usually less expensive to eat dinner as an MAP guest than to select items from the menu on an à la carte basis.

Other variations in meal service include whether the hotel offers *table d'hôte* (a set menu at a fixed price) or serves *à la carte* (with a choice of individually priced items from a menu). À la carte dining, where one may order whatever one wants from the menu, is offered only on very deluxe tours.

Special Facilities and Service. Hotels follow the lead of their guests in determining what is a frill and what is a necessity. For example, even strict budget properties in most climates usually have free swimming pools. But kiddie pools, tennis courts, beach clubs, saunas, game rooms, nightclubs, golf courses, racquet clubs, health clubs, room service, and having both indoor and outdoor pools are all special features that are reflected in room rates. One new trend is to charge a daily resort fee, even if guests do not use the amenities and which many guests resent having to pay for if not using. Travel professionals must communicate the hotel rate, taxes, and all additional fees to their clients.

TABLE 6.4 Meal Plans

EP: European plan No meals are included. This is typical in the United States and many big cities around the world. Many U.S. hotels, however, now offer coffee in the room or in the lobby, and there is a trend toward offering continental buffet breakfasts.

CP: Continental plan A light breakfast is provided, but the quantity and contents vary with local customs. For example, in the United States, France, Italy, and Spain, it is likely to include croissants or bread, jams, and coffee or tea. In Germany and Scandinavia, other items would be added, such as a buffet of meats, cheeses, cereals, fruits, and even boiled eggs.

BP: Bermuda plan A fully cooked breakfast is provided but no other meals. Generally speaking, hotels that offer BP are resorts.

MAP: Modified American plan (or demi-pension) Breakfast and one other main meal, usually dinner, are included. In many countries, dinner is the midday meal. MAP is popular in the resorts of the Bahamas, Bermuda, the Caribbean, and Mexico. Some hotels limit choices from the menu for MAP guests; diners who want a specialty, such as lobster, pay a surcharge. Some U.S. hotels give MAP clients a coupon valid for a meal in a specific dining room up to a specified dollar amount; guests pay for anything beyond that limit.

AP: American plan (or full board or full pension) All three meals are included. Ranches, spas, and resorts that are isolated, or at which clients spend almost all their time, usually offer AP. Cruise ships and all-inclusive resorts offer AP, although they may not use the term.

Hotel companies are vying with one another to provide useful technology for business travelers. Most provide high-speed Internet access in the rooms. Even Marriott's least expensive brand, Fairfield Inns, offers fax and copy services. Many hotels have an office center on their ground floor with computers, printers, copy machines, and various business supplies. Most of these features are complimentary, but others, such as teleconferencing and clerical service, are arranged and paid for as needed.

Quality of service also makes a difference. If a hotel offers round-the-clock room service or a *concierge*—a staff member who provides information and other help to guests—then the extra attention is likely to show up in the price of the room.

Price Level and Currency Value. The general price level in an area also influences room rates. Many things besides hotel rooms are more expensive in New York and Tokyo, for example, than in Durham, North Carolina, or Milwaukee, Wisconsin.

For lodgings overseas, the room rate also varies with fluctuations in the currency exchange rate. For clients who pay a hotel bill in U.S. dollars, the exchange rate used will be the rate in effect on the *day of payment*, not the day of booking. Many international hotels require full pre-payment at the time of booking, which locks in the currency exchange rate at the time of that booking and payment. If a hotel advertises a rate in U.S. dollars, this amount reflects the exchange rate on the day the brochure or advertisement was printed and is not guaranteed. Travel counselors should quote rates in the local currency, if possible, and explain them to travelers. For those who pay an international hotel by credit card, it's the day the transaction clears the bank that is pertinent.

Length of Stay. Some hotels offer discounts for long stays, such as a week or more. If a client is staying for a week, a lower rate should at least be requested. *Day rates*, which are available for those not staying overnight, are sometimes used for meetings, by people in the middle of long international trips, or by those who need to stay long after the check-out time.

Day and Season. If the demand for rooms fluctuates greatly with the date, the price of a room is likely to change as well. Many of the most popular vacation destinations have great seasonal fluctuations in demand and, therefore, in room rates. Sometimes the fluctuation depends on the weather at the destination, and sometimes on the weather that clients are trying to escape (such as northern winters).

Often the busy and expensive seasons for hotels are the same as the peak seasons for airfares. In particular,

- For almost the entire Caribbean and the beach destinations of Mexico, peak demand runs from approximately December 15 to April 15. Prices during this time may be double the rates during the rest of the year. Demand is usually lowest during late spring and autumn (hurricane season).
- European beach resorts are most popular in the summer (especially August, when entire countries, it seems, go on holiday). Lower prices prevail during the rest of the year, but the weather is just barely warm in many areas and may be rainy.
- During the summer, when business travel slows, major European cities may be less crowded, but small tourist towns or resorts will be packed.

European beaches, such as this one in Portimao, Portugal, are most crowded in August.

CLOSE-UP: SELLING TO THE BUDGET-MINDED

One night, a call was made to the toll-free number for a hotel chain that owns a downtown hotel in one of the nation's largest cities. The following conversation occurred:

Customer: "What would the rate be for a single room for January 27 and 28?"
Hotel chain reservationist: "Let's see. I can get you the rate of $115, um, oops, no. We can offer a rate of $95 for those nights. Would you like to place a reservation?"
C: "Do you have any weekend rates or packages?"
HCR: "Yes, we have a promotional weekend rate of $89. Can I book that for you?"
C: "No, not at the moment. I was just checking rates right now and will call back."
HCR: "OK, one second. Oh, you know, on that Saturday night I can offer you the supersaver rate of $69 and then make a separate reservation for the promotional rate of $89 for the other night. How's that? Would you like to hold that? And I can transfer you to our travel club. Once you're a member, you get a 5 percent rebate on all hotel reservations with us as well as $20 in free gas coupons."

When so many rates might be charged for a room, how can you be sure your rate is not too high? Here are some techniques for helping a client get the best rate:

- If you are dealing with a corporate client, be sure you find out ahead of time about any specially negotiated corporate rates.
- Determine in advance if your client is a member of AAA (American Automobile Association), AARP (American Association of Retired Persons), or another organization that may make the client eligible for a discount. Many hotels have a special rate or immediately discount the

rate 5 to 10 percent for members. Many give a special senior rate even if guests are not members of AARP.
- Ask for the rate first to establish a starting point. You might say something like, "What is the least expensive rate for the nights of _____?" or "Could you please quote the lowest rate available?"
- Ask for specials, corporate rates, packages, or discounts for weekends, off-season times, or lengthy stays. Often, the hotel reservationist will not offer discounted rates unless asked about them.
- Compare each discount. A weekend package rate may be lower than a corporate or AAA discount.
- Insist on the least expensive type of room if that is what your client desires. Some upscale chains pitch their more expensive rooms very aggressively. If you ask for the best rate on a standard room, you might still be given the rate for a deluxe room. But if you reject that rate, you will quickly be given the lower one.

Preferred supplier agreements (discussed in Chapters 1, 13, and 16) can also yield better rates. Agencies too small to establish these relationships on their own may get similar benefits by joining a consortium (a group of companies that pool their resources).

Sometimes better prices can be found by talking, not to the hotel, but to hotel consolidators or to hotel representative firms or by checking bargain sites online. You will discover with experience which sites really offer bargains and which are simply marketing devices.

Be sure that searching for a deal is worth the time to your agency. The room, after all, may not be commissionable, and clients looking for a bargain may not be willing to pay a service charge to the agency.

Peak seasons should be checked, not guessed at. For example, Bermuda's seasons are more similar to European than to Caribbean seasons. In Cambodia, southwestern China, and many other countries, the best seasons for travel depend greatly on the timing of the monsoons.

Demand and prices may also vary with the day of the week. Rooms at resorts are likely to be in demand on the weekends, so rates are higher then; the resort may offer special packages for midweek stays. In contrast, hotels that cater primarily to business travelers offer very low weekend rates or special packages that may include meals, drinks, or other extras at a large discount.

Special Rates. Besides promotional rates, hotels have special rates for guests who come as a group or who are members of certain groups.

- The *corporate rate* is sometimes offered to all business travelers, sometimes only to listed corporations, and sometimes to anyone who asks.
- The *negotiated corporate rate* is a rate that has been negotiated with a company or its affiliate or association. The hotel hopes to become that company's automatic choice for lodging; the company generally guarantees that it will rent a minimum number of room nights per year.
- A *group rate* represents a discount offered to a group that uses a certain number of rooms on the same night. As many as 20 rooms or as few as five might be required to qualify for a group rate, depending on the season and projected occupancy rate.
- A *net or noncommissionable rate* does not include any commission. This is the amount the accommodation is expecting to receive in full. Agents have the opportunity to mark up these rates or add a service fee. Net rates are common when booking through consolidators and when booking group space.
- A *prepaid rate* is typically a discounted rate that is offered by paying the total amount of a reservation in full at the time of booking. These rates are usually the most restrictive in terms of changes and cancellations. Most are non-refundable. Many European hotels offer these prepaid rates with discounts as high as 20% off their standard rates.
- The *Run-of-the-House (ROH)* rate is a flat rate that the hotel may offer to a travel agency for its clients. It would apply to any of its available rooms, whatever their location, at time of check-in with the understanding that the client will receive a stated minimum type of room or better if the upgrade is not available. Although the ROH rate is often offered for groups, it is not a wise policy to accept unless all members of the group can be upgraded. Group tour members are not happy clients if some receive better rooms than others when all are paying the same group price.
- The *convention rate* may reflect the largest discount. This reflects the fact that competition for meetings and conventions is keen because they typically use so many services at the hotel, giving the hotel many opportunities to increase revenue (particularly from the bar and catering services).

In addition, many hotel chains offer *frequent-guest programs,* which reward repeat guests with bonuses, such as a free room night, services, merchandise, and discounts. Hotels have innumerable tie-ins with airlines' frequent-flyer plans and with car rental companies.

Accommodations designed to provide a unique atmosphere include
- ✔ Bed-and-breakfasts.
- ✔ Inns.
- ✔ Overseas: paradores, pousadas, ryokans, pensions, and minshukus.
- ✔ Private home rentals

Types of rates charged by lodgings include
- ✔ The rack rate.
- ✔ Special rates for groups: the corporate rate, negotiated corporate rate, group rate, run-of-the-house (ROH) rate, and convention rate.

- ✔ Promotional rates that respond to changes in anticipated demand.

Other important factors influencing the price of a room include
- ✔ The location of the property.
- ✔ Room characteristics, such as its location in the lodging, size and furnishings, and number of beds and occupants.
- ✔ Special facilities and the quality of service.
- ✔ Competition in the immediate area.

Selling Accommodations

■ HOW DO HOTELS SELL THEIR ROOMS?

■ WHAT DO TRAVEL COUNSELORS NEED TO KNOW WHEN THEY MAKE A HOTEL RESERVATION?

The selling of accommodations has become a very sophisticated business. As we discuss in Chapter 9 (on marketing), hotels have found new ways to fine-tune their services to meet the changing needs and expectations of their guests. Thanks to powerful software and the Internet, hotels have also been able to target and communicate with potential guests in new and more effective ways, and many travelers now book their own hotel reservations directly online without the help of travel counselors.

Despite the Internet, travel counselors remain an important source of sales for the hotel industry for two reasons. First, travel counselors are effective promoters of hotels.

Second, travel agencies are a relatively inexpensive way for the hotel industry to promote and distribute its product. Hotels do not pay a commission to an agency until the guest completes a stay (or pre-pays a non-refundable reservation in full); commissions average 8 to 10 percent. Many strict-budget properties do not give commissions on sales, and some corporate sales are also noncommissionable.

For travel agencies, the relationship with hotels is sometimes testy, often because of lost commissions. If a client changes his or her arrival date, the hotel creates a new booking, information about the agency is deleted, and no commission is received. Similarly, if a client receives a lower rate when checking in than the originally quoted rate, then the hotel creates a new booking, and again the agency receives no commission. In addition, some commissions are lost simply as a result of mistakes in keeping track of millions of hotel rooms. Many agencies are turning to the pre-paid hotel rates to guarantee the processing and payment of their commissions.

Four Seasons Hotel Seattle

99 Union St
Seattle, WA

Rates: $$$$$

Phone: 1 206-749-7000
Fax: 1 206-749-7099
Toll Free: 800-332-3442
Web: http://www.fourseasons.com/seattle

Check in Time: 3:00PM
Check out Time: 12:00 PM
Number of Floors: 10
Total Number of Rooms: 147

STAR Rating: ★★★★★   Amenity Rating: ✓✓✓✓

Location and History

Located across First Street from the Seattle Art Museum, a block south of Pike Place Market, in a superb location for both business and leisure travelers, this hotel shares the top of Seattle's luxury heap with the more traditional Fairmont.

This hotel is set on a prominent corner plot, atop a bluff overlooking Puget Sound and the market area. The sleek 21-story bronze tower is topped with 11 floors of multimillion-dollar condominiums. With just 130 rooms and 13 suites, this formidable Four Seasons offshoot has the feel of a boutique-hotel, yet its facilities and service operate at a pace that puts the competition on alert.

Property Overview

The hotel's superbly designed modern interiors forgo any gimmicks, and regular updating keeps everything in impeccable condition. Thanks to Four Seasons' rigorous training programs and dedication to style and comfort, this refined hotel has become a city landmark.

Throughout the hotel, Pacific Rim and classic contemporary accents blend with satisfying results. Amid familiar crisp, modern lines, the designers' prominent use of natural regional elements lends a unique Northwest flair that provides what many design-hotels these days lack: a sense of place.

Also of note is the hotel's special relationship with the Seattle Art Museum. The hotel displays a revolving selection of the museum's works throughout the public areas and in a number of suites. The hotel's impressive permanent collection also honors regional artists.

Valets, bellhops and doormen work in unison under a wide stone porte cochere to swing open doors and assist with luggage. In keeping with the artistic flair of the hotel, the entrance is marked with museum-quality sculpture and landscape art.

Polished volcanic basalt rectangles line the lobby walls. The hall's crisp, angular surfaces and bold modern art are broken up with interesting organic features. The futuristic fireplace, adjacent to the reception counter, provides bench seats in the form of a cantilevered cedar trunk.

Goldfinch Tavern, a dining-room-meets-social-center laid out in modern gallery fashion, has gained a large local following. The rooms' buoyant art and colorful, alternating light displays complement the ever-changing views of Puget Sound through window-walls. All meals are served a la carte from attentive staff. The menu is Pacific Northwest.

This is by no means a resort, but recreation is varied for an urban locale with the city's highest real estate prices. The fourth floor harbors a heated, outdoor infinity lap pool with impressive bay vistas that give swimmers and sunbathers the feeling of being on a cruise ship.

Glass windblocks allow guests in the adjoining outdoor whirlpool tub to enjoy spectacular sunsets, and the flickering fire pit adds a touch of romance.

The small but well-equipped gym benefits from the same views. Both guests and residents are privy to the well-designed spa, which boasts saunas and a tranquil private lounge. A lobby shop sells local confections and opens to the street.

Accommodations

The accommodations are among the largest in the city, with the smallest City View rooms measuring 450 sq. ft.
Built with an emphasis on residential comfort, the units' well-crafted cabinetry, thoughtful lighting and custom furnishings

FIGURE 6.3 Hotels on the Web: An Example

Suppliers' websites, such as the one shown above, are just one source of information online about hotels. The excerpt shown here comes from Northstar Travel Group, which provides candid information about hotels and cruise ships worldwide. The service requires a subscription.

For travel agencies, the accommodations market represents a potential source of growth. If you are a travel counselor, how do you go about tapping this market? In this section, we look at some basic tasks involved in selling accommodations, as well as some problems frequently encountered by customers.

Recommending the Right Hotel

At the Broadmoor in Colorado Springs, Colorado, at the foot of the Rockies, guests can enjoy priceless art treasures from Europe and Asia in its halls and grand rooms. The resort was founded in 1918 by a couple who made a fortune in gold and copper mines. The Grand Hotel Suites of Raffles in Singapore contains rare prints, fine Persian carpets, and 14-foot ceilings. Opened in 1887, Raffles is noted not only for its Old World opulence but also for a history of famous and adventuresome guests.

These are just two of the world's legendary hotels. You might want to visit them, but if you were a travel counselor, would you recommend them to your clients? Matching the accommodation to the client is one of the most challenging aspects of travel counseling. The task requires knowledge of both hotels and clients.

Learning about Lodgings. The sheer number of lodgings complicates the task of finding the right hotel. A first step is to know the major companies, their brands, and the characteristics of those brands. (Look again at Tables 6.1 and 6.2.)

Second, to decide whether to recommend a particular hotel, travel counselors should know

- *The type.* For example, is it a bed-and-breakfast? A motor hotel? A luxury resort?
- *Location.* For example, is it on the beach or a mile away? Downtown or in a suburb?
- *Food service.* Is there a restaurant on the site? Room service?
- *Amenities.* Are there recreational opportunities? Entertainment? A courtesy van? A concierge?
- *Price.* What is its price segment? Are the features comparable to those at other lodgings for this segment? What discounts and packages are available?
- *Special advantages.* Do the rooms themselves offer anything extra? Is there a special attempt to meet the needs of business travelers or families or seniors?

Where would you go to find this information? Northstar Travel Group owns two key references: *Hotel & Travel Index* (travelweekly.com/Hotels) and *STAR Service Online* (starserviceonline.com). See Figure 6.3.

Hotel & Travel Index, which is online, has been an information source for more than 70 years. It uses a 10-tiered hotel classification system (refer to Table 6.3). It has details on more than 130,000 hotels, and its content is updated daily.

STAR Service Online provides hotel information and editorial commentary on 10,000 hotels worldwide. They employ an international network of travel professionals who visit each property and write about their experience. They allow travel counselors to send customized reports to clients with their logo, photo, and contact information.

Even these two resources could not adequately cover all the world's lodgings. Guidebooks and tourist offices have filled the information gap for years; today, GDSs and the Internet offer other options. For example,

Stay positive. You have called only five hotels, so many possibilities remain. Contact the tourist bureau in New Orleans. If it can't book a room for you, it can certainly tell you where to try.

Persistence is key. When you call a hotel, don't just ask for space. Say something specific about your clients—perhaps why they want a room or their flexibility about dates. A pleasant attitude, even a little humor, helps. If none of this yields a room, ask the reservationist to suggest another hotel that might have space.

Check tour operators. Often, they will be holding space in hotels that are sold out. If the tour operators don't have space, they may try to get it, and a tour operator will have more clout with the hotels, or you may be able to sell the client two spots on a tour operator's package, which, of course, includes the New Orleans hotel stay.

How far away are your clients willing to stay? (Accommodations may be available a half-hour or hour from town.) Does your agency send a lot of clients to a particular hotel chain? (A call from the chain's hotel manager to the New Orleans hotel may free up a room from the hotel manager's emergency inventory.) What are your clients willing to pay, and what kind of room are they willing to accept? (Often, space is available at the very highest and at the very lowest price. Also, during certain events, local people rent out their homes.)

BedandBreakfast.com provides more than 10,000 listings of bed and breakfasts, country and urban inns, guesthouses, lodges, cabins, historic hotels, small resorts, guest ranches, and farmhouse accommodations. You can search the site by various categories, such as location, amenities, or special needs.

Many travel professionals (and travelers) rely on websites, such as TripAdvisor, to learn about different properties and the experiences of previous guests. There are several websites available that provide reviews. It is important to discern the information as it applies to the needs of your particular client. Online booking tools, like ABC Global Services and CCRA, also allow you to learn about hotels and use filters to narrow down the hotels to those most suitable for your clients.

Learning about Clients. Along with knowledge about lodgings, travel counselors need an understanding of their clients. What matters to them? WiFi in a room may be more important than the soap. Vacation travelers complain most about service; business travelers complain about hotels that book more guests than they have rooms.

With information like this, though, you are still left with the question of whether a particular accommodation will suit a specific client. An individual client cannot be understood simply through data about market segments. In fact, from one trip to another, the client's motivation, needs, and expectations may well change. A client may want a budget hotel for an overnight stay on one trip and then, a few months later, something luxurious for a vacation. It is always important to qualify your clients by asking questions to best understand their needs and requirements for that particular trip.

Regarding any potential lodger, travel counselors should, of course, know who is traveling and when and where lodgings are needed. But they should also understand

- *The purpose for the trip.* Is it for business? Pleasure? To visit family?
- *The clients' needs and requirements.* For example, do they need smoking or nonsmoking rooms? Do they need cribs or babysitting services? Would they appreciate the brighter lighting and large-button telephones that some hotels offer in rooms for senior travelers? As we discuss in Chapter 11, some hotels now offer special services for elderly guests as well as for business travelers, children, the disabled, singles, and women.
- *The clients' preferences.* For example, do they expect to eat at the hotel, to play there, or to be entertained there? Or do they prefer to get away from the hotel? The more adventurous may wish to stay at a monastery in Tibet or in rooms above a pub in Ireland, whereas others may feel comfortable only in a familiar Holiday Inn. Asking clients what hotel they enjoyed in the past can shed a lot of light on what lodging is likely to suit them next time. Keeping a record of your clients' past travel and their lodging experience is important when helping them with future travel plans.

Contacting a Hotel

Once a hotel is selected, it can be contacted directly (by GDS, the Internet, letter, phone, or e-mail) or indirectly (through a repping firm, consolidator, or tourist bureau). The best method depends on circumstances.

Many travel agencies still make most of their hotel bookings through GDSs, and most hotel chains have a direct link to GDSs so that counselors see exactly what the hotel's own reservationists are seeing. Of course, some lodgings (such as some budget hotels and unusual properties) are not listed in GDSs.

Increasingly, travel agencies are booking hotel reservations directly on the supplier's website. Many hotel companies (Marriott and Hilton are two examples) now provide a "best-rate guarantee" for those who book on their sites. Travel agencies protect their commissions by making the reservations through the travel-agency section of the hotel's site.

The old-fashioned way of communicating in writing is sometimes best. Letters or e-mails are useful when booking very small hotels months ahead if the staff does not speak English well enough to handle a phone conversation comfortably. This includes properties that may not participating in online or GDSs.

The more upscale the hotel is, the greater the likelihood that a telephone call will be worthwhile because reservations tend to be more complicated for deluxe hotels. Toll-free numbers may connect either to the hotel chain or to the hotel itself.

Making a regular long-distance call to contact a hotel is sometimes appropriate despite the cost. For example, sometimes you can obtain a room by calling the hotel directly—even though both the GDS and a call to the hotel's toll-free number indicated that the hotel was sold out—because the hotel was holding a few rooms in reserve. Most international hotels have English-speaking personnel available, especially during regular business hours. (Keep time differences in mind.)

Contacting the hotel by e-mail offers advantages, particularly for complex reservations and especially for groups. An e-mail allows counselors to make sure details are correct; something as simple as the client's name, for example, can be misconstrued over the phone. Also, sending e-mail or a fax avoids language and time zone problems. The receiver will have time to get translations, if necessary, and the message can be sent and received anytime.

Sometimes, instead of using any of these methods to contact the hotel or hotel chain directly, it makes sense to contact a hotel representative firm, consolidator, or tourist bureau. Hotel representative firms handle many of the hotels that are not members of chains and do not have toll-free numbers. Consolidators sometimes offer lower prices or have rooms available when the hotel says it is sold out; many are on the Internet. (Most travel agencies deal only with consolidators that are on their *preferred* list or that they know are reliable.) Also, some tourism offices and convention bureaus have reservation systems to simplify accommodation bookings in their area. They operate much like hotel representatives, but payments are made directly to hotels.

Making a Reservation

When making a reservation, travel counselors should be prepared to give the following information:

- Client's full name as it appears on ID (or passport, if an international booking).
- Number of people in the party.
- Ages of children or listing as senior citizens (if eligible for rate reductions).
- Type of room desired (such as location, view, or amenities).
- Number and type of beds.
- Club memberships, such as membership in the hotel's frequent-guest program, a motor club, or AARP, which may entitle the guest to a discount or special service.
- Special requests, such as wheelchair-accessible rooms, cribs, or rollaway beds.
- Dates of arrival and departure.

- Time of arrival. (As we discuss later, this information is crucial.)
- Type of payment, and names and numbers of credit cards.

One client's name is sufficient when booking one room and usually sufficient for more than one room. But booking separate rooms under separate names has advantages. Clients can then receive their own confirmation numbers and can give their own names if they arrive separately. Counselors will have separate reservations for tracking commissions. But each separate booking also creates extra work. If one member of a family or small group is booking for everyone, one reservation and name may be enough. If the other people are known and might prefer the reservation in their own names, book them separately.

All reservations carry a confirmation or reservation number; it should be carefully noted, along with the reservationist's name and the date if the room was booked by phone. The rate, tax and service charges, and commissions due to the agency should also be noted. Be aware that commissions are paid on the hotel rate only, not on taxes and service fees.

As a travel counselor, you must recap with the client all fees associated with this booking.

Group Reservations

The mechanics of making a reservation for a group are in many ways the same as for an individual, but there are some differences. For example,
- Even the largest group may be booked in one name, but individual names (the rooming list) must be supplied by a specified date before arrival.
- The hotel will require a deposit and signed contracts. Watch carefully for a nonrefundable deposit and dates.
- The group rate quoted may include the agency's commission, or it may be a net rate, which means it does not include a commission. If the rate is net, the agency adds its own markup.

Usually, hotels have a separate department or specialist to handle reservations for groups. Travel counselors should become thoroughly comfortable making individual reservations before handling groups.

Many group reservations are made as part of a tour. The rates will be net, and the discount will depend on the size of the group, the hotel's occupancy, and the buyer's negotiating skills. Ask about a free room for the group leader and the number of sold rooms required for granting a complimentary one.

Other group reservations are made for conventions, meetings, and seminars. Large groups with many special needs are generally handled by specialists—*meeting planners*—who deal directly with the hotel, negotiating rates and conducting on-site inspections. Hotels are often booked years in advance for conventions and other meetings. This is a growing market, and we discuss it further in Chapter 11.

Dealing with Policies and Problems

How long is a reservation held? If travelers have reservations, are they certain to get rooms? And can they cancel without penalty? Most hotels follow the same general policies regarding these issues.

Guarantees and Late Arrivals. Most hotels have a **hold time,** the deadline for holding the room without payment. The traveler must arrive by the hold time to secure the reservation. After that time, the reservation is canceled, and the room may be given to the first person who arrives. If the traveler arrives later and a room is still available, no doubt the hotel will be glad to provide it; but if the hotel is full, it is under no obligation to do so.

The hold time is generally 4:00 p.m. or 6:00 p.m., but it can vary and should always be checked. All times refer to the hotel's clock.

If the traveler is planning to arrive or might arrive after the hold time, the reservation can be held by paying a deposit on a credit card for the room; the reservation is then *guaranteed for late arrival.* If the room is guaranteed by a deposit, the traveler may arrive at any time; the room will be held because it has been paid for. Be sure that clients understand that if they fail to appear, they will be charged for one night.

Some hotels ask for a credit card just to hold a reservation. In effect, these hotels are making all reservations "guaranteed."

If travelers have guaranteed reservations and wish to cancel, they can usually do so without penalty by calling before the hold time. But policies regarding cancellation time vary and should always be checked. Some resorts, for example, require that the cancellation be made days or even weeks in advance to avoid a penalty. Cancellations, like confirmations and reservations, are assigned a number, which should be carefully noted.

Overbooking. Hotels know that a certain number of guests with reservations will not arrive. Deposits or guarantees do not solve the problem because clients sometimes dispute these charges, and hotels then have a difficult time collecting them from credit card companies. To be assured of a full house each night, hotels overbook their rooms, much as airlines overbook their seats. They calculate how many rooms to overbook for specific days of the week and seasons. Sometimes, though, they miscalculate and end up with more confirmed guests than rooms.

The same result may occur, not because of overbooking, but because of *overstaying.* Guests do not always check out when they say they will. Most local laws state that innkeepers have the right to request a guest's departure if the room is needed for an incoming guest, but most hotels are reluctant to evict paying guests.

What happens to the unlucky confirmed guest when the hotel has no rooms available? The policy varies, but typically the hotel tries to substitute nearby accommodations of equal or better quality. This is called *walking the guest.* Some hotels pay the entire price for the substituted room; usually, though, the hotel pays the difference if the new room costs more. It also provides free transportation to the substitute hotel. The hotel urges guests to transfer back as soon as space is available, and it again pays for transportation. It's wise to advise the clients to arrive earlier in the afternoon, if possible, or to call the hotel during the day if it looks as though they may be late.

CHAPTER WRAP-UP

CHAPTER HIGHLIGHTS

Like many other industries, the accommodations industry has been marked by the expansion of chains at home and abroad. At the same time, market segmentation has produced wide choices for travelers. In fact, the variety of lodgings and rates creates a constant challenge for travel professionals trying to help travelers make wise choices. This chapter provided the background necessary to meet that challenge. Here is a review of the objectives with which we began the chapter.

1. **Identify the major trends in how accommodations are owned and operated and describe some key market segments.** Lodgings may be owned and operated as independent properties or as one of many properties that are affiliated through chains, franchises, management contracts, or membership organizations. The dominant trend is away from independent properties and toward consolidation. Around the globe, many lodgings are part of chains, which, in turn, are part of large hotel companies. In order to capture a large market, some hotel companies establish many brand names, each of which is designed to appeal to a particular market segment. Markets can be segmented by the purpose for traveling, by current needs, and by location, as well as by price. Based on price, market segments include strict budget, economy, budget luxury, mid-priced, first class, and luxury accommodations. Private room and home rental options are changing the landscape of the accommodation market.

2. **Describe key types of lodgings and characteristics that affect the price of a room.** U.S. lodgings can be classified into the following key types: motels, commercial hotels, convention hotels, airport hotels, all-suites, resorts, spas, all-inclusives, bed-and-breakfasts (B&Bs), private room and home rentals, inns, lodges, casinos, and hostels. Abroad, minshukus, paradores, pensions, pousadas, and ryokan are significant types in certain countries.

   Many characteristics distinguish one accommodation from another and can affect the price. Location is most important, but other key factors are special facilities and services (a concierge, for instance) and characteristics of the room—its location within the lodging, its size and furnishings, the number of beds and occupants. Sometimes, the length of stay and meal plan have an effect. The season, the day of the week, and the demand of the moment are also important. Applying yield management, hotels project an occupancy rate and may vary their prices accordingly on a day-to-day basis.

   The price to a particular guest will also vary depending on whether the guest pays the rack rate or is eligible for a corporate rate, negotiated corporate rate, group rate, convention rate, run-of-the-house (ROH) rate, or special promotional rate. Hotels often quote net rates for a group; the agency then adds its own markup to the quote.

3. **Outline the roles of hotels and travel counselors in selling accommodations.** Hotels have fine-tuned their services in order to increase sales, and increasingly they sell rooms to the public on the Internet either directly or through consolidators. But travel agencies remain an important source of sales for the lodging industry. To be successful in tapping this market, travel counselors must know how to match the client with the right accommodation. They need to know how to find information about specific hotels, understand their clients' needs, and learn which methods to use to contact hotels.

4. **Identify the information needed when making a hotel reservation.** Whether the reservation is made with the hotel, hotel chain, or hotel representative firm (rep firm), the travel counselor should be able to provide the name, number of people in the party, number and type of beds necessary, date and time of arrival, date of departure, age of the client, membership in any program or club that might qualify the client for rate reductions, any special requests, and the manner of guaranteeing the reservation, if necessary.

   The travel counselor should also be sure to check the cancellation policy and hold time and determine whether the reservation should be guaranteed for late arrival. The confirmation number should be carefully noted. But despite the travel counselor's best efforts, a hotel might walk the guest as a result of overbooking by the hotel or overstaying by other guests. Last, but not least, counselors should always verify whether the hotel will pay commission on the booking, and, if not, they may need to add a service fee to compensate.

KEY TERMS

A list of key terms introduced in this chapter follows. If you do not recall the meaning of these terms, see the Glossary.

adjoining rooms
airport hotel
all-inclusive
all-suite
American Hotel and Lodging
    Association (AH&LA)
American plan (AP)
bed and breakfast (B&B)
Bermuda plan (BP)
boatel
brand
casino
chain
château, castle, and villa
commercial hotel
concierge
connecting rooms
Continental plan (CP)
convention hotel
convention rate
corporate rate
demi-pension
dine-around plan
dude ranch
European plan (EP)
extended-stay hotel
franchise company
frequent-guest program
full board
full pension
group rate
guaranteed for late arrival
hold time
hospitality industry

hostel
hotel consolidator
hotel representative firm
inn
lodge
lodging
management contract
market segment
membership organization
minshuku
Modified American plan (MAP)
motel
motor inn
negotiated corporate rate
net or noncommissionable rate
occupancy rate
parador
pension
pousada
prepaid rate
properties
rack rate
rep firm
resort
retreat-style accommodation
rondavel
run-of-the-house (ROH) rate
ryokan
self-catering rental apartment
spa
tented camp
tourist court
tree lodge
walking the guest

REVIEW QUESTIONS

1. Why would one hotel company operate under many names?

2. Why is the choice of accommodations sometimes more complicated than the choice of transportation?

3. What features is a business traveler likely to look for in a hotel? What features are likely to appeal to a vacationer touring by car?

4. Which factors most affect the cost of a hotel room?

5. Name several of the different meal plans that hotels may offer and how they may vary in different countries.

6. When and why would you go first to the Internet to find information about a hotel where your client wants a room?

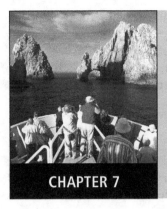

Cruises

CHAPTER 7

OBJECTIVES

After completing this chapter, you should be able to

1. Describe the key types of cruise lines and other ships available to tourists.

2. Identify the most popular cruising areas of the world.

3. Outline the key attractions of life onboard a cruise.

4. Explain major benefits and possible disadvantages of the typical cruise.

5. Name the factors that determine the cost of a cruise.

6. Describe latest trends in the cruise industry.

OUTLINE

THE MODERN CRUISE INDUSTRY
- How did the cruise industry help to create a growing market for travel by ship?

DESTINATIONS: CRUISING ITINERARIES
- What are the most popular destinations for cruises?

LIFE ON A CRUISE
- What do cruises offer passengers onboard?

SELLING CRUISES
- What are the potential benefits and drawbacks of cruising?
- What is the correct booking procedure?

"Follow the sun," the ad might say. "Awake each morning to see new vistas. From sumptuous food to Broadway shows and a spa, you'll find everything you want on our incomparable ship."

Taking a cruise like this is a dream vacation for millions. *Cruise ships* are all-inclusive floating resorts that move from port to port. For travelers, they offer constant pampering, a chance to sample the life at different ports, and opportunities for both relaxation and excitement. Cruises are also convenient. The price of the cruise covers transportation, accommodations, meals, most entertainment, and more, and passengers can visit different places without constantly packing and unpacking. In this chapter, we look at the industry that provides these services, the cruising experience and how cruises are sold.

The Modern Cruise Industry

■ HOW DID THE CRUISE INDUSTRY HELP TO CREATE A GROWING MARKET FOR TRAVEL BY SHIP?

Since the 1970s, cruising has been one of the fastest growing segments of the travel/tourism industry. Shipyards are building a world-wide fleet of new ships as fast as they can keep up with the demand. Travelers who have cruised in the past are returning to participate in new and exciting itineraries, while those who have never cruised before are finding a wide selection of tempting ocean and river trips to start them on a lifetime of cruise vacations.

The growth in cruising did not just happen by chance. The cruise lines themselves have been key in creating a profitable market for cruising.

The Cruise Lines

When the first nonstop passenger flights crossed the Atlantic from New York to Europe, the death knell sounded for the luxury ocean liner. The growth of jet travel forced shipping lines to retire the ships that had carried millions

---

CLOSE-UP: CAREERS WITH CRUISE LINES

Positions in the cruise industry are more plentiful onshore than aboard ships, but opportunities abound. Onboard, all employees are referred to as crew, and most of the positions are like those at resorts. Typically, they are contracted for six months. Hours are long, accommodations are tight, and privacy is almost nonexistent. But because crew members do not have to pay for room and board while on the ship, they can pocket a tidy sum. Shoreside positions are like those for hotel companies or tour operators, with interesting positions in marketing, sales, reservations, operations, and finance. Most shoreside opportunities are at the cruise line's headquarters office, most of which are in Florida for cruise lines geared towards the U.S. cruise market. Many other onshore positions can be found around the globe.

ONBOARD POSITIONS

■ **Position** Youth counselor

Description Watching passengers' children and conducting youth activities are the responsibility of the youth counselor. The hours are long—from 8:00 a.m. to late into the evening. The position generally requires working for three to six months at a time, followed by four to six weeks off.

Qualifications Cruise lines look for people with experience as camp counselors or with a background in education or child care. Having taken some college courses in physical education or childhood development helps. Certification in CPR and first aid is usually required.

■ **Position** Cruise staff

Description A person in this position does everything to entertain passengers, from being a costumed character to playing bingo or giving lectures.

Qualifications Gregarious people, perhaps with a background in entertainment, are suited for this position. It does not require prior cruise experience.

■ **Position** Future cruise reservations manager

Description The primary responsibility of this manager is to sell future cruises to the passengers. (If a travel agency booked the passenger on the current cruise, the agency will receive the commission for the future booking made onboard.)

Qualifications Extensive knowledge of the cruise line's products is required. Previous travel industry or sales experience is preferred.

ONSHORE POSITIONS

■ **Position** Sailing coordinator

Description This shoreside position brings responsibility for making all travel accommodations for air and sea passengers (airline, rail, hotel, transfers) and for maintaining and updating passenger records.

Qualifications This position requires at least one year of experience as an airline reservationist or as a travel counselor with GDS experience. Strong organizational skills, a good command of the English language (both written and oral), and the ability to work in a fast-paced environment are also needed.

■ **Position** Reservations manager

Description Supervising the reservations staff is the heart of this job. The reservations manager is responsible for developing procedures, implementing training, and motivating people, as well as for gauging demand in order to schedule staff efficiently. The manager must also keep other departments informed about booking volume.

Qualifications Prior background as a reservationist and some management experience in a call center are necessary for this position.

■ **Other positions** Agency marketing manager/sales representative/account executive, airfare coordinator; analyst, revenue management; barber; cabin steward; documentation agent; entertainer; fitness trainers; hairdresser; host/hostess; hotel manager; nurse; photographer; pricing analyst; purser; reservations agent.

from continent to continent. Some lines began to focus on shipping cargo; some went out of business; others created the modern cruise industry.

The industry began to take shape in the early 1960s when some shipping lines converted their ocean liners into cruise ships. Later in the 1960s, new companies developed year-round cruises to the Caribbean and introduced ships specifically designed for cruising. In the 1970s, Carnival Cruise Lines became the first line to market cruising as a vacation experience rather than as a way to get from one place to another.

The new era in cruising was marked by the founding of the *Cruise Lines International Association (CLIA)* in 1975. It promotes cruising through public relations and advertising as well as by training travel counselors. In 2006, it merged with the International Council of Cruise Lines (ICCL), a sister entity created in 1990, dedicated to participating in regulatory and policy development for the cruise industry. Today it is the world's largest cruise association, with a membership of 60 of the principal global cruise lines, dedicated to the promotion and growth of the cruise industry. CLIA represents more than 95% of the global cruise capacity.

Since the 1980s, cruise lines expanded their market by offering travelers new itineraries and new activities, as well as discounts. They repackaged cruises into vacations that could appeal to a wide range of the public. They also invested in a huge building boom, putting colossal new ships to sea. Meanwhile, cruise lines themselves were being bought, sold and consolidated. *Parent cruise companies* often own several cruise lines. The Carnival Corporation & plc, an American and British cruise company, is the world's largest operator, with more than 100 vessels across 10 cruise lines.

The parent cruise companies have created brands of cruise lines (Table 7.1), much like the hotel brands discussed in Chapter 6. By selecting destinations, activities, ship designs, and themes, they create an identity for a cruise line that will appeal to particular segments of the market. For example, Carnival owns not only Carnival Cruise Lines—which offers popularly priced, resort-style cruises—but also other brands, including the somewhat sedate Holland America; the deluxe, elegant Cunard line; and Seabourn, a cruise line known for its smaller ships and luxurious amenities.

CLIA categorizes the lines into the following major types:

- *Contemporary, resort-style brands.* These offer midsize to huge ships, rich with activities, in a generally casual style at a moderate price. For example, Carnival's newest ships *Vista* delivered in 2016, and the *Horizon* delivered in 2018, strive for a beach-party atmosphere with fun for the entire family. These ships have a capacity of almost 4,000 passengers. Another contemporary brand that continues to deliver new ships is NCL, designing large ships with amenities that appeal to all types of travelers in a casual atmosphere.
- *Premium brands.* These lines feature midsize to large ships with the extensive diversions offered by resort-style brands plus some upscale features, such as art collections and gourmet-style cuisine. One example is Celebrity's *Eclipse* with five specialty restaurants and onboard classes, among other amenities. Other cruise lines in the premium brands include Princess Cruises and Royal Caribbean, to name just two.
- *Luxury brands.* Unparalleled personalized service, a spacious environment, exotic ports, and luxury on small to midsize ships are offered by the luxury brands, such as Silversea Voyages, Seabourn, Azamara, Oceania, and Crystal.
- *Specialty/expedition brands* (also called *niche brands*). These lines offer cruises with a distinct focus; most emphasize discovery of the cultures of their destinations. Prices range from moderate to deluxe.

■ *Value brands* (also called *traditional brands*). These lines offer the standard features of a cruise at a more economical price than other brands, typically on small to midsize ships. Hurtigruten Cruises, famous for its Norwegian fjords cruises, is an example.

The Ships

The old language of the sea is still used to describe cruise ships (see Figure 7.1). Thus, the front of the ship is the **bow** and the back is the **stern;** anything toward the front is **fore** and anything toward the rear is **aft.** Speed is measured in knots (one **knot** is equivalent to about 1.15 land miles per hour). Round windows are *portholes,* kitchens are *galleys,* and ramps by which passengers get on and off ship are *gangways.* The vessels are always referred to as *ships,* never as boats. Those who sell cruises need to use these correct terms.

Comfort, Health, and Safety. Seasickness is one tradition of the sea that modern cruisers can usually avoid. All cruise ships have **stabilizers,** which are devices that extend from both sides of the ship and minimize roll. **Roll** is the ship's side-to-side movement; it is the primary cause of seasickness. (The ship's movement up and down is called **pitch.**) Because of the efficiency of modern stabilizers, most passengers will be perfectly comfortable a fair distance from each side of midship.

To minimize other potential hazards at sea, travelers rely on governments to make and enforce regulations. However, cruise ships are not subject to U.S. laws when they are at sea. Each cruise ship has a **country of registry;** the ship operates under the maritime laws of that country. U.S. laws require that ships registered under the U.S. flag be built in the United States and operated by American crews, which is an expensive proposition. Operators save huge sums by registering ships under the flags of other nations. When a company registers its ships under a foreign flag in order to avoid the regulations or taxes of its home country, it is said to fly a **flag of convenience**.

Whatever its country of registry, ships that serve U.S. ports must meet certain health and safety requirements. For example, they must follow the **Safety of Life at Sea (SOLAS) regulations**. These are rules established by the International Maritime Organization, which is part of the United Nations. The rules cover the configuration of ships and equipment and are designed to prevent and control hazards, such as fires.

In addition, the U.S. Public Health Service regularly checks and grades the cleanliness of ships sailing from U.S. ports in order to minimize the risk of disease on the ships. Under the *Vessel Sanitation Program (VSP),* any ship that has a foreign itinerary, carries 13 or more passengers, and calls on a U.S. port is subject to unannounced twice-yearly inspections. The Summary of Sanitation Inspections, commonly called the **green sheet,** is posted on the website of the Centers for Disease Control and Prevention (www.cdc.gov). Ships with unacceptable scores, however, are not stopped from sailing.

Finally, the *International Council of Cruise Lines (ICCL),* which merged with CLIA and represents most of the largest cruise lines serving the North American market, sets guidelines regarding medical care onboard cruise ships. For example, the guidelines state that cruise ships should provide reasonable emergency medical care, adequate infirmary care, and a medical staff competent in life-support techniques and cardiac care. The medical staff should be able to administer emergency first aid and to diagnose, stabilize and facilitate the evacuation of seriously ill or injured persons to the nearest onshore hospital.

TABLE 7.1 The 29 Global Cruise Lines Belonging to CLIA

Cruise Line	Web Site	Ships	Comments
Aida	www.aida.de	13	One of the most modern and eco-friendly fleets
AMA Waterways	www.amawaterways.com	20	Rivers of Europe, Russia, southeast Asia, Africa
American Cruise Lines	www.americancruiselines.com	12	Various U.S. rivers and the Eastern and Western seaboard for the U.S.
Avalon Waterways	www.avalonwaterways.com	22	Europe, China, Egypt, Galapagos. Part of Globus family of brands
Azamara Club Cruises	www.azamaracruises.com	2	Europe, Asia, Panama Canal, Atlantic Crossings, less-traveled Caribbean
Carnival Cruise Line	www.carnival.com	26	Alaska, Canada, New England, Caribbean, Mexican Riviera, Panama Canal, Australia, New Zealand
Celebrity Cruises	www.celebritycruises.com	14	Alaska, Bermuda, Pacific Northwest, Canada, New England, Caribbean, Europe, South America. They also have smaller expedition ships for unique adventure itineraries.
Celestyal Cruises	www.celestyalcruises.com	2	Mediterranean and Caribbean. Formerly known as Louis Cruise Lines.
Costa Cruise Lines	www.costacruises.com	15	European style, Europe, Russia, Baltic, South America, Dubai, Asia, Seychelles, Madagascar
Crystal Cruises	www.crystalcruises.com	2	Virtually everywhere; 25 percent international guests. Voted best large ship line by *Condé Nast Traveler*
Cunard Line	www.cunard.com	3	Worldwide itineraries, British tradition since 1840, unique lecture series, trans-Atlantic crossings again
Disney Cruise Line	www.disneycruise.com	4	Caribbean, Mediterranean, Baltic; emphasis on families and children
Emerald Waterways (part of Scenic Luxury Cruises & Tours)	www.emeraldwaterways.com	14	Sails on six European Rivers, the Nile in Egypt, the Volga in Russia, and the Mekong in Southeast Asia.
Holland America Line	www.hollandamerica.com	15	All seven continents, will mark 150 years of service in 2020
MSC Cruises	www.msccruisesusa.com	16	Italian style and service; world destinations with stops in Malta, Balearics, Ukraine, Portugal, South Africa
Norwegian Cruise Line	www.ncl.com	17	World destinations, originator of freestyle cruising, array of cruising options
Oceania Cruises	www.oceaniacruises.com	6	Country club elegance; Down Under, India, Africa, Southeast Asia, Black Sea, and more
Paul Gauguin Cruises	www.pgcruises.com	1	Year round in Tahiti, French Polynesia, South Pacific; onboard water sports marina
Pearl Seas Cruises	www.pearlseascruises.com	1	Canadian Maritimes, Great Lakes, New England, Caribbean, Central America
Ponant	www.ponant.com	7	World destinations, elegant yachts, French inspired.
Princess Cruises	www.princess.com	17	Sailings to all seven continents, home of the original "Loveboat," which was used in the 1970s television series of the same name
Regent Seven Seas Cruises	www.rssc.com	4	All-suite ships, 300 worldwide destinations, upscale educated clientele over age 45
Royal Caribbean International	www.royalcaribbean.com	26	Major destinations, itineraries from three to 14 days, home of megaships *Allure* and *Oasis of the Seas*
Seabourn Cruise Line	www.seabourn.com	6	Top-rate, small-ship cruise company voted #1 by *Travel and Leisure* readers in 2011
SeaDream Yacht Club	www.seadream.com	2	Ultra-luxury mega yachts, seven-day sailings to Greek Islands, Mediterranean, Caribbean, Croatian coast
Silversea Cruises	www.silversea.com	9	Worldwide destinations, small ultra-luxury vessels able to put in at smaller ports
Tauck River Cruises	www.tauck.com	4	Themed cruises, multigenerational; several ships chartered from other cruise lines.
TUI Cruises	www.tuicruises.com	17	All audiences; calls in ports in northern Europe, the Baltic Sea and the Mediterranean in summer and Canary Islands, the Orient, Asia, the Caribbean and Central America in winter.
Uniworld Boutique River Cruise Collection	www.uniworld.com	21	500 departures on 30 itineraries on 11 rivers in 20 countries including Europe, Egypt, China
Windstar Cruises	www.windstarcruises.com	6	Operates 4- and 5-masted sailing ships, carries 145–312 guests, couples oriented. Water sports.

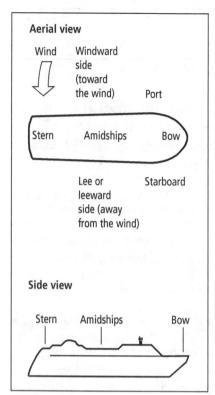

FIGURE 7.1 Shiptalk

Here are some of the basic terms used to describe locations on a ship.

Note that these guidelines are limited. There might be no surgeon onboard, and medical equipment might not be current. Furthermore, there is no agency to enforce the guidelines or to certify that a cruise line follows them.

Comparing Ships: Size and Age. Nothing can quite compare with the sight of a huge cruise ship slipping gracefully away to sea. Each ship has its own personality, but age and size represent key differences among ships.

Although modern ships offer the latest in technology, comfort, and amenities, some travelers prefer older ships. Their rooms are more varied in size, their histories can be fascinating, and their characters are distinctive.

The size of a cruise ship may be cited in terms of the number of possible passengers, the number of **berths**, or its **gross registered tonnage (GRT)**, which is the amount of enclosed revenue-producing space. **Megaships** measure at least 70,000 GRT and hold more than 1,600 passengers. One example is Royal Caribbean's *Allure of the Seas*. Its GRT is 225,282, and it carries up to 6,296 passengers and 2,384 crew members.

Is bigger better? On large ships, motion is reduced to a minimum. Large ships also bring economies of scale, so they offer amenities that smaller ships cannot match. Also, the extra space on megaships permits attractions and activities unthinkable a few years ago. For example,

- Norwegian Cruise Line's *Norwegian Epic*. Built in 2010 as a 155,873 GRT vessel, its 19 decks hold 4,100 guests, double occupancy. There are 20 different dining options on board, a sports complex with climbing wall and full-sized basketball court, and a spa offering a wide range of treatments, including teeth whitening and Botox.
- MSC Cruises *Fantasia*. The 137,936-GRT ship debuted in 2009 and carries a maximum of 3,900 passengers. Italian-owned and -styled, it attracts many Europeans as well as Americans, particularly couples and families. The casino offers free gaming lessons.
- Cunard's *Queen Mary 2*. Launched into service in 2004, this 151,000-GRT beauty has a maximum guest capacity of 2,620. In addition to its cruise schedule, it offers transatlantic service between Southampton and New York. Unique on-board lectures, a book club, workshops, performances, and other intellectual/cultural offerings are provided by representatives of London's Royal Academy of Dramatic Art, the Royal Astronomical Society, and the Juilliard School of Music.

Currently, all major cruise lines serving the U.S. cruising market are building ships that will feature exciting amenities to offer their clients. New ships are being released several times each year, providing additional marketing and sales opportunities for travel professionals. Each of these ships varies significantly. It is important to know the differences among the cruise brands and the ships they offer.

Despite the excitement of megaships, some travelers prefer smaller ships for the more intimate, quiet atmosphere. Small ships also can visit destinations that are inaccessible to large vessels because of the depth of the harbor or the dockage space. Because a small ship may have more room per person, it can feel more spacious. One measure of spaciousness is the **space ratio,** which is the ship size in GRT divided by the number of passengers. A space ratio of 50 is luxuriously spacious; a space ratio of 20 might feel crowded. For example, one crew member to every three passengers would not provide the personal service that one crew member to every 1.5 passengers would.

The cruise lines continue to expand their fleets with ships large and small. Ships not distinguished by their large size are likely to feature unique destinations, innovative programs designed for special market segments, or an unusual degree of luxury. Trends include Internet access for passengers and the dine-around option in several onboard restaurants.

The Cruise Market

Once upon a time, only the rich took cruises. Cruise lines exploit this old association, presenting cruising as an opportunity to experience unique luxury. But they have also made cruises affordable to a broad range of travelers. Because cruise prices include transportation, accommodations, and food, the cost compares well with that for land-based vacations.

Who are the people taking cruises? People of all ages and incomes can be found on cruises, and the numbers of cruisers increase every year (see Figure 7.2).

This variety among cruisers is matched by the variety among cruises. Look again at the description of the types of cruise lines in Table 7.1. As we noted earlier, the parent cruise companies have aimed to create cruise lines for different market segments. As a result, today, there is a cruise for almost every budget and for almost every age. For example, many cruises offer services that appeal to young clients. Some promote a party-like atmosphere and offer special singles get-togethers. Ships that cater to families offer children's fares, babysitting services for a fee, and special events and programs for children.

There are also cruises for all interests. Specialty or **niche cruises** on specific sailing dates might feature jazz, blues, country-and-western, and oldies' rock cruises; sports and celebrity cruises; and adventure, heritage, gourmet, mystery, and chocoholics cruises. There also are several cruises geared towards the lucrative LGBT market.

Cruise companies aim to accommodate different lifestyles. Most cruises still have one or two nights when women wear formal clothes and gentlemen wear dark suits or even tuxedos, and the typical cruise seeks to preserve the tradition of elegance set by luxury ocean liners. But new ships have become increasingly informal. Casual dress is normal during the day; for most dinners, passengers dress as they would in a good restaurant back home. On large ships, passengers can choose from multiple restaurants and dining rooms to find the atmosphere and dressing standards they prefer. There are sailing cruises that require little more than a bathing suit all day and a cover-up for the evening.

Cruises of different lengths tend to differ in price, clientele, and atmosphere. More than half of all cruises last from six to eight days. The longer the cruise, the more expensive it is and, generally speaking, the older the clients. Long cruises are also more likely than short ones to have a formal atmosphere and to emphasize service, ports, and gourmet cuisine. Short cruises of three or four days tend to attract those looking for pure escape; they exude an informal, often partylike, atmosphere and serve to attract the client who then may book longer, more expensive trips in the future.

Other Ship Travel

Besides traditional cruises, other forms of travel by ship are also popular. The main options are yachts, large sailing ships, freighters, ferries, and the newest favorite, river cruises.

Yacht Charters. *Yachts* are boats used for private pleasure excursions. On a typical yacht charter, groups of four to 10 people hire the boat for a certain

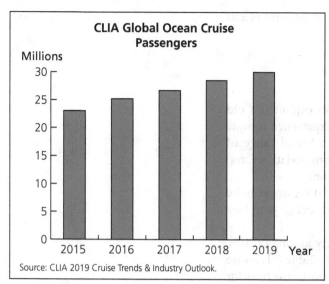

CLIA Global Ocean Cruise Passengers

Source: CLIA 2019 Cruise Trends & Industry Outlook.

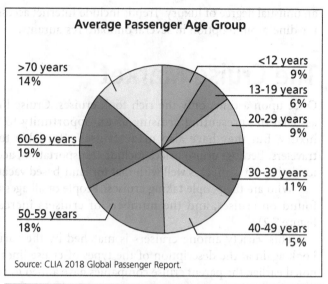

Average Passenger Age Group

Source: CLIA 2018 Global Passenger Report.

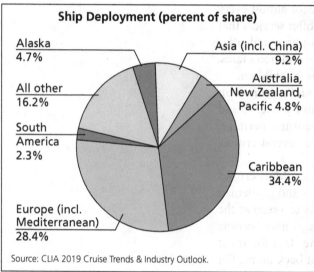

Ship Deployment (percent of share)

Source: CLIA 2019 Cruise Trends & Industry Outlook.

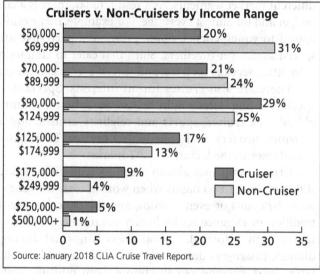

Cruisers v. Non-Cruisers by Income Range

Source: January 2018 CLIA Cruise Travel Report.

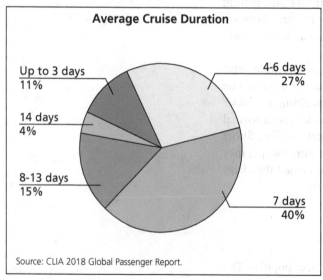

Average Cruise Duration

Source: CLIA 2018 Global Passenger Report.

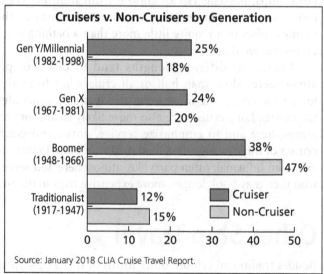

Cruisers v. Non-Cruisers by Generation

Source: January 2018 CLIA Cruise Travel Report.

FIGURE 7.2 Who Is Cruising?

Cruisers include a broad range of people of various ages and income levels. And the popularity of the family cruise, including children, teenagers, and grandparents, often alters the statistics.

number of days. They choose the itinerary, subject to the advice of the operator and the crew. A professional crew sails the boat and cooks the meals.

Experienced sailors may charter yachts that they sail themselves, without a professional crew; this is known as a **bareboat charter.** The boat operator requires evidence of sailing experience and expertise; some operators give a written exam or conduct a trial at sea. If the prospective skipper and crew pass the tests, they receive their boat complete with charts, safety equipment, and everything necessary to sail.

Many large yachts migrate seasonally. The Caribbean season begins around Thanksgiving and runs through April; peak time is Christmas week. The Mediterranean season begins in mid-May, peaks in July and August, and ends in October. New England charters are at their height in July and August; the season runs from June through Labor Day. The Moorings offers both bareboat and crewed yacht charters in a variety of world destinations. Katarina cruises offers crewed charters in Croatia, which has become a very popular destination for yacht rentals.

Sailing Ships. Large sailing ships with multiple sails are called **windjammers.** For example, Star Clipper's 227-passenger *Royal Clipper* has five masts and 42 sails. Windjammers are large for sailing vessels but much smaller than cruise ships and usually less luxurious.

Informality is the hallmark of windjammer cruises. Passengers may help sail the ships and often pick up a smattering of nautical knowledge. But note that windjammer cruises are not charters. Berths are sold to the public on a per-person basis, and the operator determines the itinerary.

Some large sailing ships are computerized and use both sails and motors; they are classified officially as **schooners.** They take advantage of modern technology without sacrificing the beautiful lines of a sailing vessel. Windstar Sail Cruises and Club Med have been offering cruises on schooners much like traditional cruises. Passengers can enjoy swimming pools, casinos, and other amenities in a very informal atmosphere.

Freighters. Ships that have the principal purpose of carrying cargo are called **freighters,** but the typical freighter may also carry passengers. Most are modern vessels with stabilizers, climate control, and some amenities.

Most freighters take up to 12 passengers. The cabins are comfortable, the food is varied, and the table conversation may be entertaining, depending on who the other 11 passengers are. But onboard activity is limited. Passengers should take plenty of good books, plan their own shore excursions, and pack hand-washable clothing. Freighters are best suited for people with time to spare, few fixed commitments, and the ability to stay friendly with eight to 10 other people in fairly close quarters for many weeks. Ports on the itinerary are those desirable for cargo purposes, not necessarily ones that tourists may prefer. Freighters are usually not suitable for those requiring serious medical attention.

Ferries. Around the world, *ferries* carry passengers, vehicles, livestock, and supplies across bodies of water on regular schedules. The trips take from a few minutes to several days, although most take less than a day. Ferries can be as small as a rowboat or as large as a small cruise ship. But unlike cruise ships, ferries act simply as a means of transportation; the price does not include food, accommodations, or other activities. Service is what you might expect on any public transport.

Sometimes ferries are the only practical way to get to a destination. But travelers also take ferries by choice rather than necessity. Some construct entire vacations around ferry travel along the Alaska coast, the Norwegian coast, or the Greek islands. Hong Kong has some of the most famous ferry trips in the world, notably the *Star Ferry* that travels between Hong Kong Island and Kowloon and is used daily by many commuters.

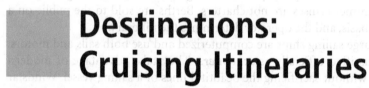

Destinations: Cruising Itineraries

■ WHAT ARE THE MOST POPULAR DESTINATIONS FOR CRUISES?

Most cruises last three to 14 days, but travelers can cruise for several months if they choose. However, most cruisers seem to be selecting cruises that last seven days.

Today's cruise ships average about 16 knots; thus, they have a maximum daily range of about 450 to 550 miles (724 to 885 km), which is about the distance from Boston to Washington, D.C., or from San Francisco to San Diego. They visit ports in every corner of the world. When a harbor is too shallow or too crowded for a ship to dock, passengers go from ship to shore and back on small boats called *tenders.* The cruise might allow several days or just a few hours onshore.

To fill the growing number of ships, cruise lines have added service from new originating, or *embarkation, points.* They have also expanded the destinations they visit, or *ports of call.* Each year cruise lines offer new itineraries.

Traditional Cruising Areas

According to CLIA, the most popular destinations for cruise ships have been the Caribbean, the Mediterranean and Europe, Alaska, and Mexico. Other popular cruising areas include Panama Canal crossings, Bermuda, and Asia. Newly popular areas include the Adriatic Coast from Venice, Italy, to Dubrovnik, Croatia. The cruise lines continue to visit new ports and offer unique itineraries. This is meant to keep their repeat cruisers coming back for more cruise experiences.

The Caribbean and Bahamas. When people talk about the Caribbean, they often mean not only the islands in the Caribbean but also the Bahamas, which are islands in the Atlantic (see Figure 7.3). The largest percent of the cruising public visits the area.

Cruise-goers prefer one-week trips in the Caribbean to cruises of any other length. But two- to four-day cruises are also very popular, particularly for first-time cruisers. Many islands are close enough to one another for ships to visit one island all day and sail on to another at night. Many itineraries are offered, but here are three popular types:

■ One-week cruises of the *eastern Caribbean*, including San Juan, Puerto Rico; St. Thomas (one of the U.S. Virgin Islands); St. Croix; and the Dominican Republic. The familiar American ports of San Juan and St. Thomas are especially popular with first-time passengers. San Juan provides Las Vegas–style entertainment, and St. Thomas has duty-free shopping and beautiful beaches.

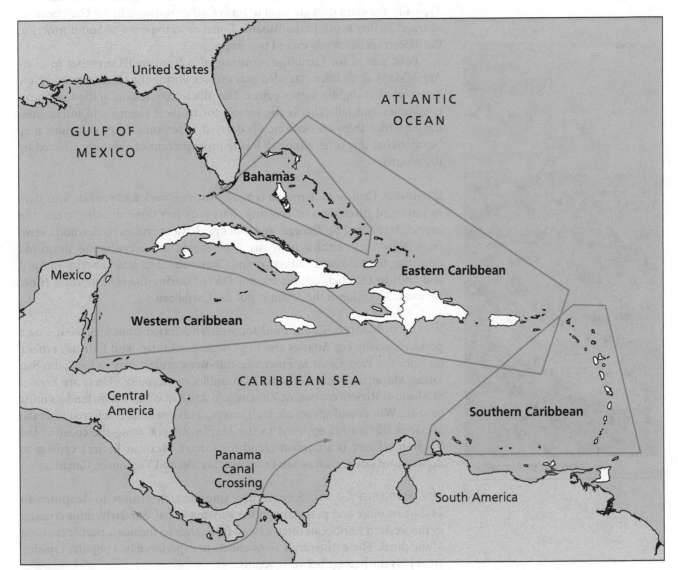

FIGURE 7.3 Cruising the Caribbean and the Bahamas

Cruise lines carve dozens of itineraries out of the four regions of the Caribbean: western Caribbean, eastern Caribbean, southern Caribbean, and Bahamas. (To find the specific islands the text mentions, see a map of Middle America and the Caribbean in an atlas.)

- One-week cruises to the *western Caribbean,* including Jamaica, the Cayman Islands, Key West, and Mexican sites, such as Cozumel and Tulúm, near Cancún. A fun atmosphere and the cultures of Jamaica and Mexico are highlights of these cruises.
- One-week cruises to selected islands of the *southern Caribbean,* such as St. Maarten, Antigua, Martinique, Saint Lucia, Barbados, Grenada, Curaçao, and others. Different southern Caribbean itineraries offer varied attractions—from opportunities for shopping and nightlife to islands with an unhurried atmosphere and a hint of the exotic. This itinerary makes an excellent second or third Caribbean cruise. Typically, the one-week cruises to the southern Caribbean will depart from San Juan, Puerto Rico, where the longer itineraries can depart from other ports, such as Ft. Lauderdale and Miami. Both Eastern and Western Caribbean cruises depart from a variety of ports, including Miami, Ft. Lauderdale, Charleston, Tampa, Galveston, and New Orleans, just to name a few.

Several cruise lines offer Caribbean itineraries lasting 10 to 12 days. Typically, the extra days are used to push farther eastward in the Caribbean or to travel farther south to the Panama Canal or to the coast of South America. Caribbean cruises rarely exceed two weeks.

Peak season for Caribbean cruising runs from mid-December to mid-April. Many ships offer extended gala cruises during the Christmas and New Year period at slightly higher prices. The official low season in the Caribbean is summer and fall. This is the season for tropical storms and hurricanes, during which ships are occasionally delayed or rerouted. Steep discounts may be offered at this time, although less than 10 percent of ships are affected by these storms.

Bermuda. Cruises to Bermuda typically last one week and provide four days in port and three days of cruising. Bermuda has three docking areas: the capital, Hamilton; St. George; and Dockyard. Most cruises to Bermuda leave from New York, although we are now seeing some cruises to Bermuda departing from Boston, Baltimore, and Charleston. The season begins in April and ends in October; cruises are not offered during the cold months. Note: Bermuda's location is the Atlantic, not the Caribbean.

Western Mexico. Cruises sail for western Mexico from U.S. West Coast ports, especially Los Angeles and San Diego. Brief three- and four-day cruises go from the West Coast to Ensenada; one-week cruises may call at Cabo San Lucas, Mazatlán, Puerto Vallarta, Manzanillo, or Acapulco. These are known as Mexican Riviera cruises. At Zihuatanejo and Cabo San Lucas, tenders must be used. Winter and spring are high season. This coastline is referred to as the Mexican Riviera (as opposed to the Mayan Riviera along the coast of the Yucatán). There is a current trend for longer Mexican Riviera cruises to depart from ports, such as San Francisco, Seattle, and Vancouver, Canada.

The Panama Canal. Some cruise lines stretch cruises to Acapulco to 14 days or more and pass through the Panama Canal. Similarly, ships cruising in the western Caribbean often extend itineraries to include a partial crossing of the canal. These itineraries allow clients to experience two popular cruising areas plus the passage between oceans.

Transit through the Panama Canal takes a full day and is usually done during daylight hours for maximum effect. Early in the morning, a ship pilot boards the ship to navigate the intricate locks. Meanwhile, a lecturer describes the canal's history.

Traveling through the Panama Canal

South Pacific/Asia. Some long cruises originating in Los Angeles or San Francisco call at Honolulu and then sail on to Tahiti or New Zealand and Australia, or to Singapore, Hong Kong, China, and Japan. Travelers can also take cruises to China or the South Pacific from ports such as Osaka, Hong Kong, Singapore, or Sydney. Usually cruises in the South Pacific take at least two weeks; often these are segments of a world cruise. Only occasional departures are offered. Paul Gauguin cruises offer year-round itineraries within Tahiti and French Polynesia, giving clients the opportunity to explore the area on seven-day and 10-day voyages. The cruises depart from Papeete, which is a nine-hour flight from Los Angeles.

Alaska. On cruises to Alaska, passengers can be pampered on the most deluxe of ships, or they can select a no-frills trip that emphasizes learning about the people, history, and geography of the area. *Inside Passage* cruises travel along the coast of Canada's British Columbia to ports of southeastern Alaska. The ship is never out of sight of snowcapped mountainous land. Highlights include the spectacular scenery of Glacier Bay; the once-rowdy frontier town of Skagway; the capital city, Juneau; Sitka, with its Russian history; and the modern Canadian cities of Vancouver and Victoria. The Inside Passage season runs from mid-May to late September. Combining an Alaska cruise with a land tour has become very popular in recent years. Several cruise lines offer the opportunity to spend a few days experiencing Denali National Park and surrounding areas, either prior to, or after their seven-day inside passages cruise. This provides clients an opportunity to see the best of Alaska both by land and sea.

Canada and the U.S. East Coast. During the summer, ships sail from New York and Boston and call at Canadian ports in Nova Scotia, Prince Edward Island, and Québec, as well as at New England ports, such as Bar Harbor, Boston, and Newport. The crossing between New England and Nova Scotia can be rough. Smaller ships may also call at places along the New England coast, such as Gloucester, Nantucket, Martha's Vineyard, Portland, and New Bedford. In the autumn, several lines add special cruises for viewing the colorful fall foliage. Other cruises visit southern ports, such as Savannah, Charleston, Hilton Head, St. Augustine, and small cities along the Chesapeake Bay.

The Mediterranean. Popular cruise stops for the western Mediterranean include Cannes or Nice on the French Riviera; Barcelona, Spain; the islands of Malta and Sicily; and Naples and Livorno, Italy (see Figure 7.4). A one-week cruise might depart from Venice and call at Corfu in the Adriatic Sea, Palermo in Sicily, Valletta in Malta, Costa Smeralda in Sardinia, Portofino in Italy, and Nice in France. Genoa, Italy, is an ideal port of embarkation for a circle cruise of eastern and western Mediterranean ports.

The eastern Mediterranean offers some of the world's finest ports. Cruising lasts from April to October. One arm of the Mediterranean, the Aegean Sea, is "Europe's Caribbean." It offers an abundance of small islands within easy sailing distance of one another. The islands are the sites of legendary civilizations; they also provide beautiful beaches and a relaxed lifestyle. There are regular departures from Piraeus, the port of Athens.

Cruises that touch the coast of Turkey usually spend a day at Istanbul and include a stop to visit the ancient ruins of Ephesus from the ports of Izmir or Kusadasi. Because St. Paul is said to have preached here, many religious groups market these itineraries as "In the Steps of Paul" cruises. Stops at other ports can be brief and are affected by tidal conditions.

ON THE SPOT

You are on your first six-month contract as an assistant on the cruise director's staff, and you have been assigned to help sell tours at the port-excursion desk. At one port of call, passengers invariably come back complaining that the all-day tour of the island was too long and not worthwhile. When passengers on the next cruise ask you about the same tour, what do you do?

If the reactions have been consistent, you should not recommend this tour, even though part of your job is to maximize revenue for the ship. You don't need to criticize the tour. Just point out that it is a lengthy one and sing the praises of one of the shorter trips.

In addition, it might be a good idea to probe the reactions of those who took the tour. What part bored them or made them feel that the trip was too long? And be sure your cruise director or another manager is aware of the reactions to the long tour.

Cruises are also available during the summer from Southampton, England, into the Mediterranean or down the coast of Portugal to North Africa and the Canary Islands. These cruises range in length from one to three weeks.

Several of the luxury cruise lines can call on ports that are smaller, less touristy, and can provide a more intimate experience for their clients. While the price may come at a slight premium, the experience many times can far outweigh the hustle and bustle of the busier ports.

FIGURE 7.4 Major European Ports and Cruising Areas

This map shows only key destinations mentioned in the text.

Northern Europe. Popular cruises in northern Europe cover the North Cape or the Baltic. These cruises are generally 14 days long.

The North Cape of Europe is the geographic and scenic equivalent of Alaska. From a port such as Copenhagen or Hamburg, the cruise heads up the Norwegian coast as far as Tromsø and Hammerfest in Lapland. Here cruisers see Norway's mighty fjords; in late June and early July they enjoy the "midnight sun," which never dips below the horizon. Cruising season runs from June to late August.

Other cruises head into the protected waters of the Baltic Sea and call at major port cities, such as St. Petersburg, Helsinki, and Stockholm. Each Baltic stop offers a multitude of sightseeing and shopping possibilities, in contrast to the simple quiet of North Cape towns.

South America. South America offers a variety of cruise experiences. A trip along the east coast can combine calls on Forteleza, Recife, and Salvador de Bahia with stops at the notorious Devil's Island and at Rio de Janeiro for Carnival. A trip around the tip of South America that includes Tierra del Fuego, Falkland Islands, Beagle Channel, and Cape Horn attracts naturalists and adventurers alike. An interior exploration of the Amazon as far as Manaus, Brazil, has been popular for several seasons. And, occasionally, cruise lines have given up their annual winter around-the-world itineraries for interesting itineraries around the South American continent with stops in Chile, Peru, and Ecuador. Adventure cruises to Antarctica sail during South America's summer to the white continent of Antarctica, primarily from Ushuaia in southern Argentina.

Nontraditional Cruises

Wherever there is a body of water, somebody is likely to be sailing across it. Experienced cruisers in particular may be interested in some of the many options beyond the traditional cruising areas.

The Grand Tour (The World Cruise). Some upscale ships offer a return to the golden era of the Grand Tour. One cruise from January through April takes passengers through the Atlantic, Indian, and Pacific Oceans, crossing the equator twice and stopping at 38 ports, from Zanzibar and Ushuaia to Acapulco and Hong Kong.

Clients who cannot afford the time or money for a complete world cruise might purchase segments of an itinerary. For example, one 96-day cruise goes from Fort Lauderdale to Los Angeles by way of South America, Africa, and Asia—but clients can book just parts of the cruise, such as a 28-day segment from Fort Lauderdale to Buenos Aires, or a 90-day trip from Fort Lauderdale to Honolulu, or even shorter segments. The World Cruise usually is a winter cruise.

Theme Cruises. For years, cruise lines experienced slow periods during late September through November, post-Christmas into January, and again from late April through early May. To attract passengers during these times, cruise lines began offering cruises with special themes—such as preholiday shopping sprees, Improv at Sea Comedy, fall foliage tours, celebrity guest sailings, Murder Mystery at Sea, ethnic festivals, and beauty and fitness programs. Bookings are now sometimes difficult to obtain during these once-slow seasons. Several cruise lines offer cruises geared towards the LGBT market.

Repositioning Cruises. Cruises in Europe, Alaska, and Bermuda are not offered during cold months. As the cruising season draws to a close in one area, ships can be seen sailing away. For example, in the fall, ships sail from Mediterranean and European ports to the Caribbean and South America. And although cruises operate year-round in the Caribbean and western Mexico, many ships relocate from there during the summer. Rather than sail empty with a skeleton crew, cruise lines market these seasonal migrations as *repositioning cruises.* These trips combine ports of call that are not part of a ship's usual itinerary. The same phenomenon takes place along the U.S. West Coast. In fall, ships relocate from Alaska down the coast through the Panama Canal. In the spring, the ships return from their winter season in the Caribbean, through the canal and back up the coast to Alaskan or Western Canadian waters.

Repositioning cruises offer an ideal opportunity for veteran cruisers to try an unusual itinerary with their favorite ship. The trips frequently feature special themes and entertainment. Often cruise lines also give substantial discounts on repositioning cruises, especially on luxury ships.

Transatlantic Crossings. Several lines offer crossings between Europe and the United States. Many of these trips are actually repositioning cruises. Travelers can choose a crossing as short as six days, taking a Cunard cruise from New York to Southampton, England, or perhaps as long as 23 days, taking a cruise from Fort Lauderdale to Lisbon.

River Cruises. A phenomenon that has developed in recent years is the popularity of river cruising. As megaships have become larger and larger, many cruise passengers have become enamored of the opposite trend—small ships plying the world's great rivers in style. Four particularly popular river cruise companies—AMAWaterways, Avalon Waterways (part of the Globus Family of Brands), Uniworld River Cruises, and Viking River Cruises—have created a new type of cruise experience somewhat akin to a floating tour. Several new river cruise companies have become part of the market and should not be overlooked. The river cruise market is quickly changing and growing and should be well researched on behalf of the travelers' needs and wish lists.

Passengers buy a total package of airfare to and from the ship, cruise accommodations, meals, onboard lectures, light entertainment, and sightseeing/shore excursions. Unlike traditional cruises, the basic shore excursions are not an additional cost. Passengers are close to the shore, and stops are frequent. For those wishing to see a great deal of an area, these offer an alternative to motor coach tours.

Most of these cruises began on the rivers of Europe— the Danube and the Rhine, which is famous for the vineyards and castles lining its banks, the Rhone through the heart of Provence, and the Mosel, which connects with the Rhine in western Germany. The completion of the Rhine-Main-Danube canal in 1992 joined the Rhine/Main and the Danube to create a single waterway from the North Sea all the way to the Black Sea, opening European river cruising to a great many new itineraries.

A Danube River cruise at Budapest, Hungary

In addition to Europe, river cruise companies have now expanded their offerings to include Egypt (the Nile), China (the Yangtze), Russia (the Volga and inland canals), Vietnam (the Mekong), and others. In addition to river cruise ships, even smaller vessels, such as *cabin cruisers* (power boats with living accommodations), sail the Thames in England and slow-moving *barges* (flat bottomed boats) cruise the inland waterways of France.

Being educated on the different river cruise options is important to matching your clients to the right cruise. For instance, only a few river cruise companies accept children on their itineraries, while other river cruise companies have created itineraries that are both engaging and fun for children. Some river cruises attract clients in the more mature demographic, while others are marketing towards Gen X and Gen Y travelers. River cruises provide a great value for your clients and great earning potential for travel professionals, but being knowledgeable about the options is important.

Special-Interest Cruises. Every cruising area offers a culture that appeals to particular tastes and interests, but some lines go further and design cruises to appeal to people with specific interests. The subjects can be varied: a jazz or big-band dancing cruise or renowned guest lecturers speaking on topics ranging from the habits of polar bears to the causes of the 1929 stock market crash. It also could be a cruise to a specific spot in the middle of the ocean to watch an eclipse or to anchor in Rio's Guanabara Bay for Carnaval.

Sometimes such cruises are referred to as *adventure cruises* or even *expeditions* when they are venturing to new areas or are highly specialized in scientific inquiry. They usually appeal to passengers with time, money, and deep intellectual curiosity. The ships are often small, accommodating between 90 and 250 people, and feature world-famous experts and lecturers in a given subject. Companies such as Lindblad Expeditions, partnering with National Geographic, and a British company, Swan Hellenic, are examples of companies providing specialized cruises.

✔ CHECK-UP

Peak seasons for cruising are
✔ In the Caribbean, from mid-December to mid-April.
✔ Along the Inside Passage of Alaska, from mid-May to late September.
✔ In the Mediterranean, from April to October.
✔ In Scandinavia, from June to late August.

Nontraditional cruises include
✔ Theme cruises.
✔ Repositioning cruises.
✔ Transatlantic crossings.
✔ River cruises.
✔ Special-interest and adventure cruises.

Life on a Cruise

■ WHAT DO CRUISES OFFER PASSENGERS ONBOARD?

For many experienced cruise passengers, the ship is their true destination. Ports of call are a secondary consideration; they take a cruise for the way of life onboard.

Accommodations

Deck plans of a ship show the locations of cabins and public rooms; Figure 7.5 gives an example. A cabin amidships is the ideal location for passengers prone to seasickness. An outside cabin may have a porthole that looks out over the ocean; inside cabins have no access to natural light. Note, though, that portholes cannot be opened to allow fresh sea breezes into cabins. In fact, on older ships, caps are sometimes secured over the portholes on the lowest decks to make them safe for rough seas.

Cabins, which are sometimes called *staterooms* or simply *rooms*, are smaller than comparable hotel rooms, but cabin size varies from ship to ship. Large cabins have both a sleeping area and a separate living space. Many ships have cabins with large bathrooms and extra-large doorways to accommodate wheelchairs. (For a discussion of the accessibility of cruise ships for those with wheelchairs or other special needs, see Chapter 11.) Many cabins, especially on new and upscale ships, have private balconies or verandas. Some cruise lines offer ships that are comprised only of suites.

The typical cabin has two lower twin berths; new ships and some refurbished ones offer double, queen-size, and even king-size beds. In some cabins, beds convert to sofas during the day or recess into the wall. Families or young people traveling as a group may prefer the cabins with upper berths recessed into the walls above twin beds; the berths can be pulled out to provide sleeping accommodations for two additional persons. Those electing this option should be carefully advised as to how crowded the cabin will be when all four beds are used. Newer ships are being designed with cabins designed for families, some of which include multiple sleeping areas and more than one bathroom.

Passengers with a typical cabin can expect small closets, a dresser with mirror, a toilet, a washbasin, and a shower. Usually, only expensive cabins have tubs. Luxury ships offer amenities, such as hair dryers, minibars, refrigerators, in-room safes, and terry bathrobes, depending on the stateroom category or resort refurbishing. Most ships offer radio or limited-channel television in the cabins. Nevertheless, most cruise cabins are never as spacious as hotel rooms.

Food Service

Cruise ships are famous for the quantity and quality of their food. The reputation for cuisine varies from ship to ship, but all offer an abundance of opportunities to eat.

A traditional dining room onboard has tables for six or eight, but many ships accommodate requests for private tables for two or four. Usually, passengers receive their table assignments after they board, but some cruise lines preassign tables. Large ships often schedule two sittings in the dining room; passengers indicate their preference for first or second sitting. Early-to-bed and early-to-rise passengers as well as families with young children will probably prefer the first sitting. Those who plan to dance or gamble the night away will probably prefer the second sitting. Ships with only one sitting are considered more gracious as service is less rushed.

Norwegian Cruise Lines (NCL) pioneered changes in how cruisers dine. Its Freestyle Cruising program does away with assigned seats and designated times for dining. Its ships have up to 10 restaurants each, and passengers choose where and when to eat. As a result, they may have to wait in line to dine, but many of the restaurants take advance reservations. Several other cruise lines now offer flexible dining times, providing travelers more freedom and flexibility to enjoy their cruise experience.

Some cruises now have 24-hour restaurants. Most will arrange private parties; deliver continental breakfasts, sandwiches, and cocktails to cabins by request around the clock; and accommodate most special diets (salt-free, fat-free, and so on) if notice is given well in advance—at least two weeks ahead of sailing—so the chef can provision accordingly.

The variety of food is impressive. On many ships, menus include light fare and heart-healthy choices. Many feature an array of casual eateries, such as pizza and burger joints, small supper clubs, and ethnic restaurants. Some of the larger ships may have as many as 20 different onboard dining options.

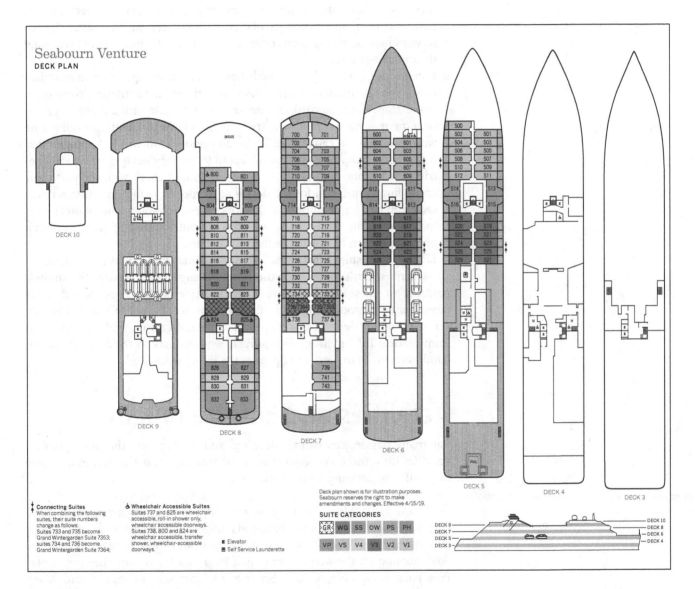

FIGURE 7.5 Deck Plans: A Sample

Shown here is the proposed deck plan for the *Seabourn Venture*, scheduled to launch in 2021 (image subject to change without notice).

Other Services

On most cruises, passengers can find an array of services:

- *Infirmary.* The ship's doctor provides treatment for routine medical problems and is on call for emergencies. Hours and fees are posted in the daily news. Cabin calls are a costly extra.
- *Duty-free shops.* Open daily while the ship is at sea, these shops sell gifts, clothing, souvenirs, tobacco, candy, and necessities.
- *Beauty salon and barber shop.* These facilities are usually open whether the ship is at sea or in port. Facials and manicures are usually available.
- *Laundry.* Laundry and dry cleaning can be left with the cabin steward for a fee; this service normally takes two days. Some ships have free self-service laundries.
- *Religious services.* Some ships offer Jewish, Catholic, and interdenominational services; others offer only interdenominational services. Services for particular religions or sects are offered on holy days, such as Easter. Special services may be arranged on some cruises for couples interested in renewing their marriage vows.
- *Communications.* Each ship publishes a daily newspaper that summarizes news, sports, financial information, and shipboard activities. Nowadays, major ships have onboard Internet services available with a range of prices, or some may have complimentary WiFi. Purchasing or renting a cell phone with international capabilities is also an option. Onboard technologies that use satellite equipment may be subject to temporary outages of any satellite-connected shore-side service. Passengers should check with the particular cruise line in question for full details as to specific communication services each ship has. Some ships have developed new technology that allows guests to communicate with other guests throughout the ship by using their cell phones, without having to use their data plans.
- *Library.* Most ships offer a small library that may include DVDs for rent.

On most cruise lines, it is the **hotel manager** who ensures the smooth running of all services. The manager's office is chiefly responsible for passenger accommodations and (like the front desk of a hotel) offers banking services, safety deposit boxes, postal communication, and customs and immigration information. The **purser,** who reports to the hotel manager, handles financial matters and operates the information desk.

Activities and Entertainment

For many passengers, eating, sleeping, and relaxing are the most popular activities on cruises. For anyone who chooses a more active life, most cruise ships offer an amazing array of activities.

Onboard Fun. When the ship is at sea, shops and casinos are open, as is the library, the card room, intimate bars, and lounges featuring soft music. Most ships also have a cinema and discotheque. Passengers can also jog around the deck, try skeetshooting off the stern, or drive golf balls into the ocean. They might play Ping-Pong, bridge, bingo, chess, Scrabble, backgammon, or shuffleboard. Many ships offer a sauna and a gymnasium. There is usually no charge to use exercise equipment or attend aerobics classes. Many upscale cruise lines feature full-service spas with a complete menu of services, such as aromatherapy, hydrotherapy, and herbal wraps for a fee. The spas are usually run by outside companies. For example, the *Queen Mary 2* features Canyon Ranch, with facilities in Tucson,

Arizona, Lenox, Massachusetts, and Las Vegas. It is suggested that clients book spa/beauty services ahead or immediately upon boarding and query the price of services at that time.

A captain's welcome-onboard cocktail party, gala farewell dinner, and theme night (a masquerade, talent show, and so on) are traditional events on cruise ships. Most ships have a large ballroom or lounge for dancing and for shows featuring professional entertainers. Larger ships offer theaters with revolving stages, retractable domes over swimming pools, 18-hole miniature golf courses, and nightclubs 15 decks above the sea. Entertainment rivals Las Vegas revues. An entire deck may be devoted to the casino or shops. New ships even have water parks, laser tag, and other activities for the more adventurous traveler. There is something for everyone on the new mega-ships that have been debuted recently.

The cruise director and staff arrange a nonstop flow of activities from dawn to dusk and beyond if the ship is at sea for all or part of the day. While the ship is in port, limited activities are featured for those who do not wish to go ashore. Classes may be offered on topics as varied as dancing, flower arranging, tennis, and photography. Figure 7.6 shows an example of the schedule for a day aboard one ship. Passengers are free to choose as many or as few activities as they please.

Usually, a talk each day familiarizes passengers with the attractions of the next destination. Topics include history, major sights, shopping hints, optional shore excursions, and local customs. Long cruises or those with an emphasis on a certain theme or destination often have experts as guest lecturers.

Excursions. Shore excursions run the gamut from two-hour city tours to extravagant overnight adventures exploring the depths of the Amazon. They are conducted by local tour operators under contract with the cruise line. On some cruises, passengers may purchase all shore excursions as a package. The cost of the package is considerably less than the sum of the components purchased separately. However, shore excursions purchased onboard cruise ships vary greatly in quality and value.

Some travel counselors excel at pre-booking private shore excursions or activities for their clients. Several river cruise companies and adventure cruise companies include most shore excursions in the cruise package. For some excursions, individuals can make their own arrangements. But if several cruise ships are in port, they may find that tour operators have booked all available transportation onshore, as well as all tickets to local attractions.

Onboard Expenses

Although the price paid for a cruise covers accommodations, meals, entertainment, and many activities, passengers do incur other expenses. Tipping is one important addition to the cost.

Usually, shipboard tips come to at least $12 a day per person. Ship's officers are never tipped. Bar personnel, wine stewards, and cocktail waiters are tipped the normal 15 percent whenever a tab is paid. Tips to the dining-room steward, the busboy, and the cabin steward are normally given at the last dinner or the evening before leaving the cabin. On long cruises, however, tips are given every week or every two weeks, not just at the end of the cruise. Some cruise lines advertise a no-tipping-required policy, but passengers may want to recognize outstanding service. Most cruise lines provide passengers with tipping guidelines. In fact, many cruise lines, depending on their nationality, automatically put tips on your shipboard bill to simplify matters. Check with individual cruise lines as to their policy.

Other expenses not covered by cruise prices that may be incurred onboard include

- *Personal expenditures.* Passengers pay extra for purchases in shops, certain medical expenses, and casino gambling, as well as for the use of special facilities (such as the beauty salon and spa) or certain sports equipment or activities.
- *Liquor and soft drinks.* On most lines, passengers pay for wine at dinner, other alcoholic beverages, specialty drinks, soft drinks, and even bottled water to take onshore. Many river cruises make it a habit to have coffee and bottled water available throughout the day on a self-service basis.

Refreshing Morning

6:00 a.m. – Noon
The Wake Show!
Wake up with Kelvin & Matt – Channel 21, Crew's Choice

6:00 a.m. – Onwards
Daily Brainteasers & Sudoku
Available in the Library, Deck 5 Midship

6:00 a.m. – 10 a.m. approx.
Scenic Cruising in Tracy Arm (Weather Permitting)
During our time in Tracy Arm, there will be a commentary on deck, Horizon Court & Channel 35 of your stateroom television with Naturalist Julius Talarica

7:00 a.m. – 10:00 a.m.
Up Close & Personal
Watch out for our Photographers on the open deck this morning as we sail through beautiful Tracy Arm

7:00 a.m. – 11:00 a.m.
Tracy Arm Outpost
Binoculars, cold weather gear, books, souvenirs, sundries and much more. Lido, Deck 14 Midship

9:00 a.m. – Arrival
Fine Jewelry Silent Auction – Day 2!
Learn how to bid on our private collection of Fine Jewelry. Deck 7 Midship

10:00 a.m.
Body Sculpt Boot Camp
Aerobics Studio, Deck 15 Fwd

10:00 a.m. – Noon
Bridge Play & Lecture with Donald Hennigan
Vivaldi Dining Room, Deck 5 Midship

10:15 a.m.
Free Seminar: "Arthritis & Back Pain Relief"
With Sarah Licensed Acupuncturist. Hearts and Minds, Deck 7 Fwd

10:15 a.m. Zumba Time!
Another chance to Zumba. Wear your workout clothes. Club Fusion, Deck 7 Aft Crew's Choice

10:30 a.m. Ice Carving Demonstration
Neptune's Reef & Pool, Deck 14 Midship

11:00 a.m.
Knitting & Crochet Get-Together
Crooners Bar, Deck 7 Midship

11:00 a.m. $60 Texas Hold'em Tournament
Followed by a $1/$2 No Limit Cash Game. Register with the Casino Cashier from 10:30am. Grand Casino, Deck 6 Fwd

11:00 a.m. Free Seminar: "Non-Surgical Facial Rejuvenation"
With Dr. Jariel. Hearts & Minds, Deck 7 Fwd

11:00 a.m. How to Get Around & What to See in Juneau & Skagway
Last minute VIP cards, coupons, and maps for Juneau and Skagway. Atrium, Deck 5 Midship

11:00 a.m. – 2:00 p.m. Reindeer Chili Cook-Off
Calypso Pool, Deck 14 Midship

11:15 a.m. $1300 Snowball Jackpot Bingo Crew's Choice
Could go in 53 numbers, plus 3 other cash prizes. Cards available until 11:15 a.m. Club Fusion, Deck 7 Aft

11:15 a.m. Morning Trivia with the Cruise Director's Staff
Explorers Lounge, Deck 7 Midship

11:30 a.m. Free Seminar: "Secrets to a Flatter Stomach"
Aerobics Studio, Deck 15 Fwd

FIGURE 7.6 Sample Morning Schedule from the Sapphire Princess' Daily Activity Newsletter

This schedule of the activities available illustrates a typical first-day schedule for cruisers.

- *Shore excursions.* Unless specifically stated to the contrary, shore excursions are an option that passengers may purchase before or during their cruise.
- *Dining.* Several cruise lines charge for dining at specialty restaurants, and some also charge for in-room dining. This varies based on the cruise line.

Policies for paying for onboard services and purchases are usually stated clearly in brochures and on the cruise line's website. Most ships establish a credit account for passengers as soon as they board the ship; then passengers sign for these services onboard. Passengers who do not have credit cards may be required to deposit cash with the purser at the start of the voyage to cover onboard purchases. Accounts are settled at the purser's office at the end of the cruise. Cash, credit cards, or traveler's checks are usually accepted.

✔ CHECK-UP

Typically, onboard expenses not covered by a cruise fare include
- ✔ Tips.
- ✔ Personal expenditures.
- ✔ Liquor.
- ✔ Shore excursions.

Usually, passengers must pay extra for certain services, including
- ✔ Cabin calls from the ship's doctors.
- ✔ Dry cleaning.
- ✔ Videos.
- ✔ Herbal wraps.

Selling Cruises

- WHAT ARE THE POTENTIAL BENEFITS AND DRAWBACKS OF CRUISING?

- HOW MUCH DO CRUISES COST?

CLIA statistics point to the potential for continued growth in cruise sales, which can represent more than 60 percent of many travel agencies' vacation sales volume and, therefore, good cruise sales personnel are very valuable to most travel agencies. For the agencies, cruises represent a very profitable market, and if the client has been properly counseled, a cruise booking often requires only one phone call or GDS entry by the agent. Furthermore, the commission paid to the travel agency on the sale is based on the total cruise product, which includes meals and entertainment—items not normally commissionable on the typical land vacation.

Acquiring Expertise

Although cruises are sold online, the vast percentage of sales comes through travel agencies that have special cruise departments or counselors (either onsite or often home-based) specializing in cruises. There are many cruise-only agencies. Selling cruises requires expertise. Often, the seller must overcome clients' misconceptions, and the sheer number of ships and itineraries can be overwhelming to clients and counselors alike.

Fortunately, opportunities for learning about cruises abound.

- CLIA offers training programs for selling cruises; they are described in Chapter 16.
- Some cruise lines offer training videos, seminars, courses, and webinars on how to sell their products. A cruise line may reward travel counselors who complete its courses by designating them as certified sales experts and listing them on its website.
- Travel counselors can also learn about specific ships by taking part in familiarization trips, ship inspections, trade shows, and "cruise nights" offered by cruise lines.

Even if you take advantage of these educational opportunities, it is next to impossible to know every cruise ship afloat. The names, itineraries, sizes, schedules, and services of ships and cruise lines change constantly. One strategy for dealing with this problem is to choose a preferred supplier for each category of cruise line and learn its ships intimately.

Travel counselors should also be familiar with the websites of the major cruise lines; these offer a wealth of information. But don't expect the website to have all of the best price information. The cruise lines phone, e-mail, or fax information on discounts and special promotions to cruise specialists. Usually the websites of cruise lines steer the general public to consult a travel agency, but many do take reservations directly.

CLOSE-UP: ON THE JOB WITH HILLARY PENNELL, AGENCY MARKETING MANAGER FOR A CRUISE LINE

Hillary Pennell works as an agency marketing manager—often called a sales representative—for a deluxe cruise line that has five ships. Her territory consists of three states, and much of her job is on the road.

"I started out as an intern at a travel agency while still going to travel school. After graduating, I took a job in reservations with a tour wholesaler. A year later, I moved into marketing and sales with that company. I was basically the inside sales representative. We sold exclusively through travel agencies, so I dealt mainly with them; at the same time, I was learning about advertising and marketing. Since then, I have been a sales representative for an airline and now a cruise line.

"This isn't an entry-level job, but you can move into it fast if you prove yourself. My main job is to help my distributors sell my product. That means getting travel counselors to fill our ships. My main duty is to differentiate my product from the others. I explain to travel counselors—so they can explain to their clients—what makes my cruise line different, what experiences travelers are going to get that they won't get on another cruise line.

"One key way I do this is to give ideas to the counselors on how to sell our ships. Of course, what I learn from one agency is strictly confidential. But I can share general ideas on how to promote, advertise, and sell, hoping they take the ball and run with it. Of course, I give the most help to those who most help themselves.

"I may spend one day a week working in my home office catching up on any emails and phone calls, making appointments and doing paperwork. The rest of the time is usually spent visiting agencies or meeting with home-based counselors. I try to make more and more of my calls have a specific purpose. I also try to make an appointment to see the manager or speak to the counselors in a group.

"I start out by telling them anything new that is happening on our side—new ships debuting, new policies—and reviewing past innovations they might have forgotten. Then I ask them what is new with them. The more they talk, the more I listen—and see if I can glean something that will help. Otherwise, we take a few minutes just to socialize and make that bond stronger.

"A certain number of evenings during the year, I spend at trade shows, conducting our own cruise seminars, and attending cruise shows or cruise nights that agencies or their cruise specialists put on and that feature our cruise line in particular. I escort a couple of familiarization cruises a year also. On these, we'll choose some of our top agencies and those we think have potential.

"Our side of the business is going to have a lot of growth and opportunity. I plan to be a big part of it. I want to show agencies and their associated home-based cruise counselors how they can be a big part of it also."

The websites for most cruise lines have a special section reserved for travel counselors; access requires an agency's IATAN (International Air Transport Association) or CLIA number. This section often includes

- Information on commissions, discounts, marketing materials, and group bookings.
- Information on how to arrange group transfers or special gifts for clients.
- Information on how to set up cruises for meetings or incentive travel.
- Booking or reservation forms.
- The capability of taking reservations online, directly on the cruise line's booking engine.
- Sign-ups for an e-mail newsgroup.
- Details on who's who in the sales department and how to reach them.

For finding information on the thousands of smaller ships, ferries, and boats that ply the seas of the world, the Internet is almost indispensable. Almost every shipping company has a website. However, travelers must recheck schedules when they arrive at a destination, and often tickets must be purchased locally.

Understanding the Benefits and Drawbacks of Cruising

A first step in selling cruises is to identify which travelers are likely to enjoy a cruise. What do cruises have to offer them, and what are the drawbacks of cruising?

The most important benefits of cruises include the following:

- *Relaxation and entertainment.* The sea has a romantic allure. The combination of the constant gentle movement of the ship, the brisk sea air, and the unhurried pace makes a cruise relaxing. Passengers are insulated from anything that reminds them of everyday responsibilities. Everything is within easy walking distance, including good restaurants and evening entertainment. Also, passengers unpack and pack only once. They can be as busy or as lazy as they like. Those who travel alone are never at a loss for opportunities to socialize.
- *Prepayment.* Because most expenses are prepaid, clients can accurately predict the cost of their vacation and avoid carrying large sums of money.
- *Service.* Cruise ships pamper passengers with personal service and gracious touches. The crew anticipates as many of the passengers' needs and desires as possible.
- *Variety of destinations.* On a typical cruise, passengers cannot explore destinations in depth. But they can get a taste of different locales while enjoying the convenience of returning to the same lodging each night. In one CLIA study, 50 percent of cruisers said that they expected to return to a destination they visited during their cruise for another type of vacation. The cruise provided a preview of possible destinations for future vacations. Several cruise lines now offer overnight stays in ports, providing travelers even more time to immerse themselves into the destination.
- *Value.* Although cruises may look expensive at first glance, their cost compares favorably with that of many resorts and other prepaid vacations and package tours. The base price for a land-based vacation is likely to be lower than the price of a comparable cruise, but the base price for the land-based vacation often does not include essentials that are covered by the cruise's price, such as meals and entertainment. Furthermore, cruises can

offer intangibles unmatched elsewhere, such as the romance of the sea, the atmosphere on the ship, and the chance to meet other vacationers onboard. The result, for many clients, is that cruises give them the best value for their money.

Not everyone is a good candidate for a cruise. Poor candidates include the following:

- Although seasickness can usually be avoided, those who fear storms or the sea should try a different kind of vacation.
- Those who dislike waiting in lines or being in crowds are likely to find a large cruise irritating. People who tend to be claustrophobic should avoid extended cruises and small ships; once at sea, there is nowhere else to go.
- Travelers who are eager to study the world and its peoples in depth may be disappointed by a typical cruise. While ashore, passengers may have time to do little more than take a standard sightseeing tour, visit a beach, or check out local markets and stores. A typical cruise allows only fleeting impressions of the destinations visited.

Matching Clients and Cruises

Notice that the short time spent at each destination can be either a benefit or a drawback, depending on a person's viewpoint. Even among people who enjoy cruises, attitudes and preferences vary greatly.

Knowing the client is one key to success in selling a cruise. For example, travelers who fear they might feel claustrophobic on a typical cruise might enjoy a short cruise or a megaship. If one member of a couple is ardently pushing for a cruise while the other is reluctant, a short cruise might represent a workable compromise. Another choice might be a cruise that focuses on a special interest that both people share.

Different clients weigh various factors differently. Sometimes, the client's own location is important. Caribbean cruises are most popular among clients from the U.S. northeastern, mid-Atlantic, and midwestern states. Cruises of western Mexico are especially popular with people from the U.S. West and Rocky Mountain states.

To other clients, the ship itself is key. Some passengers develop an affection for a particular ship and return to it year after year. Some eagerly await inaugural cruises so that they can be among the first to sail on a new ship. One client may be looking for elegance onboard; another, for excitement.

The right cruise for an individual client is likely to depend on the itinerary and its length and on the ship itself and its size, style, and service. All these factors also influence the cost of a cruise, and sometimes their importance depends on their effect on cost. It is said that cruises may be classified into four types: (1) those with limited budgets and limited time; (2) those with ample budgets but limited time; (3) those with ample time but limited budgets; and (4) those with ample budgets and ample time. There are cruises for each type.

The Price of a Cruise

The prices quoted by cruise lines are for one person sharing a cabin with another. Singles pay a charge called a *single supplement* and occupy a cabin that is built for two. However, some lines allow those traveling solo to avoid paying the single supplement if they are willing to share a cabin with another traveler of the same gender. In that case, they pay the **guaranteed share rate;** if no other single traveler books, they still pay this lower rate. Unfortunately, many cruise lines do not offer those traveling alone an attractive single occupancy rate; it may be as high as paying for two. Many agents will suggest that a single traveler find a friend or family member to travel with them and, thus, share the cabin and the cost. Some cruise lines are designing cabins for the solo traveler, providing the traveler an opportunity to avoid paying the single supplement. The cruise lines are recognizing the value of solo travelers.

If a third or fourth person shares a cabin, it costs the cruise line very little extra; therefore, the **third/fourth person rate** is very low. Dividing the total cost among all three or four persons in a cabin can reduce the cost for all. Third and fourth passengers occupy upper bunks that retract into the wall during the day. Cruise prices are often compared by the *per diem* (daily) cost per person. In general, the price of a cruise depends on its length, the season, the ship, the cabin, discounts, and the location on the ship.

Length of Cruise. To some extent, the number of days devoted to a cruise determines its price.

The Season. Shoulder and offseasons are known as the **value seasons.** Value-season prices can be as much as 20 percent less than regular prices.

The Ship. A ship that offers more space and more crew members per passenger generally is more expensive. Luxury cruises may have as many as one crew member for every one and a half or two passengers.

The efficiency of a ship's design also influences price. For example, new ships built specifically for short cruises usually have many small cabins, are fuel-efficient and require fewer crew members than older ones. As a result, their fares may be lower than those for cruises on other ships.

CLOSE-UP: SELLING CRUISES BY DEALING WITH OBJECTIONS

Selling a cruise begins with knowing the client and the product and using that knowledge to find a good match between the client and a cruise. No matter how much you learn, though, a client's lack of knowledge may create problems. Because many people are unfamiliar with cruises, they will probably have questions, misconceptions, and objections about any recommendation, however good it may be.

The most frequently heard objections from clients include the following:
- I'll get seasick.
- It's too expensive.
- I don't like dressing up.
- I'll feel stuck.

The facts that address each of these concerns are discussed in the chapter. To present them effectively, try these guidelines.
- Remain positive, not defensive. The objection is not about you personally.
- Listen to the objection carefully, without interrupting.

- Before countering the objection, show that you understand it by paraphrasing it. (For example, "A lot of people worry about that. Getting seasick certainly would spoil things.")
- Then give clear, practical solutions to the problem.

Suppose, for example, that your client is concerned that bad weather could spoil a cruise. In fact, the captain uses radar to avoid storms whenever possible, but cruises are vulnerable to bad weather. When rough seas cannot be avoided, they can cause physical discomfort and make movement around the ship difficult. Even prolonged rain or cloudiness can sharply reduce the passengers' enjoyment of a cruise despite the multitude of indoor activities available.

How, then, could you respond to the client's concern about the weather? You might say that—because of the size of ships, their technology, and indoor activities—weather is no more a factor than it is on any trip, and note that cruisers are more satisfied with their vacations than any other type of traveler.

Herbert and Eva Robertson, both retired, had long dreamed of taking a cruise. After talking with you, looking at brochures, and talking some more, they had almost decided on a cruise to the Caribbean with a quoted price of $1,299. Then Herb called with new doubts. They had just seen an ad for a trip to the Caribbean for $599, he said, and it looked like a better deal. What would you say to them?

A wise sales counselor gets clients thinking value rather than price as soon as possible. A hamburger at a fast-food chain costs much less than prime rib at a good restaurant, but many people choose the prime rib every day; they are putting a value on the cuisine, atmosphere, and service. In this case, not only may the cruise give much greater value, but the price might even turn out to be less.

Since Herbert and Eva have dreamed of taking a cruise, it probably offers greater value to them than sitting in one place on an island. Discuss the price with them so that they understand the two options. For example, what will three meals a day cost them in the Caribbean? And will they be able to order whatever they want at all these meals? What if they want entertainment on several days and evenings? If you add cover charges, drink minimums, and taxis or other transportation, the sum is substantial. The total costs of the two trips will probably end up somewhat similar.

To make the sale, remind them of why they wanted to take a cruise, and mention additional benefits. Would they like to unpack only once and yet visit four or five destinations? Would they like to have meals and entertainment just steps away from their door? Would they like to travel with a large group of like-minded fun-lovers? If you have determined their wants and needs correctly, they will find the cruise an excellent value.

The Cabin.

Size, design, and special features of the cabin influence price. For example, bathtubs and balconies may add to the cost. The location of a cabin is also important.

- Usually, the higher the deck is, the more expensive its cabins. Higher decks tend to be closer than lower ones to most public areas; lower decks are closer to the engine room and may be noisier.
- The cost of a cabin is also dictated, to some extent, by its proximity to the bow or stern of the ship. Most people prefer a cabin midship, which is usually more convenient to public areas and may offer a smoother trip, so these cabins cost a bit more.
- Outside cabins are more expensive than inside cabins of comparable size and comfort. For budget clients who don't mind not having a window or porthole, an inside cabin can save them money.

Discounts.

Agencies that simply sell cruises for the rates listed in brochures are not likely to be competitive. Discounts come in many guises.

- Most cruise lines offer discounts if passengers book soon after the cruise is open for booking, usually from six to 12 months in advance. The price might gradually rise toward the brochure rate during the first few months of booking, or the discount might simply end at a certain date.
- Cruise lines may also offer discounts close to the date of departure when there is excess space.
- Typically, cruise lines offer to help travel counselors promote group tours, and they may give discounts for groups with 10 to 15 passengers. They also may offer a free berth on the cruise segment only to the group leader, based on volume.
- Agencies obtain group rates from cruise lines that the agencies can offer to the general public on certain dates; sometimes a broad selection of dates is available to the agency and its affiliated counselors.
- Discount brokers also offer attractive rates. They advertise their toll-free numbers and websites in newspapers and magazines.
- In addition to discounts, some cruise lines offer additional perks to make it appealing for travelers to confirm their reservations. These perks can include onboard spending credits, free specialty dining, beverage packages, future cruise credits, and so much more. The cruise lines are getting creative in offering multiple amenities to attract more travelers.

Additional Costs

Beyond the quoted price of a cruise, passengers must pay for the onboard expenses that we discussed earlier—tips, personal expenditures, liquor, and shore excursions. In addition, two other costs should be considered when evaluating the total cost of a cruise: (1) port charges, fuel surcharges, and fees and (2) transportation to and from the embarkation point.

Port Charges.

Port charges are fees assessed by the cruise line that cover fees charged by governments or port facilities for the use of a port. Cruise lines may also include as port charges various fees for services, such as handling baggage and security on the gangway. A seven-day cruise might bring $120 in port charges.

Not all quoted prices include the port charges. Since 1997, most cruise lines serving the U.S. market have agreed to include these charges in their advertised prices, as part of the settlement of lawsuits. But occasionally, port charges are omitted from advertised prices. Also, cruises that operate in other parts of the world may not follow this policy. It's always wise to query the cruise line on this matter. It's also a good idea to ask if there have been any fuel surcharges or additional costs since the cruise price was published.

Air/Sea Packages. Passengers also need transportation to and from the embarkation point. Most fly to it. They might arrange and pay for their travel to the port on their own and pay a *cruise-only rate* for the cruise itself. But to provide incentives for people to book cruises, cruise lines offer special *fly/cruise* arrangements. These *air/sea* packages come in three varieties.

- The cruise line organizes an air charter between major cities and the port of embarkation.
- The cruise line gives passengers an air credit. Passengers then choose their own air itinerary, class of service, and route. If their chosen flight costs more than the air credit, they pay the difference. Some passengers may elect to use their own frequent-flyer miles.
- The cruise line negotiates a schedule and rate with the airline and pays for round-trip air service to the embarkation point. Passengers have little or no say in the airline or schedule. Any desired changes should be made through the cruise line's air desk as soon as possible; sometimes changes incur a fee.

When passengers buy an air/sea package, the cruise line is responsible for getting them to the ship. If delays or cancellations prevent them from making a departure, the cruise line will fly them to the next port, issue refunds, or do whatever is necessary. In contrast, when passengers make their own flight arrangements, they are responsible for getting to the ship on time, and no refund is given for missing the ship.

Transfers to and from the airport and pier are included in air-sea packages purchased from cruise lines. Passengers who buy their own air transportation have the option of buying round-trip transfers from the cruise line—an option that is usually more economical than paying taxi fares.

Making the Reservation

To reserve a cruise, travel counselors should have the following information:
- Names of all travelers (with names exactly as listed on passports).
- All travelers' complete birthdates, proofs of citizenship, passport numbers, and dates of expiration.
- Ship, date, and city of departure.
- Preference for type of cabin. Counselors should help clients choose the general type of cabin they prefer. But it's best if the client does not select a specific cabin or location because it is very likely the cabin will not be available. Typically, cruise lines assign cabins within a particular category on a first-come, first-served basis, starting midship and working toward the bow and stern.
- Preference for first or second sitting in the main dining room.
- Preference for a smoking or nonsmoking cabin—unless the entire ship is smoke-free, which most are that serve the U.S. cruising market.
- Any special occasions the client is celebrating.
- An indication of whether the client is a repeat cruiser on this ship or line. If he or she is a past cruiser for a particular cruise line, it is important to get a loyalty number. This may provide your client with preferred pricing, discounts, and additional amenities.
- Prebooked shore excursions desired, when available.
- Package choices, if any, for before and after the cruise.

Some travel counselors still book cruises by calling the cruise line's toll-free number, but they can make bookings in other ways. They can book most cruise lines on GDSs. Agencies that sell many cruises usually have a direct link with the cruise lines' computers. As a result, the agency's computer shows almost the identical information available to a reservationist for the cruise line, and the agency can book and confirm cabins and prices instantaneously. Many travel counselors book reservations on the cruise line's website once their agency has registered on the site.

Reservations should be made as early as possible to secure the best rates and cabins. The exception occurs when clients want to gamble on obtaining steep discounts during the last few weeks before departure. But if the cruise line foresees a full ship, there will be no discounts, and clients will be left with the highest prices and least desirable cabins, if any. For group bookings, reservations should be made with the cruise line's *group desk* eight to 20 months in advance. Cruise lines generally give group space as a **spread**—that is a range of cabins in various price categories. It is rare to obtain a **block** of cabins for a group all at the same price.

When a cruise is reserved, the cruise line cites an **option date,** which is the deadline for payment of a deposit. It also states the date for final payment and the total for each payment, including port charges and air taxes.

Travelers sometimes obtain a **guaranteed rate,** which means the cruise line promises they will receive either a cabin in their requested price range or an upgrade at no additional cost. In no instance should travel counselors tell clients that an upgrade is guaranteed.

Serving the Customer

Because cruising is associated with pampering and luxury, many travel counselors perform special services for cruise clients. They may purchase a bon voyage gift, such as a bouquet, which the cruise line places in the client's cabin, or a bottle of wine, which the waiter presents at dinner. Special requests to a cruise line should be made by telephone or computer, but a follow-up e-mail to the line helps ensure that the request is met.

For many cruisers, information may be a more important service. Counselors should

- Supply all cruise passengers with information about U.S. customs and immigration regulations (discussed in Chapter 2).
- Be sure clients understand that cruise lines reserve the right to change an itinerary, at the captain's discretion, without refunding passengers. Changes are usually dictated by weather or political events.
- Be sure passengers are aware of the limitations of onboard medical care. Those with medical conditions should consult their physicians. (Many travel counselors have their clients sign a disclaimer indicating that this information has been communicated to them.)

Travel counselors might also recommend that clients ask their doctors for advice about medication for seasickness. Dramamine, Marezine, and Bonine are over-the-counter drugs taken orally before sailing to prevent seasickness. Drowsiness is often a side effect of these drugs. Sea-Band is a band worn on the wrist that prevents motion sickness through pressure; no side effects have been reported. Sea-Band is drug-free and is endorsed by CLIA.

Clients are also likely to welcome information on destinations, independent sightseeing, tipping, shopping, and dressing. They frequently ask for advice about what to wear in the evening; because fashions do change,

ON THE SPOT

You are an assistant on the cruise director's staff on Wonderland Cruises. On every sailing, at least one passenger asks you a question such as, "Where do I find the best marijuana on an island?" or "Can you take some of my luggage through U.S. Customs because I'm over the exemption?" How do you respond?

Needless to say, if you respond positively to any of these questions, you will not only jeopardize your job but perhaps risk a fine or worse. Clients like these are not likely to appreciate a lecture. Have some boilerplate answers ready, such as, "I'm sorry, but I can't help you with that request. I much prefer my onboard cabin to spending time in a local jail cell!"

counselors should consult the individual line at the time of booking. Clients can also be given advice about how to arrange special events, how to avoid lines, which onboard activities they might enjoy, and how to avoid certain tourist traps or dangers at destinations.

Travel counselors can also enhance their clients' cruise by booking shore excursions for them in advance—if the cruise line permits—which increases the chances that clients will be able to take the excursions that match their interests. And the travel agency may earn a commission on the excursions (which does not happen if clients book the excursions through the cruise line after they're aboard). Travel counselors can book these excursions through experienced receptive ground operators who specialize in the destination. (Chapter 8 discusses tour operators.)

Many clients check the Internet before calling or stopping at an agency, and travel counselors should be familiar enough with the offerings there to know what their clients are seeing. Clients who spend a lot of time online may appreciate receiving e-mail with attachments of stories from various sites about their destination. Whether you search the Internet for appropriate information for your clients or refer to the sites of a handful of cruise lines with which you work frequently, nothing beats your ability to kindle excitement in clients and to find just the right itinerary and ship to meet their needs. Clients will find that calling you with their questions and comments is better than their staring at a computer screen in the long run, and direct contact builds the rapport between you and the clients.

Providing service for your clients doesn't end when they set sail. It is important to reach out to your client when they return home. Some agents like to send welcome home gifts to their clients. Others like to talk on the phone to learn what went well on their cruise and whether they can help plan their next cruise. It is important to have personal touchpoints with all your clients returning from any trip you planned and arranged.

Where Is the Cruise Industry Headed? As the cruise industry matures, it is becoming ever more popular and diversified. Though it has been dominated by the North American market in the past, globalization is increasing as more international passengers enter the market. Expectations are for continued interest in the return of some transatlantic crossings, expedition and exploratory style itineraries, small-ship offerings on the world's rivers and inland waterways, and megaships with their many onboard offerings. More focus also is foreseen for special markets, such as families, singles, retireds, active travelers, and LGBTs. (See Chapter 11 for a discussion of specialized sales).

CHAPTER HIGHLIGHTS

Here is a review of the objectives with which we began the chapter.

1. **Describe the key types of cruise lines and other ships available to vacationers.** Cruise ships are all-inclusive floating resorts that move from port to port. The cruise industry helped expand its market in part by creating different brands of cruise lines that could appeal to people of almost every income, age, or lifestyle. As a result, the lines fall into five main types: resort-style, premium,

luxury, specialty/expedition, and value brands. The ships themselves help create the brand. Recently built ships include megaships. Because of their size, megaships can provide amenities, attractions, and activities unthinkable a few years ago.

In addition to traditional cruise ships, vacationers also travel in smaller river cruise ships, windjammers, schooners, yachts, freighters, ferries, and tenders.

2. **Identify the most popular cruising areas.** The Caribbean/Bahamas is the most popular area. Peak season there runs from mid-December to mid-April. Four other popular areas include the Mediterranean (with cruising from April to October), Europe (from June to late August), Alaska (with Inside Passage cruises from mid-May to late September), and Mexico year-round.

3. **Outline the key attractions of life onboard a cruise.** Cabins vary greatly, but cruises generally are famous for their personal service and for the quantity and quality of their food. Many ships now offer alternatives to the traditional dining room, including restaurants as well as casual eating spots. Most cruise ships also provide a nonstop flow of activities, but passengers are free to choose to do as much or as little as they wish. On most ships, passengers can also find an array of useful services—such as an infirmary, duty-free shops, beauty salon and barber shop, laundry, religious services, a daily newspaper, and access to other forms of communication.

4. **Explain benefits and possible disadvantages of the typical cruise.** A cruise offers opportunities for both relaxation and entertainment. Prepayment alleviates financial worries and allows vacationers to predict the cost of the trip. Pampered personal service is found on most ships. The ship itself and the ability to visit many ports of call while unpacking only once are added benefits. Possible disadvantages include the fact that calls at port do not allow enough time to get an in-depth feel for the area or its culture. Also, bad weather can make a cruise miserable, and some people find cruises too confining. Seasickness is another potential problem, although cruise ships have stabilizers to minimize the ships' roll, and pharmacies sell several over-the-counter remedies.

Of course, whether a feature of a cruise is a benefit or a drawback depends on the individual traveler's perception, and travelers evaluate the importance of different features differently. The right cruise for an individual client is likely to depend on the itinerary and its length; on the ship's size, style and service; and on the cost.

5. **Name the factors that determine the cost of a cruise.** The length of the cruise, the timing (for example, during a value season or high season), and the ship itself all influence the price. The number of people per cabin also has an effect. Solo passengers can avoid paying a single supplement by taking the guaranteed share rate sometimes offered on some cruise lines; families or groups can save by taking advantage of the third/fourth person rate. Characteristics of the cabin—such as its size, design, feature, and location—also influence the price as do current world events and competition from other cruise lines.

The quoted price covers accommodations, meals, choices of entertainment at night, a full program of daytime activities, and transport to each port on the itinerary, as well as a ship's newspaper, special events, and other amenities. Some important costs, however, are usually not included in the price; these include port charges, tips, personal expenditures, liquor, and shore excursions. Transportation to and from the embarkation point may also add to the cost. Many travelers, however, save money by obtaining fly/cruise packages from the cruise lines, as well as discounts on the fare.

6. **Describe new trends in the cruise industry.** Many new ships are entering the market, including extremely large ships with a wide selection of onboard sporting activities as well as many small vessels suitable for river and canal cruising. Larger ships are offering dine-around possibilities in specialty restaurants, ranging from

elegant, more formal service to quick snack-type spots. Internet access for passengers is now available on many of the newer ships.

Today's itineraries include new destinations previously not reachable. Passengers reflect many nationalities today other than American, particularly European and Asian. Nevertheless, 50 percent or more of travelers departing U.S. ports are North Americans, departing not only from Miami and other Florida cities, but also New York, Boston, Galveston, and California, as well. Lastly, a number of travel agents are choosing to specialize in cruise sales and often are home-based, many of them continuing to work well into their retirement years.

KEY TERMS

A list of key terms introduced in this chapter follows. If you do not recall the meaning of any terms, see the Glossary.

adventure cruise
aft
air/sea
bareboat charter
berth
block
bow
cabin
country of registry
Cruise Lines International Association
   (CLIA)
cruise ship
deck plan
embarkation point
expedition
ferry
flag of convenience
fly/cruise
fore
freighter
green sheet
gross registered tonnage (GRT)
guaranteed rate
guaranteed share rate

hotel manager
knot
megaship
niche cruises
option date
pitch
port charges
port of call
purser
repositioning cruise
roll
Safety of Life at Sea (SOLAS) regulations
schooner
single supplement
space ratio
spread
stabilizer
stern
tender
third/fourth person rate
value season
windjammer
yacht

REVIEW QUESTIONS

1. Which cruises attract older clients? Wealthier ones? Those with families? Why?

2. What costs are not usually included in the price of a cruise?

3. How does river or canal cruising differ from ocean cruising?

4. Why might one purchase shore excursions in advance?

5. Why might clients prefer an inside cabin?

6. Where would one find information on ships to be launched next year?

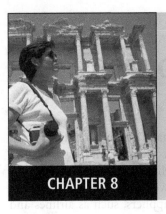

CHAPTER 8

Tours and Packages

OBJECTIVES

After completing this chapter, you should be able to

1. Identify at least five types of tours and packages.

2. Describe the key components of tours and packages.

3. Explain the tour contract and the responsibilities and liabilities of tour operators.

4. Discuss key criteria for selecting a tour operator.

5. Identify benefits that tours offer travelers and travel counselors.

OUTLINE

A WORLD OF TOURS
- What are the main types of tours and packages offered to today's travelers?

CREATING AND EVALUATING TOURS
- What are the most important variations in the components of tours?
- What issues are covered by the tour contract, and what are the responsibilities and liabilities of the tour operator?

SELLING TOURS
- How would you choose a tour operator?
- What benefits do tours offer travelers and travel agencies?

If you are in the market for a home computer, you might select and buy each component separately—monitor, printer, keyboard, drives, and scanner. Or you might avoid a lot of work by buying the entire system as one package.

In much the same way, many travelers turn to tours and packages. Through one operator, they buy various trip components—transportation, accommodations, meals, sightseeing, and other features. A **tour** offers a package of features for purchase as a single unit and is prepaid by the traveler before departure. The traveler is not given a breakdown of the price of each component and does not pay at each hotel, restaurant, or event.

The traveler might, for example, buy a tour that includes a flight to Miami, Florida, and the use of a rental car for a week—or a tour that includes a flight to London and a motor coach trip with a guide meandering all over England and Scotland for two weeks with stays at 10 hotels. In the typical case, tour operators or tour wholesalers assemble the components of the tour, buying features from suppliers, such as airlines, car rental companies, and hotels, and then marketing them as a package. The vast majority are sold to the public by travel agencies and their counselors, although a number are also available online.

The world of tours offers a wealth of opportunities for travelers and travel professionals alike. For travelers, tours offer bargains, convenience, security, and expert guidance. For travel professionals, the tour industry includes a fascinating range of career opportunities; the Close-Up on Careers in Tours describes a few of them. In this chapter, we consider the variety of tours available, how the components are put together, and how they are sold.

A World of Tours

In the early 1840s, an Englishman named Thomas Cook became the first to organize a group of travelers for a tour. For decades, he and his son took British travelers all over Europe, Africa, and the Middle East.

The process of taking people on tours, however, has become far more sophisticated than in Cook's time. It involves suppliers, such as airlines and hotels, as well as ground operators and destination management companies, which sometimes coordinate the operation of tours at the destination. Key jobs are performed by tour operators, tour wholesalers, and travel agencies, although their roles often overlap.

In fact, the terms *tour wholesaler* and *tour operator* are often used interchangeably, but strictly speaking, we can distinguish between them.

CLOSE-UP: CAREERS IN TOURS

Careers in tour operations offer some of the best opportunities in the travel industry for fulfilling dreams of traveling to exotic places and doing adventurous things. The amazing variety of tour companies includes those that specialize in international travel, escorted travel by groups, tours for inbound travelers, adventure and special-interest tours, travel for specific markets, such as museum societies, and more. Companies other than tour operators (such as hotels, tourism bureaus, cruise lines, and motor coach companies) often have departments for tour operations. Positions in tour operations use just about every background and specialty, but the biggest growth is in quality control, marketing, and e-commerce.

■ **Position** Sales agent/tour consultant/reservationist

Description The person in this position books tours, usually by telephone and most often for travel counselors. Duties include eliciting information in order to make recommendations, suggesting ways to combine the tour with other travel, determining tour costs, and discussing deposits and cancellation policies. Communicating with other departments about bookings and handling complaints from customers are also part of this job.

Qualifications This is sometimes an entry-level position. It requires study at a travel school or two years' experience as a travel agent or experience for one year with a tour wholesaler. It also requires excellent communication skills, a personable telephone manner, knowledge of geography, computer literacy, and ability to follow through on many details.

■ **Position** Quality assurance manager

Description The quality assurance manager troubleshoots complaints and problems and then incorporates corrective measures in tour products and procedures. To improve customer service and efficiency, the person in this position also works to implement customer evaluation processes, increase awareness of quality concerns within the company, and improve interdepartmental communication.

Qualifications The star performer in reservations or customer service usually assumes this role, but a company also may go outside the industry to hire someone who has completed college and postgraduate programs in quality assurance.

■ **Position** Group sales representative

Description This position specializes in travel by groups and has responsibility for planning, packaging, and selling air and motor coach tours. Specific duties include helping clients by designing and costing out a suitable itinerary, working with overseas offices and vendors to obtain services, sending written proposals to clients, booking, maintaining communication with clients, assisting in creating promotional materials, working with the operations coordinator on travel documents, preparing profit/loss analyses, and working with the customer service department to resolve complaints.

Qualifications Qualifications include study in travel school or two years in a tour operation or four years in another facet of the travel industry. Excellent communication skills, a pleasant telephone manner, an understanding of geography, and the ability to work as part of a team are also needed.

■ **Position** Product development manager

Description This manager creates tour packages. Duties

(continued on next page)

Typically, a ***tour wholesaler*** assembles the components of the tour into a package and pays a commission or offers a net rate to the tour seller; the wholesaler leaves tour operations to others. In contrast, ***tour operators*** not only assemble the package but may also operate aspects of the tour, own facilities or vehicles used on the tour, and employ personnel, such as escorts and drivers (see Figure 8.1). Tour operators may also sell directly to the public, and some own travel agencies. For simplicity, we use the term *tour operator* to refer to either wholesalers or operators.

The lines between tour operators and travel agencies are also blurred. Much as tour operators sometimes act like travel agencies by selling to the public, some travel agencies create, operate and sell their own tours.

Each year, thousands and thousands of tours and packages are sold. The reasons for this popularity are many because tours themselves come in many shapes and sizes to satisfy the varied needs of travelers.

Types of Tours

There are tours that will take you to Antarctica or the wilds of the Amazon for weeks with expert guides—and other tours that offer only a rental car and a weekend at a Las Vegas hotel. Because they are so varied, tours can be classified in many ways. One significant distinction is whether tours are marketed to the general public or to specific groups. Group tours include:

- Tours arranged for ***affinity groups,*** people who share a particular interest, age, or background and belong to a club, team, or other organization.

CLOSE-UP: CAREERS IN TOURS (cont.)

include conducting research on destinations and site inspections, planning logistics, creating the itinerary, negotiating for space and rates with suppliers, costing, keeping track of sales and clients' comments, and analyzing competitors' programs. The job may also entail participation in producing brochures, marketing, and training sales agents.

Qualifications Tour companies look for three or more years' experience with a tour operator and knowledge of the destination as well as personal contacts with hotels, attractions, and ground handlers. The position also requires creativity, the ability to follow through on details, and sensitivity to travelers' preferences. Analytical skills are an asset.

■ **Position** Tour manager/escort/director/leader

Description This person leads a tour group and is responsible for the well-being of the guests, handling any emergencies, and providing information. Typically, the tour manager conducts a particular series of tours within a specific area for months at a time. This is often a contract position.

Qualifications This position requires specialized knowledge about a destination and its people—the history, economy, politics, geology, geography, flora, and fauna. It requires leadership skills, common sense and

resourcefulness, the ability to remain calm in an emergency, good communication and organizational skills, attention to detail, the stamina to make it through long days, and enthusiasm for doing the same tour over and over for months. Tour companies look for experience in travel-related customer service, such as customer contact in the hospitality industry. They may also expect a specific educational background and language skills.

■ **Position** Director of tour escorts

Description This position is responsible for supervising the staff of tour guides—hiring, training, scheduling, briefing, and managing them in the field (which can be far-flung points throughout the world). Other duties include preparing reservations and instructions for each tour departure, writing tour manuals and routings for tours, and being on call 24 hours a day to deal with emergencies.

Qualifications This position is usually held by a person with managerial ability who has spent years in the field as a tour manager.

Other positions Business analyst; client services specialist; costing coordinator; district sales manager; manager of database marketing, planning, and analysis; product coordinator; step-on guide; tour guide; webmaster.

- *Convention tours,* designed for members of associations or corporations who are attending a convention, trade show, or similar gathering.
- *Incentive tours,* offered as a prize or reward to employees of a company, usually for productivity or sales performance.

Tours can also be divided into *custom-designed tours* and *prepackaged tours.*

Custom-Designed Tours

Until the 1960s, many travelers had their arrangements custom made to fit their individual requirements. Transportation, hotels, and other features of a trip were selected and bought in advance for the traveler, just to fit that person's needs. Today, a custom-designed tour is often called an **FIT.** The initials originally stood for "foreign independent tour"; nowadays, the term is used whether the tour is foreign or domestic. It is usually applied only to trips taken for pleasure, even though arranging a complicated business trip is often like arranging an FIT. Some travel professionals view the FIT acronym unofficially as 'free independent traveler.'

The market for FITs has been rather small. Because FITs are individualized, their packagers cannot obtain volume discounts from suppliers. As a result, FITs are more expensive than prepackaged tours. Generally, FIT wholesalers require that an FIT consist of at least three destinations and accommodations for at least six nights plus transfers and sightseeing at each destination.

FITs are usually more expensive than ready-made tours because they are custom designed to the traveler's dates, needs, interest, and specifications. This would be analogous to having a suit custom designed and tailored for you versus buying one off the rack at a department store. Designing FITs is time and labor intensive and requires an experienced employee to successfully operate such personalized trips. For some clients, creating an FIT is the way to create a unique and custom travel experience that can't be found elsewhere. FIT travel can be a good revenue stream for agencies with luxury travel clients.

As booking engines become increasingly powerful and sophisticated, the limitations on custom-designed tours seem to be easing. Some booking engines allow *dynamic packaging,* which is the ability to quickly put together a travel package involving multiple components (such as air, car rental, and hotel) from a variety of sources and offer it at a single price. A dynamic packaging tool gives you a direct connection to suppliers, providing access to the real-time availability and prices of the travel products. It allows you to obtain the components at net prices, add an appropriate markup and offer the package at a single price, hiding the price of components (**opaque pricing**).

Although the market for custom-designed tours may be growing, when we refer to "tours" in the following pages, we are talking about prepackaged tours. Depending on their structure, prepackaged tours can be classified as independent, hosted, or escorted, as the following sections explain.

The Independent Tour

For some people, the word *tour* evokes images of ruthless early-morning awakenings, regimented sightseeing, and unceasing hustle and bustle. An **independent tour,** however, has no group and no tour leader, and independent

---

FIGURE 8.1 Steps of a Tour

Traveler

Travel Agency

Online agency, brick-and-mortar agency or home-based agent

Tour Operator

Puts together tours and packages, markets them to the public and to the travel agency community. Buys possible tour inclusions below—either directly or through a ground operator/destination management company (DMC).

Possible Tour Inclusions

- Hotels
- Airlines
- Rail
- Motor Coaches
- Meals
- Local City Tours
- Social Events
- Tour Leaders
- Local Step-On Guides
- Baggage Handling
- Taxes, Some Tips
- Airport Transfers
- Miscellaneous

tours are very often called *packages* or *vacation packages*. They usually offer the traveler very good value because the operator gets excellent bulk rates from suppliers. If the traveler is willing to fit his/her plans into the operator's offer, such as choice of hotels or airline, the total trip package price is usually considerably less than trying to do it on one's own.

Participants travel independently; they may depart and return any day and can adjust the tour length to suit themselves. They may not even realize that they are on a tour. But it is a tour because participants buy some arrangements in advance as a package: They receive vouchers for the arrangements from the travel agency and give the vouchers to suppliers, such as hotels.

These independent packages may include many components of a trip or only a few. Many provide only transportation to a destination, round-trip transfers from the airport to hotel, and accommodations at one hotel for the number of nights the participant chooses. This kind of package is popular in resort areas where vacationers want only to relax and in cities that have public transportation and popular sightseeing tours.

Other packages include car rentals or stays at multiple hotels or both. The advertised car is usually compact or economy size, but participants may pay to upgrade it. When hotels are part of the package, participants often choose from a list of hotels with varying prices. They may arrive any day of the year (although they may pay surcharges during especially popular periods), and they may extend their trip by paying a fixed rate for each night beyond the number specified for the tour. They set their own pace and arrange each day to suit themselves.

A *fly/drive* package includes air transportation, a car rental, and a number of hotels. Often participants can stay at any of a specific chain's properties. Fly/drives are suited for travelers who wish to tour a particular region, stopping at a different place every night or two and enjoy the freedom of driving themselves. But, here again, the tour is pre-sold and pre-paid by the traveler, who does not pay each hotel or service during the trip.

The Hosted Tour

On a *hosted tour,* individuals travel independently, but a host is available at each destination to help them arrange activities. The *host* is a representative of the tour or ground operator. Typically, hosted tours include basic sightseeing or entertainment and offer optional arrangements for purchase.

Often, participants in a hosted tour may arrive on the day of their choice, choose from a range of hotels, and adjust the length of their stay. Some hosted tours include more than one destination. In each city, participants normally receive round-trip transfers from airport to hotel, one sightseeing tour to orient themselves, and the services of a host.

Other hosted tours offer less flexibility. On some, participants take a chartered flight and must stick to the dates selected for the flight. But even though they arrive together, the participants spend the tour as independent travelers, not as a group.

What does the host do? On most hosted tours, the host greets the participants when they arrive, gives them a brief orientation, and lets them know when he or she is available for further assistance. Usually, the host does not accompany travelers on any sightseeing tours. The typical host can be found at the desk in the lobby of each hotel on the tour. When the host is not at the hotel, tour members can receive help by calling the tour operator's local representative. In some instances, hosts can be found on cruise ships helping to coordinate groups on behalf of a tour operator.

The Escorted Tour

On an *escorted tour,* participants travel together as a group and are always accompanied by a professional *tour escort,* who is responsible for ensuring that the tour goes smoothly. Participants enjoy a structured program of sightseeing, meals, transportation, and accommodations. Details and difficulties are taken out of their hands.

Movement characterizes escorted tours. Unlike independent and hosted tours, escorted tours usually move from one place to another every one to three days—usually by motor coach. Participants do not select specific hotels; instead, they choose a tour whose cost is based on a specific grade of tour—such as budget, economy, classic, or deluxe (see Figure 8.1). During the tour, they stay as a group at hotels of the grade selected by the tour operator.

Tour escorts (also called *tour managers, tour leaders,* or *tour directors*) are usually gold mines of information, but the term *tour guide* is often reserved for local specialists on particular topics. Guides (sometimes called *step-on guides*) often join escorted tours briefly to conduct sightseeing of a city, museum, or art gallery. In fact, many cities require that locally licensed guides lead all sightseeing tours, for example, in Florence, Italy, or at the Palace of Versailles.

People who do not want to compromise may not enjoy escorted tours. If the motor coach is leaving, tour members must be ready to leave—even if they would rather sleep or shop an extra hour. A well-run tour tries to anticipate and meet each individual's needs, but an escorted tour limits the traveler's options by its nature. Traditionally, from the moment an escorted tour departs, participants travel together.

CLOSE-UP: ON THE JOB WITH SANDY JOHANSEN, TOUR ESCORT

Sandy Johansen, a teacher, applied in February for a position as a tour escort during the summer. The tour company could not guarantee how much work it could offer her, but it scheduled Sandy for two training sessions in April and a couple of one-day training tours on Saturdays in May. Sandy did well on the training tours.

"I just loved it. Of course, what really helped was working with an experienced tour manager who let me ease into things. I greeted people, learned their names, introduced them to each other when I could, and found out a little about them if there was time. Trying to learn their names was hard for me. I wish they had had name tags, but Happy Seniors Tours didn't use them, at least on this tour.

"I checked off their names on the manifest and kept track of who had not arrived yet. At the same time, I tried to overhear what Jan, the regular escort, was telling our motor coach driver. I was probably the most nervous when I was getting on the microphone to introduce myself. It was one thing to talk to travelers individually and another to see all 33 of them seated and looking in my direction. But Jan made it easier, and once I heard my voice going out there—well, I knew I'd be able to do this. It might just take a little getting used to.

"I studied the itinerary, which was an all-day wine châteaux tour in California. Jan mentioned in earlier training that I wouldn't be expected to know it all—a guide at each of the three vineyards would be the expert, and I could learn along with everyone. Whatever I did know was a bonus.

"Jan gave me a few prepared things that I could point out on the way to the first winery. Our coach also had television monitors at various intervals, and we played a tape about winemaking to get everybody in the mood; I made the announcement before the tape. Jan had a few good jokes related to what happened on the last tour to someone who got a little carried away with the winetasting. The clincher was that we might be picking that person up this time because he never made it back to the bus. I think the real moral of the story was, 'If you're not back, we're leaving!'

"In any case, it worked out well. Teaching will be a breeze when I go back in September—if I go back. I guess I will because the number of tours slows down dramatically in the late fall. But in a few years, who knows?"

Recently, many tour companies have made their tours more flexible in order to suit independent-minded travelers. Some offer *modules:* Instead of a full two-week escorted tour of Australia, for example, the traveler might be able to choose certain segments, such as three days in Sydney, three days in Melbourne, and four days on the Barrier Reef. Other tour companies have created options for their clients during the tour where they can choose from a list of one, two, or three different activities happening at the same time. This provides travelers an opportunity to customize their tour.

In other ways, too, tour operators are blending the categories of tours as they compete for travelers. Some independent tours, for example, now include escorts or hosts for city tours as optional elements.

Special-Interest Tours

Competition for travelers is the basis for another trend: the development of *special-interest tours,* designed for people with an interest in a particular topic or activity—such as photography or skiing, scuba diving or Russian, baseball or Buddhism. One family might choose a Working Cattle Drive tour, where they learn to ride horses, get to sleep in a lodge, and gather around the campfire at night. Another might tour southern China for InspirAsians Cooking School, learning secrets from local chefs and tasting local delicacies.

Special-interest tours provide exceptional opportunities for both traveler and travel professional. What is it worth to take cooking lessons from a famous French chef or to travel with 20 other people who share your love of butterfly collecting? On a special-interest tour, the expertise required of the tour operator and the tour leader will be more in depth and focused.

One type of special-interest tour is the *adventure tour,* which focuses on outdoor physical activity—horse or camel riding, biking, backpacking, canoeing, or sailing. Adventure tours are often classified as hard or soft. **Hard adventures** feature strenuous activity (for example, kayaking or mountaineering), remote locations, or risk. **Soft adventures** involve physical activities that offer little physical challenge or danger, such as walking from inn to inn or river rafting on a mild river. Tours that appeal to an interest in the environment—*ecotours*—are also popular. An ecotour may consist of trips to view natural wonders, such as unusual birds or waterways, or trips in which participants work to repair environmental damage. The International Ecotourism Society (TIES) defines *ecotourism* as "responsible travel to natural areas that conserves the environment and improves the well-being of local people." Many ecotours are also classified as adventure tours.

Other special-interest tours include

- Ski, dive, golf, or tennis tours at hotels with all the equipment, staff, and services needed. They also offer special courses or well-known instructors.
- Cultural tours, which may focus on art, architecture, history, anthropology, or similar subjects.
- Tours to special events, such as the Olympics, music and theater festivals, Mardi Gras, Oberammergau—the list grows every year.
- Religious tours, which visit shrines and are often led by a clergy member.

Gourmet, winetasting, horticultural, gambling, shopping, and photography tours are among the many other types of special-interest tours offered. Many of these special-interest tours are led by key figures with a following and are referred to as **Pied Pipers**.

FIGURE 8.1 An Escorted Tour

The luxury travel company, Abercrombie & Kent (abercrombiekent.com), offers private tours and small-group adventures on all seven continents. Its Resident Tour Director® guides the journey from start to finish with help from specialist local guides.

Source: Reprinted by permission of Abercrombie & Kent.

✔ CHECK-UP

Putting together a tour may involve work by a host of travel professionals, including
✔ Suppliers.
✔ Tour wholesalers and tour operators.
✔ Travel agencies.
✔ Ground operators and destination management companies.

Two basic types of tours are
✔ Custom-designed tours.
✔ Prepackaged tours, which may be independent, hosted, or escorted.

Popular types of special-interest tours include
✔ Adventure tours, with hard adventure or soft adventure.
✔ Ecotours.

Creating and Evaluating Tours

■ WHAT ARE THE MOST IMPORTANT VARIATIONS IN THE COMPONENTS OF TOURS?

■ WHAT ISSUES ARE COVERED BY THE TOUR CONTRACT,
AND WHAT ARE THE RESPONSIBILITIES AND LIABILITIES OF THE TOUR OPERATOR?

Successful tours require the combined skills and resources of many people. What do they consider in choosing the components of the tour, and how are the pieces put together?

Components of a Tour

If you were developing a tour, what would you include? Obviously, the answer depends on the intended market. Some tours offer a minimum of elements; others are all-inclusive. Table 8.1 outlines variations to consider.

Transportation. Most tours include transportation as part of the package. We discussed a *fly/drive*, which combines air transportation and a car rental. An *air/sea* or *fly/cruise* combines air and ship transportation; a *rail tour* includes transportation by train; a *motor coach tour* uses buses to carry tour participants from destination to destination to visit major attractions. Many tours also include transfers to and from airports, hotels, and rail stations.

Itineraries. Years ago, most tours packed in as wide an area with as many stops as possible. Today's tours are more likely to aim for an in-depth exploration of a smaller area.

For escorted tours, going from site to site within countries is a large part of the trip's enjoyment, but the hallmark of a good tour is a relaxed pace. A trip that changes hotels every night takes a lot of energy. Long stays at key destinations distinguish deluxe tours. As a rule, tour operators avoid more than 10 hours of travel or 350 miles (563 km) in a day, and they average substantially fewer miles per day.

For any intercontinental trip, consider time zones and jet lag when judging an itinerary. The day of departure, the day of arrival, and the departure day on the return often amount to lost days for clients. An eight-day, seven-night tour to Europe, for example, might consist of only five days of touring. When comparing tours, travel professionals must take into account the number of travel days and the actual number of tour days that are included in the price.

Tours tend to use one of three types of itineraries:

■ A *circle itinerary*, which brings travelers back to their starting point via a different route. Passengers experience varied sights and places throughout, without retracing their steps. This approach suits tours that aim to cover a broad area, such as "Highlights of Central Europe."

■ An *open-jaw itinerary*, which begins and ends in different places. For example, a "Highlights of Italy" tour might visit Milan, Venice, Florence, Pisa, and Rome—without returning to Milan. This type of itinerary works well when returning to the starting point would mean retracing steps or visiting less desirable locations.

TABLE 8.1 Components of Tours

Component	Special Features
Transportation	Air travel: type and class
	Departure point
	Airline
	Ground transportation: type and class
	Transfers
Itinerary	Number of stops
	Time spent at each stop
	Amount of time traveling
	Amount of leisure time
Accommodations	Class of lodging
	Location of lodging
	Choice of room types
	Location of rooms
Meals	Number of meals
	At restaurant or hotel
	Choice of meals and meal plans
Other	Sightseeing: included or optional
	Special events: number and kind
	Side trips
	Luggage handling
	Luggage allowance
	Tips: Included or optional
	Leadership

■ A *hub-and-spoke itinerary,* which is an increasingly popular approach. Travelers set up their base at a hotel in one city for several days and take day trips into the surrounding area, thus avoiding packing, unpacking, and moving baggage. They might also spend one night away from the home base. The hub-and-spoke approach allows travelers to explore a region in depth. For example, on a "Highlights of France" tour, travelers might be based in Paris and take day trips to the numerous sights within striking distance of the City of Light, such as Versailles or Giverny.

Accommodations. Proximity to sightseeing attractions, transfer services, parking for the motor coach, and handicapped accessibility may all be important in selecting hotels for a tour. Hosted and independent packages usually offer participants a choice among several hotels in different price ranges. On escorted tours, participants stay together at a hotel. Thus, hotels selected for escorted tours must be able to register groups efficiently, serve group meals, and (because all tour participants pay the same price) provide similar rooms for everyone in the group.

Meals. Tour operators can cut their costs substantially by requiring tour participants to pay for their own meals or by adjusting the kind of meals offered. A tour operator that includes five dinners and five lunches is offering more than an operator that includes 10 breakfasts. A tour operator that permits an unlimited choice from the menu (à la carte) is offering more than an operator that arranges a set menu or limited choice. (Look again at Table 6.4, for a description of various meal plans.)

Escorted tours typically start after breakfast on the first day and conclude before dinner on the last. When meals are included in the tour but not provided at the hotel, participants are usually served at well-known restaurants. Often the restaurant provides special tour menus (table d'hôte) or limits choices to four or five entrées. Deluxe tours may offer à la carte dining where the guest may order anything he wishes on the menu.

Sightseeing. Tours usually include some attractions that are standard tourist draws, such as Walt Disney World Resort, Busch Gardens Tampa Bay, and Universal Orlando Resort in Florida. On an independent or a hosted tour, travelers generally receive sightseeing vouchers and admission tickets ahead of time or pick them up at the first stop on their trip.

On an escorted tour, attractions might be added during the tour, depending on the interests of the group. Most attractions are prepaid, and the tour escort will have tickets or vouchers for members of the tour. Sometimes these must be obtained at the attraction itself, in which case, the tour escort precedes the group and pays the admission fee.

Tour operators can significantly lower the cost of a tour by reducing the number of attractions included. An escorted itinerary that includes phrases such as "Balance of the day at leisure" or "Today you are free to explore" may reflect such cost cutting. But the result may actually suit many travelers. They may like the idea of having free time and independence and prefer not paying for a constant schedule of activity. If they wish, they can purchase optional sightseeing tours on the spot.

Tour operators can also lower costs by selecting lesser-known attractions. Again, travelers may prefer this cost-cutting option. Going to lesser-known areas, rather than traditional tourist hotspots, may provide a better chance to experience the local culture and obtain an in-depth look at a destination. Increasingly, vacation packages and tours incorporate nontraditional sightseeing, such as visits to local farms and walking tours.

Other Components. The fare for some tours includes services—such as baggage handling—or covers tips, service charges, or taxes. Some tours also offer items, such as flight bags, free drinks, or other gifts—elements that might be of little value to many travelers.

Price. Whatever the components of a tour, travelers are likely to weigh them against its price. A small percentage of tours are quoted per couple (the most obvious are honeymoon packages). But the vast majority of prices are given *per person, double occupancy*, which means that each person pays this price when sharing a room with another. Single occupancy prices are higher, sometimes much higher; the additional price paid by a person traveling alone is called the **single supplement**. A few tours try to find a roommate for a traveler who does not wish to pay the single rate. When the tour operator will not guarantee a roommate, the traveler may have to pay the single supplement, often referred to as a **forced single**.

Developing and Operating Tours

Planning and Negotiating. Whatever a tour's components, its creation begins with planning, as Figure 8.2 indicates. Ideas for a tour come from many sources, including customers, but having exciting ideas does not ensure success. Market research should be a key component of the planning stage. It can help both to generate ideas for tours and to test the viability of ideas.

FIGURE 8.2

Developing a Tour

The process of creating a tour involves the chain of linked steps outlined here. Any break in the chain can make the tour a failure.

Step 1: Planning
The idea for creating a tour might come from market research, a customer, inspiration, or just about anywhere. The planning process might involve steps, such as site inspections and market research. It's wise to allow a lead time of one year.

Step 2: Negotiations
Secure the services of suppliers. Negotiate prices and create an itinerary.

Step 3: Costing
Determine the cost of each component of the tour. Add in all the costs of promotion, sales, and overhead to determine net cost. Mark up the net cost to establish the price.

Step 4: Promotion
Produce a brochure and Web page. Promote the tour through advertisements, direct mail, group presentations, or a Pied Piper.

Identifying the needs of the target market and evaluating what a destination has to offer to meet these needs are crucial tasks.

In recent years, market research has often encouraged specialization. Tour operators and agencies may specialize by concentrating on tours for certain demographic segments—seniors or the youth market, for instance—or on certain destinations—such as the South Pacific or Costa Rica—or on special interests. Specialization can be the key to success, or even survival.

Negotiations with suppliers are the second step in creating a tour. Hotels and other suppliers typically reduce their prices for tour operators when the operators have generated a predetermined volume of business; tour operators make their money by selling the same tour to many clients. Once prices have been negotiated, an itinerary is created.

Setting the Price. Next comes the process of establishing a selling price for the tour. To set the price, some tour operators first calculate how much each participant in the tour will cost them. To this cost the tour operator adds a markup sufficient to cover all promotional costs, staff salaries, commissions it must pay to travel agencies selling the tour, and other overhead. Finally, the operator adds a markup to allow a profit, setting the price for the tour.

Determining the cost of a tour, however, is an art, and it often requires a great many assumptions and estimates. A motor coach, for example, costs a tour operator a flat fee no matter how many people take the tour, but its cost per participant depends on how many tours are sold. Tour operators can economize on their costs by adjustments in four main areas: meal costs, hotel quality and location, length of stay in principal cities, and sightseeing.

Promoting the Tour. Promotion is the fourth step in developing a tour. Tour operators produce brochures, catalogues, and websites describing the features, terms, and conditions of their tours. These are important sales tools.

Usually the front of a brochure describes the tour operator's credentials and experience along with key characteristics of tours and explanations of terms used in the brochure. The main section of the brochure lists each tour and describes its itinerary, highlights, and costs. (Some operators put the costs at the end or in a special insert.) At the back are the terms and conditions of the contract between the tour operator and the traveler.

Websites for tours generally present the same information as brochures. They must be well designed, so they are easy for people to understand and to navigate when they are looking for specific information. The websites of many tour operators allow you to print or e-mail an electronic version of their brochures. Sometimes the operator has created these e-brochures by adding information to a *template*.

Once brochures and Web pages are produced, the tour operator promotes the tour through selected advertising media. The promotional campaign might include some combination of commercials on radio or television, advertisements in newspapers or magazines, ads and links on other websites, mailings and flyers, and presence in the social media—all depending on the clientele one is trying to reach.

After the Sale. The job of tour operators does not stop with the sale. They are also responsible for:

- *Documentation.* Incoming reservations must be processed; invoices for passengers' final payments must be issued; tickets, vouchers, baggage tags, and so on must be sent to all confirmed participants.
- *Operation.* The components of the tour must be coordinated by a tour manager, escort, host, or ground representative.

- *Relations with suppliers.* All suppliers must be given correct and final information, such as the names and special needs of participants, their passport data, and rooming arrangements. Payment schedules must be established and followed.

The Tour Contract

In the back of their brochures, operators must disclose the provisions of the contract with travelers. The details of this contract are extremely important to both the traveler and the seller. The following are five key issues.

Items Not Included. How many meals are included on the tour? (Clients need to budget for those not included.) What sightseeing is included? What is "optional" or "suggested"? (Clients need to budget for independent sightseeing or for extra, optional tours.) What tips, if any, are included?

Unless a brochure clearly states that a feature is included, assume that it is not. Many tour operators state explicitly what is not included.

Deposit and Payment Schedule. For prepackaged tours, the payment schedule is usually as follows:
- All tour operators require a deposit to hold a reservation more than a few days. The deposit must be received by the tour operator within a specified time (often seven to 15 days) after the reservation is made, or it will be canceled.
- The balance, or final payment, is due no later than 30 to 60 days before departure, or as specified in the brochure.

After the deadline for final payment has passed, tour operators usually still accept reservations, with full payment due immediately if space is still available.

The procedure is different for FITs. Usually the FIT wholesaler/operator requires a nonrefundable deposit before beginning work and then sends a suggested itinerary and a cost quotation to the travel counselor. Once the client accepts the itinerary and the price, the FIT operator secures confirmations of all arrangements, and the deposit submitted earlier is credited against the tour purchase.

Cancellation and Refund Policy. Tour operators reserve the right to cancel a tour before departure. The cause may be political events, social conditions, or weather. Escorted tour operators also cancel tours when there is an insufficient number of participants for a particular date; their cost for hotel accommodations, sightseeing, and the motor coach is based on a minimum number traveling together.

If clients cancel before departure, they are usually liable for a **cancellation penalty,** particularly if the cancellation is made close to departure. To cover this penalty, travelers can obtain *cancellation insurance* through the tour operator or through an insurance agency; see Chapter 11 for a discussion of this and other types of insurance.

If part of the tour is canceled by the operator, clients are typically entitled to a refund for the value of the portion missed. Most tour operators reserve the right to substitute tour elements with or without notice. If the substitution lowers the quality of an element, the client receives a refund for the difference between the costs of the original and the substituted element, either on the spot or after returning home.

ON THE SPOT

Mr. and Mrs. Sargent have just returned from a cherry blossom tour of Washington, D.C. They walk into the travel agency with itinerary and sales brochure firmly in hand. With barely a word of greeting, they explain their mission. "Look at this! In black and white, clear as day, the brochure promised that we'd 'see such historical monuments as the Washington, Lincoln, and Jefferson memorials.' But we rode right by them on the bus! The driver wouldn't let us off to see them! We want a refund. At least a partial one! This is outrageous." If you were the travel counselor, what would you say?

First, you should be sure to hear the Sargents out completely without interrupting and to show that you understand their complaint and sympathize with their point of view. Do not argue. But do remind them that you had gone over the itinerary and brochure with them before the trip and that neither mentions stopping at or visiting the monuments. A lot depends on your agency's policies for dealing with dissatisfied clients. But generally speaking, no refund would be made under these circumstances.

That is why it's important that clients understand before purchasing the tour the difference between seeing or viewing a place (as from the outside in passing) versus visiting a place (as going inside with the admission fee paid by the tour operator).

Once the tour is under way, most tour operators reserve the right to expel tour participants for due cause—without compensation.

Limitations on the Operator's Responsibility and Liability. Tour operators point out that they cannot be held responsible for the actions of airlines, hotels, bus companies, or any other supplier or its employees. They also disclaim responsibility for any loss, damage, or delay caused by events outside their control or by tour participants.

Status of Fares and Rates. The tour brochure describes whether costs differ according to seasons or departure dates. Most tour operators set their rates for an entire year.

Some tour operators quote prices for the tour plus airfare from large cities. Almost all operators also have *land rates*, which are rates that exclude transportation costs between the traveler's home and the start or end of the tour. Land rates apply for the effective dates covered by the brochure and typically do not change if the tours are within the United States and are quoted in U.S. dollars.

For tours outside the United States, the land rates are also usually quoted in U.S. dollars, and most tour operators reserve the right to adjust prices if currency fluctuations affect them. Once final payment has been received, most do not impose any surcharge to cover currency changes. However, airlines may incur fuel surcharges up to the time air tickets are issued.

✔ **CHECK-UP**

If a tour operator wants to economize, key possible targets are
✔ Meal costs.
✔ Hotel quality and location.
✔ Length of stay in principal cities.
✔ Number of sightseeing attractions.

Essential information in a tour brochure includes
✔ What is included in the tour and covered by the price and what is not included.
✔ The deposit and payment schedule.
✔ The operator's cancellation and refund policy.
✔ Limitations on the operator's responsibility and liability.
✔ The status of the fares and rates published in the brochure.

Selling Tours

■ HOW WOULD YOU CHOOSE A TOUR OPERATOR?

■ WHAT BENEFITS DO TOURS OFFER TRAVELERS AND TRAVEL AGENCIES?

Each tour is a unique product, and brand-name tour companies are few. The public often needs help making decisions concerning which tours and operators are best. Thus, it is not surprising that only a small percentage of travelers book tours online. There are so many tours to choose from, and so much is riding on those choices, that the travel counselor is likely to remain important in selling tours for years to come. The travel counselor's task is to choose among tour operators and tours in order to satisfy the client's needs.

Choosing Tour Operators

There are more than 2,000 tour operators in the United States. In Canada, there are fewer tour operators, however, all travel agents have options to book any tour operator in the world. There are tour companies specializing in international travel, domestic escorted travel, inbound travel, and adventure travel, as well as travel for specific markets, such as travelers with special needs, LGBTs, families, teens, students, or museum societies.

Out of all these possibilities, travel counselors must find tour operators that can be trusted to provide all arrangements as advertised and to offer substitutions of the highest possible quality, if unforeseen circumstances arise. Obviously, the tour operator selected should be experienced, reputable, and financially stable.

Membership in Professional Organizations. One measure of a tour operator's quality is whether the operator has met the standards for membership in professional organizations. Two of the best known are the United States Tour Operators Association and the National Tour Association.

The *United States Tour Operators Association (USTOA)* is a professional association for worldwide tour operators that conduct business in the United States. Its motto, "Integrity in Tourism," requires members to adhere to the highest standards in the industry. Members also must demonstrate ethical and financial responsibility in their business conduct in order to instill confidence in their financial stability, reliability, and integrity.

Among USTOA's goals are to:
- Educate the travel industry, government agencies, and the public about tours, vacation packages, and tour operators
- Protect consumers and travel agents from financial loss in the event of an active member's bankruptcy, insolvency, or cessation of business
- Foster a high level of professionalism within the tour operator industry
- Promote and develop travel on a worldwide basis

The National Tour Association (NTA) is the leading business-building association for professionals serving customers traveling to, from, and within North America. Its 700 buyer members are tour operators who buy and package travel product domestically and around the world. Its seller members (500 destinations and 1,100 tour suppliers) represent numerous travel products and have access to many networking opportunities.

Additional Criteria. Answering several questions can help you narrow the field of tour operators to the most promising candidates.
- *Is the operator known for consistent operation?* Does the tour operator have a history of canceling scheduled departures or raising prices between the date of reservation and departure?
- *Is the operator a specialist?* Operators that specialize in particular markets tend to know their product in depth.
- *How long has the operator been in business?* In the travel business, longevity may be a meaningful measure of quality. The older tour operators have established relationships with their suppliers over the years, and clients on their tours receive preferential treatment. Certain tour operators—because of their contacts, their experience, and the repeat business they provide—can insist on special arrangements and considerations for their clients.
- *Is there a strong relationship between the operator and the travel agency?* Clients benefit from close relationships with better accommodations,

superior service, and acceptance of last-minute changes or payments. If the operator is a preferred supplier, travel agencies may also benefit by earning higher commissions.

In Canada, there are consumer protection bodies, such as the **Travel Industry Council of Ontario (TICO)**, British Columbia Consumers Protection (BCCP) and, in Québec, the Office de la Protection du Consommateur (OPC). These regulatory bodies ensure that consumers are protected if the tour operator does not provide services as promised or if the tour operator files bankruptcy.

Identifying the Benefits of a Tour

Selling a tour requires that counselors have a solid grasp of how the features of a tour might translate into benefits for their clients. Some clients may be interested in purchasing a tour just to save money on airfare; others may want a particular destination or a chance to socialize with people of like interests.

Chapter 10 discusses how you can determine which features of a trip a particular client is likely to perceive as benefits. In general, however, tours offer four key benefits:

- *Known costs.* Tours are prepaid, and additional travel costs can be calculated with fair accuracy in advance. As a result, tour participants need to carry less money with them than other travelers and often are protected against unfavorable currency fluctuations or other unexpected expenses.
- *Savings.* Tour operators negotiate discounts from suppliers. As a result, prepackaged tours can be significantly less expensive than the same trips arranged by individuals.
- *Guaranteed entrances.* Tour operators make block purchases of tickets to attractions and events to ensure that their clients have access. Individual travelers may find it impossible to obtain tickets that are available to tour participants. Tour participants also can avoid lines for some attractions.
- *Reliable sightseeing features.* Tour operators use their long experience to design tours that provide tried-and-true sightseeing attractions and other activities.

Other benefits depend on the format of the tour. For example, independent tours enable clients to obtain the benefits of volume discounts and prearranged guaranteed rates without sacrificing independence and flexibility. Escorted tours require clients to sacrifice some flexibility, but their disadvantages are matched by other benefits, such as

- *Security.* On escorted tours, hotels, restaurants, and attractions are chosen with security in mind.
- *Peace of mind and relaxation.* Travelers feel safer with escorts along. They know that if problems arise, the escort is there to help. And they do not have to worry about getting from the airport to attractions or waste time each day finding hotels. For many people, escorted motor coach tours are the most relaxing form of transportation. When the motor coach starts in the morning, the sightseeing begins; when the motor coach stops, it is magically in the right place for a visit, a meal, or an overnight stay. Border crossings, airport arrivals and departures, hotel check-ins, and baggage are all handled by someone else.
- *Efficiency.* Escorted tours are carefully planned by people who know the area intimately in order to make the best use of time and know which dates and times certain sites are closed.
- *Expertise.* Clients are assured that the operator knows where to take them and that local advice and assistance are available for special tastes. The

escort or tour director often points out customs, traditions, and unusual phenomena that independent travelers miss.

- *Sociability.* People on escorted tours can meet and socialize with fellow travelers with the same interests. Many become lifelong friends.

In short, escorted tours provide structure and security, which may be especially desirable on trips to exotic locations. Thus, it is not surprising that a high percentage of leisure travel in Africa, Asia, and South America involves escorted tours. (Hosted and independent tours are popular at beach destinations in the Bahamas, the Caribbean, and Mexico.) The features of escorted tours are also likely to be seen as benefits by first-time travelers abroad, by dependables, and by older travelers.

Helping Clients Choose a Tour

The selection of tour operator for a client is of utmost importance. While some travelers may feel comfortable enrolling with an unknown operator online, most do not know how to select a reputable operator and, if left to their own devices, may select a fly-by-night company that looks beautiful on a website but is lacking in substance.

Matching clients with the right tours is not easy. Operators' brochures and catalogues are indispensable tools both for learning which tour would suit which client and for selling the tour to the client. The Close-Up on Selling the Right Tour includes tips on how to use them to select tours. On many of the websites for tours, you can ask for lists of tours that meet certain criteria—such as tours to a certain destination or tours with a particular theme or tours of a certain type—thus making it easier to narrow your search for a suitable tour.

In theory, travel counselors should know the details of every tour in every brochure in their offices and be able to lead the client deftly through the features of each. In practice, travel counselors must limit their detailed knowledge to the offerings of the tour operators whose products they sell frequently. Developing preferred supplier relationships (as discussed in chapters 1 and 13) simplifies this job. However, in some cases, these operators may not offer a tour that matches the traveler's needs, and the counselor may offer a tour with some other well-known operator that does not have a preferred supplier arrangement with the travel agency.

Ultimately, it is the client's trip, and the choice of the tour is the client's. But here are a few steps that can help clients make a wise choice.

- Offer clients one or two choices that seem to match their desires.
- Highlight points unique to that trip in order to help clients examine and compare the components of the tour.
- Go through all the details to make certain the clients understand them.
- Take the initiative to summarize the provisions of the tour operator's contract, although clients should be encouraged to read each part of the contract. In particular, review what each tour does and does not include, the deposit and payment schedule, the cancellation policy, the limitations on the operator's responsibility and liability, and the status of fares and rates in the brochure.

Once the tour operator and tour have been chosen, the booking requires just a toll-free call to the tour operator or an entry at a computer. Many tour operators can be reached through GDSs, and almost all have websites.

Electronic booking bypasses the possible nuisance of being put on hold, but it does not allow for questions.

Benefits to Travel Agencies

Selling tours offers important advantages to travel agencies. It allows them to provide clients with time-tested products that give good value for the price. Other benefits to travel agencies include

- *Speed and efficiency.* The features of a tour can be purchased from a single source—the tour operator. Dealing with a tour operator may require only one telephone call, one written communication, and one payment. The operator prepares the documentation.

- *Maximum earnings.* Selling tours may increase commissions. The price on which the tour operator pays a commission typically includes the cost of items that clients would otherwise pay for out of their pockets at the destinations, such as meals, special events, tips, and taxes. In addition, agencies can earn higher commissions from tour operators based on the volume of bookings made.

- *Objective advice.* Operators specialize in particular destinations, and they know their territory. They can provide travel counselors with advice about accommodations, sightseeing, climate, culture, and current trends.

Operating their own tours is also an attractive option to some travel agencies. Doing so allows them to add their own markups instead of being dependent on suppliers' commissions. But agencies should be careful before operating their own tours. It is a complicated, time-consuming, and risky business. Usually, the costs for staff and promotion must be incurred before a single sale is made. Also, one must often place advance deposits with hotels and airlines in order to hold space, thus requiring cash flow. Agencies should first work with experienced operators, "sell into" existing tours, have tour operators dedicate a tour for a specific group, and then learn the ropes by operating small local tours.

CHAPTER WRAP-UP

CHAPTER HIGHLIGHTS

In this chapter, we outlined basic facts and concepts needed to find one's way through the ocean of information about the multitude of tours. Here is a review of the objectives with which we began the chapter.

1. **Identify at least five types of tours.** Tours may be divided into those marketed to the general public and those intended for members of specific groups, such as affinity groups. Tours may also be classified into custom-designed tours, or FITs, and prepackaged tours. Depending on their structure, prepackaged tours are classified as independent, hosted, and escorted tours; independent tours are very often called packages or vacation packages. On both independent and hosted tours, participants travel independently, not as a group; but on hosted tours, a host is available to help travelers at each destination. On escorted tours, participants travel as a group and are accompanied by tour escorts. Many tours of various types are special-interest tours, designed to appeal to people interested in a particular topic or activity.

2. **Describe the key components of tours.** The major components of tours are transportation, itinerary, lodging, meals, and sightseeing. Typically, the components are packaged by a tour operator or tour wholesaler for sale by a travel agency; however, some travel agencies also package tours, and some tour operators sell their tours to the public themselves. Tour packagers usually obtain the components at reduced prices from suppliers and add a markup to the total cost to establish the selling price. The price is usually given per person for double occupancy. Tour packagers can economize on their costs primarily by adjusting meal costs, hotel quality, the length of stay in principal cities, and sightseeing.

3. **Explain the tour contract and the responsibilities and liabilities of tour operators.** Tour operators publish their contract with tour participants in their brochures, catalogues, and websites. They set out what is included in the tour, the payment schedule, the cancellation and refund policy, the status of fares and rates, as well as limitations on the operator's responsibility and liability. Many operators explicitly state in their brochures what is not included in the tour. Tour contracts vary, but generally they require a deposit; final payment is usually due at least 30 to 60 days before departure. Tour operators reserve the right to cancel a tour before departure, and most reserve the right to expel tour participants for due cause without compensation. Prices may vary with the date of the tour, and, for tours abroad, most operators reserve the right to adjust prices to reflect currency fluctuations. Reliable tour operators accept responsibility for fulfilling the terms and conditions described in their brochures. But they disclaim responsibility or liability for the actions of suppliers and for any loss or delay caused by passengers or by events outside their control.

4. **Discuss key criteria for selecting a tour operator.** The ideal operator is experienced, reputable, and financially stable. The operator's membership in professional organizations, such as USTOA or NTA, its relationship with the travel agency, its reputation for consistent operation, its specialization, and its longevity are specific factors worth considering when choosing an operator.

5. **Identify benefits that tours offer clients and travel counselors.** For most clients, benefits include knowing the cost before the trip and receiving a good price, assured entrances to attractions, and reliable features. Tour guides provide additional benefits on hosted and escorted tours. Of course, benefits vary with the traveler and the type of tour. For many travelers, escorted tours provide additional benefits, such as security, peace of mind, an efficient use of travel time, and opportunities to socialize. For travel counselors, the advantages of selling tours include the speed and efficiency of booking many elements through one source, the income generated for the time expended, and the advice available from expert operators.

KEY TERMS

A list of key terms introduced in this chapter follows. If you do not recall the meaning of these terms, see the Glossary.

adventure tour	package
affinity group	Pied Piper
cancellation penalty	single supplement
ecotour	soft adventure
escorted tour	special-interest tour
FIT	step-on guide
fly/drive	tour
forced single	tour escort
hard adventure	tour guide
host	tour operator
hosted tour	tour wholesaler
independent tour	Travel Industry Council of Ontario
land rate	(TICO)
National Tour Association (NTA)	United States Tour Operators
opaque pricing	Association (USTOA)

REVIEW QUESTIONS

1. What are the differences between an independent tour and a hosted tour?

2. What does the price of a tour usually exclude?

3. For some participants on escorted tours, enjoyment of the tour depends on the tour escort. Why?

4. Clients often object to the high cost of traveling as a single. How would you deal with this objection?

5. What can travel counselors do to keep clients booking with them rather than directly on the Internet, and how can travel counselors harness the Internet for tour sales?

Part 3:
Marketing Travel

Chapter 9
Marketing

Chapter 10
Making a Sale

Chapter 11
Specialized Sales

Marketing

OBJECTIVES

After completing this chapter, you should be able to

1. Outline the marketing process and name the four Ps.

2. Summarize key decisions that a travel business must make about its product.

3. Describe the major forms of promotion.

4. Identify the distribution system and selling sites most often used by travel businesses.

5. Describe pricing strategies frequently used by travel suppliers and travel agencies.

OUTLINE

THE MARKETING PROCESS
- What are the basic components of the marketing process and the marketing mix?

WHAT TO SELL: DEFINING THE PRODUCT
- What decisions must travel businesses make when they define their product?

HOW TO SELL: PROMOTING THE PRODUCT
- How do travel businesses promote their products?

WHERE TO SELL: SALES AND DISTRIBUTION CHANNELS
- How do travel businesses get their products to buyers?

HOW MUCH TO CHARGE: SETTING THE PRICE
- What pricing strategies are most often used by travel sellers?

Chapters 4–8 focused on the principal products and services that the travel industry sells to the public. But before travel companies can sell anything, they must decide what to sell, to whom to sell it, what price to set for it, and how to sell it. These decisions are part of *marketing*—a series of decisions and actions taken by a seller to create a match between consumers' preferences and a product. Notice that consumers are at the heart of the process.

The changes in travel agencies, starting in the 1990s, illustrate marketing decisions at work. At the start of the decade, travel agencies maintained traditional offices and depended on airline sales for their survival. Agencies rarely charged clients directly; the agencies received almost all their income from commissions from suppliers. Then the slide in commission rates began, and many travel agencies faced financial disaster. Additional challenges soon followed as the Internet gave travelers a new way to arrange travel directly. Would travel agencies go the way of buggy drivers and shoeshine stands?

In short, travel agencies faced a severe challenge to their marketing methods. Like all businesses, they had to find ways to match what they wanted to sell with what consumers wanted to buy, and to do so in a way that produced a profit—or go out of business. Many small neighborhood agencies closed or consolidated into larger agencies. However, a great many defied the doomsayers by surviving, and **they** survived by changing. The industry began by emphasizing service and by selling more tours and packages, cruises, rental cars, and hotel rooms—decreasing its reliance on airline sales. Agencies set up websites to promote themselves and began leveraging social media. Greater numbers of independent agents began working from home offices. Also, charging fees became more common practice.

Travel agencies no longer limit themselves to serving the surrounding community. Many have developed a clientele across the state, country, and even overseas. With Internet and smartphone technology, forward-looking counselors use e-mail, social media, and evolving communication tools to expand their reach and stay in front of clients and prospects.

The changes made by travel agencies demonstrate concepts of marketing that affect all travel sellers—from airlines to tour operators, hotels, theme parks, and dozens of other travel-related entities. In this chapter, we consider the basic elements of marketing, beginning with an overview of the marketing process.

The Marketing Process

■ WHAT ARE THE BASIC COMPONENTS OF THE MARKETING PROCESS AND THE MARKETING MIX?

Developing a marketing plan is critical to the success of any business. A *marketing plan* selects a target market and describes how to handle four basic characteristics of the business, called the *marketing mix* or the *four Ps:* product, promotion, place, and price (see Figure 9.1). In other words, the marketing plan should answer four basic questions:

1. What product will we sell?
2. How will we promote it?
3. Where—at what place—will we sell and distribute it?
4. At what price will we sell it?

Conducting market research is a first step toward answering these questions.

Product	**Promotion**	**Place**	**Price**
What travel products will we sell? Will we specialize in some type of travel? What level of service will we offer?	What image are we promoting? How and where will we advertise? What public relations activities will we undertake?	Where do we want to sell? In an office? On the telephone? On the Internet? At home?	What price range of travel will we sell? What fees will we charge?

Target market

FIGURE 9.1 Components of a Marketing Plan

A marketing plan describes the marketing mix and the target market. Thus, it defines the product to be sold, how it will be promoted, its price, and the place of sale.

Market Research

At the center of marketing is the relationship that businesses build and maintain with their customers. Thus, the basis of marketing is an understanding of the customers' needs and wants and is an attempt to find ways to satisfy them. As the world changes, customers change, so it's imperative agents research their market and actively listen.

As the name indicates, **market research** is the gathering and analyzing of information about consumers and products. Even a small company can do useful market research. For example, travel agencies and tour operators can ask new clients to fill out a form about their preferences and interests. They can ask clients returning from a trip specific questions to discover what was most liked and disliked about the trip.

Sources of Information. The information used in market research includes both primary and secondary data. *Primary data* consist of information that a company collects, like the results of questionnaires sent to clients, traffic, and pageviews at an agent's website, or social media insights. *Secondary data* consist of preexisting information, such as data in reference books, on the Internet, and surveys conducted by research firms.

Test marketing—experimenting with an idea by introducing a product or service on a limited scale—is another form of market research. For example, cruise ships might offer special sailings to a limited number of people before the official inaugural sailing of a new ship to test the services provided. Similarly, agents can use tools like Facebook Groups to float ideas about new services or itineraries they are considering selling.

Uses of Market Research. Information gained from market research is useful at each stage of the marketing process, beginning with market segmentation. Recall that *market segmentation* categorizes people into potential target niches. (Table 9.1 reviews key forms of market segmentation.) Research on market segmentation might tell a local travel agency, for example, that its community includes many middle-aged people and many golfers but very few wealthy people or students.

Market segment research allows a company to identify populations who might serve as target markets and form the basis for a marketing plan. Many companies have discovered their company serves several different submarkets, each needing separate travel products and a separate marketing plan. An adventure tour company that begins serving a young, extremely active clientele may find its marketing plan needs to change as its clients grow older, raise a family, and ultimately want less strenuous destinations and itineraries.

TABLE 9.1 Types of Market Segmentation

Type	Defining Characteristics of Segment
Demographic	Age, sex, race, income, and so on
Psychographic	Attitudes, interests, and beliefs
Location	Distance between client and travel company—in town, out of state, overseas
Usage	Purpose (business, leisure, VFR, meetings, and incentive travel)
Price	Different ranges (e.g. budget, luxury, ultra luxury)

A company that specializes in honeymoons may discover it needs to develop new travel products and marketing plans to include anniversary or vow renewal trips. Research also helps a company identify trends that might affect its market, such as :

- *Demographics.* Changes in birthrate, family size, divorce rate, and the average age of a population are all examples of demographic change. These changes may point to coming trends in the demand for certain types of travel. Recent demographic changes in the United States, for example, include a rise in the average age of the population, an increase in the number of elderly people, and an increase in the number of people with a Hispanic background. The U.S. Census Bureau is a good source for such information.
- *Laws.* For example, specific laws dictate how services and products can be advertised, how contests must be structured, and who can gamble.
- *Politics.* Unrest in a country affects both business investments and travel.
- *Economics.* Rates of income growth, inflation, unemployment, and consumer debt, as well as changes in how consumers spend their money, all influence a business' costs, revenues, and ultimate profitability. By definition, discretionary travel is sensitive to changes in the economic climate.
- *Technology.* Advances in transportation may open up new destinations; advances in computers and communications may influence what and how clients buy and how businesses can market their services.

A company cannot control trends, but if it pays attention to market research, it can spot them and adapt to them. Wise travel sellers, for example, see the growing number of people over age 45 as an opportunity to market cruises and overseas travel to clients in their peak earning years. They are certain not to rely too much on travel to one area, such as the Middle East, in case of political turmoil. They view technological change as an opportunity to change tactics or strategy faster than their competitors.

Research is also key to monitoring and improving a company's performance. Do employees have ideas for improving how they do their jobs? Are customers satisfied? Why or why not?

Customer Relationship Marketing. As business competition has heated up, obtaining feedback and following up on it in order to improve customer service have become essential to survival. For example, surveys of female business travelers led Wyndham Hotels to add library-style pubs for after-work drinks. Hotels and cruise lines often use guest comment cards and surveys online to obtain feedback from their customers; then they can adjust their services based on that feedback. To encourage their customers to participate in surveys, airlines and car rental companies award bonus points to frequent flyers or frequent renters who complete the surveys.

Information from surveys can be easily collected, sorted, analyzed and retrieved rapidly, thanks to computerized databases. With a sophisticated database of a travel agency's clients, for example, you might select the names of all clients who (1) live in a zip code of mostly affluent people, (2) have recently flown overseas, and (3) are interested in winter sports—and then put these names on a mailing list to receive information about European ski resorts. This is a simple example of ***customer relationship marketing.*** Using the information gathered and compiled in a database system, businesses contact customers with promotions and services that match their clients' preferences and interests. The focus is on serving their clients' needs while building relationships rather than making individual sales.

Marketing Strategies in a Changing Industry

Decades ago, businesses usually followed a *product-oriented marketing strategy:* They sensed that a product would be profitable, and then they looked for customers to buy it. For example, a tour operator might decide that it could offer motor coach tours profitably, so it developed the tours and then searched for customers.

Today, a second type of marketing strategy is more common: a *market-oriented strategy,* which is also called *customer-oriented marketing.* Companies first define the needs of a target market and then try to develop a product to meet those needs.

Suppose the manager of a travel agency hopes that expanding into the sale of group tours will help the agency stay competitive and successful. Should the agency begin with a tour and then try to find a buyer, or start with a group that wishes to go somewhere? In the first approach, the manager might have a team develop a tour and then try to find a market for the tour. But this product-oriented strategy stacks the odds against the would-be operator. Great amounts of advertising and effort might be necessary to identify and reach a market segment with unserved needs that would be met by the new tour. Travel professionals today are more likely to favor a customer-oriented strategy.

Focusing on the Customer: The Four Cs. The focus on customers can be seen in the changing marketing methods and strategies used by the travel industry. As its customers' needs and expectations have changed, each sector of the industry has adapted. Table 9.2 summarizes these changes. Many of them have been discussed in earlier chapters; others will be discussed as we explore the elements of the marketing mix in this chapter.

You might have noticed that the four Ps describe the marketing mix from the seller's point of view. Some marketing experts have suggested a way of looking at the marketing mix instead from the customer's point of view. The result is the *four Cs:*

Four Ps	**Four Cs**
Product	Customer value or solution
Promotion	Communication
Place	Convenience
Price	Cost to the customer

Today's view of marketing can be summed up as the delivery of customer satisfaction at a profit.

The emphasis on customers is reflected in the development of **customer relationship management (CRM),** a strategy that combines personalized service and technology to meet the specific needs of customers, enabling businesses to provide excellent service and build lasting relationships with their clients, thus increasing customer loyalty.

For example, Ritz-Carlton employees provide memorable experiences to their guests by treating them as individuals. They record specific guest preferences in the company's CRM/database, which holds individual customer preferences accessible by all hotels in the worldwide Ritz chain.

A special customer request at one Ritz-Carlton is then accessible at all its hotels in a database.

A request made today in Atlanta for feather pillows will be initiated without an additional request being made in the Ritz-Carlton in San Juan months later. Technology helps the company build stronger relationships with its guests. These preferences also can assist in creating better and more personalized marketing.

Coordinating the Elements. Whatever marketing strategy is devised, decisions about product, promotion, place, and price must be coordinated if the strategy is to succeed. Suppose you run a travel agency that sells deluxe tours at an office in a pricey neighborhood. If you promote your tours by putting flyers on car windows and jingles on alternative rock radio stations, you are probably wasting your money. You might be better off buying social media ads targeting users living in affluent regions or zip codes.

Like the pieces of a jigsaw puzzle, all parts of the marketing mix must fit together. They must be blended into a coordinated program designed to achieve the marketing objectives. In the rest of this chapter we look at each part of the marketing mix.

TABLE 9.2 Adapting to Changing Customers

Travel Sector	Recent Marketing Methods and Strategies
Travel agencies	Less dependence on air sales; more attention to tour packages, cruises, rental cars, and hotel rooms Both "bricks" and "clicks" points of contact with customers Emphasis on service Specialization More home-based agents Charging service fees to customers
Airlines	Cost cutting by major carriers Successful business model by low-cost airlines
Ground transportation	Addition of features to cars in rental fleet Increased number of luxury and SUV vehicles in rental fleet Increased availability of light rail, high-speed trains, and specialty rail
Accommodations	Consolidation of ownership but increased variety of brands for targeted market segments Increased use of guest comment cards and Internet surveys to identify changing needs More features and services that provide convenience to business travelers at commercial hotels and that cater to the needs of families at resorts Increased use of technology to help personalize services and build a loyal customer base
Cruise lines	New and varied products that appeal to different market segments Promotion through varied media with multiple points of contact
Tour operators	Increased flexibility and variety of products Changes in the length and focus of tours to meet a variety of needs

✔ CHECK-UP

Elements of the marketing process include
✔ Market research.
✔ Identification of market segments.
✔ Selection of target markets and a marketing strategy.
✔ Development of a marketing plan.
✔ Ongoing market research to monitor trends and performance.

A marketing plan includes decisions about
✔ The target market.
✔ The product.
✔ The product's promotion.
✔ The place to sell the product.
✔ The product's price.

What to Sell: Defining the Product

If you were in the business of selling cruises, you might wonder whether you should sell large contemporary ships, expedition cruises, or river cruises. Should you offer only standardized offerings, or should you offer additional inclusions, like pre- or post-trip stays? Should you also sell passport services and travel insurance?

These are the types of questions that a marketing plan should address regarding the first *P*—the product. Airlines, for example, must select the routes they will fly; hotels define the amenities they will offer; cruise lines create itineraries. Similarly, travel agencies must determine the range, mix, and level of products and services they will offer. To remain competitive, businesses of all types must keep developing and refining the products they offer.

The Range and Mix of Products

As travelers change, travel sellers must alter their product mix in order to survive. In recent years, for example, more travelers wanted a chance to experience "authentic" (also called "immersive") experiences. Successful tour companies responded by developing more contacts that could connect their clients with local chefs or with families who own vineyards and restaurants, and they would take their customers behind the scenes at major tourist sites.

Similarly, car rental companies responded to the changing expectations of their customers by adding features and special equipment to their vehicles. They also increased the number of SUVs, sports cars, and luxury vehicles available.

To determine the range and mix of their products, companies use *segment analysis,* an evaluation of the profitability of different products and services. Which ones bring in the most income relative to the amount of time spent handling the transactions? By providing an answer, segment analysis helps companies decide how to allocate their resources efficiently.

The recent history of travel agencies demonstrates the importance of decisions about the range and mix of products. Little more than a decade or two ago, travel agencies churned out airline tickets as fast as fingers could fly over computer keys. Hotel and car reservations were sometimes an afterthought, and many felt that selling tours and cruises just slowed them down. The number of air tickets sold was the name of the game. When the airlines eliminated commissions, travel agencies had to adjust in many ways, including focusing on a more profitable range and mix of products sold. They put more emphasis on selling cruises and tours, luxury travel, and customized experiences to specific types of travelers (look again at Table 9.1).

Developing expertise in special types of travel was one frequent response. For example, an agency might specialize in

■ Particular destinations, such as Las Vegas or Hawaii, western Europe, or the Caribbean.
■ Particular demographic groups, such as seniors or families, upscale or budget travelers.
■ Particular interests, such as golf vacations, safaris or scuba diving.

- Particular types of travel, such as corporate travel.

Specialization is not an all-or-nothing proposition. Basically, a travel agency may meet the challenge of determining what it will sell in three ways.

- It may operate as a general agency but concentrate on certain products.
- It may develop *niches,* or specialty markets, such as adventure travel, premium cruises, upscale travel, or budget travel. The agency sells a wide range of products, but it aggressively markets certain types of travel arrangements in these specialty areas.
- It may deal with one type of travel to the exclusion of all others, developing a marketing plan that prepares it to succeed through sales only in this niche. Some agencies that take this approach still provide other services when it's profitable and when they are appointed to receive commissions from the supplier. Many do not; incentive houses (which arrange only incentive travel) and cruise-only agencies are examples.

Many agencies still sell a complete range of travel arrangements—air, rail, auto, hotel, tour, cruise—plus insurance and perhaps miscellaneous products. But being all things to all people is increasingly difficult. Large agencies tend to create special departments to deal with specific types of travel. When many agencies are close to and competing with each other, the tendency increases for each to specialize.

Ultimately, agencies need to sell products and services they can be proud of and that will provide a reasonable profit.

The Level of Services

While a travel agency decides which travel products it will offer for sale, in fact it is only helping travelers to lease these products temporarily. Suppliers provide the air seats, cars, and hotel rooms. Travelers can call suppliers or go online in order to book these products themselves. When they go instead to a travel agency, they are purchasing the agency's time and expertise; the agency is providing services that should give the travel products their highest possible value.

What services are travelers looking for from a travel agency? Surveys show vacation travelers are likely to be especially interested in

- Help in getting the most value for their money.
- Assurance that they will get high-quality accommodations and services on the trip from reputable operators.
- A trouble-free trip.
- A counselor available to help if things go wrong.
- Unbiased opinions from a knowledgeable professional.
- Service that saves them time.
- Personal contact with a professional.

In effect, the travel agency sells a counseling service that is only as good as its counselors. The agency's success depends on providing a consistent level of service, so training and quality control are vital.

How much time should an agency's travel counselors devote to looking for bargains or checking the quality of a product? Should the agency promise that someone is available 24 hours a day in case something goes wrong? In short, what level of service should the agency's counselors give clients? If ABC agency plans to sell mainly discount-priced trips, then offering a lot of frills is not likely to be profitable. If an agency sells a deluxe product mix, then it should offer a high degree of personal attention—perhaps including limousine services and premium travel gifts free of charge. The level of service provided should mesh with the agency's overall brand and marketing plan.

Specialization by travel agencies
✔ May be carried out to varying degrees.
✔ May focus on particular destinations, demographic groups, interests, or types of travel.
✔ Allows counselors to offer travelers detailed, professional knowledge.

The level of service provided by a travel agency should
✔ Be consistent from one travel counselor to another.
✔ Mesh with the marketing plan.

How to Sell: Promoting the Product

■ HOW DO TRAVEL BUSINESSES PROMOTE THEIR PRODUCTS?

Very few products or services sell themselves. They must be promoted. *Promotion,* the second *P,* consists of efforts to communicate information about a product or service to the market. It includes

■ Advertising, whether in print, online, or through social media.
■ Sales promotions, such as discounts, bonuses, and contests.
■ Public relations.
■ Person-to-person selling.

All the elements of promotion should help to create a perception of the company and its offerings—an *image*— consistent with the rest of the marketing plan. A travel agency emphasizing corporate travel with deluxe arrangements should not aim to convey a family vacation image.

How does a business create an image? Many elements can contribute. Carnival Cruise Lines promotes its "Fun Ships" with advertisements that are festive; Royal Caribbean's advertising emphasizes the "royal" treatment its passengers receive through personal service and pampering. Or consider a California travel agency for upscale leisure travelers. It builds its image through

■ Its name. It describes itself as "cruise and tour consultants."
■ The design and atmosphere of its office, which features teakwood and classical music.
■ Its staff 's appearance. Their usual attire is relaxed but chic—yet they have been known to don tuxedos and elegant dresses for cruise nights and safari clothing for consumer seminars on Africa.
■ Its advertising. It uses highly selective direct mail, word of mouth, and its website.
■ Its treatment of clients. The agency offers its clients chilled canapés and a choice of beverages; it has a substantial wine list. Counselors meet with clients privately without interruption.

Besides defining an image, a company must also determine the mix of promotional methods to use. Will it rely mostly on person-to-person selling by representatives, or will it attract customers mainly through advertising? How and where will it advertise? Should it devote significant resources to special promotions (such as contests) or to public relations? Each of the many methods of promotion has benefits and disadvantages, which we look at next.

Direct-Mail Advertising

Many companies use some type of **direct mail**—letters, postcards, flyers, brochures, questionnaires, or newsletters distributed through the mail. Mailing lists are compiled from the company's own records, from local directories, or from mailing-list companies.

As discussed in earlier chapters, brochures represent an important form of promotion for travel suppliers, such as tour companies and cruise lines. By making the products more tangible to buyers, the brochures become an essential sales tool for travel agencies that sell the supplier's products. Thus, brochures include enticing photos, a list of the products' features, and a translation of those features into possible benefits for the buyers.

Direct mail can be more expensive than other forms of marketing, but it offers several advantages.

- It can contain far more information than any other kind of advertisement.
- It stands alone, unlike newspaper advertisements, which compete with other ads for the consumer's attention.
- It may be kept around for days before being discarded, and the recipient may pass it on to others.
- It reaches identifiable segments of the total market. For example, a travel agency might send a special announcement just to those clients who have taken a cruise or to everyone who has not taken a trip in the past year. The piece can be tailored to the audience and its needs.
- It can be sent whenever the company needs to advertise, with little lead time.
- Its effectiveness can be measured by including a promotion code or return-reply envelope with the mailing.

Figure 9.2 includes some tips for making direct mail effective. Newsletters can be especially informative. Of course, newsletters can be sent electronically, and the same principles and techniques apply whether they are sent via direct mail or digitally.

Newsletters may include many types of reports to stimulate interest and confidence and to build a company's image. For example, a travel agency's newsletter might include reports from staff members or clients about recently visited destinations and news about staff members who have completed special training courses or fam trip experiences. It might encourage clients to contact a staff member who has specialized knowledge or recent experience with a particular kind of travel. And it can be used to announce upcoming trips.

Here are some tips for writing effective newsletters:

- Make sure the company name is front and center and/or the most visible text on the page.
- Place your full contact information where it can be spotted easily by your readers.
- Use the word *you* as often as possible and ask questions directed to readers to draw them in.
- To give the newsletter direction and interest, target its content around the ideal clients.
- Provide crisp, eye-catching images and compelling captions.
- Be sure to give readers advance notice of upcoming or future group trips.
- Use lots of white space to make the newsletter more appealing and inviting.
- Where appropriate, incentivize customers by providing discounts or other benefits for subscribers only.
- Be sure all hyperlinks are current and functioning.
- Publish newsletters regularly for maximum impact.

ABC TRAVEL
GOING OUR WAY?

25 | APRIL -2019 | VOL. 3

You can reach us at:
www.abctrvl.travel
(800) 555-5555 &
info@abctrvl.travel

Budapest is one of the most captivating cities in world at night. Call today about a special ABC Travel Group Danube river cruise, May 2020.

SUMMER'S COMING

Have you booked your summer vacation yet? Cruise cabins and resort rooms are filling up. But we've got some great vacation ideas and values to share. Page 2

APRIL IN PARIS

Last April, we sent Sarah and Jeff Smith on a romantic 6-night stay in the City of Lights, reserving exclusive candlelit dinners and 25th anniversary photos on the Seine. Page 3

RIVER CRUISING

We recently joined partner AmaWaterways on a Rhone River, wine-tasting cruise — perfect for your Grenache palate. Come join our owner Anne, in pictures and words. Page 4

OUR SERVICES

Another crazy winter is over, and we cannot tell you how happy we are being able to recommend **Travel Insurance** to our clients.

When the March Noreaster impacted thousands of flights up and down the U.S. Atlantic coast, our clients were able to cover extra hotel nights, meal expenses and a variety of other costs from the storm disrupting flight schedules.

Did you know that ABC Travel can get you discounts for your transfers to and from 100s of airports in the U.S., Mexico and the Caribbean? Let us take care of all of your **Ground Transportation** worries.

Finally ready for that first international trip? ABC Travel knows all of the **passport and visa requirements** and deadlines to send you off on that first incredible journey abroad. Call us.

A. **Ensure company name and contact information is visible**

B. **Use *you* frequently**

C. **Use crisp images**

D. **Keep sentences short**

E. **Ask questions**

F. **Ask for response**

G. **Use lots of white space**

H. **Stress benefits and emotions**

FIGURE 9.2 Making Direct Mail Effective

This sample newsletter illustrates a few guidelines useful in all forms of direct mail.

Consumers usually take nine to 11 days to respond to a campaign sent via first-class mail. Mailings to repeat customers should be sent four to six times a year; general-response mailings should be sent twice a year. Mailings that arrive midweek have the best chance of bringing a response.

Print Advertising

At one time, print media (newspapers and magazines) were prime outlets for paid ads, for example, accompanying editorials in Sunday travel sections. Today, much of the budget for this kind of promotion has gone to the Internet. Most newspaper Sunday travel sections are fairly slim, and most travel magazine ads are not affordable for the small advertiser—only for major suppliers, such as cruise lines, hotel/resort chains, tour operators, and government tourism offices.

Therefore, a company must decide carefully where to spend its limited travel/tourism budget. Choices include online advertising, print media advertising, targeted direct mail, and tabletop exhibits at community events or consumer expos. Some companies use a mix of several methods. Viking River Cruises, for example, uses frequent repeat mailings of brochures to past passengers, magazine ads, social media, and webinars to educate travel counselors on how to sell its diverse itineraries.

Ads in newspapers and magazines are all forms of *print advertising*. Two key differences among print ads—how long the publication lasts and its audience—help determine which is best for different purposes.

Newspaper readers tend to throw a paper away after reading it. Thus, newspapers are typically best used to deliver a specific message of short-term relevance—for example, to advertise a particular tour or departure—and to motivate readers to contact a company immediately.

Unlike newspaper ads, advertising in phone books reaches only the people who are looking for the service. This advertising is rarely used any more because the same information can be quickly found online. Also, advertisements in the yellow pages must be valid for a year. These ads are therefore useful for making general statements about service, experience, and expertise.

Most magazines conduct research to determine the tastes and lifestyles of their readers and are designed to reach specific market segments. Thus, advertisers know with some certainty who the magazine's readers are and which market segments are likely to see their ads. A travel agency might advertise in *Travel & Leisure* magazine, which the general public reads, but not in *Travel Weekly*, which travel sellers read. Travel suppliers, such as tour companies and cruise lines, might advertise in both.

For travel agencies, **cooperative advertising** can be an effective way of using print advertising; it is an arrangement in which travel suppliers or distributors (particularly cruise lines and tour operators) share the cost of print advertising with travel agencies. The supplier's or distributor's advertisement includes the travel agency's name and address as a contact for reservations. However, such cooperative opportunities are increasingly rare unless the agency has a strong booking history with the supplier.

Radio and Television Advertising

Few travel agencies use radio as an advertising medium, and virtually none use broadcast television, mostly due to the expensive nature of marketing through these channels. These media have the potential of reaching a large audience, but, especially in the case of broadcast television, they have two drawbacks.

- The audience tends to be diverse, including many people outside the target market.
- More problematic is the cost, a combination of the advertising rates charged, the need for repetition, and production costs.

A typical radio or television advertisement lasts only 30 to 60 seconds and cannot be easily saved and found again. Only repetition ensures that a radio or television advertisement will register in the consumer's consciousness. In small towns, radio may be no more expensive than other forms of advertising, despite the need to air the commercials repeatedly. But in large metropolitan areas, the cost of repeating radio advertising most likely exceeds the average travel agency's budget.

One type of effective radio advertising can be when a popular disc jockey acts as a *Pied Piper* and announces that he will lead a group of listeners who share a common interest, such as Big Band music, on a cruise. Broadcast television is usually even more expensive, not only because of the high rates charged to advertisers but also because of production costs. Viewers measure television advertisements by the standards of professional advertising agencies that handle multimillion-dollar accounts. Amateur television advertisements seldom measure up.

Production costs are also high for advertising on cable television, but some larger agencies may be able to afford to advertise in small cable markets. Many cable companies offer help in preparing commercials aimed at local subscribers. Advertising on cable can be targeted to particular segments of the market. There are cable television channels directed at travel aficionados, sports fans, culture buffs, news junkies, and other segments.

DVDs for home use provide another way to reach potential clients. Tour operators and cruise lines sometimes produce videos to send directly to clients or to be distributed by travel agencies.

Advertising Online

The Internet—searchable and available 24 hours a day, every day—quickly has become the principal marketing tool for most advertisers. Many people see it as a social tool, a library, or a game room. But it is also a place for distributing products (discussed in the next section) and an advertising medium.

For every traditional method of advertising, the Internet offers an electronic counterpart, plus additional options. For example,

- The Internet version of television advertising is streaming videos, complete with high-quality audio and visual components that can be delivered at a fraction of the cost of television ads.
- If radio is your medium of choice, the Internet offers live radio programs that include advertising opportunities in both audio and text formats. Travel Talk Radio (www.traveltalkradio.com) is just one example. There also are podcasts—radio-like shows that can be accessed through the Internet—or podcast apps.
- The Internet's version of direct mail is *e-mail marketing*, where consumers have agreed to receive e-mail advertisements and promotional messages direct from travel suppliers or a travel trade news service, such as

The Internet offers a wealth of streaming videos.

Travel Research Online (TRO) and Travel Market Report. E-mail is considered by most marketing experts to be the most effective form of marketing today because content can be customized for individuals by their preferences, and success can be measured through digital "bread crumbs" left by those who respond to an email.

Electronic brochures, websites, banner advertisements, listings in search engines, and links to other websites are a few of the other popular forms of online advertising. We will examine the two most common forms in this section: hosting a website and linking from other sites.

Establishing a Web Presence. Few travel sellers can do without a website. Consumers have been trained to validate a company's credibility by their web presence, and an attractive website helps convey a company's brand and offerings. Some travel sellers design their website mostly to build awareness. Others expect their site to generate new business. Some sites are designed to increase client' satisfaction or provide clients with the ability to book all, or just a few, elements of a trip on their own.

The content and complexity of a website depends on the company's goals, but here are a few general guidelines.

- Websites should be professionally designed. They should reflect the company's overall image, be pleasant to look at, and be easy to navigate (see Figure 9.3).
- Websites must be constantly monitored and updated, or they could detract from a company's brand.
- Inquiries from clients at the website should be answered quickly. What "quickly" means depends on the company's strategy and products, but 24 hours is generally seen as the maximum.
- Other marketing should direct clients and prospects to the site, as discussed in Chapter 3.
- The narrower the market niche and the more specialized the product or service, the greater the chances are that the site will attract interested buyers. For some specific comments about the steps involved in establishing a website, see Chapter 14.

Linking from Other Sites. Most successful airlines, tour operators, and other travel sellers are linked to dozens of websites. If you look up travel information on Frommer's site, you will be a click away from hotel providers, tourist bureaus, or travel gear manufacturers, for example. Many wholesalers, tour operators, and tourist offices also give links to lists of travel counselors. These counselors typically have paid for the listing through certification programs, relationship building, and sometimes via advertising dollars.

Many companies find that Web links (both paid and unpaid) are their most effective method of online advertising. Search engines, like Google, will elevate a site's visibility based on the quality and number of third-party, authoritative websites that link to a site. Carefully chosen reciprocal links can (1) enhance the content for the company's own visitors and (2) bring in visitors from other sites that feature a link to it, increasing the company's marketing reach.

Once travel agents understand the key market segments they are trying to reach and define what the agency wants to sell, choosing the right mix of marketing channels can be more effective. Effective promotion of a business uses multiple media for advertising, as well as other forms of promotion.

Public Relations

Compared with advertising, public relations is usually a less obvious type of promotion. Any activity conducted to establish recognition and respect within the community is a form of ***public relations.*** When a newspaper lists a company as the sponsor for a charity event or reports that a company employee has won a community service award, the company's efforts at public relations have succeeded. To gather publicity, companies must perform a variety of tactics to engage journalists and the media.

Hosting special events is a complicated but productive form of public relations. Companies either sponsor or participate in events, such as a golf tournament or a benefit fashion show. Some travel agencies hold regular travel nights where they show films, present speakers and promote related travel arrangements. Travel sellers also participate in consumer events, such as wedding/bridal shows or local chamber of commerce small business expos.

Like other forms of public relations, hosting a special event can help establish a travel company's image. Often these events provide a means of identifying market segments interested in a particular kind of travel and of better defining the target market. Sometimes they also present opportunities for person-to-person selling.

Suppliers often cooperate with travel agencies to produce special events. A cruise line, for example, might work with a travel agency to organize an event

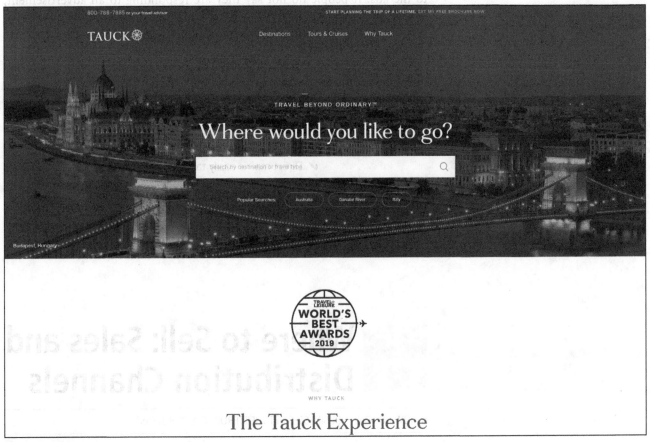

FIGURE 9.3 Advertising on the Internet

Hosting a website is one way of using the Internet to advertise a company. The Tauck home page is pleasant to look at (especially in color) and easy to navigate.

Source: Reprinted by permission of Tauck.

known as a cruise night and share the costs of refreshments, decorations, invitations, and door prizes. Representatives from the agency and the cruise line would offer information about cruising itineraries, life onboard, and specific cruises.

Personal Selling

Salespeople are also elements in the promotional mix. As part of the marketing plan, businesses decide how much of their resources they will devote to selling face-to-face and how much to other promotions. Whatever the answer, the salesperson can be an important part of the marketing effort.

Consider the case of travel counselors. Through constant contact with clients, they can gather vital information about tastes, trends, and attitudes. In short, travel counselors conduct informal market research every time a client answers a question. Both counselors and management know what sells, but front-line counselors can detect subtle shifts in why it sells and who is buying it. That knowledge might suggest a new promotional approach.

By evaluating advertising effectiveness, travel counselors also can help ensure its efforts are not wasted. Counselors should know what products their agency is advertising. If, for example, an agency has run a cooperative ad with a cruise line, it can be prepared to deal confidently with clients who respond to the ads. If people do not say they are responding to an advertisement, counselors should ask if they saw a particular ad. By logging the number of responses and the number of bookings, an agency can measure the effectiveness of the advertising.

At the end of the marketing process, travel counselors and other front-line salespeople in travel companies ensure the ultimate success of the marketing plan. Their selling makes the marketing plan work.

✔ CHECK-UP

Four of many possible considerations in selecting a medium for advertising are
- ✔ How long the message is accessible.
- ✔ How targeted the audience can be.
- ✔ Whether it is consistent with the desired image.
- ✔ What the cost is.

Each form of advertising has its advantages:
- ✔ Direct mail is easily targeted to a specific audience.
- ✔ Newspaper advertising produces immediate responses.
- ✔ Radio and television ads usually have a large audience.
- ✔ Websites are available 24 hours a day.

Where to Sell: Sales and Distribution Channels

■ HOW DO TRAVEL BUSINESSES GET THEIR PRODUCTS TO BUYERS?

Once you have a product or service, how do you get it to the public? Do you sell it directly or through an intermediary? And where do you locate the points of sale and distribution? Must travelers come to buy your product in person, or can they make the purchase over the phone or online? These questions all address the third *P* of the marketing plan—place (also known as *point of sale*).

Distribution Channels

Many travel suppliers answer the question of place by using a *dual distribution* system: they sell to the public both directly themselves and indirectly, through travel agencies and other intermediaries. Their marketing plans should indicate how much emphasis to give to each of these channels.

One reason for dual distribution by suppliers is the nature of travel inventory. A supplier's inventory is highly perishable; today's airline seat or hotel room cannot be sold tomorrow. The supplier must make the product as available as possible, so most, if not all, suppliers maintain direct booking channels.

During the 1990s, the growing popularity of toll-free numbers and the Internet made it easier for suppliers to sell directly to the public, bypassing travel agencies. As a result, travel agencies continue to face direct competition from the suppliers they sell. In fact, suppliers are tempted to do all the selling themselves if commission expenses get too high. And many retail travel agencies are loathe to sell products from suppliers who are competing with them, in effect, selling on both sides of the fence.

CLOSE-UP: ON THE JOB WITH JOHN ABRUZZI, WEBSITE SPECIALIST

Twenty years ago, the positions of Web designer and Web programmer would have drawn a blank on the radar screens of most travel employers. Most of these jobs are filled by people who learn computers first and then apply their skills to the travel industry. John Abruzzi is one who kept learning in both fields and became his company's Internet specialist.

"I was just getting into the travel business in the early 1990s. CRSs had been in travel agencies for about 15 years, and I relished the opportunity to practice what I learned in travel school. Within a few months, I was turning out tickets, itineraries, invoices, boarding passes—you name it. Within a year, no one could produce them as fast as I could. Little did I know I'd soon be doing computer work that barely existed when I went to school.

"It's up to me to monitor and operate our agency's website. It just fell naturally in my lap because I'd been keeping up with the Internet in the mid-1990s and had my own home computer.

"One of the major things I do is make constant changes in the information on our site. We run specials from preferred suppliers, consolidators, and lately even from airlines.

"The specials change constantly, and I have to keep our site fresh so clients will keep coming back to look. We also have our travel counselors' pictures on the site, information on where they've traveled, what their field of expertise is, and even personal information if they wish to share it. As soon as people return from a trip, I add that to their 'résumés' and write a feature for the website.

"I also help other counselors create custom-made brochures with the software we have. It's hard to believe that instead of giving clients the same brochure that a tour company prints in the thousands, we can print one in color with the client's name on it—and we can print only the particular tour or cruise and the date those clients are considering.

"I route website inquiries. People can e-mail us for a reservation, general information, a brochure, or other requests. I decide who gets the request and check that the client gets an answer within four hours. Often the client gets an answer even faster. I answer a lot of them myself.

"One of our goals is to get clients on the phone as soon as possible because then we can learn much more quickly which clients are qualified buyers. You can hear the tone of their voice, give them an idea of price and decide if they are serious buyers. We try to hook them right away by emphasizing the special expertise a particular travel counselor has, something they couldn't get anywhere else.

"Our website might not look like it provides a lot of direct bookings, but it already produces a lot of repeat and word-of-mouth business. A lot of the time, clients will later e-mail or phone, or their friends will. We haven't been tracking this, except informally, but we know quite a bit of this business is there—people who first saw the site and now call or e-mail. Then again, some repeat clients book right on the site.

"It seems as though the Internet is such an advanced tool, but I keep reading that its integration into the world of business has only just begun. I'm going to make sure I'm in the forefront of new developments."

Consider the airlines. The two primary reasons airlines paid travel agencies a commission to sell their products at one time were (1) to increase their marketing reach and (2) to use travel agencies as a sales and reservations staff that was far less expensive than hiring employees. In the last 20 years, however, they have developed a more economical distribution channel: the Internet.

Many travel suppliers still prefer to pay commissions to travel agencies rather than employ large sales and reservations staffs of their own. And many still advise consumers to "See your travel agent." Furthermore (as discussed in Chapter 3), consumers still value the unbiased information, convenience, and personal service, travel agencies provide, as indicated by the high percentage of sales booked by travel agencies.

Selecting a Retail Storefront Site

Like other elements of the marketing mix, the site for an office or retail outlet should be consistent with the rest of the marketing plan. For example, locating a deluxe cruise agency in the poorest area of town is likely to be a mistake. But today, decisions about the place of sale and distribution involve far more than the location of a building. Answering the question of place also means deciding the extent to which the company will use an office or retail outlet, telephone, Internet, or other type of location as the site for selling.

The airlines again provide an example. They still sell to the public from airline ticket offices, but the major carriers have closed most of them. Today, airline tickets are sold at airports, at ticket machines, over the phone, online, and—of course—through travel agencies.

Similarly, travel agencies have decreased their reliance on walk-in business at retail outlets. In fact, a great deal of selling occurs outside the travel agency's office. Corporate sales often take place in the office of the client corporation. After this initial sale, primarily to set up the contract and the ground rules, the client company's employees rarely visit the agency; the account is serviced over the phone or online. Similarly, group travel may be sold at the agent's or decision maker's home or at the headquarters of the group buying the trip. Outside sales agents may do most of their sales at a client's home, their own home offices, or even over coffee at a local café.

The Home-Based Office.
Increasingly, the home is an attractive choice for the site of an office. Sales representatives or account representatives for travel suppliers frequently work out of home offices. Often, their company's headquarters is far from their sales territory, and business is conducted at the clients' place of business.

Sales representatives at cruise lines, tour operators, and airlines have huge territories and rarely manage to visit agencies spread so far and wide, preferring to keep in contact with agency clients by phone, e-mail, and educational webinars. The cost of using traditional offices and retail space is high, and technology now allows people to perform many tasks that once had to be done in a traditional office setting.

Travel professionals working at home fall into three categories:
- Employees doing some or all of their work at home, using e-mail, web meeting services, and Internet calling services like Skype.
- Part-time or full-time independent contractors, working for themselves.
- Independent entrepreneurs, operating their own businesses.

By using home-based independent contractors, companies save many costs, including Social Security taxes; employee benefits, such as health insurance,

Account representatives frequently work out of home offices.

vacations, sick days, training, and pensions; and office space and office equipment. They may also save the cost of contributing to their state's funds for workers who are disabled or unemployed. But to avoid violating tax laws, the company must be certain these individuals are truly independent contractors, not employees in disguise. Chapter 14 discusses the criteria that the U.S. Internal Revenue Service uses to determine whether a person is an independent contractor, as well as details involved in establishing home-based offices.

The Internet. The growth in home-based offices owes a lot to the Internet. A web presence can serve not just as an advertising medium but also as a company's store, or as one of its stores. In other words, the Internet can be a place of sale and distribution in one of two ways: (1) as the sole location for a company's sales or (2) as an alternative point of a sale.

To use the first strategy and succeed without a brick-and-mortar location, a company must have wide recognition or must affiliate itself with other well-known, well-respected companies. The number of travel reservations booked online continues to grow, but the more complex the transaction, the more clients want to talk to or meet a live person. To satisfy clients" needs, travel sellers need to occupy both cyberspace and a piece of real estate—a *bricks-and-clicks strategy.*

The more specialized an agency is, the better its chances of gaining the trust of clients to use its website and book components other than air, hotel, and car. Travelers planning to take a bicycle trip in Vietnam, for example, will look online for advice, web content, suppliers for such trips, and sometimes for a travel counselor who specializes in that kind of experience. When they find one, they may eventually book a trip—but not until they have called or e-mailed several times with questions and feel confident about the company or the counselor.

Who is or is not likely to book online? Candidates for booking online are those clients who are very familiar with air pricing for their most frequent routes, are certain of the hotel and rental car they want, prefer a simple package of trip elements, and/or need no extra travel assistance.

However, frequent business travelers are likely to turn instead to travel counselors to book their arrangements for several reasons: They make frequent changes to their travel plans and often need assistance before departure or in transit, their travel arrangements involve numerous details, and their time is very limited.

Leisure travelers are most likely to rely on travel counselors if they are seeking advice on a tour or cruise or if they are not familiar with the many possible choices in the marketplace—the companies, their travel offerings, reputations, and personalities. Also, when consumers realize the time and knowledge required to compare all of their options and to understand how these options do and don't meet their particular needs, they turn to agents.

This portrait of today's sales and distribution channels suggests two simple conclusions for travel counselors: to attract clients, they should provide multiple means of contact—in person and by phone, e-mail, or website—that are most convenient to travelers, and they should provide clients with additional valuable services, above and beyond simply making a reservation.

✔ CHECK-UP

Key questions about sales and distribution channels include
✔ Whether to use dual distribution, selling both directly and through intermediaries.
✔ Whether to use multiple sites for sales, such as retail offices, the telephone, and the Internet.
✔ How much to emphasize each site if multiple sites are used.

Travel buyers are good candidates for booking online when they
✔ Are very familiar with airfares.
✔ Know what hotel room and car they want.
✔ Do not need other travel management services.
✔ Trust the website host.

How Much to Charge: Setting the Price

■ WHAT PRICING STRATEGIES ARE MOST OFTEN USED BY TRAVEL SELLERS?

To customers, the pricing of a product or service is likely to be the most visible marketing decision. Most businesses buy a product at one price, add a markup, and sell it at the resulting higher price. But how high should the markup be? How is the price determined? Prices, the fourth *P*, reflect a basic marketing decision: Will the company compete on the basis of price, or not?

Pricing Strategies

A company can use two basic pricing strategies.
■ It can treat a product as a commodity and sell it at a price that is the same as, or lower than, its competitors' price. Recall that a *commodity* is something that has a specific value. Gold is a commodity because at a given time an ounce of gold has almost exactly the same value anywhere in the world.
■ A company can aim to differentiate its product by offering something that its competitors do not, and then sell the product at the same price as competitors do—or at a higher price. For example, a beautifully crafted gold necklace is not a commodity; its value is determined by how beautiful and worthwhile people deem it to be, and the seller prices it accordingly.

The second strategy is the one more often used by travel suppliers. Chapters 4–8 discussed the prices that suppliers charge for hotel rooms,

Upscale clients pay more for individual, personalized services.

cruises, and other products. Suppliers generally aim to distinguish their product from others and price it in a way that meets the needs of particular market segments. (Look again at Table 6.2.) Deluxe art tours and windjammer cruises, for example, reflect attempts to offer products that differ from other tours and cruises.

Travel Agencies and Pricing. What about travel agencies? For years, their pricing practices presented an exceptional case. They earned their profits, not from markups, but from commissions, mostly from airline tickets, and the airlines set the commission rate and the final price. Most agencies treated their services as commodities. Each travel agency had the same price for the same product. But the elimination of base commissions for domestic flights forced travel agencies into new marketing strategies.

In order to survive, travel agencies had to find sources of income other than commissions. Since 2002, almost 95 percent of travel agencies charge fees for some or all of their services. (For details about these fees, see Chapter 13.) Many agencies had feared that clients would not be willing to pay fees for their services; after all, clients had long thought of travel agencies as working for them for free. But travelers have accepted these fees and demonstrate a high degree of loyalty to their travel counselors even when they move away or change their travel habits and style.

Most travel agencies now aim to differentiate themselves from the competition and price accordingly. This pricing strategy obviously must fit with the rest of the marketing plan. For example, if an agency's target market is an upscale clientele, it might offer limousine service, personally deliver documents for a vacation, set up golf tee times, offer trips with unusual luxuries—and set the price accordingly. But if its target market is student travelers on a budget, the travel agency would not provide those extras, opting instead to offer, with cheerful efficiency, low-budget trips that give good value. In both cases, the price and the service meet the needs of the target market.

Lessons from Airlines. It is easy to oversimplify pricing strategy and its effect on marketing. One might think that low prices require a company to have low costs and that low costs mean a low level of service. But the experience of airlines in recent years shows that business is far more complicated.

After 9/11, the airlines faced a general downturn in the economy, a reduction in passenger loads, and rising fuel costs. Many of the major carriers took drastic cost-cutting measures. They reduced schedules in many markets, eliminated meals on most flights and laid off thousands of employees. New services were introduced that further reduced the cost to the airline. For example, self-check-in kiosks at airports eliminated the need for some airline personnel, reducing airline labor costs. Still the major carriers lost money.

While the major carriers—referred to as *legacy airlines*—were struggling financially, low-cost airlines were able to thrive and grow. Examples of successful low-cost U.S. carriers are Southwest, JetBlue, Frontier, and Spirit. RyanAir is an example of a successful regional low-cost European carrier. But low-cost doesn't necessarily mean less service. In fact, the most successful low-cost carriers focus on providing excellent customer service to their passengers. JetBlue, for example, offers leather seats and Direct TV on its flights and prides itself on hiring employees who are service- oriented and highly motivated.

The factors that contribute to the success of the new business model of the low-cost airlines include

- Lower prices, making them attractive to consumers.
- Improved cost efficiency due to using a new single type of aircraft (reducing airplane maintenance, training, and labor costs).
- Service efficiency, by empowering employees to provide good customer service.
- Scheduled service to routes that are profitable.

Surviving and Thriving with Competitive Pricing

Price competition among businesses sometimes leads to dubious methods. For example, if you advertise your lowest price and that price is in fact available for only a few restricted items, which you know will sell out very quickly, is that honest? Often only a very thin line separates advertising your lowest price and practicing a *bait-and-switch,* which means advertising something that is generally not available. Bait-and-switch methods are deceptive, unethical, and usually illegal.

Travel counselors should take action against suppliers that practice a bait-and-switch, but they should also be sure to distinguish it from legitimate pricing practices. For example, counselors should be able to explain to clients the difference between a restricted airfare and a bait-and-switch. In the first, the product is available if you meet the restrictions; in the second, the product is unavailable no matter what you do.

For travel agencies, being successful in an environment of stiff competition requires that the agency and its travel counselors

- Be more resourceful and efficient than the competition in searching out the best price from suppliers. Even those traveling super-deluxe want value for their money. Being able to give clients the best value for their dollar is a service they will pay for.
- Be able either to offer a lower price than competitors or to differentiate the agency's services (by offering more services or more knowledgeable counselors or unique products or a unique style, for example), then sell the

value of the higher-priced product.

- Establish communication and confidence between client and counselor.
- Keep current with new marketing ideas, new markets, and new technology.
- Offer something that others cannot. In other words, find a niche and specialize. (See Chapter 10 for more ideas on specialization.)

CHAPTER HIGHLIGHTS

Professionals in all sectors of the travel industry deal, in varying degrees, with marketing. Understanding marketing and staying focused on the consumer in all business processes is key to success. In this chapter, we considered the basic elements of marketing; here is a review of the objectives with which we began the chapter.

1. **Outline the marketing process and name the four Ps.** The marketing process aims to create a match between consumers' preferences and a company's products. Making that match requires knowledge not only about products but also about consumers' changing needs and expectations. To gain that knowledge, businesses rely on market research. Based on that research, they develop a marketing plan, which includes the selection of a target market and decisions about how to reach that market. In other words, it includes decisions about the marketing mix, or four Ps: product (what product is to be sold), promotion (how the product will be promoted), place (where it will be sold), and price. Each of the four Ps must mesh with the others.

2. **Summarize key decisions that a travel business must make about its product.** Travel businesses must determine the range and mix of travel products they will offer for sale as well as the level of service they will provide. Segmental analysis provides a tool for determining which products and services are most profitable and should be emphasized. Many travel agencies find that, to be competitive, they must specialize, developing their own niche. Ultimately, however, travel agencies are selling their service to customers.

3. **Describe the major forms of promotion.** Advertising, sales promotions, public relations, and person-to-person selling are the major forms of promotion, and each has a place in the travel industry. Advertising uses many media, including direct mail, newspapers, yellow pages, magazines, radio, television, video, social media, and the Internet.

   Each form of advertising has advantages and disadvantages. Direct mail can be tailored to a specific audience, easily changed, and it can convey much information. Newspapers can deliver a specific message of short-term validity, but they are discarded quickly. The yellow pages attract only interested consumers. Consumers tend to keep magazines longer, and most are more narrowly targeted than newspapers. Radio and television advertising needs repetition to register with consumers and usually are expensive compared with other forms of advertising. Advertising on the Internet is constantly available, but the messages can be easily lost amid the mass of information. The most common ways for travel businesses to advertise on the Internet are by having a website and by linking to other websites. Cooperative advertising with suppliers is a popular way for travel agencies to increase their advertising cost-effectiveness.

4. **Identify the distribution system and selling sites most often used by travel businesses.** Many travel suppliers use a dual distribution system, selling directly to the public and through intermediaries. Most travel agencies

traditionally used retail outlets as their place of sale, but today, many sales occur in client offices, over the telephone, in the seller's home, and online. The Internet may be used as the sole location for sales, but more often it is an alternative point of sale, as part of a bricks-and-clicks strategy. Decisions about how to use a website, like other marketing decisions, should be consistent with the rest of the marketing mix and integrated with the overall marketing strategy.

5. **Describe pricing strategies frequently used by travel suppliers and travel agencies.** Travel suppliers usually aim to distinguish their product from others and then sell the product at the same price as competitors or even at a higher price. But the price must be selected, so the particular product at that price meets the needs of particular market segments. A low price does not necessarily mean a low level of service, as low-cost airlines have demonstrated. Most travel agencies now aim to differentiate themselves from their competition and price their services, so the price and service meet the needs of their target market.

KEY TERMS

A list of key terms introduced in this chapter follows. If you do not recall the meaning of these terms, see the Glossary.

bait-and-switch	marketing plan
cooperative advertising	market research
customer relationship marketing	niche
direct mail	promotion
dual distribution	public relations
four Ps	segment analysis
legacy airlines	

REVIEW QUESTIONS

1. What is the relationship between a travel agency and a supplier?

2. What are the distribution channels for airline tickets? What benefits can travel agencies offer the consumer that other distribution channels cannot?

3. What makes up a company's image?

4. Name three effective methods to advertise travel. How or when would each be most effective? Name one disadvantage of each.

5. Under what conditions are consumers likely to book online without other contact with the supplier or travel agency?

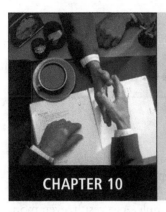

CHAPTER 10

Making a Sale

OBJECTIVES

After completing this chapter, you should be able to

1. Describe the agency-supplier relationship, which limits the agency's potential liability.

2. Describe the skills that provide a foundation for effective communication by salespeople.

3. Identify eight steps in making a successful sale.

4. State five questions involved in qualifying a client and three ways to close a sale.

5. Discuss the responsibilities of a travel counselor after the sale has been made.

Good salespeople are made, not born. Successful selling comes from knowledge about what is sold and from skills, such as asking the right questions. Both the knowledge and the skills can be learned by almost anyone who is motivated to become a successful salesperson.

The successful seller depends on certain techniques, but not on a prepackaged presentation, because each client is different. Some clients make quick decisions and focus on the big picture. Others move slowly, considering every option and everything that could possibly go wrong. Furthermore, the sales presentation must vary with the destination, the product, and the client's needs. The business traveler who wants a flight to a meeting in Phoenix, the young family searching for an inexpensive way home to Atlanta for Thanksgiving, and the retired couple eager to explore museums in eastern Europe—each of these travelers needs something different from the travel seller for their needs to be met effectively.

Variations in selling is the topic of Chapter 11: Specialized Sales. In this chapter, *Making a Sale*, we examine characteristics that are shared by almost all selling situations, primarily in an office. We look first at the relationship between the seller and the buyer and at the keys to successful communication, an important part of any sales situation. Then we focus on the basic steps in selling and essentials of customer service. These steps may need to be modified when selling a travel product by telephone, e-mail, and other non-traditional office situations.

The Sales Relationship

The job of selling travel is shaped by the fact that the product is intangible. Unlike a car or jewelry, travel arrangements cannot be felt, heard, tasted, or tried before buying. You cannot kick the tires of a tour. Buyers may spend thousands of dollars on a product they cannot sample. As a result, even more than other salespeople, those who sell travel must try to make the product or service as tangible as possible and to establish their credibility with the buyer.

The Sellers of Travel

Selling occurs in all facets of the travel industry. Airlines and railroads, motor coach and car rental companies, hotels and cruise lines—these and

---

CLOSE-UP: ON THE JOB WITH TOM MCLAUGHLIN, OUTSIDE SALES AGENT

Tom McLaughlin works for a medium-size travel agency that recently affiliated with a large chain. Tom was the agency's first outside sales agent. It now has eight full-time travel counselors and six outside sales agents.

"As an outside sales agent, I work strictly on commission and am responsible for my own clients. My agency gives me all kinds of support. When I go on vacation, I know my clients will be well taken care of by someone at the agency; I have access to mounds of information; I attend weekly meetings; I feel like an important part of a team.

"I'm a full-time agent like any other, but technically I am not an employee—I'm an independent contractor. I make my own hours and handle my clients the way I want. As long as my clients are taken care of, the agency is happy. I follow their office procedures, of course.

"When I began, I received 40 percent commission, but as I proved myself and built up my volume, I got 50 percent. Recently, we changed the commission split to 55 percent for me and 45 percent for the agency. Now the agency has a written commission scale for all outside agents.

"I go into the office three days a week and work at home the rest of the time. I have GDS access at home and can queue in a reservation to the agency, and it does the ticketing. I concentrate on tours, cruises, and custom-made trips, along with groups.

"I give clients I know my home phone, so they can call me direct. This can get a little out of hand sometimes, but if I really want some privacy, I can always have the call go to voicemail. I got a call from clients one time who arrived in Mexico, and the hotel had no record of them and no room. They had paid in full, and I had sent the hotel the payment. I was glad I could be there for them. I talked to the manager, explaining that I had used this hotel for clients before and that I had sent the payment. The manager gave them a room and later found the reservation misfiled—the name was misspelled. My clients probably could have taken care of this themselves with some persistence, but they didn't go on vacation to worry about this.

"I'll do whatever it takes to get clients. I often meet with them in the agency in the evening after the office is closed. Actually, I prefer this if they have a major vacation to plan. There are no distractions, and everyone can relax and talk as long as needed. I have some coffee, tea, or wine ready. I'll deliver documents right to their home if they wish. Again, it gives me a chance to build a personal rapport.

"Theoretically, I could take all kinds of discount trips, but I don't have the time. I usually plan my own fam trips as part of my vacation. I once spent the whole day in Cancún walking from hotel to hotel taking notes on them.

"Sometimes I take a total vacation and just sit by a lake. I've seen a lot of the world, but there is a lot left to see in the future. My clients are getting interested in places not even heard of 10 years ago. I'll try to get there first."

other suppliers all hire salespeople. Some take calls from consumers and travel counselors; others are sales representatives (like the one described in Chapter 7) who go out to travel agencies and other organizations to familiarize them with their company's products in hopes of future sales.

Travel sellers may work inside an employer's office or in their own home-based offices, or both. They may be salaried employees or *independent contractors*—people who are not employees but are self-employed, working under contract. Independent contractors are not subject to the same rules and control as employees, and many do not receive the same benefits, such as paid vacation time, sick days, health insurance, or pensions. Chapter 14 discusses some of the special challenges and opportunities that come with working out of the home and with being self-employed.

To some suppliers, the travel agency is a buyer, but travel counselors, of course, are also sellers—they sell to the general public. And, as mentioned earlier, many suppliers sell directly to the traveler, bypassing the travel counselor. The Close-Up on Careers sections in Chapter 1 described some of the specific sales positions in travel agencies. There are leisure and corporate travel counselors, and **outside sales agents**—people whose job is to bring new clients to the agency, attracting customers outside the agency's existing clientele. Outside sales agents for suppliers are called business development managers (BDMs).

Unlike most retail sellers, travel agencies normally maintain no inventory. Sometimes, the agency pre-purchases blocks of airline seats, hotel rooms, and so forth for resale; but, usually, agencies place an order only when the client decides to buy. As a result, travel agencies do not risk money acquiring products they may be unable to sell. But the lack of inventory also has a disadvantage: The agency must usually check with a supplier before selling anything. The agency does not control the inventory; suppliers do.

To some extent, travel suppliers also control who may sell their products. As we discussed in Chapter 1, through the conference system, certain groups of suppliers—such as IATAN (International Airlines Travel Agent Network), ARC (Airlines Reporting Corporation), and CLIA (Cruise Lines International Association)—appoint agencies to sell their products.

The Buyers of Travel

Economists talk about travel as being a *discretionary* purchase because the demand is *elastic* and *price sensitive*. In other words, people tend to travel less when budgets are tight and to travel more during periods of prosperity, or when prices are slashed or when an obviously good value is offered. For individual travelers, however, trips are often not discretionary but necessary. A person traveling on business, for example, often has no choice, and people often feel obliged to travel to attend various family gatherings. (Grandchildren may have done more for the travel industry than the Wright brothers.)

Based on differences such as these, we identified three main types of travel in Chapter 1: *vacation and leisure travel; corporate* or *business travel* (any trip purchased by a business and made for the purposes of the organization); and *VFR travel* (travel to visit friends or relatives). For each type of travel, clients are likely to have different needs.

Discovering those needs can be particularly challenging in the case of leisure travelers. The challenge comes in part from the sheer variety of needs and motives. Leisure travelers may be looking mainly for rest or for intellectual stimulation, for a change in routine or for a religious experience.

They may be hoping to meet new friends or to learn more about a specific field by joining a tour led by an expert. Table 10.1 describes some of the many specific activities and benefits that people look for when they take a leisure trip.

Beyond conscious purposes like these, travelers may also be influenced by subtler needs. For example,

- A need for *social status* leads some people to travel to a particular destination or to stay at a particular hotel because many of their friends have been there. The same need leads others to travel where none of their friends has been so that they will stand out as leaders.
- A need for *self-esteem* motivates some travelers to stay at deluxe hotels where they will be treated with deference and motivates others to search for unusual destinations or opportunities for learning.
- A need for *self-actualization* leads some people to select travel without concern for what others are doing but with the aim of fulfilling themselves, whether that means trekking alone in the Himalayas, going to cooking school in Tuscany, or traveling to Peru to help in a shelter for the poor.

TABLE 10.1 Motives for Leisure Travel

Motivator	Examples of Possible Destinations
Gambling. Because gambling is now legal to some extent in more than 30 states, it is less likely than in the past to be the sole motivation for travel far from home.	Casinos have proliferated in many states, so riverboat casinos and motor coach tours to local gambling attractions are other possibilities. Despite the increased competition, Las Vegas remains the major gambling destination. Internationally, Monte Carlo (on the French Riviera), many Caribbean islands, and cruise ships offer opportunities for sub-segments of the gambling market.
Shopping. All but the most remote destinations offer shopping, among the top activities of domestic and international travelers, here and abroad.	Shopping tours can be organized to almost anywhere, from the local outlet mall, to European Christmas markets, or Hong Kong. North American malls known as tourist attractions include the West Edmonton Mall in Edmonton, Canada, and the Mall of America in Bloomington, Minnesota.
Religion. For some, religious beliefs require a visit to particular regions or sites. For others, it is an opportunity to visit sites of cultural significance.	The Vatican is a key religious destination. Others include Israel, Lourdes, France, and shrines or special places of worship in many locales.
Sun. The urge to get away from cold, gloomy weather to find some place warm is reason enough for many consumers to travel.	The sunny climates of Florida, California, Mexico, and the Caribbean attract millions of warm-weather sun-worshippers every year.
Food and drink. A desire to sample different cuisines or restaurants is often a secondary reason for traveling, but an interest in taking gourmet or winetasting tours may also be the primary reason for a trip.	Destinations are becoming increasingly adept at developing culinary and beverage clusters that attract travelers. Cruises and certain tour companies also are developing vacation itineraries and experiences. Winetasting tours to the Napa and Sonoma Valleys in California and to French vineyards are very popular.
Entertainment. The chance to sample the nightlife of a city sometimes stands on its own as a reason for traveling.	Las Vegas, Hollywood, New York City, New Orleans, Paris, and Rio de Janeiro are a few of the standouts that can satisfy the party crowd.
Arts. People will travel halfway around the world to experience great art and architecture firsthand. Music, opera, dance, and theater all form separate travel niches.	New York and London are especially known for theater tours. Italy attracts opera buffs; Austria, lovers of classical music.
History and culture. Many people travel in order to trace their own roots or to learn about the past by visiting museums or historical sites.	Ellis Island in New York is of particular interest to the American descendants of immigrants who want to trace their past. Those with broader historical interests might be drawn to the archaeological sites and ruins in Greece, Mexico, Peru, Egypt, or Rome; presidential libraries; Colonial Williamsburg in Virginia; the Freedom Trail in Boston; or battlegrounds of the Civil War.

(continued on next page)

In short, people with differing motives and needs are likely to be satisfied by different destinations, accommodations, and activities. The successful salesperson learns the products of key industry suppliers, such as tours, cruises, and resorts and is able to ascertain which company's product would be a good match for a particular client's needs.

The Contract between Buyers and Sellers

Ideally, a sale involves a partnership between the buyer and the seller in which the needs of both are met. The buyer obtains something he or she wants; the seller gets the sale. Neither pressure nor manipulation is needed. Reality, of course, often varies from this ideal.

TABLE 10.1 Motives for Leisure Travel (cont.)

Motivator	Examples of Possible Destinations
Collecting countries. In this age of "Instagrammable" moments, travelers want to see how many countries they can have stamped in their passports and posted on their social media handles.	Don't forget to route these travelers through Liechtenstein and Monaco on that European trip. Try San Marino and Andorra as well.
Meeting people. Travelers may want to meet the people who live at a destination. Others may hope to travel with newfound friends—a motivator that clients do not always mention but that subtle questions may uncover.	Tours for singles are one possibility. For those wanting to meet people at the destination, consider countries, such as Ireland, that are known for being friendly to travelers. The Bahamas is one of many countries that has a "People-to-People" program: The Ministry of Tourism will arrange for travelers to meet Bahamians with interests similar to their own.
Personal challenge. For some people, a trip alone to a foreign land constitutes a challenge. For others, this motivation may translate into a desire for an adventure, such as climbing a mountain or rafting down dangerous rapids.	The possibilities obviously depend on the particular challenge. For whitewater rafting, for example, opportunities include going down the Colorado River through the Grand Canyon, the Zambezi River in Zimbabwe, or rivers in West Virginia, Idaho, Costa Rica, and Chile. Dude ranches in Arizona, Colorado, Montana, and Wyoming provide a challenge many travelers enjoy.
Ecotourism. Broadly defined, this motivation includes the desire to see nature's variety and beauty.	Costa Rica, Belize, the Galápagos Islands, African safaris, and national parks all over the world offer opportunities to satisfy this desire.
Sightseeing. Some people derive satisfaction just from knowing that they have seen famous places for themselves. Many tours are purchased based on the number of sights that will be seen.	From the classic Grand Tour of Europe, to river cruises that stop in famous cities, to the theme parks of Orlando, Florida, and monuments and museums of Washington, D.C., there are so many sights and sounds attracting travelers to destinations and regions.
Special events. There is an endless list of special events and festivals that bring people together, from those famous around the world to local arts and crafts fairs.	Prime candidates include annual Mardi Gras or Carnival celebrations, particularly in New Orleans, Rio de Janeiro, and Trinidad; the sites of the Summer and Winter Olympics; the Passion Play in Oberammergau, Germany; and tennis matches at Wimbledon, England.
Getting away from it all; relaxation. Someone with a quiet job may consider an action-packed vacation to be the best way to get away from it all; someone with a stressful, exhausting job may want to go somewhere and lie in a hammock for a week.	It is important to note this motivation but then also to determine the type of destination and activity that will meet the client's needs. For those most interested in peace and quiet, a secluded Caribbean island might be the answer.
Active sports. Skiing, golf, tennis, scuba diving, and windsurfing are among the physical activities that many people enjoy. They will travel for the chance to indulge in a particular sport or for the opportunity to experience it in new and unusual settings.	Switzerland as well as Aspen and Vail, Colorado, should satisfy skiers. Ireland and Myrtle Beach, South Carolina, have much to offer golfers. Some places offer travelers the chance to learn a sport; for example, resorts in the Caribbean teach scuba diving.

Occasionally, written contracts regulate the relationship between travel buyers and sellers. For example, car rental companies present a contract for signature. But most contracts are implied. The purchase of an airline ticket, implies assent to the airline's contract with passengers, as discussed in Chapter 4. Tour operators and cruise lines state their contracts in their brochures.

Similarly, the contract between a travel counselor and a client is usually considered to be implied. Basically, the counselor is responsible for

- Confirming reservations, sending deposits, checking times and schedules, issuing correct documents, and so forth.
- Protecting the clients' best interests by negotiating on their behalf with suppliers for the best possible arrangements at the best possible price.
- Verifying clients' citizenship if they are traveling to other nations and notifying them about necessary documents, such as passports and visas.
- Conveying other needed information—such as cancellation charges and change fees, any negative information about the contracts with suppliers, financial instability among tour operators or suppliers, risks associated with the destination, and the need for travel insurance.

Beyond these responsibilities, however, the contract for services exists between the client and the *supplier*, except when a travel agency is operating its own tour. The travel counselor usually is only an agent of the supplier and is not responsible for the actions of the supplier.

Travel counselors should make sure that clients understand this relationship. By disclosing the agency-supplier relationship, travel counselors may limit potential liability. They can protect themselves further by publishing a *consumer disclosure notice* (see Figure 10.1). The notice should be prominently displayed, inserted in client materials, or printed on invoices, ticket jackets, or itineraries. Agencies seeking additional protection ask that clients sign a disclosure or disclaimer. Some offer their disclaimers online at their websites.

No disclaimer, however, can protect a counselor who is negligent. A disclaimer of responsibility for the actions of suppliers does not release the travel counselor from responsibility for checking suppliers and arrangements carefully. A counselor who spots inaccuracies in brochures, for example, should draw the client's attention to them. By offering the brochure to the customer, the salesperson is taking responsibility for its truthfulness. By misrepresenting the supplier's product or by being a party to the supplier's misrepresentation, the travel counselor can become legally liable for any problems that the client encounters. We discuss the legal and ethical responsibilities of travel professionals further in Chapter 16.

Note that the management of many travel agencies may have already selected certain suppliers as preferred suppliers. These are suppliers that the agency management prefers its agents to use when possible for two reasons. One is that they may have arranged for the supplier to grant the agency a higher rate of commission than the basic 10 percent. The second reason is that they trust the selected supplier and may have worked with them over the years, with the supplier having a track record of giving the agency and its clients superior service.

In the rest of this chapter and the next, we focus on the various steps involved in selling by travel counselors. The variety and flexibility of their products relieve them, to a great extent, of the need to pressure customers. The customers want to travel. The travel counselor only has to find the right experience to match them with and persuade them to buy.

Sellers of travel include
✔ Sales representatives from suppliers who sell directly to the public.
✔ Sales representatives from suppliers who sell to travel agencies.
✔ Travel counselors who sell to the general public.

Buyers of travel may be planning
✔ Vacation or leisure travel.
✔ Business or corporate travel.
✔ VFR travel.

The relationship between buyer and seller
✔ Ideally results in a sale that meets the needs of both.
✔ Involves a contract, whether written or implied.

Learning to Communicate

■ WHAT SKILLS DO SELLERS NEED TO COMMUNICATE EFFECTIVELY?

Selling is basically just a particular type of communication. If you communicate well, you are at least halfway on the path toward success in selling. Like other types of communication, effective selling requires the ability to (1) create a good relationship, (2) ask questions and listen actively to the answers, and (3) present ideas or information.

Creating a Relationship

The keys that unlock the door to effective communication are the desire of other people to talk with you and to trust what you say. Unfortunately, first impressions often are lasting impressions, and a bad first impression can permanently block development of this relationship. Here are some tips for creating an impression to encourage rapport with customers.

■ Greet customers when you meet face-to-face. Make eye contact and smile. Stand to introduce yourself and extend your hand to welcome them; perhaps direct them to a seat. If you cannot greet clients immediately because you are on the phone or with another customer, acknowledge their presence and let them know you will be with them soon. No one likes to feel ignored.

■ Look at your workplace from the customer's viewpoint. Is it tasteful and neat? Does it put clients in a relaxed mood? Does the decor whisper of far-off places?

■ Place the client's chair next to yours, if possible, not across the barrier of a desk. Offer the customer a cup of coffee.

■ Look at your own appearance. Is it professional?

■ If your first contact with a customer is through your website, what message does your homepage convey? Is it easy for them to understand what services you provide and what your value proposition is for them?

■ If your first contact is via phone or e-mail, you want to convey an especially friendly, personal impression, in the hope of leading the customer to more discussions or a face-to-face meeting. Many sales today are made without the client and customer ever seeing one another.

Beyond creating a good impression, establishing a link with your customer will be easier if you

- Begin and end each conversation with a smile. Emotions are often infectious.
- Use the customer's name frequently.
- Don't waste time. If you do not know an answer, offer to research the issue and get back to the customer. Keep frequently used resources close by.
- Use a moderate tone of voice. Adjust it to the speed at which your customer talks.
- Be positive and empathetic. Try to view clients' interests through their eyes. You may never have skied, for example, but if you can imagine the thrill of skiing down the slopes and the taste of hot chocolate in front of the fireplace, you can get excited about the experience.
- Inspire trust by being prepared.

Asking Questions and Hearing the Answers

For the salesperson, questions give structure to the sales process. Before asking any question, you should have in mind where the answer will take the conversation. By asking effective qualifying questions but letting the client do the talking, you can lead the conversation toward the desired end.

Three types of questions are useful in different circumstances.

- *Close-ended questions* invite precise answers like "Yes" or "No" or simple facts. They narrow the possibilities and yield specific information.
- *Open-ended questions* invite answers that include the facts, opinions, and/or feelings the client thinks are relevant. Open-ended questions typically begin with what, how, or why; for example, "What do you have in mind?" "What kind of vacations have you enjoyed before?" "Why do you like the idea of a cruise?" These questions encourage people to open up, perhaps revealing their attitudes, tastes, preferences, and needs as they discuss the topic.
- *Feedback questions* confirm details that have emerged in the conversation. For example, "So you want a resort with a very sociable feeling, where you can meet people. Is that right?" The other person can simply respond, "Yes," offer minor corrections, or object.

Questioning, of course, should never sound like cross-examination. Effective questioners try to

- Weave their questions into the conversation.
- Combine different types of questions.
- Reflect the client's own language in their questions.
- Phrase questions to elicit a positive answer.
- Limit their own talking. Clients must be allowed to talk freely, even as you guide the conversation into relevant areas.

The purpose of asking questions is to hear the answers, but research suggests that the average listener grasps the significance of only about 25 percent of what was said. Effective listening requires effort. Here are some tips for hearing what another person actually says.

- Shut out distractions. Don't take incoming calls while with a client.
- Don't interrupt, even if the person pauses for a long breath.
- Take notes.
- Keep an open mind. To avoid missing what clients are saying, don't let what they say or how they say it irritate you, and don't jump to conclusions.
- Use verbal and nonverbal signals to indicate that you understand and are paying attention. Nodding, eye contact, and phrases such as "I see" all indicate that you are listening.

- Listen for inflections and watch the client's *body language,* which consists of nonverbal signals, such as facial expressions, posture, and gestures. These nonverbal signals reveal attitudes and biases; Table 10.2 describes some examples.
- *Recap*—that is, review key points of the conversation.
- Get the client's contact information. Don't let someone leave your office or end a telephone conversation without doing so.

Presenting Ideas and Information

Beyond questioning others to gain information, effective communicators also present their own information persuasively. They know how to make their points both clear and appealing. Here are some techniques that will help you do the same.

- Adopt the words and style used by your listener. Avoid using jargon the other person might not understand; use everyday language instead. Does your listener really know what round-trip transfers are? He or she will surely understand if you say, "You will be taken from the airport directly to your hotel and back again at the end of your stay in time for your flight."
- Elicit feedback throughout your presentation, mixing questions with your comments. For example, you might ask, "Does that sound good to you?"
- Be prepared with two ideas, but present only one idea at a time.
- Do whatever you can to make the intangible tangible. Use words that create mental pictures; give examples; use visual aids if possible.

In the next section, we describe how to apply these techniques to the challenge of selling travel.

TABLE 10.2

Body Language in the United States

Defensiveness
- ➤ Holding arms crossed in front of chest
- ➤ Crossing legs tightly
- ➤ Interposing a shoulder or an object, such as a handbag or papers

Frustration and aggression
- ➤ Making a clasped fist
- ➤ Holding wrist of fisted hand
- ➤ Holding fist to chin

Thoughtfulness, attempt to reach a decision
- ➤ Touching chin or cheek
- ➤ Stroking chin
- ➤ Pinching bridge of nose

Readiness to buy
- ➤ Nodding and smiling
- ➤ Leaning in with a relaxed arm and open hand
- ➤ Leaning back and relaxing

✔ CHECK-UP

Successful communicators know how to
- ✔ Create rapport with listeners.
- ✔ Ask effective questions.
- ✔ Listen carefully.
- ✔ Present ideas and information clearly and persuasively.

Some of the elements needed to develop rapport include
- ✔ Developing a good impression through your appearance, surroundings, and manner.

- ✔ Showing interest in the other person.
- ✔ Demonstrating empathy.
- ✔ Inspiring trust.

Three types of questions are
- ✔ Close-ended questions.
- ✔ Open-ended questions.
- ✔ Feedback questions.

Steps in Selling

- WHAT STEPS SHOULD SELLERS TAKE TO MAKE A SALE?

- HOW DO SELLERS QUALIFY CLIENTS, AND HOW DO THEY CLOSE A SALE?

Every salesperson needs to know what to say, when to say it, and how to say it. So far, we have considered how to say things effectively. In this section, we focus on what to say in a sales presentation and when to say it.

In a general way, the steps in selling outlined in Chapter 1 provide the answer; they lay out a framework for progressing toward the sale. Figure 10.2 reviews these steps.

Good salespeople follow a structure similar to the one spelled out in Figure 10.2, but they vary it as necessary to respond to individual situations. Sometimes, for example, clients know exactly what they want, and you can go directly from step 3 to step 7, closing the sale and recapping, which means moving the customer to make a purchase commitment. Often, steps in the cycle must be revisited. For example, you might go from recommending a product (step 5) to overcoming obstacles (step 6) and then back to recommending a product (step 5).

Steps 1–3: Acquiring Information

"Hi, do you have any information on Mexico?" Most conversations between a travel counselor (whether in person or via digital communications like Facebook messenger or e-mail) and a client start something like this. Travel counselors should view these requests as evidence of a desire to travel. If you simply answer the questions without initiating your own presentation, you are doomed to frustrating days with few sales. In this case, for example, you might say something like,

> Yes, we certainly do. What got you interested in Mexico? What part have you been thinking about visiting?

Step 1: Identify Customers. Of course, not everybody who contacts you is ready to make a purchase. Counselors need to *qualify* the client; that is, determine how ready and able the client is to make a purchase. Thus, a first goal of the sales presentation is to ask five **qualifying** questions:

1. When would you like to go?
2. Do you know exactly where you would like to go?
3. How many are in your travel party, and who are they?
4. How long do you plan to be away?
5. What kind or class of service do you need? You might answer this question by saying, "What kinds of hotels do you usually like to stay in? Should we look for the same type this time?" or "Is this a special occasion?"

Besides indicating whether the person qualifies as a potential customer, these questions should elicit information that will help you narrow the search for the services the customer needs. By starting with these questions, you can avoid getting involved in long, inconclusive discussions or confusing the client with too many possibilities.

Occasionally, clients immediately announce precisely what they want, or they are eager to book the trip once they have answered the initial questions. In these cases, there is no reason to linger on other selling steps; in fact, you may lose the sale if you do not move to the closing. Confirm the information you have received and be certain that the proposed arrangements meet the customer's needs. If they do, close the sale and recap (step 7).

The Budget Question. Some salespeople like to add a sixth qualifying question, one about the budget, such as "How much do you want to spend?" or "Do you have a total budget in mind?" The answer allows the seller to focus quickly on the appropriate arrangements. Also, asking about the budget helps the salesperson avoid embarrassing or alienating customers by suggesting arrangements that cost far more, or far less, than they intend to spend.

But there are good reasons for avoiding or postponing a question about budget. Many people overestimate the cost of travel and do not have a clear picture of what they want. Others understate how much they will spend in an attempt to get the best deal. Further, what clients are willing to spend ultimately may depend on the value offered for the money. In short, the client's initial response to a question about budget may be misleading.

There is no single best time to deal with the budget question. Usually, hints come from the fifth qualifying question, about the class of service, and other signals throughout the conversation. Your recommendations (step 5) can reflect those hints even though you have never explicitly asked about their budget. But if no definite signals come through indirectly, you might ask about it once you have built trust (step 2) with the client, or you might recommend choices from two price ranges, explain the differences, and pick up on the client's needs there.

Step 2: Build Trust. At each step, salespeople should be developing and maintaining links to their customers. It is especially important to begin winning client trust early in the sale. The techniques discussed earlier for creating a relationship will establish the foundation for trust.

At this point, you can also ask customers about their previous travel experiences, what areas they are most interested in, and what they most enjoy.

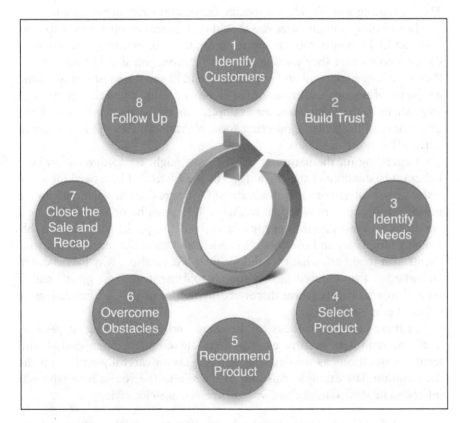

FIGURE 10.2 Steps in Selling

Not every sale requires these eight steps, and sometimes the salesperson must cycle back through some steps. But understanding these steps and keeping them in mind should help you learn to communicate effectively with clients, to meet their needs and to make the sale. While these basic steps work well in a face-to-face selling situation, the travel counselor will have to modify them if selling by telephone or e-mail.

In short, show that you care about their feelings and ideas. For example, in the course of a conversation with the young man who asked about Mexico, it might be appropriate for the travel counselor to say,

> *Mmm, yes, that part of Mexico does have some great beaches. It sounds as if you've done some thinking about it.*

Try to develop trust in a way that comes naturally to you, with sincere statements. Select one of the client's statements with which you can identify. Remember that trust is inspired by self-confidence, and self-confidence comes from being up to date about what you are selling and from knowing the answers, or where to find the answers.

Step 3: Identify Needs. Usually client answers to qualifying questions do not disclose everything you need to know. To pinpoint client needs more precisely, you must ask additional questions.

Chapters 4–8 identified many of these questions. Recall, for example, the discussions of what travel counselors should ask when selling an airline ticket (in the Close-Up: On the Job with Nadia Jones in Chapter 4); when qualifying a client for a car rental (in the Close-Up: On the Job with Frank Sciata in Chapter 5); when finding lodging for a client and making a reservation (in the Close-Up: Selling to the Budget-Minded in Chapter 6); and when making a cruise reservation (Close-Up: On the Job with Hillary Pennell in Chapter 7). These questions should give you specific facts about your clients' needs.

In addition, in many cases you should elicit more personal information to understand the clients' motives, needs, and wants. For example, if your clients do not know where they want to go for a vacation, you should find out why they are taking a vacation and what they would like to do. Most travelers have a mixture of reasons and motives. For clients who just know they want to go somewhere in the Caribbean, for example, you might ask them to rank the importance of the beach, sightseeing, food, nightlife, and shopping in order to narrow the choice of islands.

Depending on the nature of the trip, you might try to develop an even richer understanding of the client. Is he or she motivated by a need for social status or self-esteem or self-actualization? Or where does the client fall on the psychographic spectrum shown in Figure 1.3? Does he or she tend to be a venturer (outgoing, confident, eager to lead the pack) or a dependable (valuing familiarity and comfort)? To understand these characteristics of your clients, you might ask what they did for their last vacation, why they chose it, and whether they enjoyed it. "My friends told me it was just great!" and "I wanted to visit before it was discovered by hordes of people" indicate quite different personalities.

In these early steps, focus on the client and avoid making suggestions until the complete picture emerges. Ask close-ended, open-ended, and feedback questions as we described earlier. Listen carefully and recap the conversation. For example, this step in the sale to the young man who was interested in Mexico might end with the travel counselor saying,

> *OK, so let me review this. You're planning to go in late January for eight or nine days, and you want one of the quieter beach locations, one that is fairly new. You don't need a lot of fancy nightlife, but you want at least something to do at night, and you do want a nice place to stay because you need a real mental break. Does that sound about right?*

Step 4: Select a Product

So far, our hypothetical travel counselor has greeted the client, qualified him and learned a great deal about what he wants and needs. What next?

Experienced counselors may have just the right recommendations for a trip, but even those who do not know what to recommend should be able to make the sale. They can look for help from several sources, including

- *Colleagues.* Professionals in all fields regularly consult one another, especially through closed Facebook groups and other online communities.
- *Reference materials.* Check in print, online, or on other media.
- *Clients.* Many agencies solicit and file clients' reactions to their trips. Also, do not be afraid to ask well-traveled clients for their opinions about destinations and suppliers.
- *Suppliers.* Good tour operators and DMCs try to help travel counselors match clients to their tours and packages, many of which are extremely cost-effective for the client and both time- and labor- saving for the counselor.

As you consider what arrangements will suit a client, remember that not even the wealthy want to be overcharged. Clients seek a price that represents a good *value*. Value, of course, is subjective. To the couple who want to celebrate their 25th wedding anniversary by returning to their honeymoon hotel in Hawaii, even a very high price may represent an excellent value. Low-cost arrangements that do not meet a client's needs do not represent good value. Sometimes clients may be willing to compromise or eliminate choices because of the price, but they should understand what they are sacrificing.

Many clients say they are looking for a deal. A deal does not mean a low price; it means an excellent value for whatever price is paid. A great price for a week in Hawaii that buys a motel-like accommodation in an urban area three blocks from the beach may or may not fit a particular client's needs. Clients get a deal whenever they get excellent value for their money and receive the product that serves their needs and wants.

Usually suppliers prominently advertise their lowest fares or rates. Clients may not note the restrictions that apply. For example, the lowest hotel and car rates are often available only on certain days; the lowest-priced tours, only at the least desirable hotels; and the least expensive cruises, only on certain sailings and for few cabins. Counselors should check and explain the restrictions and suggest alternatives if the client cannot meet them.

Step 5: Recommend a Product

Once you are confident that you know what a client wants and that your suggestions will meet those desires, make a recommendation confidently and enthusiastically. In the case of the man who wanted to go to Mexico, the counselor eventually suggested a choice: either Ixtapa or Huatulco, described the features and benefits of each, and then let him decide. Clients who are reluctant to choose ("Well, which one do you recommend?") can be gently urged in the direction that you think might be best.

When presenting recommendations, give each possibility its due. Do not eliminate all options. At some point, the real world—in which there are full flights, full hotels, full tours, and full cruises—will intrude. No recommendation should be so exclusive that the client will cancel the trip if one element cannot be booked.

To make your recommendation persuasive, remember to avoid jargon. For example, you might have read a magazine article about Huatulco when it was first being developed as a new resort and say,

Huatulco is a new tourism development with new properties. Growth of its infrastructure is just in the inception stage. There are likely to be availabilities for your clients.

But when you give the same information to your customer, you might say something more client-focused:

Huatulco may have that fresh feeling you're looking for. It's growing more popular, but right now it's still quiet and pristine. Let's see if there's something available.

Furthermore, to ensure your effectiveness, incorporate the client's own statements or refer to them. Use your words to paint a picture of your recommendation, as Figure 10.3 describes.

Also, use maps, brochures, videos, and social media when applicable. In fact, maps are absolutely necessary when planning a wide-ranging itinerary. Remember that brochures paint a rosy picture and that the camera can mislead. Streaming videos can either whet travelers' appetites at an early stage or keep them enthused later. Printouts from websites can also keep interest up and may help finalize a sale.

These visual aids are just that—aids. They need to be used at the right time; they are not a substitute for your presentation. Bring out a limited number of brochures (probably two at most), ones that are appropriate and familiar to you and for companies with which your agency has a track record and a preferred supplier relationship. For more specific advice on using brochures and other visual aids, refer to the discussions in chapter 8.

One other guideline is important when presenting a recommendation: Link the recommendation to the benefits the client seeks. This is worth some further comment.

Translating Features into Benefits. Clients may be impressed by features, but they will not be motivated to purchase them unless the benefits are clear. As we discussed in Chapter 1, a *feature* is an inherent characteristic of a product or service; a *benefit* is the positive result that a feature brings to a particular client. Effective salespeople translate features into benefits, as Table 10.3 illustrates.

Personalize this translation by restating the client's wants and needs and then relating the specific benefits of features to those wants and needs. For example, a travel counselor might say, "You mentioned that you'd like a relaxing vacation on a beach. This place has its own private beach, giving you the tranquility you're looking for."

Different people may buy the same product because of different features and benefits. For example, one person chooses a particular cruise in order to relax; another, because it stops at interesting ports. Even a single feature can offer varying benefits to different people. Some travelers take a half-day sightseeing tour of Hong Kong because they do not want to try to find places on their own; others do so because they want a quick orientation to the city before they begin their own exploration. Emphasize the benefits appropriate to the individual. Knowing which benefits to suggest to each client comes from careful qualifying and active listening.

FIGURE 10.3

Selling a Recommendation

"If your client imagines himself on a trip," writes Marc Mancini, "he's more likely to actually take that trip." You can help clients imagine themselves on a trip by painting mental pictures that put clients at their center. Here are some tips for how to create such pictures.

- **Use visual words to give form to the picture.**

  "When you see this magnificent ship in port, you'll know you're about to begin a very special experience."

- **Stress your enthusiasm.**

  "I was really excited when I found it."

- **Use action words to make the picture move.**

  "You can play volleyball in the sun and enjoy food prepared by a world-famous chef as you sail up the coast."

- **Comment on the picture, describing exactly the benefits it brings.**

  "I can get you a cabin with its own veranda. That way, you can have your own private view of Alaska's amazing scenery as it passes by."

- **Elicit other senses to make the picture real.**

  "When you get to Glacier Bay, you'll have the incredible experience of hearing huge chunks of ice thundering into the water right in front of you. And there's nothing to compare with that bracing air."

Source: Adapted with permission from Marc Mancini.

Dangers to Avoid. What you do *not* say to your customers is also important. Among statements to avoid are

- *Exaggerations, overgeneralizations, and lies.* Avoid saying things like "It's the greatest value in New Orleans"; "It's always lovely at this time of year"; "You don't have to worry about malaria because you'll never catch it in a week." Do not generalize about things you know nothing about: "This hotel is just great. I'm sure you're going to love it."
- *Guarantees of enjoyment by referring to another client's experience:* "I know you'll enjoy this trip because Mr. and Mrs. Jones did." Mr. and Mrs. Jones may have liked it for reasons totally unimportant to the current client.
- *Guarantees of anything beyond your control,* such as the weather, the service, or even the client's reaction. "You'll love it" is a dangerous expression.
- *Apologies for circumstances beyond your control.* Constant apologizing creates the same effect as constant negatives. It also implies that you are responsible to some degree.
- *Overpromises.* If you say you are going to do something, do it.
- *Knocks on the competition.* Clients might mention that another agency did not give good service. The comment should not be answered directly, and your next sentence should focus on the client's needs and perhaps the kind of good service he can expect from your company without denigrating your competitor.
- *Use of the phrase "No problem."* This phrase suggests that no great effort will be taken because none is needed. But also avoid giving the impression that the trip is extraordinarily difficult or likely to be mishandled.
- *The word "cancel."* Instead, suggest that clients can change reservations should the need arise.

Once you have recommended two or three suitable options (don't overload your clients with too many product choices) and communicated features as well as benefits, you will need to check to see which, if any of your recommendations appeal to your customers. This check pulls together details from the conversation and resolves any confusion. It reduces the possibility that a disappointed client may later accuse the seller of not having explained things clearly. An accurate summary of the recommendations also starts the client toward saying "Yes" and can lead easily into an offer to book the trip.

This conversation may uncover disagreements or objections; resolving these is the next step, step 6. If the client agrees with your summary of the conversation so far, you can proceed to step 7, closing the sale and recapping, or you can suggest upgrading or adding to the arrangements.

TABLE 10.3 Translating Features into Benefits

Features of a Convention Center	Possible Benefits
Small and independent site Unique design and furnishings Intimate atmosphere	Personalized service
Remote location Encourages camaraderie Refreshing tranquility	Few distractions On-site recreation activities for families and free time
All meals included	No need to search for restaurants No need to monitor budget for meals
Daytime and nighttime activities	Wide variety of things to do both day and night Can be as active or lazy as you like

Selling Up and Cross-Selling

If the client agrees with your recommendation, you might increase the scope of the sale with a little effort, through selling up and cross-selling. *Selling up* means upgrading, changing to a more expensive or inclusive version of a product. For example, you might suggest

- An upgraded hotel or an upgraded hotel room. If a client is paying $1,500 for a trip, would an upgraded hotel room with a view of the ocean for $150 more be worthwhile? Clients often splurge on lodging. Many clients will be disappointed later if you did not offer better accommodations.
- An outside rather than an inside stateroom on a cruise, or a cabin on a higher deck or with a more central location.
- Larger rental cars for people who may need the extra space.
- First-class or business-class airfare to those already paying a high nondiscounted fare.

Clients who enjoy their trip may grumble about the cost of things in general but will give you credit for helping them plan a fantastic trip. Suggest an upgrade. Clients will appreciate it.

Cross-selling—selling additional products or services—is another way of increasing a sale while providing more service. Ask simple questions, such as "Do you need a hotel room when you arrive?" and "Do you need a car when you arrive?" Clients may not even be aware that you can arrange tickets for attractions in advance. Or they may forget to ask for services and then make arrangements on their own later, resulting in lost commissions for the agency and often higher costs for the clients.

Other opportunities for cross-selling include

- Travel insurance, discussed in Chapter 11. Every client is a candidate for some type of travel insurance.
- Transfer service from an airport to a hotel or ship.
- City and local tours.
- Tickets for theaters or museums, restaurant reservations.
- Stopovers en route to or from the destination. A poor air connection can sometimes be made into a stopover that enhances the entire itinerary.
- Shore excursions for cruise passengers—some private or personalized to meet clients' specific interests.
- Supplementary products and services, such as passport pictures, luggage, and travel books. Many travel agencies offer these items in their offices or in conjunction with suppliers.

Step 6: Overcome Obstacles

Be prepared for obstacles in the form of objections to your recommendations. When they arise, take a positive attitude and avoid becoming defensive. Listen carefully and evaluate the objections.

Sometimes objections arise from the client's ignorance, prejudice, or misunderstanding of a recommendation. In these cases, try again to explain the recommendation. At other times, objections arise because of real problems with the recommendation. In these cases, suggest alternatives.

Sometimes objections are hidden. For example, if you end a conversation by offering clients exactly what they want, and they still seem unwilling to commit, price may be the principal objection. Suggest ways in which the cost could be reduced without sacrificing too many benefits.

Often, clients feel they must consult a spouse or traveling companion before committing. Fully describe the arrangements and their benefits so the client can explain the trip positively to others; then set a date to call back.

Sometimes, after objections have been met and resolved, a customer still resists. Several kinds of resistance need to be recognized. One is guilt. Sometimes clients suddenly feel guilty about spending money on themselves. By reviewing how the suggested arrangements meet their needs, you can help them overcome any guilt. And as an antidote to price shock, focus on value by stressing benefits.

Resistance also may be a maneuver by the client. Some clients view the conversation as a kind of negotiation and look for one last concession. They need to feel they had the last word and struck the best possible deal. As a result, they might raise last-minute objections in the form of requests for impossible guarantees or unusual services. Generally, these objections are not serious; consider them a signal to move forward and offer to book.

Clients also may resist a recommendation because they feel pressured. Most people prefer to delay decisions, especially those that cost money. Some counselors think they are doing their clients a favor by advising them to go home and think it over. Given such advice, most leave. But making a decision is usually followed by a great sense of relief and expectation.

If a client raises unexpected resistance that seems to spring from a desire to postpone a decision, stress that the decision has been reached by mutual agreement. Point out how the arrangements meet the client's needs. Explain that a decision now can avoid disappointment later. In this way, you can help clients overcome the last psychological barrier to a decision.

Step 7: Close the Sale and Recap

Surveys indicate that salespeople fail to ask for the client's business in up to 90 percent of all sales situations. Perhaps they worry about appearing pushy. Yet a missed sale benefits neither buyer nor seller. To **close** a sale requires two separate decisions: when to do it and how to do it.

When to Close. Unfortunately, the right moment to close is often unclear. Table 10.2 on body language included several key *buying signals*, signs that the customer is ready to make the purchase. Signals that the client is *not* ready to buy include

- Frowning and avoiding eye contact.
- Leaning back with arms crossed in front.
- Fidgeting.
- Refusing to touch or look at marketing collateral, flipping idly through it, or reading it very closely (indicating a need for more information).

But far more sales are lost by delaying the closing than by offering to book too soon. Clients are often ready to commit before salespeople attempt to close the sale.

You might offer to book several times and learn much from the attempts. Indeed, counselors may uncover objections or questions only when they try to close the sale. It's good to closely document these interactions for your personal reference.

If a client cannot answer essential questions even after careful questions and recommendations, offer a tentative or conditional reservation (Table 10.4). Then set a date by which the client must confirm the conditional arrangements and offer to contact the client on that date. Note, however, that some promotional fares prohibit the use of conditional reservations.

Your manager has forwarded an e-mail to you that came to your agency's website. He doesn't know the client, Frank Jefferson, but Frank states that he wants to go to Cancún in three weeks and wants the trip booked immediately. What should you do?

Recognize that you do not have enough information to begin a sale. Your best bet is to see if you can contact Mr. Jefferson by phone, assuming he left a number. Failing that, reply to his e-mail and ask him to call you immediately or to e-mail you a number where he can be reached. With time so short, you'll need to make contact immediately in order to complete steps 2–5 in the sales cycle. What exactly is three weeks? In other words, when does he really want to go? How many people are going? What hotel will you help him choose? It sounds as though steps 1, 6, and 7 will be easy, but you can't take them for granted either.

How to Close. There are techniques, procedures, and even specific phrases that can be used to close a sale effectively.

- *Offer to book.* For example, you might say, "Well, what if we see if space is available and hold a conditional reservation while you decide?"
- *Give choices.* You might ask, "What do you think? Do you want to leave on the week of the 12th or the 19th?" or "Well, did you decide on the El Sol or the La Maya hotel?" Do not state the choice as "Would you like to book the cruise or not?"
- *Ask for the preferred method of payment.* "Will that be check or credit card?" A form of the alternate-choice technique, this approach should be used when you are fairly certain of the booking.
- *Compliment the client.* "I think you've made a very good decision in picking the package to Fiji." If the client has not yet made the decision, he or she will let you know. Otherwise, you may proceed with the booking.
- *Put a clock on the client,* indicating a time limit. "Get it while supplies last" and "Last day of the sale" are popular advertisements in other businesses; equivalent statements in the travel industry are often literally true. If the client does not book now, the space may not be available tomorrow, or the price might be different.
- *Check availability.* Nine times out of 10, what is available now might not be available tomorrow. Thus, this approach leads into the technique of putting a clock on the client.

Book while the client is there. If you determine availability via your computer or speak to the supplier on the phone while the client is present, your information gains credibility. If there is any change from the information in an ad or brochure, hearing it firsthand helps. For example, while on the telephone to the cruise line, you might say to the client, "The $599 lead price is currently sold out. They have two cabins left in the $649 category. Shall I put a hold on one for you for a few days to protect you?"

Recapping. TAn important—but often overlooked—step is recapping what terms you and the client have agreed upon. Although you may be repeating most of the same information, the client will be reassured that all details are arranged and that all concerns have been addressed. You should have a conversation like this:.

"Mr. Smith, let's go through this and be sure we have all our information together. Your limo will pick you up on Monday, January 28th, at 5:45 a.m. at your house and take you to Boston Logan Airport. Your American Airlines flight 3124 will depart at 8:00 a.m. Eastern Time and will arrive at DFW Airport at 11:15 a.m. Central Time. You will have a two-hour layover in the Dallas airport, and your American Airlines flight 4567 to Cancun will depart at 2:10 p.m. Central Time. You will arrive at Cancun International Airport at 3:45 p.m. Your pre-paid transfer will be waiting for you outside the airport once you go through customs. The name of the company and driver will be on your documents. You are staying at the Cancun Palms Hotel. You are checking in on Monday, January 28th and will have a beach-view room. Your checkout date is February 2nd. You will take the 8:00 a.m. hotel shuttle to the Cancun airport. Your American Airlines flight 8796 will depart at 11:02 a.m. and arrive at DFW Airport at 1:56 p.m. Central Time. You will have a layover of approximately 3½ hours. Your American Airlines

flight will depart at 5:30 p.m. and arrive in Boston Logan Airport at 8:36 p.m. You will catch a cab to return home."

End your sale on a positive note. Thank the clients for their time, assure them that the purchase (if made) is a good one, shake hands, use their names, and be prepared to follow up with a phone call, note, or e-mail if needed.

Step 8: Follow Up

Once the sale has been closed, each detail must be processed and monitored. This may be as simple as creating an invoice and itinerary or as complicated as carrying out many steps for each part of a long itinerary. In all cases, processing must be done in an exact and timely manner.

Even the most conscientious person will occasionally make a mistake. Mentally walk through the client's itinerary day by day. Check everything twice, particularly documents arriving from suppliers. Some common mistakes include

- Routing clients into one airport in a certain city and out of another without realizing it. Clients may arrive at Orly Airport in Paris with a connection departing from Charles de Gaulle Airport on the other side of the city.
- Making a car or hotel reservation for the wrong day. Clients who depart New York in the evening on November 1 will require a car rental or hotel reservation in London on November 2, the day the flight arrives.
- Assuming that clients know passports are required for overseas travel.
- Failing to mention the need for a visa or proof of citizenship.

Charles de Gaulle Airport, pictured above, is 16 miles (25 km) northeast of Paris; Orly is 8.1 miles (about 13 km) south of the city.

Complicated itineraries require a file for correspondence and documents. Even if all communications and reservations were handled via the computer, and a complete electronic file exists, most agencies require a hard-copy file to be kept on bookings. Once the trip is over, the file becomes the reference once the current online reservations are wiped out. The records of previous trips constitute the most basic data for the agency's marketing research.

TABLE 10.4 Dealing with Unanswered Qualifying Questions

Qualifying Questions	Response If Question Is Not Answered
Where?	Review needs with the client. Provide more information. Make suggestions. Set up an appointment for the future.
When?	Make transportation reservations (air, cruise, and so on) on the most likely dates, provided there is no cancellation penalty.
How long?	Make definite reservations for outbound transportation, and reserve on the most likely return date, or leave the return temporarily open if that option is allowed.
When and how many?	Make reservations for the greatest number likely to travel. It is always easier to cancel one person from a party than to get a duplicate booking for another traveler later on.
What kind or class of service?	Ask more questions. Provide more information.

Processing the sale and record keeping are just the most obvious tasks necessary after closing the sale. Successful people in all facets of business know "It isn't over 'til it's over." And in the travel industry, it isn't over even when it is over. Once the sale is made, you must work to keep it made. Also, clients may cancel or change their reservations. And once their trip is completed, follow-up is essential: Contact the client; discuss the trip; be sure the client was satisfied. Be sure your client's name and contact information go on the agency's mailing list. Ask for referrals and even pique their interest in next year's trip. Repeat and referral clients are the lifeblood of a successful agency.

In fact, giving good customer service by following up, keeping in touch and anticipating a client's needs often separates the successful counselor from the average one. The extra thought shown to a client or the prompt handling of an unexpected problem may earn the client's loyalty for years to come.

Serving the Customer

■ WHY DOESN'T THE SELLER'S JOB END WHEN THE SALE IS MADE?

Clients are longing for good service, and most are willing to pay for it. They will be loyal to salespeople who go the extra mile. The possible services that travel counselors might provide leisure travelers, for example, are limited only by their imagination; a few include
- Providing destination information from national tourism offices.
- Saving and offering articles about their destinations, from both print and online sources.
- Sending birthday, anniversary, or welcome-home cards.

It is up to the travel agency or supplier to develop a marketing strategy that defines and supports the services that salespeople are expected to provide, as we discussed in Chapter 9. Not all companies choose to emphasize customer service. Whatever the company's policies, though, customers are likely to expect certain basic benefits from a travel agency; these are our focus in this section.

Following Through

In the travel business, a sale may last several weeks or even several months. Clients often pay deposits months ahead of time to ensure space on popular trips; final payment on major trips is usually required 60 days before departure or even earlier.

Keeping in touch with the client throughout this process is a subtle but effective reminder that the agency is keeping an eye on the client's plans. In many cases, there may be information from the supplier, visa forms, or receipts to send to the client. If there has been no contact for a month or two, drop a brief note or e-mail or a brochure or newspaper clipping about the destination.

Most of these interactions can be automated through your agency's CRM, providing triggers for you to follow-up based on the client's reservations and trip requirements or sending reminders automatically.

Be sure to tell clients when documents and tickets are expected. If they are not received by that date, check with the supplier to make sure they are on their way and then call to reassure the client. If you wait for the client to call, you may lose some of the client's confidence, especially without a ready answer.

Customers must also be advised of their responsibility to obtain visas and immunizations and to be aware of restrictions that might affect their freedom of movement. Always identify who sets these requirements (a government, an airline), and tell clients how they can easily comply. Some travel agencies provide all clients with an information packet about these requirements (discussed in Chapter 2) and the places to contact with questions or problems. Exceptional agencies go further and provide travel tips and checklists of tasks to complete in preparation for a trip. The tips can include information about the weather, clothing and packing recommendations, suggested readings about the area, and foreign currency and exchange rates.

Whenever clients visit an agency, whether or not they book, they should walk out with at least three items: (1) your card, (2) collateral stamped with the agency's information or rates and notes on the agency's letterhead, and (3) a clear understanding of what is going to happen next. Are you going to call? Are you going to send information? Perhaps you and the clients agreed that they will e-mail you with a decision. Maybe you will be calling them to set up a second appointment, by which time you will compile a list of recommendations. Perhaps they are going to send you a deposit. Whatever is agreed to as the next step, follow up on it—whether or not the clients do.

Dealing with Changes

Additional services may be necessary when clients want to change or cancel aspects of their booking. Changes are part of every travel counselor's daily responsibilities. In fact, the ability to make changes quickly and efficiently is one of the basic reasons consumers—especially business travelers—use travel agencies.

Clients may choose to add arrangements, exchange one arrangement for another (such as a change in departure date or class of service) or cancel without rebooking. Before altering arrangements, make sure the changes are in the client's best interests. In particular,

- Ask the reasons for the changes.
- Restate the benefits of the original choice.
- Quote rates for the new favorite.
- Inform the client that the new choice may not be available.
- Never cancel a reservation until the alternative has been confirmed.

Changes may also be involuntary. Insurance can protect the client's investment in the trip in many cases; it is discussed in Chapter 11. A cancellation or change may be necessary because of

Listening courteously can help defuse the situation when a client complains.

- *Strikes.* Usually, alternatives that provide the same, or virtually the same, arrangements are available. Because an airline strike affects many travelers, speed is vital to secure alternative arrangements for your clients.
- *Bankruptcies by suppliers.* Travel counselors have the responsibility to choose suppliers carefully to protect the client. Whenever possible, clients should pay for travel by credit card so they will not be charged for services they do not receive.
- *Political upheavals, epidemics, and natural catastrophes like earthquakes and hurricanes.* Travel counselors should stay current on political upheavals and threatening weather forecasts. As discussed in Chapter 2, the State Department provides information about current conditions around the world.

Many agencies have specific policies and procedures to help counselors decide how to deal with these situations.

Occasionally, an emergency develops while the client is traveling. In most instances, tour operators, airlines, or U.S. foreign service officers take the lead in aiding affected passengers. U.S. embassies and consulates are charged with the responsibility, within reason, of helping citizens who get into trouble while traveling abroad. But, in some cases, it is the travel agency's duty to help. The agency may be the only contact that a cruise line, airline, or tour operator has for a client who becomes seriously ill or dies. Travel counselors may need to help relatives make arrangements to transport a sick client or a client's remains back home.

The American embassy or consular office will know local requirements and costs for such arrangements and will send an official to mediate with the host government. The Citizen's Emergency Center in Washington, D.C., can help contact U.S. officials abroad.

Handling Complaints

Travel counselors are likely to have little or no control over the elements of a trip once the client departs. Still—along with flight attendants, customer service representatives, hotel desk clerks, the cruise director's staff, and tour directors—they are part of the front line that receives the full force of customers' complaints.

Clients are likely to complain whenever they find discrepancies between what they thought they had bought and what they received. The source of the problem might lie with the supplier, the travel counselor, or even the client. Whatever the source, the counselor should listen to the complaint.

When faced with a complaint,

- Be courteous. Courtesy often defuses complaints; rudeness provokes them. Remember that clients who honestly report problems are valuable sources of information about suppliers and destinations.
- Listen carefully to the client's full explanation of what occurred. Before assigning blame, hazarding guesses, or apologizing, obtain all the facts and clarify uncertainties by asking questions about the relevant circumstances.
- Take detailed notes.
- Make a strong effort to help your client feel the complaint is being taken seriously and try to empathize with the client's disappointment.
- Restate the complaint to show it has been understood.
- Explain what action can be taken.
- Process the complaint *in writing* with the supplier concerned, copying in the client.
- Never admit responsibility for whatever went wrong without first discussing the complaint with the agency manager. Offering a small sum of money could be interpreted as an admission of responsibility.
- Follow through on the promised action.
- Inform the client of the resolution of the problem.

Even if the client is temporarily satisfied, refer any complaint through appropriate channels, preferably put it in writing to the appropriate supplier with full, detailed information. If possible, take steps to see that the problem does not recur.

CHAPTER WRAP-UP

CHAPTER HIGHLIGHTS

Seldom will a salesperson use all the techniques discussed in this chapter for one client; many can be adapted to fit the client and type of sale. In the next chapter, we discuss how to vary the selling process to suit particular types of sales. Here is a review of the objectives with which we began the chapter.

1. **Describe the agency-supplier relationship, which limits the agency's liability.** Travel suppliers sell their own goods and services through travel agencies or directly to the public. Travel agencies act as intermediaries, selling the supplier's goods and services to the public. The supplier controls the inventory and, in some cases, uses a conference system to appoint those who may sell its products. Contracts among the parties in these transactions may be written but usually are only implied. In most cases, travelers are contracting for services directly with the suppliers. The travel agency is not liable for the actions of suppliers, but it is responsible for conveying necessary information to the client.

2. **Describe the skills that provide a foundation for effective communication by salespeople.** To communicate effectively, it is important to be able to make a first impression that encourages the development of rapport and then to establish a link with the client. Successful communication also depends on the ability to ask effective questions and to listen carefully. Questioners should use close-ended, open-ended, or feedback questions as the circumstances require. Listeners should

watch the speaker's body language and recap the conversation. Finally, effective communicators must be able to present their information persuasively; it helps to avoid jargon and elicit feedback.

3. **Identify eight steps in making a successful sale.** The first three steps basically help the salesperson acquire information: (1) identify customers, (2) build trust, and (3) identify needs. The next steps are to (4) select product, (5) recommend product, and (6) overcome obstacles. During this process, the salesperson looks for opportunities for selling up and for cross-selling. Both the client's body language and his or her comments help the salesperson determine when to attempt to close the sale and recap, which is step 7. The final step, step 8, is to follow up.

4. **State five questions involved in qualifying a client and three ways to close a sale.** The basic questions in qualifying a client are When? Where? Who? How long? and What type or class of service? To close a sale, the salesperson might simply offer to book the trip or set a time limit on the decision or present a choice that assumes the client is making a purchase. Additional methods include asking for the preferred method of payment or complimenting the client in ways that assume the sale has been made.

5. **Discuss the responsibilities of a travel counselor after the sale has been made.** After a sale, travel counselors must ensure that the sale stays made and that the client is satisfied with the result. Service earns loyalty from the client. Besides processing and monitoring the sale precisely and keeping records, travel counselors might provide extra services by sending additional information about a destination or even surprise gifts. More basically, though, they should follow up on the sale, keeping in touch with clients and informing them of their own responsibilities. Counselors should also be prepared to deal with any changes or emergencies and to handle complaints.

KEY TERMS

A list of key terms introduced in this chapter follows. If you do not recall the meaning of these terms, see the Glossary.

body language
close
close-ended question
cross-selling
feedback question

open-ended question
outside sales agent
qualifying
selling up

REVIEW QUESTIONS

1. What can you do to develop rapport with a client?

2. What are the advantages gained by asking the five qualifying questions?

3. What would you do if you were not sure what to recommend to a client?

4. How could you find out how much clients want to spend on a trip?

5. What types of objections do clients make, and how should a travel counselor treat them?

6. At which steps in the sales process could you use e-mail to enhance your chances of success?

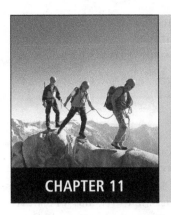

CHAPTER 11

Specialized Sales

OBJECTIVES

After completing this chapter, you should be able to

1. Describe three key variations in selling situations that travel sellers must adjust to.

2. State four principles to follow when selling a trip to a group.

3. Discuss the distinctive characteristics of business travel.

4. Describe the special challenges involved in arranging meetings and incentive travel.

5. Identify the main types and benefits of travel insurance.

6. Name three specialties prevalent in the travel industry.

All clients have different needs. Some require special meals for religious reasons; some need kennels for their pets. There are clients who are looking only for an airline ticket at a good price and others who are hoping for inspiration in choosing the trip of a lifetime.

Whoever the client is, the salesperson must adapt the sales techniques used to suit the client and the situation. Is selling travel to a 70-year-old different from selling to a 20-year-old? How is selling to a group different from selling to individuals? This chapter addresses these and similar questions, examining the special needs of different clients and situations.

Customizing Sales and Service

■ WHAT ARE THE KEY DIFFERENCES IN SELLING SITUATIONS THAT TRAVEL SELLERS SHOULD RECOGNIZE?

Many travel companies and many travel professionals specialize in selling to clients with particular needs or interests. But even specialists must deal with

OUTLINE

CUSTOMIZING SALES AND SERVICE
■ What are the key differences in selling situations that travel sellers should recognize?

SELLING TO GROUPS
■ How does selling travel to a group differ from selling travel to individuals?

SELLING BUSINESS TRAVEL
■ How does selling business travel differ from selling leisure travel?

MEETINGS AND INCENTIVE TRAVEL
■ What special skills and functions are involved in arranging meetings and incentive travel?

SELLING TO SPECIALTY MARKETS
■ What are some of the specialty markets, and what skills or approaches are helpful in marketing to potential participants?

OFFERING TRAVEL INSURANCE
■ How does offering travel insurance benefit both the seller and the buyer of travel, and what are the major types of travel insurance?

people who have varying needs and problems. To be successful, travel sellers—whether they are travel counselors or airline reservationists or sales representatives for suppliers—should be prepared to recognize some key variations in the demands of selling situations.

Variations in Purpose

Perhaps the most basic variation in travel is the one introduced in Chapter 1. Recall that travel can be classified into three types based on its purpose: *corporate,* or *business, travel* (any trip purchased by a business and made for the purposes of the organization); *vacation and leisure travel;* and *VFR travel* (travel to visit friends or relatives). For each type of travel, clients are likely to have different needs.

Leisure and Business Travelers. Consider the differences between leisure travelers and business travelers. Here is a list of some common reasons people have for leisure travel:

- To get rid of stress.
- To enrich their perspective on life.
- To bring the family closer together.
- To do what they want, when they want.
- To feel alive and energetic.

In contrast, some key reasons for business travel are

- For sales calls, purchasing, and consultation.
- To handle internal company business.
- To solve problems.
- For training, conventions, or other meetings.

Because they have such different reasons for traveling, selling to business travelers is very different from selling to leisure travelers. The majority of leisure travelers ask for advice on many issues. Business travelers often know exactly what they want; most seek advice only about airlines, hotels, and car rentals. We look at business travel in detail later in this chapter.

VFR Travel. Sometimes, VFR travel is lumped together with leisure travel, but selling VFR travel can be very different. Often, VFR travelers need only transportation. Their plans have neither the complexity of some pleasure trips nor the urgency of many business trips. Usually they are most interested in getting the best fare possible that aligns with their schedule.

When VFR travel is discretionary, it may be very sensitive to price. If an airfare sale suddenly reduces ticket prices, Aunt Minnie in Missoula may get a visit. If prices are high, Aunt Minnie may have to wait a few months.

Some VFR travel, though, is not seen as discretionary by the traveler. People often consider holiday travel obligatory, for example. Clients who put off their planning for holiday travel may have to pay premium prices in order to travel at peak times, and they may be very willing to do so. Families with school-aged children must plan their vacation around school breaks, which also can result in premium prices.

Travel counselors who book VFR travel should be prepared to deal with the special situation of unaccompanied minors traveling by air. Travel counselors must inform the custodians or parents of the procedures and legalities that must be followed at the airports.

Travel counselors should also be ready to help families come together when there is a medical emergency or death in a family. Because they typically do not

This special-interest group went trekking on Mt. Kilimanjaro.

have advance notice in these situations, travelers could end up paying full coach fares. Travel counselors can help them obtain a lower fare by checking for the *bereavement fares* that are offered by some airlines. To qualify for this fare, the traveler needs documentation of the situation that the airline can verify. Travel counselors should compare the airlines' policies and provide the family with advice about the best fares and schedules and the required documents. Some airlines offer last-minute discounted fares that many times are lower than the bereavement fares, so it is wise for the counselor to check.

Finally, travel sellers who are interested in giving good service to VFR clients might alert them to air sales to cities where they have friends and relatives whom they visit frequently. Travel counselors might also record information about clients' preferences, if any, for car rentals and hotels.

Variations in Interests

Even among leisure travelers, travel sellers must adjust their sales techniques to a tremendous range of interests. Some travelers just want to lie on a quiet beach; others want to dance 'til dawn or challenge a mountain or contemplate medieval masterpieces.

Increasingly, leisure travelers want to get something specific out of their vacations. The number of bookings made by travel agencies for *special-interest trips*—travel planned around a specific theme such as a sport, casinos, hard or soft adventure, and so on—continues to grow. Chapters 8 and 10 outlined some of the many interests that can be the focus of vacations (see Table 10.1, in Chapter 10).

Some people believe that only those who share a special interest can arrange a successful special-interest trip. Scuba divers are unlikely to book a trip with someone who does not know what a PADI certificate is; trekkers will expect advice on how to choose between Tibet and Patagonia for their next journey. Certainly, it helps to be personally involved in the special interest, or at least to learn a great deal about it. Sellers who know the basics in the field or are active participants will find it easier to empathize with clients and to establish credibility.

Variations in Special Needs

Beyond their purposes and interests, travelers differ in yet another way: demographics. They may be young or old, single or married, for example, and these characteristics often bring with them certain needs.

Single people, for example, may be particularly interested in tours, cruises, or resorts that make a special effort to offer opportunities for singles to meet other singles. Or they may be especially interested in finding accommodations without the single supplement (the higher rate often charged to those occupying a hotel room or cruise cabin by themselves) or in finding suppliers that help singles find roommates to avoid the extra charge.

Honeymooners are another example. Even in difficult economic times, honeymoon travel remains relatively stable. Newlyweds are rarely willing to forgo a honeymoon of some sort. Working on honeymoons is often very time-consuming, but couples who have had memorable wedding trips are excellent sources of repeat business and will speak glowingly of their experience to family and friends, all of whom are potential clients.

Members of some religious groups may also have special needs. They may want to attend services on a particular day or at a particular time each day. They may ask for special diets. They may not be able to travel on certain holy days. If the travel seller senses that a client is interested in any of these topics, it does no harm to ask if there are any other special observances. Clients who request particular foods may have other needs that they do not think of expressing.

There are many other travelers with special needs and products to fulfill their needs. Let's examine a few of the specialties.

Senior Citizens

Senior citizens, those 65 years of age or older, are a large and growing part of the traveling population. What do seniors look for when they are traveling? Some may be eager to return to destinations they loved in the past. Comfort, safety, and pacing are especially important to many. They might prefer rooms close to elevators, for example, and want meals that conform to special diets. Also, compared with people of other ages, a high proportion of senior citizens travel in groups, enjoying the camaraderie as well as the luxury of having someone else worry about many travel details.

But stereotyping is dangerous. People tend to underestimate the stamina and interests of senior citizens. The next senior citizen who calls may be more adventuresome than most 30-year-olds. Many are sophisticated, energetic travelers who have visited many destinations and are looking for new itineraries. And the coming generation of seniors is expected to be more active and more widely traveled than their parents and grandparents. Tour operators typically provide an activity level rating for each of their tours. While this can be useful, not all operators are consistent in how they rate their tours. It is important that both the travel sellers and travelers read the itineraries carefully.

Travel sellers should be prepared to ask seniors the same qualifying questions that they ask other clients, but they should also be ready to determine whether seniors are interested in the special services available to this age group. For example, are they interested in senior discounts? In group travel that caters to seniors? In cruise ships that offer promotional nights for seniors? In the special rooms that some hotel chains provide? For example, some hotels offer rooms for seniors that have bright lighting, large-button telephones, lever-style handles on doors and sinks, and grab bars in showers.

Family Travel

The importance of family travel as an area of expertise that brings success to travel counselors cannot be overestimated. Many travel suppliers offer services designed to have special appeal to families and to meet the needs of children. For example,

- Car rental companies have car seats (infant, toddler, and youth) available when requested in advance.
- Airlines normally preboard families with young children and on flights with meal service can serve children's meals if requested in advance. Baby strollers fit between the aisles in the cabin and can be stowed in the overhead bins, beneath the seat, or in the baggage compartment. Flight attendants can heat milk for babies.
- Some cruise lines and resorts offer special activity programs for children. The parents are then free to leave them for almost the entire day, if they wish. Most cruise lines offer babysitting services subject to the availability of crew members. Some resort hotels in Hawaii offer children ages five through 12 activities such as boogie boarding, ukelele playing, lei making, and hula dancing. Other resort groups have family camps with age-appropriate sports activities. For sellers of family travel, it is important that they research and know which cruise lines and resort brands are geared toward family travel. This can have a dramatic impact on the overall travel experience for both the children and parents.

Many suppliers provide special rates for children accompanying their parents. Cruise lines frequently accept the third and fourth occupants of a cabin at considerably reduced rates or do not charge for them at all. Some hotel chains allow children under age 18 to share a room with their parents at no charge. Airlines frequently offer discounted fares to children flying with a parent. (For more on these discounts, see Chapter 4.) For international travel, however, it is important for travel counselors to advise their clients that children traveling with only one parent or with grandparents may need a notarized letter from parent(s) authorizing the guardian to take the child out of the country. Each country has specific requirements as it relates to preventing child abduction.

Travelers with Disabilities

Nearly one-fifth of all Americans have some type of disability. By the broadest definition, *travelers with disabilities* are those who have impaired mobility and require special arrangements—such as people who are blind or deaf, confined to wheelchairs or stretchers, mentally challenged, very elderly, extremely obese, or in need of oxygen or a respirator. In the United States—thanks to the 1986 Air Carrier Access Act and the 1990 *Americans with Disabilities Act (ADA)*— people with disabilities have the right to access the same services as those without disabilities. The ADA does not cover air travel. In 2018, the *FAA Reauthorization Act* was introduced and mandates the development of the *Airline Passengers with Disabilities Bill of Rights*, a plain-language description of disabled passengers' existing legal protections. On non-U.S. airlines, IATAN (International Air Transport Association Network) regulations provide rules regarding accessibility similar to those in the United States.

The *Society for Accessible Travel and Hospitality (SATH)* estimates that about 83 percent of Americans with disabilities are potential travelers. They represent a tremendous opportunity for travel professionals who understand and respond to their needs.

Accommodations can be made for travelers with disabilities, including trips to Angkor Wat in Cambodia.

Travel Agencies. Making travel arrangements for people with disabilities may take extra time, but that time is more than compensated for by repeat and referral business from satisfied clients.

Travel sellers should be careful not to stereotype travelers with disabilities. Many persons with disabilities choose adventurous, physically demanding trips. The qualifying questions described in Chapter 10 must still be asked, but travel counselors must also be able to identify unusual requirements. They should ask questions frankly and, if possible, speak directly to the travelers—not to companions or assistants.

Travel counselors who make arrangements for travelers with disabilities should check with each supplier as far ahead as possible. If suppliers are given sufficient notice of clients' needs, these clients can go almost anywhere. The following sections briefly summarize the services and challenges that travelers with disabilities, particularly those in wheelchairs, often encounter when traveling.

Air Travel. Generally speaking, travelers with disabilities prefer as much space as possible. On planes, first-class seats are ideal. In the coach section, aisle and bulkhead seats may be best because they provide the most legroom. Sometimes airlines can leave the middle seat in a row of three empty if a special-needs passenger is occupying one of the others. Seating in emergency exit rows is limited to those with the most potential to operate the emergency exit and to help evacuate the aircraft. On most planes, travelers with disabilities find it difficult or impossible to use the small bathrooms, but, on larger wide-body aircraft, there is typically at least one bathroom designed to accommodate Narrowmatic wheelchairs.

The airlines provide many services for special-needs passengers. They might offer advance boarding, a wheelchair, storage of canes and crutches, an escort, special meals, and fully reclining seats. Service animals may travel in the passenger cabin free of charge on domestic airlines; however, some countries quarantine all arriving animals. Policies on what constitutes a service animal varies by airline. Travel sellers should be aware of the policies and procedures that surround this need.

The airlines provide some services automatically, but others must be requested, sometimes up to 48 hours in advance. Computer codes for special service requests (SSR) and for information on other services (OSI) alert the airline to the client's requirements. For clients with wheelchairs, travel sellers should ask whether the wheelchair is self-propelled or battery-operated and note special arrangements needed for battery-operated chairs. Travelers will be switched to an "aisle chair" at the airport unless their chair fits through aircraft aisles. In either case, the wheelchair is then stored.

Rail Travel. Amtrak schedules provide information about the accessibility of rail stations. Amtrak promises that
- Help is available for boarding and detraining.
- On each train at least one coach car has accessible seating and accessible restrooms.
- Trains with sleeping cars have at least one bedroom that is accessible.
- Service animals are welcome onboard at no charge.
- Meals and beverage service will be brought to the passenger's seat.

Reservations and special requests for passengers with disabilities should be relayed as early as possible. Only a limited number of accessible spaces are available on each train. To ensure an accessible space, you must make a reservation for the accessible bedroom accommodation, transfer seat, or wheelchair space (even on an unreserved train). Accommodations can be reserved for passengers with mobility impairments until 14 days prior to departure; then the accessible bedrooms are available on a first-come, first-served basis. Amtrak supplies a Special Services Request Form for noting pertinent details about services being requested, and it has discounts for passengers with disabilities.

On international railroads, accessibility and services vary widely. Travel counselors should consult the U.S. offices of the rail lines for information and should be sure that help will be available for your clients at the stations.

Car Rentals. With about 48 hours' advance notice, some major car rental companies can provide cars with hand controls for physically challenged drivers, often at no extra cost. If transfer from the terminal to the car is difficult, the car can be waiting outside the baggage claim area (if airport regulations permit), or a van with wheelchair accessibility may be provided to transfer the passenger to the rental car. Some companies specialize in renting vans designed to carry one or two wheelchair-bound travelers and up to five other passengers. Some small cars, particularly in Europe, do not have room for a wheelchair in the trunk.

Motor coaches. By law, new U.S. motor coaches must be accessible to people with disabilties, and motor coaches must store wheelchairs and help people with impaired mobility to a seat. Old coaches, however, are not required to add special equipment.

Nevertheless, local transportation systems generally have wheelchair lifts, and long-distance companies, such as Greyhound, have now added services for travelers with disabilities. For example, with 48 hours' notice, you can request a coach equipped with a wheelchair lift. Greyhound provides assistance with boarding and deboarding, with luggage, with transfers, and with the storage and retrieval of mobility devices. Greyhound also extends a 50 percent discount for personal care attendants who are traveling with physically challenged passengers, although there are restrictions.

Tours. U.S. tour operators are required to serve those with disabilities to the best of their ability. An increasing number of operators specialize in tours for travelers with disabilties and use motor coaches with lifts and enlarged baggage compartments. Tour packages of all kinds—from trips to Disney

A client calls, wanting to fly with her husband to Nassau and stay at a hotel on Paradise Island. She informs you that her husband uses a wheelchair. What will you ask her? What arrangements will you make?

Ask the same questions you would ask of any client. You may find much of what you need to know by asking about the couple's past travels. In addition, ask what kind of help her husband needs. Can she help him from the chair to his seat, or will an airline attendant be needed? What are the dimensions of the chair? Does it fold up? Ask if there are issues you have not addressed that you should know about.

Book the flight accordingly. If you are not certain of the codes needed for requesting wheelchairs, call the airline. If booking a transfer, contact the transfer company directly and describe the needed services. When booking the hotel, don't depend on a simple statement that it has an accessible room; ask for a detailed description. Does it have ledges and sills to get the chair over, or does it have ramps? How wide are the doors? What are the bathroom facilities? Call and reconfirm all details a day or two ahead. Special arrangements often must be double-checked because personnel sometimes change, people get busy, and the information might be sitting somewhere unread. Recheck everything and get confirmation of the services in writing and the names of the people you spoke to.

World to African safaris to around-the-world air tours—are available from operators that have expertise in serving travelers with disabilities. Care must be taken to ensure that the special accommodations provided are appropriate to meet the various and specific needs of each client.

Hotels. The Americans with Disabilities Act requires that new hotels must be accessible to those with disabilities and that existing hotels must do everything that is "readily achievable" to make their rooms and all public facilities accessible.

What makes a hotel or a room accessible? The entrance must be level or provided with a ramp. If no accessible rooms are available on the ground floor, elevators must be large enough to accommodate a wheelchair. In the hotel room, light switches, thermostats, air-conditioning controls, and locks must be low enough to be reached from a sitting position. The bathroom must have a tub with safety bars and be able to accommodate a wheelchair, whether the door is open or closed. The bed should be the same height as the wheelchair to permit easy transfers, and there should be a bedside telephone. For the deaf and hearing-impaired, U.S. hotels are required to provide equipment, such as text telephones and flashing lights for alarms and doorbells.

Of course, for travel abroad, conditions in each country must be checked carefully. Some small European hotels have only very small elevators with narrow entrances, many steps, and other situations that are not compliant with the ADA requirements prevalent in the United States.

Cruises. Because cruise lines are technically owned by non-American companies, they traditionally have not been covered by U.S. laws, such as the Americans with Disabilities Act. Nevertheless, courts have ruled favorably on lawsuits that aimed to force the cruise lines to comply with the act. Progress has come slowly, but most cruise lines are improving accessibility, and a growing number offer programs, facilities, and services for passengers with disabilities.

A statement that a cabin or certain public rooms are "accessible" leaves many unanswered questions. Exactly what public areas are or are not accessible? How are port calls handled? What are bathroom facilities like? What is the staff's attitude toward serving passengers with special needs?

Some cruise lines require passengers with disabilities to be accompanied by a person without disabilities.

The potential difficulties for people with disabilities on cruises are numerous. Narrow cabin doors and narrow passageways may restrict the ability to maneuver wheelchairs around the ship. Only the latest ships provide some cabins designed to accommodate the needs of wheelchair-bound passengers. At some ports where seas are rough, transporting wheelchair passengers to tenders may be impossible. Many cruise lines require that passengers with disabilities be accompanied by a person without disabilities, and many refuse to accept the very elderly or passengers with a history of illness without a doctor's certificate. Most ships will not carry animals of any kind, including service animals, and quarantine regulations apply at foreign ports.

If the difficulties can be reduced, however, cruises provide distinct advantages for travelers with disabilities. The proximity of restaurants, entertainment, planned activities, and open deck space increases their independence. For the travel seller who is able to satisfy the client's needs, a repeat customer is virtually assured because the cruise passenger and the passenger with disabilities are statistically among the most loyal clients.

Travel sellers adjust their sales techniques in light of
- ✔ The purpose for the trip.
- ✔ The client's interests.
- ✔ The client's special needs.
- ✔ The situation.

Unlike leisure travelers,
- ✔ Most business travelers seek advice only about airlines, hotels, and car rentals.
- ✔ VFR travelers often require only transportation and sometimes view their trip as obligatory.

Demographic groups that may have special needs include
- ✔ Singles.
- ✔ Members of certain religious groups.
- ✔ Senior citizens.
- ✔ Families with children.
- ✔ Travelers with disabilities.

When selling to clients with disabilities, travel counselors should be sure to
- ✔ Avoid acting on the basis of stereotypes.
- ✔ Ask the usual qualifying questions.
- ✔ Ask about other requirements.
- ✔ Be aware of their clients' rights to accessible facilities as guaranteed by federal law in the United States.
- ✔ Plan to check with each supplier and to relay reservations and special requests as early as possible.
- ✔ Plan to spend extra time and effort in handling arrangements for travelers with disabilities.

Selling to Groups

■ HOW DOES SELLING TRAVEL TO A GROUP DIFFER FROM SELLING TRAVEL TO INDIVIDUALS?

Travelers with disabilities and senior citizens are important potential customers not only as individuals but also as members of groups. Thousands of clubs and organizations—from the local gardening club to the high school French club to a support group for divorced fathers—as well as businesses are potential buyers of group travel. Selling travel to groups can be a lucrative part of your business. Just as some travel sellers focus solely on selling cruises, some focus solely on group travel.

Making the Sale

If you are selling travel to a preformed group, here are four suggested steps.
- ■ First, construct a profile of the membership. Selling travel to a group requires careful consideration of the group's makeup. Draw a profile of the average member in terms of age, economic status, background, interests, and whatever other factors may have led the person to join the group.
- ■ Second, design a trip for the average member. Use the profile to help determine the approach to take, the choices to offer for destinations, and the special needs to consider. Developing relationships with your preferred suppliers will help with the process of building the trip.
- ■ Third, establish a working relationship with the key decision maker who will act as your contact with the group, communicating the group's desires to you and relaying information back to the members. This person may be a Pied Piper—someone whom others will follow, whose opinions others will respect. Extend VIP treatment to this person. Selling a concept to one person may produce a trip for a group of 40.

- Fourth, based on the profile of the average member, prepare one option to sell. You cannot expect a group to reach agreement in an open meeting if they are given a random selection of suggestions. Before the presentation, complete the preliminary work of establishing a destination, travel dates, estimated price, and availability. You can expect to make some revisions to the plans early on in this process until the key decisionmakers and their group members can reach a consensus.

Making Travel Arrangements

Ensuring the availability of arrangements and accommodations for a group may require as much as a year's lead time. Some destinations require an even longer lead time, especially if you are planning group travel around a special event, such as the Olympics. Arrangements for groups are different from arrangements for individuals in several ways.

- Most suppliers have departments that specialize in handling group business, and reservations for group travel usually go through these specialists.
- Group bookings have special payment procedures and cancellation penalties. Generally, all arrangements for group travel must be completed at least 30 to 60 days before departure—sometimes earlier.
- Discounts, upgrades, special amenities, and incentives, such as complimentary trips or tickets, are often available for groups. For example, a hotel may offer an upgrade to a suite; an airline might offer a special discount or a free seat for each specified number of paying customers.

Anyone arranging group travel should negotiate with suppliers for these special benefits of group travel. The arranger will also need to draw up schedules for reservations, deposits and final payments from participants, payments to suppliers, mailing of rooming lists to hotels, and issuance of tickets.

Travel counselors can take care of all of this, putting the entire travel program together themselves. But this means dealing with hundreds of details. It requires experience, organization, and great energy.

An alternative is to use a tour operator. The operator then takes care of making arrangements for hotels, restaurants, guides, museums, local transportation, and so on. The travel counselor concentrates on selling the trip to the group and on handling details related to communication, documents, payments, pre-trip meetings, and instructions for group members.

When travel counselors use tour operators for group travel, they have two choices:

- Book into an existing program. A travel counselor might book a scheduled departure or request a separate departure for the group for an existing tour. If too few people sign up for the trip, it may be possible to switch members to a regular departure of the tour with that same company.
- Have a tour operator put together a custom-made trip for the group. This option is often used. The cost is usually higher, but the result may be a trip that most closely meets the group's interests and, thus, gives high value for the money.

When an existing tour is booked for the group, the agency receives the tour operator's usual or negotiated commission rates. For custom-made group travel, suppliers usually quote *net rates* (without commissions). To set the price for these trips, the travel agency must add to the net rates all the other costs involved in the trip and its planning: tips, taxes, promotional costs, complimentary trips for the group's recruiters, and any other special items. On top of this, the agency adds a markup as its profit.

How much should the markup be? The answer depends on many factors: complexity of planning, competition, and the expertise of travel counselors, to name a few. One rule of thumb is that when an agency does most of the planning for a fairly complex trip, the markup should be at least 20 percent on the net. When a tour operator does most of the planning, custom-making the trip for a group, the agency's markup might be as low as 10 to 15 percent.

✔ CHECK-UP

When selling to a group,
✔ Prepare a profile of the average member.
✔ Establish a close relationship with a key decision maker.
✔ Prepare one option to sell.

In arranging travel for a group, travel counselors might
✔ Put the entire trip together themselves.
✔ Book an existing program.
✔ Have a tour operator put together a tailor-made trip.

Selling Business Travel

■ HOW DOES SELLING BUSINESS TRAVEL DIFFER FROM SELLING LEISURE TRAVEL?

According to the U.S. Travel Association, in 2018, domestic travelers spent over $282 billion on business travel, with $126 billion of that on meetings and conventions. For many travel businesses, this is a very appealing market. Compared with leisure travel, business travel tends to be far steadier in several ways.

■ Business travel (also referred to as corporate travel) varies less than leisure travel during the year.
■ Business travel is less sensitive to changes in the economy. When economic growth slows, many companies tighten their belts and reduce travel, but not as much as leisure travelers do. In fact, some businesses increase travel in difficult times.
■ Business travel is also less sensitive to changes in price. If travel costs rise, most businesses try to pass the cost on by raising their own prices.

Furthermore, corporate travel can generate other business. For example, client companies may turn to their corporate travel agencies to arrange meetings and incentive travel, and business travelers may turn to the travel counselors who arrange their business travel for their VFR and leisure travel.

Businesses handle their travel in varying ways. Some have their own corporate travel departments. Travel managers in these departments work for the corporation, not a travel agency. Some companies go to a general-purpose travel agency or to a **commercial agency,** which is a travel agency that specializes in business travel. And in some companies, a travel agency is hired to establish an onsite office within the company to handle travel arrangements. Success in this attractive market requires the ability to appeal both to the ultimate customer—the company paying for the travel—and to those traveling.

Amy Markell works for a travel agency whose clients include large corporations. She and another counselor work as a team and are assigned one very large and three very small companies. Most of her day is spent with a headset on; it frees her hands to use the computer while talking with clients on the telephone.

"I don't think I was even very aware of business travel when I was studying to be a travel agent. The people I deal with generally know where they want to go, when, and often how. Sometimes it's cut-and-dried. Other times, they have never been to a city and want you to suggest hotels. Regardless, I always try to add something special. How much a taxi will cost from the airport, if there is a current show or exhibit going on, how to get hockey tickets—things like that, especially if I know something about what my client is interested in.

"And I do know a lot about my clients. Their computer profile contains not only all their credit card information, addresses, phone numbers, airline seat and hotel room preferences, likes and dislikes, and special needs, but also anything else that I can pick up about them. So, if I know they particularly liked a Broadway musical one time, I might be able to suggest something in Los Angeles another time. Even if they go to the same city week after week, you try to do something to personalize the transaction, even if it's just a comment on the itinerary like, 'Wow! Podunk again! You must be excited!' You have to use good judgment and know your client. It's the little-mint-on-the-pillow idea:

People don't book the hotel to get that little mint, but it symbolizes the care and personal attention that the hotel is going to give them in a lot of other ways.

"About half the time, we don't even talk to the person traveling. We're dealing with the assistant or colleague who makes the reservations. Then, not only do we want to add some personal touch for the traveler, but we also want to keep a good relationship with the person making the reservation. We always want to make him or her look good, especially if the person being booked is the boss.

"OK, there's the downside, too: travelers who can't make up their mind or who change their mind. They cancel; they change. It gets a little frustrating. But maybe their work keeps changing. My agency doesn't just look at how much dollar volume I book but also at how many transactions I perform. If I book and cancel a ticket and have to issue a refund, that's two transactions and maybe no money earned (we have to give all the commissions back). If I did my job well, that's not my fault. It's up to the agency to decide if this company's travel is worthwhile. The agency might have to renegotiate the contract or raise the company's service fees.

"We're a fairly large agency and have just joined up with one that operates coast to coast. There's room for advancement. I haven't tried yet, but now I'm ready. We have international specialists, and I think that's what I would like to move to first."

Needs of Business Travelers

In many organizations, travel connotes prestige, and many business travelers enjoy the experience. Often, though, business travelers travel because they must. Their travel is sometimes accompanied by stress, is usually filled with hard work, and often leaves no time to enjoy the place visited. Business travelers take pride in the fact that they are traveling for important reasons, and they focus on the business they must accomplish. They are likely to buy from travel professionals who help them keep this focus.

Among the key needs of the business traveler are

- *Prompt service.* In business travel, "prompt" is likely to mean confirming reservations while the client is on the phone, calling back within an hour, or finalizing arrangements before the day is over.
- *Absolutely correct arrangements.* The correct car rental company must be booked, the preferred seating on the plane reserved, the frequent-flyer number recorded, and so on. Excuses for inaccuracies are not acceptable.
- *The ability to change reservations at a moment's notice.* In the business world, plans change frequently.
- *An environment suitable for concentration on business.* For example, business-class sections on airplanes and airport club lounges offer the

quiet, comfort, and service that allow business people to work during and between flights. Many hotels offer time-saving breakfast buffets and rooms away from noisy guests.

- *Special services to enable them to conduct their business.* Examples include access to WiFi, as well as help obtaining translations or preparing presentations.
- *Physical and psychological pampering.* Business travelers may want exercise facilities or swimming pools to relieve stress. They may look for luxuries to keep their morale high.

The Company's Travel Needs

Even the best service to individual business travelers may not be enough to retain a company's travel business; the company's needs must also be served. Of course, those needs vary, just as do those of individuals. But the cost and efficiency of travel are likely to rank high on a company's list of concerns. Keys to meeting these concerns are negotiations with travel vendors, record keeping and analyses of travel expenses, and development and enforcement of travel policies.

Negotiations with vendors assume importance in part because many special rates and amenities are available for corporate travelers. Many suppliers are willing to offer favorable rates to win the business of these frequent travelers. A specific company may negotiate with a supplier (with or without the assistance of a travel agency) for a discount available to all of that company's travelers when they use that supplier's services; this is known as a *company-negotiated rate.* In addition, travel agencies negotiate for discounts known as *contract rates;* these are rates available to all business travelers who book the supplier's service through that travel agency.

Record keeping is another tool for controlling travel costs. With the help of computers, it is easy to keep records of travel expenses that categorize those expenses in myriad ways—by traveler, destination, supplier, activity, time period, and so on. Thus, the company can see just how its money is being spent and spot inefficiencies.

Analysis of travel costs can help a company design effective travel policies. For example, one company might decide that only employees at a certain level are allowed to fly first class or that frequent-flyer awards are to be turned over to the company, rather than used by the employee.

Travel Agencies and Business Travel

Travel agencies have long provided companies with services, such as offering a toll-free line available 24 hours a day for assistance. But, today, commercial agencies must also offer more-sophisticated services; they are, in effect, in the business of travel management. They are selling an array of services to help companies manage their business travel—from reservations and ticketing to vendor negotiations, expense management, and travel policy development.

Sometimes the desires of the company and the traveler clash. For example, the company might require employees to take the flight with the lowest fare if it gets them to the destination before 9:00 p.m. If the lowest fare requires a connecting flight, the traveler might ask instead for a nonstop flight. The travel agency must follow the company's policy unless it receives approval to meet the employee's request. It is the company, not the traveler,

Suppose you are a commercial travel counselor and one account that you handle is Rollaway Blinds. Travelers at the company hint that they could find lower fares on the Internet than you get them— and Rollaway Blinds wouldn't have to pay the fees to your agency. What can you do to win their confidence and satisfy their complaint?

These travelers may be unaware of the other services that your agency is giving the company, such as expense reports, assistance with setting travel policy, and savings from negotiated rates. They may not know that many Internet fares cannot be changed without penalty. And they probably are not the ones making the decision about where Rollaway Blinds books its travel. But because they are complaining (and most such travelers wouldn't worry about what the company is paying), keep your ears open. Maybe they have a hidden complaint that they aren't sharing. Also, be sure to notify the appropriate person at your agency of the comments that you are hearing; he or she might want to meet with the decision makers at Rollaway. Travel agencies must be prepared to prove their value to the companies and travelers they serve.

that has hired and is paying the agency. Still, if the company's travelers become dissatisfied with the agency, word is likely to reach the company's decision makers, who may soon choose another agency. Ultimately, the individual traveler's needs must be met, too.

Usually a contract spells out the arrangement between the travel agency and the company. The contract specifies the services that the agency will provide and how quickly those services will be delivered. It usually reflects or incorporates all or part of the company's travel policy, such as when flights with the lowest airfares must be selected. The contract also states what management fees or service charges are to be paid to the agency.

Handling Corporate Accounts. Selling a travel agency's services to a particular company might require only a call from the agency's owner, manager, or corporate sales manager asking for the company's business. Or the sale might require many sales calls over the course of months or even years, with skillful use of all the selling techniques discussed in the previous chapter.

Once a travel agency has a company's business, the corporate counselor must give great service in order to keep the account sold. The advantage of working with business travelers is that they know where and when they want to travel. Often, they prefer a particular airline, car rental company, or hotel chain. Furthermore, they may repeat the same trip several times. Corporate counselors, therefore, face fewer decisions than leisure counselors, and they seldom need to apply the selling techniques discussed in Chapter 10 in full force.

But speed, accuracy, flexibility, skill at phone communications, and professionalism are especially important when handling corporate accounts. Usually, corporate travel counselors must do a high volume of business for the agency to make a profit. They must also be prepared to make frequent and speedy changes in travel arrangements. And the corporate counselor might handle all the arrangements on the phone, without ever meeting the traveler. The business traveler may never visit the agency. In fact, even on the phone, the commercial counselor often will be dealing with an assistant, instead of the traveler. Thus, corporate travel counselors must be very good at telephone communications.

Using Technology. The corporate counselor who can provide a high quantity and quality of service is likely to be one who is comfortable with the latest technology. To serve business travelers efficiently, for example, information about their preferences is kept in a profile maintained by a database system, like the one shown in Figure 3.1. The client profile might include

- Office, home, and billing addresses and phone numbers.
- Billing preferences and credit card numbers.
- Seating preferences.
- Information on membership in frequent-flyer and other frequent-traveler programs.
- Preferred hotels, types of rooms, and special requests.
- Preferred car rental company and type of car.
- Special airline meal requests.

Much of the information about a client remains the same for every trip. Once it has been entered into the system, one or two keystrokes can move many lines of information into a client's reservation. Each GDS has its own proprietary name for these profiles, such as Star from Sabre.

Commercial agencies also have software that can create reports about almost any aspect of travel that a company wants to track: who traveled; how many times they traveled; their average hotel rate, airfare, and car rental cost; how many times they used discount fares; and so on. Companies have come to expect this kind of analysis.

In addition, self-service booking systems on the Internet are fast becoming an essential feature offered by corporate travel agencies. These systems allow business travelers to make their own reservations on a site that is customized to reflect the company's travel policy. For instance, preferred airlines may appear more prominently, and only those hotels with which the company has contracts might be presented. These booking systems are set up and managed by travel agencies, and travel counselors are available on the phone to handle questions, problems, and special arrangements. Even small agencies can service corporate accounts that make bookings online through GDS products or online services, such as Travelocity, Expedia, and Orbitz; the agency then provides fulfillment and added services for a fee.

✔ CHECK-UP

For the travel counselor, serving business travelers is unlike selling to leisure travelers in that
✔ Their travel is not discretionary.
✔ The traveler's employer as well as the traveler must be satisfied.
✔ The counselor might deal only with an assistant, not with the traveler.
✔ Details regarding the services to be rendered have usually been agreed to, often in a written contract.
✔ The business traveler often has distinctive needs.

Among the services often provided by commercial agencies are
✔ Reservations and ticketing.
✔ Document delivery.
✔ A 24-hour toll-free line for assistance.
✔ Negotiations or assistance in negotiations with travel vendors.
✔ A computerized record of various employees' travel expenses.

Meetings and Incentive Travel

■ WHAT SPECIAL SKILLS AND FUNCTIONS ARE INVOLVED IN ARRANGING MEETINGS AND INCENTIVE TRAVEL?

Despite teleconferencing, videoconferencing, and the Internet, businesspeople still feel the need to meet face-to-face. In addition, scientific, educational, religious, and charitable associations, political and special-interest groups all hold *meetings*, meaning association- or corporate-sponsored events with an overnight stay.

The industry associated with meetings is huge, and it is growing. It arranges conventions, trade shows, exhibitions, and other meetings, as well as incentive travel programs. The *Meeting Professionals International (MPI)* organization—which has more than 17,000 members and is represented in over 22 countries—promotes the industry, along with other associations, such as the *Events Industry Council,* the *Center for Exhibition Industry Research (CEIR),* and the *Society for Incentive Travel Excellence (SITE).* These groups provide information, educational programs, and forums for identifying and solving problems.

Meetings and Conventions

Table 11.1 defines the major types of meetings. The suppliers for meetings include companies that provide the physical facilities as well as those that provide the many services used at meetings. The buyers include affinity groups and associations, promotional and marketing companies that are putting on conventions and trade shows, as well as businesses. They may be holding a meeting to train employees or consumers, to introduce or sell products, just to exchange ideas, or for any of a host of other reasons.

Although small meetings can be set up by any agency with an eye for detail, large or frequent meetings are usually handled by specialists called meeting planners. ***Meeting planners*** act as intermediaries, conveying to suppliers the wishes and requirements of the sponsor of the meeting. These experts may work for meeting planning companies, hotels, exposition centers, or the corporations holding the meetings or conventions. Sometimes they work for divisions of large travel agencies that manage business travel; others are independent contractors. Planners involved in large conventions often work as much as five years in advance, selecting the convention city, booking convention centers and a spread of the city's hotel facilities.

Meeting planning involves much more than the usual travel arrangements. The field is both specialized and broad. The job may involve signing up a former president for a speech, choosing the right wines for attendees, and traveling to analyze locations. Depending on the size and duration of the meeting, as well as the buyer's wishes, the functions of the meeting planner might include the following:

- Clarifying the goals and requirements of the meeting.
- Selecting the site and facilities and negotiating for their use.
- Budgeting for the event.
- Arranging transportation.

TABLE 11.1 Major Types of Meetings

Type	Description
Clinic	A group session that offers counseling or instruction on a topic
Conference	A meeting designed to exchange views or to settle differences
Convention	A large formal meeting of members, representatives, or delegates of an organization, profession, or industry
Exhibition or exposition	The public showing of goods and services as part of a large meeting
Lecture	The exposition of a subject by a speaker before an audience
Panel	A discussion by a group of persons in front of an audience
Symposium	A formal meeting intended for the discussion of a particular issue
Trade fair or trade show	The public showing of goods or services in displays and booths, often open only to members of a profession or industry
Workshop	A meeting or series of meetings for educational purposes in which a small number of participants interact and exchange information

- Handling reservations and housing.
- Working with a hotel's group sales department to coordinate the meeting.
- Planning guidebooks, documentation, and registration procedures.
- Planning and managing the setup of function rooms and exhibits.
- Managing food and beverage service.
- Selecting speakers and booking entertainment.
- Scheduling publicity.
- Developing programs for guests and families.

Incentive Travel

Thousands of companies, large and small, use travel as an incentive. They might offer a trip as a reward to employees who have contributed to successful marketing efforts or to dealers and distributors who have achieved a certain level of sales. The trip itself may be strictly for pleasure, or it may combine business and pleasure.

Incentive programs sometimes offer trips to individuals, but most incentive programs offer group trips. In most programs, spouses or other guests are allowed to accompany the qualifying employee. Resorts, spas, and cruises are popular choices. To succeed as an incentive, the trip must be a very special experience, with every detail carefully planned.

Arranging activities at the destination requires creativity and close collaboration with suppliers. Theme dinners, parties, special sporting events, and sightseeing might be included. Usually the host company expects some attractions and activities to highlight the company's own goals and activities and to foster corporate loyalty. For example, suppose top salespeople for a company in the fashion industry are on an incentive trip to Ecuador or Bali. An exhibition featuring handmade clothing by local artisans might be created exclusively for them in a country market town when few other tourists are present.

Arranging this type of travel takes expertise and experience. The trip itself is part of a broader motivational program, and its objectives must be clear, realistic, and quantifiable. (Is the main goal, for example, to boost morale and loyalty by encouraging cooperation? Or to boost performance by encouraging competition?) Those arranging incentive travel must shift their focus away from how to sell travel and concentrate on how to use travel as a motivational tool to meet the goals of a specific group. (How high should the standard be, for example, for receiving a reward? Should it be set so that most of those eligible will win or so that only a few will win? How valuable must the reward be in order to work as an effective motivator?) It's important to understand that the trip participants cannot buy their way into the trip. The only way they can qualify to go is to meet the employer's requirements—usually by meeting a predetermined sales quota during a specific period.

Agencies that specialize in this field are called *incentive houses*.

Adventure Travel Specialist

One of the most popular specialties in today's travel world is *adventure travel*, also sometimes called *active travel*. As more and more travelers look for outdoor activities and have a love of nature, these companies have developed and offer a wide range of choices.

For the very active, companies offer *hard adventure*, which may involve mountain climbing, hiking 30 miles a day, and sleeping under the stars. For those who have slowed down a little in life, there is *soft adventure*, perhaps some daily exercise followed by a bit of village browsing, a glass of wine by the fireplace, dinner and overnight in a cozy inn. And *cultural adventure* is for those who still like to learn, get off the beaten track, and meet interesting people but whose energy and activity level is limited. Strenuous physical participation is not required.

Counselors do not necessarily need to be adventure travelers themselves to sell this specialty but should know which companies work with travel agencies and which don't and be familiar with the various companies and their particular products as well. For example, some companies may offer multi-sport vacations while others have itineraries that focus on one type of sport, such as bicycling trips.

It's also important to know the terminology and safety rules and regulations involved. For example, if selling a dive trip, a counselor must understand that, for health reasons, a client cannot fly within 24 hours of the last dive. And the counselor should know the difference between a shore-based dive vacation and a live-aboard one and be able to screen clients for proper dive certification requirements.

Travel counselors need enough knowledge about diving to know that a client cannot fly within 24 hours of the last dive.

Adventure trips should be sold only with well-known, reputable companies, and such trips are not necessarily inexpensive. Involvement in the adventure travel sector of the industry is a specialty worth considering. A good resource to learn more about adventure travel is the *Adventure Travel Trade Association (ATTA)*.

Cruise-Only Specialist

Many employees and independent contractors in the travel industry specialize in selling cruises. With the huge number of ships at sea, just learning all you need to learn to sell cruise travel well is a challenge unto itself without learning to sell tours, rail travel, air travel, and all the other sectors. In fact, most successful cruise counselors do not represent all cruise lines; they carefully select a handful of the companies they would like to promote and concentrate on their offerings.

Often the companies and ships they sell will depend on their clientele and their expectations—whether it's a young couple off on their first weekend party cruise all the way to a wealthy, retired couple on an around-the-world winter cruise aboard an upscale cruise line. Of course, many of these successful cruise salespeople take cruises themselves, often as leader of their own small groups on board. They try to learn the personality of certain ships and become familiar with the itineraries and practices of the cruise lines they represent. They also develop pleasant working relationships with the cruise line office personnel to be able to service their clientele's special needs and requests.

Some are employees of a full-service retail travel agency, others may be owners of a cruise-only franchise, and still others may simply be independent contractors, perhaps working from their home. Many tend to be mature, retired or semi-retired travel veterans who have built a following of clientele through the years (see previous Close-up: On the Job with Lance Hendry).

Other Popular Specialties

Several other specialties within the travel industry may be considered. One is termed **ethnic agencies**—travel agencies or tour companies that specialize in travel for persons of a particular ethnic background or language. In some large U.S. cities, such agencies abound for the Spanish-speaking or Chinese-speaking market. Obviously, employees must be bilingual and know the travel products of interest to this market. Many so-called "ethnic travelers" simply buy airfare to and from their native country at key holidays or to visit family. Often, the agency has negotiated special airfares with certain airlines serving these destinations.

Another specialty company is the **inbound travel** company, often referred to as a receptive travel company or destination management company (DMC). These are companies, or subdivisions of other companies, that specialize in individual travelers, or most likely groups, arriving from other parts of the country or from abroad. A second language, a knowledge of one's own city and its attractions, and a sensitivity to the needs and customs of international travelers are a plus for employment in this segment of the industry. Many of these companies are affiliated with their city's convention and visitors' bureau.

There are also specialists in romantic travel, often billing themselves as **honeymoon specialists** but, in reality, handling much more than honeymoons. They usually market themselves with wedding shows and magazines and focus their knowledge on resorts and cruises that are particularly appropriate for the honeymoon couple. Many also offer renew-your-vows trips, anniversary trips, or destination weddings. They must have expertise on the legalities, rules and regulations governing marriages abroad.

Some cities may also have agencies or key employees who are adept at counseling their **LGBT** (lesbian, gay, bisexual, and transgender) clientele. They must know which destinations are LGBT-friendly and which are not. Agents working in this field are often heavily involved in community events in their own hometown, such as Gay Pride activities.

Other popular specialties include niche markets for solo travelers, women travelers, religious tours, and culinary experiences, just to name a few.

Offering Travel Insurance

■ HOW DOES OFFERING TRAVEL INSURANCE BENEFIT BOTH THE SELLER AND THE BUYER OF TRAVEL, AND WHAT ARE THE MAJOR TYPES OF TRAVEL INSURANCE?

For a payment, or *premium,* travelers can obtain insurance (also known as travel protection) against many of the risks associated with traveling. Some travel counselors feel uncomfortable offering travel insurance because discussing the topic tends to emphasize everything that might go wrong on a trip. But there are three reasons for overcoming this hesitancy. First, clients have a right to know that they can protect their investment in a trip, and they may hold a travel agency liable for any losses incurred if insurance is not offered. Second, in many instances, travel insurance protects the travel counselor from liability. Third, insurance sales can improve an agency's profitability.

In Chapter 5, we discussed car rental insurance. Here we describe other types of travel insurance, when they are needed, and how they are sold.

Types of Insurance

Specialized types of travel insurance can be purchased separately, in combination, or as part of a travel package. Besides car rental insurance, there are four basic types: (1) flight, (2) travel accident and health, (3) baggage and personal possessions, and (4) trip cancellation or interruption.

Flight Insurance. Accidents that occur in connection with air travel are covered by *flight insurance.* Coverage begins when the client leaves home and includes the ride to the airport. The coverage is in effect until the completion of the confirmed flight itinerary. Coverage is extended if scheduling changes by the carrier create delays beyond the client's control.

The benefits paid by flight insurance range up to $1 million for accidental loss of sight, limb, or life that occurs while the insured is on airport premises or is riding as a passenger on a flight or on other forms of transportation used by an airline to transport passengers, such as transfer buses. In the case of death, benefits are paid to the *beneficiary,* a person chosen by the insured at the time of purchase.

Travelers may receive flight insurance automatically as a benefit when tickets are charged on certain credit cards. Otherwise, clients may buy flight insurance from travel agencies, from the airline, from tour operators, from cruise companies (on air/sea programs), or from insurance companies that sell it from booths and machines at airports. The premiums for flight insurance many times is quite inexpensive. The coverage, though, covers only their flight and not their entire travel investment.

Travel Accident and Health Insurance. Whereas flight insurance is bought frequently but collected on rarely, the benefits from **travel accident and health insurance** are often needed. It protects the insured in case of accidents (whether travel-related or not) and sickness at all times while away from home. In some cases, travelers' existing health insurance already protects them in these situations. Neither Medicare nor most private health insurance policies, however, cover the cost of medical care abroad.

Most travel accident and health policies do not cover the cost of medical evacuation, and they do not give benefits in cases of illness or death caused by acts of war or by "dangerous activities," which include such sports as mountain climbing, skiing, and hang-gliding. (People who plan activities like these may want to purchase additional special insurance. Also, travelers can buy additional policies that cover emergency medical transportation, which includes evacuation to the nearest medical facility or home.) Many policies also exclude preexisting medical conditions unless purchased within a specified time frame from when the trip deposit was first paid. Travel insurance companies have different policies and premium costs, based on the coverage type and whether preexisting conditions are covered or not.

Baggage and Personal Possessions Insurance. For protection in case their baggage or personal possessions are lost, stolen, or damaged while traveling, clients can buy **baggage and personal possessions insurance.** It picks up where the responsibility of an airline, motor coach company, or other carrier ends. Normally, only items owned by clients and taken for personal use are covered. Some policies also cover items borrowed just for the trip. Benefits are payable at actual cash value, up to specified limits. The value on clothes is usually based on the value of used clothing, not new replacement value. One premium covers all family members.

There are very specific exceptions and limitations to the coverage provided by this insurance, and clients should read the policies carefully. Most insurance companies limit the amount they will pay for loss of jewelry, furs, currency, or cameras. Clients should be made aware of the procedures required for reporting a loss in order to ensure payment of their claims.

Many homeowner's insurance policies cover loss of or damage to personal possessions even away from home. Unlike most homeowner's policies, however, baggage insurance rarely has a deductible and often covers mysterious disappearances. Some companies offer coverage for emergency purchases that must be made when baggage is delayed or lost.

Trip Cancellation or Interruption Insurance. Many clients already have some form of health, accident, and personal possessions insurance, but travel agencies are among the few sources of *trip cancellation or interruption insurance.* It reimburses clients for (1) nonrefundable prepayments if they must cancel a trip for a reason covered by the policy and (2) any nonrefundable portion of their trip and the cost of transportation home should they have to discontinue a trip. It will also pay for transportation back to a group if clients remain behind temporarily because of an accident or illness covered by the policy.

The reasons for cancellation that qualify for coverage vary with the policy. Most policies provide reimbursement in cases of sudden illness, accident, or death in the family. Some policies also cover cancellations when clients are summoned for jury duty, served with a subpoena, or forced to vacate their home for some reason. Some offer coverage for weather and other natural disasters; this coverage reimburses the client if the natural disaster prevented the airline or other supplier from providing service. A change in plans for personal or financial reasons ordinarily is not covered. Canceling a trip for *fear* of a hurricane, for example, is not covered.

Some insurance companies allow trip insurance to be bought up until the day before departure. Others require that the policy be purchased when the trip is booked or before cancellation penalties take effect.

Trip cancellation or interruption protection should be offered to all clients. The amount that clients should purchase depends on the greatest possible loss that can be anticipated.

In offering trip cancellation, be sure to clarify if the coverage is an actual refund of the client's monies paid or if it is just an offer to grant the traveler the same trip at a later date (usually within a year). Cruise lines often invoke this policy.

Coverage for Bankruptcies and Defaults. The possibility that a travel supplier might declare bankruptcy or become insolvent represents yet another risk. Customers might receive compensation by filing a claim in bankruptcy court—but the refund may be small and slow in coming. For fuller protection, some travel insurance policies offer coverage against defaults. As discussed in earlier chapters, however, protection also comes from

- The consumer protection plan of the United States Tour Operators Association (USTOA). The USTOA $1 Million Travelers Assistance Program is solely for use in reimbursing consumers for tour payments or deposits lost in the event of a) a USTOA Active member bankruptcy; b) a USTOA Active Member insolvency; c) a USTOA Active Member cessation of business; d) failure of a USTOA Active member to refund consumer deposits or payments within 120 days following its cancellation of a tour(s) or vacation packages(s) or its material failure to complete performance of a tour(s) or vacation package(s).
- Payment by credit card. Usually, if customers can provide documentation, credit card companies ensure that they do not pay for services not received.

The Role of the Travel Counselor

A travel counselor may offer travel insurance (also known as travel protection) to their clients. Should a client have a specific question about the policy or coverage details beyond the information provided in the insurance quote, the travel counselor should direct the client to the insurance company to ask further questions. While travel insurance can be quite profitable for an agency, there are many nuances to insurance policies about which the experts at the insurance companies are better equipped to answer, reducing potential risk and liability for the travel counselor.

Travel counselors offer insurance from two types of sources. First, insurance companies appoint travel agencies to offer their policies. The commission from the insurance companies to the travel agency usually runs between 20 and 35 percent. The agency's management usually selects the insurance company the agency will use and all counselors use that one company.

Second, tour companies and cruise lines offer insurance to those booking their tours and cruises, and travel counselors can offer this insurance when they sell the tours or cruises. But offering insurance from these sources has two drawbacks. First, clients are not protected if the tour company or cruise line offering the insurance goes out of business. Second, the commission rate for the insurance sale is the same as for the rest of the package, which is likely to be only 10 percent. However, compared with insurance from insurance companies, insurance from tour or cruise companies may be less expensive for the clients, and processing these insurance sales requires less of the counselor's time. To address this last issue, some insurance companies now allow travel agencies to issue insurance policies online. Many of these relatively inexpensive insurance offers from the tour or cruise company itself are not always true third-party insurance but merely a waiver and/or credit for future travel.

Although it is dangerous to generalize, some form of travel insurance is likely to be very desirable for

- Any tour, cruise, airfare, or other item with high cancellation penalties.
- All charter arrangements.
- All escorted tours when baggage may be left out overnight for early-morning pickup.
- People with conditions or responsibilities that might hinder their departure at the last minute.

Giving a client a brochure or fact sheet that describes travel insurance may be sufficient to constitute an offer of insurance for legal purposes. Of course, referring to insurance or recommending it during the sales presentation, whether in person or by telephone or e-mail, is more effective and more clearly an offer in a legal sense. If insurance is offered and refused, that fact should be noted in the client's file, and the client should be asked to initial a spot on the final invoice indicating that the offer was refused. This can help protect you and your agency.

Whenever insurance seems advisable, travel counselors should

- Advise clients to check their existing health and homeowner's policies and their credit card agreements to see what coverage they already have. (Clients may, for example, want to insure their baggage only for the amount of the deductible on their homeowner's policy.)
- Check all suppliers' cancellation penalties and refund policies.
- Present all the options as clearly as possible and allow clients to determine what is best.
- Be sure the client is aware of what is and what is not covered by the insurance.

CHAPTER HIGHLIGHTS

To succeed in selling, travel professionals must respond to the needs of particular individuals and the demands of specific situations. This chapter outlined some of the important variations in these needs and situations. Here is a review of the objectives with which we began the chapter.

1. **Describe three key variations in selling situations that travel sellers must adjust to.** Travel sellers must adjust to differences in the purpose of trips, differences in the interests of travelers, and differences in the special needs of travelers. For example, travelers with disabilities may have special requirements, such as rental cars with room for a wheelchair, bathrooms large enough for wheelchairs, hotels with accessible entrances, or accommodations for a service animal. Families may need babysitting services or special activities for children. Members of some religious groups follow special diets and restrict their activities on certain days.

2. **State four principles to follow when selling a trip to a group.** Learn all you can about the makeup of the group. Target the presentation to the average member of the group. Establish a strong relationship with the key decision maker in the group. Select a specific trip to promote.

3. **Discuss the distinctive characteristics of business travel.** Two clients must be satisfied: the company and the traveler. For the company, commercial agencies offer many services that help the company manage travel and reduce costs. Individual business travelers are likely to be especially interested in receiving prompt service with accurate arrangements, being able to change their travel arrangements quickly, and having an environment suitable for working during the trip. They are also likely to be interested in having access to services that enable them to conduct business and to relieve stress during the trip.

4. **Describe the special challenges involved in arranging meetings and incentive travel.** Meetings and incentive programs involve a host of details. Meeting planners act as intermediaries between suppliers and the host of the meeting. Their functions depend on the size and duration of the meeting and the wishes of the buyer, but they might involve just about anything from clarifying the goals of the meeting to selecting wines or speakers. Those involved in arranging incentive travel face the additional challenge of learning to think of a trip as part of a motivational program.

5. **Discuss some of the other specialties within the travel industry that have become popular, such as adventure travel, cruise-only agencies, ethnic agencies, inbound travel, romantic/honeymoon specialists, and LGBT specialty companies.** The market has become splintered into many additional specialties, including adventure travel, one of the largest, offering hard adventure, soft adventure, and cultural adventure trips. Another niche is cruise-only agencies, which concentrate on selling the cruise experience only. Some agencies have particular expertise for specific ethnic groups, particularly the Latin-American market and the Chinese market. The reverse face of outbound travel is inbound travel, sometimes called receptive travel, specializing in arrangements for incoming visitors. Honeymoon experts also are a popular niche as are companies that cater to the LGBT market.

6. **Identify the main types and benefits of travel insurance.** Key types of travel insurance are flight insurance, travel accident and health insurance, baggage and personal possessions insurance, and trip cancellation or interruption insurance.

Travel insurance protects the client's investment in the trip, protects the travel counselor from many forms of liability and earns the travel agency a sales commission. Failure to offer insurance could render the agent liable should the client be harmed in some way that insurance would have covered.

KEY TERMS

A list of key terms introduced in this chapter follows. If you do not recall the meaning of these terms, see the Glossary.

Airline Passengers with Disabilities Bill
    of Rights
Americans with Disabilities Act (ADA)
baggage and personal possessions
    insurance
commercial agency
ethnic agencies
FAA Reauthorization Act
flight insurance
honeymoon specialist
inbound travel

incentive house
LGBT travel specialty
meeting
meeting planner
Meeting Professionals International (MPI)
Society for Accessible Travel and
    Hospitality (SATH)
travel accident and health insurance
travelers with disabilities
trip cancellation or interruption insurance

REVIEW QUESTIONS

1. How do the needs of the business traveler differ from those of other travelers?

2. Name two things to remember when dealing with the following travelers: (a) travelers with disabilities, (b) seniors, (c) families with children.

3. What forms of transportation appear to be most adaptable to the needs of travelers with disabilities?

4. What would you emphasize about a travel agency in order to inspire confidence in its ability to handle group arrangements?

5. You have booked an escorted tour for clients who want to buy health and cancellation insurance for the trip. You can add the insurance to the reservation with a simple click of the mouse. Should you take this step?

6. Name several specialties mentioned in this chapter and specify one or two that appeal to you and why.

Part 4:
The Travel Workplace

Chapter 12
Communications

Chapter 13
Money Matters

Chapter 14
Home-based Agents

Chapter 15
Finding Employment

Chapter 16
Building a Career

Communications

OBJECTIVES

After completing this chapter, you should be able to
1. Outline the advantages of the major methods of communication in the travel industry.
2. Describe at least four guidelines for selling travel on the telephone.
3. List five situations in which a travel counselor should communicate by letter.
4. Review at least five guidelines each for effective letter writing and use of e-mail.
5. Understand how digital communications are impacting agents' interactions with sales prospects and clients.
6. Describe four methods of interoffice communication.

Like highways to truckers or stocks to Wall Street, communication is key to the travel industry. Clients' needs and dreams; the details of schedules, itineraries, restrictions, and rates; the characteristics and attractions of destinations—these and other facts and ideas must be passed back and forth among innumerable people in the travel industry. Success depends on effective communication.

Chapter 10 (Making a Sale) included tips on how to communicate, but that discussion focused primarily on face-to-face communication in selling situations. Is communication different when you are not face-to-face? Are different skills needed when you are communicating with a colleague rather than a client? This chapter addresses those questions by examining the many types of communication that occur from a distance—through phone conversations, e-mail, and letters—as well as interoffice communications.

OUTLINE

METHODS OF COMMUNICATION
■ What different methods of communication do travel professionals use, and why?

COMMUNICATING BY TELEPHONE
■ How does communicating and selling on the phone differ from face-to-face communication?

COMMUNICATING IN WRITING
■ When is it best to communicate in writing?
■ What are the keys to writing effective letters and e-mails?

INTEROFFICE COMMUNICATIONS
■ What are the key methods of communication within travel offices?

Methods of Communication

■ WHAT DIFFERENT METHODS OF COMMUNICATION DO TRAVEL PROFESSIONALS USE, AND WHY?

When people communicate face-to-face, much of the message is unspoken; in fact, some claim that words carry only 7 percent of the communication. The tone, volume, speed, and inflection of the voice—all influence how the words are interpreted. *Body language*—facial expressions, posture, and gestures—is often even more important.

When communication is not face-to-face, many or all of these nonverbal cues are lost. On the telephone, the listener cannot see the smile or the frown on the speaker's face; all of the cues usually offered by body language are lost. In e-mails, both body language and voice cues that are available in person and on the telephone are missing. The words themselves must do all the work of communicating. As a result, developing rapport may be more difficult than in face-to-face meetings, and misunderstandings can easily crop up in these other forms of communication. But these communication methods are obviously essential.

How do you select which method of communication to use? Begin by knowing the best way to communicate with specific people. Do they use e-mail? Do they dislike talking on the phone? Do they have trouble understanding your written communications? Whenever possible, use the method with which they tell you they feel most comfortable. Don't assume everyone is as savvy about new electronic methods of communication as you are. Many seniors do not use computers at all or use them only on a limited basis.

When dealing with clients, travel counselors are likely to use several methods of communication—perhaps a face-to-face meeting, phone contact, and e-mail contact. In addition, consumers increasingly expect to be able to communicate digitally with travel companies through services like Facebook Messenger and Twitter. Each method has advantages in particular situations. Whenever give-and-take is needed or one party wants to gauge the other's reactions to suggestions, a phone call is probably best. When accuracy, detail, and permanence are needed, which usually is the case in conducting travel business, communicate in writing. Letters give a personal yet official touch to communications. When a letter would be too slow but something in writing must be sent or the person cannot be reached on the phone, an e-mail or other digital communication provides an alternative.

Despite the speed of e-mail, delivery by the U.S. postal service or a private company is sometimes the better option. In particular, when confidential material is a concern, when the material is bulky, or when the sender wishes material to be tracked and signed on delivery, overnight delivery by the U.S. Postal Service's express mail or by a company such as FedEx is likely to be the best delivery method. They both offer guaranteed overnight delivery of items of nearly any size, track the material and provide notification of delivery. If mailing passports, always send them by a secure method that can be tracked.

✔ CHECK-UP

Compared with face-to-face communication,
✔ Visual cues from body language are missing in phone conversations.
✔ Visual cues plus auditory cues from the tone of voice are missing in written communications.

Written communications offer the advantages of
✔ Accuracy, detail, permanence, and proof of exactly what was communicated.
✔ Giving senders the flexibility of making the communication at any time.
✔ Giving recipients the flexibility of reviewing the communication carefully and responding at their convenience.

Communicating by Telephone

■ HOW DOES COMMUNICATING AND SELLING ON THE PHONE
  DIFFER FROM FACE-TO-FACE COMMUNICATION?

The telephone has been so much a part of everyday life for so long that it may seem odd to talk about how to use it, but, for travel professionals, it is a tool that is worth learning to use effectively. Before looking at some specific situations, we consider general guidelines for communicating clearly and persuasively on the telephone.

Telephone Tips

Communicating on the telephone is different from communicating face-to-face. Telephones tend to decrease the volume of the voice, make it drag, and raise its pitch. To compensate,

- Speak a little more loudly than usual.
- Speak very clearly and do not slur words; enunciate.
- When speaking, be sure not to have anything in your mouth.
- Be sure to minimize any background noise.
- Lower the pitch of your voice if it is normally high.

  The absence of in-person interaction and body language presents even more of a challenge to effective communication on the telephone than changes in the voice. You must make your message clear and interesting without the help of eye contact, nods, and other gestures. You need to read between the lines to understand the other person's reaction without cues from his or her body language. The following steps should help:

- Smile. When you smile, the tone and pitch of your voice change, and the caller can hear it. (Try saying "Hello" while keeping a straight or dour face and then say "Hello" while smiling, and you will hear the difference.)
- Make a special effort to concentrate. Take notes and avoid distractions. Do not do anything else, including eating, drinking, smoking, or chewing gum.
- Let the other person know you are listening by at least saying something like "OK," "Uh-huh," or "I see." Remember that he or she cannot see that you are paying attention.
- If you are doing most of the talking, pause every minute or so or ask a question to be sure the other person has a chance to talk.
- Listen for the other person's tone of voice. It will often tell you when the person is interested or has objections.
- Plan ahead when you make outgoing calls. Know the purpose of the call, the questions you need to ask, and the objections you might encounter.
- Have pen and pad ready to deal with incoming calls. Keep frequently used references nearby.

  To avoid wasting time on telephone tag, try these guidelines:

- Call busy people early in the morning, midweek, and midmonth.
- Ask when the best time would be to return the call and record it for future reference.
- Leave detailed messages so others can help relay your information.
- When leaving a message, be sure your callback number and name are spoken clearly.
- Be available when you tell others you will be.

■ Remember to take into account any differences in time zones.

Also, do not use a speakerphone unless it is necessary to include others in the conversation and you have asked the caller's permission.

Using Voice Mail

Often the first contact clients have with a travel business is by telephone, and that first call can create a lasting impression. Today, that first impression is likely to come through *voice mail*, an automated phone-answering system that handles incoming calls. Voice mail irritates some people who do not like talking to machines. But voice mail saves time and reduces errors, offering convenience and efficiency for both callers and businesses. Callers never reach an unanswered phone; they are always able to leave detailed messages.

Here are some tips for using voice mail.

■ The greeting should be short and professional. Everyone is sorry they missed everyone else's call; you don't need to state the obvious. If you are making a voice-mail greeting for a personal phone, you might include information about when you can be reached.
■ The menu of options should not be overly long.
■ Answer your phone yourself when possible.
■ Check voice-mail messages frequently and return all messages.
■ When leaving a voice-mail message, state the reason for your call as briefly as possible, but convey the facts necessary for the other person to be ready to answer you or to act on any instructions you give them. Speak slowly and distinctly. When you leave your phone number, speak even more slowly so the person can write the number without replaying the message multiple times.
■ If you are a home-based counselor, your taped response should sound professional and not have the sounds of children or pets in the background.

Handling Incoming Calls

At some time or other, everyone is likely to serve in effect as a receptionist, fielding calls and transferring them to the person the caller is seeking. Here are some basic rules of telephone courtesy when answering a phone.

■ Answer the phone by the third ring. Most people hang up after the fourth or fifth ring. Answering promptly reduces office noise and tension, eliminates distractions, and pleases the caller.
■ Use a standard greeting such as "Good morning" or "Thank you for calling." Then identify the company and give your name (and the department, if applicable).
■ Ask the caller, "How may I help you?" or "How may I direct your call?"
■ Ask the caller's name and use it in the conversation if possible.
■ If taking a message, ask the nature of the call and help the caller yourself if possible. The message should include the caller's name, telephone number, and the day and time the call was received.
■ If you must put the caller on hold, explain why and ask permission ("That line is busy. May I place you on hold?"). Wait for the caller's response before hitting the hold button. Try to get back to the caller within 30 to 45 seconds. If the hold will be lengthy, estimate how long the caller will have to wait and ask whether he or she wants to continue to hold or would rather leave a message. Thank the caller for holding.
■ If you must transfer a call, tell the caller you are transferring and say why.
■ When the call is complete, thank the caller and let him or her be the first to disconnect.

Selling by Telephone

Even on the phone, sellers should follow the eight steps in the sales cycle discussed in Chapter 10. Many of those selling travel by phone are sales agents for airlines, hotels, car rental companies, tour companies, and cruise lines. They may not give clients the amount of counseling and time that travel counselors typically do, but they do follow the sales cycle.

Reservationists need to establish rapport with a smile in their voice, seek out information from the client, make recommendations, handle objections and close the sale—and they usually need to do so quickly. Even though others in the company may handle follow-up communications with the buyer, reservationists often are judged by the number of sales made.

In much of the travel industry, those handling phone reservations will be dealing with people they do not know or hardly know. Those working for very large suppliers seldom talk to the same client twice. In contrast, travel counselors try to use the telephone to begin a lasting relationship. They aim to receive a large percentage of their phone calls from repeat clients—people whose needs and preferences they know and who they know will buy.

Clients who phone travel agencies range from *shoppers*—people who merely want information and are not ready to discuss their plans in detail— to *buyers*—those who are already prepared to book. Experience in asking qualifying questions helps counselors distinguish the buyers from the shoppers. Most experienced counselors will not spend time with callers unwilling to give their names, phone numbers, or details about their possible trip. Spending hours with shoppers can be as counterproductive as losing a sure sale from a buyer. But keep in mind that today's buyers were yesterday's shoppers. Many skilled counselors excel at converting shoppers into buyers.

Selling by phone brings some special challenges. Remember that you may have to give extra feedback to clients or ask for more feedback from them to compensate for the absence of body language cues. Pay special attention to the other person's tone of voice; it may tell you if the person is ready to buy or is too busy or tired to discuss the trip. Because you cannot use brochures, pictures, maps, or other visual aids, stress benefits that clients can visualize and paint verbal pictures. Double-check and then check again to make sure the picture got across.

Some callers can be difficult to understand because they lack fluency in English, have a heavy accent, mumble, or speak too rapidly. Don't pretend to understand anything that you don't get. Ask them to start over and to speak slowly.

Selling by phone brings special challenges.

Note that selling via phone can have advantages as well as drawbacks, especially when you do not have all the answers to questions or are not certain what recommendations to make. It is much easier to tell clients you will call them back than it is to ask them to wait in your office or to return the next day. Plus, they won't be able to see the puzzled look on your face.

Videoconferencing or *teleconferencing* puts the visual element back into the communication process: You can see people and their reactions as well as hear their tone of voice. Using videoconferencing is increasingly commonplace with businesses. Services, such as Webex, FreeConferenceCall.com, and GoToMeeting, offer free trials and low-cost plans, allowing people to work together anytime, anywhere. These services work on any computer or compatible mobile phones. Skype also is a good choice when you need to communicate with people.

When handling incoming calls,
✔ Answer the phone by the third ring and greet the caller.
✔ Take accurate and complete messages.
✔ Be as considerate as possible if you must put the caller on hold.

Those selling by telephone should
✔ Follow the same sales cycle used in face-to-face selling.
✔ Take special care to qualify clients.
✔ Pay special attention to the client's tone of voice.
✔ Remember to compensate for the absence of cues from body language, lack of visual aids, and voice distortion on the phone.

Communicating in Writing

- WHEN IS IT BEST TO COMMUNICATE IN WRITING?

- WHAT ARE THE KEYS TO WRITING EFFECTIVE LETTERS AND E-MAILS?

Unlike a phone call, written communications can be sent at any time without disturbing the recipient, and the recipient can take the time to give the message a studied and accurate response whenever convenient. The message can be saved and referred to later. But compared with face-to-face communications, written ones lack not only visual cues to meaning but also auditory cues and the nuances of back-and-forth interaction. Getting one's idea across clearly takes great care. That is why writing well is a skill, sometimes even an art.

There are times when only writing will do.

Business Letters

A letter is the best way to communicate whenever accuracy and some formality are necessary. For instance, a tour operator might phone or e-mail to request a certain number of rooms be reserved for a group; the reply might also come by phone or e-mail. But the reservation will be confirmed by letter or contract. A business letter is generally best to confirm contracts, to introduce a company or personnel, to make or answer a complaint, to ask for payment, and to thank people for their business or services.

For travel counselors, for example, using a letter is usually best in order to
- Request or confirm changes or additions to standard arrangements from suppliers, such as a request to have king-size beds or to join a tour on its second day.
- Explain or confirm complicated or detailed arrangements to the client.
- Advise the client of important information, including deadlines for future payments, visa requirements, and so on.
- Make a record of agreements and details as protection against a client's misunderstanding or future liability.
- Seek refunds on behalf of a client.
- Thank the client for a reservation.

- Promote sales.
- Welcome the client home from a trip.

Sometimes, for people you deal with regularly, e-mails can be used instead of business letters for these purposes. Experience will tell you when that is the case. Figures 12.1 and 12.2 show examples of letters.

Whatever its purpose, the fundamental rule of business correspondence is to communicate information as briefly and clearly as possible. Organization is key. In addition, through its appearance as well as its content, a letter should help convey an image of professionalism. Attention to spelling, grammar, and neatness enhances that image and boosts the credibility of the statements in the letter.

In order to meet these goals, try to follow these guidelines.

- Limit letters to one page whenever possible.
- Try to avoid sentences with more than 17 words.
- Use short paragraphs.
- Use active verbs; for example, "We recommend," not "It is recommended."

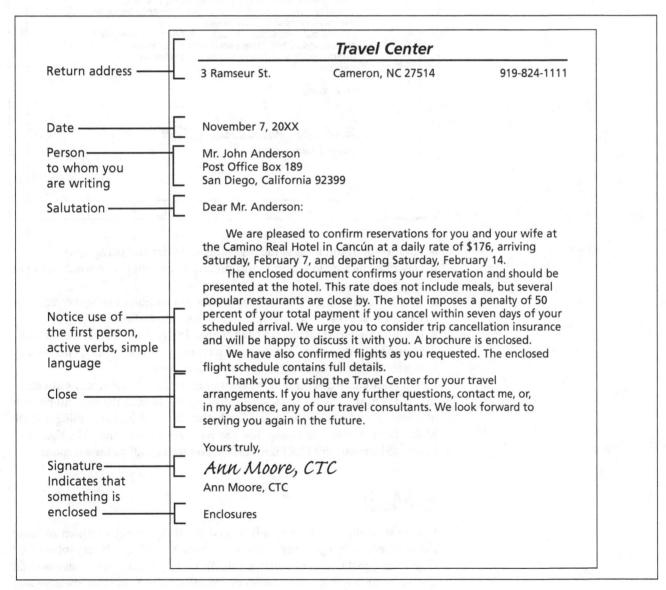

FIGURE 12.1 Sample Letter to a Client

FIGURE 12.2

Sample Letter to Suppliers

Travel Center

3 Ramseur St.   Cameron, NC 27514   919-824-1111

August 10, 20XX

Ms. Judy Daugherty
Accounting Department
Funway Tours
6259 Griffiths Boulevard
Minneapolis, Minnesota 55469

Dear Ms. Daugherty:

Our clients, Mr. and Mrs. William Murray, were booked on your Acapulco Plus one-week tour arriving July 18. Because of overbooking, they could not be given their prepaid accommodations in the Hotel Contessa until July 20. They spent two nights in the Santa Maria Hotel on the understanding that they would receive a refund equal to the difference between the room rates at the two hotels.

By our calculation Mr. and Mrs. Murray are entitled to a refund of $48. Please send your check to my attention. I am enclosing copies of all relevant documents.

Yours truly,

Roberta Fairbairn, CTA

Roberta Fairbairn, CTA

- Put the important ideas at the beginning of letters and paragraphs.
- Describe rules, requirements, and procedures in your own words. Do not merely quote a source.
- Avoid jargon such as "Unfortunately, your reservation came up no rec."
- Use the first person ("I" or "we") rather than "this office."
- Use simple, straightforward language. Instead of "Please remit your remuneration," write "Please send payment." Rather than "This agency regrets this inadvertent error," write "We are sorry."

In addition, when sending marketing letters, catch the reader's attention immediately and ask for a response. Most people look at the top and bottom of a letter for a few seconds to decide whether they will bother reading it at all. Make the first sentence strong, use the recipient's name and title, sign your name, add a postscript (P.S.) if necessary, and set a deadline for a response.

E-Mail

Strictly speaking, *e-mail* is simply a method of delivering a written message electronically. It brings many of the advantages of sending a letter—plus speed close to or equal to that of a phone call. An e-mail message is noninvasive and almost instantaneous, and it allows recipients time to review the message and respond at their convenience. It is also less intrusive than a phone call.

E-mails can be received instantaneously or take a few minutes to a few hours to be received. ***Instant messaging*** is a form of e-mail where the sender and the receiver see each other's messages instantly. You respond immediately as in a conversation, and you can immediately clarify or modify what you say. Instant messaging is used for both personal communications as well as in business, typically for interoffice communication. Sending text messages between cell phones is another vehicle for communicating brief messages instantaneously.

Guidelines for E-Mail. Find out whether e-mail is a person's preferred means of communication and the frequency at which he or she accesses an e-mail account. If not daily, you may wish to call for important decisions.

Even if a face-to-face meeting or a phone call is the preferred option in a situation, it may be desirable to send an e-mail late at night or early in the morning. The e-mail can always request that the client phone you.

If you decide to send e-mail to a stranger or someone with whom you are doing business, follow these guidelines.

- Use meaningful, brief subject lines. Many business e-mails are unopened because the subject line has no message, an inadequate message, or may appear to be spam or a virus threat.
- Be concise and simple. People may receive dozens of e-mails (or more) a day.
- Don't neglect spelling and grammar just because e-mail is quick and easy. E-mail to clients is a form of business correspondence, and it shapes clients' impressions of your competence and reliability. Before pushing the "Send" button, proofread carefully and use autocorrect tools.
- Use words, not capitals, to emphasize your ideas. Capital letters are interpreted as shouting at the recipient.
- When writing international e-mails, consider the culture of the recipient. Being overly friendly or informal can be interpreted as a lack of respect or insincerity. Err on the side of caution. Use formal titles and keep a formal tone until you are invited by the recipient to use a less formal title or his or her first name. Keep in mind that the recipient's first language may not be English. Avoid regional idioms, symbols, acronyms, and jargon.
- Learn how to use attachments and links. Lengthy information may be clearer in an attached file than in an e-mail message, which has less formatting. However, many e-mail users will not open unsolicited attachments because they may contain viruses. A link provides quick access to additional information while keeping the e-mail message short and the file size small.
- Send unsolicited information only if you have some basis for thinking the person will appreciate receiving it.
- Always include your contact information (company name and website address, along with and your name, title, phone numbers, and address). This is called your e-mail signature block. (See Figure 12.3.)
- Carefully read e-mail messages before sending them to be sure they are clear and cannot be misinterpreted. Like other forms of written communication, e-mail is not accompanied by your smiling face or pleasant voice.
- Don't be offended if clients state tersely what they want. Assume a smile on their faces.
- Answer all e-mails within 24 hours, at most. The faster you can answer, the better. If you don't have the answer the person is looking for, e-mail immediately to say when you will have it.

Legal and Security Issues. Remember that e-mails leave a permanent record. Clients will likely hold you accountable for what you promise to do in writing. Furthermore, recipients of your e-mail can print, copy, and forward it. Your e-mail may be seen and read by others who are not a part of the original e-mail thread.

Also, your e-mail correspondence can be monitored by your employer. Laws vary regarding ownership of e-mail, but typically your employer owns all e-mail sent and received through the company's computers.

Confidential information should not be sent via e-mail unless security features are set up on your computer system. It is crucial that you know whether the e-mails you are sending are *encrypted* (scrambled into a secret code so that they cannot be read by anyone other than the intended recipient) over a secure connection. When in doubt, do not send confidential information, such as credit card numbers, via e-mail.

Using Auto-Responders. *Auto-responders* reply to incoming messages automatically, without the need for human intervention. They range from basic to "smart" programs with advanced capabilities. An auto-responder can be set to respond to all your e-mails while you are out of the office, telling the sender whom to contact in your absence and when you will return.

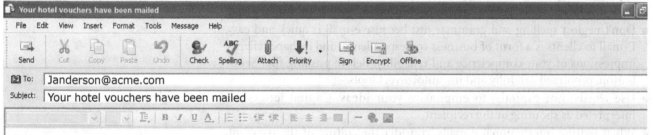

Dear Mr. Anderson,

We are pleased to confirm your hotel reservations for you and your wife for your trip to Cancun arriving February 7 and returning February 14th. I express mailed your hotel vouchers along with a brochure of the Camino Real hotel via U.S. mail today. Your package will be delivered to your home tomorrow.

If you would like to view complete details about the Camino Real Hotel in Cancun, simply click on the following link www.camino-real-cancun.com. This website provides detailed information regarding the many amenities that this resort has to offer, room features, and restaurant services.

Mr. Anderson, you and your wife will need to show your valid U.S. passports when checking in for your flight and complete a tourist card to enter Mexico. I have enclosed two tourist card forms in the package I sent, so that you both can fill them out in advance.

Thank you for using the Travel Center for your arrangements. If you have any further questions, contact me, or, in my absence, any of our travel consultants. We look forward to serving you again in the future.

Best regards,

Ann Moore, CTC
Ann Moore, CTC
Travel Counselor, Travel Center
Website: www.travelcenter.com
e-mail: ann.moore@travelcenter.com
Phone: 919-824-1111

FIGURE 12.3 Sample Business E-Mail

Notice that this sample e-mail contains a descriptive subject line, a link, and a signature.

Building Business Relationships. With the right clients, e-mail gives travel counselors an ideal way to keep in touch during the weeks or months before a long trip and for follow-up after a trip. They should follow up and keep the connection, even with prospects who did not buy from them. Remember, though, that *spam*—unsolicited e-mail—is unethical and, in some cases, can violate laws and cause the sender to be fined. Only send business e-mails to individuals who wish to receive them.

Businesses should give clients the choice and the opportunity to opt in and opt out of e-mailing lists. They should ask clients and potential clients what type of e-mails they would like to receive. Would they like to receive a monthly newsletter or notification of special promotions and sales? Do they want to receive information regarding their special interests, such as news and special pricing for skiing, sports events, festivals, and so on?

E-mail services, like Constant Contact and Mailchimp, and marketing automation tools, like HubSpot, can manage e-mail lists for agencies and independent agents.

Like other technology, e-mail used properly provides tools that allow you to improve communication and your efficiency. It can help you keep in close communication with clients, provide personalized service, strengthen business relationships and build customer loyalty.

Digital Communications

New tools are reshaping communications. Like the travel industry itself, communication tools are constantly evolving. The increasing acceptance of *chatbots*, Facebook Messenger, and other social media platforms for engagement between customers and travel vendors is impacting communications during the planning of a trip, during a journey, and after a client has returned home.

According to Conversocial's "State of Digital Care in 2018," 81 percent of consumers said "their expectations for digital customer service are higher today than they were a year ago." Some 57 percent of respondents to the survey said they would stop doing business with a brand because of a poor digital customer service experience.

In a separate report from SimpliFlying, a U.K.-based airline marketing consulting firm, 43 percent of airlines said their 2018 social media strategies were focused on improving customer service. Meanwhile, 44 percent of airlines were shifting financial resources from traditional call center operations to social media.

Mastering the skills to use digital communications tools effectively and understanding the unique dynamics they present are important for the success of a travel business.

Planning and booking travel. As previously mentioned, e-mail is an extremely popular tool for travelers to use during the planning and booking stages of a trip. In 2018, e-mail and phone dominated the communications methods for home-based travel agents, used in bookings by about 90 percent of the respondents to Phocuswright's 2018 U.S. Travel Agency Distribution Landscape report. In a leisure retail storefront, phone is slightly more popular than both e-mail and walk-in, face-to-face conversations, with all three methods used by about 90 percent of agents. Phocuswright said e-mail is even more popular for corporate travelers.

But approximately one-third of home-based advisors told Phocuswright their customers use tools—like text messaging, WhatsApp, and similar platforms—to book their travel.

A heavy reliance on digital communications presents many challenges in trying to interpret what two or more parties are trying to say. But there are additional issues digital communications present.

For example, credit card companies and regulators have security compliance standards for the sharing of sensitive, confidential information via electronic means, like e-mail. *The Payment Card Industry Data Security Standard (PCI DSS)* requirements allow for the use of e-mail to transmit credit card information, but only if data in those e-mails is protected (encrypted). However, services like WhatsApp offer end-to-end encrypted messaging and are growing increasingly popular for businesses for the transmission of credit card data. To read the requirements and for more information on the standard and how to maintain a secure environment for sensitive information, go to https://www.pcisecuritystandards.org/.

Customer service responsiveness. Another area where travel companies are relying heavily on digital communication is servicing clients while on their journey. Consumers, having already installed apps like Twitter and Facebook onto their phones, have ready access to the public social media handles of their favorite travel companies while they are traveling, and they are using them.

For example, in fall 2017, when a volcano erupted on the island of Bali, forcing an airport shutdown, many of the thousands of stranded travelers reached out to their carriers via Twitter. Staffing up their social media customer service reps, some carriers used the medium to communicate public updates about flight schedules, while also using Twitter's direct message feature to help rebook individual travelers.

In fact, when Conversocial looked at major air carrier responsiveness through Twitter—examining data over a period in which there were no major events (e.g. delays and cancellations)—they found the average response time to client inquiries was 20 minutes, and, 92 percent of the time, carriers responded in under an hour.

Another tool that consumers are using while traveling is Facebook's messenger app. When someone opens a Facebook business page, the messenger tool automatically opens, perhaps with an out-of-office message or a question inquiring what the user is looking for.

Facebook and third-party providers are incorporating artificial intelligence into the messenger feature so a consumer can have a conversation with the tool, which, over time, learns how to provide relevant and accurate answers to the inquiries and direct the inquiry to the right person for follow-up. More and more business websites are installing these *chatbots*—technology used to simulate conversation, or chatting, between people online, often enabled by artificial intelligence. Chatbots can increase a travel company's ability to serve more of its clients more efficiently—especially when a company is small and growing, like an independent travel agency.

The tide has turned for travel companies. Consumers are increasingly expecting all their travel vendors to be monitoring their social media handles and smartphone apps 24/7, whether they are a large airline, an independent boutique hotel, or a home-based travel agent.

Managing customer complaints. Finally, travel suppliers need to be conscious of the fact that, when things go wrong, travelers also have ready access to platforms to air their grievances and potentially damage a company's reputation. More and more, travelers are using their own social media handles, as well as the Facebook business pages of travel industry vendors, to call out suppliers who they feel failed to deliver on their service promise.

A series of 2017 viral videos about various air carrier service issues dominated media coverage for months. During the Bali volcano eruption, consumers expressed their dismay openly with carriers who were not communicating regularly about airport and flight schedule changes.

Many of these incidents became major issues because the carriers tried to publicly deny any culpability as the event unfolded. Others took too long to contact the aggrieved parties privately to mitigate their public attacks.

Some basic steps for travel companies to take to quickly resolve situations and protect their reputation include:

- Accepting the complainant's feelings and sense of dissatisfaction publicly; don't publicly dispute their verbalized experience.
- Confirming and providing facts that can be discussed publicly (e.g. a flight was or was not delayed two hours due to a thunderstorm; a hotel did walk customers on a specific date because it was oversold).
- Apologizing publicly for a complainant's dissatisfaction (e.g. "We're sorry you have experienced an inconvenience during your trip.")
- Directing the resolution phase of the conversation to an offline/less public communication channel (e.g. direct telephone call, Twitter's direct messaging tool).
- Monitoring the platform for any ongoing discussions about the incident, either from the original complainant or from other travelers who may have been similarly impacted.
- Ensuring that all communications deal only with the facts (i.e. keep emotions out of the conversation) and that only authorized, trained employees conduct these communications; these two actions are critical because everything is in writing, which can be shared publicly by the complainant or used in a court of law.

While digital communications tools are a mainstay in the travel industry today, travel companies and all employees engaged in client communications need to learn the basic skills of how to deal with the public. The growth in use of these platforms and tools still under development will continuously challenge travel industry employees to learn and master new skills.

Regardless of which written communication method you choose, it should be sufficiently formal to appear to be professional, even if it has a friendly touch. Communication methods, such as texting, are best left to very casual situations.

Occasionally, handwritten notes lend a gracious touch to what otherwise might be cold correspondence. They are appropriate to thank someone for hosting you or referring a client to you, for example.

All written communication, in whatever format, should exhibit proper spelling and grammar. Two excellent reference books on writing should be on your bookshelf: *The Elements of Style* by William Strunk Jr. and B.B. White (MacMillan Publishing Co., Inc.) and *The Associated Press Stylebook*, edited by Norm Goldstein.

Two essential elements of an effective business letter are
✔ Organization
✔ Clear and concise writing

E-mail has the advantages of
✔ Being almost instantaneous.
✔ Being noninvasive.
✔ Allowing recipients to review the message and respond at their convenience.

Digital communications are increasingly being used to
✔ Meet travelers' higher customer service expectations
✔ Transmit sensitive, confidential information
✔ Resolve client complaints

Interoffice Communications

■ WHAT ARE THE KEY METHODS OF COMMUNICATION WITHIN TRAVEL OFFICES?

Although most travel employees use e-mail for interoffice communications, GDSs permit users to place messages, reminders, or instructions in storage (on *queue*) for coworkers or others on the system. The queue system is still the official way that rates on complicated itineraries are transmitted, schedule changes are announced, and other changes are communicated between airlines and travel agencies. A permanent record of who accepted the message and what action was taken resides in the PNR (passenger name record; see Chapter 4).

Most businesses in all sectors of the travel industry schedule regular staff meetings. These meetings enable employees and managers to discuss office procedures and propose changes. Upcoming promotions, recent advertisements, and the manager's plans can be discussed. Meetings may also offer opportunities to boost morale or plan responses during crises. Travel agency staff meetings provide an opportunity for counselors who have recently returned from trips to brief their colleagues on destinations.

Manuals provide another method of interoffice communication. In every office, there are certain tasks and problems that everyone should be handling in the same way, as well as certain questions that come up over and over again. Describing official policies and procedures in a manual helps ensure consistent service to customers and fairness to employees. It also eases the task of training new employees. In addition, having a manual provides legal advantages by proving that certain policies are part of standard operating procedures.

Manuals should review

■ Policies and procedures relating to customer service.
■ Personnel policies regarding dismissal, performance appraisals, liability, and outside employment.
■ Pay issues relating to bonuses, holidays, lunch and break times, overtime, and comp pay.
■ Vacation time and benefits, including fam trips in the case of travel agencies.
■ Health care, including insurance, pension plans, dental and eye care, and sick days.

Many manuals also describe the company's history, mission statement, and code of ethics.

CHAPTER HIGHLIGHTS

This chapter has outlined some basic guidelines for clear communication, the cornerstone of a successful travel business. Here is a review of the objectives with which we began the chapter.

1. **Outline the advantages of the major methods of communication in the travel industry.** Travel professionals are likely to communicate face-to-face, over the phone, by letter, and by e-mail. Which method is best depends on both the situation and the preferences of the people involved. Many nonverbal cues are lost when communication is not face-to-face. Unlike written communications, a phone call allows people to gauge each other's reactions. But written communications offer accuracy, detail, and permanence. Phone, e-mail, instant messaging, and fax have the advantage of speed. Letters give a personal, yet official, touch to communications.

2. **Describe at least four guidelines for selling travel on the telephone.** Follow the steps in selling used in face-to-face interactions but be prepared to compensate for the lack of visual cues. Smile through the phone, give feedback and paint word pictures. Listen very carefully, take notes and review details frequently. Be prepared also for voice distortion. Speak slowly and clearly, and vary your pitch. Remember that both you and the other person may be more easily distracted on the phone than in person; concentrate.

3. **List five situations in which a travel counselor may want to communicate by letter.** A letter to the supplier is a good way to request special services and to seek refunds. A letter to the client may be the best way to state agreements, explain trip details and payment schedules, and say "thank you" for the reservation.

4. **Review at least five guidelines each for effective letter writing and for effective use of e-mail.** The organization of a letter is key to its effectiveness. Place important ideas at the beginning of each paragraph and letter. Keep sentences and paragraphs short and simple. Use short, clear statements and avoid jargon. Use your own words, not quotations of rules and procedures. Limit the letter to one page, if possible. (These principles also apply to e-mail.)

   For effective use of e-mail, find out whether the people you communicate with use e-mail and whether they check for messages regularly. Be concise and simple. Do not let the ease and apparent informality of e-mail lead you to neglect good writing techniques. For international e-mails, consider the recipient's culture. Learn how to use attachments and links. Check e-mail messages before sending them. Answer e-mails promptly. If you do not know the recipient's e-mail system, use plain text format. Become knowledgeable about security on your e-mail system. Do not spam people. Expect to use digital communications and to provide digital customer service with your clients.

5. **Describe four methods of interoffice communication.** GDSs permit people to place messages, reminders, or instructions on queue for coworkers or others on the system. E-memos can circulate quickly in an office and are often the best way to transmit information. Meetings not only allow the staff to discuss office procedures, propose changes and announce news but also offer an opportunity to boost morale and plan responses during crises. Manuals emphasize more general and long-term issues; they help ensure consistent service to clients and fairness to employees.

KEY TERMS

A list of key terms introduced in this chapter follows. If you do not recall the meaning of these terms, see the Glossary.

chatbox
instant messaging
Payment Card Industry Data Security Standard (PCI DSS)
videoconferencing
voice mail

REVIEW QUESTIONS

1. What do you think is the ideal way to answer a phone in an office?

2. The text suggests situations in which a business letter is appropriate. Can you suggest any others?

3. List one situation in a travel business for which each of the following forms of communication would be most desirable: (a) a face-to-face meeting, (b) a phone call, (c) a business letter sent through the mail, (d) a fax, (e) an e-mail, (f) digital communications.

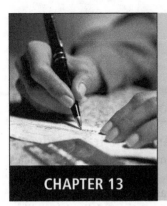

Money Matters

After completing this chapter, you should be able to

1. Describe three types of expenses and two types of financial statements.

2. Outline how suppliers receive their payments and how travel agencies receive their commissions and other earnings.

3. Identify three benefits of preferred supplier relationships.

4. List at least five sources of income for travel agencies, key expenses, and major strategies used by agencies to hold down expenses and increase income.

5. Describe precautions that should be taken when accepting credit cards and checks.

6. Discuss the relationship between customer service and a travel agency's success.

THE BUSINESS OF TRAVEL
- How do travel businesses measure and keep track of their financial well-being?

TRANSACTIONS BETWEEN SUPPLIERS AND AGENCIES
- How are funds transferred among suppliers, travel agencies, and travelers?
- What are the benefits of preferred supplier relationships?

THE ECONOMICS OF TRAVEL AGENCIES
- How do travel agencies manage to be profitable?

TRANSACTIONS WITH CLIENTS
- What do travel counselors need to know about handling documents and money?

CUSTOMER SERVICE AND THE BOTTOM LINE
- What is the relationship between customer service and financial success?

If you are a call-center reservationist, how long should you spend on each call? If you are a hotel manager, should you hire new employees for the busy season or have current ones work overtime? If you are a travel counselor, how much time should you spend with a client planning a deluxe cruise? Should you send a package of brochures by priority mail, use a cheaper, slower method, or suggest the customer look at the supplier's online brochure on its website?

Day by day, the impact of the answers to small questions like these adds up, shaping a company's reputation for service, as well as its expenses, its income, and ultimately its profitability. Collectively, these decisions are just as important as those made by the president of a travel company. Whatever their position, travel professionals should be thinking not only of how their actions fit into the company's marketing plan but also of how they affect its financial status. They should understand where a company earns its money and how it spends it. If they are front-line salespeople, such as travel counselors, they must also have a detailed knowledge of how to handle the documents and money that pass between sellers and buyers. This chapter aims to provide the foundation for that knowledge.

Chapter 13: Money Matters **325**

The Business of Travel

Consolidation and specialization have marked the travel industry in recent years. Airlines, hotels, car rental companies, and travel agencies have come together to form larger companies, and parts of the industry targeted increasingly specialized markets, such as seniors, women, families, outdoor adventurers, cruisers, and more. Other agents specialized in selling specific companies or products, such as groups, academic study trips, and sports events.

The period following the 9/11 terrorist attacks produced nervous travelers and increased security, along with increasing costs associated with new security measures. Other events included the war in Iraq, the U.S. recession, government deficits, rising fuel costs, and disruption caused by terrorism and more frequent, severe weather. The travel industry has had to adapt and is still trying to find its way.

The decisions that travel company owners, managers, and entrepreneurs have had to make required a clear picture of their company's financials and how the consumer's travel dollar flows through the industry's various intermediaries and suppliers.

CLOSE-UP: ON THE JOB WITH CLAUDIA KEMPTES, AGENCY MANAGER

Claudia Kemptes is the manager of a travel agency in a prosperous suburb of a major city. Its business is split almost equally between business and leisure travel.

"Even though our agency is larger than most, I still wear many hats. Sometimes I'm in personnel, doing occasional hiring and keeping my agents happy. Then, I am the advertising and public relations department. I start the new agent training, but after the first day, I delegate that to one of the other agents. Another key area I am in charge of is finances. Everything else depends on this. If we don't make money, eventually we are out of business.

"Our agency has a computerized accounting system. Every transaction that an agent does is entered into the system. This enables me to look at how the agency did by the year, quarter, month, week, or even by the day if I want.

"I can keep track of our accounts receivables — who owes us money. I have one agent who tracks that. If she has any doubts about whether this money is going to be paid or it is taking too long, she notifies me immediately.

"Once we know we have business coming in, my key job is to see how the agents are doing. Each agent must handle a certain amount of business. We have seven inside agents, including both vacation and corporate. If we total all our expenses, our salaries, and our expected profits and divide by seven, then we know how much commission each agent needs to earn from the business she or he handles. Those who bring in more get a bonus. We work with those who bring in less to get them up to speed.

"Actually, the formula is a bit more complex than this. It isn't divided into seven equal parts. Some agents who have been with us for a while earn a higher salary and have a higher goal. Others are newer and have a lower goal. We also have two part-time agents who are judged accordingly. And then there's me; I still handle some clients, but not that many. My job is to oversee everything and plan for the future, so my salary is listed as an expense.

"We stress cruises and tours as much as we can. We earn the most income from these compared to the amount of time we have to put in. And we stress our preferred suppliers because their overrides will give us more commissions to meet our goals. But mainly we stress what is in the best interest of our clients because we know that is what will make us best off in the long run. I've been in the business almost 11 years and have been the manager for almost three. We're ready to change as the industry changes so that we can be around for a long time."

Income and Expenses

To plan and control their businesses wisely, people need accurate and timely information about where their money is coming from and where it is going—their income and expenses.

Customers may be the ultimate source of most of a company's revenues, but it is important to track the types of purchases that produce income so the profitability of different products can be analyzed. For a travel agency, for example, major sources of revenues are likely to include supplier commissions and service fees they may charge customers. These fees partially compensate agencies for products that do not pay commissions, as well as for the expense of services that add client value. For cruise lines, revenue comes not only from the purchase price for a cruise but also from onboard revenues—from shore excursions, casino spending, bar sales, and so on. For many segments of the travel industry, income is seasonal. Tour operators may shut down completely during some seasons. Airlines, hotels, cruise lines, and travel agencies all must plan around seasonal peaks and valleys.

Expenses are the cost of goods and services used in the process of earning revenue. For anyone trying to control costs, it is important to identify three types of expenses: fixed, variable, and semi-variable.

- *Fixed expenses* are costs that remain unchanged during a specific period despite changes in the volume of business. Rent, insurance premiums, GDS computer leases, salaries, subscriptions to reference books, industry magazines and furniture are all fixed expenses.
- *Variable expenses* are costs that increase and decrease directly and proportionately with changes in business volume. Commissions to outside agents and corporate dividends, for example, should increase when business is good and decline when business is slow.
- Semi-variable or *mixed expenses* are costs that change in response to a change in business volume, but they change by less than a proportional amount. Some part of the cost is fixed for a certain time, and another part changes with volume. Semi-variable expenses include electricity, telephone service, and advertising.

Financial Statements

Usually, recording the daily transactions that create revenue and expenses—checks issued, deposits made, interest payments, and so on—is the job of *bookkeepers.* Analyzing how these transactions add up is the job of *accountants.* Is the company bringing in enough money to update its equipment? Does it have enough cash on hand to weather a slow month? To provide this analysis, accountants produce many types of financial statements that paint the fiscal picture of a company, including the income statement and the balance sheet.

Income Statements. An *income statement* summarizes revenues earned and expenses incurred for a particular period (see Figure 13.1). It answers the questions

- How much money came in, and where did it come from?
- How much money went out, and where did it go?
- Does the income minus the expenses yield a net loss or a net gain (profit) for that period?

Balance Sheets. The income statement (Figure 13.1) is used to prepare the *balance sheet* (see Figure 13.2); it shows the financial position of a business at a particular time and may compare it to the business's position at the same time of a previous year. The balance sheet indicates

- *Assets,* which are usable resources, such as cash in a checking account, money owed to the agency by clients (accounts receivable), office supplies owned by the company, and furniture.
- *Liabilities,* which are claims that other companies or individuals have against the company. For example, it may owe money to a bank, salaries for days that employees have already worked, or payroll taxes.

Palmetto Travel
Income Statement for 20xx

Revenues

Domestic air commissions	$ 0
International air commissions	141,134
Consolidator air commissions	50,072
Service fee on air and domestic rail tickets	156,989
Tour, package commissions (with overrides and FIT markups)	133,791
Cruise commissions (including overrides)	32,829
Hotel commissions	61,915
Car rental commissions	12,532
International rail commissions	2,733
Travel insurance commissions	11,711
Commission on miscellaneous sales	31,246
CRS Sharing	3,000
Total Revenues	$637,952

Expenses

Salaries	$343,000
Outside agent commissions	146,387
Rent	35,211
Computers (including GDS fees, hardware, and maintenance)	2,921
Advertising	2,649
Phone	10,742
Utilities	5,680
Furniture and equipment	5,230
ARC, CLIA, and other fees and subscriptions	3,799
Depreciation	3,793
Insurance	26,609
Taxes	5,438
Interest expense	5,000
Office supplies	8,495
Postage	1,926
Miscellaneous expenses	454
Total Expenses	$607,334

Net Income (excess of revenue over expenses)	$ 30,618

FIGURE 13.1 A Sample Income Statement

Palmetto Travel is an imaginary small corporate agency.

- *Equity*, which is the excess of assets over liabilities. Depending on how the company is owned, the equity may be called *owner's equity* or *stockholders' equity*.

The rule in preparing balance sheets is that a change in the amount of assets necessitates an equal change in the amount of liabilities plus equity. Thus, the sum of all assets is constantly equal to the sum of all liabilities and equity. If liabilities exceed assets, the owner must inject more capital soon.

What does the balance sheet tell you? It can allow an accountant to answer questions such as

- Does the company have enough money on hand to pay its bills and meet unexpected needs for cash?

Nirvana Travel Balance Sheet—December 31, 20xx

Assets

Current Assets		
Cash	$50,000	
Accounts receivable	15,000	
Prepaid expenses	500	
Total current assets		$ 65,500
Long-Term Assets		
Tangible assets:		
Furniture and fixtures	$10,000	
Equipment	5,000	
Automobiles	3,000	
Total tangible assets		$ 18,000
Intangible assets:		
Goodwill	$ 5,000	
Leasehold improvements	3,000	
Total intangible assets		$ 8,000
Total Assets		$91,500

Liabilities and Capital

Current Liabilities		
Accounts payable—ARC	$35,000	
Accounts payable—other	6,200	
Advance client deposits	5,000	
Total current liabilities		$ 46,200
Long-Term Liabilities		
Note payable	$ 5,000	
Total long-term liabilities		$ 5,000
Capital		
Invested capital	$25,000	
Retained earnings	15,300	
Total capital		$ 40,300
Total Liabilities and Capital		$91,500

FIGURE 13.2 A Sample Balance Sheet

A balance sheet shows a company's assets, liabilities, and equity on a particular date. Unlike this sample balance sheet, some include information about the company's financial position at an earlier date for comparison.

- Is the company using its assets efficiently?
- Is the company generating enough cash to meet long-term liabilities? Will the company be able to stay in business for the foreseeable future?
- How profitable is the company?

An introductory course in accounting describes how to use a balance sheet to compute numbers that answer these and other questions.

Cash Flow. Neither the income statement nor the balance sheet reports directly on another important indicator of a business's status, the *cash flow*—the pattern of income and expenditures that determines the availability of cash. In an ideal world, income would always precede the expenses associated with it. In the real world, companies must pay salaries and other expenses even if their customers have not yet paid money owed. Because of slow periods, even a profitable company may lose money for a particular month or quarter.

Most companies prepare a report called a *statement of cash flows*; it shows how much cash the company generated over a period of time and where it went. The statement shows the company's ability to pay its short-term obligations when due, and the data helps anticipate cash flow needs.

Cash flow is vital to a company. Companies have been forced into bankruptcy, not because they were not doing well or did not have bright futures, but simply because they had no cash to meet current expenses. Furthermore, money on hand is worth more than the same amount promised for some future date because money on hand can be invested in any number of ways to produce income.

✔ CHECK-UP

Expenses are classified as
✔ Fixed.
✔ Variable.
✔ Semi-variable (or mixed).

Two basic financial statements are the
✔ Income statement, which summarizes a company's business activities over a period of time—its revenues and expenses.
✔ Balance sheet, which indicates a company's financial position—its assets, liabilities, and equity—for a particular period.

Transactions between Suppliers and Agencies

- HOW ARE FUNDS TRANSFERRED AMONG SUPPLIERS, TRAVEL AGENCIES, AND TRAVELERS?

- WHAT ARE THE BENEFITS OF PREFERRED SUPPLIER RELATIONSHIPS?

The flow of money in the travel industry can get complicated. Suppose a client books with a travel agency a trip that includes flights, rental cars, and hotels. How do the suppliers get their payments, and how does the travel agency get its commissions from the suppliers?

When suppliers work with travel agencies, suppliers may receive payments in four ways:

- Directly from clients.
- From credit card companies.
- In the form of checks from travel agencies.
- Through ARC (Airlines Reporting Corporation).

Travel agencies receive their commissions from suppliers in three ways:
- Through ARC.
- By deducting commissions before sending payments to suppliers.
- By checks from suppliers.

Thus, ARC plays a large role in the flow of payments through the travel industry. Recall that, as discussed in Chapter 4, ARC is an organization owned by major airlines that regulates the sale of airline tickets by appointing those who may sell them. (To review the requirements for obtaining an appointment, look again at Chapter 4, in the *Interline Agreements and ARC* section.) ARC also issues standardized numbered forms, called **accountable documents**, that serve as tickets, and it operates a centralized system for processing sales. Hundreds of airlines worldwide, as well as an expanding list of other suppliers (such as Amtrak), participate in ARC's system for processing sales, which we examine in the next section.

Payments and Commissions through ARC

The *Area Bank Settlement Plan* is the system set up by ARC through which participating suppliers receive payments for sales by travel agencies. Each travel agency pays the ARC suppliers weekly by electronically filing a mandatory *ARC report*, which is an accounting of sales. (The report is also called an *air report* or *sales report*.)

The ARC report is usually prepared by the travel agency's bookkeeping staff or by a designated employee, usually a Certified ARC Specialist, or CAS. ARC requires a business to have a CAS Qualifier on staff to receive an ARC appointment. To become a CAS, you must complete an application and pass the CAS test. All CASs must take the test and be recertified every four years.

ARC's *Industry Agents' Handbook* fully describes the procedures involved in the Area Bank Settlement Plan. Figure 13.3 outlines how the system works. It may be accessed at www.arccorp.com/iah.

First, customers pay the travel agency for the airline ticket or other accountable document with cash, check, or credit card. The travel agency deposits cash and checks received from clients into the travel agency's own bank account.

Within two days after the end of each business week, the agency submits an ARC report via computer to ARC's clearinghouse in Arlington, Virginia, so filing for the previous week must take place every Tuesday. (Currently, Sunday is the last day of the business week.) This process is called *Interactive Agent Reporting (IAR)*. The software for IAR, *Interactive Plus,* can be downloaded at no additional charge. When an agency uses IAR, its daily ticket sales are transmitted from their reservations systems nightly to IAR, which prepares the weekly sales summary daily, allowing the agency to verify transactions and correct any errors. Note that voiding of any air tickets must be done by 23:59 (11:59 p.m.) of the following business day, except for Fridays, Saturdays, and Sundays, which can be voided on Monday.

The ARC report itemizes all the travel agency's sales to ARC suppliers. It also contains adjustments. For example, the ARC report shows the commissions on credit card sales deducted from the cash amount the agency owes the airlines, as well as adjustments for tickets refunded directly by an airline. It also includes adjustments for *credit memos* and *debit memos;* these are documents sent by a supplier when a travel agency has reported incorrect amounts for commissions or fares.

The ARC processing center acts as a collection point for ARC reports and disburses money to the appropriate suppliers. It calculates the total amount due the suppliers and presents a demand for that money (called a *draft*) to the travel agency's bank.

The amount withdrawn from the agency's bank account equals cash sales minus commissions from both cash and credit card sales. Thus, commissions remain in the travel agency's bank account. The commissions are calculated on the **base fare**—the fare shorn of all taxes. Most ARC travel agencies process their service fees paid by credit card through ARC.

The ARC bank then disburses the money to the appropriate suppliers. It also forwards credit card billings to the credit card companies, which pay the suppliers.

In short, the travel agency reports its sales each week to ARC, and ARC withdraws money from the travel agency's bank and pays the suppliers. Thus, whether clients pay or not, the agency pays for a ticket within a week of issuing it. To protect against miscalculations by the area bank, the agency tells the bank each week the maximum amount to be withdrawn from its account.

After the area bank has processed all transactions, an *agency sales summary* is accessible on the Internet (over a secure connection), usually within three days after the ARC report was submitted. (For an extra charge, the agency can receive a paper version of the summary in the mail.) Along with other information, the sales summary itemizes all the travel agency's sales to ARC suppliers with a breakdown of commission, tax, and net remittance for each transaction. The travel agency reconciles its weekly ARC report with

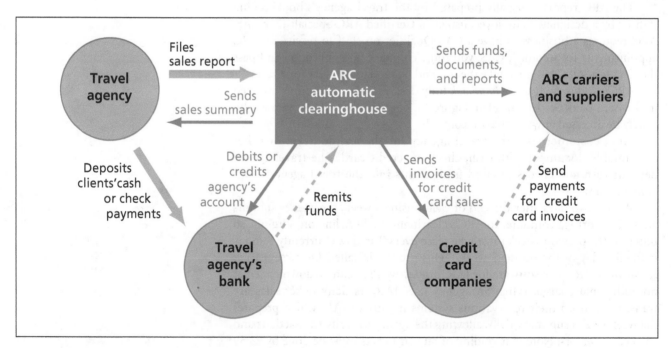

FIGURE 13.3 ARC Settlement Plan

This diagram shows what happens to payments that come to an agency for travel with ARC suppliers. The agency receives its commission immediately because ARC leaves the amount of the commission in the agency's bank account.

ARC's agency sales summary to correct its bookkeeping or to request an adjustment from ARC or an ARC supplier.

Agency Payments by Check

To pay suppliers for services not covered by ARC documents, travel agencies send checks to suppliers. These checks are usually for the *net amount;* in other words, agencies deduct their commissions before sending checks to suppliers. Deposits and taxes complicate the process.

- If clients pay a deposit, no commission is taken from the deposit. The total commission is deducted from the final payment.
- No commission is received on taxes if the taxes are calculated separately and added to the package. If taxes are not listed separately but included in the cost of the package, the commission is still taken on the entire package. For example, a tour company will include hotel taxes as part of the stated cost of a package and, in effect, pays a commission on them.

Suppose the cost of a tour package, including taxes, is $549 and the commission rate is 12 percent. Twelve percent of $549 is $65.88, and it is deducted from the final payment. The transactions might go as follows:

1. The client pays a deposit of $100 to the agency to hold the reservation.
2. The agency deposits the check.
3. The agency sends an agency check made out to the tour company or to its escrow account for the full deposit, $100. (An *escrow account* consists of funds or other property that is held by a third party, such as a bank, until specified conditions are met for its release.)
4. The client makes the final payment of $449.
5. The agency deposits the check.
6. The agency calculates the payment due the supplier by deducting the commission of $65.88 from $449 and sends a check for that amount, $383.12, to the tour company (or its escrow account).

Notice that the agency sends the deposit in full to the tour operator and later submits a check to the tour operator for the balance, less the commission. A record of monies received and disbursed on behalf of a client should be part of the client's file.

As another example, suppose a cruise air/sea package is $1,499 and the commission rate is 10 percent. Port taxes are $109, for a total cost of $1,608. The commission, however, is 10 percent of the quoted cost of $1,499, which comes to $149.90. The sequence of transactions might be as follows:

1. The client pays a deposit of $200 to the agency by check.
2. The agency deposits the check.
3. The agency sends a check for $200 to the cruise line.
4. The client makes the final payment of $1,408 by check.
5. The agency deposits the check.
6. The agency deducts the commission of $149.90 from $1,408 and sends the cruise line the net amount, $1,258.10.
7. The taxes are passed from the cruise line to the governments involved.

For payments overseas, a company may calculate the dollar equivalent of the foreign amount owed and send a check drawn on its U.S. bank account, but the amount sent will seldom be exact because exchange rates vary daily. The solution may be to send a check in the local currency. International currency specialists write drafts in local currency drawn on foreign banks. Local banks also provide this service, but they charge more for it. For more information, speak with the international department of your bank or other exchange service, such as your stockbroker.

You are the night desk clerk and the
bookkeeper for a motel in a growing
chain that hopes to establish good ties
with the increasing number of travel
agencies planning road trips. Your
manager has asked you to iron out
agencies' complaints that they have not
received their commissions or have
received only partial commissions. Your
preliminary look at the records suggests
that agencies are requesting commissions
for guests whom they did not book or
who checked out early. What do you do?

Agencies seldom request commissions for
guests they did not book, but they might
not know that a client did not stay for the
time originally reserved. Did the guests
change to a different rate or date?
Whoever made the change perhaps
neglected to note that the original
reservation was agency-generated. If the
agency has a booking number or name
for the reservation, you should be able to
prove this fact and pay the commission.
Determining the facts when guests seem
to have checked out early may be more
difficult. For example, the guest may have
changed rooms. See if the client is listed
as having "arrived" again on the same
day—a stay that the computer might list
as a walk-in, which would generate no
commission.

Checks from Suppliers to Agencies

If clients pay suppliers themselves, or if clients pay non-ARC suppliers by credit card, the supplier sends the travel agency a check for the commission. The agency must keep careful track of these commissions due. Chapter 12 included suggestions for how to make effective requests for late commissions.

Most suppliers pay commissions in a timely way, but a few become notorious for slow payment or no payment. In some cases, the failure may reflect a simple oversight. But an overdue payment could mean the supplier is in financial difficulty—a fact that the agency will want to know immediately.

Preferred Supplier Relationships

Regardless of how suppliers pay commissions to agencies, most suppliers offer *overrides*, or bonus commissions, to agencies that meet various sales goals or move clients to the supplier's products. For example, a tour operator might offer
- A 1 percent override after the travel agency has sold 25 tours in the same year.
- A 2 percent override after the agency has sold 50 tours in the same year.
- A 3 percent override after the agency has sold 100 tours in the same year, or perhaps the override is based on dollar volume.

The program might be published for all agencies, or it might be negotiated privately between particular agencies and the tour operator. Establishing such an override usually results in the preferred supplier relationship discussed in other chapters.

Preferred supplier relationships bring benefits to both suppliers and agencies. Suppliers gain, in effect, a motivated, knowledgeable salesforce. It is a workforce that gets paid only when it is successful. Travel agencies gain the possibility of earning higher commissions. Agencies also gain other tangible benefits. The preferred supplier may support its marketing with joint or co-op advertising campaigns, special sales seminars, priority status for familiarization trips, and added client amenities (e.g. champagne welcomes at hotels and resorts).

Ideally, an agency chooses the best suppliers for its clients. By concentrating on preferred suppliers, the agency's employees can more easily develop in-depth knowledge of the products they sell and direct relationships with supplier employees. These personal contacts may be invaluable in helping travel counselors resolve issues for their clients or in assisting the agency during travel disruptions. But preferred supplier relationships also can create ethical conflicts, which are discussed in Chapter 16.

✔ CHECK-UP

Key elements of the Area Bank Settlement Plan include
- ✔ The ARC report, which is sent by the travel agency each week and accounts for all sales of airline tickets and other accountable documents.
- ✔ The area bank, which receives the ARC report from the travel agency, withdraws money from the travel agency's own bank, and sends payments to the appropriate suppliers. It also puts commissions from credit card payments into the travel agency's account.

When travel counselors obtain commissions by pre-deducting the commission from a check being sent to a supplier, no commission is taken on
- ✔ Deposits.
- ✔ Taxes that are calculated separately and added to the cost of a package.

The Economics of Travel Agencies

For many years, the economic health of travel agencies was tied to the commissions earned from airline ticket sales. The elimination of those base commissions and the public's use of the Internet to book travel posed immense challenges. In earlier chapters, we examined how new marketing strategies met those challenges; our focus here is on financial operations.

Income and Expenses for Travel Agencies

Travel agencies today derive their income from numerous sources:
- Commissions on sales of transportation, accommodations, cruises, tours, insurance, and other travel components.
- Override commissions.
- Fees and service charges.
- Markups on net charges.
- Miscellaneous amounts from passport photographs, travel guidebooks, luggage, travel accessories, credit for bookings on GDS contracts, and any other services or products the agency decides to provide.

Commissions. Commissions used to account for the largest share of travel agencies' income, but this share has fallen dramatically and is likely to slide further. That said, commissions continue to be a high portion of revenue for travel agencies. Rates vary dramatically for different travel products. For example, it can range from 5 percent on a cruise line you do not have a preferred relationship with, to 16 or 18 percent on travel insurance. Many agencies also rely heavily on client fees.

Independent agents who work through a host agency usually split their commissions with the agency. The split varies. Independent agents may keep as little as 5 percent of the commission or as much as 100 percent. It all depends on the level of revenue independent agents bring in and the contract they make with the Host Agency. It is important for Independent agents to do their research with each host.

Overrides. Overrides are so important; often they determine whether an agency survives. If an agency handles a gross volume of $2 million worth of commissionable business and its commissions average 10 percent, it earns a net of $200,000. If an agency's travel counselors concentrate on preferred suppliers, it might earn an average override of 1 percent on that gross volume of $2 million. The agency therefore earns an extra $20,000, increasing its gross earnings 10 percent. If its previous profit was $20,000, the profit now becomes $40,000. In other words, a 1 percent override can result in a 100 percent increase in profits. Well-run agencies can earn an average of 3 percent or more of gross volume on overrides if they sell the right suppliers' products. Of course, it may not always be possible to sell the service of your agency's preferred supplier if the client chooses another supplier. A skilled travel counselor can often solve this.

Fees, Service Charges, and Markups. Many travel agencies now assess client transaction fees, a growing percentage of a travel agency's revenue, and that percentage is expected to continue rising. Agencies that charge fees should have clear policies concerning when they are imposed, how much they will be, and when they can be waived. (See Table 13.1.)

Some agencies charge a fee on all transactions; some find that the commissions paid for most tours and cruises negate the need for fees for these bookings. Certainly, any service for which the agency is not receiving a commission warrants a service charge. Those can include items, such as trip cancellation, helping clients with restaurant reservations, booking non-commissionable air tickets, hotels, and some adventure trips.

Travel agencies also gain revenue through markups on net rates. For example, they can apply markups when they create tour packages, taking on at least some of the functions of a tour operator, or when purchasing net airline tickets from a consolidator.

Miscellaneous Income. Some travel agencies offer services, such as passport photos, currency exchange, and visa services. To differentiate themselves from competitors, some offer home-security services, pet sitting, grocery delivery for the client's return home, or other special services. Some large firms are becoming one-stop travel stores that offer luggage, guidebooks, leisure wear, videos, and other travel-related products. Many more agencies are going in the opposite direction, offering just a few unique services related to their specialties.

Expenses. The expenses of a travel agency are at least as varied as the sources of income. Salaries and the taxes and benefits related to salaries, however, are by far the largest expense.

Strategies for Success

How do the expenses and sources of income add up for travel agencies? Since 2000, the number of ARC-approved U.S. travel agencies has declined

TABLE 13.1 Sample Travel Agency Service Fee Schedule

Service	Fee
Cruises, packages, tours	No fee
Standard domestic airline ticketing service	From $29 per ticket
Standard international airline ticketing service	From $39 per ticket
Ticket exchange	From $60 per ticket
Special circumstances (includes coupons, certificates, upgrades, mileage tickets, paper tickets)	From $60 per ticket
European Rail passes	No fee (rush fee $29)
International rail tickets/reservations	$29 each
Hotel or car only (with no air or rail)	From $25
Travel insurance (with no other travel product)	From $20
Accounting record research	From $25

Actual fees are at the discretion of the individual travel agency. All agency fees are nonrefundable. These fees are in addition to any charges imposed by individual airlines/suppliers.

significantly, from about 23,000 in 2004 to about 12,000 agency locations in late 2019. The average sales at each location have risen, however, and a majority of existing travel agencies are profitable.

Cost-Benefit Analysis. Cost-benefit analysis is one tool entrepreneurs use to hold down expenses and ensure profits. A cost for something that sounds like a frill, such as flowers or gifts for clients or counselors, may be worthwhile if it results in repeat bookings and low staff turnover. In light of cost-benefit analyses, some agencies stopped selling airline tickets after most stopped paying commissions—thus eliminating expenses associated with ARC and reducing computer costs—and then focused on a niche market or on the sale of more-profitable products, such as cruises. According to one CLIA study, on average, selling a cruise earns an agency more than twice as much per hour worked as selling a land package. Thus, it is not surprising that most agency owners and managers emphasize cruise sales.

Part of the decline in agency locations is based on a large number of mergers and acquisitions. Large agencies have bought small ones, and equal-size agencies have united to form larger ones. With size come economies of scale, as well as negotiating leverage with suppliers, which can enhance commissions and overrides.

Consortiums. Many U.S. travel agencies are small and independent, with only one location. Most survive in part because they have entered into some kind of partnership—perhaps as a member of a network, co-op, or *consortium*, which is an association of agencies that retain their independent identities but pool their resources for certain purposes.

Some consortia have quite a large membership across the United States and Canada. Others may be smaller and regional in nature. Travel agency management decides which consortium the agency will join, and the individual counselors in the agency are asked to become expert in and sell that consortium's preferred suppliers to assure the maximum benefits for the traveler and profit for the agency. The counselors do not hold individual memberships.

In addition to the preferred supplier relationships available through the consortium, agencies are offered a menu of possible services to which they may subscribe, depending on the agency's needs and budget. Those range from marketing resources, technology, customizable websites, database programs, client newsletters, access to research, and staff training (through seminars, conferences, and online webinars).

Well-known consortia include Signature Travel Network, MAST Travel Network, Ensemble Travel Group, Travel Leaders Network, Western Association of Travel Agencies (WESTA), and Virtuoso. Some specialize in upscale travel products, and their agencies often garner top honors in travel magazines like *Travel+Leisure*.

Most agencies—like most U.S. businesses—have also used another strategy in recent years to lower expenses and earn a profit: reducing the expenses associated with employees. How much employees cost relative to the revenue they produce is a key factor in agency success. In recent years, travel agencies, like businesses in other industries, have cut benefits (such as health insurance and vacation time) and minimized salary increases for most employees. In addition, travel agencies have reduced labor costs by significantly changing their model to focus on bringing in independent contractors who work solely through commissions. These types of relationships bring income to an agency while adding little to the agency's fixed or variable expenses. To learn about the work of independent contractors and home-based agents, see Chapter 14.

Key elements in a travel agency's financial picture are
✔ Commissions, fees, and overrides.
✔ The cost of employees, which is the largest single expense of travel agencies.

Important trends in the economics of travel agencies in recent years include
✔ Consolidation.
✔ Increased membership in joint marketing organizations.
✔ Specialization.
✔ Increased hiring of commissioned salespeople.

Transactions with Clients

■ WHAT DO TRAVEL COUNSELORS NEED TO KNOW
ABOUT HANDLING DOCUMENTS AND MONEY?

As conduits between clients and suppliers, travel counselors assume the role of trustees, charged with protecting the financial interests of their clients and their suppliers. In their transactions with clients, they handle both valuable documents and large sums of money.

Accountable Documents

Several of the documents handled daily by travel counselors with ARC-appointed agencies fall into the category known as *accountable documents*—that is, forms issued by ARC that the travel agency must account for. Each accountable document is numbered. If the document is not to be used, the travel counselor must write "VOID" on it. Records of voided documents must be kept for at least two years.

Airline tickets are the principal type of accountable document. As discussed in Chapter 4, most airline tickets are electronic tickets now. If the trip is canceled, e-tickets must be voided, refunded, or exchanged like any other accountable document.

However, agents may still encounter clients who insist on paper tickets. That may occur if the client will be traveling in less-accessible regions of the world where the locals are unfamiliar with e-tickets and perhaps cannot access them by computer. However, paper tickets can require an extra charge by the airline concerned.

Another type of accountable document is the **miscellaneous charges order**, or **MCO**. It records deposits and full prepayments for transportation, tour packages, supplemental charges, accommodations, or additional collections. A clear description of the type of service for which it is issued must be indicated on the MCO.

These documents are like blank checks to those who know how to use them, and they should be handled with as much care as cash. ARC has specific rules about where accountable documents may be kept.

Invoices and Receipts

Travel counselors also handle vouchers, invoices, and receipts. A **voucher** is any document used to confirm arrangements, identify clients, or indicate payments made. An **invoice** indicates the amount due from a client and constitutes an implied contract between the agency and the client for services rendered in exchange for payment. **Receipts** are invoices that indicate an amount paid and the method of payment.

An invoice must be clear and concise and avoid abbreviations unfamiliar to clients. Besides the amount due, a standard invoice may also carry notices and advice to the client that limit the agency's liability. Additional information on an invoice varies with the agency, but often invoices include the serial numbers of tickets or vouchers and some indication of the itinerary.

GDSs can generate invoices or itineraries, or agents can put all this information into a document called a *computerized itinerary/invoice* or *layman-language invoice* (see Figure 13.4). The GDS takes the booking information from the client's PNR (passenger name record) and translates it into easy-to-understand language. It also allows the travel counselor to indicate details of the itinerary and payments, and it can include standard notices or advice to the client, such as a reminder to reconfirm international flights.

In short, computerized itinerary/invoices can itemize the complete details of a client's trip. The information can then be automatically transferred to the agency's accounting system, allowing agencies to track sales and unpaid commissions easily. Thanks to these documents, vouchers are usually unnecessary these days.

Handling Payments from Clients

Usually most travel agencies do not release tickets or other documents until they have been paid for. Agencies encourage corporate clients to use a credit card. But a few corporate clients pay through a central financial office and must be billed.

Travel counselors should scrupulously follow an agency's rules for handling payments. In general, cash should be counted and recounted and a receipt prepared in the client's presence. Personal checks, company checks, and credit cards require even more care because they can be forged, stolen, or invalid for other reasons. One agency manager describes the consequences.

> *Just think, if we accepted one bad check for $500, we would have to sell $5,000 worth of commissionable travel to make the commission back just to break even. That means 11 times the work, and we wind up with no income at all. Actually, we lose big time because I am paying everyone's salary and overhead to do the business.*

Following are guidelines for handling credit card payments and checks.

Credit Cards. Most travel agencies prefer receiving payment by credit card, and a large majority of ARC sales are by credit card. Suppliers largely dictate policies for accepting credit cards. For example, most airlines accept the major credit cards, such as MasterCard, Visa, and American Express. A few issue their own credit cards (called *airline cards*) for paying for travel-related services. ARC's *Industry Agent's Handbook* lists the forms of payment accepted by specific airlines, and CRSs indicate if a particular credit card payment is not acceptable to the airline being used.

INVOICE

Quality Travel Solutions
6304 East Ensenada Street
Mesa, AZ 85205
602-614-6679

John Smith
1234 Wishing Welll Lane
Silver Spring, NY 10000

Invoice: 1241
Travel Consultant: Don Capparella
info@qualitytravelsolutions.com
http://www.QualityTravelSolutions.com

PASSENGERS

	DOB		DOB
John Smith	01/01/1970	Julie Smith	12/12/1972

Hilton Hotels	Depart: 01/18/2020	Return: 01/24/2020	Conf: 013456754		
				Sub-Total:	$ 1,374.00
				Taxes:	$ 137.00
Hotel Details				Total:	$ 1,511.00
Hilton Hotel. Times Square. Executive King room Confirmed.				Payments:	$0.00
$229 per night, plus taxes and fees.				Balance:	1,511.00
Changes and cancellations must be made 24 hours in advance of check-in time. Check-in time is 4:00pm					

Carnival	Depart: 01/24/2020	Return: 02/02/2020	Conf: WRTGFV		
				Sub-Total:	$ 4,200.00
				Taxes:	$ 0.00
Cruise Details				Discount:	$ 200.00
10-Day Eastern Caribbean Cruise from New York City. Cabin #6011. Late seating confirmed. Cruise fare, gratuities, and transfers have all been paid in full.				Total:	$ 4,000.00
				Payments:	$4,000.00
				Balance:	0.00

Notes From Travel Consultant:

Please reconfirm your hotel reservation 24 hours prior to arrival. Advise the hotel if you need a late arrival check-in.

Start getting excited! The final payment for your cruise has been made. Make sure you have all necessary documentation prior to travel. We highly recommend you purchase travel insurance protection.

Seg. 1 Total: $ 1,511.00
Seg. 2 Total: $ 0.00

Invoice Balance: $ 1,511.00

*Quality Travel Solutions * Don Capparella * 6304 East Ensenada Street * Mesa, AZ 85205 * 602-614-6679 * info@qualitytravelsolutions.com **

http://www.QualityTravelSolutions.com

FIGURE 13.4 Computerized Itinerary/Invoice

This is an example of a short computerized itinerary/invoice. A more complete itinerary may also be sent to the client.

Some travel agencies become *credit card merchants* themselves. In other words, like a store or restaurant, they accept credit cards on their own behalf, and may set their own policies for accepting credit cards. But they still must pay the credit card company a percentage of each sale.

ARC has set up a system—the *Travel Agency Service Fee (TASF)* program—that allows agencies to accept credit card purchases for non-ARC items, such as service charges, and to process them through the Area Bank Settlement Plan for a 3.5 percent fee. This program eliminates the need for agencies to have agreements with each credit card company.

Agencies that accept a credit card on behalf of a supplier may be liable for any problems the supplier encounters in collecting payments unless the following steps are taken:

1. Ask the cardholder for proof of identification by showing a picture ID. Only the cardholder whose authorized signature appears on the back of the card may sign for a charge; cardholders cannot authorize a spouse or a child to use their cards.
2. Ensure the card has not expired.
3. Ensure payments made over the phone or through other remote means meet the card company's "card-not-present" rules.
4. Compare physical signatures with the signature on the credit card when possible.
5. Obtain the credit card company's authorization (through the computer or over the phone) and show an approval code on the charge form.

Travel agencies typically accept credit card payments over the phone only if the client is known and trusted or if doing so is part of a legal agreement between the client and agency. Take care not to give cash refunds for tickets originally charged to a credit card and to credit refunds only to the credit card that was used for the purchase. Occasionally, thieves try to charge tickets to a stolen credit card and then resell the tickets. Suppliers and travel agencies are reluctant to reveal much about these problems for fear of giving ideas to potential thieves, but ARC provides educational seminars and other training to help reduce credit card fraud.

Checks and Traveler's Checks. Checks require careful handling. Unless an agency has a different policy,

- Do not accept a personal or company check from anyone, regardless of how much identification the person produces, unless (1) you can hold the tickets or other negotiable documents until the check clears the bank or (2) you know the person and are willing personally to cover payment if the check bounces.
- Do not accept second-party checks (checks with a name and address different from the bearer's).
- Do not accept checks larger than the amount due and then give change.
- Write the client's address and phone number, as well as driver's license number or other proof of identity, on the back of the check.

Some agencies use a check verification service (such as TeleCheck) to verify that the client's account has sufficient funds to cover the check. Another option is an electronic funds transfer, which credits one account (the agency's) and debits another (the client's) automatically by computer.

For traveler's checks, precautions similar to those for personal checks are needed.

- Write the client's address, phone number, and proof of identity on the back.
- Never accept pre-signed traveler's checks. Have the client sign them again in your presence and be sure the signature matches that on the proof of identity.

- Accept checks only from reputable, recognized companies.
- Be willing to give some change for traveler's checks; but if the value of the checks far exceeds the amount of the actual sale, advise the client to cash them at the nearest bank.
- If in the United States, be certain that the checks are in U.S. dollars rather than Canadian or other funds.

These rules should be followed in a matter-of-fact way to preserve the client's goodwill. If the situation is properly handled, few clients will take offense. Those who take offense are usually people you do not want as clients anyway.

✔ CHECK-UP

Key documents that travel agencies prepare for clients are
- ✔ Airline tickets.
- ✔ Other accountable documents—MCOs.
- ✔ Invoices.
- ✔ Receipts.
- ✔ Computerized itinerary/invoices.

Procedures that reduce the chances that a travel counselor will accept a bad check include
- ✔ Holding tickets or documents until the check clears.
- ✔ Refusing second-party checks.
- ✔ Refusing to give change for checks larger than the amount owed.
- ✔ Verifying the identity of the person signing the check.

Customer Service and the Bottom Line

■ WHAT IS THE RELATIONSHIP BETWEEN CUSTOMER SERVICE AND FINANCIAL SUCCESS?

Money has been the topic of this chapter, but concern for the bottom line must be balanced with attention to customer service. Many services and actions that do not pay off in the short run may do so in the long run if the company's plan is to gain repeat clientele and a reputation for impeccable service.

What does this mean in the case of travel agencies? Travel counselors should analyze the services they render: Will the service bring in extra income now or create a good chance that the client will return next month or next year? Is it in keeping with the image and reputation that the agency seeks?

When faced with specific decisions about service (which clients should receive "Welcome Home" cards, which get flowers or wine in their stateroom, and which get an extra hour of consultation?), travel counselors will find some answers addressed by the agency's policies. But good customer service is an art, not the science of following procedures. Sometimes a counselor does something for a client just because it feels right or spends time sharing ideas because that is why the counselor went into the travel industry. Special occasions when no reward is sought can be the ones that make lifetime clients.

Repeat clients are key to financial success. It costs a good deal of money to find new clients. In contrast, superb customer service leads to repeat clients and creates word of mouth that brings in new customers at little or no additional cost.

CHAPTER HIGHLIGHTS

To work effectively, travel professionals should understand how their activities influence their companies' financial well-being as well as how to handle the documents and money involved in transactions. This chapter provided the foundation for understanding these issues. Here is a review of the objectives with which we began the chapter.

1. **Describe three types of expenses and two types of financial statements.** Expenses are classified as fixed (which are costs that do not depend on the volume of business), variable (which are costs that are proportional to the volume of business), and semi-variable or mixed (which change by less than a proportional amount as the volume of business changes). An income statement summarizes revenues earned and expenses incurred for a particular period. A balance sheet shows the financial position of a business at a particular time, indicating the business's assets, liabilities, and equity.

2. **Outline how suppliers receive their payments and how travel agencies receive their commissions.** Suppliers receive payments directly from clients or their credit card companies, through ARC's Area Bank Settlement Plan, or in the form of checks from travel agencies.

    Travel agencies receive commissions in three ways. First, for the sale of accountable documents for services from ARC vendors, such as airlines and Amtrak, commissions are handled through the Area Bank Settlement Plan. Each week, the agency sends an ARC report to an area bank, accounting for all sales of accountable documents. The area bank withdraws the money due suppliers from the travel agency's bank account; thus, the agency retains the commission once the client's payment is received.

    Second, when clients pay the travel agency for services not covered by ARC suppliers by cash or check, the commission is pre-deducted from the check that the agency sends to the supplier as final payment. The commission is taken on the total package but not on any separately stated taxes.

    Third, when clients pay suppliers directly and when they pay for non-ARC services by credit card, the suppliers are supposed to send the commissions to the travel agencies at a later date and need to be carefully monitored to ensure that they do.

3. **Identify three benefits of preferred supplier relationships.** Suppliers gain a dedicated, knowledgeable workforce that only gets paid when it is successful. For agencies, preferred supplier relationships make it easier to provide in-depth knowledge to clients, simplify the task of promoting products, provide personal contacts that can help solve problems, and give them the opportunity to earn override commissions, which have a huge financial impact.

4. **List at least five sources of income for travel agencies, key expenses, and major strategies used by agencies to hold down expenses and increase income.** Commissions on some airline tickets, car rentals, hotels, cruises, tours, rail travel, and travel insurance are major sources of agency income. Other revenue sources include overrides, fees, and service charges, markups, and miscellaneous income, such as money from the sale of travel guides and other travel-related items. Expenses are varied, including fixed expenses such as rent, variable ones such as postage, and semi-variable expenses, such as telephone and office supplies. But salaries and the taxes and benefits tied to salaries are the largest expense for travel agencies. A cost-benefit analysis helps businesses make

decisions that will maximize income and minimize expenses. Frequently used strategies for ensuring or enhancing profits are consolidation, membership in consortia, specialization, and reducing the expenses associated with salaries—through paying employees on a commission basis and through increased use of independent contractors.

5. **Describe precautions that should be taken when accepting credit cards and checks.** A person accepting payment with a credit card should always ask for a picture ID, check the card's expiration date, where possible ensure the customer signs the charge form and that the signature matches the one on the credit card, get an authorization code, and write the code on the charge form. If a personal check is being accepted, proof of identity should be received and noted on the check. Second-party checks should not be accepted, and change should not be given for checks larger than the amount owed. Tickets and other negotiable documents should be held until the check clears. Whether a credit card or check should be accepted in the first place, however, depends on the agency's policies.

6. **Discuss the relationship between customer service and a travel agency's success.** Giving service costs money, and not every service is worth the expense to a business. But services that do not pay in the short run are sometimes worthwhile in the long run. High-quality service leads to repeat clients—who are key to an agency's financial success—and can create word of mouth that brings in new customers.

KEY TERMS

A list of key terms introduced in this chapter follows. If you do not recall the meaning of these terms, see the Glossary.

accountable document	escrow account
ARC report	income statement
Area Bank Settlement Plan	invoice
base fare	miscellaneous charges order (MCO)
cash flow	receipt
consortium	voucher

REVIEW QUESTIONS

1. What can an individual travel counselor do to help control company expenses?

2. What can an individual travel counselor do to increase company income?

3. Why do companies need cash readily available?

4. If a company were to hire one new employee, what extra expenses might be incurred?

5. Why are override commissions important to a travel agency?

6. How has technology eased the agency's job of collecting income?

7. How do travel agencies make money by selling air tickets?

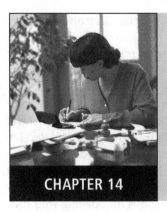

Home-Based Agents

Many home-based agents wonder why they didn't set out on their own sooner. Their earnings may exceed what they would have made working for someone else or paying the high overhead costs of maintaining a traditional brick-and-mortar agency, and they thrive in their new freedom to make business decisions and pursue specialties that match their interests and skills.

It is difficult for a beginner to open his/her own home-based company without previous experience working in the travel business. Those who seem to be the most successful are those with a number of years' experience in travel behind them. Many getting close to retirement age wish to continue in the trade in a specialty, such as cruising, religious tours, family trips, and other niches, which can be very successful.

Still, even travel professionals with years of experience may not be suited to going independent. Some people are surprised by how much they miss the office environment and interaction with coworkers. They also miss the support of departments of experts, such as accounting and tech support to call on when things go wrong. Some people discover too late that they do not have the discipline or ambition to work on their own. Some discover that they do not like the risks of owning their own businesses.

The Travel Institute gratefully acknowledges the contribution and expertise of Andy Ogg, CTIE, an industry authority on home-based travel agencies. This chapter would not have been possible without the help of Ogg and his long history of sales, marketing, and education delivered on the Ogg Marketing Group's platforms.

Fortunately, there are several large host agencies that offer start-up assistance for new agents who lack specific travel industry experience but have a strong desire to enter the industry as a home-based travel agent. Many offer mentors who will help you establish your business plan and marketing plan and help you launch your business.

Being independent means that you are responsible for all aspects of your business and must weather its ups and downs. What skills do you have that will help you to operate a successful business? How can you strengthen and develop the skills you have and acquire new ones? How do you get started? How do you build a network of support for your business? Should you work with a host agency or join a consortium—an association of home-based agents and other industry associations? What are the legal considerations for opening your own travel business? This chapter will examine questions such as these.

It's important, if leaving an employee situation and going out as an independent, that there be a clear understanding with the employer one is leaving as to whose clients belong to whom. Will the clients remain with the agency and be serviced by someone else on the agency staff? Or will the employee who is leaving be able to take past clients along?

Of course, this chapter is only an overview of the opportunities, issues, and considerations faced by home-based agents. You can find more detailed information in Tom, Joanie and Andy Ogg's *How to Start a Home Based Travel Agency* (Ogg Marketing Group © 2020).

Opportunities for Home-Based Agents

■ WHAT ARE THE OPPORTUNITIES FOR HOME-BASED AGENTS?

The Trend toward Home-Based Work

Many factors contribute to the growing numbers of travel professionals who work at home. In fact, this change in the travel industry reflects trends in the U.S. economy in the past two decades. In many industries, several developments have encouraged businesses to use people who work outside traditional offices while also encouraging people to work at home.

For example, advances in technology have made it possible for people to conduct business from almost anywhere while keeping in touch with a central office. Businesses have intensified their cost-cutting efforts as they aim to remain competitive. They may try to save not only on salaries but also on office space, Social Security taxes, pensions, health insurance, workers' compensation, and so on.

In many parts of the country the increased hassles associated with commuting—whether in the form of increased transportation prices or rising commuting times—make home-based work more attractive to employees. The search for a better balance between work and family life makes home-based options alluring to many.

Changes specific to the travel industry have boosted the growth in home-based work among travel professionals. These include the declining importance of air tickets as a source of travel agency income, a shift to pay-for-performance models of compensation, and the emergence of many niches within the travel market, as well as changes in the expectations of travelers and in travel distribution channels.

The changes in travelers' expectations and travel distribution channels are especially significant. Today's travelers have embraced the opportunity to obtain travel services through multiple forms of contact—in person, on the phone, by e-mail, or through a website or *social media* channels, such as Facebook Twitter, LinkedIn, Instagram, Pinterest, Nextdoor, and other social media platforms. Meanwhile, through the integration of Global Distribution Systems (GDSs) with the Internet and online booking engines (discussed in Chapter 3), travel distribution channels have evolved so that travel professionals can provide a full menu of services even if they are not linked with a traditional agency.

Types of Home-Based Agents

Travel professionals working at home fall into three categories:
- Employees doing some or all of their work at home. Using the phone, e-mail, and the Internet, they can stay in close touch with the home office.
- Part-time or full-time independent contractors.
- Independent entrepreneurs who operate their own agencies.

Home-Based Employees. Many travel agencies, like many other businesses, can now be flexible about when and where many of their employees perform their jobs. Opportunities have increased for agency employees to *telecommute*, conducting business out of their homes while staying in touch with the agency's office through the phone and online.

Which agency employees can work from their homes? Job responsibilities at a travel agency may allow not only travel counselors but also those working in Web design, social media marketing, accounting, and sales representative positions to work at least partly from a home office. Working from home is an especially attractive option to *outside sales agents,* people who bring new clients to a travel agency. Outside sales agents may be employed by an agency or may work as independent contractors.

Independent Contractors. An *independent contractor* is a self-employed person who is paid by a business to provide certain services. By using independent contractors instead of hiring its own employees, a company saves the cost of paying for benefits, Social Security taxes, office space, office equipment, and other costs, as discussed in Chapter 9. But to avoid violating tax laws, the company must be certain that it truly treats these people as independent contractors, not employees in disguise.

What is the difference between an employee and an independent contractor? Independence is essential. According to the criteria set by the Internal Revenue Service, a business cannot impose control over the independent contractor's time or require certain sales levels. Independent contractors must be free to work where and when and how much they choose. They also must be free to conduct business with whomever they choose; a business cannot require that an independent contractor work exclusively with that company.

The criteria set by the IRS also limit the support that a company can give to an independent contractor. Independent contractors may have a desk at the host agency, but the IRS requires that agencies charge independent contractors a fee for any desk space in the agency's office. Independent contractors must pay for their own supplies, reference materials, and other "tools of the trade" necessary to conduct business, as well as for training. Table 14.1 summarizes the major criteria that the IRS uses to determine whether a person is an independent contractor or an employee. To determine whether you are classified as an independent contractor under the laws of your home state, see www.irs.gov or IRS Publication 1779 and consult an attorney.

In the travel industry, independent contractors are often travel counselors who choose to become affiliated with one or more *host agencies*. The host agency gives them a means of obtaining domestic airline tickets, override commissions, marketing support, operational support, clout, and credibility.

CLOSE-UP: ON THE JOB WITH SARA MCLAREN, AT-HOME AGENT

After graduating from a two-year college, Sara McLaren enrolled in a 10-week travel program and became a full-time travel counselor. Eight years later, when she got married, she was one of the most productive people in her office. A year after that, with her first child due and hopes for another, she decided to quit, but after a talk with her manager, she became an "at-home agent" instead.

"My manager, Dolores, introduced me to the possibility that I could work at home. I was skeptical. How would I set up an office at home? And where would I find the time to manage the kids, the house, and the agency work?

"Dolores assured me that I could have GDS access just as if I were in the next cubicle at the office. And she assured me that the agency would work with me. I could take in as much work as I thought I could handle and could stop taking in new clients whenever I wanted. I decided to give it a try and am still doing it three years later.

"Much of my morning is filled with feeding the family and getting the kids involved in something. I try to get to my computer, check my e-mail, and turn the phone on by 10:00 a.m., but sometimes it is a bit later. The pattern for the rest of my day consists of alternate bouts of work and attention to the children as needed. At 2:30 on the dot, we all go out for a walk, whether we feel like it or not and no matter how busy I am. I will often work into the evening.

"Wednesday mornings we have a staff meeting at the agency. It's as important for me to be there for business reasons as it is for me to keep in touch with my colleagues on a personal level. I've hired a neighbor to come in and stay with the kids while I attend the meeting. She also comes in on the rare times that I go out to lunch with a client or my mother.

"The agency paid for all my computer hookups and expenses, and I furnished our third bedroom as an office. I produce a little over half of the volume of business that I used to do in the office, and I am compensated accordingly. I am trying to better that by increasing my efficiency without lessening the attention I give to my family.

"There are distinct advantages and time-saving opportunities. I put on a pair of jeans and a top, stride barefoot to my computer, and my commute is complete. My coffee cup and snacks in the refrigerator are always an arm's length away. No traffic, no gas stations, and no time wasted. I may be making 40 percent less, but I certainly save money on clothes, dry cleaning, gasoline, and taxes. And if I decide to go to the pool for an hour in the summer, for all my clients know, I am busy on other calls. One downside is that on days when my printer needs a new ink cartridge or for some reason I can't get online, I've got to solve the problem myself.

"Most days you couldn't tell me from any other agent if you were on the other end of the phone. Commercial accounts might call me five times a day, or I might be scrambling to get a room in a sold-out convention area in New Orleans. If I am really going to be inaccessible during the day, the agency picks up my calls. Yes, there have been times when a client has heard baby cries in the background, and I laughingly remarked, 'I'll bet you can tell that I'm working from home.' I figure that when the kids go off to school, I might decide to get to my computer earlier in the morning, but I'll continue my regimen of a long walk in the afternoon or a stop at the pool in the summer."

A formal written contract should be signed between the independent contractor and the host agency. The contract specifies the commission split, which varies but typically is 70 percent to the independent contractor and 30 percent to the host agency for sales made by the contractor. Some agreements allow contractors to retain 100 percent of their commissions while paying the host agency a fee for each transaction. Host agencies may charge a monthly fee to the independent contractor to cover expenses, such as agency-supplied GDS connections, invoices, and other supplies.

Owners of Home-Based Travel Agencies. Home-based agents who do not affiliate with an agency are a growing sector of the travel industry. These business owners make all the decisions for their businesses. They work completely independently and deal directly with suppliers. Operating a travel agency from the home is more complicated than using the home as the base for work as an employee or independent contractor with a host agency.

Relationships with the Industry: ARC, GDSs, and IDs

If you are on your own, how do you maintain relationships with the rest of the industry? How do you shop for travel products and book them for clients?

One key decision is whether you will sell airline tickets. In order to issue airline tickets, agents must obtain an ARC appointment (see Chapter 4) or have an ARC-appointed agency issue their airline tickets for them. Host agencies usually provide home-based agents with remote access to their GDS and the ability to issue airline tickets with the host agency's ARC number. Home-based agency owners who decide to obtain ARC accreditation in order to issue airline tickets must follow the procedures set forth by ARC in the same way that a retail storefront agency does. As discussed in Chapters 4 and 13, ARC has very specific requirements regarding bonding, financial condition, reporting and bank accounts, security requirements, and personnel training and experience. Accredited agencies are given an ARC number that is

---

TABLE 14.1 Who Is an Independent Contractor?

Criterion	Employees	Independent Contractors
Behavioral control	Work hours that are set by the company	Determine for themselves which hours to work
	Are hired or fired by the company	Contract to work
	Are trained by the company	Provide their own training
	Are supervised by the company regarding how and where they work	Work independently, where they please
Financial control	Are paid a salary	Are paid commissions
	Are guaranteed their pay	May incur either a profit or a loss
	Are reimbursed for expenses	Pay their own expenses
Relationships between the parties	Work exclusively for one company	May contract with other companies
	Receive employee benefits such as health insurance	May or may not be eligible for employee benefits

Note: The criteria described here are the major ones used by the Internal Revenue Service to determine whether a person is an independent contractor. For additional details, see IRS Publication 1779 and www.irs.gov.

TABLE 14.2

Identification Numbers of Home-Based Agents

1. CLIA membership number
   www.cruising.org.
   Issued by CLIA (Cruise Lines
   International Association.

2. Registered Seller of Travel.
   Issued by your state—if required by
   law.

3. TRUE (Travel Retailer Universal
   Enumeration) www.ccra.com, issued
   by CCRA.

4. VTC (Verified Travel Consultant).
   Issued by ARC (Airlines Reporting
   Corporation).

used throughout the travel industry to identify them as bona fide sellers of travel in order to receive commissions and travel benefits.

Due to the expenses and limited profitability of issuing airline tickets, fewer agencies are choosing ARC appointments. Most home-based agencies do not concentrate on making domestic airline reservations. For international air reservations, they most often book consolidator tickets that do not require ARC appointments or GDS access. If selling tours and cruises, they often have the tour company or cruise line handle the client's air as well.

GDSs provide a quick, easy, efficient way of shopping for airfares and making reservations with many types of travel suppliers. But obtaining GDS access is no longer a stumbling block for independent agents. All major GDS companies have a variety of products that provide access to their systems through the Internet. Many non-ARC independent agents serve their clients well without direct access to a GDS. Most non-airline travel suppliers let travel counselors make reservations directly with them through a special "agent" section of their websites or by calling toll-free.

If you choose to deal directly with suppliers without using a host agency, you should consider ARC's Verified Travel Consultant (VTC) program. This program allows agents who do not issue air tickets and who meet other criteria to be recognized by, and receive commissions from, certain travel suppliers and organizations by using the ARC number issued to individual VTCs. Verified Travel Consultants also receive the VTC Tool Kit, which contains resources and tools.

If you do not have an ARC number or if you are a Verified Travel Consultant, you will want some other identification number certifying that you are a professional travel seller. Table 14.2 lists numbering systems recognized by major travel suppliers to identify professional travel agents who are entitled to receive commissions for their sales and qualify for travel discounts and benefits. Each has its own requirements for membership.

Networks of Support

Both independent contractors and home-based agency owners face special challenges because they are on their own. Independent contractors no longer have colleagues on hand for on-the-spot advice; nor can they rely on supporting departments for accounting, marketing, or computer expertise.

Home-based agencies lose the opportunity for walk-in business. Success will probably require an existing network of potential clients, specialization in a particular type of travel, and links with a traditional travel agency or with a host agency. Many independents join a consortium to increase their buying power, to qualify for override commissions, and to take advantage of the additional support that these organizations offer, as discussed in Chapter 13. Many are members of CLIA.

Becoming an active participant in travel industry organizations and taking advantage of opportunities for continuing education will help independents to build a network of support. There are many educational opportunities that we have discussed throughout this textbook; additional educational opportunities are discussed in Chapter 16.

The evolution of home-based travel agents has progressed, and some of the niche associations that were focused on home-based travel agents—like NACOA, NACTA, and OSSN—have either been absorbed or ceased operation. (NACTA is now known as the ASTA Small Business Network.) This change is due in large part to the growth of host agencies that offer extensive programs and administrative support to those who want to launch a home-based travel business. Also popular are local and regional agency groups that meet in support of one another and draw interest from home-based travel agents.

Home-based travel professionals may be
✔ Employees who telecommute.
✔ Independent contractors.
✔ Home-based agency owners.

To be considered independent contractors by the IRS, individuals
✔ Must be free to work where and when and how much they choose.
✔ Must be free to conduct business with whomever they choose.
✔ Must pay for their own supplies, reference materials, and other "tools of the trade" and must abide by the IRS rules.

✔ Must pay for the space if they have a desk at a host agency.
✔ Must have a written contract if they work with a host agency.

To increase their chances for success, independent agents should
✔ Become active participants in travel industry organizations.
✔ Take advantage of educational opportunities within the travel industry.
✔ Join an association of home-based agents.

Setting Up Your Business

■ WHAT SHOULD HOME-BASED AGENTS DO IN ORDER TO SET UP A BUSINESS IN A PROFESSIONAL MANNER?

■ WHAT SPECIAL TASKS FACE INDEPENDENT CONTRACTORS AND HOME-BASED AGENCY OWNERS WHEN THEY ESTABLISH A BUSINESS?

Successful businesses are usually those that are well planned. A key question to consider is whether there is a market for what you have to offer. Marketing research, which is discussed in Chapter 9, can help you answer this question. Let's suppose you have determined that you have the skills and personality to work on your own and that there is a market for your services. What's next? You should devote the time and effort to develop a business plan. Unfortunately, many choose to skip this important step.

The Business Plan

A *business plan* is a summary of what is expected from a business effort, including the level of income, benefits, and investment, along with a statement of mid- and long-term goals. Following are some basic elements of an informal business plan:

■ *Your expectations.* For example, how long do you expect to take to generate income? Do you expect to work part-time or full-time? Do you expect eventually to obtain all of your income from this business?

■ *Your business concept, or the profile of your business.* What is its niche? What is the competition? You may want to specialize in two or three niches to cushion your business for seasonality and unpredicted marketplace changes.

- *A mission statement.* It should clearly communicate your company's purpose.
- *Specific objectives.* Based on your expectations, you can identify specific goals that will direct your efforts and help you set priorities for your activities.
- *Projections for the business.* What income do you project for the first year? For the first three years? What expenses do you project? Do you need outside funding?
- *Your name.* Choose a name that is descriptive of your business's focus. For example, "World Diving Cruises and Tours" is much more descriptive than "Suzy's Travel Shoppe."

If you need outside funding or loans, you should create a formal business plan. There are many books and computer programs that can help you do so.

Legal and Accounting Requirements

Turn to the experts to help you set up your business correctly. In particular, find a good attorney and accountant who specialize in small businesses or travel agencies.

An attorney's advice and assistance should help with the following:

- *Establishing and filing a Fictitious Business Name Statement* (DBA, or Doing Business As) with the appropriate government officials (county and state). Typically, you must file forms with the county recorder's office and place an announcement in a local newspaper for a specified time.
- *Choosing the type of business you will establish: sole proprietorship, partnership, Subchapter S corporation, corporation, or limited liability company (LLC).* Evaluate the benefits and drawbacks of each type. Most home-based agencies are established as sole proprietorships; however, the trend is toward establishing a subchapter S corporation for the liability and tax benefits.
- *Obtaining the proper business license.* Check with your city hall or county officials to determine if a local license is required to operate a business from your home. Some states require travel sellers to register with the state attorney general's office.
- *Evaluating your business insurance needs.* Your attorney can explain your liabilities and the type of insurance you will need. For example, **errors and omissions and general liability insurance** provides coverage if you are sued by a client for a mistake or negligence. You may purchase insurance through an insurance company.
- *Preparing disclosure forms.* A disclosure notice is a written statement that identifies the information you have communicated to clients and is signed by clients. (Figure 10.1 shows an example.) A disclosure notice should include receipt of documents, the responsibilities of the seller, cancellation and refund policies, and offers of insurance. Ask your attorney to evaluate the disclosure forms that you plan to use. Disclosure forms are meant to prevent legal problems, but they only help if you keep the client's signed notice on file.
- *Reviewing your contracts.* Have an attorney look over your contracts with a host agency (if you choose to go that route) as well as any contracts that you have prepared for suppliers.
- *Complying with Seller of Travel Laws.* Check with your attorney to make sure you are in compliance with the Sellers of Travel Law. These consumer

protection laws are designed to protect residents of its state, and the laws apply to any Seller of Travel who sells to residents of the regulating state.

An accountant's advice and assistance should help with the following:

- *Assessing the tax implications* of the type of business that you have selected (sole proprietorship, partnership, and so on).
- *Evaluating your business plan.* An accountant can give you advice about the format and content of your business plan.
- *Setting up your books.* Your accountant can help you set up reports needed for funding requests and taxes as well as an accounting system. There are many good accounting programs designed for small businesses that you can customize; see the discussion in Chapter 3.
- *Opening bank accounts.* Most home-based travel agencies set up two checking accounts for their business: a trust account for client funds and a checking account used for operating expenses.
- *Establishing a merchant account.* If you are planning to charge service fees or provide any services or products in addition to those purchased from travel suppliers, you will need to set up a merchant account with the major credit card companies. You may want to use a service (such as First Data Corporation) that will set up a merchant account with multiple credit card companies and provide the capability to process charges over a secure connection online. This also allows you to accept customer credit card charges via your website. If you are working with a host agency, you may opt to use its merchant account.
- *Setting up a federal tax ID number.* An employer identification number (EIN), also known as a federal tax identification number, is a nine-digit number that the IRS assigns to business entities. EINs are used by employers, sole proprietors, corporations, partnerships, nonprofit organizations, trusts and estates, government agencies, certain individuals, and other business entities. Sole proprietors may use their individual Social Security numbers for tax reporting, but suppliers may view an EIN as more professional.
- *Using a limited power of attorney.* Some independent agents use a limited power of attorney as authorization to process phone orders charged to the client's credit card in order to protect themselves from disputed charges. It does provide limited protection and should be reviewed by an attorney.

Your Office

Setting up a home office requires time, effort, planning, and money. The investment is worthwhile for a space that gives you a professional atmosphere and convenient access to the required tools of the trade. Here is an outline of the basic elements that you are likely to need for a well-equipped home office.

Stationery and Business Cards. Use a professional-looking logo on everything—from letterhead and envelopes to brochures and business cards. A graphic designer can create a unique logo that will project a professional image for your business. Also, be sure to carry your branding into your digital footprint.

Office Space. In order to take tax deductions for the expenses of a home office, the IRS requires that an area of your home be set aside for "exclusive use" by your business. The dimensions of the office are used to calculate the percentage of your home that is for business use. You may then be able to

A well-planned office makes work easier.

deduct that percentage of home expenses (such as mortgage payments and electricity) as a business expense.

Setting aside an area of your home exclusively for your business has psychological as well as financial advantages. It helps you and your family separate personal activities from business tasks and is likely to make it easier to reduce the noise and distractions that inevitably occur in a home. Having an area set aside exclusively for your business is likely to make it easier to efficiently store and organize everything you need to conduct your business and is a way to let your family know when you are working.

Office Furniture. You will need a desk with enough space to conduct business effectively, a comfortable office chair, shelves, and file cabinets.

Office Equipment. Here is some advice about the telephone and computer equipment that you are likely to need.

- Install a phone line under your business name, or consider a Voice-Over-IP service, such as Ring Central or Google Voice. These services allow you to set up multiple extensions, follow you wherever you choose to work and e-mail your voice messages to you. These services can work in conjunction with a land line or independently of one. They also can include toll-free numbers for a small monthly fee. Many agents use their cell phone as their primary communication tool. Having the ability to text, call, email and use other communication apps—such as Snapchat, Whatsapp, SKYPE or social media—all from one platform is essential if you are selling to the under-40 crowd.
- Answer your phone with a professional greeting and record a voice-mail greeting that identifies your business and your hours of operation.
- If you need to purchase a new computer, consider investing in a laptop; they have enough memory and storage capacity to meet everyone's needs. Mobility is especially beneficial to home-based agents who may be meeting clients at locations away from their home offices and may need to keep in touch with customers or perform business tasks while traveling.
- When setting up your account with an Internet service provider, also known as an ISP, consider the high-speed access options available in your area.

- Word processing software is a must-have for letters, flyers, and other marketing and promotional materials. In addition to the desktop options in Microsoft Office, many agents choose **cloud** options, such as Google Docs or Zoho.com. Those are websites with software programs that are stored on the cloud. They can be accessed via desktop computer, smartphone, or tablet, such as Apple's iPad or the Kindle Fire. The sites offer much of the same features as traditional software packages for much less, but there are limitations to the features, and a careful evaluation should be conducted to make the right choice for your business needs.

In addition to word processing options, an accounting program is necessary. Choices include desktop software, such as Quicken or Quickbooks by Intuit, and a Web-based option, such as Freshbooks.com or LessAccounting.com. Those are not programs designed for travel agencies, but they use accounting standards adopted by many Certified Public Accountants, which can be useful when preparing taxes. Your CPAs probably will use an accounting system they are fully integrated with and will recommend the one you should use.

Website design software also comes in many varieties. Desktop programs, such as Adobe's Dreamweaver, have an easy-to-use graphical interface, but the learning curve can be steeper than Web-based content management systems, such as WordPress, and cost can be a consideration. WordPress is free and available as an add-on to most website-hosting packages. WordPress powers an estimated 70% of the world's websites at this time.

If your business also will use online media for marketing, then you will need software to handle layout, graphic creation, photo and video editing, and tools for creating professional level content. As an example, Adobe's Creative Cloud offers an assortment of tools for this purpose.

Depending on the number of office machines you install, you may need to add electrical outlets to your home office. If additional outlets are required, put them on a separate circuit breaker and invest in a good surge protector.

Your Website

A website is especially important for home-based travel agencies because they lack a physical storefront. You may want to develop a site on your own, but many companies specialize in creating, hosting, and maintaining websites for travel agencies. Here is an overview of the steps to take to establish an online presence for your business.

1. *Determine the purpose and the goals of your online presence.* Do you want your site to act as an electronic brochure and advertisement? Do you want to provide additional services to your clients online, such as destination information, or even the capability to make reservations on your site? Once you have defined your goals, you can work with the site designer to include the features that meet those goals.
2. *Register your company's domain name.* Your URL should be as close to your business name as possible. To find out if your chosen domain name is available, go to www.internic.com. Go to www.icann.org for a list of accredited domain name registrars.
3. *Choose a hosting company.* A reliable hosting company is the foundation of your Web presence and your e-mail. When choosing a hosting company, look for one that offers a service guarantee and the option of an online database. Some offer Web-based design packages, such as WordPress or Joomla, for free. Those programs are database-driven, meaning there are

ON THE SPOT

You are a travel counselor who just gave your business card to a friend of a friend. She mentions that she's planning to go to the Caribbean for her honeymoon and expects that she and her fiancé will check the Internet and reserve the trip themselves and save some money. How would you respond?

You almost always want to respond to a person by finding an area of agreement. "Yes, it's amazing what you can do on the Internet," you might say. "We keep a file of some of the best honeymoon hotels in the islands in our agency computer. I'd love to tell you about the ones our clients have raved about, to make sure you don't book at one they were disappointed with. If you two would like to get together with me next week and describe your dream getaway, I can tell you which ones might fit."

If she seems responsive, follow up with, "What day would be best for you?" If she seems reluctant, you might ask for her phone number or e-mail address. You want to keep as personal a connection as possible, so a meeting or phone number is better than an e-mail address. Your object in the future will be to have another face-to-face meeting to plan her honeymoon—hardly a trip she would want to leave to chance.

not pages to upload, but the design and the content are separate for ease of changing the design or making text updates via a Web browser. HostGator.com, GoDaddy.com, and many others offer nominal hosting packages that include everything an agent needs to get started. There also are cloud-based web development tools that require no knowledge of HTML such as Wix, Weebly, Jimdo, and many others. These tools allow you to build excellent sites.

4. *Develop and design the site.* Using HTML editors, or Web-based services, such as WordPress, novices can create and maintain Web pages without learning HTML coding. However, many Web designers and Web-development firms will design and maintain your site for you, for a fee.

   If you need to give your customers the ability to make reservations through your website, you can obtain tools for online booking through (1) a travel-specific technology company, (2) a GDS, (3) a travel supplier's booking engine, or (4) an agency network or consortium.

5. *Maintain the site and plan for growth.* Websites must be constantly updated, maintained, and improved. Anticipate and plan for the maintenance and growth of your site in a way that works in harmony with your marketing plan.

6. *Evaluate the effectiveness of your site and adapt to changing needs.* For each goal that you defined in step 1, you need to develop a method of measuring your success in achieving it. Measure, track, and evaluate the effectiveness of your site on a regular basis. You must be willing to adapt your online presence to the changing needs of your customers. Surveys and feedback forms on your site are valuable tools to help you make this evaluation. In addition, most Web-hosting companies provide access to reports, called *log analyses,* that contain important information about the visitors to your site. They track information, such as the number of hits, page views, and unique visitors to help you evaluate the success of your site.

   One free service worth noting is Google Analytics, which gives comprehensive reports and evaluations of where traffic comes from on a website and how it finds your website through keywords.

7. *Use search engine optimization (SEO).* One way to increase the traffic to your website is through SEO, which means finding ways to have your website appear as high as possible in search results. Different ways to do that include placing key words throughout your site and having fresh content that is updated frequently.

8. *Keep your customers coming back.* Interesting and up-to-date content keeps customers coming to your site. Base the content of your site on your knowledge of your customers. Give them something of value. Make the site as interactive and as customer-friendly as possible. Ask your clients for suggestions about how you can better serve them. Don't be afraid to try something new. Your site can be an effective way of earning your clients' trust and loyalty.

9. *Consider a blog.* A blog is an extremely effective way to connect with your site visitors in a personal way and showcase your unique qualities and experience. It can give your website visitors a sense of trust that can be lacking in the faceless world of the Internet. Blogs also give you conversation starts in social media, such as Facebook, Twitter, and Pinterest and can be one part of a full online marketing plan.

Working with a Host Agency

If you are an independent contractor seeking to work with a host agency, you must first complete two tasks: selecting a host agency and signing a contract with that agency.

Selecting the host agency partner that is a good fit with your business is a key decision. You may choose a local retail agency that has experience working with independent contractors, or you may select an independent contractor network that specializes in working with independents.

Although a neighborhood agency may be convenient, the location of the agency is less important than other features and benefits provided by the host agency. When searching for a host agency, you may consider resources like findahosttravelagency.com or hostagencyreviews.com. When evaluating a host agency or independent contractor network, consider the following issues:

- *Specialization.* Is the host agency compatible with your business and marketing plan? Does the agency specialize in the products and services that are your business focus? If it does, it will have preferred vendor programs, offering support and overrides that will benefit your business.
- *Training.* What training programs does this agency provide? Does it typically work with experienced agents who require little training? Or does it focus on new entrants to the travel industry and provide extensive training? What level of training do you need?
- *Support.* What level of support does the agency provide? Does it provide quality control of bookings and automated access to a GDS with technical support? If a problem arises with your customer, will the agency provide help through relationships it has built with suppliers' representatives?
- *Experience.* How many years has the agency been in business? Does it have experience working with independents? How many independent contractors does the agency work with now? How successful are they?
- *References.* Ask for a list of references and contact them. Check with the Better Business Bureau to see if it has unresolved complaints filed against the agency. Check industry references and independents already working with the agency.
- *Professionalism.* What memberships in travel industry associations does the agency hold? Does the agency carry errors and omissions insurance? How professional are the owner, manager, and agents who will be working with you?
- *Compatibility.* Can you work well with this group, including the agency owner, manager, inside agents, and other independents? Is your respect for them reciprocated?
- *Benefits.* What travel benefits will the agency extend to you? Will you qualify for discounts on travel and be eligible for fam trips?
- *Finances.* What are the total costs, and what do you get for your money? What is the commission split for your sales for you and the agency? How are overrides handled? Do you get the same commission split for overrides?

Note that many host agencies do not allow non-agents to work on live GDS systems for at least 12–18 months.

A written agreement that states the terms of your relationship with the host agency or independent contractor network and that clearly identifies you as an independent contractor is required by the IRS. Without this written agreement, the IRS considers you to be an employee of the agency. If you intend to serve as an employee, a written employment agreement between you and the agency should be prepared and signed. An attorney should look over any contract before you sign it. A variety of sample contracts are available through the Travel Professional Community and some of the industry associations. Table 14.3 shows important components that should be included in your contract.

Establishing Relationships with Suppliers

If you are setting up a home-based agency focused on a niche, one of your first tasks is to establish and begin building relationships with carefully chosen suppliers. Research and choose suppliers that you know you can trust—ones that can deliver services in the specialties you have chosen. Focus on creating a network within your niches. You must be prepared to prove yourself as a professional who can help your suppliers' bottom line by delivering substantial sales.

Fully develop your network for each of your chosen niches. For example, if you choose cruises as a specialty, become a CLIA member. Once you are a member, you will have access to resources to help you sell more cruises. These include a listing in their Cruise Expert Locator plus free classroom, online, and DVD sales training. Establish relationships with suppliers that specialize in shore excursions so that you can offer your clients a unique and high-quality product with expanded services. Join a cruise consortium to obtain access to overrides, special commissions, and extra services for your clients so that you can maximize your profitability and increase your client loyalty. If you follow a similar process for each of your chosen niches, you will soon develop a complete support network for your business.

TABLE 14.3 Elements Needed in Contracts for Independent Contractors

Parties to the agreement. Clearly identify all parties to the agreement, including Social Security numbers and mailing addresses.

Purpose of the agreement. Define and state the purpose of the agreement. Be as specific as possible.

Term of the agreement. Define a specific length of time (term) in which the agreement will be valid. You may want to include a rollover clause so that the contract can be automatically renewed at the end of the term. For example, "the agreement shall be month to month and will automatically renew at the beginning of each new month." Always include a statement that allows for termination of the contract by either party for any reason. For example, "this agreement may be canceled by either party for any reason, with or without cause, with 60 days' written notice of intent to cancel."

Duties of the parties of the agreement. Describe the specific duties of both parties. Be as thorough and complete as possible. If the agency has verbally stated that training or support will be provided, include the details of what will be provided in the agreement.

Independent contractor statement. The agreement must clearly state the working relationship between you and the agency, identifying you as an independent contractor and not an employee. Include characteristics of the relationship that further define you as an independent contractor, such as nonexclusivity; your paying for "tools of the trade"; your freedom to work where, when, and how much you choose; and the risk of profit and loss.

IRS reporting. The agreement must state that all commissions paid to the independent contractor will be reported on an IRS 1099 form and that the independent contractor is responsible for reporting and paying taxes.

Commission split or other remuneration. The exact details of the commission split, the override split, charges or fees due to the agency, and the timing and method of payments to the independent contractor should be specified. The agreed-upon method of resolving disputes over commissions and payments should also be clearly defined.

Ownership of accounts. A clear, concise statement of who owns the accounts that the independent contractor brings into the agency will eliminate problems when the relationship between the independent contractor and the host agency has ended. This is a common area of dispute that should be agreed upon at the outset of the relationship.

Payment for services. Details of the collection of funds and the policies for holding client funds need to be clearly defined. How are clients' checks and credit card charges processed and handled? Does the independent contractor collect a client check and then issue a business check to the host agency? What is the procedure for handling bounced checks or denied credit card charges? How and when are commissions paid when the client uses a credit card for payment?

Indemnification. *Indemnification* means protection against or compensation for damage, loss, or injury suffered. Your agreement should contain an indemnification clause that specifies in what circumstances each party will indemnify the other from loss created by errors and omissions. For example, if the host agency issues an airline ticket for the wrong date, the agency should be responsible for the expenses incurred to correct the situation; however, if the independent contractor made the error, he or she should bear the expense. Defining resolutions for these issues in advance goes a long way in ensuring that each party acts in the best interests of the other.

(continued on next page)

TABLE 14.3 Elements Needed in Contracts for Independent Contractors (Cont.)

Miscellaneous operating and service fees. Both parties need to agree upon charges that the independent contractor will pay to the agency to perform tasks that service their clients but do not create revenue, such as reissued tickets, voided tickets, coupons, and frequent-flyer tickets. Any additional fees should be clearly identified in the written agreement.

Travel benefits. The complete extent of travel benefits the independent contractor will receive and the procedure for obtaining these benefits should be specified in the written agreement.

Compliance with local, state, and federal laws. The written agreement should include a statement that both parties will comply with all local, state, and federal laws during the term of the contract.

Miscellaneous clauses. Your attorney may suggest specific wording and clauses that should be added to the agreement—for example, which state laws apply if the host agency and independent contractor are located in different states, which party will be responsible for paying attorney fees if there is a dispute, and other specifics that should be explicitly stated and agreed upon by both parties.

Note: This list is not comprehensive. For a more detailed list with explanations, see Ogg Marketing Group, How to Start a Home Based Travel Agency, published in 2020.

✔ CHECK-UP

To set up a home business, you should
✔ Develop a business plan.
✔ Obtain expert advice from an attorney and an accountant.
✔ Invest the time and money to create a professional, convenient office space.
✔ Establish a website.

✔ Consider whether to work with a host agency if you are an independent contractor.
✔ Establish relationships with suppliers if you are an independent agency owner.
✔ Establish a support network.

Growing Your Business

■ HOW DO HOME-BASED AGENTS EXPAND THEIR BUSINESSES?

Now that you have all the components in place for your business, you need to bring in customers and grow your business. As with all aspects of your business, purposeful and careful planning is required to ensure that your marketing efforts are effective. You will need to define your market, establish a marketing budget and design a marketing plan to achieve the objectives in your business plan. Business growth requires finding the right marketing mix and differentiating your products and services from the competition.

The Marketing Mix

Chapter 9 explains why developing a marketing plan is critical to the success of any business. A *marketing plan* selects a target market and describes how to handle four basic characteristics of the business called the *marketing mix* or the *four Ps of marketing:* product, promotion, place, and price. Although each home-based agent creates a marketing mix based on his or her business goals and budget, here are some common choices made by home-based agents:

■ *Product.* Most home-based agents specialize in a type of product or activity, a type of client (target market), or a destination. Product choices tend to be focused on internal yields and complexity.
■ *Promotion.* Many home-based agencies use a combination of methods of promotion. A review of Chapter 9 will remind you of the many forms of

TABLE 14.4

Marketing Tips for Home-Based Agents

■ **Tip 1: Look around you.**

Look to your right, look to your left. Your next client is only three feet away from you. Whether you are standing in line at the grocery store or sitting in the bleachers at a little league baseball game, that person next to you is a potential client. Start a conversation; tell people what you do. Pass out your business cards and give them to your family and friends to pass out for you. That is an inexpensive way to advertise your business.

■ **Tip 2: Promote yourself.**

There are lots and lots of travel agents out there, and there is the Internet. How do you compete? Promote your customer service. People want the best value for their money, and they want to feel that someone cares about their vacation. Be accommodating; meet your clients where and when it is convenient for them. Let them know you are there whenever they need you. Deliver their travel documents in clever, creative ways. They will appreciate it and will share your name with others.

■ **Tip 3: Don't be a couch potato.**

Clients will not just show up on your doorstep. You have to go out and find them. Become involved in local organizations, such as the Chamber of Commerce. Volunteer to work on community or church events. Join a networking group in your area. Advertise in church and school bulletins. Wear a shirt or jacket or carry a tote bag with your logo and agency name when you attend functions. Be visible in your community.

Source: Nancy Kist, CTC, president of Career Quest Training Center (www.careerquesttraining.com).

promotion that travel sellers can use. Consider your target market when choosing promotion methods, in addition to your budget.

■ *Place.* Although their offices may be in their homes, many home-based agents conduct business over the Internet, make "house calls" at clients' homes or businesses, or even meet clients at a local café. They may also conduct travel seminars in meeting rooms of hotels or public libraries.

■ *Price.* Some home-based agents specialize in upscale, luxury travel; others provide products and services in a variety of price ranges. Although most home-based agencies cannot compete by offering the lowest price, they provide value to their clients. Often, they can deliver extra services through personal attention to each client and through expert knowledge of their niche.

Whatever your marketing mix, develop a capabilities brochure that describes and promotes your business. Include a mission statement, a list of the services you offer, the benefits that you provide your clients, and your credentials as an expert. Consider adding testimonials from satisfied customers and the professional organizations that your business belongs to. Also include any guarantees that you offer to ensure that your customers are satisfied. See Table 14.4 for some additional marketing tips.

Differentiating Your Services

Independent agents are actually in a better position than many large companies to deliver personalized, customized service to individuals. As we discussed in Chapter 9, travel sellers across the globe are striving to become more skillful at delivering personalized service through customer relationship marketing and customer relationship management.

Customer relationship marketing enables companies to use information about the individual's preferences and interests to create effective marketing. They build, maintain and use customer databases that include information, such as an individual's travel patterns and preferences, demographic information (age, gender, income level, and so on), hobbies and interests, and more. Based on this information, businesses can customize market offerings, services, programs, and messages. *Customer relationship management (CRM)* is a strategy that weds personal attention and technology in order to provide personalized service and build lasting relationships with clients.

Contact management software has evolved to allow you to keep track of your customers and prospects in ways never before possible. Among effective programs are online services, such as PipelineDeals.com (Batchbook.com's replacement) and SalesForce.com, which allow you to synchronize your e-mail, mobile phone, and other points of contact into one place. They also can run reports, as well as sort, filter, and e-mail directly from the program or connected third-party applications. Using the data that comes in, you then can send targeted offers and make calls to people who have expressed an interest in that destination, niche, or supplier. Most also are compatible with online services that perform specific functions, such as Freshbooks.com for invoicing, Mailchimp.com for e-mail blasts, and Shoeboxed.com for expense management. ClientBase is a popular database program for travel professionals.

Managing the relationships that you have built with your customers is essential to the success and growth of your business. If you keep your customers' needs as your focus, you will keep your customers loyal and your business growing.

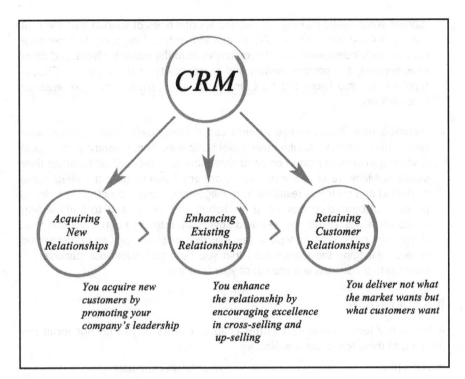

Customer-relationship marketing is crucial.

CHAPTER HIGHLIGHTS

Here is a review of the objectives with which we began the chapter.

1. **Distinguish three types of home-based agents.** Employees of agencies may work out of their homes. Home-based agents may also be nonemployees who work as independent contractors. The IRS has several criteria for distinguishing employees and independent contractors. Basically, independent contractors must in fact be independent—free to establish where, when, how, and with whom they work and limited in the support they can receive from a company. Some independent contractors work with a host agency; they must have a written agreement stating that they are not employees of the agency. There are also a growing number of independent home-based travel agencies.

2. **Discuss the importance of developing a business plan and seeking professional advice when setting up your own business.** A business plan is a summary of expectations from a business effort, including the level of income, benefits, mid- and long-term goals, and investment. Without a business plan, activities are likely to lack direction, decreasing the chances for success. Developing a business plan helps the business owner to keep clear objectives in mind and to set effective priorities. It is extremely important to invest in the services of an attorney who specializes in the travel industry and small businesses in order to obtain advice about legal issues and to check the wording of contracts, insurance policies, and other documents. An accountant who specializes in setting up small businesses or travel agencies can provide valuable information and advice about setting up the books and tax reporting.

3. **Identify the issues that should be considered when selecting a host agency or suppliers.** To determine if a host agency is a good match for your business, you should consider the host agency's specialization and preferred

supplier agreements; training offered; the specific types of support that the host agency will provide, such as GDS access and technical support; its experience working with independent agents; references from the industry, clients, and other independents; the professionalism and compatibility of the suppliers. Choose suppliers that you know and trust, and focus on suppliers within your areas of specialization.

4. **Describe how home-based agents can differentiate their services and grow their businesses.** Like other travel businesses, home-based agents should develop a marketing plan in order to determine how they will differentiate their business. Many travel businesses today are emphasizing customer relationship marketing and customer relationship management, using technology in order to provide customized, personalized marketing and service and to build lasting relationships with clients. Home-based agents are often in a better position than many large companies to achieve this marriage of technology and personalized service. Managing the relationships that you have built with your customers is essential to the success and growth of your business.

KEY TERMS

A list of key terms introduced in this chapter follows. If you do not recall the meaning of these terms, see the Glossary.

business plan	independent contractor
cloud	social media
CCRA	telecommute
errors and omissions and general liability insurance	Verified Travel Consultant (VTC)

REVIEW QUESTIONS

1. What actions can home-based agents take to project a professional image of their company of one?

2. Outline the steps to take when establishing an online presence.

3. What industry organizations are especially helpful to home-based agents, and what type of services do they provide?

4. Why must sellers of travel acquire an identification number that is recognized by suppliers? Describe the numbering systems available to independent contractors.

Finding Employment

If you have completed a travel program, are pleasant with people, and are willing to work hard, the travel/tourism industry needs you! Nevertheless, finding the position you want may require skill and effort. Both those who are new to the employment market and those who are changing careers and entering the travel/tourism industry for the first time will probably begin with an entry-level position. Our focus in this chapter is on how to obtain one of those positions; jobs further up the career ladder are discussed in Chapter 16.

Preparing for the Employment Search

■ WHAT STEPS SHOULD YOU TAKE TO PREPARE FOR YOUR EMPLOYMENT HUNT?

■ WHAT SHOULD YOUR PORTFOLIO AND RÉSUMÉ INCLUDE?

■ HOW CAN YOU FIND POSSIBLE OPENINGS?

In the years before the popularity of the Internet, newspapers advertised travel/tourism positions extensively, as did industry magazines and special employment agencies dedicated to this segment of the work force. That is not the case today. Now most entry-level employment opportunities are found by a concerted effort on the part of the seeker. This includes a variety of methods, such as networking, researching extensively about potential companies, applying cold to companies of interest, or being an intern.

No two people and no two positions are precisely the same; neither are any two searches. Still, following certain steps can increase your chances of success, no matter what position you are looking for. A first step is to prepare yourself for the search by clarifying your goals and possibilities. What types of positions exist, what type of position do you want, and what are your strengths as a potential employee?

Evaluating the Possibilities

In previous chapters, we described many different positions in the industry; Table 1.1 listed more than 60. You probably meet the requirements described for many of these positions. One way to sort through the possibilities is to classify them into three types: (1) nonpersonal phone work, (2) personal intermediary of services, and (3) in-person supplier of services. Almost all positions that handle reservations fall into the first category, nonpersonal phone work. These jobs are not *impersonal*; you are expected to be friendly and personable. But they are *nonpersonal* because you will probably never talk to the same person twice. You are trained to sell and reserve a particular hotel, airline, car rental, cruise line, or tour. You hang up and, seconds later, take your next call. Your employer monitors how pleasantly you treat callers, how accurately you give them information, and how often you sell your company's product. When you take off your phone headset and walk out the door each day, you can usually forget about the job until the next day. On the other hand, you do not get the satisfaction of seeing a person's travel through to the end or of developing relationships with clients. Some people find that the work becomes repetitive and the pressure fierce.

The second category—personal intermediary—includes almost all jobs in travel agencies as well as many positions as representatives of suppliers. In these jobs, no two days are alike. You are expected to develop and maintain a personal rapport with clients. You are personally responsible for creating and keeping repeat customers. You gain satisfaction from meeting your clients' needs, but you are likely to feel that the job never ends. Tasks are extremely varied. You must be able to organize your work and assign priorities.

The third category—in-person supplier—refers to the people who deal with travelers while they are traveling. Flight attendants, airport ticket agents, tour guides, cruise activity leaders, and front desk personnel at hotels are examples. You deal with clients face-to-face. You are on your feet, perhaps on the move, throughout the day. Most of these jobs take a lot of energy. They are ideal for people who do not want to stay behind a desk, who want to be out in public, and who enjoy dealing with people in person.

Whatever type of employment suits you, particular companies and specific positions offer varying advantages and disadvantages. One might offer a nice starting salary but little chance of advancement; another might provide challenging responsibilities but a tense work environment. What is most important to you?

- *Think experience.* You might view your first year on the job as a paid internship. You may wish to take whatever position becomes available in order to gain experience.
- *Think career.* If you view this first position as a stepping-stone, the opportunities for advancement may be the most important characteristic to evaluate.

- *Think salary.* If you expect to remain in the same position for several years, consider its earnings potential. Is the pay at the prospective employer equivalent to that at similar companies?
- *Think benefits.* Both tangible and intangible benefits may be much more important than an extra dollar or two an hour. Tangible benefits might include travel, vacation pay, health insurance, profit sharing, and so on. Intangible benefits may be even more important. Does the atmosphere of the company match your style? Will you be comfortable there? What type of training will you be given? It is usually better to take a position with a company that has a specific training program than one that trains haphazardly or expects you to learn on the job. Large companies probably have a formal training program whereas small retail agencies may not.
- *Think location.* Travel agencies and hotels are located almost everywhere, and most small towns are within reach of an airport that may need personnel. Also, cars are rented at all airports and in many towns without airports. Small, receptive tour companies may be located in any area that receives tourists. But large reservations offices, often referred to as **call centers**, are located only in certain cities. Unless you are willing to relocate, your choices and your chances for advancement might be somewhat limited by location.

As you research, you'll find that, while there is still opportunity for employment in this huge travel/tourism industry, there may not be the openings you'd like as a travel counselor in a retail travel agency. You'll need to look at the industry as a whole and, perhaps, get an introductory position in

---

CLOSE-UP: ON THE JOB WITH MEGAN MATTHEWS, TRAVEL AGENCY INTERN

Megan Matthews spent a year and a half at a four-year college and then switched to a travel school. Her friendly attitude, excellent grades, and ambition resulted in her immediate hiring after graduation. She chose a medium-size agency that is increasing its emphasis on leisure travel.

"I learned a lot in travel school. After the first week, I realized I had an awful lot more to learn, but now after three months I feel I'm making great progress. Luckily, my manager helps me and answers a million questions even when she is busy. When she isn't very busy, she leads me through the steps so I can find the answer myself.

"I'm called an 'intern' right now. Let me explain because there are two kinds of interns. The first is a person who is still in school and is sent for some on-the-job training (usually unpaid) at a travel company. At our agency 'intern' is what they call a new agent for the first six months. After that, we're expected to be 'productive agents,' which, at first, means making enough sales to at least pay our salary.

"The agency's job description for new agents includes greeting walk-ins, answering the phones, steering clients to the travel counselors they want to talk to, answering simple questions, sorting all the mail, and doing the filing. For me, the manager has added working on a website. She mainly wants to see if we can develop inbound business from

overseas to our area but also wants something for current clients to look at.

"When the agents get very busy, I also research prices at hotels or for cruises by making calls or checking online. I've had to run to the office supply store, and I've delivered documents with the owner's car. Actually, I enjoyed getting out of the office and doing that.

"I canvass my family and friends on trips they might take. I don't really do it to get their business, although that's a good possibility, but so I can practice. I search out the best fares and schedules and then call and give them the information. They've had some questions, so I researched further. When I get new clients, I'll be ready for them.

"The agency is going to have me work particularly on Vegas packages and Disney World when I take clients because I've been to both. So, I've been studying the brochures and seeing what other counselors book for clients. It's amazing what you learn just by hearing experienced counselors talk to clients.

"Soon I'll be doing trips all over the United States and then North America. And the rest of the world had better look out after that because here I come."

one of the other sectors, such as at a hotel or a tour operator, for example. Then with a year or so of work experience, it's possible to move on from there. Any sector of the broader tourism industry is a good starting point.

Begin planning your job search while you're still taking travel classes; don't wait until that magical moment when you receive your graduation certificate. And be sure to appraise yourself realistically. You may find you'll have to forgo certain employment possibilities if your life does not permit you to relocate to another city, work irregular hours, get by the first year on minimum wage, or perhaps drive to and from the airport in the middle of the night.

Assessing Yourself

If you do not recognize all your positive qualities, you obviously cannot present them to a potential employer. Here is one way to conduct a self-assessment that will allow you to present yourself in the most favorable way.

Take out some paper or start typing a list of your qualifications and qualities, including

- Skills (for example, being able to book PNRs (passenger name records) in a GDS, build websites, speak another language, or figure out complex airfares).
- Destination knowledge (maybe you know a lot about the major Caribbean islands and their highlights).
- Talents (ballroom dancing, a memory for names and faces, leadership ability—everything counts).
- Interests (outdoor sports, the arts).
- Personal preferences (working together with a team, having a lot of variety in your work).
- Accomplishments (receiving a perfect attendance award, being recognized for charitable work).
- Personal travel, if any (including domestic and international).

List as many of your qualities and qualifications as you can and then set the list aside. If additional entries come to you, jot them down. After a few days, reexamine your lists. Can you add to them? Check the curriculum of your travel program. Have you listed all the areas you mastered and skills you developed during the program? Talk to your friends and relatives to determine whether you have overlooked any qualities and qualifications. Now read over your lists. As you go about your job search, remember all you have to offer.

Most likely, you will also think about negative qualities as you do this exercise. Perhaps you have few contacts, you lack self-confidence, or you tend to ignore other people's opinions. Think about how you can either overcome these drawbacks or transform them into positive characteristics. Write down a plan for doing so and follow it. Do not dwell on your shortcomings; everybody has some. Some may be fairly easy to overcome (such as lack of contacts); others may take longer. In the meantime, think about your positive qualities.

Developing a Portfolio

To be ready for any situation in your job search, prepare a complete portfolio. Every component of the portfolio should be available in both print and electronic form. It should include

- The original of your *résumé*, which is a summary of your qualifications and work experience.
- The original of a list of personal, educational, and professional references.

- Diplomas from all schools attended.
- The final transcript from the last school you attended—if you had good grades.
- Any special certificates or awards.
- Samples of your work, such as itineraries, school projects, or tests.
- Two or three extra copies of your résumé and list of references.

Everyone needs a good résumé. Although résumés do not by themselves win jobs, a poor one will usually eliminate you from consideration. The goal of the résumé is to gain an interview and then to serve as a convenient summary.

Figures 15.1 and 15.2 show sample résumés. Notice that their formats are

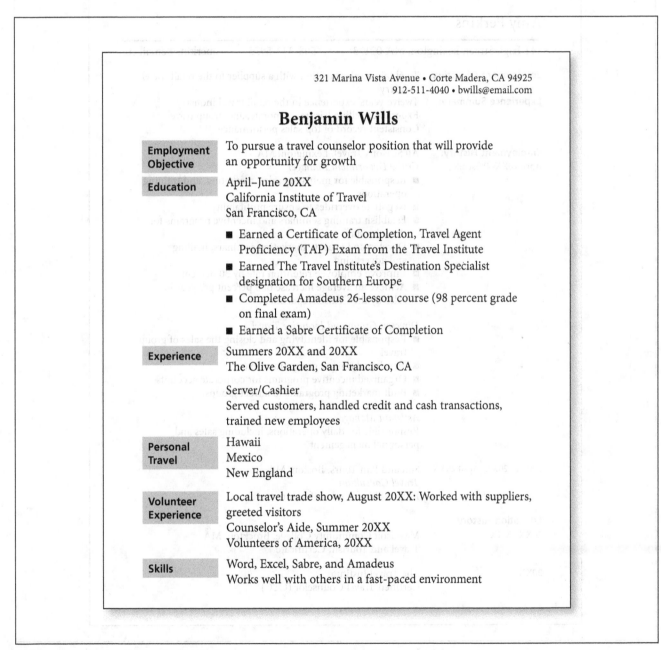

321 Marina Vista Avenue • Corte Madera, CA 94925
912-511-4040 • bwills@email.com

Benjamin Wills

Employment Objective
To pursue a travel counselor position that will provide an opportunity for growth

Education
April–June 20XX
California Institute of Travel
San Francisco, CA

- Earned a Certificate of Completion, Travel Agent Proficiency (TAP) Exam from the Travel Institute
- Earned The Travel Institute's Destination Specialist designation for Southern Europe
- Completed Amadeus 26-lesson course (98 percent grade on final exam)
- Earned a Sabre Certificate of Completion

Experience
Summers 20XX and 20XX
The Olive Garden, San Francisco, CA

Server/Cashier
Served customers, handled credit and cash transactions, trained new employees

Personal Travel
Hawaii
Mexico
New England

Volunteer Experience
Local travel trade show, August 20XX: Worked with suppliers, greeted visitors
Counselor's Aide, Summer 20XX
Volunteers of America, 20XX

Skills
Word, Excel, Sabre, and Amadeus
Works well with others in a fast-paced environment

FIGURE 15.1 A Sample Résumé

This sample résumé is for a candidate with no previous experience in the travel industry; therefore, he elected to describe his travel education first. Another option if you have no experience is to emphasize your skills.

slightly different: Each résumé is structured to highlight different points. Similarly, you should adjust your résumé so that the emphasis suits the positions you are applying for. If you are applying for diverse positions or in different types of companies, you should prepare more than one résumé. Store them on your computer and customize for each company you apply to.

Amy Perkins

111 High Street, Lexington, MA 02173   508-332-5955   aperkins@email.com

Employment Objective:	To obtain a sales position with a supplier to the retail travel industry
Experience Summary:	Twelve years' experience in the retail travel industry Experience selling leisure, corporate, and group travel Consistent record of top sales performance

Employment History:
April 20XX–Present

All Seasons Travel, Lexington, MA
Cruise Department Manager
- Responsible for managing sales, marketing, and training operations
- Negotiate overrides to ensure profitability
- Establish training seminars and incentive programs for the sales staff
- Develop and execute marketing seminars, mailings, and advertising
- Improve employee retention rate by 30 percent
- Achieve an average increase of 5 percent per year in sales by the Cruise Department

Director, Group and Incentive Travel
- Responsible for identifying and closing the sales of group travel
- Developed unique group travel events
- Organized incentive programs for corporate accounts
- Built marketing programs to attract groups

Assistant Manager
Responsible for daily operations, including sales and personnel management

January 20XX–April 20XX

Sun and Fun Tours, Boston, MA
Travel Consultant
Responsible for sales of leisure travel

Education History:
20XX–20XX

Massasoit Community College, Brockton, MA
Travel and Tourism Certificate

20XX

The Travel Institute
Certified Travel Counselor (CTC)

FIGURE 15.2 A Sample Résumé

This sample résumé is for a candidate who has worked for two travel companies. Notice that she featured her experience and accomplishments in these jobs and placed her schooling at the end of the résumé.

Guidelines for Résumés. Many résumés are only one page. However, if you have extensive relevant experience, a two-page résumé is acceptable It might follow a conventional structure such as the following:

- *Employment objective.* Keep your statement of the objective somewhat general so you do not limit your possibilities.
- *Work experience.* For each job you have held, gather the following information: beginning and ending dates of employment, company name, complete address and phone number, job title, and short description of your duties. List the positions in reverse chronological order, putting your latest job first. Remember, customer service is paramount for most travel jobs. If you have experience dealing with the public, emphasize it. To some employers, experience waiting on customers at Burger King might be the most meaningful item on a résumé. Do *not* list every short-term job you have held since childhood.
- *Education and specialized training.* List the names and complete addresses of schools, dates attended, degree or diploma received or credits earned, honors, and awards. Also list specialized training, such as computer classes, GDS training, destination seminars, certifications from The Travel Institute [TAP, CTA, CTC, CTIE] and travel suppliers, certificates of completion from Sabre or other GDS courses, and language courses. If you are finishing travel school and have little work experience, you might list your educational background before your work experience.
- *Skills and accomplishments.* List your skills. Use descriptive, active words, and list accomplishments that apply those skills. Emphasize the most valuable areas of your experience and be specific. For example, "Managed seven-person team at Burger King for eight months. Absenteeism was 30 percent lower than the average team. Was offered position of day manager." Quantify accomplishments whenever possible. Also include any volunteer work.
- *Personal travel.* Extensive travel to other countries should be noted, especially for jobs with travel agencies.

Usually, a line stating that references are available is no longer included on résumés, nor are the actual references listed on the résumé itself. Employers assume you will produce a separate list of references when requested. Prepare a list of work, educational, and personal references on a separate page. Make sure each person listed has agreed to be a reference and knows he or she may be called. Include telephone numbers and e-mail addresses.

To make an effective presentation in the résumé, use short paragraphs. Avoid exaggerated claims, unnecessary information, repetition, jargon, slang, and abbreviations.

The appearance of the résumé matters, too. Use wide margins. Avoid gimmicks, such as unusual paper or fancy lettering, but highlight the most important points by using bullets, underlining, or bold print. Finally, have someone else proofread your final copy and be sure to use spell-check.

Preparing a Digital Résumé. Many employers require an online application and a digital résumé. They often will have a **résumé builder** on their websites, in which each user fills in the blanks with contact information, skills, experience, and so on. Employers might ask you to upload a copy of your résumé and cover letter. Or, they might ask you to e-mail your documents. If you use e-mail, the cover letter should constitute the body of the e-mail, not be attached separately. You should even include your résumé in the body of the e-mail unless you have received permission to send the résumé as an attachment and have verified that the recipient can open it. Many companies have strict policies against opening attachments from unknown senders.

Finding Current Openings

Most job openings are offered by employers to people they know, people who are recommended to them, or people who contact them directly. If any of your friends or relatives know someone in the travel industry, they may be able to help you. Try *networking*—using personal contacts to make business contacts and to advance in the business world.

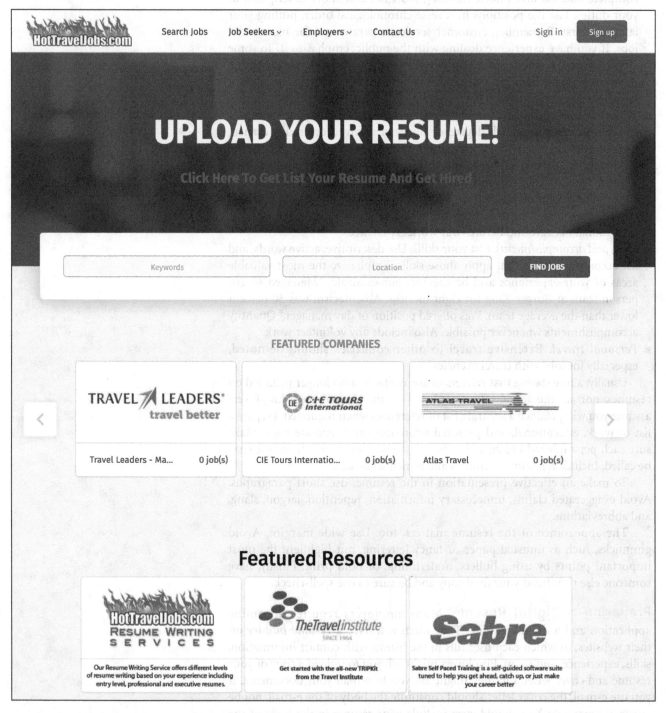

FIGURE 15.3 Submitting Digital Résumés

Job listing sites like HotTravelJobs.com allow applicants to submit digital résumés for multiple open positions.

If you are professional in your approach to school or your current job, then your instructors, employers, fellow students, or coworkers will be able to help you make contacts. Your classmates are your first network. As each classmate finds a job, that person becomes a contact for the others and can provide information about what is happening in his or her company. Also, your travel instructors have a multitude of contacts in the industry.

The placement department of your educational institution may help you find a job, but do not depend on it alone. The department may be helping a hundred other students. Once the placement department gives you information, follow up on it and let the placement people know the result.

Also consider any guest speakers in your classes. Did any of them impress you? Did they tell the class to contact them? If they passed out business cards, they are inviting you to keep in touch. Call and reintroduce yourself.

Use information interviews to develop your network. An *information interview* is one in which you are seeking knowledge about an industry or company. It should not be a disguised attempt to get a job. Many of these interviews do bring job offers or information about job openings, but never bring up the subject first. Many people will be gracious in giving you their time.

The larger the company, the more likely a phone call is the way to get started in the right direction, but many travel agencies and tour operators are small entities. Often a personal visit is your best chance to make an impression. Many jobs are obtained by people who just show up at an office with their résumé and ask to fill out an application. Timing and luck are important. Treat the visit just as you would an interview; it may turn out to be one. Dress professionally. Do not take it personally if people do not have time to talk with you. Ask for the name of the person to contact by phone or mail.

Also, call employment agencies and ask if they handle travel positions. Describe clearly the type of positions you are looking for, and do not be steered into others. Employment agencies that specialize in the travel/tourism industry usually concentrate on finding experienced superstars or in filling higher management positions, but these people may have some of the best contacts in the industry. Private employment agencies earn money only when an applicant is hired. Make sure that the company, not you, pays the fee. Temp agencies that may send you to work in a company temporarily are, at times, a good way to get your foot in the door.

Check online. A large percentage of all employers now use the Internet for job posting and recruiting. Many companies have employment information on their websites. Often the sites list available positions, describe how to apply, and say where to send a résumé or application. Also check popular job-listing sites (such as Monster.com and Indeed.com) as well as online employment services that specialize in travel (such as HotTravelJobs.com and Travel Placement Service at TravelPlacement.com) and the Job Search area on the website of the **International Council on Hotel, Restaurant, and Institutional Education (CHRIE)**. See Figure 15.3. Most positions listed by online services require experience, but, by reviewing them, you can learn what employers are looking for and can pick up the general tenor of the business and the jargon that is used.

Many online services will help you create an e-résumé that includes searchable keywords and will send your résumé to potential employers—for a fee. At ASTA's Job Board, job seekers register online, and an advanced matching engine automatically notifies them every time a new job is posted that fits their skills and experience. Also, applicants can give permission for employers to search their résumés.

Other sources of information about job openings include libraries and state employment services. The listings at state employment services cover only a fraction of job openings, but job counselors may give you fresh ideas. In some places, these services offer classes on interviewing and résumé preparation, job-search libraries, or computerized job listings.

✔ CHECK-UP

Three types of positions in the travel industry are
✔ Nonpersonal phone work.
✔ Personal intermediary.
✔ In-person supplier.

Qualities and qualifications to consider in a self-assessment include
✔ Skills.
✔ Knowledge.
✔ Talents.
✔ Interests.
✔ Personal preferences.
✔ Accomplishments.

Applying for a Position

■ WHAT CAN YOU DO TO INCREASE THE CHANCES THAT YOUR APPLICATION FOR A JOB WILL SUCCEED?

If you are reading this book, we assume that you like travel and that you like working with people; these are two essentials for getting a job in the travel/tourism industry. As we discussed in Chapter 1, for an entry-level position you also need an ability to speak and write clearly, to handle basic math, and to learn. Beyond these fundamental ingredients, what makes a successful candidate for a travel job?

Employers look for (1) intangible qualities, such as personality, attitude, and friendliness; (2) experience; and (3) travel education. Although most employers prefer someone with experience, they know that people with education and intangible qualities will turn into top-notch performers quickly. People who have all three characteristics have the best chances. Throughout the job application process, highlight your strengths in these three areas, beginning with your cover letter.

The Cover Letter

If you hear about a job opening that interests you, respond with your résumé and a *cover letter*, which is a letter of introduction that accompanies a résumé and is designed to obtain an interview or an application form. And because many openings are not posted, approach companies cold anyway with a cover letter. A good cover letter creates a positive impression and makes a prospective employer want to talk to you. It not only describes your talents but also says how they will benefit the company. The more you can customize your letter to a specific company and to a specific person, the better the chance that your letter will stand out.

To create a successful cover letter, follow the guidelines for business letters described in Chapter 12. Keep the sentences, paragraphs, and letter short.

Proofread carefully. The following structure is usually effective:

- In the first paragraph, state the position you are seeking and where you saw the ad; Figure 15.4 shows an example. If you know anything about the company, use that knowledge to describe why you would like to work there.
- In the second paragraph, refer to your enclosed résumé. Do not repeat the information in the résumé, but you can explain, elaborate, or supplement that information. If applicable, explain how you meet all the requirements mentioned in the ad. Present evidence to support your claim.
- In the third paragraph, point out some job-related personal qualities and accomplishments. Be positive but not cocky.

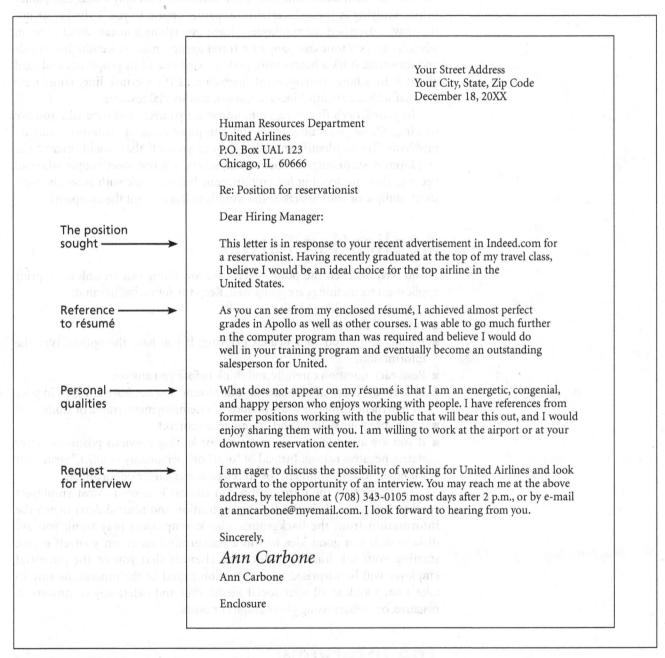

The position sought

Reference to résumé

Personal qualities

Request for interview

Your Street Address
Your City, State, Zip Code
December 18, 20XX

Human Resources Department
United Airlines
P.O. Box UAL 123
Chicago, IL 60666

Re: Position for reservationist

Dear Hiring Manager:

This letter is in response to your recent advertisement in Indeed.com for a reservationist. Having recently graduated at the top of my travel class, I believe I would be an ideal choice for the top airline in the United States.

As you can see from my enclosed résumé, I achieved almost perfect grades in Apollo as well as other courses. I was able to go much further n the computer program than was required and believe I would do well in your training program and eventually become an outstanding salesperson for United.

What does not appear on my résumé is that I am an energetic, congenial, and happy person who enjoys working with people. I have references from former positions working with the public that will bear this out, and I would enjoy sharing them with you. I am willing to work at the airport or at your downtown reservation center.

I am eager to discuss the possibility of working for United Airlines and look forward to the opportunity of an interview. You may reach me at the above address, by telephone at (708) 343-0105 most days after 2 p.m., or by e-mail at anncarbone@myemail.com. I look forward to hearing from you.

Sincerely,

Ann Carbone

Ann Carbone

Enclosure

FIGURE 15.4 A Sample Cover Letter

This job candidate has a lot of good things to say, but notice that she gets to the point of the letter and also sells herself in the first two sentences, in case the personnel manager does not have time to read a four-paragraph cover letter.

- If the position was advertised and the ad asked for a salary history, use the fourth paragraph to meet this request. Give a salary range that you believe overlaps the company's range. Keep your comments about salary general. Note that an acceptable salary is negotiable, and avoid stating exactly what you currently earn.
- In your final paragraph, ask for an interview and give your e-mail and telephone number. Close with a positive statement that encourages a response.

Send a résumé to a company even though you do not know whether it has any job openings. In this case, the résumé should be accompanied by a type of cover letter called an **application letter** or *unsolicited cover letter*. Take the time to learn something about the company. Carefully assess companies before applying to them. If certain companies appeal to you, (whether or not they have advertised for employees), learn everything you can about them in advance. If it's a tour company or a travel agency, read its website backwards and forwards. If it's a hotel chain, perhaps visit one of its properties and read about it in a hotel management magazine. If it's a cruise line, familiarize yourself with its various itineraries, ships, and special features.

In your letter's first paragraph, introduce yourself and state why you are writing. Show you know what the company does, its interests, and its problems. Try to identify something about yourself that would interest the employer. A surprising number of employers will not meet people who call because they are looking for employment but will talk with someone who seems unique or who has taken the trouble to learn about the company.

Application Forms

If you have reached the point where you are filling out an online or print application form, things are going well. Keep the following in mind:
- Don't leave anything blank.
- Follow all directions.
- Use black ink and your neatest printing. If you have the option, type the information.
- Read each question carefully and think before you answer.
- Be sure the information matches your résumé. Do not leave any gaps in your employment history. Include periods of unemployment, travel, or study.
- Make sure your spelling and grammar are correct.
- If you are asked to state your reason for leaving previous positions, never state a negative reason. Instead of "quit" or "personality conflict," write "left for better job environment" or "received better career opportunity."

Take care that the information you submit is correct. Most employers conduct background checks. If your application and résumé don't match the information from the background check, employers may think you are dishonest. It is a good idea to run a background check on yourself before starting your job hunt to reduce the chances that you or the potential employer will be surprised by information found in the process. Be sure to take a hard look at all your social media sites and delete any controversial, negative, or embarrassing photographs or posts.

The Interview

On average, it costs thousands of dollars in time and training to bring a new person into the staff of a travel company. An interview represents your best opportunity to show that you are worth that investment. You should be selling your abilities to the employer, showing that you are the ideal solution to the employer's problem (needing a good employee). Put your best foot forward, showing your strong points honestly. Dishonesty or even insincerity is likely to backfire.

Preparing for an Interview. Sometimes an employer calls to arrange the interview; sometimes an employer writes and asks the job applicant to call to arrange it. This initial phone contact might be used to screen applicants. In fact, whenever you talk with a representative of the company, be prepared for a mini-interview. Have your résumé handy and be prepared to answer questions. Be as professional as possible. Eliminate all background noise and give the person on the phone your undivided attention. Use your best phone manners and English, have a pen and paper ready, and do not hesitate to ask questions or directions.

Before the interview, be sure you find out its exact time, the name and title of the interviewer, and the name and address of the company. Prepare thoroughly. In particular,

- If you are unsure of the company's location, go there the day before, if possible.
- If you live far from the company, be prepared to say how you would get to the job. Do not allow a potential problem to eliminate you from consideration.
- Learn everything you can about the company (its brochures, destinations, properties, ships, price points, and itineraries, for example). Check its website and read about it in trade publications.
- Be prepared to take tests.
- Prepare any questions you may wish to ask.
- Be prepared to answer all questions.

"Tell me about yourself." "What is it about this position that interests you?" "What do you expect from the company you work for?" "Why should I hire you rather than someone else?" These are all *open-ended questions* frequently asked by interviewers; Table 15.1 lists others. Be ready to take advantage of the opportunity that open-ended questions present. Before the interview, plan key points that you want to get across about yourself. If you are applying to a European air consolidator, for example, be ready to emphasize your knowledge of major European airports. Prepare examples to prove your points.

You might prepare further by becoming a beginning expert in some niche in the market. Keep current by reading the trade publications of whatever field you are most interested in. Or come to the interview with a list of possible prospects, including any organizations you belong to that might have potential clients. Employers love to hear how you are going to help sell their products and services.

Like an athlete getting ready for a game, you should prepare for an interview and then relax. Look at the interview as a conversation and an opportunity to learn about the company and for the company to learn about you. The least that can happen is that you make a contact and find out more about your future.

Avoiding Elimination. When there are many candidates for a position, the interviewer's first task is not to choose the best person but to narrow the field. The best person may be eliminated because of a crucial early mistake. The following guidelines will help you avoid that fate:

- Be on time. In fact, be 10 minutes early.
- Call if you are going to be late or if you cannot report for the interview. You should have a very good explanation, but be aware that this may eliminate you anyway.

ON THE SPOT

Jason Jackson is a recent graduate with little work experience and none in travel. He is attending a group interview for positions at Sea Gull Airlines. When the interviewer calls out his name, she asks, "I notice you have no experience in this type of position. Why should we hire you over someone with experience?"

Jason might answer, "First, I believe I can be productive very quickly, and I will be committed to doing so. If you look at my school records and recommendations, I think you'll see that I've always done so in the past. Our instructors emphasized the importance of enthusiasm and love of what you're doing, and I certainly have those. After all, everyone must start somewhere without experience. Second, because I have no travel experience, I have no baggage or bad habits you would have to undo or deprogram. Travel is going to be my career, and I am going to give my all to the company that helps me get started. I hope that's Sea Gull Airlines."

Note that Jason never would have been invited to the interview if the airline wasn't ready to hire beginners. What's most important here is not the answer itself but how Jason handles the question and if he is prepared for the interview. A good candidate will be ready to pounce on an open-ended question like this one.

- Dress appropriately. Regardless of the style of dress in the office, dress professionally and conservatively for the interview.
- Go to the interview by yourself.
- Smile, be friendly and be polite. Assume that you are being observed from the time you enter the parking lot until the time you leave. Many interviewers will ask receptionists or others their impression of a candidate.
- Fill out forms neatly and completely.
- Greet the interviewer, introduce yourself, and offer a firm handshake. Do not sit down until you are offered a seat or until the interviewer sits down.
- Have good posture and positive body language.
- Be enthusiastic and ask pertinent questions.
- Speak clearly and correctly.
- Stress your sales ability, even if in a different field.
- Don't immediately ask what benefits exist.
- If applying to a retail travel agency, perhaps mention the possibility of your bringing a personal following of clients to the agency.
- Don't schedule yourself too closely. If the interviewer would like you to stay a bit and meet some of the key people, you don't want to refuse because you have another appointment or a baby-sitter waiting.
- Bring your portfolio with you and present it.
- Bring extra copies of your résumé and references.
- Ask for the interviewer's business card at the end of the interview. Thank the interviewer and the receptionist.

You may be asked to participate in a remote or video interview. The same guidelines apply.

Remember that the company is not looking to spend thousands of dollars on someone who will soon quit. Emphasize your commitment to a travel/ tourism career. Whatever you do, be confident.

TABLE 15.1 Frequently Asked Interview Questions

Topic	Example
Previous work experience	Why did you leave your previous job?
	What did you dislike about your boss?
	How did you deal with the pressure?
	What did you like about your job? Dislike?
Education and interest	What did you like most in your travel program?
	What course gave you the most difficulty?
	Will you be taking other courses?
	Do you have any certifications?
	What do you do in your free time?
	Do you have a hobby?
	How do you think your education prepared you for this job?
	What leadership roles have you held?
	Where have you traveled?
Work style and preferences	How do you feel about overtime?
	Do you like working alone?
	How well do you work with a team?
	What kind of supervisor do you prefer?
Personality	What five words best describe you?
	What are your strong points? Weak points?
	What do you see yourself doing five years from now?

Selling Yourself. If you are applying for a position that involves meeting and serving the public, the impression you make on the interviewer amounts to a test of how well you would perform on the job. A successful interview should be a pleasant experience for both you and the interviewer.

Whatever the position you are applying for, the interview resembles a sales situation. In fact, you may be asked to participate in a mock sales call. Much as a salesperson needs to develop rapport with clients and understand their needs, you should put yourself in the interviewer's shoes and ask yourself what is important to the company. Focus on issues that are relevant to the company and to the job opening. Show that you understand today's business environment and the challenges it poses to the company. Be positive about the working environment.

Also, be prepared to turn any of your liabilities into positive characteristics or at least to neutralize them. Do not bring them up unless the interviewer does or unless they are obvious. Younger people emphasize their energy; older people emphasize their experience.

Illegal Pre-employment Questions. It is illegal for an employer to ask certain questions of a job applicant. Unless employers can demonstrate that applicants' ability to perform a job depends on the answer, employers are not legally allowed to ask about gender, race, religion, marital status, number of children, disability, or current economic status. They may ask if you have been convicted of a crime or if there are felony charges pending against you—but not about an arrest record. Legally, you may be asked if you are a citizen of the United States—but not whether you (or your parents or spouse) are a naturalized or native-born citizen. And you may not be asked what country you are a citizen of. The employer is allowed to ask about your age only to determine whether you are old enough to work legally.

Of course, pointing out that a question is illegal is not likely to help your chances of being hired. (Reporting an employer to the authorities won't put you on the top of the candidate list either, but it may help future job seekers.) You might try to address the concern of the question without answering it directly. For instance, if an interviewer asks the illegal question, "Do you have plans to raise a family?" the interviewer's concern is whether you will stay with the company. A response that affirms your commitment to the position would probably satisfy the interviewer.

Asking Questions. An interviewer expects an intelligent applicant to ask questions. For example, unless the topics have already been covered, it would be appropriate for you to ask

- What are the daily responsibilities of the position?
- What is the most important responsibility?
- What is a typical day like?
- What qualities are you looking for in the person who fills this position?
- Is training provided?
- To whom would I report?
- With whom would I be working?
- Are there advancement opportunities?
- What other skills are required?
- When can I expect to hear from you regarding the position?
- What is the next step in the process?

If you have traveled extensively, you are at an advantage. And if you find that the company has a large program to a specific area, Mexico, for example, be sure to emphasize that you know Mexico well and feel you would be able to sell it well—both its wonderful seaside resorts and its historic Aztec and Mayan sites. And being bilingual is a definite plus!

Questions regarding salary, benefits, travel opportunities, and so on should wait until the second interview or the job offer.

Interviewing is a two-way street. You will be evaluating the company as much as it is assessing you. Are you and the company a good fit? Can you picture yourself working here? Would you enjoy doing the work the employees do?

Following Up. As soon as the interview is over, take time to send a brief thank-you letter to the person who interviewed you, as well as to anyone who referred you or paved the way for the interview. Be prepared for additional interviews with different people. If you have not received feedback from an interview after approximately 10 days, you may write an e-mail or call to ask about the status of the position.

Lastly, do not become discouraged if you do not obtain the exact job of your dreams for starters. Broaden your field and consider applying in affiliated fields, not just travel agencies and tour companies. A year or two of experience working in the hotel/restaurant field or at a car rental company is excellent experience for starting your career and then perhaps transferring laterally into your first choice.

Group Interviews

Many airlines and other large companies like to give group interviews. You should prepare for a group interview as you would for a one-on-one interview. Keep in mind that the interviewer may be watching how you react throughout the session. The interviewer wants to see if you are friendly and interact well with others.

The interview may offer several opportunities for you to ensure that you will be remembered. Plan a statement introducing yourself that indicates why you would be an effective employee and that shows you know something about the company. There is a good chance the interviewer will ask for volunteers to answer the first questions. Those who are ready will be remembered for their initiative. Sometimes the interviewer asks applicants to sell something to the group; how you handle yourself is usually more important than what you say. Even asking for the interviewer's card at the end of the session or having an excellent question may earn you a place in the interviewer's memory.

Remember that the interviewer is not only looking for outstanding candidates but also eliminating people from consideration. First impressions count, and negative ones will disqualify a candidate. Do not do anything to eliminate yourself. Your goal is to get to the second interview, which will be one in which your chances for success are good.

CHAPTER WRAP-UP

CHAPTER HIGHLIGHTS

Résumés, cover letters, and interviews all represent opportunities for you to introduce yourself to prospective employers. How to take these and other steps in a way that will lead to an entry-level job was the focus of this chapter. Here is a review of the objectives with which we began the chapter.

1. **Design a plan for your employment search.** Begin with an evaluation of the type of position you are looking for and of your own strengths. The creation of a portfolio and a hunt for job openings are logical next steps, followed by preparation of a cover letter or application letter. Eventually, these steps should lead to an interview.

2. **Describe the items to include in a job-seeking portfolio and in a résumé.** A résumé, a list of references, school diplomas, transcripts, certificates or awards, and samples of work make up a portfolio. Each component should be prepared in both print and electronic form; many employers require that applications and résumés be submitted electronically. Traditional and e-résumés follow the same structure. Career objective, work experience, education, skills, and accomplishments are the key features of a good résumé. The best order depends on the specific position, the type of company, and the applicant.

3. **Identify at least six sources of information about job openings.** Networking is one of the most productive sources. Online ads, a school's placement office, information interviews, employment agencies, state employment services, and online services, such as the one sponsored by ASTA, also provide information about openings. In addition, positions may be discovered by searching online for the names of companies and then phoning or visiting them.

4. **Discuss at least three keys to a successful job interview.** Preparation is one key. It should include learning about the company, going over sample questions, and planning key points to convey. Courteous, professional behavior (such as being on time and dressing appropriately) is another key to success; it is needed to avoid early elimination from consideration. During the interview, it is important to be confident, to focus on issues that matter to the interviewer, to emphasize one's strengths, and to ask intelligent questions. And every interviewer should be acknowledged with a thank-you letter.

KEY TERMS

A list of key terms introduced in this chapter follows. If you do not recall the meaning of these terms, see the Glossary.

application letter
call center
cover letter
International Council on Hotel, Restaurant,
    and Institutional Education (CHRIE)

networking
résumé

REVIEW QUESTIONS

1. Name three characteristics you would consider in evaluating a potential employer.

2. Describe how you are going to overcome or transform one of your weaknesses as a potential employee.

3. What are four parts of an effective cover letter?

4. List four behaviors at an interview that might eliminate an applicant from serious consideration.

5. Outline steps you would take to use the Internet in your employment search.

CHAPTER 16

Building a Career

OBJECTIVES

After completing this chapter, you should be able to

1. Suggest at least four ways to ensure success in a new job and four steps to take to prepare for advancement.

2. Outline a path for advancing in a travel/tourism career.

3. Identify at least four ethical responsibilities of travel professionals.

4. Describe how to develop your skills and knowledge as a travel professional.

Your first day on the job will be the first day of the rest of your career. Where will you go from there? This chapter suggests some destinations and directions. After discussing how to meet the challenges of a new job, we examine how to build a successful career in the travel/tourism industry. We conclude with a closer look at two keys to success and professionalism: ethical behavior and continuing education.

OUTLINE

SUCCEEDING ON THE JOB

■ How can people in the travel industry increase their chances of success in a new job, and how can they prepare for a better position?

CAREER PATHS IN THE TRAVEL INDUSTRY

■ What steps make up the career ladders for travel professionals?

ETHICS IN THE TRAVEL INDUSTRY

■ What ethical dilemmas are most likely to face travel professionals, and what principles should guide their reactions?

CONTINUING EDUCATION FOR TRAVEL PROFESSIONALS

■ Where can travel professionals obtain the continuing education and training to build their careers?

Succeeding on the Job

■ HOW CAN PEOPLE IN THE TRAVEL/TOURISM INDUSTRY INCREASE THEIR CHANCES OF SUCCESS IN A NEW JOB, AND HOW CAN THEY PREPARE FOR A BETTER JOB?

The New Position

The first step toward success in a new job is to have appropriate expectations and attitudes, enthusiasm, a willingness to learn, and patience with yourself as you encounter new situations. With these, you can begin to establish yourself and earn credibility and respect. The following are tips for starting a new position.

- Make all your first impressions good ones. Always be on time. Notice how those around you dress. At first, you might dress slightly more formally than you think is expected.
- Don't pretend to know something when you don't. Ask questions. Realize what you don't know; then learn it. Admit mistakes and look at them as opportunities for learning. Let your mistakes be errors that result from taking initiative, not from being immature or impatient.
- Look for a *mentor* in the company, a person who serves as an unofficial teacher, counselor, role model, and advocate. Your mentor should be someone who can give you advice, whose knowledge and character you respect, and who will appreciate your eagerness to learn.
- Be a team player. Help out colleagues whenever possible.
- Demonstrate initiative. Successful people do things on their own and watch for opportunities to do more. Be involved. Don't wait for things to happen.
- Have a positive attitude. Be optimistic and cheerful. When something goes wrong, take it as a challenge to find a solution. Love your work and work hard at it.

Table 16.1 presents some examples of failures and successes in carrying out these tips.

Striking a balance between prudence and initiative can be especially difficult when you begin a job. Remember that every company has its own *corporate culture*—its own set of values, beliefs, priorities, and practices. In one company, for example, people may saunter in anytime between 9:00 and 9:15 a.m. and no one cares; in another, if you are consistently five minutes late, you may be fired. The policies and procedures described in the company manual may differ from the reality in many ways, large and small. You may be told, "Well, when Sally isn't here, we check with Joe even though we're supposed to check with Dottie because Dottie is always tied up on the phone with clients."

Most likely, you will need to learn the elements of the corporate culture piece by piece over the first few months. Be prudent at the beginning and

TABLE 16.1 The Professional versus the Order-Taker

Unsuccessful New Employees Say	Successful New Employees Say
Their lines are always busy; this is a waste of time. I'll never get through.	Does this phone have automatic redial and speed dial? We've got to get through.
They'll never answer. What a waste of time.	I think I'll open all the mail while I'm on hold.
How should I know that's the way I was supposed to do it?	Sorry. I never really learned how to do this before. Do you have time to show me?
I've finished my job.	I finished filing faster than I thought. Can I make some calls and help you research those rates?
Sorry, that fare is all sold out.	Sorry, that airfare is sold out, but I can get you a lower fare for a flight that leaves the next day.
So, do you want to make this booking now? Client: "Thank you." Counselor: "No problem, no problem."	Which can I reserve for you, the 10th or the 12th? Client: "Thank you." Counselor: "It was a pleasure to serve you. See you again."

operate according to the manual or the practices of your coworkers. Eventually, you may decide that it is worthwhile to challenge existing procedures. But don't try to change things overnight. Remember that (1) your coworkers have been doing the job for a lot longer than you have, (2) it is human nature to resent criticism from a new person, and (3) there is bound to be a lot going on in the company that you do not know about yet.

Your Next Position

Many people are happy in an entry-level position for many years and become very valuable to their companies. Others are eager to move into positions with more status, responsibility, and earnings. You will have to gauge the possibilities for advancement with your first employer. Changing jobs, sometimes a number of times, is an accepted part of the travel industry and sometimes necessary to advance. Some people have found it necessary also to change companies or transfer to different sectors within the travel industry to help propel their career.

If you are interested in moving up the career ladder, your first step is to establish yourself as being excellent at whatever you are doing. Find positive ways to stand out. For example, volunteer to take on extra work or to help organize a company function. When the opportunity arises to talk with a supervisor, don't be shy about describing your accomplishments.

Maintain and extend your networks. Your coworkers and managers are potential members of that network. Make a special effort to be friendly to those whose personalities do not mesh with yours and avoid office gossip.

Also, join and take an active part in local industry associations. In previous chapters, we described many of these nationwide organizations, such as ASTA (American Society of Travel Advisors) and MPI (Meeting Professionals International). They offer opportunities not only for networking but also for learning. Other smaller groups often can be found on a local level, providing an opportunity for travel professionals to share experiences and hear speakers on a variety of industry-relevant topics. There also are many ways to network online, including professional platforms like LinkedIn or other social media groups geared toward your profession.

Remember to keep your portfolio and résumé current. Add anything you accomplish to your portfolio. Mention seminars, trade shows, courses, and any other experiences that have added to your expertise. Did a client write a letter of praise and thanks? Cherish and protect it.

Above all, be professional. A *professional* has learned a body of knowledge, mastered skills needed for a certain occupation, and demonstrates a commitment to the standards of that occupation and the interests of his or her clients. People have no trouble knowing when someone is or is not being professional. Professionals treat others with respect, follow through on commitments and take responsibility for their work. Professionalism requires both ethical behavior and continuing education, and we take a closer look at both of these topics at the end of the chapter.

Skills to Develop

Continuing development of your skills and knowledge is essential to professionalism and to career advancement. Take advantage of on-the-job training and personal travel. Learn another language, attend a webinar on a popular destination, or take classes toward a business degree. Just keep learning and gaining new experiences. You can continue your education on your own; take advantage of educational opportunities offered by organizations in the travel industry, take courses at a college or university, or attend seminars or webinars from industry suppliers.

Which skills are most likely to help you as you advance in the travel industry? Chapter 1 described general skills required for entry-level positions (in interpersonal relationships, language, math, technology, and the ability to learn). To perform professionally in the travel industry, you will need not only to build on those skills but also to develop others, such as those listed below:

- *Business communication.* Every travel professional should refine and develop communication skills constantly. This includes both written and verbal skills. They cannot be stressed too much.
- *Organization.* Travel professionals manage massive amounts of information. The ability to determine which information is relevant and to obtain up-to-date information when it is needed is crucial.
- *Time management.* Many jobs in the travel industry require the ability to perform multiple tasks simultaneously while meeting deadlines. Travel professionals need skill at assigning priorities to tasks to manage their time well.
- *Negotiation.* Travel professionals negotiate daily. To be successful, you need to communicate effectively and to offer creative ideas for solving problems.
- *Understanding consumers and trends.* In order to deliver excellent customer service, travel professionals must develop skill at understanding their clients' needs and motivations and at noticing shifts in patterns of consumer spending and travel.
- *Planning and crisis management.* To advance in the travel industry, you should be able to manage crises effectively. Planning how to deal with problems is one of the best ways to ensure that you will be able to handle a crisis. Good planning also allows a business to remain competitive.
- *Embracing cultural diversity.* Increased knowledge about different cultures will help the travel professional overcome problems that cultural differences can bring, especially as the workplace and business interactions become more culturally diverse.
- *Staying current.* The travel industry is renowned for constant change. Failure to prepare for and adapt to change leaves your success up to chance. If you try to avoid managing change, change will manage you. If you expect and accept change, then change will become not an obstacle but an opportunity. That includes staying current on new travel products, policies, and any world events that may affect travel.

✔ CHECK-UP

A corporate culture
✔ Includes values, beliefs, priorities, and practices.
✔ May be inconsistent with the policies and procedures described in a company manual.
✔ Is not a formal structure and is learned piece by piece.

Professionalism requires
✔ Mastery of the body of knowledge and skills required by the specific occupation.

✔ Commitment to the standards of the profession.
✔ Commitment to the best interests of clients.

Implicit in professionalism is a willingness to
✔ Abide by ethical standards of conduct.
✔ Engage in continuing education and development of skills.

Career Paths in the Travel Industry

■ WHAT STEPS MAKE UP THE CAREER LADDERS FOR TRAVEL PROFESSIONALS?

You have succeeded in your first job. You have an excellent reputation, an extensive network, and an up-to-date résumé. You have developed your skills and attended numerous seminars. Now you want a new job with more status, pay, and responsibility. What is your next step?

No one structure describes all companies in the travel industry, and there is no one set of steps that constitutes the career ladder for all companies. The Close-Up: Careers in Chapters 1 through 9 described many positions, including the principal entry-level jobs. Here we outline some of the key opportunities for advancement in the industry.

Travel Agencies and Home-Based Offices

The smaller the travel agency, the more likely it is to be family-owned and to have people entrenched in positions. Medium-sized to large agencies or agency chains usually provide more opportunities for promotions. To keep current, travel counselors should read trade journals, such as Travel Weekly, Travel Agent, and TravelAge West.

Travel counselors in small to medium-sized travel offices might advance by steps to lead agent, assistant manager, or manager—if these positions become available. They are more likely to advance by becoming better travel counselors—able to handle more clients, to do so more efficiently, and to contribute to a higher profit margin for the agency, which may, in turn, qualify them for higher earnings as salary increases often are tied to increased sales and agency profit.

For counselors with several years of experience, other options for advancement are
- To work for a mega-agency. A mega-agency is likely to have many specialized jobs and levels of management.
- To work as an outside sales agent.
- To work as an independent contractor.
- To start their own travel agency.

Striking out on your own has obvious attractions as well as risks. Chapter 14 discusses the benefits, problems, and steps involved in starting your own agency or setting up as an independent contractor.

For any of the career paths we have described, your best chance for success as a travel counselor is to specialize. Just as travel agencies need to carve out market niches, individual counselors should select an area, or a few areas, of specialization. Figure 16.1 outlines steps to take in establishing a specialization.

Earlier chapters described types of specialization. They include
- *Particular kinds of travel based on an activity or interest,* such as adventure trips, ecotours, and different kinds of sports tours. If you earn a reputation as the one counselor in your community who knows about the specialty, your success is likely to be guaranteed for a number of years.

FIGURE 16.1

Developing a Specialization

Everyone has interests that can be developed into sales specialties that will enhance a career. These five steps have proved to be a successful path for counselors to follow.

Step 1: Look at Your Interests and Select A Potential Specialty.
What do you do with your spare time, or what did you enjoy doing as a child? What vacations have you enjoyed? What trips do you most enjoy working on? Do you have a special skill?

Step 2: Check Out the Niche.
Survey existing clients. Are they part of the potential market? Is there enough interest to justify the specialization? How much will it cost to penetrate the market? What volume of sales could be expected? Is the market adequately served now? If not, why not? How will your service differ from already available services?

Step 3: Educate Yourself.
Read as much as you can. Take fam trips related to the specialty. Contact related tourist boards and magazines. Consider courses offered by The Travel Institute, ASTA, CLIA, and other professional organizations. Learn about relevant suppliers.

Step 4: Develop A Marketing Plan.
Identify your potential clients and the marketing mix you will use to reach them. Don't overlook less expensive types of promotion. Check your database for people who have expressed interest in the specialty. Send newsletters and press releases. Consider ways to use your website and the Internet. Arrange speaking engagements or theme nights. Attend events and exhibitions. Get involved with organizations related to the specialization.

Step 5: Stay Fresh.
Monitor the market through trade publications. Take trips. Keep in touch with tourist boards and suppliers. Ask your clients for feedback.

- *Specific demographic or affinity groups,* such as particular ethnic groups, specific age groups, disabled travelers, honeymooners, LGBTs, doctors, or firemen. To develop this kind of specialization, you also form bonds with the group. One travel counselor who became an LGBT specialist reported that her first step was to join the International Gay & Lesbian Travel Association (IGLTA). She wrote to all the suppliers on its membership list, studied their brochures, started running weekly ads in a local LGBT newspaper, and bought guidebooks from the local LGBT bookstore.
- *Specific geographic areas.* Pick the place about which you are or would like to become most knowledgeable. Make yourself known as the specialist in that area for your agency, your city, or even nationwide.
- *Cruise travel.* Some agencies work only on cruises; many others sell a range of types of travel but have cruise departments. Some counselors focus solely on oceangoing cruises, while others have built niche markets by selling only river cruises. If your specialty is cruises, do not look just for cruise-only agencies as possible employers; most successful agencies want to emphasize cruise sales.

These specializations are not mutually exclusive. For example, if you decide to specialize in an ethnic group, you would establish a network within that ethnic community, attend community events, learn about its culture and develop expertise in destinations popular with that group. If you specialize in a geographic area, the specialty might take longer to develop than others because you might have to build your market one client at a time, but you can combine this specialty with others. A specialist in Italy, for instance, might also become expert in trips devoted to art, wine, or cooking; a specialist in Latin America might develop expertise in ecotourism or Mayan culture. Cruising is a field with almost endless opportunities for specialization—adventure, family reunions, the Greek islands, and more.

During the coming decade, leisure travel is expected to grow more than business travel. But if you want to advance and increase your earnings quickly at the outset of your career, consider concentrating on business travel. Large commercial agencies often call themselves *travel management companies* and include many specialized jobs, such as corporate account manager and customer service agent (see the Close-Up on Careers with Travel Agencies in Chapter 1 for sample job descriptions). Sales representatives keep business coming in; negotiators make sure suppliers are giving the agency the best possible rates and overrides. In addition, Web specialists handle bookings online or keep the agency's website updated; systems administrators respond to users' calls to the help desk; database administrators provide technical support and maintenance for computer networks. In addition, companies often have separate departments for group sales, incentive travel, and convention and meeting coordinators.

Online Travel Agencies, GDSs, and Virtual Careers

Online travel agencies (OTAs), such as Travelocity, Expedia, and Orbitz, need people proficient in computers and people familiar with air reservations and other sectors of the travel industry. A combination of computer and travel knowledge can put you on the fast track.

Many small online companies have locations all over the nation. Most online travel companies, including airline reservation centers, hire fulfillment companies to provide customer service, and reservation services through call centers in the United States and other countries, such as India.

A growing number of careers in the travel industry—beyond just online agencies—focus on electronic communication. Every sector of the travel and tourism industry has an electronic component. Many companies are looking for people within the travel industry who have computer and Internet skills, rather than hiring technical experts who are unfamiliar with the industry. Thus, there are many opportunities for travel professionals who would like to specialize in e-marketing, Web design and maintenance, database management, distribution systems, Web-based applications, and customer relationship management (CRM).

GDSs (global distribution systems) have been the traditional employers of travel professionals specializing in computers. Travel computer specialists may begin their careers by working at a GDS help desk and move into sales and then management. Due to the growth of OTAs, opportunities with GDSs are quite limited.

However, because computer specialization now extends to all sectors of the travel and tourism industry, you may begin your career with computers in any sector of the travel industry.

Tourism and Destination Management

Careers in the tourism industry range from dealing with activities (festivals, gambling, skiing, music) to promoting single attractions to marketing entire nations as destinations. Opportunities exist in destination management companies (DMCs), government tourist offices (GTOs), and convention and visitors' bureaus (CVBs). (See the Close-Up On the Job with Mandy Hallet in Chapter 2 regarding careers in destination management and promotion.) Career paths may begin with behind- the-scenes support jobs and move to highly visible positions planning events. Working for DMCs, GTOs and CVBs can be a great area of the industry to explore for travel professionals interested in living abroad.

Airlines

In recent years, the airline business has been volatile. Many employees have moved from one carrier to another because they wanted to look for advancement or because their employer ceased operations or cut its workforce.

Those who work in the reservations office of an airline might seek advancement by applying for openings in specialty areas, such as the agent desk, tour desk, group desk, or computer help desk. Supervising and training positions are logical promotions. Another path is to move into sales, advertising, or marketing. For example, you might aim to become a district or regional sales manager, often referred to as a business development manager.

If you work at the airport as a ticket agent, gate agent, or customer service specialist, you might aim for supervisory roles, such as schedule coordinator, shift manager, or airport station manager (who manages the day-to-day operations of an airline at a particular airport).

Flight attendants can advance to become senior flight attendants, supervisors, or training instructors. If flight attendants decide to end their flying days, they have a good chance of securing a position in other areas of the airline. They often make excellent travel counselors or tour leaders.

Accommodations

Because of its large size, the hotel industry is likely to have more job openings and more opportunities for advancement than other segments of the travel/tourism industry. Those who want to take advantage of these opportunities need to gain expertise in areas, such as room inventory management, housekeeping, facility maintenance, and food and beverage sales. These can be studied in hospitality courses and hotel training programs. AH&LA (American Hotel & Lodging Association) can help you stay in touch with changes in the industry.

Many top-grade hotel chains are dedicated to promoting from within and have programs to help their personnel advance. Supervisory and assistant managerial positions may be the obvious steps after an entry-level job. The resident manager (also known as general manager) at some properties not only supervises all hotel operations, departments, and personnel but also is the principal contact with guests to resolve special issues and build goodwill. Usually the resident manager completed study at a hotel school or a hotel management program and rose from a front-desk position to assistant manager or executive housekeeper.

At many resorts, you can combine hotel skills with an interest in a specialty. For example, gambling resorts, spas, and western ranch resorts need people who know the special features of their operations.

Ground Transportation

Because ground transportation is often sold as part of a travel package, many jobs in this travel sector involve vendor relations and marketing relationships with other segments of the travel industry. Generally, positions related to yield management and computer-based distribution and marketing are growth areas. Fleet acquisition and logistics offer fascinating career paths. For example, the fleet manager for motor coach companies monitors and allocates equipment used for charters, tours, and regularly scheduled service and figures out how to get equipment where it is needed in the most efficient way.

In car rental companies, rental agents who excel may move up in the management structure at a particular location—perhaps from shift manager to station manager to city manager. But advancement might require relocating to another city. Becoming a district manager and then being promoted to regional manager are logical steps. Other opportunities are available only at the company's main office, where operations, sales and marketing, and management and administration functions are performed.

For careers in passenger rail travel, future opportunities depend not only on market forces but also on changes in government funding. Advancement within Amtrak may be slow, but longevity and dedication may pay off. Amtrak prefers to promote people from within its system and people who believe strongly in rail travel. Those in reservations might look for advancement in supervisory roles, training, and sales, much as with the airlines. Management positions are possible for those who further their education. Attendants might look to advance to onboard chief (the supervisor of the train's onboard crews).

Cruises

Because of the impressive growth of cruising, chances for advancement are excellent for those who are ready to seize opportunities. Land-based personnel might move into specialized areas, such as capacity control, group sales and reservations, air/sea operations, and air/sea ticketing. Most positions are in U.S. port cities, and many of these are in Florida. Watch for openings in supervisory or managerial positions, marketing, and sales. Account executives or sales representatives who are stationed in different parts of the country can make excellent salaries. Most of them have a large sales territory and usually work out of their homes. A lateral or upward move might take you into cruise-only travel agencies. Expertise and sales ability could lead to an excellent position in one of these companies.

For ship-based personnel, possible career moves into specialized areas are much like those for hotel personnel because a cruise ship is a floating resort. Travel management, hotel, financial, or ship experience might lead to the position of purser or even hotel manager (called *chief purser* on some lines). These positions are responsible for the passengers in almost all respects: overseeing cabins, handling the guests' finances and securing their valuables, handling the ship's other income and expenditures, making sure the ship complies with local documents and regulations, and much more. Those involved in entertainment and activities might aspire to be assistant cruise director or cruise director. Shipboard experience as part of the cruise staff is the best preparation for these jobs. Note that shipboard experience can be on board the ship, wherever it may be. On the other hand, working for a cruise line's headquarters will require your moving to that location, most often Florida.

Tours

Wholesalers tend to be larger companies than tour operators, which are often small operations in the United States. Even some large tour operators are family-owned and -operated, which means the number of upper-level positions is limited. The best opportunities lie with the largest domestic tour companies. High growth has increased openings, particularly in product innovation and quality control. Every company is seeking to promote itself on the Internet, providing opportunities for those knowledgeable in e-commerce.

To advance in a career in tours, you might take one of three general paths.

- If you start as a tour guide or tour escort, your advancement may come by working more often, with larger groups, or on more prestigious tours. Successful escorts work well with diverse people and get to know the inner workings of the product. Thus, many can rise to high levels in the company when they decide to "come in from the cold" and work in the company's home office.
- If your entry-level position is in the office, your career path might involve moving into groups, sales and marketing, or operations (that is, keeping track of clients and vendors and communicating with them).
- If you are committed to working on tours and have something special to offer, you might start your own operation or begin a new program for an existing tour operator. New destinations, activities, and ideas are needed constantly. Ski instructors, river-raft enthusiasts, art teachers, ranch hands, ecotourism experts, chefs, musicians, animal lovers—all might involve themselves in starting or helping to build tour programs for an existing tour operator.

Travel counselors increase their chances of advancement by selecting an area of specialization, which might involve
✔ Particular kinds of travel.
✔ Specific demographic or affinity groups.
✔ Specific geographic areas.
✔ Cruises.

Career paths in the travel industry
✔ Vary from one sector of the industry to another.
✔ May require a willingness to change locations or change companies or both.

Ethics in the Travel Industry

■ WHAT ETHICAL DILEMMAS ARE MOST LIKELY TO FACE TRAVEL PROFESSIONALS, AND WHAT PRINCIPLES SHOULD GUIDE THEIR REACTIONS?

Professionalism implies a commitment to ethical behavior, which means following certain principles of proper conduct. In fact, ethical behavior is often in the long-term best interests of a company and an individual. If you earn a reputation for unethical behavior, you forgo the trust of clients and ultimately are likely to lose business as well. But these considerations about whether a behavior will pay off have nothing to do with ethics.

There are ethical standards and ethical dilemmas in every facet of business life, from hiring and firing to relations with colleagues and customers. A company may establish policies that encourage or discourage ethical behavior, but ultimately, each individual is responsible for acting ethically.

Sometimes the ethical choice is difficult to determine. No law prohibits many unethical behaviors. It is not against the law, for example, to tell outsiders about a client's travel plans or to neglect to cancel space that you know will not be used, but, usually, these acts are considered unethical by most travel industry professionals.

One aid in determining the ethical course of action comes from codes of ethics published by professional associations. ASTA's code, for example, states that "all ASTA members pledge themselves to conduct their business activities in a manner that promotes the ideal of integrity in travel and agree to act in accordance with" the principles of the code (see Table 16.2).

Often, however, no rule clearly defines what should be done in a particular situation. For a great many situations, you can determine what is ethical only by consulting your own conscience and by asking, Is this action fair? Is it just? Will it harm anyone? In this section we look at some of the situations that most frequently raise ethical questions for travel professionals, and particularly travel counselors.

Confidentiality

Duties to preserve confidentiality protect and restrict travel agencies, travel counselors, clients, and suppliers. A salesperson should not disclose information gained from a client to anyone except others in the industry who need that information in order to provide services. (By requesting services, the client has given implied approval for these disclosures.) Clients' travel plans should not be discussed outside the office, and information about their plans should not be given over the telephone to anyone except those clients.

Similar restrictions apply to information given to an employer. Travel professionals should never discuss with the public the cost of travel benefits received from suppliers, and supplier representatives should treat information about travel counselors as confidential.

Travel Benefits

Anyone actively engaged in the travel industry and meeting certain minimum requirements may be eligible for benefits and discounts offered by hotels and resorts, sightseeing attractions, airlines, cruise lines, and many other travel companies. People who misrepresent themselves as active travel industry employees and do so in order to obtain these benefits are guilty of unethical conduct. It is also unethical to encourage or help others to misrepresent themselves.

TABLE 16.2 ASTA Code of Ethics

Preamble:

Travelers depend on travel agencies and others affiliated with ASTA to guide them honestly and competently. All ASTA members pledge to conduct their business activities in a manner that promotes the ideal of integrity in travel and agree to act in accordance with the applicable sections of the following principles of the ASTA Code of Ethics. Complaints arising under this Code should be filed in writing with the ASTA Consumer Affairs Department.

...

1. **Accuracy.** ASTA members will be factual and accurate when providing information about their services and the services of any firm they represent. They will not use deceptive practices.

2. **Disclosure.** ASTA members will provide in writing, upon written request, complete details about the cost, restrictions, and other terms and conditions of any travel service sold, including cancellation and service fee policies. Full details of the time, place, duration, and nature of any sales or promotional presentation the consumer will be required to attend in connection with his/her travel arrangements shall be disclosed in writing before any payment is accepted.

3. **Responsiveness.** ASTA members will promptly respond substantively to their clients' complaints.

4. **Refunds.** ASTA members will remit any undisputed funds under their control within the specified time limit. Reasons for delay in providing funds will be given to the claimant promptly.

5. **Cooperation.** ASTA members will cooperate with any inquiry conducted by ASTA to resolve any dispute involving consumers.

6. **Confidentiality.** ASTA members will treat every client transaction confidentially and not disclose any information without the permission of the client, unless required by law.

7. **Affiliation.** ASTA members will not falsely represent a person's affiliation with their firm.

8. **Conflict of Interest.** ASTA members will not allow any preferred relationship with a supplier to interfere with the interests of their clients.

9. **Compliance.** ASTA members shall not have been convicted of a violation of any federal, state and local laws and regulations affecting consumers. Pleas of nolo contendere, consent judgments, judicial or administrative decrees, or orders, and assurances of voluntary compliance and similar agreements with federal or state authorities shall be deemed convictions for purposes of these provisions.

Responsibilities of All Members

1. **Notice.** ASTA members operating tours will promptly advise the agent or client who reserved the space of any change in itinerary, services, features, or price.

2. **Delivery.** ASTA members operating tours will provide all components as stated in their brochure or written confirmation, or provide alternate services of equal or greater value, or provide appropriate compensation.

3. **Credentials.** An ASTA member shall not, in exchange for money or otherwise, provide travel agent credentials to any person as to whom there is no reasonable expectation that the person will engage in a bona fide effort to sell or manage the sale of travel services to the general public on behalf of the member through the period of validity of such credentials. This principle applies to ASTA members and all affiliated or commonly controlled enterprises.

Conclusion

Failure to adhere to this Code may subject a member to disciplinary actions, as set forth in ASTA's Bylaws.

Source: Adapted with permission from ASTA.

This type of misrepresentation became a business of its own in the 1990s, when companies popularly known as **card mills** began selling travel agency credentials. Card mills advertise for outside sales agents as if they were bona fide travel agencies, but they provide minimal support and training. They pay members a fee for each new person recruited. Training often focuses on how to recruit new members, not on travel products and how to sell them. Some people pay the initial fee and join simply to use the identification cards in order to take advantage of discounts on travel that are intended for bona fide travel professionals.

These card mills may harm the traveling public, the suppliers who offer the discounts, and professional travel counselors whose reputation they cheapen. ASTA, IATAN, and the Association of Retail Travel Agents (ARTA) have all been working to stop this abuse of travel agent credentials.

Misrepresentation and Disclosure

Deceptive advertising is unethical. The facts in an advertisement should be clear and complete. It is unethical to advertise services that are not available or that are so limited that very few can obtain them (in other words, bait-and-switch schemes). When services are limited, the advertiser should clearly spell out the limitations. Also, there are truth-in-advertising practices as they relate to promoting travel services at discounted prices. The cruise industry has started to crack down on agencies discounting their prices, so all agencies have an equal opportunity to sell their cruises. Some cruise lines have revoked permission for some agencies to sell their cruises because of this unethical practice.

Similarly, it is unethical for salespeople to misrepresent a product. For new salespeople, it is easy to misrepresent a product unintentionally, through inexperience or over-eagerness. Salespeople should avoid overgeneralizations such as: "Oh, it's just great on that island; everyone loves it."

Failure to disclose facts necessary for the client to make an informed decision is also unethical. The fact that a client does not know enough to ask the right questions does not alter the salesperson's responsibility to disclose vital facts. Travel counselors are ethically obliged to warn clients about facts such as code-shared flights and drawbacks of a destination. In fact, the U.S. Department of Transportation now requires that travel agencies give travelers information in writing about a code-shared flight or a flight listed as "direct" that actually requires a change of planes.

Ticketing

Travel counselors are contracted to sell suppliers' services according to the suppliers' rules and regulations, and counselors must make a good-faith effort to follow and enforce those rules. Certainly, they should not tell clients how to circumvent the regulations. But when clients find their own way around the rules, the ethics of the situation sometimes become murky.

In particular, the rules regarding discount airfares have created difficult situations. Many travelers learn how to manipulate these rules with no help from travel professionals. Back-to-back ticketing and hidden-city ticketing are two examples.

In **back-to-back ticketing**, the client buys two discount tickets and rearranges the departures and returns. The practice occurs when the cost of

ON THE SPOT

Mr. Dehere, a frequent business traveler, has a meeting that ends two hours before his departing flight. He is not certain he will make it to the airport for this flight, but he says he really needs to get on that flight, if possible. If he doesn't make it, he will be even more desperate to get on the next flight. So, he asks you to make a reservation for him on both flights. What should you do?

This is clearly a case of doublebooking. Savvy clients know that they can pick up the phone, call the airline, and doublebook themselves. Mr. Dehere might want to engage in this unethical practice on his own, but you should not violate the airline's rules by doublebooking (nor should you encourage him to do so). Urge him to reserve the later flight. He can then try to make the earlier flight and see if a seat is available.

two discount round-trip tickets is less than the cost of one round-trip ticket at full fare, but the discount tickets have restrictions that the client cannot meet. For example, a client might want to make a round-trip flight to New York but be unable to meet the restriction on the discount fare that calls for staying over on a Saturday night. So, the client buys two discount round-trip tickets for different dates and then uses just one leg of each ticket in order to complete his trip.

In *hidden-city ticketing*, a client who wants to go to City Y buys a ticket for a flight from City X to City Z with a connection at City Y because the fare for a ticket from City X to City Z is less than the fare from City X to City Y. The client actually gets off the plane when it lands at City Y. For example, to go to Atlanta from Chicago, a client might buy a ticket for a Chicago-to-Orlando flight with a connection in Atlanta—and get off at Atlanta—because the airline has a special discount fare for the Chicago-to- Orlando flight. This practice only works for travelers not checking luggage.

The airlines argue that these practices violate ticketing agreements. Many travel counselors complain that it is not their job to police clients' requests. But if travel agencies practice back-to-back or hidden-city ticketing, they risk incurring fines from the airlines and even the loss of their ARC appointments. Travelers who are found to be using this practice risk having their return ticket cancelled and future flying privileges on that airline revoked.

To understand and comply with all rules and restrictions, travel counselors always should check the websites of the U.S. Department of State (state.gov), IATA (iata.org), ARC (arccorp.com), and individual airlines.

Reservations

Ethical considerations also limit reservation practices. It is unethical
- To try to book travelers who have already made reservations or paid for travel with another agency.
- To book reservations that you do not intend to use and then cancel them at the last moment to open space for standby passengers or those hoping for an upgrade.

You should cancel, in a timely manner, all space that clearly will not be used, and you should book only one reservation that a client can use at a time. Booking two reservations for an individual at the same time is called *doublebooking* and is unethical. But if clients ask you to doublebook far in advance and for only a very short time, so that they can confer with others, the ethics of the situation are less clear. Many agents feel ethically correct in doing so even though they are technically violating a supplier's regulations.

Selecting Suppliers

Some agencies could not survive without the override commissions given by preferred suppliers. As an employee, the travel counselor has a duty to concentrate on these preferred suppliers. Ideally, only companies that are leaders in their fields, providing value and service, have been selected as preferred suppliers. Thus, in principle at least, by selecting preferred suppliers the travel counselor is meeting the needs of both the agency and the client.

In practice, preferred supplier relationships obviously raise the possibility that the interests of the agency and the client will conflict. Disclosure helps: The agency should make a list of preferred suppliers available to clients. In

ON THE SPOT

RentUsNow is offering travel counselors a free car rental for a week if they make 10 bookings with it this month. Your agency approved the contest, and you would certainly like that prize for your upcoming vacation. It's the end of the day on the last day of the month, and you have sold nine rentals for RentUsNow so far. Now a client calls and wants a rental. You determine that for this location, renting from Top Rentals, which is just as reliable as RentUsNow, would save the client $15. Which supplier do you select?

Your client's best interests must come first. But before giving up on RentUsNow and the prize, you might try calling the company and asking it to match the other supplier's price, or you might offer your client a $15 rebate check (which you would pay for personally), explaining your reason for wanting to book with RentUsNow. If neither strategy succeeds, booking with RentUsNow would be unethical.

any event, the travel counselor has an obligation to help the client choose the service or supplier best suited to that client. If the preferred supplier does not meet that test, the travel counselor should recommend a supplier that does, even though the result is a lower commission.

Gifts, prizes, awards, and contests offered by suppliers to travel agencies or directly to travel counselors may also tempt counselors to put their own interests ahead of the client's. Given the fact that employees in many businesses and governments are not allowed to accept any gift worth more than $25, the policy of offering gifts worth $100 or more is questionable. Agencies should set clear policies regarding their employees' participation in reward programs. The counselor, in any event, has an ethical obligation to serve the client's interests.

Fiduciary Responsibilities

If you are a travel counselor, once a client gives you money, you are considered the guardian of those funds. You have an obligation to try to deal only with reputable suppliers, and you have a specific duty to disburse the funds as the client intended. This means doing so in a way that meets deadlines and other requirements of the supplier. By the same token, the supplier has an ethical duty to guard funds entrusted to it toward a particular end. It is unethical to risk a client's funds on other purposes when there is a chance those funds may be lost before the client's trip.

In some states, these responsibilities are regulated by requirements that travel agencies or suppliers place client funds in escrow accounts under certain situations. (Recall that an *escrow account* consists of funds or other property that is held by a third party, such as a bank, until specified conditions are met for its release.) In a sense, an operator should consider all client funds "in escrow" until the trip has been completed.

Government Regulation of Travel Sellers

The higher the ethical standards of those in a profession, the less need there is for laws and regulations by government. But even if travel professionals adhere to the highest standards, frauds and other unethical behaviors may be carried out by people outside the travel industry. Many travel organizations, such as ASTA, try to prevent or uncover these problems, but they persist.

When an industry's attempts to police itself fail, government may provide a last line of defense. For example, in 1999, the Federal Trade Commission (FTC) established Operation Trip Trap to stop unethical companies from fraudulently tricking consumers (mainly teens and seniors) into thinking they had won trips they had not won.

In addition, a number of states either have laws licensing or regulating travel sellers or are considering them. Their chief aim is to protect consumers from scams and from losing their money if a travel seller goes out of business. These laws often require that travel sellers register with the state in some way and either post a bond or contribute to a consumer restitution fund. Some of these laws require travel professionals to prominently display their license number in their agency and on their business cards. ASTA offers a course on travel agency relationships and the law.

Continuing Education for Travel Professionals

■ WHERE CAN TRAVEL PROFESSIONALS OBTAIN THE CONTINUING EDUCATION AND TRAINING TO BUILD THEIR CAREERS?

Effective travel professionals are always learning. Four types of continuing education might enhance your career:

■ *College or university education.* In the travel industry, top positions in particular may require completion of courses that teach advanced business, marketing, or management skills. George Washington University in Washington, D.C., has been known for decades for its Master of Tourism Administration program. There also are several travel/tourism certificate programs available for industry professionals who have undergraduate education in a different field of study.

■ *Industry education,* which includes seminars, trips, and specialized courses. We examine some of these opportunities later in this section.

■ *General education,* which includes keeping current with events on the international scene and in the business world. Your personal travel is one invaluable resource. The travel, business, and international news sections of your local newspaper and of national papers, such as *The New York Times* (in libraries and online), will often include valuable reports. Subscribe to at least one of the trade publications listed in earlier chapters. Consumer publications, such as *Condé Nast Traveler*, *National Geographic Traveler*, and *Travel + Leisure*, as well as travel videos, guidebooks, and travel literature, can round out your education.

Keep in mind that you can pursue each of these types of education using the Internet. If you take a class online, in most cases you will be able to study when and where you want. But the advantages of this freedom prove to be disadvantages to many. Being able to study "whenever" can become "never." Choose a specific place and time for study or look for online courses that present seminars at scheduled times or that set a strict schedule of assignments that must be e-mailed to the instructor.

Educational Resources of the Travel Industry

Suppliers are a tremendous source of educational opportunities. At their seminars, you can learn about the company and the industry, make contacts with others, and enjoy yourself—at little or no cost. Many suppliers also offer online training, webinars, and certification programs focused on sales techniques, destinations, and product offerings.

Discounted trips, familiarization trips, and ship inspections offer unique and enjoyable opportunities for learning. On *discounted trips*, you join with others to sample a company's service or tours; these trips may require little of you other than sampling the services as any traveler might. A true *familiarization* (or *fam*) *trip* is a working trip: You travel with a group of other

---

CLOSE-UP: ON THE JOB WITH TALULA GUNTNER, TRAVEL AND TOURISM EDUCATOR

Talula Guntner, CTC, is a professor emerita of travel and tourism and teaches tourism online as an adjunct professor from her home in North Carolina for Northern Virginia Community College. She has also been the director of a proprietary travel school. She holds a B.A. in elementary education and library science from Columbia College, an M.A. in education and human development with a specialization in travel and tourism, and an Ed.S., the latter two from the George Washington University. The following are excerpts from an interview by Kate Rice for *Travel Professional* magazine.

Kate Rice: "Travel became your passion early on. Why?"
Talula Guntner: "I guess it was just seeing there is so much more of the world than what I knew about firsthand. A guy I dated in college would ask me how I knew there really was an Arizona if I had never been there. He would talk about how he wanted to touch the pyramids to see if they were real. Now, I have actually been inside a pyramid and know they really do exist, not just in pictures.

"I've been to the jungles of Ecuador, visited Mount Bromo in Indonesia at sunrise, ridden a donkey to the top of Santorini, gone horseback riding in the water in Jamaica, gone tubing through a cave in Belize, and stood on a glacier in Alaska.

"In 1969, when I was an elementary school librarian, I went on one of the tours to Europe—'If This Is Tuesday, This Must Be Belgium,' a 30-day tour of Europe for $850. That's what really sold me on travel. I quit teaching and did outside sales. Of course, I had no training. I didn't know what I was doing, so I had to go back to teaching.

"Then I moved to Washington, and a woman who just did groups hired me. I had no training, but I kept myself a lifelong learner. I was always going to seminars and conferences. I got my CTC and then found out that, at that time, your CTC counted toward a third of your master's degree at George Washington University. So, I went back and got my master's in education and human development. If I got it now it would be a master's of tourism administration. All this time, I was working in the industry.

"When I got into the business, there weren't even training schools, not even six-week schools. Now you can get a doctorate in business at George Washington University with an emphasis in travel. And there's such opportunity out there.

"We need to encourage people to join our industry; we need to add good people to it. I speak to schools all the time—elementary schools, high schools. When I speak to students I tell them to look at travel. It's important to do work you enjoy; you don't need to wait to retire to enjoy life.

"We have a lot of what I call the chronologically gifted, people who are retiring [from another industry] or people who realize that they just don't want to be tied to a computer all day and that they want to deal with people more.

"Now in travel, there are so many different things to do. You can have two or three careers in travel—a car rep becomes a cruise line rep; the cruise rep becomes a travel counselor.

"Travel has enriched my life. I have made lifelong friends in the industry and through travel. I have been privileged to share some of what I have learned with my students. It is rewarding helping people enter such an exciting field. If I had my life to live all over, there is very little I would change besides marrying my husband earlier, taking more trips, and saving more money so I could travel more!"

---

travel professionals on a specially arranged itinerary and are expected to participate in all scheduled functions and to learn as much as you can. In some cases, an accompanying spouse or another person may come along; in other cases, that is not allowed. The airlines, hotels, tour operators, or other suppliers involved count on your participation to warrant their sponsorship of the trip. Active attendance at events is your most important "payment" for the trip. Suppliers should make clear the level of participation expected, ensure that participation is worthwhile, avoid overburdening participants and monitor who participates.

The tourist boards of many countries offer special training programs. The Magic of Mexico programs are some of the best known. Other educational opportunities come from professional organizations. For example, ASTA holds seminars in cities and online on a variety of subjects, as well as some home study courses.

Numerous organizations provide advanced training programs, and some certify travel professionals who complete the requirements of a program. For example, ARC (Airline Reporting Corporation) offers a number of self-paced tutorials and virtual classes.

CLIA (Cruise Lines International Association) offers one of the best-known training programs. Its certificate program has two levels: *Accredited Cruise Counselor (ACC)* and *Master Cruise Counselor (MCC)*. The program includes classroom training, sales and marketing seminars, cruise conferences, exams, ship inspections, and cruises. Employees from many parts of the industry benefit from CLIA's one-day seminars and courses offered in cities throughout the country and aboard ships.

Among the many other examples of certificate and training programs are:

- Advanced training for the hospitality industry is available from the International Council on Hotel, Restaurant, and Institutional Education (CHRIE), an organization devoted to education and training for the hospitality and tourism industry, and from the American Hotel & Lodging Association (AH&LA), which conducts an educational institute that offers training in all facets of the hotel industry.
- Organizations, such as the Global Business Travel Association (GBTA) and the Association of Corporate Travel Executives (ACTE) can help you remain current with developments in business travel. For special training related to meetings and incentive travel, the Convention Industry Council (CIC) offers the *Certified Meeting Professional (CMP)* certificate, and the Society for Incentive Travel Excellence (SITE) certifies members who complete its requirements as *Certified Incentive Specialists (CIS)*.
- The National Tour Association (NTA) awards a *Certified Tour Professional (CTP)* certificate, and the Association of Destination Management Executives International (ADMEI) offers a *Destination Management Certified Professional (DMCP)* designation for successful completion of their programs.

Programs from The Travel Institute

Certifications, specializations, and other training resources are also available from The Travel Institute, an international nonprofit organization that aims to increase professionalism within the travel industry and to create standards of excellence for all travel professionals. Since 1964, it has been the premier educational resource for members of the travel industry at all stages of their careers. A trusted partner to industry organizations and educational institutions, The Travel Institute educates hundreds of thousands of travel professionals through introductory training, certification, specialist courses, webinars, and more.

This textbook prepares you for the first of a series of professional credentials offered by The Travel Institute: the *Travel Agent Proficiency (TAP®) Test.* This exam is designed to confirm that students new to the industry can demonstrate a mastery of travel industry basics. By taking and passing the TAP Test, you will earn the nationally recognized TAP credential. This credential can be used during your application process when applying for your IATAN Accreditation, and, once approved, provides access to the IATA/IATAN ID Card program. Passing the TAP Test also reduces (by six months) the work experience required to complete the Certified Travel Associate designation.

The *Certified Travel Associate, CTA®* program is designed and delivered strategically to help you grow travel sales, enhance your value to clients, improve efficiencies, increase marketability and, of course, earn more! The CTA course's thought-provoking, self-paced, and layered curriculum provides the knowledge and tools travel professionals need to achieve the next level of success in their travel careers. The program covers 15 areas of study and takes you through an in-depth learning experience delivered in a variety of blended learning formats, such as: knowledge application activities, case studies, expert tip reviews, audio and visual enhancements, and knowledge checks. The prerequisites for the CTA are a basic understanding of the retail travel industry, plus a minimum of 12 months' industry work experience at the completion of the course. Following successful completion of the CTA program, continuing education is required to keep this certification current and maintain its value. Benefits of earning the CTA designation may include: a higher earning potential due to the ability to match the right customer with the right product; greater credibility and marketability based on the commitment to professional development; increased job and personal satisfaction; and access to a digital credential for online validation and marketing purposes.

The *Certified Travel Counselor, CTC®* program builds on the knowledge gained in the CTA program and prepares you to effectively meet the workplace and industry demands of travel managers and supervisors. This online course teaches you new skills that can be put into practice immediately. This course helps you set the groundwork for obtaining the best position for your company and enables you to handle complex business and operational undertakings. In addition, it helps you: better understand your bottom line; develop strong employees, co-workers, and partnerships to ensure a cohesive team; gain confidence to build a strong company and a promising future by finding new ways to do business and get the most from your staff; and learn how your staff and colleagues think, operate and interact, as well as how to get the best results from all players. The prerequisites for the CTC are a minimum of five years' industry experience, plus the CTA designation. Following successful completion of the CTC program, continuing education is required to keep this certification current and maintain its value. Benefits of earning the CTC designation may include: increased effectiveness through knowledge and understanding of your management style; greater team successes due to application of the skills learned; greater advancement opportunities; better understanding of your clients' personalities and "hot buttons"; and access to a digital credential for online validation and marketing purposes.

The *Certified Travel Industry Executive, CTIE®* program offers the high-demand skills needed by leaders to drive excellence throughout their organization. A leader needs to be focused on goals aligned with his or her company and have a team that understands these goals and is committed to achieving them. The CTIE program is rooted in this concept and helps executives advance far beyond the "being in charge" mentality. This online course teaches you new skills that can be put into practice immediately and help you: learn your own executive manner/approach in an effort to make you more effective and capable of properly applying the organization's core values and resolving challenges and obstacles along the way; discover your negotiating style and the styles of others to build effective negotiating strategies; develop strong co-workers and employees to ensure a cohesive team for all; gain the confidence to build a strong company and a promising future; find new ways of doing business and getting the most from your staff; and understand how your employees and co-workers think, operate and interact, as well as how to get the best results from all players. The prerequisite for the CTIE is a minimum of five years' industry experience. Following the successful completion of the CTIE course, continuing education is required to keep this certification current and maintain its value. Benefits of earning the CTIE designation may include: increased effectiveness through knowledge of your leadership style; increased professional and personal satisfaction due to your "change-agent" approach; greater results in organizational growth and talent development; greater advancement opportunities; and access to a digital credential for online validation and marketing purposes.

The *Destination* and *Niche Market* courses are designed to provide a travel professional with the tools and knowledge needed to be successful in various industry segments. In addition, there are individual courses on *Business Planning* and *Financial Planning*, as well as *Business Ethics*. Courses are added regularly. Visit www.thetravelinstitute.com for a complete list.

The *Travel Introductory Program, TRIPKit*, is designed for someone brand new to the travel industry—someone who has the desire to become a professional but needs both the textbook knowledge and practical application to get started. The TRIPKit curriculum contains a comprehensive collection of essential tools for entry-level professionals. It includes this textbook as well as another textbook, *Exploring the World*, and their supporting workbooks to help you master the fundamentals of the travel industry and provide information on career options and trends. Separate study guides and videos supplement the applications covered in the textbooks. TRIPKit also includes a TAPTest Voucher, a six- month membership with The Travel Institute, and the *Insider Insights* video series—an online component that tackles the practical, real world scenarios you'll face as a travel agent every day. There are no prerequisites for TRIPKit. The benefits of completing TRIPKit may include: higher earning potential due to greater industry knowledge; more informed career decisions based on a better understanding of industry segments; greater credibility and marketability based on commitment to professional development; and an industry-recognized designation with a passing score on the TAP Exam.

The *Basic* and *Premium Access Membership* products provide access to a variety of education options, including webinars and online content on varied topics. This type of access allows travel professionals to immerse themselves in learning and expertise available from The Travel Institute as well as from industry veterans and experts delivering on-demand webinars, podcasts, blogs, white papers, articles, and self-paced specialist courses. While membership is not a requirement for most of our products and services, the affiliation does provide an array of valuable benefits, whether you are just starting out or have been in the industry for years. In addition, membership demonstrates your commitment to learning and to a higher standard for yourself and the industry. Basic Member Access includes: all live training webinars; five free archived training webinars; access to the members-only online lounge; 10% discount on products; and the *Friday Five* business tips blog. Premium Member Access includes all the benefits of basic access membership plus: all archived training webinars; access to the members-only online lounge; all destination specialist courses; the *Business Planning* course; the *Financial Planning* course; all destination and niche market courses; and the entire library of content on various business topics.

All of The Travel Institute's education programs can be completed through self-study, group study, or online. Regardless of which program you choose, The Travel Institute's programs provide essential knowledge at each stage of your travel career.

Prospects

For travel professionals ready to learn and to adapt, this is a time of opportunity. Experts offer varying predictions about what will happen to specific segments of the travel industry in the near future. In the long run, each segment is likely to grow, although the jobs of travel professionals will change.

Travel itself will also change. Globalization is shrinking the world and making it more homogeneous. The Nepalese wear their jeans while sipping Cokes and watching YouTube videos. International basketball stars arrive in the United States while American players go to Europe. And wherever people are, they can get a Big Mac. Yet the variety of distinct human cultures persists as individuals struggle to keep their unique identities intact.

A hundred years ago, only a tiny percentage of people could get to even the most accessible places around the globe, and many places were inaccessible. A hundred years from now, will there still be reasons to leave home? Will the 21st century end up being one in which people can go everywhere but where there is nowhere worth going to? We think not. Instead, it will offer travel opportunities undreamed of a century ago. Physical presence in a different place will still trump any form of virtual or cyber presence.

Like other citizens, travel professionals have a role to play in determining tomorrow's travel paths. They can influence how the peoples and environments of destinations near and far are treated. In fact, some argue that travel professionals have a special ethical obligation to help protect the cultures and environments of the destinations they profit from, and many companies offer "green" programs. Meanwhile, this is a time during which you can go almost anywhere on earth, and even travel in space, yet a time in which there are still adventuresome and culturally distinct destinations to visit.

CHAPTER WRAP-UP

CHAPTER HIGHLIGHTS

This chapter discussed the keys to making the most of the opportunities in the travel industry. Here is a review of the objectives with which we began the chapter.

1. **Suggest at least four ways to ensure success in a new job and four steps to take to prepare for advancement.** New employees especially should aim to

make a good first impression, to be a team player, to take initiative, to have a positive attitude, and, of course, to work hard. The path to success is easier for those who find a mentor and learn to understand the corporate culture. Steps to take to prepare for future advancement include establishing a reputation for excellence, extending and maintaining networks, keeping a job portfolio current, continuing to learn, and being professional. It is important for travel professionals to develop skills in business communication, organization, time management, negotiating, understanding consumer trends and motivation, crisis management, cultural diversity, and managing change. Successful travel professionals look at change as an opportunity to position themselves and their companies for success.

2. **Outline a path for advancing in a travel career.** Specific steps depend on the career and the company. Large companies often offer more opportunities for advancement than do smaller ones. Sometimes advancing in a career will require relocation, specialization, or additional formal education, whether through college courses or through programs offered within the travel/tourism industry.

3. **Identify at least four ethical responsibilities of travel professionals.** Travel professionals have a responsibility to preserve the confidentiality of information provided by clients. They also have an obligation to present clear and complete information about their products or services, avoiding deceptive advertising and disclosing all facts necessary for clients to make informed decisions. In addition, they are obliged to serve the client's interests in selecting suppliers and to act as guardians of any funds entrusted to them (sometimes by maintaining escrow accounts). Travel counselors also have a responsibility to follow suppliers' rules and regulations when they sell suppliers' services. Thus, clients' requests for back-to-back ticketing, hidden-city ticketing, and doublebooking all raise ethical questions for the travel counselor.

4. **Describe how to develop your skills and knowledge as a travel professional.** General education on your own—through on-the-job training and experience, personal travel, and reading—is one important path to professional development. College and university courses provide another route and may be necessary for some positions. In addition, suppliers and professional organizations in the travel industry offer innumerable seminars, trips, and formal courses. Among the programs offered are courses leading to certification as a Certified ARC Specialist (CAS), Accredited Cruise Counselor (ACC), Master Cruise Counselor (MCC), Certified Meeting Professional (CMP), Certified Incentive Travel Executive (CITE), Certified Tour Professional (CTP), Destination Management Certified Professional (DMCP), Certified Travel Associate (CTA®), Certified Travel Counselor (CTC®), Certified Travel Industry Executive (CTIE®), and Destination or Niche Market Specialist.

KEY TERMS

A list of key terms introduced in this chapter follows. If you do not recall the meaning of these terms, see the Glossary.

back-to-back ticketing	doublebooking
card mills	hidden-city ticketing
corporate culture	mentor

REVIEW QUESTIONS

1. What is a mentor?

2. What is meant by a company's corporate culture?

3. What are some of the factors that shape the opportunities for advancement in a company?

4. What are four skills that every travel professional should develop, and why are they important for career growth?

5. Describe three situations that would create an ethical conflict for a travel counselor.

6. List three ways that the Internet can help you continue your travel education.

Glossary

24-hour clock A timekeeping method that eliminates a.m./p.m. usage, opting for a different numeral for each hour of the day.

■ A ■

AAA See *American Automobile Association.*

ACC Accredited Cruise Counselor, training program and designation offered by Cruise Lines International Association.

accountable document A standardized, numbered form issued by *ARC* that the travel agency must account for.

Acela Express *Amtrak*'s high-speed train serving the Northeast corridor of the United States.

ADA See *Americans with Disabilities Act.*

additional liability insurance (ALI) Extra coverage for injury, death, or other liability to a third party, beyond both what state law mandates that car rental companies include in the cost of the rental and what the renter's own insurance might cover.

adjoining rooms Rooms next to each other with separate entrances and no way to go from one room to the other.

adventure cruise A *special-interest cruise* designed to appeal to an audience of similar tastes and interests, often on ships serving 90 to 250 people.

adventure tour A *special-interest tour* that focuses on outdoor physical activity. See *hard adventure* and *soft adventure.*

affinity group A club, team, or other membership organization of people who share a particular interest or characteristic (such as age or ethnic background).

aft Toward the rear of a ship.

AH&LA See *American Hotel and Lodging Association.*

Airline Deregulation Act The U.S. law that ended the government's economic control of the airlines; enacted in 1978.

Airline Passengers with Disabilities Bill of Rights The U.S. law directing the Federal Aviation Administration to create a bill of rights, protecting the rights of passenger with disabilities to fly free of discrimination

Airlines Reporting Corporation (ARC) The group owned by major U.S. airlines, regulating the sale and distribution of airline tickets. It accredits agencies that sell airline tickets; supplies documents used in selling airline tickets, rail transportation, and related services; and provides a central sales-processing system.

airport hotel A lodging built to be convenient for travelers departing on early-morning flights or for people not needing to go downtown for business.

air/sea A package that includes the cost of the cruise and flight arrangements to the port of embarkation.

Air Transport Association (ATA) The trade association formed by major U.S. airlines that represents them before governmental bodies and promotes the safety and efficiency of airlines.

ALI See *additional liability insurance.*

all-inclusive A *resort* offering a complete package of vacation activities for one price, typically including meals, accommodations, entertainment, and sports and recreational facilities.

all-suite A hotel offering rooms with separate sleeping and living areas.

altitude The elevation above sea level.

Amadeus One of the four major *global distribution systems.*

American Automobile Association (AAA) A motor club that offers members a variety of travel and motoring services in the United States.

American Hotel and Lodging Association (AH&LA) The trade association representing the lodging industry in the United States.

American plan (AP) An arrangement in which the room rate usually includes three meals; also called *full board.*

American Society of Travel Advisors (ASTA) The trade association that lobbies governments, presents educational programs, and speaks to the public on behalf of its members, including travel counselors and others in the travel industry.

Americans with Disabilities Act (ADA) An act passed in 1990 stipulating that people with disabilities have the right to access the same travel services as those without disabilities.

Amtrak The corporation that operates passenger rail service in the United States.

AP See *American plan.*

APEX fare The most frequently used discount fare for international air travel.

application letter An unsolicited *cover letter*, accompanied by a *résumé*, sent to a company when the sender doesn't know if the company has any job openings.

Apollo A computer reservation system owned by United Airlines.

ARC See *Airlines Reporting Corporation.*

ARC report A weekly accounting of a travel agency's sales of airline tickets and other *accountable documents;* also called a "sales report" or "air report."

Area Bank Settlement Plan The system by which airlines that are members of *ARC, Amtrak,* and certain other *suppliers* receive payments for tickets sold by travel agencies.

arrival tax A tax imposed on passengers entering a country.

ASTA See *American Society of Travel Advisors.*

ATA See *Air Transport Association.*

atlas A compilation of maps.

■ B ■

back-to-back ticketing The practice of buying two discount tickets and rearranging the departures and returns in order to avoid restrictions on the discount ticket.

baggage and personal possessions insurance Coverage for lost, stolen, or damaged baggage or personal possessions.

bait-and-switch The deceptive practice of advertising something that is not available.

bareboat charter A chartered *yacht* without a professional crew.

base fare Airfare before taxes, fees, commissions, surcharges.

B&B See *bed-and-breakfast.*

bed-and-breakfast (B&B) A small establishment emphasizing personal attention and offering individually decorated rooms with special character.

benefit A positive result that a *feature* brings to a particular client.

Bermuda plan (BP) A room rate including a full breakfast.

berth A bed on a cruise ship.

block A group of cabins on a cruise line all at the same price.

boarding pass A document that allows a passenger on a flight.

boatel A motel, which can be a boat, on a river or waterway for guests who arrive by boat.

body language Nonverbal signals such as facial expressions, posture, and gestures.

bow The front of a ship.

BP See *Bermuda plan.*

brand An identity associated with a company name.

bricks-and-clicks agency A travel agency with a *marketing plan* that calls for using both a website and a physical location as points of sale.

BritRail pass A *rail pass* that allows travel throughout England, Scotland, and Wales.

browser Software that provides access to material on the Internet (for example, Explorer, Navigator, and Firefox).

buffer zone The 225-mile zone extending from the U.S. border into Canada and Mexico within which the *U.S. ticket tax* is assessed.

bulkhead A movable partition that divides an airplane into compartments.

bullet train Japan's high-speed passenger train.

bumped Denied a seat on a flight even though one has a confirmed seat because the airline oversold the flight.

business class A class of service ranging between first class and coach in amenities; also known as *executive class.*

business development manager (BDM) An airline sales position that is equal to being a district or regional sales manager.

business plan A summary of what is expected from a business effort, including the level of income, benefits, and investment, along with a statement of mid- and long-term goals.

business travel Travel undertaken for the purpose of conducting business, including meetings, conventions, and *incentive travel;* also known as *corporate travel.*

■ C ■

CAA See *Canadian Automobile Association*

CARs See *Canadian Aviation Regulations*

cabin A bedroom on a cruise ship.

call center Large reservation offices maintained by airlines, hotels, and other travel/tourism companies.

Canadian Automobile Association (CAA) A motor club that offers member a variety of travel and motoring services in Canada.

Canadian Aviation Regulations (CARs) A compilation of regulatory requirements and rule governing civil aviation in Canada.

cancellation penalty A charge incurred for canceling travel arrangements after a specified time.

Canrailpass A pass offered by *VIA Rail.*

card mill A company that sells travel agent credentials to outside sales agents but provides minimal support and training.

cash flow The expenditures and income that determine the availability of cash.

casino A center for gambling, often operated in conjunction with hotels or resorts.

CCRA An organization that specializes in representing and supporting *independent contractors* in the travel industry, *outside sales agents,* and host agencies.

CDC See *Centers for Disease Control and Prevention.*

CDW See *collision damage waiver.*

CEIR See *Center for Exhibition Industry Research.*

Center for Exhibition Industry Research (CEIR) Organization that advocates for and represents the exhibition industry.

Centers for Disease Control and Prevention (CDC) Provides travelers information about health risks, specific diseases abroad, and recommended or required immunizations.

chain A group of affiliated properties that bear the same name, follow the same operating procedures and standards, and share a reservation system.

charter A specially scheduled flight reserved by a private group or *tour operator.*

chatbot Technology used to simulate conversation, or chatting, between people online, often enabled by artificial intelligence.

château, castle, and villa An upscale inn in a unique property, such as a medieval castle or an entire villa, often with amenities that include an on-site chef and private swimming pool.

CHRIE See *International Council on Hotel, Restaurant, and Institutional Education.*

Chunnel The tunnel beneath the English Channel that links England and France.

CIC See *Convention Industry Council.*

circle trip A journey that returns to the city where it began but by a different route on the return trip. It is like a *round-trip* but involves two or more *stopovers.*

CITE Certified Incentive Travel Executive designation program offered by the Convention Industry Council.

civil aviation All cargo or passenger air travel done for hire, including *scheduled service* and *charters.*

classes of service Compartments that distinguish levels of service; for example, *first class, business class,* or *coach.*

CLIA See *Cruise Lines International Association.*

climate The weather that usually prevails in a region.

close To obtain the client's firm commitment to buy.

close-ended question A question inviting precise answers or simple facts.

cloud Websites with software programs that are stored on a remote server.

CMP Certified Meeting Professional designation from the Convention Industry Council.

coach A class of service in the least expensive and most frequented compartment on an aircraft or Amtrak; called *economy class* on many international airlines.

code-sharing agreements Agreements that allow an airline to use the same two-letter code as a larger, better-known airline.

collision damage waiver (CDW) Insurance that waives the car rental company's right to charge the renter for damages if the rental car is involved in an accident. See *loss damage waiver (LDW)*.

command interface A system of communication between a computer and its user where the user types strings of keystrokes to control the computer.

commercial agency A travel agency specializing in *business travel*.

commercial hotel A centrally located hotel in a city, catering mostly to business travelers but also suitable for leisure travelers.

commission A percentage of the sale or a fee paid to a salesperson for selling a product.

commodity Something that varies little and has the same value everywhere.

commuter airline A small carrier that services one region (such as the Midwest or New England).

computer reservation system (CRS) An electronic system that links distributors and suppliers to a centralized database and is set up for making reservations; a *global distribution system (GDS)*.

concierge A lodging staff member whose function is to provide information and other services to guests.

conference system A system by which a group of *suppliers* controls the sale of their product, appointing agents to sell it and establishing a standard contract.

configuration The layout of seats in an aircraft.

confirmed A reserved travel arrangement.

connecting flight A flight that has a stop that requires the passenger to change planes.

connecting rooms Rooms that are linked by a common door inside the rooms.

connection A stop that occurs when the passenger deplanes with the sole purpose of boarding another plane.

consolidator A distribution company that negotiates with airlines to buy seats on flights at bargain rates and then resells the flight tickets.

consortium An association of travel agencies that remain independent but pool their resources for certain purposes, such as advertising and training.

construction principles Rules and guidelines for formulating the airfare for itineraries other than simple round-trips; usually used for international air travel.

consulate A regional office of an embassy.

continent One of the earth's seven large landmasses: Africa, Antarctica, Asia, Australia, Europe, North America, and South America.

Continental plan (CP) An arrangement in which the room rate includes a light or continental breakfast.

convention hotel A hotel that focuses on hosting meetings and conventions.

Convention Industry Council (CIC) A group of organizations representing the convention, meeting, trade show, and exposition industries.

convention rate A discount rate for accommodations offered to participants at meetings and conventions.

cooperative advertising An arrangement in which an advertisement by a supplier or distributor includes information about a travel agency as a contact for reservations in return for the travel agency's contribution to the cost of the advertising.

corporate culture A company's set of values, beliefs, priorities, and practices.

corporate rate A special rate sometimes offered to all business travelers, sometimes just to listed corporations, and sometimes to anyone who asks.

corporate travel Travel undertaken for the purpose of conducting business; also known as *business travel*.

couchette Sleeping accommodations on a train consisting of a compartment with six bunk beds; found on European trains.

Council on Hotel, Restaurant, and Institutional Education See *International Council on Hotel, Restaurant, and Institutional Education*.

country of registry The country from which a cruise ship is legally recorded as doing business and by whose laws and financial regulations the ship is governed.

cover letter A letter of introduction accompanying a *résumé* and designed to obtain an interview or application form.

CP See *Continental plan*.

CRM See *customer relationship management*.

cross-selling Selling products or services beyond those originally requested by a client.

CRS See *computer reservation system*.

Cruise Lines International Association (CLIA) An association that promotes cruising to both the selling agents and the buying public through public relations and advertising as well as by training travel counselors.

cruise ship An all-inclusive floating *resort* that moves from port to port.

CTA Certified Travel Associate The Travel Institute's designation and educational program designed to grow sales, improve efficiencies and increase marketability.

CTC Certified Travel Counselor The Travel Institute's designation and educational program created to prepare candidates to meet the workplace and industry demands of travel managers and supervisors.

CTIE Certified Travel Industry Executive The Travel Institute's designation and educational program offering high-demand skills needed by leaders in the travel industry.

CTP Certified Tour Professional Educational program and designation offered by the National Tour Association.

customer relationship management (CRM) A strategy that combines technology and personalized service to meet the specific needs of customers, provide excellent service, build lasting relationships with clients, and increase customer loyalty.

customer relationship marketing The use of information from databases to direct marketing efforts so that promotions and services match clients' preferences and interests.

■ D ■

database An organized collection of data.

debit memo A document issued by an airline when an agent has issued an airplane ticket not in compliance with rules and regulations; requires the agency to pay a penalty or the difference in airfare between the ticket that was issued and how the ticket should have been issued.

deck plan A diagram of the layout of a ship.

demi-pension A meal plan at a European lodging that includes breakfast and one other main meal, usually dinner, in the room rate; called *Modified American plan (MAP)* in the United States.

demographic segmentation The process of categorizing people according to characteristics such as age, sex, or marital status.

denied boarding compensation Compensation owed to a passenger who is *bumped* if the airline cannot get the passenger to his or her destination within the originally scheduled time.

departure tax A tax imposed on passengers leaving a country.

dependables In Stanley Plog's analysis, people who value familiarity and comfort and focus on everyday problems tend to visit popular places when they travel and to return to the same places each year.

destination A location that a traveler chooses to visit.

destination geography The study of those characteristics of locations that influence travel.

destination management and promotion The overall marketing of an area, whether a city, region, or other location.

destination management company (DMC) A local company that specializes in inbound travel.

Destination Specialist Site-specific educational program and designation offered by The Travel Institute.

dine-around plan A room rate including a meal plan credit for dinner at other hotels or separate restaurants.

direct flight A flight with one or more stops at which the passenger does not have to change planes; also known as a *through flight*.

direct link A seamless flow of information between a distant computer and a *computer reservation system*.

direct mail Advertising that consists of letters, newsletters, or other printed material mailed to potential customers.

discount fare See *promotional fare*.

distributor A company that acts as an intermediary between *suppliers* and travelers, helping travelers obtain the goods and services owned by suppliers.

DMC See *destination management company*

domestic air travel Flights between and within the continental United States and parts of Alaska, Hawaii, Puerto Rico, the Virgin Islands, and Canada.

doublebooking The practice of booking two reservations for a client at the same time.

double open-jaw trip An arrangement similar to a round trip that allows the passenger to depart from and return to different airports in a city or a neighboring city.

dual distribution A practice whereby travel *suppliers* sell to the public both directly and indirectly, through travel agencies and other intermediaries.

dude ranch A resort, usually in a western U.S. state, where guests can participate in horseback riding and hayrides.

duty A charge or tax.

duty-free port A port in which no duties or taxes are levied on goods.

■ **E** ■

economy class See *coach*.

ecotour A *special-interest tour* designed to appeal to those interested in the environment.

electronic reading device Lightweight, portable electronic tablets with a large storage capacity for downloading and reading books and periodicals.

electronic ticket Flight information stored in a computer but not printed on a paper ticket; also called an "e-ticket."

ELI See *extended liability insurance*.

e-mail Communication sent from one computer to another.

embarkation point The port from which a cruise begins.

embassy The office of the ambassador who represents a nation in another country.

EP See *European plan*.

equator The imaginary line that circles the globe halfway between the North and South Poles.

errors and omissions and general liability insurance A type of insurance that protects a business from a claim of alleged negligent acts, errors, or omissions in the performance of its services; also called "professional liability insurance."

escorted tour A *tour* in which participants travel together as a group and are accompanied by a professional escort.

escrow account Funds or other property held by a third party, such as a bank, until specified conditions are met for its release.

ethnic agencies Travel agencies or tour companies specializing in travel for people of a particular ethnic background or language.

Eurailpass A *rail pass* that allows unlimited first-class travel through specific European countries for a specified time.

European plan (EP) An arrangement in which the room rate includes no meals.

Eurostar The train that transports passengers through the Chunnel, the tunnel beneath the English Channel that links England and France.

Eurotunnel The train that transports cars, coaches, trucks, motorbikes, and bicycles through the Chunnel, the tunnel beneath the English Channel that links England and France.

excess baggage charge The fee that airlines (or other modes of transportation) charge for exceeding a stated limit on the weight or number of pieces of baggage that may be transported.

exchange rate The rate at which the currency of one nation can be exchanged for that of another.

executive class See *business class*.

expedition A trip taken on a small cruise ship by a group with a specific objective, such as a particular *soft adventure* or cultural or educational experience; generally features a nontraditional itinerary and expert lecturers.

extended liability insurance (ELI) Additional insurance for injury, death, or other liability to a third party, beyond both what state law mandates that car rental companies include in the cost of the rental and what the car renter's own insurance might cover.

extended-stay hotel A type of *all-suite* geared to those staying at a destination for a few weeks or more.

■ **F** ■

FAA See *Federal Aviation Administration*.

familiarization (fam) trip A trip offered to travel professionals at a reduced rate so they can inspect hotels and restaurants and sample area attractions, services.

feature An inherent characteristic of a product or service.

Federal Aviation Administration (FAA) The agency of the federal Department of Transportation that has primary responsibility for airline safety regulations and that licenses pilots, certifies aircraft as safe, and enforces rules regarding passenger safety.

Federal Aviation Administration Reauthorization Act The U.S. law that mandates the development of the Airline Passengers with Disabilities Bill of Rights.

feedback question A question that confirms details that have emerged in the conversation.

ferry A ship that carries passengers, vehicles, livestock, and supplies across a body of water on a regular schedule.

first class (1) A class of service on an airline or train that provides more comfortable travel than other classes of service, usually by providing better service, more complimentary amenities, and more spacious seating; (2) a very good to excellent hotel, but not as luxurious as a deluxe hotel.

FIT A custom-designed *tour*.

flag of convenience A term used for a ship a company registers in a country other than its own to avoid regulations or taxes.

flight insurance Coverage for accidents that occur in connection with air travel.

fly/cruise An arrangement whereby a cruise line offers air transportation.

fly/drive An *independent tour* that includes air transportation as well as car rental and permits participants to stay at a number of hotels.

forced single An additional amount that a single traveler may have to pay when a tour operator cannot find a roommate.

fore Toward the front of a ship.

four Ps The four characteristics of a business—product, promotion, place, and price—that make up the marketing mix.

franchise company A company that provides the use of a name, a central reservation system, advertising, and training.

freighter A ship whose principal purpose is to carry cargo.

frequent-flyer plan A bonus program for people who fly frequently on a particular carrier.

frequent-guest program A program that rewards repeat guests with bonuses, such as a free room night.

full board See *American plan.*

full pension Where three meals are included in the price of lodgings, usually in Europe.

■ G ■

Galileo One of the four major global distribution systems.

gateway A city that serves as the arrival or departure point for international travel.

GDPR See *General Data Protection Regulation.*

GDS See *global distribution system.*

General Data Protection Regulation (GDPR) A privacy and security law passed by the European Union; it imposes obligations on entities anywhere in the world if they collect or process personal data related to EU residents or citizens; fines and penalties are assessed for noncompliance.

geography The science that studies the earth, its features and life, as well as how these interact.

global distribution system (GDS) An electronic system that links distributors and suppliers to a centralized database and is set up for making reservations; once known as a *computer reservation system.*

GMT See *Greenwich mean time.*

Graphical user interface A system of communication between a computer and its user in which the user can control the computer by clicking on pictures or symbols that are displayed on the computer's screen.

green sheet The Summary of Sanitation Inspections of International Cruise Ships. It can be viewed on the website of the Centers for Disease Control and Prevention (CDC).

Greenwich mean time (GMT) The time at Greenwich, England, from which world time zones are calculated; also known as *universal time coordinated (UTC).*

gross registered tonnage (GRT) The amount of enclosed revenue-producing space on a cruise ship.

group rate A rate that reflects a discount offered to a group that uses a certain number of rooms on the same night.

GRT See *gross registered tonnage.*

guaranteed for late arrival Situation in which a client can hold a reservation past the standard arrival time by paying a deposit for the room.

guaranteed rate Situation in which a client is guaranteed a cabin in a given price range by the cruise line, which arbitrarily assigns the client a cabin.

guaranteed share rate Situation in which a cruise line or *tour operator* guarantees a per-person double-occupancy rate if a single client is willing to share a cabin or room with another person of the same sex; if another person is not available, the client still receives the share rate.

gulf A body of salt water bordered by a curved shoreline, such as the Gulf of Mexico.

■ H ■

hard adventure A type of *adventure tour* that features strenuous outdoor activity (for example, mountaineering or white-water rafting), remote locations, or risk.

hidden-city ticketing The practice in which clients buy a ticket for a flight between two cities with a stop at the desired destination, where they actually get off, because that ticket is cheaper than a ticket for a flight between the originating city and the desired destination.

high season The season when rates and traffic peak.

hold time Deadline for holding a room without payment.

honeymoon specialist A counselor with expert knowledge of resorts and cruises appropriate for couples and requirements for marriages abroad.

hospitality industry The industry that supplies hotel accommodations and food and beverage services.

host A representative of a tour or ground operator who helps tour participants to plan and arrange activities.

hosted tour A *tour* in which individuals travel independently but have access to a *host* to assist them at each tour destination.

hostel Dorm-like accommodations, usually open to all ages, and less expensive than some other types of lodging.

hotel consolidator An intermediary company that purchases blocks of hotel rooms at favorable prices and resells them.

hotel manager The person on a cruise ship who ensures that all passenger services run smoothly.

hotel representative firm A firm that accepts reservations and provides marketing and sales for individually owned properties; also known as a *rep firm.*

hub-and-spoke system A system by which an airline uses certain cities as connecting centers, or hubs, for as many flights to and from outlying cities as possible.

■ I ■

IATA See *International Air Transport Association.*

IATAN See *International Airlines Travel Agent Network.*

IDP See *International Driver's Permit.*

inbound travel Companies that specialize in travelers arriving from other parts of the country or from abroad.

incentive house A travel agency that specializes in arranging *incentive travel.*

incentive travel Travel offered as a prize or reward for employees, usually for productivity or sales performance.

income statement A financial statement summarizing revenues and expenses for a certain period.

independent contractor A self-employed person who is paid by a business to provide certain services. The IRS has specific criteria to distinguish independent contractors from employees.

independent tour A *tour* in which participants travel independently; often called a *package.*

inn A lodging that offers local character, personal service, and a dining room; is somewhat larger than a *bed-and-breakfast* and functions more like a hotel.

instant messaging A form of e-mail communication where the sender and receiver see each other's messages instantaneously.

interface See *graphical user interface*

interline agreement An agreement among airlines.

International Air Transport Association (IATA) An association of international airlines, whose goal is to create stability in international aviation.

International Airlines Travel Agent Network (IATAN) The organization that appoints U.S. travel agencies to sell tickets for international airlines serving the United States.

International Council on Hotel, Restaurant, and Institutional Education (CHRIE) An organization dedicated to continuing education in the *hospitality industry.*

international date line The imaginary line roughly equal to 180° *longitude* that, by international agreement, separates one calendar day from another.

International Driver's Permit (IDP) A translation of a driver's license into an internationally recognized format.

Internet The global network of computer networks that enables anyone who accesses it to communicate with any other computer connected to it.

invoice A document that shows the amount a client owes.

island A body of land completely surrounded by water.

isthmus A narrow body of land connecting two larger land areas.

■ J ■

joint fare The fare for a trip through a connecting city when the flights involve different airlines that have agreed on one published fare.

■ K ■

knot The measure of speed at sea; equal to about 1.15 land miles per hour.

■ L ■

land rate The tour rate that does not include destination airfare.

latitude The distance measured in degrees north or south of the *equator.*

LDW See *loss damage waiver.*

leeward The side sheltered from the wind.

legacy airlines Major airlines among the first in the industry.

leisure travel Travel done for pleasure in the broadest sense of the term (travel to visit family and friends is generally, but not always, included in this category).

LGBT travel specialist An agent familiar with destinations friendly to the lesbian, gay, bisexual, and transgender traveler.

lodge Historic, rustic accommodations, often found in U.S. national parks.

lodging Another term for the hotel industry.

longitude The distance measured in degrees east or west of the *prime meridian*.

loss damage waiver (LDW) Insurance that waives the car rental company's right to recover damages resulting from theft, vandalism, or collisions involving the rental car. See *collision damage waiver (CDW)*.

low season The season when rates and traffic are at their lowest; sometimes called the *value season*.

■ **M** ■

management contract An arrangement by which a hotel company manages but does not own a hotel.

MAP See *Modified American plan*.

marketing A series of decisions and actions taken by a seller to create a match between consumers' preferences and a product or service.

marketing plan A set of decisions that identifies a *target market* and determines what to sell, how to promote it, where to sell it, and at what price to sell it.

market research The gathering and analyzing of information about consumers and products.

market segment/market segmentation The process of identifying clusters of individuals who have similar needs and can form a *target market*.

MCC Master Cruise Counselor, training and designation program offered by Cruise Lines International Association.

MCO See *miscellaneous charges order*.

Mediterranean climate A *climate* with warm, dry summers and mild, wet winters.

meeting A gathering arranged by a business or other group and involves an overnight stay.

meeting planner A specialist who plans *meetings* for sponsors.

Meeting Professionals International (MPI) An association of meeting professionals that promotes the meeting industry.

meeting travel Travel to organized gatherings such as conferences and conventions.

megaship A large cruise ship measuring at least 70,000 *GRT* and holds more than 1,600 passengers.

membership organization A not-for-profit association in which individual members own and operate hotels that share a global reservation system as well as other common services.

mentor A person who serves as an unofficial teacher, counselor, role model, and advocate.

metric system The system of units of measurement based on decimals; used by most countries.

mileage system The method of determining airfares that ties the fare to the number of miles flown. Most simple domestic *round-trips* are not based on the mileage system.

minshuku A traditional-style private guesthouse in Japan; similar to a European *pension*.

miscellaneous charges order (MCO) An *accountable document* issued by travel agencies when standard ticket stock cannot be used.

Modified American plan (MAP) An arrangement in which the room rate includes breakfast and another main meal, often dinner; called *demi-pension* in Europe.

monsoon A wind system that changes direction seasonally; also may refer to the heavy rains that accompany the wind.

motel A lodging with only one or two stories, ample parking, and very limited food service.

motor coach A bus.

motor inn More hotel-like than the traditional *motel* yet catering to the auto traveler; often found in or near large cities.

MPI See *Meeting Professionals International*.

■ **N** ■

National Tour Association (NTA) The association of *tour operators, suppliers,* and destination marketing organizations that are insured and comply with the NTA Code of Ethics.

national tourist office (NTO) A government-sponsored office that works within the country to make it attractive to tourists and works outside the country to present it in the best light.

National Transportation Safety Board (NTSB) The government agency that tracks aviation fatalities, publishes annual safety statistics, investigates accidents, and recommends safety enhancements.

negotiated corporate rate A rate negotiated with a company or its affiliate or association.

Net, or non-commissionable, rate A rate that does not include a *commission*.

networking Using personal contacts to make business contacts and to advance in the business world

niche A specialty market.

niche cruise A cruise designed around a theme to appeal to the interests of a special group.

non-commissionable rate See *net rate*.

nonstop flight A flight with no intermediate stops.

no-show A person who does not show up for his or her scheduled flight but does not cancel or change the reservation.

NTA See *National Tour Association*.

NTO See *national tourist office*.

NTSB See *National Transportation Safety Board*.

■ **O** ■

occupancy rate The percentage of rooms occupied.

ocean A major division of the earth's huge body of salt water; the four major oceans are the Arctic, the Atlantic, the Indian, and the Pacific.

one-way trip A trip from an originating city to a destination city with no return to the origin.

online travel agency Usually refers to a travel agency that does business almost exclusively online but can refer to any travel agency that uses the Internet for a portion of its business.

opaque pricing A tour package of multiple components from a variety of sources bought at net prices, with an appropriate agency markup, and offered at a single price to consumers.

open-ended question A question that invites answers that include whatever facts, opinions, or feelings the respondent thinks are relevant.

open-jaw trip A trip in which the passenger either returns to a city different from the point of origin or departs for the return trip from a city other than the original destination.

open-skies policy The policy that eliminates governmental regulations in order to allow international air carriers to fly where they choose, charge what they want, and make deals among themselves.

option date The date by which a deposit or full payment must be made when a window of time exists between booking and payment.

outside sales agent A person who brings in new customers, beyond the travel agency's existing clientele. This person may be an employee or an *independent contractor*.

overbook To sell more tickets than there are seats.

override An extra payment made by a *supplier* as a bonus for a large volume of sales. See *preferred supplier relationship*.

oversold A situation in which the number of confirmed passengers who show up for a flight exceeds the number of seats.

■ **P** ■

package Two or more travel components bundled and offered at one price; often used to refer to an *independent tour*.

PAI See *personal accident insurance*.

paper ticket The conventional airline ticket, which consists of a booklet of coupons, including one kept by the passenger.

parador A traditional-style, government-operated hotel of Spain, usually in a historic building with atmosphere. (Puerto Rico also applies the term to some of its local inns.)

passenger facility charge (PFC) A surcharge imposed to pay for airport improvements.

passenger load factor The percentage of available seats on a flight that are actually sold; it can be stated for any length of time.

passenger name record (PNR) A record of a passenger's reservation information in a computer.

passport A document issued by a government to a citizen in order to establish an individual's identity and nationality and to request protection for the citizen while he or she is abroad.

Payment Card Industry Data Security Standard (PCI DSS) The standard that merchants, vendors, and financial institutions must comply with; the standard sets security policies, technologies and ongoing processes to protect payment systems from breaches and theft of credit cardholder data.

PCI DSS See *Payment Card Industry Data Security Standard*.

peninsula A body of land with water on three sides.

pension A small family-run European lodging that may be run much like a hotel or a *bed-and-breakfast*.

personal accident insurance (PAI) Car rental insurance that covers bodily injury to the renter.

personal selling Selling conducted through person-to-person contact.

PFC See *passenger facility charge*.

Pied Piper A well-known and popular leader for a special-interest tour.

pitch (1) The amount of space between one seat on a plane and the seat directly in front of or behind it; (2) the up-and-down motion of a ship.

PNR See *passenger name record*.

point-to-point tickets Fare from one *stopover* point to another.

port charges On a cruise, charges to cover fees levied by governments or port facilities for the use of the port.

port of call A stop on a cruise ship's itinerary.

pousada A government-operated, traditional-style hotel of Portugal, usually in a historic building with atmosphere.

preferred supplier relationship An arrangement where a travel agency is committed to maximizing its use of a particular *supplier;* in turn, the agency can receive *overrides*.

premium economy class Airplane seats located between business/first class and economy class.

pre-paid rate A discounted rate offered by paying the total amount of a reservation in full at the time of booking.

price segmentation The process of dividing a population into segments based on the amount they can and will pay for a product.

prime meridian The imaginary line running through Greenwich, England, that connects the North and South Poles.

professional A person who has learned a body of knowledge, mastered skills needed for a certain occupation, and demonstrated a commitment to the occupation's ethical standards and the interests of clients.

promotion An effort to communicate information about a product or service to the market.

promotional fare A lower fare offered by an airline to generate more business; also called a *discount fare*.

properties A term for the various types of accommodations in the hotel industry.

psychographic segmentation The process of categorizing potential consumers based on their attitudes, interests, beliefs.

public relations Any activity conducted to establish recognition and respect for a company or product.

purser The person on a cruise ship who handles financial matters and operates the information desk.

■ **Q** ■

qualifying The process of identifying potential clients by determining how ready and able they are to make a purchase.

■ **R** ■

rack rate The regular posted or off-the-street price of a room.

Rail Europe A company owned by Swiss and French railroads that acts as a booking agent for rail travel in Europe.

rail pass A pass that allows train travel for a specified time and region with unlimited stops and unlimited mileage.

receipt An *invoice* that indicates an amount paid and the method of payment.

record locator number Numbers or letters assigned to each air reservation, called the "reservation number" by the general public. Various forms of the term can be used for other travel components.

rep firm See *hotel representative firm*.

repositioning cruise A cruise moving a ship from one cruising area to another between seasons.

resort A hotel that is a vacation in itself, offering a variety of activities, facilities, and services.

résumé A summary of qualifications and work experience.

retreat-style accommodation Often a full complex used by companies or organizations for meetings and educational activities.

ridesharing A car service in which a person can use a smartphone app to arrange a ride, usually in a privately owned vehicle.

river A moving body of fresh water that flows from a basin to a termination point.

ROH See *run-of-the-house*.

roll A ship's side-to-side motion.

rondavel Circular lodgings in southern Africa with varying levels of amenities.

round-trip A journey returning to the same city where it began.

routing system The method of setting international airfares in which the fare depends on the specific route flown; used for most international *discount fares*.

run-of-the-house (ROH) A flat discount rate at which a hotel offers any of its available rooms, whatever their location, to members of a group.

ryokan A traditional-style inn in Japan; usually superior to *first class*.

■ **S** ■

Sabre One of the major *global distribution systems*.

Safety of Life at Sea (SOLAS) regulations Rules established by the International Maritime Organization, part of the United Nations, regarding the configuration of ships, equipment, and fire safety.

SATH See *Society for Accessible Travel and Hospitality*.

scheduled service Regularly scheduled flights, in contrast to *charter* or on-demand flights.

schooner A large sailing ship that uses both sails and motors.

sea A body of salt water surrounded or defined by land, such as the Mediterranean and Caribbean Seas.

search engine Web-based software that indexes and searches the Internet, finding and displaying Web-based sources for information requested by users.

seat width The total side-to-side space available at seat cushion or chest level.

security fee A fee established in 2001 to pay for increased security measures.

segment analysis An evaluation of the profitability of different products and services.

segment tax A tax on each takeoff and landing at U.S. airports.

self-catering rental apartment Furnished flats or apartment available in some major cities and beach communities.

selling An aspect of *marketing* that ensures that a product or service is purchased.

selling up Upgrading a client to a more expensive or inclusive version of a product or service.

shoulder season The period between *high* and *low seasons.*

single supplement An additional charge, over the per-person double-occupancy rate, for single occupancy of accommodations.

SITE See *Society of Incentive and Travel Executives.*

Skype A computer software application that lets you talk with others by voice, video, or instant messaging.

social media Electronic communication through which people interact, such as Facebook, Twitter, LinkedIn, and Pinterest.

Society for Accessible Travel and Hospitality (SATH) A nonprofit organization devoted both to promoting awareness, respect, and accessibility for disabled and mature travelers and to promoting their employment in the tourism industry.

Society of Incentive and Travel Executives (SITE) A worldwide organization of professionals dedicated to the development of *incentive travel.*

soft adventure A type of *adventure tour* that involves mild activity but little physical challenge or danger; for example, a walking tour through vineyards or rafting on a mild river.

SOLAS See *Safety of Life at Sea regulations.*

sound A long, wide body of water connecting two larger bodies of water.

spa A type of *resort* that emphasizes health, diet, and fitness.

space ratio The measure of spaciousness on a cruise ship; computed by dividing the ship's *GRT* by the number of passengers.

special-interest tour A *tour* designed to appeal to the interests of a very specific *market segment.*

special-interest travel Travel devoted to a particular interest or activity.

specialty train A train taken by passengers mainly for the experience, not the transportation.

spread A range of cabins at various prices on a ship.

stabilizer A mechanical device that can be activated from the side of a ship to minimize its *roll* and create a smoother cruise.

standard ticket A form of airline ticket accepted as valid by all airlines that are members of the *ATA.*

standby A person who wants space on a flight listed as full.

step-on guide A person who joins a *tour* briefly to conduct sightseeing.

stern The back of a ship.

stop Occurs whenever a plane lands.

stopover A planned break in a journey; occurs whenever the traveler stays at a domestic location for more than 4 hours (or 24 hours for international flights), unless the *stop* is necessitated by the airline's schedule.

strait A narrow channel of water connecting two larger bodies of water.

supplier A company that owns and provides the goods and services (including transportation, food, shelter, entertainment, and attractions) sold to travelers.

supporting businesses and organizations Entities that either provide travel-related services such as maps and travel insurance or aid or regulate the travel industry.

■ **T** ■

TAP Test See *Travel Agent Proficiency Test.*

target market A *market segment* that a seller aims to reach.

telecommute To work from a remote location and communicate with the business office via computer and other communication devices.

tender A small boat used to carry passengers from ship to shore and back when the larger ship cannot dock in a too-shallow or too-crowded harbor.

tented camp Accommodations for travelers on safari in Africa, ranging from simple to more luxurious.

TGV A high-speed train in France that travels close to 200 miles per hour.

The Travel Institute The international nonprofit organization that educates and certifies travel professionals at all stages of their careers.

third/fourth person rate The price for additional persons, after the first two, who share either a cabin on a cruise or a room on a *tour.*

through fare The fare through a connecting city when the connection involves flights by the same airline.

through flight See *direct flight.*

TICO See *Travel Industry Council of Ontario.*

tour A package of travel features sold as a single unit.

tour escort The person responsible for the smooth running of a *tour* and the welfare and satisfaction of the clients; also called a "tour manager" or a "tour director."

tour guide A specialist who dispenses in-depth knowledge about his or her particular topic on an *escorted tour.*

tour operator A company that assembles the components and operates aspects of *tours* and may own facilities or vehicles or employ personnel used on tours; may also sell tours directly to the public.

tour wholesaler A company that packages the components of *tours* for sale by retail outlets.

tourist card An entry document used by some countries in lieu of a *passport.*

tourist court Individually owned cabin accommodations built in the 1920s.

transfer Transportation between hotels and airports, docks, or railroad stations.

Transportation Security Administration (TSA) The agency of the federal government responsible for developing policies to ensure the safety of U.S. transportation, including airport security and the prevention of hijacking.

travel accident and health insurance Coverage that protects the insured in case of accidents and sickness while away from home.

travel agency A business that sells travel products and services directly to the public.

Travel Agent Proficiency (TAP) Test An entry-level competency test developed by The Travel Institute and the American Society of Travel Advisors.

travel counselor An individual who advises travelers and who sells travel arrangements to the public for *suppliers;* also known as a "travel agent."

travelers with disabilities Those travelers who have impaired mobility and require special arrangements.

Travel Industry Council of Ontario (TICO) One of several consumer protection/regulatory bodies in Canada.

tree lodge Accommodations on stilts for travelers on safari in Africa, ranging from simple to luxurious.

trip cancellation or interruption insurance Coverage that reimburses clients for nonrefundable prepayments if they must cancel or discontinue a trip for a reason covered by the policy.

TSA See *Transportation Security Administration.*

■ **U** ■

uniform resource locator (URL) The address of a website.

United States Tour Operators Association (USTOA) The professional association for *tour operators* that conduct business in the United States; members pledge adherence to a code of ethics and participate in a consumer protection plan.

universal time coordinated (UTC) See *Greenwich mean time (GMT).*

URL See *uniform resource locator.*

usage segmentation The process of categorizing potential consumers according to the purpose for which they would use a product.

USA Rail pass A *rail pass* on *Amtrak* that can only be bought outside the United States.

U.S. ticket tax A tax charged on airline tickets purchased in the United States for travel among the fifty states or in the *buffer zone* in Canada and Mexico.

USTOA See *United States Tour Operators Association.*

UTC See *universal time coordinated.*

■ V ■

value-added tax (VAT) A tax levied on a product at each stage of manufacture or distribution and included in the final price.

value season The time of year at a destination when prices are lower; sometimes called *low season* or "off-season."

VAT See *value-added tax.*

venturers The term used by Stanley Plog to describe travelers who tend to be confident and curious, to have varied interests, and to enjoy discovering new vacation spots.

VFR travel Travel to visit friends or relatives.

VIA Rail Canada's passenger train network.

videoconferencing A meeting where cameras allow participants in various parts of the country to see and talk with each other.

virtual public network (VPN) A service that provides a secure Internet connection so users can share information across insecure public WiFi.

visa An endorsement, stamp, or separate paper placed in a *passport* by officials of a foreign government specifying the conditions under which the traveler may enter the country.

voice mail An automated phone-answering system that handles incoming calls.

voucher A document used to confirm arrangements, identify clients, or indicate payments made; issued by a *tour operator,* cruise line, or travel agency.

VPN See *virtual public network.*

■ W ■

waitlisted Placed on a list of people seeking a service that is sold out.

walking the guest Practice whereby a hotel substitutes nearby accommodations of equal or better quality when it has no rooms available for a confirmed guest.

WHO See *World Health Organization.*

WiFi A wireless network that broadcasts over a particular part of the electromagnetic spectrum; short for "wireless fidelity."

windjammer A large sailing ship with multiple sails.

windward The side exposed to the wind.

Worldspan One of the four major *global distribution systems.*

World Health Organization (WHO) Provides information about vaccinations needed and health risks abroad.

World Wide Web The system that organizes information on the *Internet* into interconnected pages that can be easily presented and retrieved.

■ Y ■

yacht A boat used for private excursions.

yield The average amount of revenue earned per passenger mile.

yield management system A fare structure designed to maximize revenue.

Index

24-hour clock, 32

Photo Credits